Robert E. Speer

Robert E. Speer

Robert E. Speer

Prophet of the American Church

JOHN F. PIPER, JR.

Geneva Press
Louisville, Kentucky

Photo credits: Photo on cover and frontispiece courtesy of Presbyterian Historical Society, Presbyterian Church (U.S.A.) (Philadelphia). Photos at parts I and IV courtesy of Bryn Mawr College; photos at parts II and III courtesy of Presbyterian Historical Society.

Book design by Sharon Adams
Cover design by Lisa Buckley

First edition

Published by Geneva Press
Louisville, Kentucky

This book is printed on acid-free paper that meets the American National Standards Institute Z39.48 standard. ⊗

PRINTED IN THE UNITED STATES OF AMERICA

00 01 02 03 04 05 06 07 08 09 — 10 9 8 7 6 5 4 3 2 1

Library of Congress Cataloging-in-Publication Data

Piper, John F., 1936–
    Robert E. Speer : prophet of the American church / John F.
Piper, Jr.— 1st ed.
        p. cm.
    Includes bibliographical references.
    ISBN 0-664-50132-X (alk. paper)
    1. Speer, Robert E. (Robert Elliott), 1867–1947.   2. Presbyterians—
United States—Biography.   I. Title.

BX9225.S643 P57 2000
285'.1'092—dc21   00-41070
[B]

For all those called to ministry as missionaries of the Christian faith
and
my beloved wife Margaret Rose
and the coming generations
Kelly and Carl Pedersen, Kelsey Ann and Kylie Rose
John and Lydia Piper, John Torin and Nathaniel Frederick

CONTENTS

ACKNOWLEDGMENTS

It is a joy to be able to thank publicly those who have shared their knowledge and time so generously during the preparation of this book. Their help has led to conference presentations and journal articles, but those settings do not offer many opportunities to offer a word of thanks. This more formal setting makes it possible to acknowledge substantial debts to others.

Colleagues on the Lycoming College faculty, through committee recommendations for professional development grants and sabbaticals, have been very supportive. The college has provided travel funds, both during and between sabbaticals, to enable long-term visits to several collections of papers. President Frederick E. Blumer and Dean Shirley Van Marter were supportive of these awards. Special thanks to President James E. Douthat and the Board of Trustees for granting a sabbatical in 1998–99 which provided the time to bring this book to a conclusion. The sabbatical worked out well largely because Kathleen D. Pagana was an excellent Associate to the Dean. Diane J. Hassinger, Executive Secretary to the Dean, has been a constant source of support. Robert H. Larson, Richard J. Morris, and David S. Witwer, in the History Department, and faculty colleagues G. W. Hawkes, Ernest D. Giglio, and Owen F. Herring have shown sustained interest in this project.

Support for my project has come from a number of other sources. The American Historical Association awarded me a Albert J. Beveridge Grant for Research in American History for the summer of 1983, and the National Endowment for the Humanities awarded me a Travel to Collections grant for 1990. Princeton Theological Seminary welcomed me as a Visiting Fellow in the spring of 1984. President James I. McCord approved my request and President Thomas W. Gillespie welcomed me and helped make my stay useful. Gene P. Degitz, Vice President for Seminary Relations, helped in many different ways in the final preparations for publication. My deepest thanks to those who have provided special support for the publication of this book. They include Princeton Theological Seminary, Huntingdon Presbyterian Church, Ann Satterthwaite, Sheafe

Satterthwaite, Howard P. Colhoun, Eleanor R. Speer, Margot Speer Goudsmit, and Caroline Speer Fisher.

Robert E. Speer first entered my life during graduate work at Duke University. I thank Richard L. Watson, Jr., of the Department of History for encouraging my interest, both then and over the years. Many persons have responded to inquiries, read parts of the manuscript, granted interviews, and offered useful suggestions. My thanks to the following correspondents and readers: Robert T. Handy, Waldo Beach, James H. Smylie, William R. Hutchison, Martin E. Marty, Creighton Lacy, Bradley J. Longfield, Ann Satterthwaite, Nancy S. Shedd, William B. Miller, Charles W. Forman, R. Pierce Beaver, Norman A. Horner, Brad Spangenberg, Margaret P. Carter, John M. Currie, John H. Sinclair, Charles E. Harvey, Faye Yocum, John F. Wilson, Doug Brackenridge, James A. Scherer, Al Gendebien, Frederick L. Gifford, Wilbert R. Shenk, and Leon G. Rosenthal. Several members of the Speer family graciously granted interviews, including William Speer, Constance Speer Barbour, and Margaret Bailey Speer. Margaret, now deceased, offered me the opportunity to use many of the family's most personal possessions, including her father's Bible and the memoirs her father and mother created for Eleanor and Elliott.

Two groups of librarians have been crucial to the completion of this work. First, members of the staff of the Snowden Library of Lycoming College, particularly Janet McNeil Hurlbert, Susan K. Beidler, and Marlene L. Neece, have offered truly substantive help and encouragement over the years. Second, librarians and archivists at the key resource sites have been without exception helpful and encouraging. Louis Charles Willard, James Lenox Librarian, and more recently Stephen D. Crocco, James Lenox Librarian at Princeton Theological Seminary, were gracious hosts. Many members of the Speer Library staff have given help over the years, including John Dickason and James Irvine. William O. Harris, Librarian, Archives and Special Collections, has been very supportive, as have members of his staff, particularly Wesley Smith. My sincere thanks to the following persons: Nancy S. Shedd, Director, Huntingdon County Historical Society; Ben Primer, University Archivist, Seeley G. Mudd Library, Princeton University; Leo M. Dolenski, Manuscripts Librarian, Bryn Mawr College; Frederick J. Heuser, Jr., Archivist and currently Director of the Presbyterian Historical Society; Gerald D. Moran, Librarian, McCartney Library, Geneva College; and Martha Lund Smalley, Archivist, Yale Divinity School Library.

I am thankful for permission to quote from previously published articles in the *Journal of Presbyterian History* and *American Presbyterians*. I am also grateful for permission to quote from the Speer Family Papers in the Mariam Coffin Canaday Library of Bryn Mawr College, the Rockefeller Family Archives in the Rockefeller Archive Center, various Record Groups in the Presbyterian Historical Society, the Speer Papers in the Princeton Theological Seminary Libraries, and various Record Groups in the Yale Divinity School Library.

Editors at Geneva Press, especially Thomas G. Long and David M. Dobson, have helped me improve the manuscript.

The members of the churches I have served during the preparation of this book, DuBoistown, Nisbet, and Grace United Methodist Churches, have been very encouraging. My work at Grace Church has been shared for the last seven years by Pastor Leland Keemer; my thanks to him and his wife, Ginger. My final word of love is for my family, to whom this volume is dedicated.

INTRODUCTION

Robert E. Speer was one of the most remarkable personalities in the history of Christianity in America. Born just after the end of the Civil War, he was a member of the generation that led the Protestant churches in the first half of the twentieth century. He became the outstanding missionary statesman of his era and one of the foremost American church leaders. In a dramatic conversion experience during his college years he heard God call him to be a foreign missionary. He understood himself to be in ministry from that moment and never wavered from his call. At virtually every turn in his life he was in a position of leadership, chosen by others to be one of a small handful of spokespersons or called to the front as the leader. This book will show that in these positions he was a prophet of the American church.

His life showed a pattern from his call until his death: ecumenical settings came first, followed by denominational ones; missionary work came first, followed by nonmissionary work. He was a major figure in the Student Volunteer Movement, an ecumenical missionary organization, before he joined the Presbyterian Board of Foreign Missions. He was one of the major foreign missionary leaders in the nation before he became recognized as a prominent American church leader, before he turned his attention to issues such as ministry in wartime and the problems of racism, and before he accepted nonmissionary leadership positions both in and out of his church.

Despite this pattern, his life cannot be simply and easily divided into distinct parts. His careers, missionary statesman and American churchman, were lived simultaneously by the same man. He not only accomplished these two careers; he sustained a deep involvement in the life of his family and engaged in a variety of writing projects and speaking engagements. He always saw his life and ministry as one whole, whatever the project or event of the moment.

He began his work as a missionary statesman as one of the student leaders of the foreign missionary impulse at Princeton University (then officially known as the College of New Jersey) in 1887. Two years later he became the second traveling secretary of the Student Volunteer Movement. He was one of a triumvirate of movement leaders, with John R. Mott and Sherwood Eddy, for the next fifty years, speaking at its meetings and at the many student conferences held at Northfield, Massachusetts; Silver Bay, New York; and in other places around the nation. Called by the Board of Foreign Missions of the Presbyterian Church to be an assistant secretary in 1891, he soon became one of its senior secretaries. He remained with the board for forty-six years. In 1933 he stood at the front of the struggle to maintain the program of the board in the face of fundamentalist challenges from J. Gresham Machen, including the organization of the Independent Board for Presbyterian Foreign Missions. That same year he led the opposition to the report of the Laymen's Inquiry on Foreign Missions, because he regarded it as a challenge to the Christ-centered view of missions.

He joined many ecumenical ventures in the field of foreign missions. He was a founding member and leader of the Interdenominational Conference of Foreign Missionary Boards and Societies, and of its successor, the Foreign Missions Conference of North America. He played prominent roles at three major missionary conferences: the Ecumenical Missionary Conference in New York in 1900, the World Missionary Conference in Edinburgh in 1910, and the International Missionary Council in Jerusalem in 1928. He shared in writing the Jerusalem message. He was the central figure in the effort to extend evangelical (Protestant) missions in Latin America. He helped found and then led for twenty years the Committee on Cooperation in Latin America. In addition, he wrote and spoke extensively on foreign missions. He produced a number of biographies of missionaries and several important volumes on missionary theory. In 1910 he presented the Duff Lectures in Edinburgh, Scotland.

The international scene became increasingly complex during his lifetime. His generation witnessed growing nationalism around the world, but particularly in Western Europe. In 1885, the year he entered Princeton, King Leopold of Belgium led the European effort to carve up Africa. Many of the same European nations had already established colonies or spheres of influence in much of Asia. Missionaries were evangelists first, but they were also part of the introduction of Western civilization to the rest of the world. Speer kept his focus and the attention of his board on evangelism. Missionary leaders in the nineteenth century had adopted the formula "self-governing, self-supporting, self-propagating" for the churches newly created by the missionary movement. He placed himself squarely behind efforts to sustain and extend that policy. He stood firmly for comity among denominations in mission lands through his work with the Foreign Missions Conference, and for united churches in those lands through his own board and the International Missionary Council.

His career as an American churchman also began with his work with the Student Volunteer Movement. In 1905 the organizers of the Inter-Church Conference on Federation, which met in New York City, invited him to speak on behalf of students. He presented an appeal for Christian unity. This conference led directly to the organization of the Federal Council of the Churches of Christ in America. He attended its initial meeting in 1908 and became part of its work. In 1917 he became chairman of its General War-Time Commission of the Churches, a special commission created to develop and guide a united ministry of the churches to soldiers and their families during World War I. The ministry the churches performed became the most extensive cooperative work ever achieved by the Protestant churches in the United States. The council elected him president for the quadrennium 1920–24.

One of his important contributions to American religious life came during his service with the Federal Council and was a consequence of his commitment to the social as well as the individual gospel. During and after World War I, America's racial melting pot boiled over in a series of vicious race riots. He had from the beginning of his career been a critic of racism, especially of the way in which Social Darwinism had been used to build a case for Anglo-Saxon superiority. Much of his argument against racism had turned on its negative impact on foreign missions. However, his wartime ministry sensitized him to the degree to which racism challenged Christianity at home. As president of the Federal Council he took the lead in the formation of a new Commission on the Church and Race Relations. Set in motion by him, this commission became a leading force for racial reconciliation in the following decades.

The Presbyterian Church in the U.S.A. called on him many times for leadership beyond the field of missions, especially after 1920. It elected him moderator in 1927 as a union candidate in a time of great theological conflict between the fundamentalists and modernists. In 1928 he served on a committee of the General Assembly that considered the role of women in the Presbyterian Church. That committee proposed that women be admitted to the full ministry of the church, and he was an important figure in the effort, only partially successful, to persuade the church to agree.

He became a member of the board of directors of Princeton Theological Seminary in 1914, and continued on the reorganized board after 1929. He served as president of the board from 1937 until his death in 1947. He continued to be a leader during his retirement, teaming with George Irving in the Faith and Life Seminars, one of the first continuing education programs for clergy in America.

Robert E. Speer, at the forefront of the Christian church and its ministry, ecumenical and denominational, was a layperson. This should not be a particularly notable part of his story, since Protestant theory includes the concept of the priesthood of all believers and celebrates the laity as the church. Protestant practice has rarely matched its theory, however, and did not in the early decades of the twentieth century, even though laymen and laywomen organized a number of national movements in those years. He was the first layperson to be president of the Federal Council, and the second to be moderator of his denomination. Remarkably, church leaders of his day recognized him as one of the great preachers. When the *Christian Century* in 1924 took a poll to identify the leading preachers in the first quarter of the century, Speer made its list of the top twenty-five. He enjoyed his status as a layperson and did not appreciate being called "reverend," but as he grew older, his fellow churchmen treated him more and more like a member of the clergy.

He was widely recognized and deeply respected in the American church of his generation, but since his death he has been largely forgotten. Surveys of the history of the church in America mention him only briefly, usually solely in the context of foreign missions. Historians of ecumenism give him somewhat greater credit, but not much more space. Virtually no one has acknowledged his social gospel witness. Only those who have written about Presbyterianism have given him any serious attention.

A likely explanation for his relative anonymity lies in his conception of himself and his attitude toward his ministry. He was very modest and often withdrawn in the face of public recognition or honors. He accepted academic honorary degrees but did not use them or any titles in his personal address. He began a family history in the 1930s but refused to write an autobiography. He also turned aside the approaches of several friends when they proposed writing his biography. He took a hard line against a biography because, he claimed, it might mislead readers about his purposes and detract them from his focus on Jesus Christ. He had written many biographies, including the life stories of a number of missionaries, because he felt those stories might advance the gospel. No one could persuade him that his own story could do the same. The reluctance to have biographical materials published during his lifetime meant that his story did not get told. What appears to have been legitimate modesty has led to histories of the American church that are less than they should be because they have omitted him.

When he died in 1947 he left his family a clear message not to allow anyone to write a biography, if they could prevent it. They followed his instruction until 1952, when the 164th General Assembly of the Presbyterian Church passed a resolution to approach his family with a proposal for a biography. The resolution declared that Speer belonged to the church and that the story of his life would help extend its mission. Emma Speer, his widow, relented and granted her permission. W. Reginald Wheeler, a friend of the family who had served as a missionary to China and as a secretary of the Board of Foreign Missions under Speer, went to work. He gathered a collection of testimonies and memorials and pieced together a narrative that he titled a biography but that was really a memoir, useful as a source book. Emma and their daughter Margaret each wrote a chapter for the volume.

This biography is the first serious effort to tell Speer's story. It lifts up his life and ministry, but its purpose goes beyond that to add to the story of Protestantism in America in the first half of the twentieth century. Speer's contributions will not complete this story, but they will enhance it in a variety of ways: in terms of his personal life of faith; in the history of Presbyterianism; in filling out the story of foreign missions; in defining the roots of ecumenism; in describing the ways the American church responded to war and racism; and in exploring the emergence of women into a position of greater equality in the church.

The two main sections of this book are titled "Missionary Statesman" and "American Churchman." They are flanked by two others, a substantial first section on his life and faith, "The Standing Stone," and a much shorter final section on his ministry in retirement, "Iona." The chapters in these four topical sections are defined by both titles and themes. The titles have been taken from many of the important occasions of his life, and the themes lift up ideas that inspired him. The themes chosen for chapters 7, 10, and 11 are favorite Bible passages. The theme for chapter 2 is a phrase from the missionary leader David Livingstone, and the one for chapter 4 is from missionary mentor Henry Clay Trumbull. Chapter 5's theme is the watchword of the Student Volunteer Movement. The themes for chapters 1, 6, 8, and 12 are from favorite hymns and poems, and the one for chapter 14 is from a prayer he wrote. The themes for chapters 3, 9, and 13 come from titles of his articles and books.

His life was one whole, woven from the fabric of these many themes. Through them he made his many contributions to the American church and to Christianity around the world. They were the means by which he established himself as a prophet of the American church.

MAJOR EVENTS
IN THE LIFE OF ROBERT E. SPEER

1867   Born September 10, Huntingdon, Pennsylvania
1883   Entered Phillips Academy
1885   Entered Princeton University
1886   Joined First Presbyterian Church, Princeton
1887   Conversion experience at Princeton
        Joined the Student Volunteer Movement and signed the
          volunteer pledge
        Attended his first summer conference at Northfield,
          Massachusetts
1889   Graduated valedictorian at Princeton
        Traveling secretary for the Student Volunteer Movement
1890   Death of his father
        Entered Princeton Theological Seminary
1891   Participant in the first quadrennial of the Student Volunteer
          Movement, Cleveland
        Summer supply pastor in Bellefonte and Pottstown, Pennsylvania
        Met Emma Doll Bailey
        Left Princeton Seminary to become assistant secretary of the
          Board of Foreign Missions
1892   Wrote first books, *The Gospel of Luke* and *Studies in the Book of
          Acts*
1893   Attended the first meeting of the Interdenominational
          Conference of the Foreign Missionary Boards and Societies,
          which became the Foreign Missions Conference of North
          America
        Participant in his first General Assembly of the Presbyterian
          Church U.S.A., Washington, D.C.
        Married Emma Doll Bailey
        Began married life in Elizabeth, New Jersey
        Promoted to secretary of the Board of Foreign Missions
1894   First missionary trip, Mexico
1896   World missionary trip; contracted typhoid fever

1897   Moved to "Missionary Ridge" in Englewood, New Jersey
1898   Birth of first child, Elliott
1899   Wrote *Remember Jesus Christ*
1900   Birth of daughter Margaret Bailey
       Participant in the Ecumenical Missionary Conference,
           New York City
1901   First summer vacation at Camp Diamond
1902   Wrote *Missionary Principles and Practice*
1903   Birth of daughter Eleanor McMurtrie
1905   Participant in the Inter-Church Conference on Federation,
           New York City
1906   Death of Eleanor
1907   Birth of daughter Constance Sophia
1908   Participant in the founding meeting of the Federal Council of
           Churches, Philadelphia
1909   Missionary trip to South America
1910   Duff Lectures, Scotland
       Participant in the World Missionary Conference, Edinburgh
       Wrote *Christianity and the Nations*
       Birth of son William
       Wrote *Missions in South America*
1912   Chair of the Commission on Foreign Missions, Federal Council
           of Churches
1913   Chair of the Conference on Missions in Latin America
       Chair of the Committee on Cooperation in Latin America
1914   Member of the board of directors of Princeton Theological
           Seminary
1915   Emma chosen president of the national board, YWCA
1916   Participant in the Congress on Christian Work in Latin America,
           Panama
1917   Chair of the General War-Time Commission of the Churches
       Wrote *The Christian Man, the Church and the War*
1919   A vice-chairman of the administrative committee of the Federal
           Council of Churches
1920   President of the Federal Council of Churches
1921   Missionary trip to India, Persia, and China
1924   Chosen one of the leading preachers in America by the *Christian
           Century*
       Wrote *Of One Blood*

1925   Moved to New York City
        Member of the Commission of Fifteen of the General Assembly
        Participant in the Congress on Christian Work in Latin America,
            Uruguay
1926   Wrote *The Unfinished Task of Foreign Missions*
        Missionary trip to China, Japan, and Korea
1927   Moderator of the Presbyterian Church U.S.A.
        Member of the Committee of Four of the General Council of the
            General Assembly
1928   Participant in the Jerusalem meeting of the International
            Missionary Council
1929   Member of the reorganized board of trustees of Princeton
            Theological Seminary
1932   Emma retired from the national board
1933   Wrote *"Rethinking Missions" Examined*
        Wrote *The Finality of Jesus Christ*
        Public debate with J. Gresham Machen
1934   Murder of Elliott
1937   Retired from volunteer work with the Student Volunteer
            Movement
        Retired from volunteer work with the Foreign Missions
            Conference of North America
        Retired from the Board of Foreign Missions
        President of the board of trustees of Princeton Theological
            Seminary
        Moved to Rockledge in Lakeville, Connecticut
1939   Participant in the Faith and Life Seminars
1943   Wrote *Five Minutes A Day*
1946   Wrote final book, *Jesus and Our Human Problems*
1947   Died November 23 in Bryn Mawr, Pennsylvania; buried in
            Brookside Cemetery, Englewood, New Jersey

PART I

The Standing Stone

Robert E. Speer as a Princeton student, 1886

Bryn Mawr College

CHAPTER 1

Roots

"Blest Be the Tie That Binds"

Robert E. Speer always honored his roots. He loved his people and their land, and although he became a world traveler, he never allowed distance to separate him from them. His vast correspondence, beginning with his father, kept him current, and his frequent visits home nurtured his family ties. The people came first, but the land was not far behind. In childhood he developed a strong romantic attachment to the Juniata Valley in and around Huntingdon, Pennsylvania, and to all of the central part of the state. However beautiful and remarkable the landscape of the rest of the world, it never measured up to the land of his birth.

His father and mother, Robert Milton Speer and Martha Ellen McMurtrie, married April 26, 1864, in Huntingdon. Their union brought together the well-established McMurtrie family and the newly successful Speer family, both part of the social and economic elite of the community. They began to extend their family even as the Civil War drew to a close, and they were part of a generation that looked away from war and toward peace and prosperity. Robert Elliott—Robbie, or Rob, as his family and friends typically called him—arrived September 10, 1867, in the gracious house at 234 Penn Street, the second child and second son. He was greatly loved, but no one predicted that his life would attract so much attention that more than a century after his birth the family home would be recognized as a historical site by both the Pennsylvania Historical and Museum Commission and the Presbyterian Historical Society.[1]

The heritage he received reached deep into colonial history and included persons of local and national prominence, yet the family passed it to him quite naturally, with little effort to make him self-conscious of its importance. The ancestors were Scotch-Irish, English, and Swiss, with a strong emphasis on the Scotch-Irish. His lineage appears to go back to a Covenanter preacher named Speer who migrated with his flock from

Scotland to County Antrim, Ireland, sometime in the late seventeenth century, fleeing the persecutions led by Graham of Claverhouse. His grandfather Speer was born in Ballyrobert, County Antrim, and emigrated to Baltimore and then Shade Gap, Pennsylvania, in 1822.[2] One of his ancestors on his mother's side was Heinrich Zimmerman from the canton of Berne in Switzerland, who changed his name to Henry Carpenter after he settled in Pennsylvania. Wherever they came from, his ancestors did not remain long in the port cities of their arrival, but joined the pioneer movement to the less settled lands in the west. They made their homes in Lancaster County, Pennsylvania, and when it began to fill up, they moved farther west and south in central Pennsylvania and nearby Maryland. Descendants of these pioneers had settled in Huntingdon by the time of the Civil War.

Three characteristics marked Speer's ancestors: the success of their economic ventures; their involvement in politics; and their commitment to the Christian faith through the Presbyterian Church. They were frontier entrepreneurs with wide-ranging interests, and they were successful in virtually everything they tried. Both grandfathers were substantial landowners. Grandpa Speer "had quite a farm of rich bottom land, which under his skillful management yielded large returns." He also owned tracts of forest land, a sawmill, and a hotel and was postmaster of Trough Creek.[3] Grandpa McMurtrie worked as a merchant and ironmaster and was remembered for his "solidity" and "dignified serenity." He often sat with his older brother on a bench before his house discussing "their loans and their many farms."[4]

Politics attracted many of these forebears. One of them won a seat in the Pennsylvania Provincial Assembly in 1765 and held it through seven succeeding terms. Another, less successful one lost races for county commissioner and sheriff. Benjamin Elliott was the political star from the past. He was a delegate to the convention in Carpenters' Hall in Philadelphia in July 1776 that met for the purpose of drafting a constitution for the commonwealth, and he later served as delegate to the Pennsylvania convention that ratified the United States Constitution in 1787. He subsequently served as sheriff, justice of the peace, county treasurer, chief burgess, and county commissioner.

Scotch-Irish Presbyterianism dominated Speer's religious heritage. On his mother's side Benjamin Elliott was first on a list of subscribers underwriting the Presbyterian Church in Huntingdon in 1789. On his father's side, Grandma Agnes Cowan Speer was a faithful member of the Presbyterian Church and served the (union) Sunday school as superintendent.

One observer recalled that when any of her pupils were absent, "she would hunt them up during the week, put her arms around them, and love them back."[5] In a letter to his wife, Grandpa Speer illustrated the rigorous character of his religious tradition, but also its capacity to be interpreted by love. "My kind and most affectionate dear," he wrote, "this being the Sabbath we are lying by at Reading, Pa.—on this day [last] week we lay at Newport, Perry Co., Pa. But from conscientious scruples I denied myself the pleasure of writing to you on that day. But if we were to meet each other *on the Sabbath*, surely we would converse together without considering it a criminal offense, and I do not really see wherein it can be more criminal, *when absent from each other*, to keep up that conversation by writing."[6]

These characteristics came to a focus in Speer's parents, who were the direct transmitters of the heritage to him, and they were faithful to their traditions. They were the most important adults in his life, and his father was by far the most significant person in Robert's life until he married and established his own family. They provided him with a happy and stable home, marked by constant signs of affection and love.

His father, Robert Milton Speer, was the youngest of ten children of Robert and Agnes Speer, both of whom were Irish immigrants. He was born September 8, 1838, in Cassville, a small isolated village south of Huntingdon. He grew up a country boy and later told his children how on frosty mornings "he would rouse up a cow and then stand on the warm spot where it had lain to warm his feet."[7] He attended Cassville Seminary, a typical country private school of the day, and then taught school. In 1857 he moved to Huntingdon and began to read law in the offices of Wilson and Petriken. Admitted to the bar in 1859, he opened his law office in 1860. By then he had decided to combine the practice of law with a career in politics. In 1859 he founded and edited the *Union*, which became the Democratic party newspaper in Huntingdon County. The Civil War came to his home in August 1863, shortly after the battle at Gettysburg, when he received his draft call. Within a month he paid the $300 bounty that freed him from military service.

His mother, Martha Ellen McMurtrie, was born in Huntingdon on November 15, 1840, the eldest of eight children of Margaret Whittaker and William Edward McMurtrie. She brought to the marriage many prominent colonial ancestors who had helped build and shape Huntingdon. One observer described her as a "true helpmeet of her husband: a faithful and prayerful mother."[8] Their six children, beginning with William McMurtrie (Will) in 1865, and including Robert, Mary Cowan in 1869, Victor (Vic) in 1872, Margaret Agnes (Mig) in 1874, and Martha Ellen in 1875, were the center of their life together. Speer's earliest memory of his childhood was of a family setting, when someone carried him into his Grandpa McMurtrie's parlor "on the occasion of my Aunt Lizzie's wedding."[9]

Family Life

The Speer children grew up in the context of their father's legal and political career. In 1866 he joined his law practice to that of their uncle, E. Stewart McMurtrie, and he continued to work as a lawyer until his untimely death in 1890. He did all the court business of the partnership. By the end of his life he had gathered a substantial estate and earned reputations as an able lawyer and a successful politician. His legal renown spread outward from the Huntingdon County bar, the author of his obituary noted, largely because of "the careful preparation of his cases, his extraordinary tact in the examination of witnesses, his thorough knowledge of legal principles, and his matchless power and eloquence in the argument of cases before the court and jury. He thoroughly understood every case before he went into court with it." People also acclaimed him because they knew he was willing to defend "without fee, or hope thereof . . . the accused and friendless."[10] Speer remembered that his father prepared his cases, even the small ones, very thoroughly, gathering all the "litigants and witnesses on his side" in his law offices and going over every point with them. Years later he said he could still see him "like a lion or an eagle in the midst of them, understanding everything, piercing through to the heart of things, gathering everything together in his masterful grasp . . . , and yet so human and winning."[11]

Robert Milton was a lifelong member of the Democratic party. His political fortunes soared in 1870 when he won a hard-fought campaign against a strong Republican opponent by eleven votes and became the member of Congress from Pennsylvania's seventeenth Congressional District. He served his overwhelmingly rural constituents well enough to win reelection in 1872. He ran again in 1880, but by then Republicans had successfully gerrymandered the district to give themselves a strong majority, and he lost.[12] A delegate to the Democratic national conventions of 1872 and 1880, he was also a presidential elector on the Democratic ticket in the election of 1888. He served as chairman of the Democratic state committee in 1878. He was a true public servant, determined to accomplish the duties of his various offices. A friend described him as possessing "personal magnetism, and traits of character, that gave him wonderful influence over men. Indeed, he seemed to be a born leader of men. He was ever faithful to his friends, and he held them to him as with hooks of steel. . . . As a political leader he was sagacious, aggressive and wonderfully fertile in resources. His followers had implicit faith in his judgment and their devotion to him was never shaken."[13]

Family letters indicate that Speer's father went to Washington alone for the first session of the forty-second Congress. He made his maiden speech in early March 1871, "under the five-minute rule, against taking the duty off coal." He was surprised at the way Congress worked and told his wife she would be "amazed when you see how business is done here—You will, at first, be utterly unable to understand what is being done—the proceedings will be a complete Bable [Babel] to you."[14] She responded that the family missed him. "The little ones are very good," and then she added, "Robbie claimed my letter this evening. Won't you write him one. He asks every time, is it Mr. Robbie Ellies?"[15] Such exchanges convinced him that the separation was not good for the family, and he decided to take them to Washington for the next session.

The House of Representatives must have been a rather open and casual place in those days, for Speer recalled that he and older brother Will often went in and sat on the step in the aisle beside their father, observing him at work. One day they had a dollar and decided to buy a muzzle-loading gun. When they asked their father he consented, likely not clear about the nature of the request. The boys secured a gun, powder, and caps and then "went under the big steps of the Capitol and had a grand time loading and shooting the pistol without bullets. That night at home our mother found the pistol in our pockets and confiscated it. We never recovered it. . . . We often demanded the return of our property but we never saw it again."[16] The family lived in one of the Washington hotels, or on occasion at a boarding house. He remembered that his father took the family to the White House to call on President Ulysses S. Grant and that the president, "a short, solid, brown bearded man," shook hands with him.[17]

Two years after the family returned from Washington, Speer's mother became very sick. After extensive medical treatment she died of "pulmonary complaint" on November 12, 1876.[18] Speer loved his mother dearly but had few recollections of her. However, some of his first letters were to her the summer she went to Philadelphia for special medical care. He asked if she had seen the Centennial exhibit and told her that he had enjoyed himself at a picnic. His father wrote: "If you were not too sick you would laugh heartily to see Rob writing his letter. His hat is down on his eyes—and his face is as long as the moral law. What his thoughts are—who knows?"[19] Two of Speer's strongest memories from his entire childhood were of events that took place at the time of her death. When she was near death, she called him and Will into her room and asked them to "kneel down beside her and promise we would never touch intoxicating drink." Years later he wrote, "It has been no difficulty whatever to me to keep that promise."[20] After she died, he remembered "Father taking all of us five children into the parlor and kneeling down with us around the coffin and praying that He who promised to be a Father to the fatherless would also be a Mother to the motherless."[21] Grief piled on grief when the youngest child, Martha Ellen, her mother's namesake, died the following year of a childhood illness.

He lived with the sadness of his mother's death the rest of his life, but it did not scar him emotionally, largely, it appears, because of the remarkable envelope of love and support with which the entire family surrounded him. What the event did do was to make him very sensitive to the needs of others at times of sickness and death. "My dear John," he wrote close friend John R. Mott when his mother died, "You have had a great privilege in keeping her so long and I suppose must have known that before many years she must go on whither we that afterwards come. None the less, the loss is just as great, and greater because the passing years have knit the bonds and made the treasure richer. . . . may God comfort you and make you strong and give you peace." He added that the meaning of such "great experiences here came to me beginning with my own mother's death thirty three years ago. I have come to feel that they were to be taken as the inevitable pain of preparation of us for the larger life which is the true, and I do not grieve as I did, though I doubt not if my mother had lived until now I would grieve."[22] On occasion, especially in the early years of his work, he would make indirect public references to his mother. In a talk he gave at one of the summer bible conferences at Northfield, Massachusetts, he said: "In the central part of the State of Pennsylvania, on a little green hill that overlooks the valley of the Juniata, there is a grave. I love that spot more than any other spot on earth. There is only a white stone there, with a name on it, looking ever toward the first rays of the rising sun. And underneath the name are these words of John's: 'And the blood of Jesus Christ, His Son, cleanseth us from all sin.' There never was a human grave that less needed such words upon its stone but the words are true words for every life."[23]

The extended Speer and Whittaker families gathered around after his mother died. In particular, Louise Whittaker, called Aunt Lou, became the housekeeper and "mother," and Grandma Whittaker, or "Ma," helped out. The family arrangements resolved the most pressing problems of child care, but the tasks of being the single parent fell fully on his father's shoulders, and he accepted them, focusing most of his attention on his children's religious and educational development. The children, especially the older ones, were already on the road to maturity in these areas, thanks in large measure to patterns both parents had established.

Religious Upbringing

Religion was one thing that was not left to chance. The heritage was well established and, in addition, both Speer's parents had strong personal religious backgrounds and were active in the Presbyterian Church in Huntingdon. His mother had a conversion experience when she was fourteen; "in a quiet spring month, when there was an absence of religious excitement, alone, she entered into a covenant with God. From that hour her course was onward and upward."[24] His father was reticent about personal matters and left no record of a specific conversion experience, but much evidence that he was a convinced Christian. He was at his wife's bedside when she died and later recorded in his diary that his "dear wife fell asleep in Jesus . . . with her hand in mine. O how sad! May God help me to bear this yoke and fit me to meet her in heaven." Several days later he prayed, "O Father, give me grace and wisdom to bear my children in Thy nurture and fear—and help me to teach them to love the memory of their dear mother. Grant that the circle now broken on earth may be reunited in heaven."[25] In particular, he was a man who loved and studied the Bible. His children had an image of him "with the familiar volume in his hands, sitting in the easy chair in the corner by the window looking up the street."[26] A trustee and substantial supporter of the church, he taught a men's Bible class.

The Speers had each of their children baptized, and then enrolled them in an infants class. They had Robert baptized at the Presbyterian Church on November 6, 1869. They took the children to Sunday school and church every Sunday without fail and often attended midweek meetings as well. This was such a familiar part of their family life that Speer remembered years later the architecture and decoration of the church, with its plain front and raised dais at the rear for the choir. The inscription over the pulpit read, "Holiness Becometh Thine House, O Lord, Forever." He recalled that he used to "meditate on this with awe." The family sat in the second pew, and since no one sat in the first one, "we were the front of the congregation and our demeanor was under the eyes of all." The minister during many of these years was A. Nelson Hollifield. Although Speer remembered him well, he was "still more impressed, however, by the elders and trustees who from the low platform below the pulpit, read sermons . . . and conducted the service when we had no minister."[27]

Sunday was a very traditional day in the Speer household, spent as a day of worship and rest, just as it was in other homes and in many small towns where the Christian faith was a major part of the environment. It was Puritan in tone and content. Worship and rest were not so much enforced as they were shared experiences of the entire family, and the larger community for that matter, and therefore received as normal. Speer's parents had always spent the day with the children, and after his mother's death his father continued to keep the day for them. He remembered the Lord's Day as a family day and looked back "with unlimited gratitude to our hours as children with our father on that day, the talks then that were not possible on other days, busy as he was with his law practice and carrying loads that left no margin for recreation during the other days, but who gave himself religiously and conscientiously and with deep fatherly love to make that day a day of the home and the family."[28] "After Sunday dinner," he recalled, "we read or played in the yard, our Father entering in heartily, as time keeper in races." The day "had its own special treats of candy and books and a quiet walk in the evening."[29] It was certainly austere, but with the atmosphere of retreat came the guaranteed presence of his father, and for him that left a lifelong sweetness in his life, like the sweetness of the candy treat. Years later he reflected, "It is open to us all individually to live by the higher kind of ideals, that our fathers held up for us. A great deal of our trouble to-day is that we are relaxing those personal ideals, and that we, ourselves, are letting our own practices down a little to a level below the practices of our fathers."[30]

His parents did not consider church and Sunday school sufficient for the religious education of their children, and his father in particular developed a curriculum in religion. It included family prayers in the morning and the evening and at meals. The children were also expected to say their personal prayers before going to bed. They read the Bible on Sunday afternoons, and eventually completed the entire Bible. They had to memorize portions of it, beginning with special verses and moving on to entire books. By the time Speer left home for preparatory school, he had memorized many selected verses, the Psalms, and was into the book of Genesis. The final portion of this curriculum was the Presbyterian tradition. The children had to memorize, on Sundays, sometimes before worship, "the Infant Catechism, the Shorter Catechism and the Westminster Larger Catechism."[31] It was a rigorous discipline. He recalled that he both loved and hated learning the catechism, and many years later, near the end of his life, said that he had never met "another human being who had memorized the Larger Catechism."[32] The older children went through the entire home course; the younger children had a more relaxed version, but even softened, this was not a curriculum for the faint of heart.

The children began, at fairly early ages, to take some responsibility for their own religious development, even as they continued under their father's tutelage. Speer started to keep a more or less daily diary in 1878, when he was ten, and his entries reveal a growing interest in religion: he began to note the minister's sermon topics and texts. He bought himself a New Testament. On May 5, 1879, he led his first public religious gathering, the Monday evening prayer meeting. He attended a camp meeting that summer. What may have been his first ecumenical experience came on August 21, 1879, when he attended a Baptist ice cream social. Both he and Mig attended Methodist gatherings on occasion. On January 29, 1882, he noted that the Rev. Mr. Hollifield had resigned, and added, "I hope it is accepted." On Sunday, February 11, 1883, he wrote that the morning services were turned over to the Woman's Foreign Missionary Society. This appears to be his first exposure to the field of Christian work that was to become his own lifework. The same spring he gave evidence that the strict Sunday observance was a very conscious part of his life when he wrote on a Sunday, "Didn't dare read M.C. [*The Count of Monte Cristo*] today."[33]

He used his diary to keep track of a remarkable variety of religious and other events, and for that reason it becomes all the more important for something not found in it. It offers no hint of a significant religious experience, of what in that day, replete with camp meetings and revivals, was called a conversion experience. Indeed, he not only failed to mention such an experience, but he also did not mention church membership. The issue is not that everyone had to have a conversion experience or belong to the church, but that, given the obvious intensity of his own religious education and experience, it is strange that he left home for preparatory school in 1883 without either. Nothing in other family records explains these things. When he later decided to become a missionary, members of the family received the news as if it were a conversion experience, suggesting they were aware that he had left home without one. The final word on his religious development was that he grew in faith in the context of his home, under the guidance of his father.

All this religious training involved education, but it was considered then as now to be quite different from formal education in the academic sense. The Speers and later Aunt Lou made sure that the children had a full measure of academic experiences. The family, as part of the economic elite in Huntingdon, could afford the best education money could buy. In the years immediately after the Civil War the public education system was in transition. The Speers and most of their friends considered it inadequate and supported a variety of private schools. The Speer children all began their education in the private setting, where the parents paid the teachers and all the children from the same social group studied together. When public education began to move forward in the 1870s, the Speers became involved in the effort to lift the general level of education. They took a leadership role in the development of new academic programs and the erection of a new school building, and by the end of the decade all their children were in the public setting.

Speer and sister Mary began in "Aunt Mime's" school. She was their great-aunt Jemima Whittaker, one of their maternal grandmother's sisters, and she had a school for four- and five-year-olds in the old brick Academy building. He went from there to another school and then to the Huntingdon Academy in the new Academy building. He began at the academy in the fall of 1875, and surviving receipts indicate his father paid between $3.40 and $4.00 a term for four terms that year and the next. [34]

Once he moved to the public system, he began using his diary to track his educational experiences. He recorded that his classes during his first year or so in the public system included reading, spelling, and geography, although he doubtless studied many other subjects. The curriculum in the high school, definitely more varied and complex, included history, rhetoric, English and American literature, Latin, Greek, philosophy, music, bookkeeping, and mathematics, both algebra and geometry. [35] This was largely a classical education with a focus on preparation for a profession or college, and although it was public and open to everyone, typically only the children of the elite stayed on to graduate. He admired his teachers, especially Rachel Miller and Porter McHugh, and credited Miller with "much of my fondness for history and knowledge of it." [36]

He was in general an excellent student. His capacity for memory, honed in his father's religious program, was very useful to him in some subjects, especially history and literature. Tested in April 1883 on extracts of all the American authors, he recorded: "I knew all he asked me." [37] But his memory did not serve him as well in two other areas: Latin, where he clearly struggled, and the declamations. The declamation was the public performance of a poem or reading. Mary had a talent for these presentations and could do them with a dramatic flair. He approached them with apprehension and found them a "great cross." He remembered that he "tried Lincoln's Gettysburg Address and Whittier's John Brown of Osawatomie and others but it was a long time before I could get through a speech without breaking down completely."[38] This was the boy who as a man amazed audiences with his ability to speak for an hour or more about missions, citing statistics and reciting Bible passages, and all without a note.

His formal public schooling came to an end the summer he was fifteen. He graduated second in a class of five on June 7, 1883. The large crowd that gathered on the occasion heard him give the salutatory oration, which he titled "Tottering Thrones." He offered his audience a stinging critique of political despotism, from the ancient to the modern world, and a ringing affirmation of the American way. "Here we dwell in peace," he said. "Here no throne a despot. Here no tyrant to demand all our efforts to keep him from falling. Here we rule ourselves. . . . Our throne rests all over our country. On our throne sits the people."[39]

The Speer family encouraged or permitted the children to become involved in a variety of other learning activities. Robert learned some of his dance skills from his Aunt Clara, his mother's youngest sister, who was only seven years older than he was. She was one of the favorite people of his childhood and remained one of his strongest ties to home throughout his life. The Literary Society, which may have been based at the school but does not appear to have been part of the curriculum, sponsored debates on important topics, and Robert worked hard on them. In November 1882 the timely topic, given the recent passage of a law restricting immigration, was "Resolved, That Foreign Immigration Should Be Prohibited." He lost that one, but in January 1883 he debated "the whole crowd and won" on the topic "Resolved, That a Man Should Not Obey a Law Which His Conscience Says Is Wrong."[40] Town spelling bees were also part of the culture. He remembered one where the word "ornithorhynchus" proved too much for the competitors.[41]

Last but not least among these often informal learning experiences was the most informal and perhaps the most significant of all, his father's "law school." His father maintained a substantial library of law books, and as his reputation grew he began to attract an increasing number of young men who read law with him. Robert and brother Will read some of their father's books and spent time in discussion with the law students. The boys, strongly influenced by these experiences and their father's example, decided sometime before they left home for further schooling to become lawyers. Will attended the Hill School in Pottstown, Pennsylvania, and then Yale University, where he did some study of the law. He finished his legal education at the Albany Law School and was admitted to the New York bar in 1887. Robert was intending to study law when he felt called to the ministry, and the vocational crisis of his life involved turning away from the law.[42]

The Speers made certain their children learned their religious tradition and received an adequate education, but they also offered them freedom and space to grow with their peers. They carefully encouraged the development of what had already become a classic American trait: self-reliance. For the boys in the family, at least, this meant endless opportunities to live on and explore the land, alone and with their friends.

Life in Huntingdon

Huntingdon in the days after the Civil War was an ideal place to discover America, because almost all the major features of the nation's past and present met there. It was hardly unique in this respect, but not many towns large or small had what it could offer to those who were growing up. Located on the Juniata River in a scenic and well-forested mountain-and-valley section of the state, it was surrounded by open land teeming with wildlife and streams alive with fish. The town evolved from a frontier fort, Fort Standing Stone, used to protect early settlers from the French and Native Americans.* The fort had been built on an Oneida Indian camp that the white settlers had called Standing Stone, because of a tall petroglyph that the Native Americans had erected in the center of their camp. Huntingdon was the county seat, which meant that the legal life of the surrounding area came to a focus there. The main branch of the Pennsylvania Canal and the main line of the newly completed Pennsylvania Railroad ran through town, making it the economic center of the region. Goods and travelers moving between Philadelphia and Pittsburgh came through town, making it part of the vital national connection between east and west. Moreover, the very layout of the town, on a relatively narrow strip of land along the river, with the river and canal on the south and the nearby hills on the north, meant that virtually every resident was within a few minutes walk of the countryside. Speer grew up to

*Terms used for various racial groups reflect modern usage except where they appear in quotations or in titles.

appreciate every one of these aspects of his town and nation, from its Native American roots to its bustling business life, but most of all he fell in love with the land.

The land was at first his playground. "Boys in Huntingdon in my generation lived out of doors," he recalled, and "played anywhere—in the broad street beside our house, in the fields near town, on the hills."[43] The town was well established by the 1870s, but it was not all that distinct from the countryside. There were many open spaces not yet built up. The streets were unpaved, which meant six inches of mud or slush in the winter and three inches of dust in the summer. Play was informal, pretty much left to the creative energies of the children. Speer and his friends used the streets in the evenings for games, including "baseball, sock-ball, old cat, or 'deer,' a game of hunter and hunted whose acreage covered all our corner of the town."[44] Just down the street lay the canal and beyond it the river and the swimming holes. And not far beyond that lay the open country, some of it divided into farms owned by his father and his uncles, but much of it woods.

He learned early to fish and hunt and spent much of his free time outdoors, limited of course during the school year to Friday evenings and Saturdays. One bass-fishing companion was his uncle, Arthur McMurtrie, who must have found his young nephew something of a prodigy. Speer would walk slightly ahead and would "write on the air with my finger." When his uncle asked for an explanation of this behavior, he replied that he was trying to "rearrange statements so as to make the number of syllables a multiple of five, having noted that this gave the speech a special cadence and rhythmical vigor."[45] His typical fishing partners were his peers, especially Warren Simpson, and they went for trout or whatever else they could catch out of the river and streams. When they went overnight, as they did when they went to the Raystown Branch of the Juniata, they would camp out or, if it was fall, stay in someone's barn. He continued to fish, especially on summer vacations, for many, many years.

Two memorable experiences of his boyhood involved successful hunting trips. He hunted with Warren, Will Graffius, or Jed Cree, who was the best shot in the group. One Christmas, when he was about twelve, Speer's father gave him a 10-gauge double-barreled shotgun. He and Warren often hunted for squirrels or ducks or turkeys. He would leave his house about dawn and get Warren, who had tied a string to his toe and dropped the other end out his window so that Robert could pull it and waken him. One particular morning when he was thirteen, they got out very early and made their way to the top of Stone Creek ridge. The sun was not up yet when they came across a flock of turkeys on the road and scared them, scattering them into the surrounding woods. He had a turkey caller made from a turkey wing bone. He and Warren lay down at a fence corner, and he used the caller; a big, fat bird responded. "My heart nearly stood still as I heard it answering and then heard it coming through the fallen leaves. My father had jokingly questioned my ability to get a wild turkey and I remember my triumph and his satisfaction when I got home and marched into the office where some Philadelphia client was with him and dumped the big turkey down on he floor between them. The visitor had never seen a wild turkey before."[46]

His other great hunting success came early in the winter of 1881. A client of his father named Hiram Ross, who lived some distance from town, was a hunter and sawmill operator. In town to settle some legal question, he stayed over for Thanksgiving and took young Speer back home with him to hunt. It was very wild and difficult country. Some of Speer's friends came up later, and together they saw only one deer, a spike buck. Speer shot it as it ran past his stand. It was his only success as a deer hunter. The visit with Hiram Ross left a remarkable impression on him, and the visit, not the deer kill, became the subject of one of the most telling stories he wrote in his college career (see chapter 2).

The more he walked the land, hunting or fishing or just tramping, the more it became part of him. What he called "tramps" in the summers of 1883 and 1884 sealed his love for it. Only two weeks after he graduated from high school, he was off on the great adventure of his youth, a tramp from home to Gettysburg and back. He was joined by two close friends, Don Petriken and John Cremer. It is not certain when they devised the plan for this 200-mile hike, but shortly after school was out they began to earn money for it by picking strawberries on the Cremer farm and selling them in town. Speer earned $7 in silver, which was his share of the income from the 175 quarts of berries he picked. Although his father was not particularly in favor of the trip, he gave him $10 to help with expenses. The boys left on June 25, at least one skeptic predicting they would return before nightfall. They walked through Mapleton, Mt. Union, and Shirleysburg and made it to Orbisonia by the first night. He sent postcards home almost every day, describing the very wet conditions and the various stops.

On July 1 they reached Gettysburg, and stayed for a couple of days, on what was the twentieth anniversary of the great battle. He recorded no special ceremony and noted only that they visited the cemetery and found it beautiful. Many years later he described that visit: "The Government had not yet acquired it; there was scarcely a battle monument set; there was the field just as it had been left—barring what the husbandmen had done to it when the last gun had grown silent when the battle was gone; but the two boys who were with me and I walked up and down those hills feeling that we were on holy ground, and knowing that we stood amid great memories and impulses and ideals that we could not find on common soil."[47] Inspired and refreshed by the rest, they returned home by way of Chambersburg, Ft. Littleton, and Saxton, arriving on July 7. He marched into his father's office "brown and dirty," proud of his achievement.[48]

The trip the next summer was longer but somewhat anticlimatic and bittersweet, since only he and John were able to go, because their friend and his "closest companion," Don, was too ill with "consumption." The plan was to walk north to Sunbury and then to Danville and Eagles Mere and return by way of Williamsport and Bellefonte and Tyrone. On the North Branch of the Susquehanna River they walked part way on the old canal towpath. They found Eagles Mere, soon to become a well-known resort, "an undeveloped wilderness," and Williamsport "still a great lumber center," but the trip was not the same without Don.[49]

The tramps were maturing times, full of hard walking and good discussion. Speer remained a great walker throughout his life, with remarkable endurance even into his final years. But the most important thing about the tramps was that they made him one with the land, particularly that of his home state. He developed a mystical relationship to it. "There is something," he said, "in the state of Pennsylvania that makes her children love her with a peculiar love. . . . the sweet fields and the swelling hills of Paradise can scarce be dearer."[50] In a short story that contains many autobiographical overtones he wrote:

> About two hundred miles due west from the Delaware, and just south of the mountains of the Bald Eagle and the Warrior, which the Oneidas loved, is the center of my world. The wild goose knows it, for in his northern flight he lifts his course nearly beyond my vision, as though he shrunk from recalling to other themes a heart so filled with the memories of that spot. Perhaps his flight is high only to clear the mountain tops, for the Kishacoquillas and Seven Mountains, like peaceful brothers slumbering together, reach up into the clouds and stretch out to the north and west till they are lost in the embracing arms of the Alleghenies. . . . The little stream rising from the spring creeps off through the tangled laurels, steals warily through the darkness and solitude of the meadows, turns at last the base of an impeding ridge, and goes gaily roaring down the valley of the Standing Stone. . . . The sparkling course of the Creek of the Standing Stone is woven like a silver thread in the fibre of my life.[51]

Although he never lost his profound attachment to his native state, he later developed similar deep feelings about Northfield, Massachusetts; his

home in Englewood, New Jersey; the land around the family vacation center at Camp Diamond in northern New Hampshire; and the few acres
which constituted the family retirement home of Rockledge in Lakeville,
Connecticut.

Phillips Academy

In less than three months in his fifteenth summer his life changed greatly,
as he graduated from high school, tramped to Gettysburg, and then left
home for further schooling. His leaving was carefully planned. Will had
gone off to preparatory school and to college, and now it was Robert's
turn. In the spring he had gathered various school catalogs, including
those of Phillips Academy at Andover, Exeter, and Williston. The choice
fell to Phillips, and on September 3 he and his father left Huntingdon on
the day express for Philadelphia and then went on to Boston and Andover,
arriving on the morning of September 5.

In one sense the separation marked an important new stage of his life.
He was in a different and more demanding academic environment. He
was also off on his own, far from his people and his land. Moreover, he
was now almost entirely in the company of the social and academic elite,
and in the context of culture beyond anything available in a rustic river
town. But in a larger sense, the experiences at Andover and later Princeton,
with the one exception of his call to a missionary vocation, were more continuity than change. First, the academic transition, despite problems with
Latin, was not as significant as might have been expected, and his high
school and home preparation measured up to all his challenges. Second,
he began a regular and in-depth correspondence with his father and
others at home that constituted a continuing dialogue with them. Third,
he returned home for vacations, including the long summer ones, sustaining his home as his major point of reference. Fourth, the experiences
of his early years had been thoroughly democratic, despite private school
and some differences between "main streeters" and "back streeters." Raised
to treat people equally and to seek to meet every person on "common
ground," he did not change just because he was in a richer cultural and
more elite social context.[52] Preparatory school and college were primarily
extensions of his social and academic education in different settings, and
were not in themselves the major turning points of his life.

Phillips Academy, often called Andover, was one of the first-rate preparatory schools in the nation. Located adjacent to Andover Theological

Seminary, it benefited from the presence of graduate faculty and students. Moreover, the seminary was then in the midst of a great theological debate, and the excitement of intellectual confrontation overflowed into the academy. Seminary faculty preached Sundays in the chapel, "sermons over our heads." The only thing he could remember about chapel years later was that he had "listened reverently."[53] The academy had a three-year program—junior, middler, and senior—and divided each year into three terms, the first beginning in early September and the last ending in late June. The curriculum was strictly college preparatory. He took English, mathematics, history, and several languages, including Greek, Latin, and French. He was from the outset extremely concerned for his grades and class standing.

The second day he was on campus he took placement examinations in algebra, Greek, and Latin and to his dismay and frustration failed the Latin one. The professor placed him in the review section, and that led to a minicrisis. The version he told his father was relatively low-keyed and probably did not cause much concern. He wrote that he was "not nearly as good" in Latin, and, moreover, they "do not use the same text books here that we did in Huntingdon, nor do they translate the same. . . . I am studying as hard as I can but I don't know whether I can get along or not in Latin." The very day he sent this message to his father, he sent a much more alarming one to Will, then at Yale. If held back because of Latin, he would probably "ask papa to let me stop Latin and take something of more use and let me go here but one year," and then maybe go home to study, "and then either study for a lawyer or do something else, whatever he wants me to. . . . I don't think college does you much good any how." The problem, he told Will, was that being dropped in Latin meant an entire extra year at the academy, and he did not want to wait that long to get on with his life. "Please," he appealed to his brother, "answer right away."[54] He wrote these letters on a Sunday, his first at Phillips. He spent much of the day at church and said that it "did me more good than any other thing."[55] He acknowledged, to himself at least, that he was also a little homesick.

Within two weeks his academic life took a decided turn for the better. Latin was less fearsome than at initial prospect. As for other classes, he found them "not as hard as at first." He had occasional setbacks in his years at the academy, like the Greek exam in his second year when the teacher "asked me just what I didn't know," but typically he did outstanding work.[56] His first grade report, dated December 21, 1883, showed that he was twenty-third in a class of fifty-six in Latin, but first in a class of fifty-eight in history. History became his favorite subject and he was never anything but first in that class, scoring grades of 100 in two terms. By the time he left Phillips, he had also earned first place in mathematics once and in French three times and was near the top of his class in every subject. In his final report, given June 23, 1885, he was first in history and French, fourth in Greek, and a most satisfying fourth in Latin.[57] He gradually developed something of a philosophy of academic achievement. He worked and studied to be first in everything, but as he told his father, not for its own sake: "It is merely a matter of standing, which of itself, I think, is a most useless and undesirable thing unless it is coupled with other qualities. Many boys in our class do nothing but study hard and ceaselessly. They are digging their own graves. Others study hard and well to maintain a good standing but devote much of their time to the development of qualities of much more advantage to their possessor than a stand of one or two in his class. I prefer to be of the latter class."[58]

Religion was one of the qualities he nurtured. He continued his regular routine of church and Sunday school and joined the prayer meeting, which met twice a week. He led it on occasion, as he also did the Society of Inquiry, which met to discuss religious subjects. He heard a great variety of preachers but told his father that he found them not very good, inferior in general to those he had heard at home. Arriving at Phillips without a specific conversion experience or church membership, he was not moved to either during his stay. He also did not become alive to any particular theology, despite the debates raging around him. His spiritual life grew in straight-line continuity with his past. Only one comment from the many diary entries and letters hints at what may have been a new insight, and that is when he told his father, "Someone preached Christianity and not *about* Christianity as most of the Andover preachers do."[59]

Although he studied hard, he also quickly took advantage of many opportunities for informal learning. He joined the debating society, the Philomatheon, and participated in debates on a regular basis. In the spring of his second year he won a very close election, 48–46, for the leadership of this society, and informed his father, "It was the first time in the history of the society that a middler has been made president."[60] He entered the competition for the Draper Prize, a public speaking contest, but he was not the winner on either of his two tries. In his first year he became an editor of the *Phillipian*, the school magazine. On at least one occasion he asked his father to critique an article and commented, "The reason I write is to attain perfection."[61] Near the end of his second year he declined the chief-editorship on the grounds that he was too involved in other things.

His class elected him president for the third term of his first year. He also joined a fraternity, although he did not appreciate the "principle of secret societies."[62]

These activities, what in subsequent years would be called extracurricular, were varied but still quite similar to the kinds of things he had done in high school, only now on a larger scale. The new experience was that his peers were much more numerous and turned to him for leadership in virtually every activity in which he became involved. He was aware, of course, that he had quickly attracted a great deal of attention, but he did not seem affected by it. And he was willing, in the case of the editorship, to decline an honor.

The second day on campus he discovered something that was not part of his Huntingdon experience: football. His high school had little in the way of organized sports, but Phillips had not one but two "elevens," as well as a number of other athletic programs. He approached football slowly, aware that he was a novice, so he practiced but did not try out for either of the teams. He was growing physically, reaching five feet, eleven inches and 150 pounds that October. He began regular workouts at the gym, focusing on increasing his arm strength. He also began to play tennis. He tried out for the football team in the fall of his second year and won a place on the second eleven. They played the Harvard juniors and lost but unexpectedly defeated chief rival Exeter 11–8. The occasion brought on an outburst of school spirit that startled him as students "hugged and almost kissed each other."[63]

He enjoyed being on his own, although he struggled with a recurring sense of loneliness. He counted on and received frequent letters from home. It was no small thing when postage for an ordinary letter increased 100 percent in October 1883, from one cent to two cents. He began to keep an account book, with his father as the main source of his income. He spent $641 his first year against an income of $645. Second year expenses rose to $784. His father willingly paid the bills, but he also kept track of them. In his will the elder Speer directed his coexecutors, Will and Robert, to deduct their educational expenses from their shares of the estate, but to make no such charges against the accounts of the other children.[64] Speer kept precise financial records, a practice he continued the rest of his life, and although he was very careful with his money, he did not purposely go without needed items. He purchased his own clothes and school supplies and took care of his room and board. He also learned to do some clothing repairs, like darning stockings, but found that to be "a mean business."[65]

He had occasionally revealed a playful wit at home—like bringing the newly killed turkey into his father's office during business hours—and that part of his character now emerged more strongly. He wrote that he regretted he could not be present, "on account of circumstances over which I have no control," at the inauguration of President Grover Cleveland in the spring of 1885 and assumed that the event went off "all right without me."[66] Music was not one of his gifts. When an orchestra formed he resisted his impulse to join yet another organization, noting that "my musical talents are restricted to 'jews-harp,' 'kazoos,' 'bones,' fish horn and dinner bell."[67]

Sometime in his second year he began to consider how he might cut short his stay and move on to college, and Princeton was the only college he considered seriously. As deeply involved as he was in the life of Phillips, he was almost finished with his college entrance requirements. At the beginning of the year he had purposely chosen French over German because he would need French at Princeton. At the start of the third term in April 1885, he calculated that all he needed for college entrance was the metric system, which he had studied on his own, and Homer, which he could work on over the coming summer. All that remained was successful completion of the Princeton examinations and a letter of recommendation from Phillips. He sat for the tests at the end of June. They took him twelve hours over two days and marked a weary end to what had been a busy term. Principal Bancroft wrote a formal recommendation to President James McCosh of Princeton, certifying that Speer was leaving early in good standing and commending him as "a young man of excellent ability, high scholarship, and unblemished moral character." In a much more informal and personal vein, Bancroft told Speer that he could go "if you will send us two boys of the same sort to take your place!" He encouraged him to work for academic honors, which he was certain he could achieve.[68] Speer reflected on "the many pleasant and profitable days" that he had spent there, and added, "It will be with expectation and with thankful remembrance that I shall leave these 'hallowed halls, to memory dear.' "[69]

The Princeton Years

The Princeton years flashed by. He arrived in mid-September 1885 and immediately felt at home. Four other Phillips students were on campus, and he quickly made new friends. He met President McCosh the first week and described him as a "typical Scotchman—white beard and hair, stooping, intellectual."[70] He made the move to college without skipping a beat in academics or athletics, and he stepped up the tempo in extracurricular involvement. The uncertainty and lack of confidence that sometimes came over him at Phillips disappeared, and in its place came a self-assurance and purposefulness.

Academic work came first, and he quickly set a very high standard. Midway through the first term he stood in the first division, which included the twenty best students. His father responded to this initial success with a tribute to the virtues of college and told his son, "If I were now starting in life, I would prefer a liberal education to all the moneyed wealth of the earth. . . . Stand well in your classes—but also stand well *out of* them. Learn what is *in books,* but neglect not what is in the *world,* outside of books."[71] By the end of the semester he remained in the first division but was in the second group in two subjects, Latin and geometry. He ranked in the top four, but not first, in a class of eighty-eight.

That was the upper academic atmosphere, but his father was not altogether pleased. "You must put yourself down to earnest work," he wrote. "I fear that your thoughts are too much after light affairs and young folk's gossip. This is your period for stern study, and you should take off your coat, roll up sleeves (metaphorically) and cleave the *books.* The shotgun is not as deadly as the rifle. You must *concentrate,* remembering that there will be ample time *hereafter* for looking after other things than your books. You should stand at the head of your class, but whether you do or not, you should *thoroughly* understand what you are about, and lay deep and upon solid rock, the basis for your future. Take a *bull dog* grip of things, and go to the bottom of problems that confront you. Go forward and look *upward.*"[72] His father continued to apply pressure. "How are you prospering?" he asked in February. "Is the circle of your thoughts growing larger? Is your mental horizon extending? Are you passing from *milk* to *meat* as an intellectual diet?"[73] At the end of the first year his father advised him to reflect: "Are you as rich in intellectual food as you ought to be? Are you as strong in mental and *self* discipline as you might be? Do you know the ground over which you have come—as a careful traveler remembers every stone and tree, and brook along the path of his first journey?"[74]

He had always been a very good student, with a strong inner desire to achieve excellence. With his father urging him on, he took the two steps higher he could take. At the end of his freshman year he was in the first group in all subjects, and by midsemester of the following year he was also first in his class. "No one ahead of me," he wrote, "all behind. May I preserve that stand for Papa."[75] And he did. He never fell out of the first group in any subject, and he continued to lead his class, sharing the lead with Lewis S. Mudge on one occasion. In his junior year he received the Junior First Honor Prize and the $150 award that went with it. He won over close friend Mudge by .3 percent. He deposited the money in the bank with great satisfaction, noting in his diary on October 23, 1888, "That is my own."

The pressure to maintain the top position occasionally troubled him. During his sophomore year he felt, "If it were not for my desire to please Papa by high stand, I should enjoy my course much more," and in his senior year the need to maintain excellence in his course work distracted him at times from his various commitments to religious work.[76] Nevertheless, he was very pleased when honors came his way, and they came in large number his senior year. Specifically, he earned the right to give the valedictory oration at commencement. Much of the rest of his life, persistent rumors circulated that he and Aaron Burr had graduated with the highest honors in Princeton history. The secretary of Princeton in 1933, V. Lansing Collins, tried to pin down the truth. He found that Burr, class of 1772, graduated with no honors at all and that Speer graduated "magna cum laude, along with Lewis S. Mudge and Fred Neher." Speer had the highest grade, but, Lansing noted, the Latin salutatory usually went to the person considered the best student.[77] What Lansing did not find in the official record was that in the spring of his senior year Speer had been invited to choose between the valedictory and the Latin salutatory and chose the former, very likely with some sense of the irony of being free to accept or reject the honor named for his greatest academic challenge.[78] Whether or not the equal of Burr in intellectual capacity, Speer was the best student in his class.

Course work involved lectures, recitations, essays, and examinations. He attended classes regularly, but Princeton permitted a generous number of absences, and he took them, thirty-five the spring semester of his junior year, for example. His last two years, when he became an active spokesperson for missions, he often missed classes and would catch up by copying classmates' notes. The essays he wrote ranged over a wide variety of subjects, but most fell into the general areas of history, government, and literature. They included such titles as "Charles Sumner," "The Norman French," "Gettysburg," "The Federative Union of Capital and Labor," "The National Antipathy to the Negro," and "The National Morality."[79] In addition, he wrote short stories, speeches, debates, and newspaper articles. Little in his academic work predicted his later interest in religion.

Excellent in all areas, he sometimes reached beyond excellence in exams. It was quite common for him to score 100 on an examination, and sometimes even more. His senior year he wrote a long exam for McCosh, who was teaching metaphysics. McCosh summoned Speer to his home, asked him to read his examination to him, and posed some further questions. He then said, "Mr. Speer I will give you 103 percent on this examination and if you will stay I will make you a professor in the college."[80] Speer passed this off, considering that McCosh had a reputation for singling out the best student in each class for special attention, but he took quite seriously the invitation from Professor Alexander Johnston, proffered in late May of his senior year, to hold the political science fellowship the following year. He greatly respected Johnston but declined, because other projects were beginning to shape his future. He admired W. W. Sloane in history because he was more interested in "the philosophy of history than the facts."

He took his father's advice to stand well outside of class too. He had achieved such a combination of curricular and extracurricular success at Phillips, but that had not included being first in his class. Princeton was a more intense academic environment and required a substantial time commitment to achieve and maintain academic leadership, which made his extracurricular accomplishments stretch the boundaries of the imagination. He was in college one month when his classmates elected him freshman class president at a meeting he did not even know about. More typically, fellow students approached him, or he actively sought an office, and he held a very large number in his college career. They included, among others, membership on the lecture committee, president of the conference committee, secretary of the New England School Association, class day usher in 1886 and 1888 and grand usher at commencement and inauguration in 1888, sergeant at arms and president of Clio Hall, president of the Philadelphian Society (later the Intercollegiate Young Men's Christian Association [YMCA]), vice-president of the state committee of the YMCA, managing editor of the *Princetonian*, member of the Anti-Liquor League council, and participant in the dramatic association. He also played football throughout his college years and joined in a large number of debates and oratorical contests. The list could have been even longer, but he declined to be freshman editor of the *Princetonian*, class orator his freshman year, president of the YMCA, and captain of the football team his senior year.[81] Quite obviously his peers recognized his leadership abilities and chose him to be their leader at every turn and in every kind of activity.

He continued his football career at Princeton by joining the freshman team. He now stood somewhat over six feet tall and was strong and sturdy.

The coaches played him on the line, moving him about and finally settling on left end "rush." He was a varsity substitute his sophomore year and won his letter. A regular his junior year, he thoroughly enjoyed athletic activity and competition, but he did not always enjoy football. He filled his diaries with game scores—some of them remarkable, like those from his junior year when Princeton beat Lafayette 47–0, Lehigh 80–0, and Penn 95–0 in the championship game—and with some sharp criticisms of the game. In the fall of 1887 he grew tired of it and prayed, "May the Father help me to refuse absolutely to have anything more to do with it." Two weeks later he wrote, "Am longing for football to be over. It will be good for the American colleges when public sentiment crushes football."[82] He never really clarified his concerns, except for the amount of time football took away from his work. Most of the criticisms came after his conversion experience, when he coveted every free minute for religious activities. The negative feelings did not last, for later in life he occasionally used images from football to make a point, especially about teamwork.

A strong and effective player himself, Senator George Wharton Pepper recalled that once in a game against Princeton he picked up a fumble only to be picked up by Speer and another player, who then "tried to carry him around opposite sides of a goal post." Pepper spent several weeks in a plaster cast and added that if Speer "used the same treatment on the heathens there would have been fewer converts to Presbyterianism."[83] In a game with Penn, an unnamed player took a series of cheap shots at Speer. He finally complained to the referee, who in turn did nothing. As he later recalled, "Several scrimmages later the Penn player again resorted to his unsportsmanlike conduct and when we rose up from the scrimmage I squared off and let him have it flush on the jaw in the sight of all the players and spectators. I was immediately ordered off the field but I went off clothed with a sense of righteous indignation."[84] Creative in his studies, he also helped create a new football play, then called "boxing the tackle." In a game with Yale, he and his tackle joined to form a box around Yale's tackle and took him out of the play. The referee ruled the play illegal, but it survived to become an important part of the game.[85]

Debates were also a significant part of his college experience, and he used them quite consciously to train his voice and develop the techniques that would make him a strong public speaker. He worked on the skills beginning in high school, then doubtless because he thought they would be useful to him as a lawyer, but he intensified his efforts once he decided to become a missionary. Classmates chose him, the only freshman so honored, to participate in one of the major debates, "Ought the 15th

Amendment to have been adopted." The Fifteenth Amendment, ratified in 1870, gave citizens the right to vote regardless "of race, color, or previous condition of servitude." He won second prize, the first time in the history of that debate that a freshman had won any prize. His father welcomed the news of the success and invited him to bring the debate home for further discussion. Ever full of advice, his father added, "Exercises of this character are very useful, and you should use and improve every opportunity of the kind that comes across your path. You should *seek* occasions for extempore discussion, but not to the neglect of that severe mental discipline afforded by thorough and exhaustive written debate. You are now laying the foundation for future building, and you should lay it *so deep* that it will safely bear the needed structures of your after life. *Chew* your thoughts as you do your food, and make them a part of yourself." Speer responded that the debate was not a written one and that the aim of Princeton was "to enable one to speak from notes or without them, with the same facility and effect as from written manuscript."[86] He became something of an expert in the Princeton way and later published an often-reprinted pamphlet suitably titled *How to Speak Effectively Without Notes.*[87]

The Washington's Birthday debate his sophomore year was a painful but instructive blow to his ego. To be fully prepared for the topic, "Worker classes have grievances sufficient to warrant forming a distinct Labor Party," he went to New York City, armed with a letter of introduction from brother Will, and met and talked with Henry George, the economic and political reformer. George had just waged and lost an exciting and highly publicized mayoral campaign on the single-tax platform. He gave his young Princeton visitor a copy of his *Progress and Poverty* and plenty of ideas and useful arguments. Recounting the sad tale of his defeat, Speer wrote, "I laid out enough ground in my argument to require two hours to cover and as we had some twelve minutes each I got nowhere but I learned a lesson, which has stood me in good stead ever since." The lesson was to make his arguments "clean cut and sharp."[88] Friends tried to console him by telling him he had "brains enough for six ordinary men. That was probably the mildest way to say I did not know how to use what I had."[89] He regularly practiced his voice, working to make it stronger and fuller. After the lost debate he sought out a faculty member for advice about his voice and techniques. The professor suggested that his voice was strong enough but had a nasal twang that could be corrected with some vocal exercises, and also offered some true consolation over the defeat when he said his "bearing, gestures and manner. . . were much the best of all on Washington's Birthday."[90] His senior year was an oratorical triumph, as he won both the Baird Oration and the coveted Lynd Debate, and gave the valedictory address. When he received word of his final debate success, he gave thanks to God, but he had been training and preparing for it throughout his college years.[91]

His accomplishments in academic and extracurricular life were prodigious, but they were far from the whole story. The truly major event of his college years came in the spring of 1887: his religious conversion. Part of his call, it became the turning point in his life, directing him toward missionary work and away from a legal or educational career. It marked a new beginning for him and became so consuming that it overshadowed the rest of his college experience. He continued to be involved in competitive sports but gradually lost any real interest in them. He never became a disciple, in the intellectual sense, of any of his professors, and he rarely mentioned his academic experience at Princeton later in life. Instead, he became a student of his religious mentors, none of whom were at Princeton—people like Arthur T. Pierson, Henry Clay Trumbull, and Dwight L. Moody. He began to focus his remarkable intelligence like a laser beam on one goal and directed all his energies and resources toward it.

Little information has surfaced about how he related to his classmates outside of the considerable number of them who became his partners in Christian work after his conversion. They were typically very supportive of him. A satirical article in the *Nassau Herald* in 1889 portrayed him as the faculty favorite, very conservative socially, with a tendency to write long homilies in various Princeton publications. This may have been written in good fun, but the writing had a hard edge, suggesting that not every classmate joined in praising his many accomplishments.[92]

It is reasonable to inquire how he put all the pieces of his young life together to create one whole, how he managed to cram into his college years so many different activities, most of them in leadership roles. One key was a work ethic—his version of the Protestant work ethic—that he adopted early in life, very likely in high school and doubtless under the guidance of his father. By the time he reached Princeton, he believed, "Systematic work lessens the labor of study a great deal, so that I can accomplish much more than a good many. Regularity and application are necessary to complete the ideal student."[93] Time was precious, and he worried about wasting it. He filled his diaries with notes about activities that were unworthy of the time they took, including football and visits with young ladies. He seems to have had at least one girlfriend at home, Fannie Blandy, and others while in college, but they were more acquaintances than serious loves. The February of his sophomore year he escorted a girl home and noted that he "could fall in love with her without much difficulty." Two days later he walked Miss Townsend home and "sat before fire light and talked all evening." The very next day he found it difficult to "work after play. I must stop it. Or must I? Is not this the pleasure time? Harvests must come, but will they be poor without present restraint and monasticism of application?"[94] His conversion experience several months later put an abrupt end to walks home with girls, and he had few if any such relationships until he met the woman who would become his wife.

The other key to his success was the tranquillity Phillips and Princeton provided. The United States in those years was at relative political and economic peace, despite the Haymarket Riot in May 1886, and was involved in no international incidents. He cast his first vote for Cleveland in the presidential election of 1888, but national politics did not intrude on college life. Indeed, the outside world came only when invited, and then largely in the form of visiting lecturers and as grist for the debate mill. Theodore Roosevelt appeared on the lecture platform in January 1886, speaking on "Hunting in the West." Speer gave him "fair" marks.[95] In March 1888, Anthony Comstock lectured on the prevention of vice and "won many over."[96] The firestorms of economic depression and political unrest that hit the nation in the 1890s were not even on the horizon. Nor did the theological seminary next door seem to create much stir. As conservative as Andover had been liberal, the Princeton seminary offered chapel speakers but little controversy. There were about two hundred students at the seminary, but he told his father he had "not seen half a dozen to recognize them as embryo ministers. At Andover if you saw a theologue you knew what it was immediately."[97]

His last public word at Princeton came on June 19, 1889, at commencement. He had worked on his valedictory speech for more than a month, initially calling it "The Gospel of Liberalism" and then changing it to "The Liberalistic Temper." At first, no one planned to come from Huntingdon, not even his father, and Robert wrote tongue in cheek that he was "glad that no one is to be here to whom I should be obliged to devote myself."[98] Prospects for visitors dimmed when the great flood of 1889 hit the central part of Pennsylvania in early June. Remembered for the terror and death it caused in Johnstown and therefore often called the Johnstown flood, it did much damage along the Juniata River and destroyed the great log boom in Williamsport on the Susquehanna River. Nonetheless, he wrote the week before the festivities and encouraged his father to come, and he did.

Life in its true form, Speer told his commencement listeners, was organic. In the environment in general, all aspects of life were bound together. Princeton was a microcosm of that unity, and on this special occasion his classmates could perhaps see how "each life of us bears the impress of every other life, and the union of such influences is indissoluble forever." This important truth needed to be restated because their age had come to accept a liberalism of both mind and spirit. Their world shared in a mental awakening, characterized by many scientific discoveries, and in a tremendous increase in wealth and the enjoyment of pleasure. People claimed that in order to embrace these new ideas and things, men and women had cast off those ideas that claimed to be fixed principles and those things that were old, had in fact to throw away anything that might impede the movement forward, that might inhibit progress. Such liberalism threatened any sense of the past. It encouraged people to move "away from things that are old because they are old, and toward things that are new because they are new." Moreover, the liberalism of the age had moved to divorce reason from emotion and had left "men with a persuasion of mind without a burning conviction of heart." These divisions and separations of life in the name of rapid progress affected every area of life and thought, including scientific work, cultural life, political and social theory, and religion. Religion, for example, had come to be conceived of as "something super added to the highest life of humanity [rather] than as itself the perfect development of that life." It had become increasingly something separate from philosophy, literature, art, and science.

He acknowledged that this liberalism had become persuasive and pervasive; but, he warned his classmates, it was false. He challenged them to stand against the tide of such false liberalism and, instead, to commit themselves to the true liberalism, which "loves the past for what it has done and for what it has been" and "reaches forth to the future because it holds the promise of things to be." Progress cannot be made "by groping in the dark," but by moving forward from positions held in the past. Moreover, progress cannot be achieved unless "firm mental apprehensions" are combined with the "responsive enthusiasm of heart." True liberalism unites rather than divides and brings together religion and life, intellect and spirit. "The tendency of our times," he summarized, "in every department of life is a liberalism as rash as it is unprecedented. The emotional element of belief has been driven out by the incessant changes in intellectual assent so that conviction has become rare and enthusiasm reprobate. And this gospel of liberalism is offered us as the proper faith for an educated man—a faith here! say rather a torch flashing over the gulf of despair." He called his classmates to grasp true liberalism: "The clear duty of the educated man and of every man is to form intelligible judgments, so far as possible, from independent thought, elsewhere, on the best authority, and to adhere to them with an emotion born of conviction and proportioned to the intellectual evidence on which they rest."[99]

The speech went well. His father told him that he "had covered himself with glory" and added that some of the Philadelphia newspapers "mentioned you in a most kindly way, and I would have gathered some of them up and sent them to you, had I not felt that you cared little for such compliments, however deserved they may be."[100] The day after commencement he packed to leave, sorry to go but ready to get on with his mission. Within a week he was at Northfield for his second summer conference. He had come from a small rural town and had been blessed with a strong family and religious heritage, one that had been carefully passed on to him. Those roots nourished him, and he had worked hard and begun to build well on the foundations from the past. Fulfilling God's call was to be his life, and he looked forward expectantly.

CHAPTER 2

Call to Ministry

"To Thee I Consecrate My Life"

God's call came to Robert Speer over a period of five years, between the spring of 1886 and the fall of 1891. After it was all over, it seemed like three acts in an extended drama in which God progressively revealed his will. In process he saw each act as complete, as a turning point that reshaped his life. He left no clues at the end of each act that he had any idea of what might come next. In this sense he experienced God's call as a series of calls, each with its own dramatic quality and its own particular consequences.

The initial act in the drama was the most expected one, almost predictable: his decision to join the church. Extensively nurtured in the Christian faith, he nonetheless reached his freshman year in college without having made the public commitment that would lead to church membership. The issue was not that he did not yet know enough about the faith, but that he did not yet feel called to it. Honest almost to a fault with himself and others, he had never experienced what Presbyterian tradition called the "effectual calling." Question 31 in the Shorter Catechism, which he knew well, asked: "What is effectual calling?" The appropriate response was: "Effectual calling is the work of God's Spirit, whereby, convincing us of our sin and misery, enlightening our minds in the knowledge of Christ, and renewing our wills, he doth persuade and enable us to embrace Jesus Christ, freely offered to us in the gospel."[1]

When he arrived at Princeton, he found the religious atmosphere of the college more conservative than he had experienced in New England. He attended a prayer meeting and found the mood "almost hypocritical," but he persevered and began to lead the prayer meetings.[2] Signs of spiritual reflection began to appear in his diary in the winter of that year. On Sunday, January 10, 1886, President McCosh preached "a very good sermon," which led Speer to ask himself, "Do I do everything for my own interest? Am I completely selfish?"[3] Three weeks later Arthur T. Pierson, an evangelical with a conservative theological perspective and a leader in the missionary movement, came to speak on the Day of Prayer for Schools and Colleges. Speer attended all of Pierson's services and was both impressed and moved: "They did one good. Strengthened me."[4] Some years later he told Pierson that there were "few who can feel towards you the same grateful and filial love which I feel." He recalled the visit to Princeton and said that it was "after your sermon in the afternoon and at the after-meeting which you conducted in the evening, that I first publicly acknowledged Christ and resolved to join myself openly to His Church. During the years since, I have owed much to your unfailing interest, encouragement and confidence."[5] Pierson responded in dramatic terms that Speer had become "more like a son to me or a younger brother," and to have been so instrumental in his spiritual life made "it worthwhile to have lived."[6]

Once Speer felt the warm embrace of Jesus, he did the logical thing: he joined the church. He informed the Rev. Mr. Horace G. Hinsdale, pastor of the First Presbyterian Church of Princeton, of his intention and on Sunday, February 7, he skipped chapel and joined First Church and had communion. When he told his family in Huntingdon, they were excited. While his Ma Whittaker rejoiced, his father typically offered advice. "Deep impressions of God," he wrote, "should be received and cherished as his merciful voice speaking unto you. Heed it—obey it—and it will lead you into paths of peace, duty, usefulness, and safety. . . . We are pilgrims here—and there is a life beyond of perpetual blessedness to those who love and serve God. Open your heart to him who gave *his* life for you and make it your supreme purpose and endeavor to love and serve Him. Go to Him in prayer for guidance, and wisdom, and strength—and He will hear and help you."[7] He followed his father's suggestions but with little immediate consequence beyond church membership.

The Call to Mission

The second, and most traumatic, act in the drama of his call did not come until a year later, and it was as unexpected as the first had been expected. He did not practice the discipline of his diary very well in the fall of 1886, but, fortunately for those interested in his spiritual pilgrimage, he took up his pen again in January 1887. Almost immediately the entries carried a new note of spiritual unrest and considerable uncertainty about his personal goals. On January 12, just after he discovered that he stood first in his class, he wrote, "Three aims,—to control conversation and make peace, to think less of self, to be kind and Christian."[8] For the next two months he rode an emotional roller coaster. Despite his resolve to think less of himself, he lamented that he was not elected chair of the sophomore class reception, with the comment, "I should have had it." He won a debate in early February but did not enjoy the victory, noting that he exhibited "too much fooling and too little earnestness." A sermon titled "What Will You Do with Christ?" moved him to respond, "Choose him and love and desire and magnify." On February 22 he wrote, "Cloudy, clear, warm, cool, damp, like the struggle within me. Hot and tired of head and heart. . . . Am self-possessed but not myself." The very next day he learned he had lost an important debate and had trouble reconciling himself to it, thinking, "I have had too much success, perhaps. Perhaps I have not done right. Is not each separate human failure traceable to human sin?"

Signs of change began to appear in March. On the sixth Robert G. Wilder, just graduated from Princeton and traveling for the Student Volunteers for Foreign Missions, spoke in chapel. The very next day Speer spoke at the Philadelphian Society. It was a new experience for him, and one that led him to "the best day I ever passed in my Christian experience. It has been bright and beautiful and I have thought of God and he has been near." Although he continued unsettled, he was moving toward a resolution: "I have hours of seeming looseness of purpose. Must hand over every decision to God." On the seventeenth he heard a missionary speak and was impressed by his message, and on the twenty-fourth he wrote, "Have deeper thoughts on religious things and feel some power moving me." On the twenty-sixth he heard Wilder and John Forman, who was traveling with Wilder, speak and said, "Am beginning to think more seriously on Missions."

The call came on the twenty-seventh. He exclaimed: "Wilder, Forman, Baldwin in Neher's room from 8 to 11. I lead prayer communion. We talk. *I decide. I shall go as a Missionary to preach and to teach. Help me, O God!* Wrote to Papa. Help him, O God!" Some ten years later in a rare autobiographical note he told those assembled at the third quadrennial of the Student Volunteer Movement (SVM) in Cleveland, Ohio, that he could "see still the little room in North Middle Reunion at Princeton, where a little group of us met years ago in our sophomore year at college and faced this question, and one by one sat down at a table and wrote our names under the words: 'I am willing and desirous, God permitting, to become a foreign missionary.'"[9] The "words" were the Volunteer Pledge.

The decision ended his inner turmoil and flooded him with peace. It was the major decision of his life. The next day he wrote: "I am so gloriously relieved. All burden gone." But it was not quite so easy. He later recalled that he "used to lie awake late at night and wake early in the morning . . . re-arguing afresh night and morning the arguments by which I had first persuaded myself to turn from law to the missionary life."[10] In the midst of these second thoughts he began to reflect on the ways his decision would in fact change his life. As he explored the depth of his commitment, hopeful that he would "keep firm in this determination," he turned to the Bible. He found there answers about his call, assurances, and he discovered Paul's letters to Timothy particularly "applicable to our own souls."

The state executive committee of the YMCA, which he attended May 6 in Newark, was an important confirming event. He encountered there a young man "who had started out to save 20,000 souls and he is doing it and then going to Africa as a Missionary." The enthusiasm he experienced at the meeting inspired him, and he joyfully told his father, "It made me feel like jumping right up and shouting for the Master. I am going to get rid of the college offices I hold and go in for this. There is no work like it. The world has no work like the salvation of young men or the Evangelization of the heathen. I believe I am called to the latter. I don't see how I could get out of it, if I wanted to. God has put me there. As I look back over my short and peaceful life every important step seems to me to have been God's doing, and I don't see how there could have been any other result than the one reached. My devotion to His service, and the fullest consecration to his work."[11] By semester's end he was truly settled and could write, "Come, blessed Jesus, I say like Livingstone, 'To Thee I consecrate my life, my all—King, Father, God, My all. My Saviour and Redeemer.' "[12]

One of his major concerns as he lived through this act of his call was his father. His letters home in January had been numerous and full of relatively ordinary things, like his class standing and his debate projects, but he had also sent a signal or two that religion was attracting more and more of his attention. In early February he had told his father that the college seemed to be "striving hard to shake itself for a religious awakening" and added that he did not like the term "revival," because it inferred "the coming back to life of something which ought not to have died." The first week of March Speer had informed his father, "The claims of foreign missionary work have been pressed home earnestly to many men in this college in the last few days. The claims seem to me indisputable, but formidable."[13]

The day he signed the pledge, he had sent two letters home. The one that he wrote in the morning claimed the week had "been regular and undisturbed. I read several books, won a debate and wrote a speech." Later in the day he sent another message, this one dramatically different. "Dear Papa," he wrote, "This has been the crucial day of my life, and I have to write to you about it. Ever since a boy I have drifted toward the profession of law as my life work because I thought it was what you wanted me to do especially after Will entered Journalism, but I have come to a new conclusion today. I am going to be a foreign missionary. I have placed myself intentionally where I can not draw back. I have signed a paper. . . . I should feel ashamed of myself if I stayed in this country while millions of heathen perish daily, and 'their blood is on my head.' If it seems hard for you, . . . 'God so loved the world that he gave his only begotten son.'" He asked for his father's blessing, but he also said, "I am decided, Papa, I can't do anything else."[14] When a fellow student inquired, "What will your father say to this?" he replied, "I couldn't help it; when will *you* decide?"[15]

The letter was both a gentle explanation of the events of the day and the announcement of a final decision. Although he knew how important his study of the law was to his father, he had also signed a paper and could not retreat from his word. But he was just a college sophomore and dearly loved and respected his father, and so he longed for parental approval. As he awaited a reply, he became more and more anxious. Neher, who had also signed, had heard from home, and his mother had strongly reproached him. He pondered and prayed, "When will Papa answer? May God help us all and give us peace and show us our duty plainly and give us his Spirit."[16] His father responded about a week after the crucial day and in a decidedly cool manner, saying that he did not "now feel prepared to answer it," and proposing time for reflection. He added, "If, indeed, it be God's call, I shall be silent, however hard it will be to part with you. Search your own heart as with a lighted candle, that you may not be self-deceived."[17]

If his father's response disappointed him, he kept it to himself. Instead, he offered his father the following definition of God's call: "I think it is God's call when we feel the personal responsibility attached to obedience of His commands, and understand His promises. The sense of duty begins to disappear in the sense of privilege, and toil becomes rest, and conflict, peace."[18] His father acknowledged this the following December when he gave him a diary for 1888 as a Christmas present, and inscribed the flyleaf: "Dear Rob—March to duty—*Papa.*" Directly under this charge Speer wrote, "*I Will.* God help me."[19]

Most of the rest of his relatives were enthusiastic about his news, and immediately accepted his decision as an appropriate response to a call from God. Little brother Vic reported, "There is great rejoicing in the camp of your Huntingdon relatives, since it has been learned that you are to become a foreign missionary." Aunt Clara sent her love and support and told him that she "never knew Mother to rejoice over anything as she did over your decision, she seems perfectly happy that her prayers and hopes are to be realized. I know your Momma is rejoicing in Heaven. She always loved her 'thoughtful Rob.'"

One response affirmed him even as it raised an important distinction. Will wrote encouragingly that the decision "to enter the ministry" was a good one and that he felt he "had many traits of character that fit you for it." But, Will proposed, the call to ministry was separate from the decision to be a foreign missionary. Ministry could take many forms, and he raised the possibility that it was a little premature to define it in missionary terms "in the days of youth or the dreams of a sophomore." He prodded his younger brother with some thoughtful questions: "Do you think all the souls in the United States are saved? Do you believe the heathen in China and India have prior claims and stronger demands on you than the heathen or as bad and worse in New York and Philadelphia? Or is it that you mean to make a greater selfdenial in yourself for your self gratitude and self glory?"[20] Will's concerns did not dissuade him, but they previewed another time of decision down the road. By late spring his season of turmoil was over, and he was at peace with himself and his father.

Conversion

This second act of his call built on the first. It confirmed his Christian commitment and introduced a new dimension to it. He was now one of those set aside to preach and carry the Word to others, most likely in some other part of the world. It hit him very hard, so that he described it in terms usually reserved for a conversion experience. Typically, "conversion" is a term used to describe movement into the Christian faith. In his case he was "converted" to ministry, and the experience struck with such force because of his lifelong commitment to the law. When he had embraced Christ and the church, he had done so as a future lawyer. But this second act of the drama changed his entire life plan. Describing the event to a large gathering of students some years later, he said, "We look back to that hour when perhaps for the first time in our lives . . . there was a hand laid upon our shoulders that once was nailed to the cross, and there was lifted up before our eyes the vision of a new and larger life, and there came a new heaven and a new earth for us."[21]

During his career people occasionally asked about his conversion. One correspondent inquired, "Have you ever had a crisis experience, in which the Holy Spirit came into your life in especial fulness?" He responded, "As for myself, I grew up in a Christian home, and have never known any such critical experiences as those of which you speak, except the experience which came while I was a student in college through the surrender of legal and political ambitions, and the choice, instead, of the missionary purpose."[22] He told Presbyterians gathered for the 150th General Assembly in 1938 that Robert Wilder and John Forman, "both sons of our missions in India, were the apostles who carried the appeal of the Movement to the colleges and universities of Canada and the United States," and added, "It was through them that my own doctrine of missions came. In truth I owe them my own soul."[23]

The change in his life immediately manifested itself in a variety of new activities and ideas. He began to demonstrate a new depth of concern for others; to focus his personal study on the Bible and missionary topics; and to explore traditional Christian themes in some of his writing. Other people had always been an important part of his life, but his conversion brought him closer to some of them and at a new level of commitment. One of his first decisions after conversion was to join the Mission Band, or more accurately, he and the others who felt called created it. They met every Sunday after morning chapel to talk about a missionary topic. "We have discussed nearly every field in the world, some fields more than once," he reported a year later, "considering the history, people, country, obstacles, helps and prospects, and there is something new to be learned each time. The most interesting feature of the meetings this year has been the study of the lives of missionaries—living epistles—showing that God hath chosen the base things and the foolish and weak things and things which are despised and are not."[24]

Neher and a number of other fellow students became part of his daily concern, some finding a place on his prayer list. He hoped for them what he hoped for himself, that the initial decision would survive periods of doubt and that they would come through determined to fulfill their missionary vocation. He found these companions a great source of strength and discovered "the need and benefits of Christian Fellowship . . . more every day." His brother Vic was the other "other" person who came to the front and center of his life that spring. Vic had run away from home in defiance of their father. When Speer received news that Vic had returned in mid-May, he wrote, "Perhaps he will be better now. O Lord make him obedient to thy commands." His father wrote in early June, thoroughly discouraged about Vic; Speer responded by quoting Genesis 43:8–9, which recounts Judah's pledge to his father Israel regarding young Benjamin and includes the promise: "I will be surety for him; of my hand you shall require him. If I do not bring him back to you and set him before you, then let me bear the blame for ever." Privately he reflected, "Ought to read much Word these days, will need it."[25]

He was quite familiar with the Bible and followed the practice of reading it regularly. He used one his mother had given him and another one he received from the Presbyterian Church in Huntingdon.[26] He had marked them, identifying passages that held some particular interest for him. The missionary call plunged him into a rereading and study of the Bible. His days, apart from classes and routine activities, were filled with Bible work. He began with several of Paul's letters and then turned to Revelation. By late spring he was reading Matthew "with delight and profit and marking it."[27] He filled the pages of his diary with Bible references and quotations of favorite passages. He decided to use some prize money he won to purchase a new and larger Bible with margins for comments. When it arrived in late May, he began marking it and exclaimed, "O how I love the Word of God! It is hid in my mouth. May I do only what pleases its author divine."[28] He spent a good part of his time that summer reading and marking his new Bible. Much of this study appears to have been random, reading whole books with eyes now opened by his new experience of God. Some of it, however, was directed by his interest in better defining his particular mission. Just before he left college at the end of the term, he gave his first formal missionary address at a Sunday school, and that summer he attended his first missionary conference. The Bible study and missionary speeches, triggered by his heartwarming experience, became vital parts of the rest of his life.

After his conversion he began to write essays with definite Christian themes. In late spring he wrote about the religious events of the semester under the title "A Religious Retrospect." In reference to Wilder and Forman he said, "Two young men with the mantle of the prophets have gone up and down the land with the call of love, and young men and women have risen willingly and desirously on every side. . . . God has walked among us. We have heard his steps."[29] Over the Christmas vacation he completed an essay on the Scottish missionary and explorer David Livingstone. He also wrote an open letter "To the Student Volunteers for Foreign Missions" from "The Princeton Volunteers," about the life and programs of the Princeton Band in its first year. During the winter of 1888 he wrote a short fictional piece that he entered in the Nassau Literary Story Prize Contest. His story, "Dell Ross, My Dell," won first place, and the *Nassau Literary Magazine* published it in its March issue. The setting for the story was Hiram Ross's place, where as a young boy he had shot his first deer. In a reminiscence many years later he said he had "idealized" Ross and his family in the story. "Romanticized" might be a more accurate description, but he also included a theological message, one that seems substantially based on his religious awakening.[30]

The story recounted an event in the life of a fictional character named David Bailey, who worked in a city at a business that occupied him only in the winter months. He began to spend his summers at Fort McAlevy, along the course of the Creek of the Standing Stone. One day he wandered somewhat farther from the fort than usual and, as dusk approached, realized he was lost. Just then he broke out of the dark forest into a clearing, which turned out to be the land of a frontiersman named Hiram Ross and his daughter Dell. They lived in a humble cabin, and Hiram ran a small sawmill and hunted for a living. Hiram invited David to stay the night and then the summer. David helped at the mill, and in the evenings the three of them talked and David "learned the history of their lives, plain, simple, loving, self-sacrificing perhaps, contented, and my own life came to know more of its dignity and worth." When winter came, he left with great reluctance and with an invitation to return the next summer. And return he did, to find the clearing in the woods as peaceful and as refreshing as it was the first time. As he reached the cabin, he lightly kissed Dell and thought "it must have been right, for old Hiram smiled, and the kiss seemed to settle something."

As the summer passed quickly and fall arrived, David and Dell sat closer and talked longer. Then one Sabbath, as the time for him to leave drew near, they went to the sawmill to talk and listen to the water as it poured through the sluice that carried the logs to the saw. He was peeling some bark off a log in the sluice when his foot became caught under the log. His efforts to disengage his foot knocked loose the beam that controlled the flow of the water, and suddenly the water rushed in, moving the log forward and turning the machinery that controlled the saw. Slowly but inexorably David was drawn toward the saw, and he could not free himself. Dell tried to help but could not move the lever-pole that controlled the flow of water. She then came close to him and looked at him and smiled,

> and I knew that she had some great purpose in her simple heart; for her smile came through tears and the whole seemed to me no longer plain and sweet, but the face of an angel. It was understanding no longer, I knew now that I loved Dell Ross, my Dell; and the saw crunched its way nearer and nearer. She walked out to the end of the mill over the flood-way, paused, looked back on me a moment, and then leaped into the water. A lightning flash like a bursting sun blinded me, and the heavy thunders, something strange for October I thought afterwards, rolled horribly, ominously down the mountain sides, and Dell was gone. It dazed me for a while and the clouds grew very black, and I shut my eyes, and in a few moments, which seemed to me years, the motion stopped, the great wheel ceased its roar and the jar on the log set me free. I looked over at the gate and it was still raised, but the hole had been stopped so that not enough water escaped to turn the wheel, and Dell's body filled the hole. I reached down with a lumber hook and drew her up and forced down the gate, and sat down beside my Dell— dead. . . . "She died for me," I said. "David Bailey, she died for you."

David and Hiram buried Dell. Hiram read the Twenty-third Psalm, and David tried to find something in the Bible about how "she died for me" but could not find anything. When David had to leave, he promised to return and did every summer. He and Hiram walked and talked, and David finally learned the message of the song of the Creek of the Standing Stone, "and the word it says most is 'Dell,' and sometimes 'Davie,' and the soft echo whispers them back hand-in-hand, and I reach my hand up to heaven and I think Dell Ross reaches down, and it gives me strength to wait." But the story, as it spread, became bigger than the personal story of David and Dell. As mountain fathers told their children, "the maidens' eyes fill with tears and the hearts of the lads soften and their lives are better for it. And so it seems that when Dell died for me, she died for many, and it teaches me, David Bailey, a lesson, and gives me strength to wait in patience." The story was transparently the story of Jesus and the atonement, including the darkness of the earth at the moment of death, and the sense of strength passed from heaven to earth, from God to believers, as they waited until God came again.[31]

Speer's call to missionary ministry brought many different parts of his life together, and he increasingly focused his energies on his new goal. It generated a consuming sense of duty that he translated into a new life plan. Although he never committed this plan to paper or regarded it as absolutely fixed, he definitely decided to complete his college work, attend seminary, and then volunteer his services as a missionary to foreign lands through the Board of Foreign Missions of the Presbyterian Church.

The first national missionary organization he joined after his conversion was, not surprisingly, the Student Volunteers, since he essentially did so when he signed their pledge. He attended his first summer conference at Northfield, where he met Dwight L. Moody and many of the older missionary leaders and student volunteers. When he returned to Princeton in the fall of 1887, he was on fire for the Christian faith in general and for-eign missions in particular.[32] He began to lead missionary meetings and to accept speaking engagements in towns nearby, joined at times by other members of the Princeton Band. Some of the meetings were sponsored by the YMCA, and some were sponsored by churches and other groups. During this time he made his first visits to preparatory schools for boys and began what became a tradition of visits to schools for both boys and girls. Mission talks dominated, but he also joined in evangelistic and tem-perance meetings.

As his reputation grew, he began to receive invitations from far and wide. In January 1888 he spoke at Dwight Hall at Yale, and in March at the YMCA and the Bowery Institute in New York City.[33] In April he led a pastors' conference in Plainfield, New Jersey, and presented the claims of foreign missions to a crowd of over a thousand. That same month he received an offer to become a YMCA secretary at an annual wage of $1,200 and expenses.[34] The job did not seem to be part of his new life plan, so he declined it, but he continued to be very active on behalf of the Y. Lecture requests continued to appeal for his time his senior year, but he turned many of them down, although he did make room in the spring for speeches in Fort Wayne, Indiana, and in his hometown. That same spring he began his personal, intensive study of missions.[35]

The speeches were occasions for him to continue to explore his call, but they were also much more than that. From the very first talk he proposed not only to inform listeners but also to convert them in both the senses in which he understood conversion: to the Christian faith and to foreign missions. What may have been his first missionary volunteer came on January 28, 1888, when he "secured one person for foreign missions." The next day he and two other Princeton men "spoke for souls," and "some were born." At the Bowery Institute, two announced that "they wanted to lead new lives." For the remainder of his college career he filled his diary with the numbers and sometimes the names of those who came under con-viction during his presentations. When eight men signed the Volunteer Pledge on April 8, 1888, he wrote, "Oh! Glorious day. How He answers prayer." The following December, fourteen volunteered and seven were converted in response to his call at a meeting in Camden, New Jersey. "This has been a grand day," he wrote, "I feel that I am nothing at all and the Master all."[36]

In the spring of his senior year, he agreed to serve as chairman of the missionary committee for the Northfield conference that summer. It was his second summer conference. When he arrived on June 29, he found almost forty Princeton men there, and substantial groups from other colleges. His role was unlike that at his first conference; he was now one of the leaders, on the platform with Mott and his mentor Wilder. Mott was moved by his presentations and wrote of the occasion, "Speer is a powerful speaker. I never knew a man of his age to talk so fluently and *at the same time to put in such solid thought*."[37] Speer was moved by the response of the conference, and although he was only partly responsible for them, he carefully noted that fifty-five volunteers signed the pledge.

Call to Be a Missionary Secretary

During his senior year he decided to postpone his seminary work in order to accept an invitation from Wilder to spend a year recruiting for the newly organized Student Volunteer Movement for Foreign Missions. When he took to the road in September, he became the second traveling secretary. He was quite successful in his recruiting efforts, very likely because of his disarming and persuasive way of putting the call to foreign missions. The full range of his presentation will be discussed in depth in chapter 5, but one element was his own understanding of the call. Many Christians believed that a person had to receive a "special" call to be a foreign missionary. On the contrary, he exclaimed, every person called to be a Christian was at the same time called to be a missionary. The only people who needed special calls were those who decided not to become foreign missionaries.

His special call, in the fall of 1891, was the third act in the larger drama of his call, and it was as unexpected as the missionary call had been. The SVM leaders, particularly Mott, put pressure on him in the summer of 1890 to extend his recruiting work for a second year. He declined and said he wanted to keep the pledge, which meant finishing his education and going to the mission field. The traveling work was, in many ways, a "service which does not allow of the greatest growth. . . . I want to preach the Gospel of Christ's love and death and sacrifice, rather than of His last

command alone."[38] He stuck to his modified plan and entered The
Theological Seminary at Princeton in the fall of 1890. The following summer the New Brunswick Presbytery gave him a temporary license to
preach, and he supplied two churches in Pennsylvania, the First
Presbyterian Church in Bellefonte in June and July and the Presbyterian
Church in Pottstown in August. In his first real experience in pastoral
ministry, he kept busy in Bellefonte, "going to see people in the evenings
and preparing for Sundays and Wednesdays in the mornings." And he
loved the land: "God made everything very pretty out here. . . . Only hard
hearts could keep from praising Him for the deeds of His good Hands."[39]

One month after he returned to seminary, he received a visit from a
representative of the Presbyterian Board of Foreign Missions, who brought
a remarkable message, a new version of his call. He remembered that he
met with board secretary Frank F. Ellinwood, who invited him to leave his
theological training and join the board as an assistant secretary.[40] Startled
by the request, he nevertheless agreed to consider it and subsequently met
with a committee of the board.

When he came before this committee, which included William Booth,
Warner Van Orden, and the Rev. Joseph Kerr, he told them, "My purpose
was to go to the foreign field." A discussion ensued. They asked him if he
was willing for the board to "propose the field of service," and he said, "Of
course." They promised, if he accepted their call, to release him later if he
desired to finish his seminary course.[41] The meeting ended with the issue
unsettled. He consulted friends and teachers. His problem was that he had
signed the pledge to go abroad and had encouraged a multitude of others
to do the same, including some of his closest college friends. Could he
now stay at home? Was this his special call that qualified the general call?
Many of those he consulted told him they thought it was.[42]

He finally accepted the call and left seminary in midsemester to begin
his work with the board. Ellinwood said of his struggle to get him to join
the board: "It was with great hesitation and reluctance that he was persuaded to relinquish his purpose to spend his life on the mission field, but
it seemed clear to the Board that he was peculiarly adapted to the work of
secretary, and that he had a great mission to fulfil in arousing a missionary spirit in the younger membership of the Church. He was the youngest
man ever appointed to such a position."[43] One of his counselors had been
the elder statesman Henry Clay Trumbull, a Civil War chaplain and editor of the *Sunday School Times*, who wrote after the decision to congratu-
late him, "I am truly glad you have decided as you have. I dared not give
you explicit counsel, although I took pleasure in putting all my thoughts

on the subject at your disposal. I prayed that you might be guided by the Spirit, and I knew that that was *your* prayer. Yet all the while, as I thought out the subject earnestly and in prayerfulness, I could see many reasons why you should *take* the place as one to which God was calling you, and none why you should *decline* it."[44]

By the close of 1891 the drama of his call had reached its conclusion. He was finally settled. The second act had established the direction of his life; the third laid out the specific route he was to follow. He had became one of the volunteers who discovered as he himself had described it, "the Spirit's diversities of operation."[45] He never looked back, not even when the board he eventually came to administer fell on hard economic times, not even during the severe theological struggles in the 1930s. Though he was offered other jobs from time to time, including some very attractive ones (such as a pastorate in 1892 in one of "the very pleasantest communities" and the presidencies at several colleges, including informal approaches from Princeton), he never seriously considered changing his course.[46] He sometimes perceived such invitations as temptations. He reflected on the call from the local church: "If a temptation means a door which you ought not to enter but which it is hard to keep out of, this was no temptation, for I think God has shown me my life and way clearly thus far. But if a temptation is a call away from a line of duty to a line of greater ease and pleasure, then this is a temptation."[47]

Concept of Ministry

Accepting the call to be a missionary secretary compelled him to reflect on and reconsider the nature of his ministry. The life plan he had formulated included a theological education and ordination, commonly perceived prerequisites for ministry in his church. When he had traveled with the SVM for a year, he had simply postponed his plan. He now faced a new situation. When he decided to accept the call from the board as his special one and establish his ministry at home rather than abroad, he also decided to remain a layperson. At his interview for the position, board members promised he could later return to seminary if he wished. He never wished, at least for the record, but on several occasions he wistfully acknowledged that he did not have the theological preparation many of his mentors had. He told his foreign mission administrative colleagues in a memorial to Judson Smith in 1907 that Smith and Ellinwood had full theological training and had both been scholars, whereas he and a number

of the "younger men" had joined the work "before completing the theological course." He encouraged such men to "read enough books" in order
to keep their outlook broad.[48] He took his own advice and was an avid
reader, literally consuming books at the rate of three or more a week over
his entire career.

He not only understood himself to be in ministry, broadly conceived,
from the beginning of his secretarial work, but he also became an advocate for his vision of ministry. His idea was hardly new but was something
he adapted from the traditional Protestant concept of the priesthood of all
believers. The best and most publicized illustration of his vision was the
missionary call, where he asserted that every Christian was called to be a
missionary and hence a minister of the gospel. He struck the same note of
the ministry of all Christians time after time in public presentations and
in his correspondence. In a speech on "The Call to Christian Service,"
he exclaimed, "But, gentlemen, the call is not for men for the ministry
alone. . . . I am called not to be a minister but to minister."[49]

Although he held firm to this vision of ministry throughout his service
with the board, he did not find it easy to maintain in the face of persistent
practical and theoretical questions. No matter how often he dealt with
them, they kept cropping up. People wanted to know why he was not
ordained. It was an obvious question, since he was the only unordained
person on the secretarial staff of his board and almost the only one on any
of the Protestant mission boards. He responded to one inquiring clergyman, "I am not ordained because I am not doing the work which ordination contemplates. So far as my official relationship to the Church is concerned, it is administrative and not ecclesiastical." He added, "I preach the
Gospel at every opportunity, but I do that only because I conceive that to
be the highest duty and the highest privilege of every man who loves it."[50]
His responses to inquiries about his ministry were always direct, but people continued to be confused and sometimes perplexed by them. What
did "preaching" mean? If it meant what he did when he mounted a pulpit, then was he not assuming a typical clergyman's task? If he meant he
"preached" or communicated the gospel through his administrative work,
that was a concept beyond the reach of many of the faithful. In fact, he
meant both.

The confusion about his ministry extended to officials at Princeton. In
1910 a friend invited him to speak at Princeton chapel, and told him he
was "most anxious that you may see your way clear, or even *make* your way
clear, to accept this invitation." "You should have been on our Chapel list
years ago," he added, and then explained, "There was no personal objec-

tion on President Wilson's part but merely a scruple because of the fact that you were not an ordained minister—This, too was not his own personal scruple but rather a regard, as he thought, for the scruples of others—I felt several years ago, when I first brought the matter to his attention, that he need have had no such feelings—In fact, I know it has worked just the other way for many have wondered why we did not ask you and have criticized."[51]

So visible was he among the leaders of his denomination, most of whom were ordained, and so often did he preach in prominent pulpits, that very early in his service, people replaced "Mr." with "Reverend." He did not care for that title, but people persisted in using it throughout his life, although some switched to "Dr." after he received his first honorary doctorate. He denied the titles almost as often as they were used, but to little avail. In response to a request for a biographical sketch in 1900, he returned only the bare essentials and noted, "Perhaps I ought to say that I am not ordained, and that I have no titles, inasmuch as you give me both in the address in your letter to me."[52] In a speech before a group of laity in the early 1920s he asked, "My friends what is the church? I have a place-card here that labels me 'Reverend.' I am not reverend, I am nothing but an unsanctified layman like the rest of you, and we are the church. It is not the priests and clergy that constitute the church. We are the church."[53] Although he never stopped disliking the titles, such outbursts and objections almost disappeared after his denomination elected him moderator in 1927.

The theoretical challenges to his view of ministry often came from those who believed that clergy were either better than other Christians or had a unique calling. This was a version of the "special call" argument that he often encountered when dealing with the call to become a missionary. Those who argued along those lines had a difficult time grasping a view of ministry that did not rely on a special call. In responding to such objections, he sometimes used traditional Protestant theory and other times turned to the Bible. He directed one correspondent to Paul's argument about the value of the different parts of the body and reminded him that "every member of the body has functions just as truly assigned to it, though it be humble, as any other member of the body." He continued:

I do not believe that the divine call of a man to the ministry is any more 'unique' than the divine call of a Christian man to any other work that is assigned to him by the will of God. . . . I believe that many men go into the ministry believing that they have gained a knowledge of the divine will in a

unique and singular way; but I think also that many Christian men have
taken up other work which they believed was the will of God for themselves
under the same divine leading. Surely God has a will for every man, and it
is the business of every man to discover and do this will. I do not see why
there should need to be a peculiar method of discovering an answer in the
case of a man looking forward to any one particular service.

That was a strong case for the ministry of all believers, but he was careful
not to overstate it so that it seemed to be an argument against the ordained
ministry, which he very much supported. And so he concluded, "I would
not lower a man's conception of the ministry, I would lift up his conceptions of all other work."[54]

Although based at home and not in the technical sense a "foreign missionary," he saw his ministry in that context, and so did other observers of
the foreign missions scene. Trumbull certainly spoke for many of those
knowledgeable about missions when he said, "What two missionaries . . .
were doing more in their sphere for Christ and for souls than John R.
Mott or Robert E. Speer, who, whether at home or in their world circuits
of the mission fields, are not called missionaries, yet are always more than
missionaries?"[55] His duty now clear, he followed his father's advice and
marched to it.

CHAPTER 3

The Christian Faith

"Remember Jesus Christ"

The Christian faith dominated Speer's life. He received it as a gift from God, mediated by his family and college friends. After his conversion experience he became increasingly self-conscious about it and worked through Bible study and in prayer groups to broaden and deepen it. It was his focus and had absolute priority. Whatever he did he placed in the context of the Christian faith. Known to others as a missionary executive or an ecumenical or Presbyterian leader, and known to his family as a loving husband and father, he saw himself first and foremost as a Christian. This was the major theme of his life. It was the secure center from which he drew the energy for life and around which he lived and worked.

His faith could at one and the same time be described as the "faith of our fathers" and intensely personal. The "fathers" included his own father, who introduced him to the Bible and to the church's traditional statements of the faith, and a multitude of others, living and dead, who helped nurture him. He mentioned a great number of people in his books and letters, including in his early years missionary leader Rufus Anderson and theologian Horace Bushnell. He learned a great deal from three of the elder people of the faith of his day, Pierson, Trumbull, and Moody. Pierson had been instrumental in his decision to join the church. Of Trumbull he said, "As one who knew him as a son and who was also grateful to be his friend, I wish to speak here of his influence and character, in behalf of the multitudes of young men who knew his voice, and who trace gratefully to him to-day the unsealing and illumination of their lives."[1] Student Volunteer Movement colleagues Mott and Wilder he welcomed as brothers in helping him formulate his faith. The classroom was not one of the major sources of his faith. An exception was Hebrew scholar Henry Green, who was a member of the Princeton Seminary faculty. Typically, Speer's first and most important encounter with Green was at Northfield.[2]

Although settled enough in his beliefs by the early 1890s that he could begin lecturing, preaching, and writing about them, Speer always remained open to new ideas. An avid reader throughout his life, he read theology as well as history. After studying Karl Barth's *The Word of God and the Word of Man* in 1929, he concluded that Barth offered "an essential recovery of aspects of truth which will not be so easily lost again."[3] He commended Karl Heim's *The New Divine Order* to a correspondent in Chile in 1933. He had met Heim and described him as "a dear simple Christian and it is wonderful to think of him and what he represents in clear New Testament evangelicalism."[4]

The "fathers" were not only the elders in or proximate to his life, but also those distant in time, especially those who had created the traditional formulas of the church. He accepted the Apostles' Creed as the most succinct statement of the Christian faith, and the Westminster Confession of Faith as a more extensive one. From his perspective the creed had two important advantages. First, the early Christians believed it and accepted it as the consensus of their faith. Second, a wide variety of Christians and their churches acknowledged it, and therefore it could serve as a basis for Christian unity in the modern world. When the pastor of the Kensington Community Church in San Diego, California, requested a statement of faith for publication, Speer wrote back, "Apostles Creed enough for me."[5] He told fundamentalist J. Gresham Machen that he believed "unqualifiedly every article of the Apostles' Creed."[6]

Creeds and Confessions

He honored and used both the creed and the confession but he did not see them as fully defining his faith. They were important and useful as expressions of the faith in traditional language, but as guides rather than absolute rules. Trumbull once told him a story that he found instructive on this issue. Trumbull had grown up in Hartford, Connecticut, in the days when Horace Bushnell was a leading figure in the town. One day Trumbull stopped the great man on his rounds and had the following conversation: "Dr. Bushnell, you do not believe the Westminster Confession, do you?" "Why, yes, Henry," he said, "I do." "Well, you do not believe the Thirty-nine Articles, do you?' "Yes, Henry," said he, "I do." "Well, you do not believe the Augsburg Confession?" "Well, now Henry," said the old man, "just stop, or else name them all! I believe them all, and a great deal more." Speer interpreted: "He [Bushnell] did not mean that he was concerning himself about all the details; he just meant that the attitude of his mind was one of taking in all there was; not of seeing as little as possible, but of seeing as much as possible; and he was sure . . . that the danger that beset every man's mind was not that he would go too far, but that he would too timidly stand and drink, opening his mind to only some minimum instead of letting it go free in all the great amplitudes of fellowship with the infinite truth of God."[7]

He applied Bushnell's attitude in this story when he addressed the audience gathered in 1898 to celebrate the 250th anniversary of the Westminster Assembly. He told them he believed that the members of that historic assembly had served their generation well. The important question was how well were the leaders of the current generation serving it, how would the people in 2148 look back on the current generation? "There is a story," he continued, "of an Austrian nobleman, who, risen from the ranks of the common people, was taunted once by a group of degenerate princes because of his want of ancestry. 'Gentlemen,' he replied, 'you are descendants; I am an ancestor.' " Speer concluded, "If I must make my choice, I would rather be the ancestor of a new Westminster Assembly than the descendant of an old one. I would rather be the architect of two hundred and fifty years of future history than the product of two hundred and fifty years of great history past."[8]

While this did not mean that he felt any necessity to create a new creed or confession, he certainly felt free to do so. The first time he tried to write something like a creed, he did so quite unself-consciously in the first flush of his conversion. Using Bible passages as texts, he formulated the following statement of his new commitment:

I take God the Father to be my God.   I Thess. 1:19.
I take God the Son to be my Saviour.   Acts 5:31.
I take God the Holy Spirit to be my Sanctifier.   I Pet. 1:2.
I take the Word of God to be my rule.   II Tim. 3:16, 17.
I take the people of God to be my people.   Ruth 1:16, 17.
I take God the Comforter to be my solace.   John 14:16–18.
I likewise dedicate and consecrate my whole life to the Lord.   Rom.
   12:7, 8.
And I do this deliberately.   Josh. 24:15.
   Sincerely   2 Cor. 1:12.
   Freely   Psa. 110.
   With great joy and gladness   Luke 24:52, 53.
   And forever   Rom. 8:35–39.
"My Jesus, my King, my Life, My all, I dedicate my whole self to Thee."
                                                      Livingstone[9]

He also faced occasions that seemed to require that he put what he believed into his own words, but in a creedal form. One of those was the meeting of the International Missionary Council at Oxford in 1923. His topic was the role of doctrine in missionary cooperation, and "in order to avoid all misunderstanding," he formulated his statement of faith. Speaking in the third person, he said:

> He accepts the whole of Christianity as set forth in the New Testament. He believes unqualifiedly every article of the Apostles' Creed. No language is adequate to state his conception of Christ. He believes that He is more and greater than any words can ever express, 'the Word made flesh,' God incarnate, reconciling the world to Himself, the only Saviour, our Lord and our God. He believes in the truthfulness of the record of Christ's life, including His miracles, and rejoices with great joy in the miracle of the Virgin birth and of the real resurrection of Christ and of His future, personal advent. He believes that it is God alone who through Christ saves men, not by their characters, nor by any works of righteousness which they can do, but by His own grace through the death and life of His dear Son. As to the Bible, he accepts the doctrine of the Westminster Confession and regards its authority as supreme, not in faith only but also in the practice, conduct and relations of men.

He used this entire statement several times and later published it as part of a chapter in a book.[10] He celebrated the efforts of missionaries and the members of some of the emerging national churches to formulate new statements of faith and believed their greater unity on creedal matters was a sign of the coming reunion of the church.[11]

Faith

Creeds, ancient or modern, were very important and useful, and they reflected faith, but they were not faith itself. One of the most important books he wrote was also one of the first, *Remember Jesus Christ*. It was a series of essays, initially given as speeches at summer Bible conferences at Northfield, in which he set forth many of his most important convictions. He described faith as something Christ commanded. The imperative mood was not, he realized, something students liked. They typically preferred to be given choices, to be invited to believe. However, he pointed out that Jesus did not say, "It is a good thing to have faith," but rather directed his followers to "have faith in God." Paul agreed with Jesus in this approach.[12] What did they mean? First and foremost, Speer told his audiences, it was "a call to a personal surrender to God."[13] When Jesus told his disciples to "have faith in God," he did not mean for them to accept the doctrines he had been teaching them. He wanted them, instead, to personally "surrender their lives in the absolute confidence of an unwavering trust to God."[14] Paul said the same thing to the Ephesians when he prayed "that Christ may dwell in their hearts by faith."[15]

Faith, he concluded, was "primarily and essentially . . . a personal relationship."[16] Intellectual assent was an important aspect of faith, but it was secondary, a consequence of the primary act of trust and confidence. He cautioned his listeners, "When a child believes something which its father tells it, we call the child's acceptance an *act* of faith. But is it, except in an indirect sense? It is a *fruit* of faith. Faith is the confidence which the child reposes in its father, which leads it to believe in what the father says. But that belief is not so much an act of faith as a fruit of faith on the part of the child."[17] Ideas about faith, doctrines about the meaning of faith, were important, but they were incidental to the life lived in the faith relationship. The essence of Christian faith was "a personal relationship of living love."[18]

People approached him throughout his life, asking for help with their spiritual problems or seeking advice for loved ones. A typical request was one that came from Katherine Frazier, a plea for help for her brother in his search for truth. "Try to make him see," Speer counseled, that "faith is the activity of our trusting nature. It is love." Faith is "not to accept this or that metaphysical definition of Deity, but to yield ourselves in love to God as our Father." Invite him to study with you, he advised, and seek out together the character of God in the character of Jesus. Among the books he recommended to her for study were Bushnell's *The Character of Jesus*, Sir John Seeley's *Ecce Homo*, and his own *The Man Christ Jesus*.[19]

The Bible

The twin bases of his conviction that faith was a trusting relationship with God and not a particular creed were the Bible and Jesus Christ. They were the characteristic themes of much that he wrote. The call to work with the Board of Foreign Missions not only confirmed his vocation but also made him bold to begin to share his faith with a much larger audience. His first efforts were Bible studies, one on the Gospel of Luke and the other on Acts, published in 1892 under the imprint of the International Committee of the YMCA.[20] He followed those with another Bible study on the life of Jesus and within three years a book of essays on Jesus.[21] Although he subsequently wrote a very large number of essays, sermons, reports, and books on other topics, particularly missions and missionaries, he never stopped writing about the Bible and Jesus. The last book he wrote was about Jesus and human problems.[22]

He treated the Bible as a living book. He came to see it that way early in life, a view likely learned from his family and especially his father. After he left home, this study had been a more casual part of his life until his missionary call, and then it became a priority. He quickly reread a large part of the Bible, focusing on the New Testament. During this time he changed Bibles, finally switching from the Authorized or King James Version to the Revised Version, which was quite new when he began using it. (It was completed in 1885.) The change was not so much a turn away from the older version as an openness to new ones, an openness he exhibited throughout his life. He used the American Standard Edition of the Revised Version in his study of the Gospel of John and on occasion used the Greek New Testament in his personal study. "The King James Version of the Bible," he said, has "a sweetness of phrase in it that will never be surpassed, and its familiar turns of expression are woven into the fibre of all our thought and feeling." "But," he went on, "the reader of the Revised Version has these advantages: he knows that he is nearer to the exact meaning of what the Bible writers said and, though he does lose some of the melody of the older version, now and then he comes upon a change of language that brings out truth hidden before and flings a lane of glory across the page."[23]

The Bible study of his youth had been "study" in only the most general sense, whereas his postconversion study quickly took on the form and substance of a college course. This was stimulated by his appointment as T. H. P. Sailer Assistant in Biblical Instruction at Princeton for the academic year 1890–91, which was also his first year in seminary. Help along the way came from trusted friends like Trumbull, who advised him not to fear "that any question you may wish to ask on Bible Study, or on any other point, will not have 'a patient answer' from me, given gladly on my part."[24]

As he published his Bible studies—seven books in all by the time the last appeared in 1915—he also published his ideas about Bible study. The two premises of his program were that the study must be personal, and it must be based on a careful plan. He urged each Christian to study the Bible not only in terms of substance but also in terms of method. People might find his suggestions helpful, but they had to do the work, and that included forging a method that suited them. "Every man gathered his own manna in the wilderness," he advised, and every Christian had to do the study. And that study had to have a plan. Nothing could be gained by "mere indiscriminate, miscellaneous, unordered dipping in here and there. . . . Ezekiel's vision was a life within wheels. It combined the spirit of life and the ordered movement of wheels. It is easy for us to lose a great deal through an indefensible prejudice against methods and rules in our spiritual life."[25]

The exact nature of the plan did not matter, and just in case readers could not arrive at one on their own, he offered four possibilities. One was to read the Bible in its entirety and to reread it on a regular basis, following a scheme that would complete the reading about once a year. What he described as a "simpler" plan involved memorizing verses and meditating on them. Resorting to humor to make his point, he said that every verse in the Bible had some meaning and told of a woman who loved the verse, "At Michmash he hath laid up his carriages" (Isa. 10:28), and concluded that the Bible "will fit even the most peculiar mind."[26] Studying the Bible by books was yet another and more important way, because this helped the student to determine the authors' purposes and to discover the particular messages of the various books. When proceeding in this fashion, students needed to be careful to stick to the chosen book and not be led off into commentaries, because there was no substitute for intensive study of the Bible itself.[27] And finally, the student could work through subjects, truths, or principles, "like faith, the love of God, obedience, prayer, the Lord's return," or through characters. As to the latter, "Christ's comes first."[28]

Whatever the plan, he believed Bible study had a clear and definite purpose. In general, it was to reveal "God's personal message to our own heart and will. Each truth that we perceive is a truth to be incorporated in character. What we learn, we must be. Knowledge about the Bible is poor and imperfect if it does not bear fruit in a life of loving, joyful service of man and of the Son of man."[29] In two of his published studies directed to students he told them: "Begin, continue, and end all your study in prayer. Be willing to change your life, and to live as the Gospel may give light. Study to become better acquainted with Him, rather than to satisfy curiosity or to acquire knowledge."[30] In particular, he concluded, "all Bible-study is valuable just in proportion as it shows us the face of Jesus."[31] It helped Christians "remember that we belong to Christ," and it reminded them of their need to serve him.[32] The most helpful study was the one "which leads us to look straight at Him whom Luther called 'the Proper Man,' who was the revelation of the Father's will for every man."[33]

Bible study was an essential feature of the Christian life. Speer frequently advised people to begin or continue their study as an important part of their faith journey. "You remember I was talking to you," he wrote one young student, "about the help I thought a man could get from a loving study of the beauty of Christ. Perhaps you will be interested this Summer in working with your Bible through these studies, and I pray that they may bring you into a yet more closer [sic] and more real relationship to Him."[34] Another student received a copy of a book on Jesus from him with the advice that it might help him "in his Bible study this Summer" and the reminder that "as you know, the only way to get strong in athletics is to use the strength you already have, and the same law holds in every other sphere of life."[35] In his first letter to daughter Margaret after she entered college, he reminded her, "Don't forget your daily Bible reading and prayer. They will keep God's presence and guidance near."[36] Christians ought, he believed, to make the Bible their friend, and "to have one copy of it, surely, that is familiar and responsive to our touch, and that knows our ways and will open to what we love best."[37]

He practiced what he preached. Reflecting after retirement on his many experiences, he said, "For nearly sixty years Bible study has been for me the greatest intellectual and spiritual pleasure of life."[38] The Bible was his friend. His personal, well-worn copy fell open to the sections and passages he used most, and there were many of them. His special interests in the Old Testament included Genesis 1–15 and 35–50, Exodus 15–34, Ruth, Job 1–10, Psalms, Proverbs, Isaiah 40–66, Joel, Amos, Obadiah, Jonah, Micah, Zechariah, and Malachi. These and numerous other individual passages he marked with marginal notes in various inks indicating use over different periods of his life. The early chapters of Genesis, the middle ones of Exodus, Ruth, Joel, and the Psalms had very heavy use. Almost every single psalm received some attention and commentary, very likely because he often turned to the Psalms for his morning watch.[39]

He studied the New Testament more than the Old. The only portions not marked to any degree were Jude, Hebrews 1–10, 1 Corinthians 1–10, and substantial sections of Mark. Everything else received heavy use, roughly comparable to the heavily used sections of the Old Testament. Favorites, indicated by underlining, marginal notes, and outlines, included Matthew, John, sections of Acts, Romans, and many of Paul's other epistles.[40] He left little doubt, however, concerning his greatest love in the Bible: John. He began to work on a book on the Gospel of John as early as 1895, and when he published it twenty years later, he chose a title that revealed his opinion: *John's Gospel: The Greatest Book in the World*. He left no doubt among readers about the source of his bias, telling them that the book "springs from the unreserved and joyful acceptance of John's belief 'that Jesus is the Christ, the Son of God,' and that its humble hope is the same as John's, that others also may believe."[41] He used passages in John as bases for sermons twice as often as passages in any other book of the Bible.[42]

The Bible he used was quite large, with blank end pages as well as substantial margins in the text. He filled the open spaces with quotations, poems, outlines for speeches, and collections of scriptures for use on special occasions. The quotes, many of them about the importance of the Bible and its study, included the thoughts of Martin Luther, John Wesley, Daniel Webster, and Samuel Taylor Coleridge. He added the following words of Coleridge to the title page: "In the Bible there is more that finds me than I have experienced in all other books put together! The words of the Bible find me at greater depths of my being, and whatever thus finds me brings with it the irresistible evidence of its having proceeded from the Holy Spirit." One long essay listed questions people might raise about the Christian faith and proposed scriptural answers. For example, someone might ask how it could be that he had tried to become a Christian but had failed. He listed scriptural references that might be seen as "causes" or sources of this inquiry and other references that could be used as "cures" or answers. The extensive outlines and lists indicate he used his Bible on the lecture platforms and in meetings with students and others, as well as in personal study.[43]

At one time or another he used all of the programs for study he suggested to others, but he gradually came to focus on the study of entire books and, more particularly, of single themes. By the late 1890s the pressure of time led him to "do very little Bible study which does not bear directly upon my work."[44] He had also discovered that if he studied things that helped him personally, rather than simply topics in general, he would be able to use them in his counsel with others and therefore accomplish two things at once. After he published his study of John, he turned away from entire books and to themes or character studies. Jesus was the one personality who remained a constant attraction throughout his life. As for special topics, they varied from year to year. In 1925, for example, he worked on the title Jesus frequently used for himself, "the Son of Man." "I am trying to think out," he told a missionary friend in China, "what the significance of this phrase is in its revelation of Christ's conception, first, of His own person, second, of religion, third, of humanity. I have been going through the verses in which the phrase occurs . . . , sure that there is a great deal more in these verses than we have been accustomed to find in them, a great deal more with regard to the infinite fullness of the meaning of Christ and a great deal more with regard to God's thought about humanity and its relationship to Him."[45] In 1933 and 1934 he worked on "grace," "the love of God," and "the Kingdom of God."[46]

Bible study was a constant source of refreshment for him, like cold water on a hot day. It renewed his spirit. The controversies that swirled around the Bible during his lifetime did not affect him. Any exposition of his thought must raise serious questions about that. Speer lived through the latter half of what was almost a century of biblical criticism, a time Grant Wacker has described as "the demise of biblical civilization."[47] Although Wacker softened the finality of "demise," he nonetheless accurately suggested that by the 1920s and 1930s many Americans had lost confidence in the Bible and had come to see it as being as much a human document as a divine one, as much literature as scripture. Speer began his career in the very years his Presbyterian Church was embroiled in a great crisis involving biblical criticism. (This crisis led to the heresy trial of one of the exponents of biblical criticism, Charles A. Briggs, and to the withdrawal of Union Theological Seminary in New York from the Presbyterian fold.) Speer was very well read and knew what the biblical critics were doing. How could these events not affect him?

He seemed untouched by these currents because he was not only profoundly traditional by upbringing and inclination, but also oriented to hold the broad middle ground in most theological issues in the strict pursuit of his call on behalf of the larger mission of the church—the evangelization of the world. He could show little interest in biblical criticism because he saw the Bible as a faith document, a true witness to God's actions in humanity's time, and from that perspective essentially untouched by what the biblical critics were doing. He shared his view with the readers of his Bible studies on Jesus and Paul, both published by 1900, when he told them the studies were "sympathetic, not critical. Their purpose is wholly practical, and they pass by in the main the questions with which criticism is concerning itself."[48]

He never changed his mind on the relative unimportance of biblical criticism. The year he retired, 1937, he listed some of the things that had not changed since he had begun his career, and among them he included "the facts of our Christian history and the records of those facts in the Gospels. . . . We are not ignorant of, neither are we disturbed by, the historical and literary criticism of the early Christian documents. What the facts about Jesus Christ were they were and are. No criticism of history can alter the facts. It can alter the interpretation of the facts. It can correct any misrepresentation of the facts. But what happened happened; and we are absolutely sure that whatever changes may take place in the form of the New Testament criticism will leave us with the fact of Christ and the facts of Christ more sure and certain than ever."[49]

In the 1930s he discovered that the biblical critics, working in the glow of Barth and others, sometimes produced ideas that he found both surprising and useful. In the winter of 1933 he read Edwyn Hoskyns and Francis Noel Davey's *The Riddle of the New Testament* and realized that they made more of Jesus than he expected. The authors, he wrote, were "two of the foremost New Testament critics in England, who are as radical as any in their dealing with the gospel sources but who come out with the unequivocal conclusion that the one thing of which we can be certain is that from the very beginning the early church regarded Jesus as supernatural, a person representing the unique intervening action of God and that Jesus held this same view of Himself. The writers will have none of the old critical theory that attempted to find a purely human Jesus behind an accretion of later years."[50] Near the end of his life he summed up his thoughts on biblical criticism: "Modern criticism has not affected the value of the Bible to mind or heart in the slightest degree. One is glad for Harnack's word that the plain man may go on reading his Bible as he has always read it, 'for in the end the critic cannot read it otherwise.' But we do not need the leave of any critic. The Bible is as open to us as it is to him, and as for me, it is bread and light."[51]

When questioned concerning his beliefs about the Bible, he typically turned to the Westminster Confession of Faith and suggested that he believed what it said about the Bible. One Bible issue that became a rallying cry of the fundamentalists was verbal inerrancy. In response, Speer first quoted the confession, which said, "The Old Testament in Hebrew and the New Testament in Greek, being immediately inspired by God, and by His singular providence and care kept pure in all ages, are therefore authentical; so as in all controversies of religion the Church is finally to appeal to them." He then argued that the confession did not say "a single verbal error" invalidated the inspiration of the Bible. He concluded, "God has not deemed it essential that the 'errorless original manuscripts' should be preserved. If they are the only authentic Bible He would surely have preserved them. The Confession declares that He has so kept the Bible pure that it, as we have it, is authentical and authoritative, that the Bible that we have and as we have it is (as the Confession and the Larger Catechism say) or *contains* (as the Shorter Catechism says) the Word of

God. If anywhere in the Bible, or in the original manuscripts, there should be human error this does not invalidate its divine inspiration or authority. This is the historical and Confessional doctrine."[52]

He spent his life with the Bible. He believed Jesus also knew the Bible. Jesus had a Bible, different from the one Christians used and not likely his personal possession, but nonetheless a Bible. Jesus had made it his own by memory, and he loved it, believed it, and taught it. He also lived it, for "He saw in it the anticipated story of His life, and He fulfilled the anticipation." It was his basic resource in "times of trial, temptation, controversy and suffering." Since all these things were true, Speer concluded, "Ministers and lay people, men and women alike, need to give the Bible, in some real measure, the place in their lives which it had in the life of Christ."[53] "The minister," he told students at Princeton Theological Seminary, "is meant to be a man of one book."[54] As he worked in his study after he retired, Alexander Whyte's discovery became his own: "As I sit and write these lines I am surrounded and overwhelmed with a houseful of books of all kinds; but the longer I live and the older I grow, they are less and less in my hands, and take up less and less of my remaining time. And that is so because so few of them seem at all to know me, and to be able to speak home to me. . . . There is but one Bible. And my Bible to me is complete and supreme and alone. Till, the longer I live, the more I concentrate upon my Bible. . . . Every time I open it I find Jesus Christ in my Bible."[55] Through the years he increasingly fulfilled John Wesley's dictum: "Let me be a man of one book."[56]

Jesus Christ

The Bible was one central feature of Speer's faith; Jesus Christ was the other. Once Jesus came into his life and became the focus of it, Jesus was the context of everything Speer did. Jesus became his friend, his teacher, and in the mystical sense his great love. He once began a speech with the invitation, "Friends, I want to introduce you to my dearest friend, Jesus Christ."[57] Active and busy, frequently engaged in two or three major activities at once, as well as constantly reading and writing, friends and observers marveled at the way the many facets of his life seemed to come together, to form one whole. Jesus was the source of this unity. Jesus was part of almost everything he said or wrote. More specifically, he published twelve books on Jesus (fourteen, if two Bible studies are included) and wrote numerous other shorter pieces about Jesus, from essays to poems.

He had a unique opportunity to declare his favorite subject as a Christian and a preacher before a national audience. In 1924 the *Christian Century* polled Protestant ministers in America, asking them to choose the twenty-five whom they regard as their leaders, "the men of deepest and most prophetic vision?—the men of outstanding pulpit power?—the men whose message most vitally interprets the mind of Jesus Christ?—the pulpiteers whose thinking most deeply and potently influences the thinking of the church and the course of events in the mind of the nation?"[58] The almost 22,000 who responded selected twenty ministers, three bishops, evangelist William A. Sunday, and Speer. The list, a veritable Who's Who of American Protestantism, included Charles R. Brown, dean of Yale Divinity School; the Rev. Harry Emerson Fosdick, then at the First Presbyterian Church in New York City; the Rev. Henry Sloane Coffin, minister at Madison Avenue Presbyterian Church in New York City; the Rev. Russell H. Conwell, minister at the Baptist Temple in Philadelphia; the Rev. Ernest F. Tittle, minister of the First Methodist Church in Evanston, Illinois; and Methodist bishops Francis J. McConnell and William F. McDowell.

The *Century* invited each person chosen to "select a sermon which carries his most characteristic convictions, the message that lies nearest to his heart, the truth he most passionately desires his generation to receive."[59] Speer accepted the opportunity, but not without first pointing out that "the judgment day will show that a great many men of wider and more enduring influence were passed over by your voters. I imagine that we shall discover then that some of the most powerful persons in the world were not very widely known among men, but were very well known on high."[60] His sermon was the first in the *Century* series. He might have been expected to choose a message about foreign missions, but instead he chose his favorite subject, "The Christ Who Lives in Men."[61]

On a number of different occasions he proposed a summary of what Jesus meant to him. The most extensive effort was in book form, published in 1936 under the title *The Meaning of Christ to Me*. The more familiar statement, because editors of religious periodicals reprinted it often, he first offered to the sixth annual spiritual emphasis conference of the YMCA in Buffalo, New York, in 1930 as "What Jesus Does for Me."

> He shows me the possibility and duty of a man as to his character and his service.
>
> In the effort to attain this for myself, He does for me what I know I cannot do for myself, and what I have never found any friend, however dear, able to do for me.

He gives me a clearer moral vision and the courage to try to live by that vision.

He gives me the desire to work in the world as intensely as He worked.

He kindles me, when I grow sluggish or indifferent, to a positive and aggressive antagonism to evil within and without.

He gives me confidence in the truth and so helps me to rest, no matter what happens in the world, because I know that God and the truth must prevail.

He counterbalances, as I cannot, the variable circumstances and unequal conditions of life, and takes care of the excesses that are beyond me.

He gives me grace and strength to try, at least, things that I know are impossible, and to attempt, first of all, the things that are hardest to be done.

He helps me to refuse to do good when I know that something better can be done.

He helps me to keep on going when I have to, even though I know I cannot.

He saves me from the fret and killing of pride and vanity, and helps me to cease to care for the things that make people sick.

He helps me to keep the central things clear and not to be fogged and broken down by the accessories and secondary things.

He gives me a new and inward living principle by His Life and His Resurrection.

He reveals as sin my difference from the God I see in Him; He forgives it and deals with it and all that it involves by His Cross.

Lastly, I believe that He is Himself the principle of life and that there is another personality in me that would not be there if it had not been for Him and if it were not for Him to-day.[62]

Christians were called to "Remember Jesus Christ." The term came to him while he was on a houseboat in China, during his longest, and in many ways grandest, journey as a missionary executive. Circumstances did not permit ordinary Bible study, so he devised an alternative. Each evening he and his companions would read their Bibles together and agree on the most meaningful phrase, which they would use the next morning for their study. One night a medical missionary traveling with them was reading aloud from 2 Timothy 2 in the King James Version and came to verse 8: "Remember that Jesus Christ of the seed of David was raised from the dead according to my gospel." Speer's Revised Version translated the early part of the verse, "Remember Jesus Christ," and he later recalled that the change "sent a thrill through me as though heaven had been opened just a little."[63] He instantly recognized that the verse now said something dramatically different and more in keeping with his understanding of the gospel. To remember "that Jesus Christ . . . was raised from the dead" was to call to mind a fact of Christ's life, and while he did not diminish any of those facts, he did "not believe that the memory of any single fact of Christ's life, not even the memory of the fact that He rose from the dead, can be compared with the meaning and the joy of remembering Jesus Christ Himself." Moreover, the new way of reading the verse seemed to clarify Paul's intent. Surely Paul did not want Timothy to fill his mind with a lot of facts about Jesus or even the "doctrine of Christ's resurrection." What he wanted for his young associate was for his memory, his life, to be "filled with Jesus Christ."[64]

He realized that the new translation of the passage had exciting possibilities. It was short and easy to grasp, so simple and unambiguous that everyone could understand it, so practical that everyone could use it. Sometimes, he noted, proposals for leading a more spiritual life were complex or appeared to be mysterious, so that people were uncertain about their ability to follow them. "Remember Jesus Christ" had no such liabilities.[65] Paul laid it right out: "He means for us to saturate our memories with the earthly life of Jesus, the Son of David; he means for us to make ourselves so familiar with the story of that life and the way it went to and fro among men, the atmosphere of it, the surroundings of it, that Jesus Himself shall live again with us. Would not this be sweet? Is not this all our cry?"[66]

He proposed that the phrase be used as a "rule of life," and as such it had several attractive features. Remembering Jesus could *transform* life, so that the more a person remembered him, the more that person could become like him. Remembering Jesus could *restrain* life, and the person under such "Christ-constraint" could better lead a Christian life. Remembering Jesus could *stimulate* life, so that a person so encouraged could "go out and live a new life for Him who so made it His meat and His drink to do the will of God." Remembering Jesus was the most *sufficient* rule imaginable, capable of resolving all questions. There were those would-be disciples who were troubled by Jesus' deity or incarnation or resurrection, but if they would just remember Jesus, they would be absolutely sure to "come out where Jesus Christ is." This rule of life was so complete, he believed, "that you cannot find any circumstance or condition of life that can elude its satisfactory reach, the reach of the memory of Jesus."[67] He followed this rule personally throughout his life. He rarely gave interviews for publication, but he gave one for the *Baptist Student* in 1933. The interviewer asked: "We have in round numbers one hundred thousand Baptist students in schools and colleges of the South. If you had these before you, what would be your message to them in a single sentence? Doctor Speer lifted his eyes quickly, without the pause of a split-second his words were a flash! Remember Jesus Christ."[68]

While remembering Jesus was very important for the Christian, it implied a personal relationship with him. Speer found another Pauline phrase, "in Christ," to be an excellent description of that relationship. His extensive study of Paul led him to conclude that it meant at least two things. First, living "in Christ" was a daily testimony to the resurrection. When Paul met Jesus, he did not meet a dead teacher or a "vanished ideal"; instead, he met "a risen and living and present personal force."[69] Second, living "in Christ" was having another life within you, sharing your life with you. Paul literally lived in Christ, and Christ lived in him. The apostle's classic formulation of it was this: "I have been crucified with Christ; and it is no longer I that live, but Christ liveth in me: and the life which I now live in the flesh I live in faith, the faith which is in the Son of God, who loved me, and gave himself up for me."[70] Paul, he argued, was not speaking metaphorically, but in terms of his actual experience. It meant that the "Christian religion was a supernatural power, a supernatural life, the actual pervasion of human life by God so that there was in Christian men a real divine presence, God in Christ, God in the Holy Spirit, working in and upon the soul."[71]

He acknowledged that the experience of two lives in one was deeply mystical, but claimed that did not mean it was "unreasonable," "incoherent," or "incapable of clear and reasoned statement and explanation."[72] He found support for this interpretation of Paul in a work by Albert Schweitzer, who wrote, " 'All attempts to rob Christianity of the character of Christ-Mysticism are nothing more nor less than a useless resistance to that spirit of knowledge and truth which finds expression in the teaching of the first and greatest of all Christian thinkers.' "[73] Just as "Paul knew Christ in his heart, and sought to account for Him in his thought" with the phrase "in Christ," so too, Speer said, "true Christians will do both of these."[74] And that was possible because Paul's experience was not his exclusive possession but was open to every Christian.[75]

Although it was never easy to speak plainly of what was a mystery, Speer kept trying. In his list of what Jesus did for him, he said that there was "another personality" in him. When faced with explaining this relationship, he often turned to poetry, particularly to one of his favorite poems, *Saint Paul*, by the well-known English poet and author Frederic W. H. Myers. He was most attached to the following two verses, the first and the last of the long poem.

Christ! I am Christ's! and let the name suffice you,
Ay, for me too He greatly hath sufficed;
Lo with no winning words I would entice you,
Paul has no honor and no friend but Christ.

. . . .

Yea thro' life, death, thro' sorrow and thro' sinning
He shall suffice me, for he hath sufficed:
Christ is the end, for Christ was the beginning,
Christ the beginning, for the end is Christ.[76]

Theology and Christology

He was an outspoken advocate for faith as an experience of the living
Christ, and he turned the vast majority of his speaking and writing about
it in this direction. Although this was his primary interest, he understood
that the Christian faith included theology, or what he called on occasion
"conviction." Moreover, he acknowledged that "the conviction and the
experience are not to be separated. They were not separable in Christianity
at the beginning, and they are not separable today."[77] But his awareness of
theology did not mean that he considered himself to be a theologian. John
G. Buchanan, a good friend and a member of the Board of Foreign
Missions and of the board of trustees of Princeton Theological Seminary,
said in an obituary essay that if Speer had completed his course in seminary, he would have been a "great theologian."[78] That judgment missed the
mark, even though it was doubtless offered as a compliment. Speer was
not a theologian either by temperament or interest, and the small amount
of theological writing he did was not a consequence of the brevity of his
seminary education. It was, rather, an expression of his uneasiness with the
ability of any language to express the "operations of the mind of God." In
a most revealing letter on the subject of theological reflection, he said that
he fell back on Bushnell's "theory of language" and explained, "We have
got no terms in which to describe the infinite except finite terms, all of
them beset on every side by limitation. . . . If it be said that this view
makes a systematic theology impossible, I reply that I fear it does, in the
sense in which some would attempt to construct such a theology."
Theologies, he believed, typically led in contrary directions and became
the sources of division rather than unity. While there were those who
wished to carry on such work, he wrote, "I root my theology in what I
know of human personality," which meant he began with Jesus Christ.[79]

For Speer, theology was almost without exception Christology. When
he wrote theological essays, as he did on occasion despite the limits of

language and his own interest, he almost always wrote on some aspect of Jesus and his life and ministry. His books and correspondence reveal that he was very aware of other theological ideas and very knowledgeable about current theological developments, but he never strayed far from his focus on Jesus Christ. He expressed his perspective most succinctly in an essay he wrote in 1944 for the *Union Seminary Review*. Referring to Karl Barth and Reinhold Niebuhr, he noted that the major theological interests of the day were the doctrine of God and the nature of humanity. In each of these two areas he evaluated the developments as proper and "wholesome" reactions to what had been taking place in the recent past. The focus on the " 'otherness' of God" was a proper response to "the immanentalism or semi-pantheism that lost God in nature and forfeited the conception of God's fatherly personality which was the revelation of Jesus Christ." The focus on human depravity was a useful challenge to "the optimism and idealization of classical and modern humanism, with its false confidence and hopes." Both of the new trends were useful correctives, but as such they were in some ways exaggerations. The solution to the problem of the movement of theology from one "extreme" to another was "to be found in a different field of thought, in which the real issue of our time and of every time is to be found, namely, the field of Christology." He then argued that what Christians thought about both God and humanity depended on Jesus Christ, because "as the Son of God He revealed God to man. As the Son of Man He revealed man to himself." Therefore, he concluded, "The issues of theology as to the nature of God and of anthropology as to the nature of man depend *absolutely* on our doctrine of the Person of Christ."[80]

When dealing with Jesus in what for him was a theological mode, Speer tackled a variety of topics over the length of his career, including the incarnation, the virgin birth, and the second coming. The list is not exhaustive in any sense. He made no effort to consider every possible topic, and he did not deal with those that interested him in a systematic manner, with one possible exception, the incarnation, which he treated more or less systematically in two books, published almost four decades apart.

The traditional view of the incarnation, that God became a human being in Jesus Christ and created such a union that Christ was fully God and fully human, he accepted. When he came to reflect on it, he typically approached it from the point of view of the humanity of Christ as the way to understand better the godhood of Christ. He adopted this method very early in his career, freely acknowledging that he learned it from Bushnell's *The Character of Jesus*, and encouraged his readers to look at Bushnell for themselves.[81] His first extended work on the incarnation began as a Bible study of the life of Jesus in the Gospels, then became Bible talks at Northfield and an 1894 lecture at the Keswick Convention in England, and finally reached book form as *Studies of the Man Christ Jesus*. The title came from Paul, who told Timothy, "There is one God, one mediator also between God and men, Himself man, Christ Jesus" (1 Timothy 2:5). It conveyed Speer's thesis that, in reflections on Jesus Christ, too much attention had been paid to his deity and too little to his humanity, or as he put it, "There is no little unconscious Docetism in Christian thought still." But any effort to reduce his humanity was a serious threat to the entire Christian enterprise, for if he did not take on a real human nature, then "the incarnation would not be a real incarnation; Jesus could not have been tempted in all points as we are, and He could not have wrought out for us a salvation in any such vital sense as can alone constitute a salvation."[82]

Approaching the incarnation this way, he believed, led to a full understanding of both sides of the human-God equation. On the one hand, it revealed his deity. Focus on his human character led the student to confront the fact that "Jesus was *such* a man that He must have been more." A serious study of his humanity "excludes Him from the class of natural phenomena. Whoso begins with the acknowledgment, 'This was a righteous man,' cannot stop short of the confession, 'Surely this man was the Son of God.' " Such a serious study presents the full "Imago Christi." On the other hand, a true understanding of the incarnation lifted up Christ's humanity. Serious study of the *man* Christ Jesus revealed "an example for the Christian life." His argument ran on to say that those who looked long and hard at the man Jesus came to realize how good a man could be and came under obligation to seek to become more like him.[83]

In the several sections of his study, he examined in turn different aspects of Jesus' life and work, each revealing his perfect humanity and also leading to the conclusion that he was also divine. In the part devoted to "His Plans and Methods of Work," Speer noted how Jesus' audacious plans for a kingdom of God amazed his disciples and others and at the same time raised the issue of his deity, for "would any devout young Jew dare to declare such dreams, and yet vaster dreams, in full day unless he were more than a devout young Jew?"[84] In the section devoted to "Extraordinary Characteristics," he presented Jesus as the "perfect ideal of friendship." Not only did he teach "great masses of men what it is to live with the friendship-love. It was thus that He revealed the heart of that Father whose name is friendship-love."[85] Speer concluded his study with the assertion that the man Christ Jesus was indeed both human and God, and with what was already a characteristic of much of his spoken and written word: an appeal for commitment. In this case he challenged his readers to remember that "He is meaningless for us save as we enter into our inheritance in Him."[86]

The next time he turned his attention to a such extensive and systematic treatment of the incarnation was almost forty years later in *The Finality of Jesus Christ*, the Stone Lectures at Princeton Theological Seminary and the Gay Lectures at Southern Baptist Theological Seminary. The book was an effort to define the relationship between Christianity and non-Christian religions. (That theme is treated more fully in chapter 8 of this book.) He developed his analysis of the incarnation in the context of setting out the primitive church's view of Jesus Christ as it confronted the non-Christian religions of its time.

Speer began his argument by presenting his understanding of the essential faith of the primitive church, that "Jesus Christ was the Son of God and the only Lord and Saviour."[87] The more important question, however, was whether the modern Christian could still affirm that. The problem for the early church arose when people accepted Jesus' divinity but questioned his humanity. Speer saw that for the modern church the problem was that many of his contemporaries respected Jesus' perfect humanity, as teacher or leader, but had surrendered his deity. While the situation was different, Speer believed his solution still worked, because it cut both ways, providing arguments for both the humanity and the deity of Christ. Bushnell continued to provide the foundation of his analysis, but Speer added the ideas and illustrations of a host of his own contemporaries. He concluded that however much some modern thinkers wished to separate "the Christ of history and the Christ of experience," it could not be done without destroying the foundation truth of the gospel. In a ringing affirmation of the incarnation, he declared, "We bless God that Jesus Christ is a living spiritual presence, that Christianity is not mere historical data but an essential spirit, but we bless Him also that Christianity is historic fact, the fact of Jesus of Bethlehem, of Nazareth, of Caesarea Philippi, of Gethsemane, of Calvary, of Olivet: the fact of Christ risen and living, with us and in us forevermore."[88]

Other Theological Ideas

He wrote less extensively on other theological issues. The virgin birth occupied his attention from time to time, particularly during the controversies with the fundamentalists in the late 1920s and early 1930s. After it sur-faced as a potential issue at the General Assembly in 1927, he wrote his only long essay on it, describing his viewpoint as "the word of one believer to his fellow believers—all alike seeking to know the mind of Christ and to do His will."[89] He wrote not so much a theological statement as a series of arguments, five in number, that sustained his belief in the virgin birth. First, the Gospels affirmed it, and since they were the basic source books of the faith, they were sufficient grounds for belief in this one aspect of the faith. It was not, he claimed, reason to doubt it just because only two of the Gospels included it. After all, they did not all refer to the Sermon on the Mount, yet few if any Christians questioned its authenticity. Second, the virgin birth had been the belief of the church from the beginning. Third, in an argument borrowed from his thought on the incarnation, "Jesus was unique," and it was only reasonable that "such a life should be as different in its origin and its end as it was in its spirit and principle and manifestation throughout."[90] Fourth, Christ's work as Savior suggested such a special and miraculous origin, although it did not require it. His point was that the "Bible nowhere declares that knowledge of the virgin birth is essential to salvation," but it nonetheless was "part of the whole meaning and significance of the Gospel." Fifth, he believed in the virgin birth because any alternative view was "intolerable."[91]

He did not even hint in his essay what might have been a sixth reason for his interest, and that was the important place it gave to a woman in the Gospel account. After his death, his wife proposed such a relationship in his thought and suggested that anyone who believed the virgin birth as "wholeheartedly" as he did "was therefore inevitably a believer in an equal place for woman in the Church and in society." She concluded, "He believed that if the Saviour of the world had not been born of a woman without the mediation of a human father, women would have remained inferior to men, a mere segment of the race, a biological necessity for its preservation, instead of a normal half of it, a half that was worthy of the same dignity, the same respect and consideration that is due to each child of God."[92] He provided some evidence for this interpretation in his brief meditation "Christ and Womanhood," where he wrote the prayer: "O God, our Father, we thank Thee that Thine only-begotten Son took our nature upon Him and was born of a Virgin. . . . We thank Thee for His influence through all the centuries in protecting women from wrong, in securing justice and equality, in opening the paths of service."[93]

The second coming of Christ was as real to him as any other aspect of his faith, theological or practical, and, like the virgin birth, received special attention. The reason for this lay in part in the setting in which he first came to an awareness of what Christ's return meant. It was at Northfield the summer after his conversion. He was staying in Hillside Cottage and later recalled, "We came back to our rooms from a meeting in which some one had pointed out the New Testament passages promising the return of Jesus Christ with hearts all aglow. Life seemed altogether changed for me in that hour. I discovered that Christ was not resting back in that grave near Jerusalem; that Christ was not only sitting God-remote at the right hand of the Father, but that Christ is waiting, patiently waiting, the coming of that glad day when He is to come back again to me and to all of those who love His appearing."[94] He subsequently studied the idea, finding support for it throughout the New Testament, where he counted no less than 318 references to it. He found that the apostles had made much of it, and so had Paul, who believed he would "receive his crown of righteousness at that day." While such witnesses counted heavily, they were clearly outweighed by Jesus, who had spoken about it, promised it, and tied it "indissolubly to the Lord's Supper—'as often as ye eat this bread, and drink this cup, ye proclaim the Lord's death till He come.' "[95] Thoroughly persuaded of the great importance of Christ's return, he began to speak and write about it.

He believed that everyone acknowledged three great facts of Christianity: (1) Christ, who "came into this world by way of the manger—the great fact of the lowly incarnation"; (2) Christ, who "went out of this world by way of the cross and the open grave—the great truths of the atonement and the resurrection"; and (3) the Holy Spirit, who "came into this world as Christ's advocate to abide here as His representative." But, he added, there was a fourth fact that was as essential as the other three, as integral to the faith as any one or all of the other three, and that was "that Jesus Christ is coming back again."[96] Jesus had said so plainly: "I will come again" (John 14:3). Nothing was more certain than that Christ must return in order to "complete and fulfil His first coming."[97] The problem was that not everyone agreed with this fourth feature of the faith. There were those believers, for example, who found themselves able to relate to a "Christ of ancient history" but could not bring themselves to deal with either a "Christ of present life" or a "Christ of coming judgment." Christianity was a historical faith but not a faith of history: "We cannot well retain pure and fresh and quick our faith in the Christ who died and rose again unless we believe also in the Christ who is reigning now and who is again to come."[98]

He argued that belief in the second coming contributed many important things to the Christian faith. It promised a reunion with those who were dead. Paul had testified to this explicitly when he said that "those which sleep in Jesus will God bring with Him." The second coming was "the glorification of our human relationships, the knitting up of our severed human ties, the making permanent and eternal of our human loves and affections."[99] In addition, when he returned, he would deliver believers from both outer and inner evil, from the power of temptation from without and within. Finally, the return of Jesus made certain "the redemption of all our life." The vision had been shared by Paul in Romans, when he claimed that "the earnest expectation of the creation waiteth for the redemption of the sons of God . . . in hope that the creation itself shall also be delivered from the bondage of corruption into the liberty of the glory of the children of God," and it remained as true for contemporary Christians as it had been for Paul.[100]

One of the most important issues that swirled around the hope of the second coming in the late nineteenth and early twentieth centuries was the timing of the arrival of Christ, and what Christians were to do as they prepared for his appearance. Speer lived through one of the great ages of millennial thinking in American religious life. Some Christians, encouraged in part by the economic progress associated with the Industrial Revolution and, as the century neared its end, the amazing success of missionaries in the evangelization of the world, believed they were already sharing in the promised thousand-year reign of Christ. Other Christians, more pessimistic about both society and humanity, looked for some sure sign of judgment before the redemptive time would begin. These differences sometimes erupted into disputes between what were then called pre- and postmillennialists.

He was acutely aware of the groups and their differences and just as adamant about forging a position that would keep him free from both. He achieved this by developing a position rooted entirely in the Bible, without reference to the pluses or minuses of modern life. The Bible, he noted, used the term "millennium" only once, in the book of Revelation. As for himself, he "always" avoided using the terms " 'pre and post millenial,' believing them to be thoroughly un-scriptural." True to his word, he wrote a small book on the second coming with not a single reference to them.[101] What he called "the simple truth as we find it in the Gospels and the Epistles" was crystal clear: no one knew when it would happen. Jesus himself did not know and said so: "Of that day and of that hour knoweth no man, no, not the angels of God, neither the Son, but the Father only." Speer believed that those who proposed Jesus would come after the world was converted were talking nonsense. When, he asked, might that be, since "we have not converted a single town in America yet"?

The proper attitude of the believer toward the second coming, he said, was watchful waiting. Jesus had set the standard: "Watch, for in an hour that you think not the Son of Man cometh."[102] Such watching was to be in genuine anticipation that he might come at any time, on any given day. And when he came, Speer wanted to be able to say, "I have been waiting, Lord. The time has been long, but every day I hoped that you would come, and my joy is all delight, unmingled with any strange surprises."[103] Near the end of his life, he titled a meditation on the second coming "Watch and Wait" and crafted a prayer which distilled the essence of his thinking about it:

> O Lord Jesus Christ, we thank Thee that we have besides the story of Thine earthly life and the experience of Thy constant presence, the blessed hope of Thy coming again, when we shall see Thee as Thou art, and when Thou wilt bring with Thee all whom we love who have left our mortal sight and are safe with Thee. Forbid that we should lose the joy and strength of the daily expectancy of Thy return. May our eyes be ever toward Thy coming, not in memory of the past alone, and not alone in common human experience or in the mystery of death, but in Thy visible, personal appearing, remembering Thy most sure word, "I will come again. Watch therefore, lest coming suddenly I find you sleeping."[104]

Theological Perspective

Speer was a man of faith, a faith that was Bible-centered and Christ-centered. Although he focused most of his work, outside of the considerable body of it he devoted to missions, on the practical aspects of faith, his occasional forays into theology have led some commentators to try to place him in a particular theological context. Contemporaries typically regarded him as a theological conservative.[105] But some took other views. Many who espoused fundamentalism at first counted him in their camp, perhaps because he wrote two articles for *The Fundamentals*, but later many of those same persons rejected him and accused him of modernism.[106] A reviewer of *The Finality of Jesus Christ* dismissed it by saying it represented "the Presbyterian orthodoxy of fifty years ago." Speer responded that the criticism made "him out entirely too much of a modernist," and said that his intention in the book "was not to set forth the orthodoxy of fifty years ago but to go much farther back than that and to declare what he believed to be the orthodoxy of the New Testament," and to get "behind the times . . . wholly behind them, behind all time, and to set forth the eternal truth which is beneath time and beyond time."[107]

The consensus of his contemporaries about his theological views has not been carried forward by recent scholars. Indeed, those who have reflected on his work have had considerable difficulty agreeing about it, and as little success characterizing him theologically. Ernest Sandeen, a student of fundamentalism, called him a "conservative Calvinist."[108] Other students of fundamentalism have disagreed with that, one calling him simply a "conservative," and another a "fundamentalist."[109] Lefferts Loetscher, a historian of the Presbyterian and Reformed traditions, cited him as "a culminating product of nineteenth century evangelical liberalism, although he himself did not make that transition."[110] James Patterson, in a serious study of his missionary work, said he exemplified "nineteenth century evangelicalism." In a subsequent analysis of his controversy with Machen, however, Patterson described him variously as a "conservative evangelical" and a "moderate conservative."[111] Bradley Longfield, in a surprising contrast to Sandeen and also at variance with Loetscher, has chosen to see him as a "theological centrist."[112] Robert Handy has selected the simple term "evangelical," and so has William Hutchison.[113]

This confusion has no simple solution but at least two main sources, both of which may offer useful perspectives for evaluating Speer's theological work. First, his career spanned more than sixty years, included an active retirement, and covered more than one era of theological dialogue and dispute, including the very divisive fundamentalist controversy. Theological categories shifted, and terms had different nuances in different eras. He was an evangelical and a conservative, but in his controversy with Machen he took on a somewhat different and more complex role. Different terms fit different periods of his life, and no one formula adequately defines his entire experience. Second, and more importantly, he absolutely refused to join or be counted in any particular theological camp. He was well acquainted with some of the theologians of his day and considered at least two of them, William Adams Brown and Henry Sloane Coffin, close personal friends. But he had no interest in any theological label, or what he on occasion called "factional names." Although Hutchison has called Speer an evangelical, he has also, troubled by the seeming inaccuracy of any label, aptly proposed that he tried to "walk the tightrope of the theological center."[114] To the degree that the center was a fixed location, he was never there; but to the degree that it was a meeting

place of differing views and a potential source of their comprehension, it
was his theological home.

Speer summed up his personal attitude toward his theological position
when he spoke as president of the Federal Council of Churches and on
behalf of Christian unity to the annual meeting of the council in 1923.
He reminded his listeners that Paul had refused to tolerate even a
" 'Christian' party in the Corinthian Church," and declared there was no
reason for the modern church to repudiate his view.[115] For himself, he
utterly opposed all exclusive groups, like the fundamentalists who
dichotomized truth, claiming they had it all, but he also objected to those
who simply claimed more truth than others. He deplored the fact that in
their time no less than seven factions vied with one another, and that individuals were called, or called others, rationalists, reactionaries, radicals,
liberals, conservatives, fundamentalists, and modernists. He proceeded to
advocate all the positions, creating a litany that began, "Every Christian
ought to be . . . ," and ending with a ringing affirmation of each of them
in turn. And so he proposed that every Christian ought to be a rational-
ist, in the "readiness and ability to give a reason for the hope that is in us,"
and a reactionary, in the sense of going "back to Christ," and a radical, in
the determination to be concerned "with the roots of things," and a liberal, "a man of freedom, a believer in freedom, a preacher of freedom," and
a conservative, "a guardian of the great inheritance," and a fundamentalist, "building on the only foundation which can ever be, which is Jesus
Christ," and a modernist, "open to the ever enlarging illumination of the
Spirit who was promised as our leader into all truth, and looking for the
new heaven and the new earth."[116]

In the final analysis he used this strategy to dramatize his belief that the
"truth of God is greater than any one party can claim or any one title but
Christian can cover. What we need is a New Testament conception of its
fulness and of its communicability to the whole body alone. Only the
whole body of Christ is competent to know and experience the whole
faith of Christ." In an appeal to unity he urged his listeners to reject all
titles and to realize that the truth lay in a comprehension of them all. As
the echo of Bushnell's ideal died down, he announced his final position:
"For my part I want no label but Christian and mean to try to call no
brother Christian by any other name."[117] In this respect, at least, he was
the Bushnell of his generation.

CHAPTER 4

Family Life

"Friendship-Love"

Love surrounded and supported Robert Speer all his life. God's love as revealed in Jesus Christ he experienced as a child, and its reality expanded as he grew and remained fresh and vital for him throughout his life. Human love as shared by his family he received as a gift and in turn offered to the other families in his life. Hardly unique, but certainly fortunate, was he to find love in all three of his most important families: his birth family; the family of his wife; and the family he and his wife formed. In each case, love not only existed but abounded, both human love and divine love, for he and the families of his life never made a strong distinction between them. They collectively believed that God made all love and gave it all, in whatever form, as a blessing to be lived and shared with others.

When he left his first family to attend Princeton, he carried with him their love and affection, constantly reinforced by letters from home and during summer vacations, and he went with the personal expectation that he would one day rejoin that family, perhaps as a lawyer in partnership with his father. The missionary call changed that, and he began to realize, especially as his college years neared their end, that Huntingdon lay in his past. The fall of his senior year proved a particularly difficult time of transition. In early October he lamented, "Oh, my heart nearly overflows sometimes as I think that some day I shall have to leave the scenes I have loved at home. The friends I have loved and the life to which I had looked forward. May the Lord make me strong!"[1]

Life was also changing at home, often in painful ways. Vic's problems, which had troubled the entire family for two years, erupted again, and Robert had to step in and help try to find a resolution. Other news from home included reports that his father had suffered a "stroke of apoplexy," that his Aunt Min was "down with nervous prostration," and that his father had dissolved the law firm. Striking a rare note of discouragement, he concluded, "The world of our small lives is not serene."[2] When the traditional celebrations of Christmas fell far short of his memories, he was clearly unhappy: "We went to Ma's for dinner. Papa and Aunt Min were not there. Things are not what they used to be. I can remember when there was one long table and all were pleasant. Life has changed very, very much."[3]

The Death of His Father

The truly significant break in his first family circle came slightly more than a year later, during his term as traveling secretary for the SVM, and was the result of an event much more tragic than a disappointing Christmas holiday: the death of his father. His father was just fifty-one when he died. He had enjoyed good health in general but had experienced spells of an undefined illness for several years. In 1887 he and daughter Mary had toured Europe and had observed in several of their letters that he was feeling much better, but neither he nor anyone else in the family read in his improved condition while away any clue about the possible cause of his illness. He became seriously ill in the fall of 1889, and doctors diagnosed lead poisoning, probably from drinking water carried by lead pipes installed in his bathroom. When the local medical system could do nothing more for him, he went to New York City for special treatment. He seemed to rally after Christmas but took a turn for the worse in mid-January 1890 and died suddenly.[4] As he was the key figure in the family, even before his wife died, his death altered the family dramatically, leaving it without its longtime central focus. No one stepped forward to fill that important role, and although Huntingdon continued to be home port for those children away from home, the family had changed forever.

Speer took a two-month leave from the SVM in order to remain in Huntingdon and deal with the estate. He very likely also dealt with his own grief, although he left no record of his feelings during this time. His father was the most important person in his life, his role model and his chief correspondent, always ready with counsel and advice. The absence of any record, diary entries, or letters, may be because he was home and able to talk through his grief with other family members, or it may be a sign that the shock of the loss interrupted his regular routines. He buried the memories of his father deep, so that they rarely surfaced and then only obliquely in a reference to fatherhood in a speech or book.

Almost exactly forty years later at a family Christmas gathering, his eldest son encouraged him to create a genealogical record for his grandchildren. He began immediately, and one of the first pieces he finished was a series of "recollections" of his father. He remarked that he had a great deal of joy in the entire project, a mood perhaps inspired by finally being able to set out his feelings about his father: "My memory of him is of a powerful, wholly competent, self-contained, righteous, broadly human personality, who feared no one but God and whom nothing could divert from truth and duty; a little lonesome with his wife gone and with no friend at hand who was his equal in intellect or force; generous and high-minded, using in a small place gifts equal to vastly greater occasions but content to do work of the best and highest quality where he was, looking out meanwhile with the view of a philosopher and a historian over the life of the nation and the human movement throughout the world, and measuring it against eternity."[5]

Emma Doll Bailey

For almost two years he lived without the strong family context that had marked his entire life. He closed out his year with the SVM on a highly successful note and completed his first year of theological seminary. Then, at the student conference at Northfield in 1891, an event took place that set the stage for his next two family experiences and ultimately shaped the rest of his life. The conference organizers had invited him to lead a Bible study, and although it was only four years since his first trip to Northfield, he was already recognized as one of the leaders of the student missionary movement. The summer conferences had traditionally been open only to students at the various men's colleges, but this time someone suggested inviting students from the women's colleges. In general those plans failed, but in one particular instance they succeeded. Joining the many men that summer were two students from Bryn Mawr College, "properly chaperoned, of course." One of the women was Emma Doll Bailey of Harrisburg, Pennsylvania.[6]

Speer left no account of being impressed by her but later remembered that he had met her on the porch of the Revell Cottage. She was quite taken by him, recording his name in her diary several times, including some added emphasis on July 3, where she noted the speakers were "Brookman, *Speer*, Moorehead, Bashford." Later, after they fell in love, she wrote him an eloquent letter about her thoughts on first seeing him. Her memory highlights his status as a leader and also expresses what became their mutual lifelong conviction: God had chosen them for one another.

> I have loved you so deeply since the first instant that I saw you, that Sunday evening, in Stone Hall at Northfield. . . . The first instant that I ever saw your face, Rob, a most curious feeling came to me—you may call it a presentment [sic], second-sight, what you will, but it is quite true that when I turned and saw you, you were sitting several rows behind me, on the stairs, I think, all in a flash, just for an instant I could see out and beyond, and I felt that your life and mine were to be inseparably bound together. . . . When I saw you, you know, I had no idea who you were or any things about you, you were just one of hundreds of strange men. Do you not think it is true that such friendships as ours are formed in Heaven, and here on earth when friends meet they recognize each other? Afterward, I almost entirely forgot this feeling that I had had, and if I did think of it, knowing that you were Mr. Speer whom everyone admired, and everyone was talking about, it was only to wonder at my self, and my inconceivable presumption. So I put it away in a far corner of my heart, and would not look at it, tho' all the while it was there.[7]

The relationship between the two young people may have sparked for her that summer, but it became mutual later that year when she invited him to come and speak at Bryn Mawr. He was in the midst of reevaluating his career and had just decided to leave theological seminary and enter the work of the Board of Foreign Missions when her invitation arrived. He was receptive to the idea, since his new work involved recruitment, and as it turned out, he made two speeches at Bryn Mawr that winter. The first was in response to her general proposal to speak on some religious topic. She had informed him that her fellow students did not seem to realize the need of religion, and he had responded that such an attitude was "a trouble which affects all of us younger people—especially in colleges and seminaries—even theological ones. We do so much think of ourselves. And even among those of us who are really His, I am sure, much is lost in just this way, instead of looking steadfastly unto Jesus."[8] Shortly before the meeting she wrote again, sharing her hopes that through him "the Spirit of Truth may speak to these girls with an overwhelming power, and that from that night they may give up their lives to Christ crucified, through whom alone they can see the Father."[9]

On Sunday, January 10, he preached at the Presbyterian Church in Bryn Mawr and spoke at the college in the evening. He and Emma had some time to talk privately, and he subsequently sent her Trumbull's book on friendship, adding that it was for him good "to work each day in the strength of the knowledge that we each rely on a friendship with Him which abides as true as steel."[10] Trumbull defined friendship as "loving another for that other's own sake" and created the combination "friendship-love" as a modern translation of the biblical term *agape*.[11]

His presentation prompted a second invitation, this one from the president of Bryn Mawr, to return and speak specifically on foreign missions. Emma, as president of the Missionary Society, made the arrangements and met with him to work out some details. Up to this time his letters to her had been largely formal, but the one he wrote after this meeting had a somewhat different tone, softer and more personal, and informed her that he had "ventured to put your name on my list for prayer."[12] She responded immediately, thanking him for his prayers, and then revealed that their lives were already in a way connected. "Do you remember," she wrote, "the evening that you led the missionary meeting on Round Top at Northfield? It was at Northfield that I first realized how completely my life was lacking in all that a Christian's should be, though I had called myself a Christian for years, and it was that evening that I made up my mind that I too, from that time would have for my only object in life to be in all things well pleasing to Him who gave His life for us." She was not yet sure, she closed, whether she could be a foreign missionary, but he had helped her begin her quest.[13] Flattered? Intrigued? Definitely interested, Speer wrote the day before the meeting in the same new tone to say that he looked forward to it "and to seeing you again," adding that there was a late train from Philadelphia, and he would be happy to take it if that "would give me any opportunity of talking with you."[14]

Bryn Mawr welcomed him on Tuesday, March 1, the second time in two months, but the real consequence of the visit was a new stage in the relationship between the speaker and his hostess. They talked after the meeting and planned to meet again. He was scheduled to speak at her home church in Harrisburg, at a midweek service on the ninth, and an exchange of letters resulted in her taking some class cuts and joining him on the train trip west. Both were staying over on the tenth, she for the wedding of her brother Charles and he to catch a train for Chambersburg and his next appointment. The couple spent the few morning hours they had on the tenth on what she told her diary was a "*long walk and talk with Mr. Speer,*" north "in the shining grey mist" along the shore line of the Susquehanna River.[15] It was the most significant moment of their young relationship, for in those hours they spoke of their love for one another and promised themselves to one another.

They wrote each other immediately, exploring and trying to put into words what they felt for one another. He was at first more tentative than she, and although both possessed poetic impulses, she was the first to use them. Each used Trumbull's language about friendship. He opened with a formal address, calling her "my dear Miss Bailey," as he had previously, but within a week he switched to "my own dear Emma," and he used some version of it in his extensive correspondence with her over the next fifty-five years. He confessed that he already felt their separation, despite the fact that he knew "that the large part of a friendship like ours is superior to space and triumphs over severance but just as in the friendship which we have with Christ so also in these human ties there is the 'desire to be with' and the longing that where we are there also our friends may be." He felt encouraged that his "mind continually approves of the wealth of friendship I offered you by constantly remembering and reminding me that you did not refuse it but accepted it and gave me yours in return."[16] She opened with a poem and then admitted she was lost in wonder, love, and praise. "Yesterday," she wrote, "seems now as if it could not be anything more than a beautiful dream, our walk up the river . . . and the thought that you really care to be my friend, but I cannot tell you how happy this dream and this thought makes me. The Lord Jesus has sent some new beauty into my life each day since I put my life in His hands, and of each one I have felt my self more and more unworthy, unspeakably so of this last and most beautiful gift, of a friend—a 'friend of the first degree'—who has my friendship, too, to the fullest extent that my poor limited nature is capable of."[17]

After these initial pledges of love, letters flowed between them like the Susquehanna River in flood. He assured his "dear Emma" that their relationship was not a dream: "It is sweet like one but it is true and it will abide. Is it not, even as we are, anchored in Christ who is the same yesterday, today, and forever? And are we not longing and trusting every day to do the will of God and shall we not therefore abide forever? Let us not fear that some morning the dream will be gone. Neither let us fear, because of the deep and sudden joy, to enter freely into each other's life."[18]

He proceeded to open his life to her, in a way that he rarely did with others, ever. In a series of self-revelations he told her that his life had included many "fierce struggles," which he typically fought alone. This had made him, he acknowledged, "silent about many things," so reserved that often even his closest friends, like his former college classmate T. H. P. Sailer, could not understand him. "Perhaps I am, but I am and shall be opened all to you," for she had become part of him, and he felt free to be his true self with her.[19] She did not know him well enough yet to realize

that whatever else he might tell her about himself, this was his most profound pledge of love. And years later, when she had come to know him
almost as well as she knew herself, she discovered that he had silent spaces
that no one, not even she, could penetrate.

God, they believed, was deeply involved in their relationship; indeed,
God was primarily responsible for it, and every letter they wrote to one
another included some reference to the way God was at work in their lives.
She tended to be more brief on the point, although clearly decided that it
was God's will "that we should be one in Him," and that it was "the love
wherewith He loved His Son that is in our hearts." It was possible, she
mused, that they could have found one another without God, but "I
hardly think we could have loved each other, had we not first been His servants."[20] He had much more to say on the subject, partly because he saw
the relationship in the larger context of his call. And so he told her that he
rejoiced that they could love one another "without robbing Christ." It was
good that he was "the source and the cause and the inspiration for it," and
because of that, he was certain it would "help us to serve Him better and
to do good to men." "And I know," he added, "this will be for both of us
the blessing of our lives. So shall we learn to know God more. . . . In the
school of our affection let us learn more of Him and in the school of His
let us learn to realize more the full promise of our own."[21]

Ultimately, he believed God had moved in their lives to fulfill their
need for love and had promised them a worthy destiny, and he shared his
conviction with her: "Have you noticed in Christ's life the three loneli-
nesses of place and time and spirit? I have tasted all three. No longer can
either of us taste the worst of the third, which is the most lonely of all, for
Oh Emma, my love, our spirits are knit together—as one—not even death
shall part thee and me. With faith that God, in whose hand all life is, will
give us wisdom to act wisely and grace to act patiently and tenderly, and
thus having made us for one another's love, He will guide our steps and
prepare the way until our love find its realization and goal, my own dear
Emma, my life and my love."[22]

Falling in love, as the pair soon realized, was the easy part. The next step
was to get family—in particular, parental—approval. For a short time they
simply remained silent, but that was easier for him than for Emma. He
lived alone in New York in an apartment in University Place. Sherwood
Eddy remembered going to his room one night that spring to discuss some
spiritual problems and seeing "the striking photograph of a college girl" on
his desk. He closed his eyes to rest for a moment, and when he opened
them, the picture was gone, "and I saw that Speer did not wish to have any

questions about it."[23] Emma, however, lived in a college dormitory with a roommate, Abby Brayton, a close friend she had known for four years, and as she told him, her joy had revealed itself.[24] Also, she was from a close family who lived not far away and who were very involved in her life. Her parents, Charles and Harriet Bailey, gave her room to grow but also kept a protective eye on her. They considered her their special child. She was not only the youngest of their seven children, but she was their only daughter and, as her mother told her, "we were so desirious [sic] for a daughter, that I told the dear Lord that if we were given a daughter, we would consecrate her to His service and my dear daughter you were given to Him by us from your birth."[25]

From the outset, Robert and Emma agreed that the direct approach was best, and it worked, not only in the short term, but in the long one as well. They talked with her mother first, because Emma had a very close relationship with her, quite similar to the one he had experienced with his father. Emma spoke, and then he wrote. She reported on her conversation: "Poor dear Mother! It has taken her breath, to discover that her daughter is a grown woman, with a woman's power of giving her heart and life to whom so ever she may please. I think it had never occurred to her to think that I was old enough to love and be loved, and she had never thought of you except as a missionary, I verily believe." Her mother had the traditional objections and advised her to go slower, to write him less frequently, and to keep to her studies. But she did approve of one part of the relationship, his choice of career. Emma was relieved and found her mother "very happy with us now, for my great happiness is hers."[26]

His message to her mother was straightforward. They had met at Northfield, he told her, "in the doing of Christ's service and not in the seeking of our own pleasure. . . . We could not help it that he made us friends. We should have done wrong to be otherwise. We could not help it that we found this friendship only the confession of deeper feelings which had all the time been in our hearts. . . . And I write to you, that I may not seem desirous of concealing anything at all, to say that I do love her."[27]

Shortly after hearing from him, Mrs. Bailey broke the news to her husband, who immediately objected that his daughter was too young and then remembered that his own wife had been the same age when he had proposed. The young pair waited on her parents' decision for what seemed like an eternity, each in turn approaching her father personally, she to get his blessing and he to get his approval. In reality her father agreed to a formal engagement in less than two months. The issues were not all resolved, but gradually they agreed that Emma could leave college at the end of the term, her sophomore year, and they scheduled the wedding for the following spring.

One version of the courtship was that the "Huntingdon and Princeton friends of Robert Speer thought that no woman could be good enough for him. The Harrisburg and Bryn Mawr friends of Emma Bailey thought that no man could be good enough for her."[28] While there may have been those who held such feelings, his closest Princeton friends were not among them. Mudge, Sailer, and George Merrill wrote Emma offering congratulations. Mudge said in good humor that he was quite jealous of her, for she was "going to usurp my old place of 'wife' as we call our room mates here in Princeton," and warned her to "watch over him very carefully for he is very apt to be too good to every body and everything."[29] Moreover, if there were differences of opinion about the marriage, particularly within the two families directly involved, those were resolved in such a way that the Bailey family gladly accepted a new son. The long-term consequence of the pair's decision to be frank and open in the process was that he adopted them as his new parents, and they fully embraced him.

He was especially attracted to Mrs. Bailey, who was prominent in Presbyterian Home Missions, having been a founder and vice-president of the Home Missions Synodical Society of Pennsylvania. She also taught a large men's Bible class at her church. Not long after the engagement, he began to address her as "mother-in-love" and to sign his letters to her "son-in-love." He found her to be a woman of great faith and intellect, and they began to exchange books and ideas about the Christian faith. The day after his wedding he addressed her simply, "My dear Mother," and wrote, "There was no time in the hurry of leaving yesterday to tell you how glad and thankful I was and am to come into the peace and goodness of a mother's love again."[30] The Baileys re-formed the circle broken by his father's death, and he felt once again the full strength of family love.

The months between the engagement and the wedding, set for April 20, 1893, were filled with his work schedule and her preparations. The first two weeks of July 1892 they were in Northfield, where he spoke and she met his sisters, Mary and Mig, and had her first conversation with Mott. She also met Trumbull, and their talks brought him into their life as a couple. Trumbull had been very important to Speer in the previous few years, becoming something of a mentor and father figure. Now he assumed the same role for the two of them. They shared with him how he had, through his book on friendship, helped them find and express their love for one another. Trumbull was overcome with joy at the thought that he was "in a sense linked with you, and was a link between you, at the beginning of your new life."[31] Their exchanges with him became more frequent and more personal, as they began to refer to him as "dear father Trumbull," and he signed his letters, "Your devoted father-in-love." He confessed that although he had children of his own, he could not love any children "more dearly or more truly than I love 'you two.' "[32] The reasons for his intense feelings went well beyond the role he had in bringing them together, and lay in his growing conviction that they were an important part of God's plan for the future, a plan he could help fulfill if he assisted them.[33] As the wedding drew near, they decided to invite him to marry them. Surprisingly, the Baileys resisted the suggestion until their prospective son-in-law explained that he "knows and is a part of that which is deepest in our lives. Having anyone else marry us would seem like taking some stranger into a family secret or having some stranger do what only a member of the family should be allowed to do."[34]

Married Life

Robert and Emma were married at noon at her home, a large, prominent house on the corner of Front and Chestnut Streets, facing the Susquehanna River. A local newspaper reported that it was a "very pretty home wedding" that took place in the "exquisitely decorated" reception hall. The bride wore a traditional white gown "with orange blossoms holding her veil," and the groom was the "Rev. Robert E. Speer."[35] She was not quite twenty-one, and he was twenty-five. It marked for him the beginning of the third and final family of his life, the one that was to be his, with Emma, to form and extend. Together with her family, this provided the home base of love and security on which he built the remainder of his life.

Their union brought together families with roughly comparable proud heritages in the history of Pennsylvania. To his family tradition of politics and public service it joined her family commitment to religious leadership and economic development. Born May 15, 1872, in Pottstown, Pennsylvania, Emma traced both sides of her family to colonial roots. On her father's side she descended from a Quaker, Thomas Bailey, who arrived from Bristol, England, in 1682 to join William Penn's experiment. The Baileys later married into the Lukens family of Coatesville and joined them in the iron and steel business. Her father, Charles Lukens Bailey, had owned the Pine Iron Works at Pine Forge near Pottstown before he moved to Harrisburg, where he was president of both the Central Iron Works and the Chesapeake Nail Works. The Quakers expelled him when he married her mother, who as a Presbyterian was not considered a worthy partner, so he joined his wife's church. In Harrisburg they belonged to the Market Square Presbyterian Church, where he was president of the board of trustees. Emma later told her youngest son that his Bailey forebears "were men of iron, not only in their business, but in their souls . . . ," and added, "They were none of them distinguished, brilliant, or rich, but they all loved righteousness and were cornerstones of their small communities."[36]

Emma's mother's family was Scotch-Irish. The first member to arrive was John Elder, a graduate of the University of Edinburgh and a clergyman. After migrating to the Harrisburg area, he became pastor of the Paxtang and Derry churches. He achieved considerable reputation during the Revolutionary War as the "fighting parson" and is reported to have used his pulpit to call for a company of volunteers and to have prayed on the occasion, "We beseech Thee, through our Lord and Saviour Christ, mercifully to give us triumph, yet not ours but Thy blessed will be done. And, oh, Lord God of the Universe, if Thou are unwilling by Thy Divine Grace to assist us, do Thou stand aside and let us fight it out."[37] John's granddaughter Sarah married William Doll, of Dutch descent, and their daughter Harriet married Charles.

Emma's life had been surrounded by this cloud of witnesses and her very warm and loving family. They had nurtured her in spirit and mind, guiding her religious development and providing for her education. She made her public confession of faith in Christ at the Market Square Church on April 5, 1885, and received her first school lessons from a private tutor who came to her home. When she was ready for further education, her parents sent her to Miss Steven's School in Germantown from 1888 to 1890, and from there to Bryn Mawr College.

The newly married couple set up housekeeping in Elizabeth, New Jersey. They were very evenly matched in temperament, intellectual ability, and spiritual discernment, and even bore some physical resemblance. In describing her mother, their eldest daughter said, "She was dark and tall and had so much of the same open, handsome look her husband had that they were often taken for brother and sister."[38] If they had real differences, they never surfaced. He never raised any questions about her that could remotely be described as criticism. She became, however, sensitive to one difference between them, and although she lived with it and made the best of it, it bothered her from time to time. Her style was to talk over a problem and work out a solution in the process of the discussion, whereas his style was to think through an issue in silence. There were times when she became frustrated and felt the need for greater communication.[39] They did have individual preferences, some more significant than others. In the very incidental category, she used the King James Version of the Bible, and he took a more eclectic approach. One of the more important differences was how they wanted to spend their free time, such as it was. They were extremely busy and active people, and free time meant vacation time. She liked the sea and the resort setting, and he liked the mountains, with healthy doses of hiking, camping, and trout fishing. For much of their life she bent his way, and they vacationed at Camp Diamond in northern New Hampshire, but on occasion, and especially after the children were grown, he went with her to Seal Harbor or Bar Harbor, Maine, or she went there with friends.

Once they made the choice to live outside New York City, they set a pattern they followed until their children were grown. They continued to live in Elizabeth until 1897, when they moved north to Englewood, to a section that soon became known as "Missionary Ridge," because many people engaged in missionary work settled there. Englewood, described as "a pleasant small community on the edge of the wooded Palisades," was home for almost thirty years.[40] All five of their children were born there. They lived on Chestnut Street until 1906 and then moved their growing family to a large and spacious house on Walnut Street. This was their real family home, the one they and their children remembered best. They were active in the church and were charter members of the Shakespeare Club, which met Friday evenings to read plays. It eventually became one of their most important circles of friends. By 1925 the children had either moved away or were at school, and the house was too great a care for Emma. They moved to New York City, temporarily, they told themselves, to an apartment at 52 Gramercy Park, and then in 1927 to 24 Gramercy Park. When he returned on occasion to Englewood to get books or winter clothing, the trip made him homesick, and they finally agreed that the sensible thing to do was sell the house.[41] When the Dwight School, a day school for girls, finally bought it, they faced moving their considerable collection of possessions, not the least of which were the books.

One development that made this transition easier was a step Emma had taken, largely on her own, just after their decision to sell the Englewood house. On a trip to see their youngest son at his school, she had come upon property for sale in nearby Lakeville, Connecticut, and without consulting her husband, she had put an option to buy on it. Her decision proved to be inspired. Rockledge, which included a large house with outbuildings on about twelve acres overlooking the lakes, turned out to be their paradise. So as they were selling one home, they were acquiring another. He found it ironic that for a time they owned two houses and were not living in either of them, but he was soon caught up in the natural wonder of their country place. Emma worked on the inside, and he planted the outside with shrubs and a garden. He had never really gardened much, except for a backyard patch during World War I, but he became a serious gardener on their new land. They began to spend there what free time they had in their summers, including most of their vacation time. It became their second home until he retired, and then their home for the rest of their lives together.

The initial decision to settle in New Jersey determined one of his work habits: the trip to work. He typically walked down the hill to the Erie Railroad Station and took the train, often the 8:13, to the ferry across the Hudson River, returned on the 6:17, and hiked back up the hill.[42] He adapted to the daily travel quite easily, following a strategy for using his time wisely that he had developed on the much longer travels to and from college and in his board work. He typically carried a satchel of paperwork with him, but he usually spent his train time with books, often in the fields of history or theology or biography.[43] He rarely read the newspapers, either then or at any other time, considering them largely useless. When he read, he made note of interesting illustrations or potentially useful quotations and later copied them into notebooks for future reference. He packed his speeches and books with this gleaned material, so much so that people were in awe of him, wondering how such a busy man could read all those books. His secret was never to waste time, especially not traveling time. Friends who traveled with him discovered that he was not going to join them in idle chatter, and that he always had a book at hand.[44]

Long-distance travel became a major feature of their married life. One form of it, primarily involving him, was the almost monthly journeys to distant parts of the nation to interpret missions and raise funds, and the average of three Sundays a month speaking or preaching. Along with these regular commitments were the annual meetings of the General Assembly of the Presbyterian Church and the summer conferences at Northfield and elsewhere. Another form of travel primarily involved her, especially after 1920, in her role with the national Young Women's Christian Association (YWCA). She toured the nation almost as much as he did, visiting conferences and special meetings. Both of them took international trips. When they had married, Emma had been more experienced making this kind of trip than he was, for she had already been to Europe twice on extended trips with her family. In their first two years of marriage they went to Mexico on a mission trip and to England, where he spoke at the

Keswick Convention. In 1896 they were off on a world-circling journey that took them through Persia and China. They were in Edinburgh in 1910 for the World Missionary Conference. She also joined him at a missionary conference in Latin America in 1925, on a trip to Japan and China in 1926, and at the International Missionary Conference in Jerusalem in 1928. In 1939 they traveled together to see their daughter and her family in England. In addition, separately she made several trips with other members of the family and friends, and he made a number of other missionary trips.

Their being on the road so much had two important consequences. First, it gave them a breadth of perspective and a wealth of contacts, enriching their lives and those of their children. Second, it forced them, during those many times when they did not travel together, to remain in contact through the mails. They generated a marvelous correspondence, virtually continuous with that of their courtship and engagement. It became his practice to write her whenever he was away, often short epistles describing his day and his surroundings, but rarely dealing with work-related issues. His main message was to tell her he was thinking of her and the children and that he loved them. More than fourteen hundred such letters have survived, and although each was different, they were in a sense all the same, like the one from Lincoln, Nebraska, early in their marriage: "I have been in my room since dinner thinking over my speeches for this afternoon and evening with your picture just in front of me, but I could not stand it any longer, so I came down to the writing room to write you. I love you, love you, my own dear wife, my only one."[45] Emma responded in turn, also in longhand, with news of her day and, after they had children, stories about their adventures. He typically returned from a trip completely up to date on developments at home, an absent yet present father. Almost fifteen hundred letters from Emma have survived, in which she typically reminded him of her love: "I am thinking of you all the time, darling, and trying to remember that God loves you more than I do, and will guard you tenderly wherever you are."[46] She also shared the affection of the children: "Last evening when Elliott was saying his prayers he said, as usual, 'Bring dear Father home safely'—and then added 'As soon as you can, God.' "[47]

The letters, especially hers, offer a wealth of information about social and economic life in America over a fifty-year period, but the archivist at Bryn Mawr offered the best evaluation of them: "Indeed, one of the distinguishing attributes of this correspondence is the proof that it offers of the deep affection between Mr. and Mrs. Speer that existed over a lifetime."[48] The letters were private, of course, and their expressions of love were known only to them, but on a rare occasion he let the world into his personal life, as he did in his book *Remember Jesus Christ:* "I think very many times of the one I love best. When in the night I awake, my first thought is of her; and when early in the morning the sunrise comes stealing into the room, my first thought is of her, and constantly through the day my mind goes out to her. I think of all the sweet things she has said, of all the sweet and loving things she has done, and I do remember her. I wish I might as often and as well remember Jesus Christ."[49]

The many separations in their life, resulting primarily from his work, were not entirely unexpected. Emma's father, shortly after learning about her new relationship, had gently cautioned her to remember that "Mr. Speer's calling may keep you separate much of the time, involving more care and responsibility on your part."[50] But Emma was not really prepared for the amount of time alone, and it weighed on her, although she never saw it as a burden and rarely revealed her feelings to others. An exception was in 1922, when David Porter collected a series of letters in honor of her husband's thirty-five years with the SVM. She cooperated with the project, gave him some names of people he might write, and added, "It is perhaps the children and I, even more than Mr. Speer, who need the kindly things that his friends might say of his work. It is from knowing of the value of his service to the world that we get courage to release him for so many and such long continued absences."[51]

The large amount of travel time, even after his retirement, required them to accept what she called one of the "little ironies" of their lives. "You are the one," she wrote him "to have to go off into the world, you who so dearly love your own hearth stone, and I stay at home, I who— tho' I love home and all its beauty and holiness, of your making, do love to 'admire and see, and behold the world so wide.' "[52] The times apart never diminished their love for one another. Asked by a local newspaper reporter a few years after her husband's death what had helped her through life, she replied, "It has been through living most of my life with a wonderful . . . , a truly remarkable man . . . and through the faith which we both believed in."[53]

Their Family

Their family life, firmly rooted in their love for one another, began to expand in 1898 with the birth of their first child, Elliott, who arrived late in the afternoon on November 1. The announcement they sent to family and friends described the new baby as "a very strong, athletic young man" and said they rejoiced "in all the great goodness of our loving God to us."[54] Speer wrote his mother-in-law a special note of thanks for all her "love and goodness, especially in giving me dear Emma and letting me be your very dear loving son."[55] Other children were born two to four years apart, each greeted in turn as a wonderful and joyous gift, and each offered the same careful attention that had been given to the first. Margaret Bailey arrived at the turn of the century, on November 20, 1900, and Eleanor McMurtrie came on May 3, 1903.

The children fascinated him, and he frequently commented on their progress in his correspondence. To David Cairns, a friend in Edinburgh and frequent correspondent, he wrote, "When I saw you last, we had one little child in our home—a little boy, who will be four years old before many months now. He has now a little sister, who is just learning to walk about and to talk and the two of them furnish a faculty out-classing all theological or scientific faculties I know, in their ability to impart instruction and to promote discipline."[56] When Elliott was four, on a dark night he awakened and called out, "Is your face turned toward me, Father?" Father responded, "Yes," and Elliott said, "All right," and went back to sleep. The word of this story passed from friend to friend and finally reached Bishop W. C. Doane, who turned it into a sonnet, with these final lines: "Nor shall my heart in sorrow's darkness, fear, But rest on Thee, my Father and my Friend."[57]

"Sorrow's darkness" fell in the summer of 1906. The three children had been generally healthy, even escaping some of the typical childhood diseases. Emma had gone overseas with friends to relax and recover from a recent illness, and her mother had come to keep house and be with the family. July 4 was a pleasant day of family celebration, but the next morning little three-year-old Eleanor awakened ill. The doctors diagnosed "summer complaint," but she did not respond to treatment. Within a week she had a serious heart problem and almost died. On Saturday, July 28, two days before Emma was due home, the doctors told Robert his little girl would not likely recover. He and Emma spent the last week of Eleanor's life at her bedside, "often kneeling for hours by the little bed not knowing what moment might be the last."[58] On Monday, August 6, "the dear little girl with a little sigh went home."[59] Robert and Emma were both acquainted with loss and grief, but not of a child—their child—and they were stunned. They turned to God and one another and found great comfort there and in the love of their other two children. If there was a lesson in the tragedy, he found it in the poverty of his "spiritual vision." In reference to prayer he said, "You cite conditions. We have learned that we may think those conditions have been fulfilled, and be in error. We do not find fault with God. We discover the blindness of our best vision and the folly of our confidence in aught save the Sovereign Will and Love of God."[60]

Eleanor had called the other children "the big children," and they came to their parents' aid. Emma remembered, "The evening after she went and the next day they were with us almost all the time. If our self-control failed us for a moment, and the tears came, Elliott's arms would slip around his father's neck, and Margaret, who watched me closely, with big troubled eyes, would slip her hand in mine, and pat my hand, or put her face close to mine in silent sympathy that she had no way of expressing."[61] One way the parents handled their grief was to create "Eleanor's Book," a collection of memories and poems which they wrote out in the first months after her death.

The tragic days passed but not the feelings of loss. The board gave him time off until the end of September, but when he returned to work, he still found it hard to realize that she would not be there to greet him when he came home. He was on a trip in October when Emma wrote that she had been to Brookside, the cemetery, and could hardly bear it. "Sometimes," she told him, "one can feel superior to time and space, and live in the consciousness of Eternity, but the flesh is weak, and tonight I have had to cry-out from the deep places of loneliness and longing."[62] Eleanor's name came up in their letters, to their children and one another, for the rest of their lives. When asked about his children, he would often describe the comings or goings of the living ones and add that another "was in heaven."[63]

The family, reduced to four, soon became five again with the birth of Constance Sophia on November 9, 1907, and then six with the arrival of William on December 6, 1910. (The girls had middle names but not the boys, because Robert did not care for middle names for boys.) The parents focused much of their energy on character development, through religious training and education. Although the patterns they set did not match in either scope of information or rigor of application the home school of religion he had experienced, they did have a program and clear expectations. The family began the day with a Bible reading and prayers, which usually took about ten minutes. When guests were present, they invited them to share in this prayer time. Meals began with blessings. The children were to learn the Psalms and be able on Sundays to recite those they had memorized. The eldest daughter remembered that they were asked to read from the Bible, but never without warning, and were almost never asked to pray. The children understood that "praying was Father's business and it was our business to listen. This was not hard, for he prayed with the utmost sincerity and simplicity. God's blessing was asked on all our affairs, large and small, but never in such a way that a child could feel that his small privacy was being violated."[64] They raised them in the fellowship of the First Presbyterian Church in Englewood, where they also served, he as an elder and she on various committees and for many years as president of the Missionary Society.

The children followed a version of the educational experience of their parents, especially their father. This included some early schooling at home or in a private school, a stint in the public schools, and then more private schooling and college. Elliott set the pace, beginning with schools run by Miss Martha Banks and Miss Lucy Jackson. He went on to public school, then followed his father at Phillips and Princeton, graduating from college in 1921, somewhat later than planned because of World War I. He then attended the Theological College of the United Free Church of Scotland in Edinburgh. The Jersey City Presbytery ordained him to the Christian ministry in the Presbyterian Church. He married Charlotte (Holly) Welles, a graduate of Vassar College, shortly after he graduated from college, and they had three children: Caroline, Eleanor, and Margaret. He began his ministry in 1922 on the staff of the First Presbyterian Church of New York City with responsibilities for the work at Bethlehem Chapel in Greenwich Village, a ministry largely with Italian Americans. He left there in 1924 to become chaplain and head of the department of Bible and religious education at Lafayette College in Easton, Pennsylvania. Two years later he began his association with the Northfield schools. He served as president of the board of trustees in association with and as successor to William R. Moody until 1931. In 1932 he began his tenure as headmaster of Mount Hermon School.

Margaret, or Marnie, also attended public schools and then went to the Dwight School and Abbott Academy, the sister school to Phillips. She graduated from Bryn Mawr College in 1922, taught English at Sweet Briar College for a year, and then became a warden at Bryn Mawr. She joined the foreign mission work of the Presbyterian Church as a missionary educator in China in 1925. Once she was in the field, her father sustained a bimonthly correspondence with her for twelve years, letters full of reflections on his reading and work and a virtual diary of his life for that period.

Constance, called Pat by her family, followed her sister to the Dwight School but then chose the Shipley School and subsequently graduated from Bryn Mawr in 1930. She promptly married an Englishman, Robert F. Barbour, and they spent several years in the United States while he attended medical schools before they moved to his homeland.

William, who answered to Billy, attended public schools and the Hotchkiss School and graduated from Princeton in 1933. He became a teacher and school administrator, beginning his career with the Asheville School for Boys in North Carolina.

Each child received a full measure of encouragement, support, and, as needed, chastisement, although the family style was to seek improvement by positive reinforcement. When Speer wrote to his children, he often sounded like his own father, making suggestions and urging duty. There were two things every boy should remember, he told Elliott when he was eight: "One is that all that you are doing now is helping to form your character, that is to fix the kind of man you will be . . . ," and second, "that God sees and cares about everything that we do and that we should always do just what we know He would like to see us do."[65] When Elliott did not win the Draper Prize at Phillips, his father consoled him and added, "And please do your school work solidly and well. That is your first task. Everything else is well in its place but its place is second to school work."[66] Margaret heard from father when he received a report that she was "head of your school." "There is fame," he noted, but it "is a short lived thing and it does not reach far. Duty-doing is the one thing that lasts and that God at best remembers. And I know that is what you will always do."[67]

Communications with the younger children carried a less intense sense of duty. Pat was born the year after Eleanor died, and they lavished love on their daughter. He told a friend that she "bid fair to be as capable and energetic a little girl as Eleanor was."[68] She was every bit of that, but also her own person. Often she created games, and he recounted how one evening "she persisted in carrying out the caprice that she was my mother and I was her childy, as she called me, and it was as much as I could do to keep from laughing at the absolute consistency with which she carried out these roles."[69] When she went off to Bryn Mawr and failed to write home regularly, he wrote jokingly that if she did not reform, they would send her to a school in the remote west.[70] Billy received similar love and good-humored treatment. He was a happy baby, described by his father as the "jolliest, fattest, fastest growing little boy you ever saw," who would very likely burst his skin if he did not stop growing.[71] Height became his major feature, and as a teenager he was quite proud that he was taller than either of his parents. He shared many of his father's interests in hiking and the outdoors. One Christmas he received an air rifle and promptly became a hunter, tramping the woods nearby for bears, which were visible "if one only has eyes to see them," and squirrels. One day he shot a red squirrel, and Speer remembered that when he returned from work, "we had to sit down for some taxidermy work while I took off the skin whole. We stretched it on a board to cure it."[72] The parents were quite pleased with their children, all of them, and often told them so. They told Elliott in 1926, after the eldest two had begun their careers and as the youngest two were moving on in their education, "You and Marnie have reached just unalloyed satisfaction to mother and me and we hope and pray that Pat and Billy will follow after you."[73]

The Speer family lived an active life and gradually developed daily and yearly routines to make sure that they had some time together. When Robert was home, and that varied from month to month and year to year, he would come downstairs first and spend some quiet time alone, and then the family gathered for their prayers. After breakfast he would walk around the table, kissing each child in turn, and then kissing Emma, before he left for work. Housekeepers, often Irish, prepared some of the meals and helped with the children. The Speers hired them through the years until the last of the children left for boarding school. He returned in the evenings just in time for supper, and sometimes they had games at supper, like geography quizzes. He typically retired to his study after supper, where he often worked on the papers he brought home from the office. He would emerge about thirty minutes before he intended to go to bed, and that was the signal that he was done for the evening. He often passed around a candy treat or joined in a pre-bedtime game or told a story.[74] He enjoyed chocolates, and once thanked his sister Mig for her gift of fudge by reminding her that "it is the duty of the human race to eat up all the fudge and other sweeties that now exist or that shall in the future exist. Such things are a great danger and should be eaten at once."[75]

When he was home on a Saturday, he would sometimes play the game of Bear, which he invented for the children and their friends. They had in the front hall a great rug that they had purchased in Persia during their world trip. He played the Bear, with the rug as his base. The rules were that he could not leave the base and that the children had to try to tag him without being caught, and the ensuing chaos provided much fun.[76] Sundays at home were quieter and typically involved walks, to Brookside to visit Eleanor's grave or through the woods to Clinton Point overlooking the Hudson River. He often accompanied these walks with stories, some historical and some that he created, including "an original and highly imaginative serial about Farmer White's adventures in the Friendly

Woods."[77] He had a gift with children, his own and others, and was full of fun and good humor when with them. This part of his personality he kept largely within the home and office circles. When missionaries or church leaders who knew him in other contexts visited his home, they were typically surprised to see the "reserved Mr. Speer" frolicking with the children, and sometimes gently teasing his guests.

The summer vacation as an entire family was the highlight of the year. It was usually a month long, from early August to early September. Early in their married life they spent their free month in Connecticut with the Sailers. In 1901, he met Horace C. Coleman, who owned Camp Diamond (sometimes called Diamond Pond) in New Hampshire. From 1901 until 1925 the Speer family spent their vacation time at the camp, with occasional exceptions when he was overseas. After that they spent their summers at Rockledge, and the children, and later the grandchildren, came to visit them.

Camp Diamond was a rustic place. The family lived in a bare cabin and ate in a dining hall. The camp offered hiking, boating, fishing in lakes and streams, and miles of country roads for walking. The pattern at camp was for him to go fishing. He went alone or with other campers, usually friends he had encouraged to spend time at the camp. One such person was John Timothy Stone, who recalled that as they hiked or waded the streams, Speer was "quite prone to sing some of the famous old hymns; although he could not carry a tune, he loved the words and attempted the harmony." He was an excellent fisherman, adept at fly casting, and had several favorite flies, including " 'Montreal,' 'Royal Coachman,' 'Red Ant,' and 'Black Gnat.' " On one trip he and Stone, fishing for food for the entire camp, brought back 401 fish.[78] When Elliott and Billy got older, he took them for overnight hikes and fishing trips. They carried their equipment and plunged into the woods, often for four days at a time. They might do this every week for four weeks if the weather was right. He took the girls on separate and less rigorous trips, and when he did, he carried much of the load for them.

One of the best summers was 1912, when he was out with Elliott every week for three or four nights at a time, sleeping in a small tent or under a ready-made lean-to of branches. They fished every day all day, returning to camp at the end of each week "as dirty and weary and happy as human beings can be. I never had such glorious trout-fishing before. Elliott and I would go down the streams together in the depths of the woods, without a soul anywhere near us for miles and miles, and with the trout coming up to the flies almost at every cast, and the great forests all around us, with the wind whispering through the birches and the beeches and the spruces and the fir trees."[79]

Fishing was often spectacularly successful, as in 1904 when he caught 164 trout, but he was really following his own advice to fathers when he spent this time with his children. In a talk to young men he had advised, "Fathers should share the athletic life of their sons. They should live in the open air with them as much as they can. Camping out, or any simple life on the face of nature, is one of the best moral tonics and correctives. . . . Surely the abundant life of Christ includes all the hearty, wholesome life of His world; and fathers and sons are meant to share it, and be, in work and play, just boys together."[80] When Elliott returned from World War I, Speer took his son to camp, and they spent a month hiking and fishing and talking over the way the war had affected them. In reference to this time together, Elliott told a friend that some men took years to get the war out of them, but "I just talked with Father and it all came back."[81]

The camp was more than fishing: it became a family institution. It was their summer home, with their "own" cabin, Arden, which they rented each year, with familiar sights and sounds and smells that remained with them the rest of their lives. It was the place where their time was uninterrupted and they were together, with walks and talks and games and long conversations. They were free of all the routines of the rest of the year, free of schedules and responsibilities. For them all, but especially for Emma and the children, it became after the first few years a time of reunion with the other families, many of them clergy or missionary families like theirs, including the Hudson Taylors, the Harry Luces, the Charles Erdmans, the Robert Wilders, and the John Stones. Helen Coleman, the wife of the camp owner, first came in 1908. Her description of what she found matches perfectly what the Speer family experienced: "They seemed to be living in a community of complete contentment and faith and mutual helpfulness, such as I had never seen, and strongly resembling in some respects a little group of early Christians in the first centuries."[82]

It was all these things for Speer, but he was never without some work to do. On many of these vacations he would start, finish, or write a book, a series of lectures, or several articles. When not off fishing the streams, he would keep the morning hours to himself, working in a separate tent beside the lake, quitting promptly at lunch. He rarely carried much source material with him, using his prodigious memory to prepare his manuscripts.[83] On Sundays there were morning and evening services, and he often preached in one or both. Margaret remembers those messages as being about commonplace events of the week, full of helpful illustrations for the children as well as the adults, and often containing memorable words of wisdom, like his advice for camping in the woods: "Prepare for the worst, expect the best, and take what comes."[84]

Humor was part of his makeup and the camp setting provided many occasions for him to amuse people. On one occasion the Carrs, a local farming family, invited him to supper. He weighed himself before and after "and seemed to have gained twenty-five pounds, but no one knew then that he had slipped some old horseshoes into his pockets!"[85] He met the colorful character Owen Crimmins during his second summer and became fascinated by his tall tales, including the one about the "Dog Trout" that followed Owen home from the stream and became his pet, like a dog but in fact a trout. He eventually published his version of those stories, the most playful and lighthearted book he ever wrote.[86]

The family life Robert and Emma created was quite normal, remarkably so, given the great amount of travel he did and the length of some of his trips. The children remembered the stability and the great vacations. They also remembered, especially Margaret, one time of dramatic change. It came on a Sunday morning in December 1914. Two events took place simultaneously. A pipe had frozen and the subsequent leak had loosened the plaster, and it fell with a crash on the dining room table just as the family was preparing for Sunday school. They recalled such a minor event because at the same time someone telephoned with the news that Grace H. Dodge, the president of the national board of the YWCA, had died. Within a few weeks the board elected Emma in her place. Margaret remembered that "in the aftermath of that telephone call our lives were never quite the same again."[87] The Speer family was already going full speed and Emma's new responsibilities pushed things up a notch.

Emma's Work

Emma was a remarkable person. Robert had recognized it and it was doubtless one reason he had chosen her to be his wife. But she did not always realize it for herself, and although she accomplished much, she has never received adequate recognition for her work. She began her married life uncertain whether or not she could measure up to her husband and his high calling. She shared such feelings of inadequacy with Trumbull, and he reassured her that "God will make you a helper of his faith and his joy, and that you will have a blessing in being a blessing."[88] She wrapped her life very much in his, joining on missionary trips before the children were born and hosting missionaries and other visitors to the board at their homes. She also hosted missionary gatherings, including what came to be called the new missionaries' party, first at Englewood and then at Rockledge. If, as Trumbull argued, her husband was a missionary despite his call to remain at home, then surely she was also a missionary, as a consequence of the way she chose to live her life.

Missions was one of her major interests, but she was a multidimensional person, and she quietly and slowly forged a career of her own in work for young women. She performed many different kinds of volunteer work. Some of the tasks she took on were really jobs, but she never received, and would not have accepted, pay for them. Through them she created a career in public service.

She had developed an interest in work for young women in the spring of her freshman year, when Grace Dodge had visited Bryn Mawr and talked about the Working Girls Societies. After her Northfield experience she had requested a conference for women students, and staff members of the student division of the American committee, YWCA, had arranged one for the next year. At that meeting she confirmed what she had learned from Miss Dodge, "that there were things important and vitally interesting to be done for and with girls in our changing world."[89] So inspired, she joined the American committee and worked, during the early years of her marriage, on its student committee, feeling "a little out of my element among the dignified matrons," but gradually making her mark and becoming chair of that committee.[90] As a member of the joint committee, she participated in the planning of the union of the American committee and the international board, which took place at Old South Church in New York City on December 6, 1906, and became a charter member of the national board of the newly created Young Women's Christian Association of the United States of America. At the time she wrote, "The life of women was no longer to be lived in quiet backwaters or hidden harbors. It was moving swiftly out to sea, to be in the path of all the winds and tides, all the hurricanes and thunderclouds that were already making the horizon dark."[91]

Through her national board work and then as its president 1915–32, she worked tirelessly for the YWCA. That meant frequent trips to New York City before they moved there, additional house guests, and many visits to distant cities and colleges to meet the membership. It also required much public speaking and constant fund-raising. Her years as president included a time of tremendous growth in programming during World War I, an era of deep controversy in the industrial disputes in the early

1920s, and, as in other organizations, years of economic problems in the Great Depression. Her chief contributions were her firm convictions that women had much more to contribute to the world than they had as yet been able to give, that the association could help open up new possibilities for women, and that its programs had to remain rooted in the Christian tradition. She joined her practical organizational skills with her deep conviction that God would see her and the association through whatever difficulties they faced, and she was able to communicate such optimism to her fellow workers. She also possessed significant conflict-resolution skills and was able to work through controversies to solutions that moved the association forward.[92] When she retired, she said she had served because the YWCA "is both a Christian and a woman's movement." Her work earned her an entry in the *Dictionary of American Biography.* [93]

All through her years of service she received her husband's unqualified support and encouragement. She traveled extensively, especially in the 1920s, so much so that her trips sometimes rivaled his in both frequency and distance. "You should see the pace at which Emma is traveling these days," he told his Aunt Clara. "She is speaking in Norristown tonight, in Reading tomorrow night, in Boston on Sunday night and then goes on Monday or Tuesday to Mississippi. When I come along after her, as I did last night in Wilkes Barre, I am as a little saxophone following a symphony orchestra."[94] He was also aware of some of the issues she had to face. Commenting on a trip she made to Chicago in 1928, he said, "The Y.M.C.A. is trying to get in on the field of the Y.W.C.A. all through the country, doing girls work, which it has no business to do, and this is to be taken up in the conference this week."[95]

When she retired, John D. Rockefeller, Jr., and his wife held a dinner party in her honor that Speer described as a "lovely affair," noting, "Emma was a very shining star."[96] He looked forward to her retirement because, proud as he was of her, he was also interested in having her home more. His feelings about her absences were not much different from her feelings about his. As he considered her retirement and the many "future plans" she was making, he could not see any real relief for her or him, and told Margaret, "Aunt Vera said that from cultivating the local garden of the National Y.W.C.A. she was now to be a universal gardener. My understanding has been that the movement was to be in the reverse direction and she was going to be a Rockledge gardener but I see that I must be the Rockledge gardener while mother cultivates the Sahara Desert, and South Africa and Latin America and the small region of India."[97]

Tithing and Finance

Their family could not truly be said to have had any problems, certainly none of an interpersonal nature. They did have one continuing concern, and that was money. Speer had grown up in a frugal household and early learned to watch his pennies. From the first days he was on his own at Phillips with his father's funds, he had kept meticulous records of his expenses. He had never thought much about Christian stewardship and tithing until 1892, when he had heard Horace Pitkin, then a theological student and subsequently a missionary martyr of the Boxer Rebellion in China, read a paper on the topic at the thirteenth annual convention of the Inter-Seminary Missionary Alliance. The truth of Pitkin's analysis struck him, or as he later wrote, "It burst on me as clear as sunlight that this is the right, the privilege, and the duty of Christians."[98] Always one to act when duty called, he returned home and wrote across a page of his account book: "This man died and was buried—deep—no resurrection for *him*—and his liabilities and assets were assumed by a new and better man—as set forth as follows." What followed was an entry for a tithe account, and it remained part of his accounting system the remainder of his life.[99] He later wrote a widely distributed pamphlet on tithing, in which he argued that setting aside the first tenth of one's income marked a "distinct era of spiritual enlargement" in the Christian life. His acceptance of tithing took place before his marriage, and he and Emma began their life together as tithers. The family always tithed.

Their main financial concern was that income did not expand very rapidly. They lived, by ordinary standards, exceedingly well. But they also lived on a missionary-style income that did not expand over the years in the same way the income of others with comparable education and experience expanded. In years when the Presbyterian Church did not raise all the funds needed for mission needs, everyone, including the secretaries, took wage reductions. This meant occasions of tight money, even as the general cost of living went up. He had some inheritance from his father, and Emma eventually received a generous estate from her parents, but they tried to invest those funds, partly for the education of the children and partly for their retirement. He also had some extra income from speaking engagements and from the publication of his books. Some years that was substantial, as much as one-third to one-half of his total income, but it was also very uncertain, particularly the speaking fee, because he had no fee structure and simply accepted whatever was offered him, and then usually had to use part of it to pay his travel expenses.

Emma occasionally chafed under the circumstances because she had a different experience with money growing up. She had always had what she called "a very fair amount" of it, and what was more important, was "led by my brothers to expect as much—or more—always." But she adjusted as best she could, sometimes trying to figure out ways to save money by going without a secretary or reducing their use of maids. At the same time, her YWCA work required more help at home. The choices were rarely easy, and occasionally she used part of the principal of her investments to make ends meet. He kept the books, figuring items right to the penny at times, and she controlled the cash flow and relieved him of many of the day-to-day financial matters. Money concerns, at times troublesome, never became real problems. Emma told the children after his death that it was due to "Father's hard work, thrift, and utter unselfishness that there is a substantial sum in his estate," and that she would therefore have adequate funds.[100]

One expense he resisted for some time, long after the Ford revolution hit the country, was an automobile. He walked or took a taxi, and was reluctant to give up train rides because they were part of his study time. However, by the mid-1920s the Speer family had a car, primarily for summer use, and by the end of the decade had two cars. He was never fully at ease driving, although he claimed to enjoy it. Billy remembered that the rest of the family was not always happy to have him behind the wheel, because he "tended to regard the traffic ahead of him as though it were an opposing football team driving through which he must carry the ball. As a result, all of us, as soon as we learned to drive, always politely but rather firmly offered to do the driving."[101] One weekend in 1928 a very close friend of the family and his wife came to Rockledge to visit and were driven about by Pat. The car rode so poorly that they shortly sent Speer a check suggesting he buy a new car. There was enough money to purchase a Buick seven-passenger touring car and a secondhand Pierce-Arrow sedan. Two years later he reported to Elliott that the family had the audacity to want to sell the Pierce-Arrow. "The Pierce," he wrote, "is a noble car with a most Christian disposition. It has behaved like a perfect gentleman during these two years under a constant tirade of ridicule and abuse. . . . I cannot imagine how a Christian family like ours can show such malice, hatred, vindictive ingratitude and baseness toward this upright, faithful, devoted servant, who is ready to continue to serve us all the rest of our lives and to escort us in dignity to our graves."[102] When commercial aviation began, he continued to use the trains, although he did make occasional flights.

Tragedy

The family Emma and Robert created was full of love and was overwhelmingly happy. Their careers were marked by great success and national recognition. The children grew strong, set goals for themselves, and began meeting them, each in turn marching to his or her duty. Even Eleanor's death, tragic as it was at the time, was hardly an unusual experience in a generation in which families often lost infants and small children to childhood diseases. Sadness touched them on a number of occasions, like the death of Emma's father in 1899 and mother in 1912. Robert's brother Vic died in 1909 and his sister Mary in 1918. While they felt these losses, he grieved most deeply when Will died in 1923. He had been his good friend as well as brother, and they had kept close contact with one another through the years. No death is really timely, but these deaths were often understood, if not expected. Her father, Mary, and Will had all had long terms of illness. True tragedy struck in the fall of 1934, from a totally unexpected direction, temporarily breaking their family circle and shattering their happiness: Elliott was murdered.

The news arrived by telephone on the evening of September 14. The call came for Billy, who was home for a brief visit but at that moment out with friends. By the time he returned the call, his parents had retired for the evening, and it was his sad duty to give them the burdensome message. They dressed quickly and drove immediately to Northfield, where they heard the painful story in the small hours of the morning. Someone had worked his way quietly to the window of Elliott's study at Ford Cottage, the headmaster's home on the Mount Hermon campus. Elliott was in the study making final preparation for the opening of school on the coming Monday and had apparently just risen from his desk and turned to reach for a book on a nearby shelf when the assailant fired a 12-gauge shotgun. The shot hit him in a number of places on his right side and back, the fatal wound caused by a large slug that entered his back and tore through his right lung. Bleeding profusely, he called out to Holly as he staggered from his study into the hallway, where he collapsed. Holly's father, who was visiting, was the first at the scene. Elliott lost consciousness just as she arrived from upstairs. He slipped away about twenty minutes later, as Speer wrote his daughters, one in England and the other in China, "to be with Eleanor."[103]

The murder immediately attracted national attention. Mount Hermon was a highly regarded preparatory school for boys, and Elliott Speer was not only its headmaster but also the son of well-known parents. The *New York Times* carried the story on its front page three days running and continued updates for several months. The *Times* lead read: "Authorities were baffled tonight by a scarcity of definite clues in the gangsterlike murder of the Rev. Elliott Speer."[104] Sensationalism aside, those few words contained the essence of the story. The police rather quickly decided that the evidence suggested a well-planned murder. Speer called it an assassination. The plan, police concluded, was carried out by one person, who may or may not have been working with other persons, and who was very familiar with the Mount Hermon grounds and the work habits of his victim. But if it was, as it seemed, an inside job, the police found very few clues that they could present to a court. No weapon was ever found, despite extensive dredging operations in nearby Shadow Lake and in the adjacent Connecticut River. It had been a misty, rainy evening, and no one had seen anyone suspicious around, despite reports of a car leaving the school grounds at high speed about the time of the murder. The case became a mystery and has never been solved.

Suspicions abounded, especially at first, and the police dutifully checked out a number of leads, including the ideas that some disgruntled instructor or one of several students Elliott had recently disciplined had decided to get even with him. While those leads turned up nothing, police became increasingly interested in Dean Thomas E. Elder, especially after he presented a typed letter to the chairman of the board of trustees. The letter, which Elder claimed was from Elliott, offered Elder a substantial pay raise and praised him in such a way that it suggested he would make a good headmaster, concluding, "There is not a single phase of the work that you cannot handle as well as I."[105] The letter was unsigned.

Under intensive police questioning, Elder admitted that it was not the original letter. That, he said, had been in longhand, and he had destroyed it. Elliott's secretary told police she had never seen any such letter, and, moreover, Elliott never wrote letters in longhand. The police believed it was a forgery, and so did Speer when he examined it, but the police could never get Elder to admit it. Even if they had wrung an admission from him on this point, they had little else to go on. After several months of investigation the district attorney, Joseph Bartlett, decided he did not have enough evidence to seek an indictment and turned instead to a judicial inquest. Judge Timothy Hayes heard testimony from sixty-two witnesses and rendered his decision just before Christmas. The evidence against

Elder, however strong, was circumstantial and insufficient for a trial, the judge decided, and he concluded, "I find that the unlawful conduct of a person unknown to me contributed to the death of Elliott Speer."[106]

No other major suspects surfaced, and the case reached a dead end. There were other suspicions, some public and some private, that were the consequence of two disputes at the schools, both of which involved Elliott. They revealed deep and complex crosscurrents that may have been responsible for the tragedy. The first began in 1926 when Will R. Moody, one of the sons of Dwight L. Moody and president of the Northfield schools since 1912, became ill. The board of trustees, on which Robert Speer sat, proposed that Will move from president to chairman of the board and take a leave of absence, and that Elliott be brought in as president to work with him. Will agreed, but when he returned from his leave greatly improved in health, he found much of what he had done now being done by Elliott. Friction developed and finally led to a showdown at a board of trustees meeting on February 8, 1929. Will resigned in anger, suggesting that it was impossible to work with division of authority at the top, and adding that the problems had been "increased by the difference in age, experience, familiarity with traditions, and outlook of the occupants of the positions."[107] Robert Speer made a reasoned presentation about the choices before the board and left the meeting before the board voted to accept Will's resignation and place his son Elliott at the head of the schools.[108] All of this was done in public view, duly reported by the *Times* in bold type on its front page: "Moody Quits in Row over His Leadership of Bible Schools."[109] Moody never forgave some of those who believed he should step down, especially Henry Cutler, headmaster at Mount Hermon.[110] When Elliott moved from his work as president of the schools to headmaster, he did so as the protégé of Cutler.

The second dispute began almost as soon as Elliott assumed the role of headmaster, and it turned on changes he began to make. The *Times* reporter who wrote about his murder described a serious division at Mount Hermon between those who wanted the school to remain as it had been since the time of its founder and those who favored the changes.[111] Elliott was the youngest of any of the headmasters of the private schools in America when he went to Mount Hermon, but he had many well-informed ideas about education, gleaned from personal experience at Lafayette and during an intense year of study in Scotland and England in 1931–32. His "reforms," as they came to be called, extended to every area of life at Mount Hermon, from the modification of dorm living to reduce its "monastic" quality to the introduction of dancing, and included the

end of compulsory attendance at Sunday vesper services and the introduction of interscholastic athletics.[112] The changes, "damned changes" to
his opponents, had upset some of the school's supporters, and they had
withdrawn funds. A few campus opponents were quite vocal, while others, including Dean Elder, kept their opposition to themselves.

The two disputes were clearly related. The connecting link was the
Moody heritage, personified by Will R. Moody, and, in the minds of
many Moody supporters, openly challenged by the changes. The police
accepted the argument that someone would kill to advance his personal
status, although they could not prove that Elder had done so. But would
someone kill over other issues, like those raised by the changes? Speer may
have allowed the question to flicker through his mind. He wrote Margaret
that the murder must have been "the work of some unbalanced mind. Any
suspicions that look in other directions lead where one is unwilling to let
his thoughts go."[113] That vague reference may appear meaningless, but for-
bidden as a suspect was anyone in or having to do with the Moody family, even if only indirectly. One of his correspondents was much more
direct. Immediately after the judge's decision Henry Rankin wrote, "It
would seem as if W.R.'s jealousy of Elliott had been inherited by some
favored henchman, for any other enemy I should not think he had."[114] No
one seemed to have followed such a lead, which could have turned suspicion on someone other than Elder. Burnham Carter, who wrote the centennial history of Northfield Mount Hermon School, researched the case
extensively and wrote an unpublished novel about it, *The Devil's Chapel*,
in which he named Dean Elder as the murderer.[115]

The Family Circle

The mysterious nature of the murder evolved over a period of several
weeks and was never the primary concern of the Speer family. They
wanted the assassin brought to justice, but they were overcome by grief
and the need to deal with immediate questions, like funeral arrangements
and the care of Holly and the children. They decided to hold a brief
funeral service at Ford Cottage and to bury Elliott in Brookside Cemetery
in Englewood beside his little sister. The news spread like wildfire among
their relatives and friends, and soon they were inundated with letters and
telegrams of support and love. The outpouring helped carry them through
the shock of the tragedy. To each correspondent they sent in return a small
leaflet titled simply "Elliott Speer." It included a prayer and a word of

thanks: "This strong tide of human love helps us to realize 'the nearness of the Love Divine.' We walk in the light that streams from the Cross, that evidence in time of the meaning and power of Infinite Love, that revelation of the heart of God and His perfect forgiveness and holiness. We are more conscious, hour by hour, of the whole world's need, of those who sorrow without hope, of those who sorrow without sympathy. The way of love is the only way out of darkness into light, the only way forward through time into eternity."[116]

The Board of Foreign Missions met for a regularly scheduled meeting a few days after Elliott's death and voted words of comfort and an extension of Speer's vacation for as long as he felt he needed "to secure adequate rest for his service during the coming year and also to minister in any way to the comfort of those who may especially need his care."[117] He responded to fellow board secretary Cleland B. McAfee that the offer was very generous, but he did not think he would need extra time. As the days passed, he began to realize how much needed to be done for Holly and in regards to Elliott's estate, and he finally agreed to delay his return and told his colleague and friend McAfee, "This has been one of the loveliest days of the summer, and Mrs. Speer and I are spending it alone in quietness and in peace with its hours crowded full of this work of reconstructing life under the strange but loving will of God."[118]

He began to work through his grief by writing out an account of what had happened and then by working on a memorial book. Sitting at Elliott's desk two days after the murder, he wrote his daughters a long, detailed letter, describing the event and setting out the plans for burial. There was "no explanation of such tragedies within the reach of our thought but we can trust God and go quietly on." He added, "I cannot understand how such an evil deed as has taken him from us could be allowed by a good and loving God but He allowed it in the case of His own dear Son with adequate purpose and we must believe that it was with adequate purpose He has allowed it in the case of our dear son. . . . Life will be a wholly different thing without him but we shall care for all who were dear to him as a sacred trust and hold him fast in our hearts until we see him again."[119]

The book on Elliott began as a brief biography prepared for the formal memorial service, held at Memorial Chapel at Mount Hermon on Sunday, November 11. A crowd of more than a thousand crammed the chapel and overflowed onto the surrounding grounds. Mott offered the prayer. Speer recounted his son's early years and his ministry to the church and the schools, offering some of Elliott's educational and religious philosophy and adding some of the tributes that had poured in about his leadership. He concluded, "We have no words to measure our loss—our loss in the family circle, where he was a ceaseless joy, the loss of the Schools and the nation and the Church. His going lays on us all a holier duty to keep the sacred trust of the great tradition, to seek the light of God on our present tasks in a changing world, to see that no harm comes to these Schools into whose foundations have been built such priceless lives, to make sure that the future shall bring all that was in Elliott Speer's clear vision and brave will."[120]

Mount Hermon sent out 25,000 copies of the memorial service. By the time they were in the mail, Speer was at work on a much larger biography. He told himself and others it was for Holly and the children, but he was also working out his own grief. As he told the story of his son's life, he wove himself into many of the pages, and it became in part his autobiography. He finished the 444-page manuscript in the summer of 1935 and worked at revising it well into the fall. He must have offered it to Holly that Christmas, for he received a letter from her dated Christmas day, which said in part, "You have done a very beautiful thing—you have given to me and to our children our most precious possession. As I can not bear not to read it—so can I hardly bear to read it—You will understand I know—for you must have often felt so in writing it."[121] He considered publishing it as late as 1944 but never did, and it has remained a treasured part of the family's private history.

The family circle had been well joined over the years. Elliott's death broke it in a dramatic way. It would never be as it was, of course, but the family's love and God's love restored its unity, just as it had after Eleanor's death, and made it even stronger. The circumstances had cut back his traveling, and he and Emma were together for almost six months after that fateful September day. He eventually began to travel again and was away around Easter. She wrote that she had been thinking long about Elliott and his senseless death. "Of the Why," she said, "I have no glimmer of understanding, but this one thing I know, that life and love and truth have depths of meaning they did not have before. This clue is all I try to follow." She closed with these words, surely speaking for them both: "You are far away, but very near too, and dearer than ever in all our forty three years, most dear and great Angel. For days I have been thinking of the great phrases in the benediction: The grace of our Lord Jesus Christ, the love of God, the fellowship of the Holy Spirit. Each thought lifts one like a strong hand. Each phrase holds infinity. It is in this grace, this love, this fellowship that we are one, forever."[122]

PART II
Missionary Statesman

Robert E. Speer at 1898 Missionary Conference (2nd row, 4th from left)
Presbyterian Historical Society
Presbyterian Church (U.S.A.) (Philadelphia)

CHAPTER 5

A Student Volunteer

"The Evangelization of the World in This Generation"

The foreign missions movement and Speer's life were remarkably intertwined for half a century, beginning with his decision to join the predecessor of the Student Volunteer Movement for Foreign Missions in 1887 and ending when he retired from the Presbyterian Board of Foreign Missions in 1937. Two related but distinct contexts for foreign missions existed during this era, one of them nondenominational or ecumenical and the other denominational. Both can be traced to the founding of the modern missions movement in the late eighteenth and early nineteenth centuries, but they received a dramatic revitalization near the end of the nineteenth century—especially the ecumenical one—largely due to the emergence of the SVM and the excitement generated by its watchword: "The evangelization of the world in this generation."

He shared fully in both contexts, and that alone distinguished him from almost all of his peers. A few other leaders of ecumenical foreign missions led denominational foreign missions boards, but no other denominational foreign missions board leader also shared leadership in as many and as varied ecumenical foreign missions ventures.[1] While he firmly believed in the unity of foreign missions work and never saw the two contexts as separate, he did have a subtle sense of priority in his thinking for the ecumenical aspect. He held a global missionary vision, which he believed ultimately embraced all his work. The SVM was the foundation of all his foreign missions work, ecumenical and denominational. It marked the beginning of his career as a missionary statesman.

The primacy of the ecumenical perspective was not surprising, given his experiences. Although he was raised a Presbyterian, it was in a broad sense that permitted and even encouraged him to attend religious functions sponsored by other denominations. The emphasis of his home life was on Jesus Christ as revealed in the Bible and life, not on any particular

interpretation of him, denominational or theological. Moreover, the ecu-
menically oriented SVM mediated the most significant religious event in
his life: his conversion from law to missions and his call to be a foreign
missionary. But the movement gave him much more. It offered him his
initial experience in missions and his first job as a missionary administrator. In addition, it was one of his key institutional bases, albeit as a volunteer. As such, it served as one of his major sources of inspiration and gave
him the opportunity to work through his ideas and vision of missions. It
provided him with a truly national and international platform from which
he could share those ideas and his great enthusiasm for foreign missions
with others. In this work he attracted many of his closest lifelong friends,
along with a multitude of others who honored him as the person who was
instrumental in their own conversion and call. Moody entered his life
through the door the movement opened and quickly became one of his
most important mentors. Finally, the movement brought him to Northfield and nearby Mount Hermon, places that offered spiritual renewal in
ecumenical settings. Here he experienced both the great joy of his life when
he met Emma and the great sorrow of their lives when they lost Elliott.

The Student Volunteer Movement

The roots of the SVM predated him, but he was in important ways a party
to its founding. Those roots have been traced to two YMCA student secretaries, Luther Wishard and Charles Ober, and to Robert Wilder, who
with four other students had formed the Princeton Foreign Missionary
Society during the academic year 1883–84. But those roots might never
have produced plants and fruit, had it not been for Moody. He was a towering figure, the leading evangelical Protestant of his day, with tremendous
drawing power. Wishard understood this and had approached him as early
as 1877, trying to get him involved in the student movement, hopeful that
he could inspire an awakening in the colleges. He kept after him until the
spring of 1886, when Moody relented and agreed to sponsor a summer
conference for students at Northfield. Neither Wishard nor Moody was
principally interested in foreign missions, but neither were they uninter-
ested in them. Moody hoped the conference would serve "as a starting
point for the ultimate evangelization of American institutions of higher
education," which then in turn might "send out 'thousands of trained
Christian workers into the pulpits of our land, the foreign mission fields
and into business and the professions.' "[2]

Moody welcomed 251 students from eighty-nine colleges to his first Student Conference, most of them delegates representing their local student YMCAs. The group included Wilder, present at the special request of Wishard, and several students from other nations. Moody had been reluctant to have such a conference, because he had little experience speaking to students, but immediately found them very responsive. The loosely organized schedule featured meetings with Moody and a variety of invited speakers "for Bible study, evangelistic addresses, and discussion of methods for YMCA college work."[3] The month was half over before the two missionary addresses were given, both at Wilder's request. William Ashmore, a Baptist missionary returned from China, gave one on the topic "The work of missions is not a wrecking expedition, but a war of conquest." Pierson gave the other, titled "All Should Go and Go to All."[4]

These addresses sparked a strong response and led Wilder to request permission to speak to the assembly one evening on the missionary theme. Ten students representing ten nations, some from their own lands and some born to missionary parents, spoke about the needs of their lands for Christ, and each concluded by reciting the phrase "God is love" in the language of his country. "The Meeting of the Ten Nations," as it was called, dramatically redirected the conference toward foreign missions. Wilder reported, "Seldom have I seen an audience under the sway of God's spirit as it was that night."[5] In the few days left, one hundred students came under conviction and signed the pledge developed by the Princeton Band: "We are willing and desirious [sic], God permitting, to become foreign missionaries." The Mount Hermon Hundred, following the pattern of the famous Cambridge Seven in England, selected four of their number to visit American colleges and universities to spread the word and recruit others for missions.[6] Two of them were Mott and Wilder. The students dispersed, full of enthusiasm, but without creating any organization.

In retrospect, that failure almost destroyed the success of the summer. Academic responsibilities severely threatened the results of the conference when three of the four students realized they could not interrupt their college work. Only Wilder could go, and so he became the first traveling secretary. He persuaded John Forman, like him a Princeton graduate and a member of the Princeton Society, to postpone his seminary work, and together they toured the colleges in search of recruits. Speer was one of them, one of 2,106 volunteers, including almost 500 women.[7]

Once decided, he moved to the center of the action. He helped create the Mission Band at Princeton, went to Northfield to attend a Moody conference the next summer, and was on board when the informal move-

ment—which had called itself Student Volunteers for Foreign Missions—
formally organized in 1889 as the Student Volunteer Movement for
Foreign Missions and opened its offices at 50 East 70th Street in New
York City. His name was on the first letterhead of the movement as the
traveling secretary. Although he was the second traveling secretary, he was
the first to hold the office in a technical sense. Modest, he never claimed
any credit for organizing the movement, acknowledging that Wilder was
the man with the vision and the energy. On occasion, however, he did say
that, although he was not at the original conference, he counted himself
to be one of the founders.[8]

Even fully organized, the movement was a miniature operation, working out of a small office and with an all-volunteer staff. A recruiting rather
than a sending agency, one of its most important early decisions had been
to refer all recruits to established mission boards for commissioning and
sending. The traveling secretary was, therefore, one of the key officers,
effectively the recruiter and the connecting link between the office and the
volunteers. He moved about to the colleges and universities where mission
bands and YMCA and YWCA groups existed, offering suggestions and
support and reaching out to the many places where bands were not organized or where the seed of foreign missions had not yet been planted.

Wilder had done an exceptional job, but in the spring of 1889 he
decided the time had come for him to complete his theological studies. He
personally chose Speer and went "to Princeton and asked him to take it to
God in prayer." Although it meant delaying his seminary work, he
responded, "If God be willing I will take up your work next year. I have
not talked with any one about it, but it seems to be the way He leads."[9]
Wilder subsequently commented that Speer had "decided on what work
to do *before* he knew what would be the means of support and before consulting anyone about it because he felt that God had led him that way."[10]
Speer began in September, with financial support for expenses provided
only by the YMCA of St. Paul, Minnesota. Years later he reflected, "We
had no anxiety as to whether or not we were going to be sustained. All we
were interested in was a great cause and a chance to give our lives to that
cause."[11]

The year went quickly. He followed the pattern Wilder had established
and in ten months, with two months off because of his father's death, he
visited 110 colleges and universities in states from Maine to South Dakota
to the southern states. He kept a careful record of his work, sending general reports to Wilder and statistical ones to Mott. Some of the letters contained names of volunteers and others organizational suggestions, like the

need for a corresponding secretary in every state, and almost every one offered or invited prayer. He found the religious spirit of most of the western schools quite good, "except in State Universities where it is deplorable."[12] Early in his service he wrote from Beloit, Wisconsin, hopeful for a good year, "The work which God has enabled me to do in this state has not been great in approval due to my lack of faith and likeness of Him but still I pray that the fires I have strived to kindle may burn up fiercely this coming year."[13] He kindled well, for over eleven hundred students responded to his call. As the year closed, he wrote Mott a thoughtful note, offering a prophecy for the future, "Our God has something in store for you and me. Of that I am convinced more and more. I don't know what: may be our paths will be as wide apart as the east is from the west but He wishes us for something."[14]

No extensive accounts of the presentations he made have been found, but his notes for them have. He wrote them out on the end pages of his Bible under a number of different topics, beginning with "The Opportunity," and including "The Voluntary Demand," "The Crisis," "The Need," "Motives and Rewards," "The Bible Commands," "Call for Men," "Woman's Work," and "Final Appeal."[15] Each topic was followed by an outline that contained any or all of the following: names of famous authors; quotations from missionary leaders; biblical references; a list of nations; a collection of statistics; reasons for and against missionary work. This marked his first use of the outline method he employed the remainder of his life for talks and sermons, one that relied heavily on his remarkable memory and makes it virtually impossible to reconstruct what he said.

Although opaque as to final form, the lists highlighted some of his specific ideas and thoughts. When he spoke of "The Opportunity," for example, he told his listeners that the world was wide open and that the Bible had been translated into three hundred tongues, which meant that many of the peoples of the world would be able to accept Christ and learn about him in their own languages. "The Need" he broke up into regions of the world, like Africa and South America, and nations, including China, India, and Japan. The need in South America he defined simply as "Romanism." That marked the first time he made written reference to an area of the world he would later help expand for Protestant missions. One of the most important parts of his appeal was the one he called "Motives and Rewards." When inquirers asked, "Why go?" his first word to them was the "Love of Jesus" and his second was "John III,16." He also listed the objections people typically gave for not becoming missionaries; first on the list was the most common one: people felt they were "not personally called."[16]

A student of the movement has said, "Through the work of Robert Speer, the deity and the authority of Christ was given a central place."[17] Sometimes his strategy to elicit student interest had little to do with religion or the speaking platform. At Beloit and Otterbein, and very likely at other colleges, he used his knowledge of football to attract a crowd. He taught the basics of the game to some of the men at Otterbein and hence inaugurated that sport at their college. In 1926 Otterbein honored him with an LL.D.

When he left the formal office of traveling secretary, he did not leave the work. The movement kept him involved in one volunteer capacity or another until he retired. His service fell along two lines, so closely related that they sometimes merged, but they were nonetheless distinct. On the one hand, he helped organize the work, developing strategies and formulating interpretations on crucial issues. This work changed as time went on and as successful decisions became fixed patterns. On the other hand, he was a star recruiter, a permanent fixture at the quadrennial meetings and the summer student conferences, offering from their platforms Bible studies, lectures, and inspirational speeches, and making himself available for more personal consultations afterwards. This role changed little and stopped only when he formally retired.

The responsibility for organizing and managing the movement fell to chairman Mott, who continued in his role until 1920, and an executive committee. Speer was not an officer and therefore not involved in the formal decision-making process, but as a founder he was an important part of the wider advisory and consulting group, and he made himself readily available for any assignment. He became a member of the advisory committee in 1898 and subsequently of other oversight committees.

The Movement Evolves

The movement made some official changes in its early years, two in particular that he supported, both of which had serious theological as well as practical implications. The executive committee made the changes in response to what it described as "perils." The first was the widespread tendency of hubris on the part of both the individual volunteer and the movement. The initial enthusiasm created what Ober called a "missionary gusher" and led people "to an unwise and misleading use of the numbers."[18] Speer put it bluntly. People in the movement had talked about it as if it were a "crusade," and that exaggerated evaluation had hindered it. "[I]nstead of being allowed to carry on its work quietly and trustfully a large publicity brought unmerited praise and also unjust criticism."[19] Too much pride had both inflated the typical volunteer's image of himself or herself and had turned away others who might otherwise have been attracted to foreign missions. He supported the effort of the executive committee to play down the numbers and to offer more accurate statistics, both concerning the true number of volunteers and those who finally made it to the field. By 1894 the movement reported over 3,200 volunteers, 686 of whom had accepted a field assignment. Since many volunteered while still in the early stages of their career preparations, these numbers represented a very good result. Moreover, they were the major source for the dramatic increase in the number of new people the mission boards were sending to the field.

A second early important change also involved the volunteers, or more specifically, what they had or had not signed and agreed to do. Even as the initial wave of enthusiasm rolled through the colleges and universities, criticisms mounted concerning the wording of the pledge. The one Speer had signed said, "I am willing and desirious [sic], God permitting, to become a foreign missionary." He had not at the time regarded the phrase as debatable. The meaning seemed perfectly clear, but on later reflection he agreed that it contained, at least from the perspective of persons less persuaded, a theological flaw, or what the executive committee called another "peril."[20] In the summer of 1892 and after "exhaustive discussion," the executive committee decided to change the "pledge" to a "declaration" and to revise the wording to this: "It is my purpose, if God permit, to become a foreign missionary."[21]

Speer explained that the reason for the change was to make more room for "the leading of the Holy Spirit." He continued, "When the young people embark on an effort for doing good which seems to be clearly in line with the will of God in its spirit and inception, the subtle temptation always arises to trust to the principles implied in the character of the effort rather than to the never-failing guidance of the Holy Spirit."[22] The pledge seemed to tie the person who made it to his own will, whereas the declaration seemed to open the person who made it to the will of God. While he supported the change and believed it would be beneficial, he cautioned that it in no way diminished the importance of the pledge-declaration. He believed the movement could not have survived without it. Doubtless remembering the importance of the pledge in his own experience, he concluded, "It was necessary to ask college students to make a definite decision, and this decision must be of such a kind as clearly to express a common purpose, and of such conclusiveness as to lead those who made it to interpret thereafter what would be called Providential openings and leadings by some, as temptations to turn aside from a life to which the Holy Spirit had already directed them."[23]

He not only played a significant role in helping interpret executive committee decisions, he also joined the effort to develop three key movement ideas: the mission or volunteer band, the missionary call, and the watchword. As he worked on these ideas, he developed his own way of expressing them, and his way frequently became the stated positions of the movement. He discovered none of them, for all had antecedents, nor did he work on them alone, for others were joined to the effort to present and interpret the claims of foreign missions to their generation. But the ideas came to bear his stamp, however others also marked them, and became his major ideological contributions to the movement. He began working on all of them before or during his year of traveling, but the only one that matured enough then for him to write down and prepare for publication was the strategy of the mission band.

Mission Bands

The mission or volunteer band was an important first step for the movement, its basic organizational unit. Mott, aware that Speer had written on the Princeton Band, asked him to write an article on it, and so Speer had a draft finished in the spring of 1890. Correspondence suggested some difference of opinion between the two men over the article's final style, although no specifics were mentioned.[24] This was their first real work together, besides sharing speaking platforms, and the presence of differences, even though poorly defined, laid the groundwork for clearer and more substantial ones in the future. However, they rarely disagreed in public, so that their audiences saw them as the twin towers of the SVM and the wider student missionary movement. They never permitted their differences to disturb their deep personal affection for one another.[25] After revisions, the movement published the article as a pamphlet in its "Student Volunteer Series." Speer had initially chosen the title "The Volunteer Mission Band," but changed it simply to *The Volunteer Band.*

The pamphlet was an explanation of the idea of volunteer bands and an appeal for volunteers to form and become active in them. Although he put a great deal of his personal experience into this description, he was quick to acknowledge that the idea was not his own. He invited his readers to turn to its true source: the Bible. He reminded them, "The Lord Jesus did His Father's work by means of the little company of followers given to Him out of the world," and directed them to Proverbs 30:27: "The locusts have no king, yet they go forth all of them by bands."[26]

The volunteer band was the movement in each institution, be it preparatory school, college, or theological seminary, created for the purpose "of arousing and maintaining a personal missionary spirit and leading others to pray, and give and go."[27] Members should make every effort to keep the organization "quiet" and "unpretentious," and needed only to select a chairman and a few others to lead useful committees. An important reason for modest organizational machinery was that the band should, if possible, align itself with the existing group or groups responsible for Christian work on campus, such as the YMCA or YWCA or both, and become its missionary voice. Three important benefits followed such cooperative work: first, the larger organizations had long lifelines and could carry on the missionary work after the initial band of volunteers graduated; second, the band was not a threat to the ongoing Christian work and would arouse no jealousy if it integrated with it; and third, the larger organizations had wide audiences and could help spread the missionary appeal throughout the student body. In fact, such close working arrangements developed on many campuses.

These directives served as the introduction to the pamphlet, which Speer divided into two main topics, the nature of band meetings and the responsibilities of the band and its members. The band should meet weekly or every fortnight throughout the academic year. The meetings should be carefully planned and include prayers, which, he said, "should be definite, and believing. Our God's work moves so fast that we ought to have fresh prayers for Him each week." The topics of the meetings were very important and should be chosen with great care. They could cover the different fields of work, review the lives of famous missionaries, define the various methods of work, explain the function of the various missionary boards and agencies, outline the literature available, or cover a number of other related topics.

The specific suggestions he offered constituted his personal agenda and the movement's working agenda. When looking at a particular field, a band should study the climate, the geography, and "the customs and habits of the people, the government and all those natural things which ought to be of interest to every one especially to those who love the lost ones." It should also review the Christian work that had been accomplished, examine the methods that had been used, and then focus on the present and future needs. In this manner, "in a year any Band can circumnavigate the globe . . . and every volunteer who has made the voyage will envy them the joy of the exploration." Great missionaries suitable for study included "Carey, Martin, Livingstone, Hannington, Duff, Paton, Williams, Moffatt, and Xavier," and were often best placed in the context of their fields, because information "concerning fields and points in missionary work can best be understood and remembered by associating them in this way with a life."

The band should acquaint its members not only with evangelistic work, but also educational, medical, women's, and student association work. These suggestions indicated that from the outset the movement saw the evangelization of the world in terms of teaching and healing as well as preaching. The band should review the work of all the missionary agencies, the nondenominational and undenominational ones alike, "for there is great ignorance concerning their character and work." And if the band should at any time be at a loss for topics there were many important general ones, like "What does the Bible say about missions?, The Comparative Need and Success of Home and Foreign Missions, and The Crisis in Missions." The goal of the meetings was to sustain interest in those who had volunteered.

Self-maintenance hardly matched the world's need, and the band and its members faced some significant duties. He declared: "If those who love the Lord and wish to see His dying request obeyed do not strive while in college to awaken missionary interest, who will? In order that the great bleeding heart of our Lord Jesus may be pleased this work must be done." The band and its members could facilitate this awakening in many ways. One was obtaining and distributing the right kind of literature. Every volunteer ought to own and to have read the report of the First International Convention of the SVM, titled *The Evangelization of the World*, along with Pierson's *The Crisis of Missions* and the *Reports* of the London Missionary Conference. In addition, each volunteer should subscribe to the *Missionary Review of the World*.

Bands should encourage volunteers to give money "systematically and definitely," and each band should seek to raise sufficient funds to support its own college missionary. One important way of fixing the missionary commitment was to share it with others, and each band could help accomplish this by seeing to it that the gospel of the "world-wide Christ is preached in every Church, Sabbath-School, Young People's Society,

Y.M.C.A., College and School within its reach." In addition, every band should persuade its members to attend one of the summer student conferences. Reflecting his own experiences, Speer testified that there was no better place for coming into contact with the missionary spirit, nor for catching "the holy inspiration of a purpose to preach the Cross and Him who hung upon it to every soul before our generation sleeps. Northfield especially was not only practically the original birth-place of the Movement but it is the place where every summer it is born again."

The ultimate purpose of the band was to inspire volunteers to begin their missions where they were. It was important to get ready for the future, but if a Christian was called to be a missionary, should not that mission begin at once? He challenged his readers: "Each volunteer must work for new volunteers. Every disciple must be a disciple. Every missionary must be a maker of missionaries. Every Christian student where it is possible ought to leave behind him in college when he is graduated in a class below him, a Christian student who would not have been a Christian, humanly speaking, had it not been for his influence. So also every volunteer must leave behind him another volunteer." Making converts was never easy. Success would come only as each volunteer turned more fully to God. The band could help by inviting its members to become "an infants class." He explained: "Much pride must needs be broken down but it had best break now. And all these infant classes will form an infant school, to sit down at the feet of Him who is the great teacher of prayer. Sitting there is very sweet, and there in the school of prayer we must learn, for we know not yet how to pray as we ought." He concluded by offering a prayer for his readers: "May this coming year see the Volunteer Bands baptized with such a spirit of prayer and support that from the secret places of his communion each volunteer may come down with a face shining as the face of Moses shone and with a life that shall delight to do thy will, O God, even to the uttermost parts of the earth."

He thoroughly believed in the volunteer band and its role as a support group, but once he was out of school, he was no longer directly related to one. That remained true through the 1890s, perhaps because he was starting a new job, traveling a great deal, and developing his own family life. Shortly after the turn of the century, however, he joined not one but two small groups, both of which were essentially bands but were called prayer fellowships. In 1902 he created a small group with a focus on foreign missions, along with David McConaughy (then working with the Presbyterian Board in an effort to secure large individual gifts), David's brother James, Mott, and a few others. Meeting once a year, usually in

December, for a quiet day (Speer sometimes referred to it as a summit day), of fellowship and prayer, they remained in contact through a monthly letter, which included prayer requests.[28] Mott said: "Month by month we share with one another objects of intercession and answer to prayer. What do we not all owe to this fellowship."[29] From time to time they invited close friends with missionary interests to join them, and the group eventually included Wishard and Wilder and later Samuel M. Zwemer, Samuel McCrea Cavert, Jesse R. Wilson, Kenneth Scott Latourette, John A. Mackay, Delavan Pierson, who served as secretary, and a number of others. The group never grew beyond ten or a dozen at a time. The meetings were intensely personal, with each member in turn asking for prayers for difficult times or for blessings received. Each also shared his reading list for the past year, with comments on helpful books. Latourette noted that Speer was the most methodical in his book review-ing and added that "we always looked forward to his list as the best part of that particular portion of the program."[30] They were occasions of renewal and inspiration, and Speer attended the rest of his life.

In 1904 he became part of another fellowship group that also met annually for prayer. This group met for many years at the home of Charles R. Erdman in Princeton and then at Zwemer's home in New York City, or sometimes in a hotel there. Here Speer joined many close friends, includ-ing college classmate Mudge, Princeton Seminary president J. Ross Stevenson, and Camp Diamond fishing partner Stone. Mott and Wilder were also part of this group. The members chose specific topics for reflec-tion, including such things as "Devotion to Christ," "The Return of Christ," and "The Basis, the Limits and the Fruits of Christian Fellowship."[31] Together these bands included many of the key leadership figures in the ecumenical missionary movement and in the Presbyterian Church. They offered many informal opportunities for sharing strategies when faced with problems, as well as for prayer, and for forging ties strong enough to withstand the storms that occasionally rose against individual members and the institutions they served.

The Missionary Call

The missionary call was another crucial part of the movement, and like the idea of the volunteer band, Speer gave it its most distinctive form. In a practical sense it preceded the bands, because volunteers responding to the call created them. In the historical context, the call emerged after the

Mount Hermon meeting and became one of the major features of the movement. The line between the call before and after Mount Hermon was not drawn with great precision, because many of those issuing the new call openly acknowledged their indebtedness to those who had gone before them. This was particularly true of Speer, who traced much of his inspiration for his version of it to Rufus Anderson, who had spent more than fifty years, beginning in 1822, in one or another leadership position with the American Board of Commissioners for Foreign Missions. Speer described him as "the most original, the most constructive and the most courageous student of missionary policy whom this country has produced" and used two of his recruiting tracts, *On Deciding Early to Become a Missionary* and *Ought I to Become a Missionary?* extensively in developing his own appeal.[32]

But that did not mean that Speer, or others like Wilder and Forman, were merely popularizing the work of their missionary forebears.[33] They borrowed some themes, but the call they issued was their own, new and tailored to their generation. Unlike his article on the volunteer band, no evidence has survived that anyone in the movement asked Speer to write out his version of the call. However, when the movement issued his version of it as a pamphlet in 1901 under the title *What Constitutes a Missionary Call?* it quickly became recognized as the movement's call.[34] Circulated widely through college groups and summer conferences, it became so useful and popular that the movement reprinted it a number of times.

The version the movement published was a fine tuning of a presentation he had been working on since his year as traveling secretary, if not before.[35] At the International Student Conference in London in 1900, he had offered a brief outline of it in response to the question "What Essentially Constitutes a Missionary Call?"[36] He had been tremendously successful with it, so that the publication simply multiplied his presence and extended his success. The call appealed to students and others who were already Christian and who acknowledged that Christ had some claim on their lives, but who were uncertain about the nature of that claim. If, he told his audiences, a person asked about the nature of the missionary call, the question was a "good sign," for it "suggests that men think of the missionary enterprise as a solemn enterprise, an enterprise that is related in a singular way to God, and over which God exercises a singular care."[37] He proceeded in a straightforward and compelling way to present the call to foreign missions, dealing in turn with the perceptions and questions students had about it, and leading them to a decision. As early as the summer of 1890, he told Mott that the key lay in the appeal-decision connection: "The Volunteer Movement has succeeded in winning volunteers by a pretty clear line of appeal—a line that drives straight at decision and decision at once and yet does not ignore the Spirit's diversities of operations."[38]

The first time a person came upon Speer's version of the missionary call, he or she could be totally disarmed. Latourette, for example, was transformed by it. He reported that he read the pamphlet one summer while he was in college and the argument unsettled him. He had always expected to become a lawyer and a banker and to work with his father. He had never had "the remotest desire to become a foreign missionary. I had not even thought of becoming a clergyman." But the seed of foreign missions grew in him, and the next summer at the student conference at Gearhart he signed the declaration, "from a sheer sense of duty."[39] What startled him and many others about Speer's presentation was that it challenged their perceptions about the relationship between God's call to become a Christian and his call to become a foreign missionary.

The typical understanding of God's call was that it was twofold, a general call to be a Christian and a special call to be a foreign missionary. Speer argued that the relationship between God's calls was exactly the opposite from what people thought, and that the general call to be a Christian was the call to foreign missions. "The whole thing," he said, "reduces itself to this simple proposition. There is a general obligation resting upon Christian men to see that the gospel of Jesus Christ is preached to the world. You and I need no special call to apply that general call to our lives."[40] Students often believed that unless a voice from heaven called out to them instructions, like "China" or "India," they were free to do whatever came next in their lives. They were often stunned to receive the news: "Every one of us rests under a sort of general obligation to give life and time and possession to the evangelization of the souls everywhere that have never heard of Jesus Christ, and we are bound to go unless we can offer some sure ground of exemption which we could with a clear conscience present to Jesus Christ, and be sure of His approval upon it." It was a compelling fact, he argued, that nine-tenths of the most honored missionaries of the past, including the Anglican Henry Martyn and the Baptist William Carey, never had special calls. Even Livingstone said of himself "that he simply went out of a sense of duty." Speer challenged those who refused to become missionaries without a special call and asked if they were prepared to say "that the noblest men that ever served God in the world flew in the face of Providence because they did not have the particular sort of call you are asking for?"

One of his most telling arguments was that the demand for a special call for foreign missions was an improper use of the Bible, distorting its true message. "No man," he declared, "thinks of interpreting his Bible so in other matters. There is the command, 'Go ye into all the world, and preach the gospel to every creature.' You say, 'That means other men.' There is the promise, 'Come unto me, all ye that labor and are heavy laden, and I will give you rest.' You say, 'That means me.' You must have a special divine indication that you fall under the command; you do not ask any special divine indication that you fall under the blessing." "By what right," he concluded, "do we draw this line of distinction between the obligations of Christianity and its privileges, and accept the privileges as applying to every Christian and relegate its obligations to the conscience of the few?"

But what about "exemptions"? If everyone should go, who would stay and on what basis? He proceeded with care on this issue because he had struggled with the call of another profession and then had experienced an exemption when he accepted the call to be a foreign missions administrator. The students he faced proposed all kinds of possible "exemptions," and he argued against a number of them, using reason, humor, and satire to turn them aside. Some claimed that their inability to learn a language was a sufficient exemption. He replied that everyone except mutes had already learned one language and thereby demonstrated an ability to do so. Moreover, immersion in a culture made learning its language relatively easy. Others appealed to poor health as a sufficient cause. He answered with a story Forman told about his encounter with a man in Iowa who had suffered a sunstroke and had decided to spend his life at home. " 'Well, my friend,' said Mr. Forman,' where did you have that sunstroke?' 'I had it here in this State.' 'Now, look here,' said Mr. Forman, 'I have lived most of my life in India, and I have never had a sunstroke, and you propose to spend your life where you have already had one sunstroke and where for all you know you may have another.' " And still others argued that they lacked the spiritual qualifications. That was too easy a target, Speer said, for surely "a man not spiritually fitted ought not to go, but neither is he fit to stay. His immediate duty is to clean up and empower his life." Exasperated listeners or readers surely wondered if any exemption existed, and he finally admitted one, a special call to remain at home. Turning the whole concept of the special call on its head, he said some could stay home, for God surely wanted people "as Christian lawyers, doctors, teachers, businessmen, ministers, artisans at home," but if he wants you to do one of those things, he will call you to it with a special call, an "exemption" from the general call to evangelization.

He closed his appeal with three important topics for reflection. God called for volunteers, not conscripts, and God most wanted those who would say as Isaiah had said, "Here am I, Lord; send me." God always selected the "post of sacrifice" as the "post of presumptive duty." God called those who truly loved him. "Will you," he entreated, "look into your own heart again and make sure whether or not the call has not been there all the time? Have you been near enough to Jesus Christ to hear Him speak? . . . God forbid that we should try behind any pretext to hide from the solemn personal consideration of our vital duty. 'Go ye out into the ignorant and sinful world and preach the gospel to the lost.' " Driving to decision, he concluded, "Have you any reason for not going that you could give to Jesus Christ?"

The Watchword

The watchword, or watchcry as some called it in the early days, "The evangelization of the world in this generation," was another of the central ideas of the movement. Many leaders considered it to be the most significant one, first among equals. Evangelization was the primary issue, the key idea, the motivating factor in the life of the movement. Wilder announced what many others doubtless believed, that the movement "did not so much produce the Watchword, as the Watchword—or rather the thought behind it—helped to bring into being the Student Volunteer Movement."[41] A biographer of Mott has appropriately described it as "the beating heart of the Movement," and claimed it was "the Protestant world's most widely recognized and effective slogan."[42] Speer had nothing to do with originating it. The distant source was without question the Great Commission. Scholars have found many different, more recent sources in both England and the United States during the second half of the nineteenth century. The opening up of the world, in both Asia and Africa, generated a widespread consensus among those committed to foreign missions of the urgency of reaching the newly accessible hundreds of millions of people with the gospel. Wilder credited his father, Royal G. Wilder, then editor of the *Missionary Review of the World,* with putting together the components of the watchword, and Mott attributed the actual words to Arthur Pierson. The SVM formally adopted it when it organized.[43]

Rare was the SVM meeting without one or more speakers on the meaning of the watchword. Movement leaders chose it as the theme of their
first quadrennial in 1891 and assigned Speer and Pierson the task of bringing it into clear focus. They shared the platform one evening, the young
leader considering the watchword as "A Possibility," and the older one
approaching it from the perspective "How Made A Fact." Pierson spoke
on it again at the second quadrennial and was the foremost interpreter of
it from among the older generation. Speer presented his views again at the
third quadrennial and later published a slightly revised version of that
speech in one of his most widely used books.[44] Speer and Mott shared the
responsibility of interpreting the watchword among the new leaders.
When Mott wrote a book on the topic, he had Speer review it before the
movement published it in 1900.[45] They agreed that for the watchword to
be truly effective, it had to be the personal watchword of each volunteer,
as well as the general watchword of the movement. One commentator
accurately described them, along with Sherwood Eddy, as "defenders of
the watchword." But that commentator then continued, making a distinction without much difference, by claiming that Speer's life was the
"example of the watchword" in the context of individuals and local
churches, and Mott's life was the "interpretation of the watchword" in the
realm of the world student and ecumenical movements.[46] Other commentators have typically given Mott much of the credit for spelling out
the meaning of the watchword, one claiming it was his sense of crisis and
duty that helped propel it forward and another arguing he reinterpreted it
at the third quadrennial so as to eliminate "its millennial overtones."[47]
Neither Speer nor Mott claimed precedence as its interpreter, and they
treated one another as equals in advocating and defending it.

The final form of Speer's thoughts on the watchword appeared in
1902.[48] He divided his presentation into three parts: an introduction on
the importance of watchwords, a response to criticisms of the watchword,
and an analysis of its distinct meaning. Watchwords were important for
movements, helping to define them and serving as rallying cries. Many
important movements in history had adopted watchwords, including such
familiar American ones as "No taxation without representation" and
"Fifty-four forty, or fight." The political movements represented by these
phrases were important, but the world student movement was even more
significant, because it was "inspired by the Spirit of the Son of Man and
the Son of God," and surely should also have a watchword.[49] Moreover,
the one the movement had chosen met the basic criteria of a "religious
watchword." It was short, but not too short. There were those who wanted

to make it even shorter by eliminating either "of the world" or "in this generation." Both phrases were essential, for the one lifted up the universality of the challenge and the other the urgency of it. It was striking, phrased in such a way that "its form challenges the thought and the scrutiny of men." It was scriptural, Jesus himself calling for it when he told his disciples to "disciple all nations," "go ye into all the world," and sent them to "every creature." It proposed something heroic, beyond the capacity of anyone unless he was "clothed with the Spirit of the Most High."[50]

Yet, he noted, almost from the day the movement announced the watchword, there had been those who raised objections and offered criticisms. In particular, Edward Lawrence in his book *Modern Missions in the East* challenged it. Although Speer believed the issues Lawrence raised were unfair, he used them as a way of clarifying the meaning of the watchword. First, to the charge that it was too simple and superficial, ignoring the real difficulties of preaching the gospel to the world, Speer responded that it proposed preaching in the sense of evangelization. The movement did not recruit people to go out shouting the Word so that everyone in the world had a chance to hear it, but to share it so that they would have a chance to understand it and make a decision about it. "If some creatures cannot take it in, we shall at least do all of our part." Second, to the criticism that it ignored the aim of Christianizing the world and the proper means for doing so, he answered bluntly that it was not "synonymous with the idea of the Christianization of the world in this generation." If Christianization meant making the world Christian, that had not yet happened in the most "Christian" nations, even with centuries of effort. Christianization depended upon true conversion, but the watchword was also "not synonymous with the conversion of the world in this generation." Both Christianization and conversion were legitimate hopes of the missionary but were in the final analysis in the hands of God. Men and women offered, God alone changed. The watchword proposed the less exalted but nonetheless real task of "offering to all our fellowmen, in obedience to the command of our loving God, the gospel of the grace of the Son of Man." Furthermore, it challenged the church "to believe that her duty will not have been done—no, will scarcely have been begun—until she shall have raised up in this world an army of missionaries and native Christians large enough to secure the preaching of the glad tidings of Christ's life and death and blood to every creature in the world before they die."[51]

Lawrence's third charge was that the watchword represented some particular form of pre-millennialism. Speer flatly denied this. The key to his response was the term "particular." Everyone he knew who believed in the evangelization of the world also believed that it had something to do with the "second advent of our Lord." He certainly believed it did and confessed that he received from his "convictions as to His second advent new strength and fresh motive." But the watchword was not attached to any particular millennial view. Every Christian, whatever his or her views about the second coming, shared the responsibility of evangelization. "I do not know," he concluded, "what will come after this world has been evangelized. I do not know whether our work will be done then or not. I do not think it will. But I know that until this world is evangelized our work will never be done."[52]

Whatever watchword detractors might say, however they might try to dismiss its importance, Speer believed they could neither diminish nor destroy it, because it had too much inherent strength. It was "an appeal and a ground of appeal," and as such it conveyed three strong, positive messages. Those who took it as their own could find in it "the most true and worthy conception ever set for life in our own or any other day." A realistic way to measure it was to consider the lives of those who had accepted the missionary call in the past, like Francis Xavier, Raymond Lull, or David Livingstone. Their remarkable and often heroic efforts revealed that the watchword's challenge was "a high and holy and true and worthy aim for the life that belongs to Christ." Some argued that it was too high an aim, bordering on the fantastic and the unreal. If so, he responded, then both Jesus and Paul, who had announced it to their followers, should be charged with giving an impossible task.[53] This led him to an additional strength of the watchword, which was that "it proposes that which is distinctly feasible and possible." He believed that no long argument was needed to convey what every listener and reader knew, that the world had opened wide and that there was not "one spot" in it "where the Christian Church, if it wants to, may not go with its message of love and life of God." And the key was the "will" of the church. In the United States alone, he claimed, there were over 100,000 ordained clergy, more than enough if the church decided to redistribute them to make world evangelization a reality. "The Church of Christ," he affirmed, had "men enough" and "wealth enough." It needed will enough.[54]

Finally, the watchword set out "that which is our supreme, our primary, our imperious duty." Duty had been for him a major keystone of his life, and he built it into his argument for the watchword. He invited his audiences back to the time of Jesus and instructed them to remember not only "what Jesus Christ did," but also "for whom Jesus Christ did this." Jesus died for the sins of the world, and anyone who acknowledged that had to act so that the whole world could know it. The underlying premise was the uniqueness of Christ and Christianity and the inadequacy of any and all other religions to meet the needs of the world.[55] "Who dare stand," he asked, "in the presence of the multitudes who have only one Name given whereby they must be saved and only one door furnished through which they may go in to see the Father, and deliberately say to them: 'This gospel is ours; it is not for you'?" And the duty was to act immediately. Generations past were out of reach, and generations to come would be the responsibility of others, but "we stand face to face . . . with hundreds of millions of needy men, ignorant of the name of Jesus Christ, confronting us." The watchword was not, he concluded, a "play-word," something to be taken casually. It was the way Jesus Christ was speaking to the present generation, calling men and women to lay themselves "upon a cross," to walk in his footsteps, and to spend their lives "as Christ spent His for the redemption of the world."[56]

The work he performed on behalf of the movement, especially in helping delineate its ideas, was largely completed by the time it was a decade or so old. Although he continued to develop new themes in his student work, like his presentation on non-Christian religions at the fifth quadrennial in 1906, he spent more and more of his time with other groups. After World War I his role in the organizational aspects of the movement shifted. Even though he served on the general council, and for a short time chaired the administrative committee, he really became the elder statesman, called on to speak at the quadrennial gatherings, asked to assist with specific problems, or invited to offer a historical perspective. In 1929 the movement recognized his forty years of service and named him honorary chairman of the general council and member ex officio of the administrative committee.

Hard Times for the Movement

The postwar years were difficult ones for the movement, marked by general decline. More than six hundred student volunteers sailed in 1921, the peak year, but only about two hundred went ten years later, and the number kept falling through the 1930s.[57] In 1918 the movement provided 58 percent of the new missionaries; in 1930 it provided only 32 percent of them.[58] The numbers in 1921 disguised sea changes that were taking place, changes that had already begun to surface at the eighth quadrennial in Des

Moines, Iowa, in 1920. Mott had opened that meeting with his typical evangelical appeal, and Eddy followed in the same vein. Students later challenged Eddy, accusing him of using "worn-out phrases" and of talking "about the living God and the divine Christ."[59] Eddy scrapped his next prepared address and "spoke instead in support of the League of Nations and social reform before turning again to spiritual reform."[60] Speer, present with daughter Margaret, gave the final address. He found the "warlike" spirit of the meeting distressing.[61] It was, however, an important event in his family's life, because Margaret decided to sign the SVM pledge and give her life to God as a foreign missionary.

Things did not get much better during the next several years. Diversity of opinion became very marked at the Indianapolis quadrennial in 1924 when the movement used student-led discussions for the first time. One division that emerged in the 1920s was largely a theological or philosophical one, between those who were convinced that the older evangelicalism should remain the most important work of the movement and an increasing number who called for a refocusing of that spirit on the social problems of the world. This growing tension prefigured the open break in the ranks of missionary thinkers that took place in 1932 with the publication of *Re-Thinking Missions*, popularly known as the Hocking Report.[62] Another division was generational, with students calling for more say in the running of the movement and for changes in some of its administrative practices.

Speer became involved in these issues in both informal and formal ways, with a clear bias in favor of the traditional role of the movement but a desire to work out problems to the mutual satisfaction of all parties involved. When John Childs wrote a critique of the movement in the *Intercollegian* in 1923, calling for many changes, including the elimination of the declaration card, Speer wrote that he found the suggestions unwise, but typical of someone who had "seen just one small section of the missionary work."[63] The recurring discussion of the scope of foreign missions surfaced again in 1927 in relation to preparation for the tenth quadrennial in Detroit. He advised newly appointed general secretary Jesse Wilson that foreign missions and Christian internationalism were not synonymous, and if they were not kept separate, the Detroit meeting would be in danger of reproducing the turmoil of the one in Des Moines. He told Wilson that Christian internationalism encompassed the various social and political issues that might arise between nation states or even between the churches of different nations, but these were not foreign missions. "The foreign missionary enterprise," he said, "truly conceived is a very simple, clear, specific enterprise," and should not be confused with other things.[64]

The leadership of the movement periodically explored possible changes in structure and procedures; one such proposal distributed in 1930 would have made it subordinate to the various denominational foreign missions boards. Speer fired off a sharply worded letter to Wilson, arguing that the proposal, if implemented, would soon kill it. The scheme was too expensive, and the boards would soon scrap it, but the real problem was that it violated the nature of the movement. It was not "an office organization," but "a movement of life and action whose vitality lay in its succession of consecrated students who were going out to the foreign field and who gave themselves to touching other lives as deeply and as strongly as they could before they went themselves."[65]

The issue refused to disappear, emerging again in the midst of the debate over the Hocking Report. He convened a small and unofficial group, including Latourette, then a professor at Yale, four students, and representatives of the foreign missions boards of the Reformed Church, the Baptist Church, the Presbyterian Church U.S.A., and the Episcopal Church, to consider the future of the movement. After a "full discussion" of proposals to place the SVM under the care of various other missionary or student Christian groups, they unanimously decided the following: "that the Student Volunteer Movement as a voluntary and autonomous student movement ought not to be discontinued; that there was as great need as ever for students who were expecting to go as missionaries or for younger missionaries home from the field on furlough to carry the torch of their own missionary purpose to and fro among the students of the land."[66]

The movement created special commissions twice in the period between the world wars to deal with the many questions it faced. He served officially as chair of the commission of inquiry, created in 1925 to examine the policy, programming, and staff, and to make suggestions for changes.[67] The commission met for two days in December and considered a number of issues of vital concern to the students, including ways to increase their participation in policy making and in the program of the quadrennial meetings. He took the work seriously but found it "wearisome." Students moved on so quickly that such work had to be done over and over again, and although he tried "to keep on the watch for new viewpoints and new principles, or new light on old principles," he found it very difficult "to find much among all the effervescent irresponsibility of these present years." The students seemed pleased with the outcome, and so did he, but he also felt that he had "pretty nearly earned release."[68] That opinion hardened after he retired. R. H. Edwin Espy, the new general secretary, wrote in 1941 asking for advice. Speer generously offered to do what he could, but added, "Each generation must work out its own problems, bear its own responsibility and exercise its own judgment."[69]

Recruiter

The true gift he gave the SVM was his time, energy, and skill as a recruiter. However many committees or commissions he served on, he was its great recruiter and constant source of inspiration. He had a contagious enthusiasm for Christ and the Christlike life, and possessed a remarkable ability to challenge those in his audiences in such a way that they were moved to change their lives, either in the direction of foreign missions or for more purposeful Christian living.[70] Contemporaries used a variety of terms to describe him and his impact. Mott said he "always brought men to the point where they faced the Living Christ," and Eddy claimed that his "was the prophetic voice, speaking with searching power."[71] Mackay, who first came under Speer's spell in Scotland and subsequently became a secretary of the Board of Foreign Missions under him and then president of Princeton Theological Seminary, said he was "incomparably the greatest man I have ever known."[72]

Members of his family shared the same kind of experiences. His Aunt Mim described the reception the Huntingdon Presbytery gave him when he came to speak on foreign missions: "It is said a prophet has no honor in his own country. It was certainly not verified in Rob's case. . . . There certainly is something very winning and attractive about Rob. A magnetism that draws all hearts to him."[73] These are heady claims, well beyond verification. No effort has ever been made to quantify his influence, or that of anyone else from his generation, in religious life or without. Yet such claims were made time after time in the letters of thanks he received or the testimonies that others published about him. He never described himself in any of these terms and often tried to deny the unique character of his role, choosing instead to attribute to God or the work of others his success as inspirer or recruiter.

The primary source of such tributes was his contact with students and other young people at the SVM quadrennial meetings or the student conferences at Northfield. As his popularity grew, other groups, including the YMCA and the YWCA, invited him to their summer conferences.

Although these student meetings have been largely neglected by historians, they were an important part of American religious life for many years, a source of Christian inspiration and renewal and of recruits for missions and ministry.[74] Once begun, Speer persisted. He appeared on the platform in a major speaking role at the first twelve SVM quadrennials, which meant that twelve successive student generations heard him issue the call for foreign missions, and he rarely missed a summer student conference.

The quadrennial meetings were the major gatherings of the movement, spaced—except for the break caused by World War I—so that there was one each student generation. Those who organized those meetings planned them carefully and invited the best-known speakers, often including guests from student missionary circles in Europe, especially Great Britain. From the outset Speer's peers recognized his special platform ability and gave him a prominent place. Whatever else they asked him to do, they also assigned him to open and close the meetings, setting the spiritual tone and offering the invitation for commitment. He would prepare notes on a topic and memorize them so that he spoke without any apparent aid, except when he occasionally took a small notebook from a pocket to read a poem. Stenographers recorded his speeches, and he would review the typed scripts before releasing them for publication. Year after year he touched his audiences, always moving some of those present to decision. He was first their fellow student, later their elder brother, and finally their father and mentor. He sustained an amazingly high level of success, and if not every speech was memorable, many were truly remarkable.

The first quadrennial, held in Cleveland, attracted 680 delegates, and the second at Detroit drew 1,325. Almost 7,000 attended the eighth. Richard C. Morse, a YMCA executive, claimed that the first two drew more students than "any other undergraduate convention called together for serious discussion."[75] Speer made the closing remarks at Cleveland. Their days together, he told his fellow students (he was still in theological seminary), had been a mountaintop experience from which they would shortly have to descend, returning to "the roar and the noises and the daily tasks" that often presented "hindrances" to living the Christian life. He invited them to meet the challenges ahead by marking their lives with three things: (1) "be holy ones, even as He was holy," (2) "be men of prayer," and (3) "be in this world, more than all else, the living powers of the King." The meetings were for inspiration, but more importantly for recruitment, and so he ended his appeal by asking them "to commend unto God and the word of His grace every volunteer who, with life devoted to Jesus Christ, shall sooner or later have the rare joy of holding up the life and death and the blood of his Lord before the world."[76]

He gave other closing addresses, but the most moving one was at the second quadrennial in 1894. The Gospel of Luke, he began, recounted the story of the man with the sick son who brought him to the disciples for healing. They could not do it, and after Jesus had healed the boy, the disciples asked him why they could not. He told them quite frankly that they did not have enough faith. Speer noted that the movement had grown strong in the previous four years and that the group itself expressed so much unity and power "that some will be apt to trust too much to the Movement." Be aware, he cautioned. "We shall get most strength and most help if we do not persuade ourselves these last days that we are part of a large movement, but remember, instead, that we are part of the forsaken and the cast out Christ." Listen, he appealed, in the stillness of these moments to that Christ speaking to you as he spoke to his disciples. Hear Jesus invite you to greater faith, hear him say to you, "Follow me," "Learn of me," and "Abide in me."

But, he concluded, there was "a deeper word still," for Jesus really invited his followers, "Be I." Members of a future generation would associate such language with Martin Buber. Speer admitted that Jesus had not used the precise phrase, but "He meant it so," for it stood for the new birth in Christ. He then challenged the gathered throng:

> Fellow students, are we Christ? Is Christ re-incarnated in us? Have you been mistaken for Him? Have any of the things that we have done been mistaken for His deeds, so that men crossing our paths have said, "We have crossed the path of the Christ"? Eighteen hundred years ago He went away, but He is not away. In thousands of lives still, in the life of every one who has caught the spirit of His life, Christ lives again. And as we go, fellow students, let it not be the sense of a large enthusiasm begotten by these large numbers; let it not be the strength of a deep feeling stirred by the sweeping of His hand over the heartstrings of our lives in the days of this gathering,—let it be the living, abiding, enduring, undeparting Christ, re-living His Divine life in our lives, that shall help us to serve Him.[77]

Over 4,000 students appeared for the fifth quadrennial at Nashville in 1906, the first held in the south. The meeting had an electric quality. John B. Sleman, Jr., a Presbyterian layman, left so inspired that he immediately founded the Laymen's Missionary Movement to enlist the laity of all the churches to raise funds for foreign missions. Like the SVM it became "an expression of and a contribution to the sense of unity which characterized the missionary thrust."[78] Ernest F. Tittle, later a distinguished Methodist preacher and one of those named in the *Christian Century* poll of out-standing preachers, recalled: "I shall never forget the hush which came over that great student conference in Nashville when Robert E. Speer stood before us with watch in hand and told us, minute after minute, how many human beings in Asia and Africa were passing into eternity without hope. If only we had been there with our saving gospel before they died! Before the conference adjourned many of us had volunteered to go."[79]

He spoke several times at Nashville, including the first and last words. At the initial meeting he sounded like a revivalist when he announced that "Jesus Christ is here this afternoon more eager to give to every student that has come to this place that which we need than we are to receive."[80] In closing he became the missionary recruiter, reminding his listeners: "You and I are accountable for the lives of the men and women whom we might reach; and some day, if we have turned away from God's call and appoint-ing here to-night, their blood will He require at our hands."[81] Using his skill as illustrator, he chose a Civil War setting to drive his appeal home. Some years ago, he said, he had a layover in Salisbury, North Carolina, on his way to a southern students' conference in Asheville. There, in a small cemetery beside a church, he came upon the graves of two Confederate soldiers and on the stone of one were the words "He died for the cause he loved." "I took off my hat and stood there, and remembered the one who said, 'I am the good shepherd, . . . and I lay down my life for the Sheep.' " And then he issued his invitation: "This was the way the Master went. Shall not the servant tread it still? And here before we go, in the simple quietness of our own hearts, shall we not, each one, bow down, bending our wills beneath the will of Christ as we too lay down our lives for His sheep?"[82]

He did a great deal of his recruiting at the many summer conferences he attended. As they spread outward from Northfield to many different sections of the nation, he often tried to make them all. After the turn of the century he typically attended four or five every summer. In 1903 he spoke at Asheville (North Carolina), Lake Geneva (Wisconsin), Lakeside (Ohio), and Silver Bay (New York), as well as Northfield.[83] He became a major draw, and conference organizers came to count on him and did not hesitate to upbraid him when his schedule kept him away from their meetings. May Moody, William R. Moody's wife, could not believe that he could not arrange to be at the Northfield woman's conference one year and tried to get Emma to change his mind.[84] When he told Wilder he probably could not make an SVM meeting, Wilder replied that that was "not possible" and that he was "deeply grieved."[85]

The presentations he made at the summer conferences differed in two respects from those he delivered at the quadrennial meetings. They were less formal and on a greater variety of topics. He rarely if ever repeated himself and over his lifetime produced hundreds upon hundreds of talks. They were published in *Northfield Echoes* and, after it merged into *Record of Christian Work*, in that periodical. The *Intercollegian* published some, and others he collected in books like *The Master of the Heart* and *Remember Jesus Christ*. A sample of the titles reveals the range of interests and the kinds of conferences. At the Northfield student conference in 1892 he spoke on "The Lust of the World, The Lust of the Flesh, and The Pride of Life"; at the young women's conference in 1896, also at Northfield, his topic was "Every Human Life a Divine Mission"; at the Northfield student conference in 1905 he spoke on "The Power of Trivialities"; and at the young women's conference in 1917, the summer the United States joined World War I, he reflected on "The Call of the Hour for Missionary Enlargement."[86] In addition to speeches with titles, he led Bible studies, preached, and often led the opening and closing sessions.

He once described these conferences "as free and simple almost as was the school of Jesus on the hills and by the brooks and blue waters of Galilee."[87] They were serious times, but they were also full of spaces for recreation and good fun. The afternoons were free for games or swimming or small group meetings without specific agendas. He created a memorable occasion at one conference held the week of the Fourth of July in 1908. Called to the platform, he produced a collection of letters he claimed to have received, and he proceeded to read from them. The mother of two students at the conference wrote asking him to warn the students about the dangers of college life. "Urge them," she said, "to take more exercise. My boys are white and worn. They tell me they are all too interested in their work, that they have no time for mere physical exertion. Can you not start a movement which will do away with . . . compulsory chapel . . . so that athletic sports, now so inadequately recognized, may be given their rightful place?" President Hadley presumably wrote to ask him to recruit some men to play baseball for Yale and offered to pay $50 a month plus board. In a P.S. he added: "Don't get Harvard men. The Librarian has just had all our books nicely arranged, and we don't want any of them taken from the shelves."[88]

The SVM had an international outlook from its beginning, embracing Canada and early forging strong ties with British students. Wilder had initiated the connection to England when he had gone there in 1891,

"commissioned by the Presbyterian Board of Foreign Missions, as a special worker among young men in the interest of missions."[89] He had spoken at the Keswick Convention on missionary day and elicited an unexpectedly strong response, which led within a year to the formation of the
Student Volunteer Missionary Union. It adopted the watchword in 1896.

Speer went to England twice on behalf of student missionary work, to
Keswick in 1894 and to London in 1900, with particularly dramatic con-
sequences on the first trip. At Keswick he gave a series of Bible studies on
"The Man Christ Jesus" that took some of his listeners by storm. Temple
Gairdner, later a missionary to Egypt, wrote, "That Man still *lives*, the
Personality which, when we were shown it, burned our hearts is alive, the
same, present, our Friend and Lover. I was constrained to nestle into Jesus
as never before." Gairdner's time of decision came Wednesday evening:
"Holy Communion . . . deep impression of new era . . . Evening, Speer
simply God-inspired. Evangelization of the World in this Generation.
Never heard anything like it. Oldham and I walk up the road and give
ourselves to God."[90] Joseph Oldham became a leader in the Student
Christian Movement and the first secretary of the International
Missionary Council. Donald Fraser and Douglas Thornton, two others
who forged distinguished careers in foreign missionary work, were awakened that evening. Thornton confided to his diary, "For the first time
some ten of us at least began to realize that we individually were responsible for the Evangelization of the World in This Generation."[91] Speer
remembered Keswick as the occasion "when the fountains of the British
Volunteer Movement were opened."[92]

One constant at all the conferences he attended, large or small, formal
or informal, was his presence, in the sense that he was available for personal consultation. Some persons who carried their personal problems and
questions to him at his office at the Board of Foreign Missions reported
that they found him always willing to listen but reluctant to engage in dialogue or to offer advice, but no one remembered such behavior in the conference setting. On the contrary, there, in "interviews with literally thousands of students on the question of their life and vocation," he created a
large part of his reputation as a student worker.[93]

In 1922 friends quietly gathered tributes to him in recognition of his
years in student work. The book presented to him at the intercollegiate
conference at Silver Bay that summer contained letters from many people,
including some who had achieved substantial national reputations. Henry
Sloane Coffin wrote that he first met Speer at Northfield when he was a
Yale sophomore and "the influence which you exerted on me, and on my

fellow-students, still abides; and you have been a part of us ever since, a part we could ill forgo. . . . In these conferences no man has been heard more steadily, and none has met with a wider or a deeper response than yourself."[94] Rockefeller said: "I shall never forget the deep impression which you made upon me in one of the first talks which I ever heard you give. . . . I wish I could adequately express my sense of deep personal obligation to you for what you are, and for the influence which you have exerted and continue to exert in the written and spoken word, as well as in your daily life, for the upbuilding of Christian character in the lives of the students of the world."[95] Latourette highlighted the personal character of his work: "As I look back across the years it is not so much the memory of specific words that you have said that abides, but it is the impression of yourself. You have made God and Christ and the Christian life more vivid to me, . . . by your own life and your unfailing friendship. And after all—I suspect it is just that which you have wished to do. I thank God for you."[96]

Recruiting was not limited to student conferences but was part of all his ordinary life contacts, with students and others. From his days with the Princeton Band until near the end of his life, he visited colleges and preparatory schools, sometimes on behalf of the SVM or his board, but more often than not to talk to an association meeting or to preach in a chapel service. Always he invited the young men and women in his audiences to follow Jesus Christ. He went to so many places on so many different occasions that any effort to characterize this work must be at best anecdotal. He and Mott were at Yale during the academic year 1899–1900, and under their inspiration it "witnessed one of the most far-reaching religious awakenings ever known in the history of the University."[97] Yale awarded him an honorary M.A. at graduation ceremonies that year. After Speer conducted a day of prayer at one college, a student reportedly said: "I have been deeply impressed today. Somehow I can't but feel that Jesus looks like Dr. Speer." Speer wrote at the bottom of the letter that carried this message his response: "No—Paul alone could call men to see Christ in him—not me."[98] A student at Yale wrote in 1906 to thank him for his recent talk at Dwight Hall. "The particular point which helped me," he said, "was the idea that Christ could help a man get the bulge on his temptation *at the first*, and that he could thus *actually become a different man*."[99] Age neither dimmed his voice nor muted his appeal. He visited Wilson College in his sixty-eighth year, and a student reported to her guardians: "Dr. Speer was great this morning. His sermon was very clear and well put so that anyone could understand and follow it. . . . Too bad he isn't younger so we'd have him longer; but I never saw such a young looking man for his age."[100]

It was in the context of these visits that he received the nickname "Sobbing Bobbie."[101] Sometimes used in derision, it did not seem to impair his effectiveness, perhaps because, once students experienced his presentations, they came to see that the tears were natural and not forced. Although he was not an emotional speaker, he did not shun emotion, and if the occasion called for it, he might weep. At least two of his mentors wept in public. Professor Green at Princeton sometimes broke down at an appropriate place in a lecture, and Moody did the same. Speer often used dramatic stories, evoking missionary martyrs past and present, and there were doubtless those in his audiences who shared his tears.

Younger students held a special attraction, and he spent a great deal of time visiting various preparatory schools. Although he visited some for young women, like Abbott and Northfield, he spent much more time at those for young men, including Phillips, Hotchkiss, Lawrenceville, Mount Hermon, Kent, Peddie, Blair Academy, and the Hill School. He went to some of these regularly for years, and he spoke at Hill every year for forty-eight years, sometimes four or five times a year.[102] One school invited him to become its chaplain on a weekend basis, but he regarded that as inappropriate, given his board position.[103] Mott claimed he had a "strategy of boyhood," and believed it was "one of the most fruitful parts of his life work."[104] Speer himself never used that phrase and never offered anything that might be called a "philosophy of boy's work," but he had a lifelong interest in it. Three of his four children spent some time in such youth work, two of them as heads of prestigious schools, doubtless influenced by his interests and commitment.

This work took several forms. The Peddie School dedicated its handbook, *The Pilot*, to him in 1931–32: "In sincere appreciation for interest and help in founding the 'Y' organization of the Peddie School—the first prep school 'Y' in the world."[105] He also helped establish volunteer bands, and on at least one occasion helped dedicate a building. Most often he went to the schools to give talks or sermons, sometimes followed by a period for group or individual discussion. His topics ranged far and wide, from temptations young people faced in everyday life, like cheating and gambling, to heroes they could follow, like Martin Luther or Paul or Jesus. Always he offered some moral or religious truth, but he had the ability to phrase it in such a way that it sounded as if it came from an older brother rather than an authority figure. He rarely repeated himself, although he used some favorite illustrations in a variety of contexts. One message he gave at different places and at different times in the same place was his talk on lying. He borrowed the idea from Trumbull's book *A Lie Never Justifiable* and gave him credit for it, sometimes using that title as his own. He called it "Hate Lies" when he delivered it at Hotchkiss at the turn of the century. John G. Magee, later an Episcopal missionary to China, recalled that he "had never been moved so deeply by a sermon before and could hardly walk out of the chapel afterwards," and added that Speer "was the most important influence in my youth."[106]

Sincerely interested in what moved the young people of his day, Speer developed a questionnaire to investigate their ideas and opinions and distributed it at several of the schools. He began a book based on the responses, tentatively titled *Ideals for Boys*, but he never finished it. He did publish several collections of his talks and sermons, including *A Young Man's Questions, A Christian's Habits, Christ and Life, The Stuff of Manhood, Men Who Were Found Faithful*, and *Young Men Who Overcame*. The last two were collections of short life stories of young men, some of them missionaries, but all of them dedicated to the Christian life.[107]

Dwight L. Moody

One of the most important consequences of his decision to join the Student Volunteer Movement was that it brought him into contact with both Dwight L. Moody and Northfield. Moody became a mentor and Northfield a home. He met Moody on August 2, 1887, and heard him speak for the first time that evening in the old Stone Hall. He was overwhelmed. Moody told familiar Bible stories but made them "so vivid that they stood out before us as though they were incidents in our common life, and pouring out his great nature into ours, opening for us new doors into the reality of life and into the Kingdom of God." It was such preaching as he had never heard before, preaching that ignited his imagination, and when "that conference was over I was not sure whether I went back home on earth or above."[108] Moody became and remained the best public speaker he had ever known, "in simplicity, directness, self-forgetfulness, persuasiveness, and fervor. There was no parade, no studied art, but straightforward unaffected, convincing setting forth of his case. He was a tremendous dynamo of driving energy, with an instinct for word and action which operated instantaneously."[109] He did not try to copy Moody's speaking style, but he certainly studied him and sought ways to make the gospel come alive for his own audiences.

On occasion Speer offered tributes to Moody and celebrated his many contributions to American religious life. He typically divided his comments into two parts: Moody the man and Moody the thinker. He believed Moody was a great human being. He knew that some people, those who did not know Moody well, "thought of him as brusque, authoritative, and abrupt," but what he remembered was "his gentleness, his tenderness, the kindliness of his touch." Moody was, moreover, modest and humble, forgetful of self and always remembering God.[110] He also credited Moody as the source of some important ideas, in the practical rather than speculative sense. He told those assembled at Northfield for the D. L. Moody centenary in 1937 that Moody believed in the "uniqueness and the finality and the adequacy of Jesus Christ as the Son of Man and the Son of God," and he believed it without any reservations concerning his full manhood and his full deity.[111] At the same time, he said, Moody believed in the social aspects of the gospel, in its application to the social needs of men and women.[112] And Moody believed the Bible was as unique among books as Christ was among human beings. He claimed that Moody's theology came directly from the Bible, "and its absence of rigid consistent system caused no difficulty to him. . . . Instead of making the error professional theologians make of choosing certain texts and either explaining away or ignoring the rest, he believed the whole glorious truth."[113] Although Speer held some of these ideas—such as the individual theory of evangelism—before he went to Northfield, he acknowledged Moody's role in shaping his ideas about Jesus and the Bible and in supporting his inclination for practical thinking.[114]

Moody was drawn to Speer almost as much as Speer to Moody. Although Moody left no record of his specific feelings about the younger man, he clearly accepted him as part of the new generation of evangelists and missionaries, and so he passed the torch.[115] Moody also tried to recruit Speer for his work. Speer recollected, "In 1892 he asked me to meet him in Mr. Revell's office and wanted me to join him in Buffalo and to go with him as an evangelist to young people as Henry Drummond had done in Great Britain. What if I had gone!"[116] But most of Moody's other approaches to him succeeded. He kept inviting him back to the student conferences and other summer meetings at Northfield. In 1896 he drew him into the governance structure of the Northfield schools by persuading him to join the board of trustees. Speer served for many years as a trustee, and as vice-president of the board after 1912. The board served primarily in a consulting role. He resigned as vice-president when Elliott joined the schools but remained on the board. The one crisis he faced during his tenure involved the conflict between Will Moody and Elliott, which was discussed in a previous chapter. That issue came to a head at a board meeting in 1929 and was resolved when Will resigned.[117] But for that painful exception, his service on the board was a pleasant experience, a trust passed to him, accepted and fulfilled.

Northfield and Mount Hermon

The stream of time and energy he gave to Northfield flowed easily, because he truly loved Moody and his family and the ideals for which he and the schools stood. But the stream had other, even more personal, springs. One of them marked the place of the sealing of his missionary commitment and was his personal Galilee. In his *Memorial* to Horace Pitkin he explained the meaning of Northfield for Horace, and for himself.

> What Northfield had been to him, it was to others also—the place where life came to itself and set hard in the will to serve. The spot where this purpose crystallized and found expression became to him, as it is to many students, the dearest spot in the world. To the end, the memory of it never faded as he saw it that evening when he finally made his decision and gave open expression to it: the clump of pine trees on the side of the hill and the little birches on the top; the sun setting red and glorious on the Berkshires; the Connecticut stretching like a sinuous, silver cord up the valley; the lengthening shadows across the new mown fields; the scent of the clover and the green grass and the four hundred men lying in the hillside and thinking of the meaning and use of life, and of the light falling softly on the purpose of it, from the example of Him who nineteen centuries ago lay on the hills of Galilee; who was among men as one who serves, and who came not to do His own will but the will of His Father who had sent him.[118]

This spring ran fresh year after year as he returned in the summers and led different student groups and other generations to it, to taste for themselves and experience its nourishment. The spring of family life and love was certainly equal, if not greater. This lay hidden from Speer at first, for he met, but did not really see, Emma that first summer she attended the student conference. But soon Northfield became one of their special places, different from Diamond Camp, but a similar source of refreshment and renewal. They rejoiced when Elliott came to lead the schools, for the spring would now feed the next generation. The wounds they felt when

Elliott was murdered were deep, but the springs of Northfield had fed so much of their lives that they continued to return, drawing nourishment and giving it to others.

The Student Volunteer Movement served Speer in many ways. It gave him his start in foreign missionary work and set his early missionary experiences in an ecumenical context. And he served the movement, one of a handful of leaders who made it the premier vehicle for recruiting foreign missionaries in his generation. However, the movement and he were part of something much larger that was going on in American missionary circles beginning in the late 1880s. The missionary explosion at the end of the century has often been defined in terms of the large number of volunteers, what might be called the calculus of missions. While this was important, its significance was at least matched by a substantial change in missionary leadership. Without denying the creative ideas or capacities for service of any or all of the volunteers, most of them became volunteers when they responded to the missionary call presented by a new group of leaders. The missionary movement at the end of the century experienced an infusion of new blood on the foreign field and also received a transfusion of new blood among the leaders at home.[119]

The leaders who were retiring had been very successful in their time and were instrumental in calling forth their successors. Moody had called the student conference in 1886 and hosted its annual successors, giving his support and time, inviting Mott and his associates to positions of leadership. Pierson had shared in issuing the initial call that led to the Mount Hermon Hundred and opened the pages of the *Missionary Review of the World* to them when he became its editor. Trumbull befriended and counseled the new leaders, and as editor of the *Sunday School Times* encouraged them to write for his journal. These men endorsed and blessed the new leaders. They saw them as sons, and the new leaders in turn honored them as fathers.

Speer remembered there were those who thought the Student Volunteer Movement was "a very hair-brained [sic] and chimerical undertaking when it originated," and that the new leaders were "misguided and unbalanced young men and women when it began." But he also recalled "that little group of men, older men, who strengthened and sustained us at the beginning."[120] Trumbull had become particularly fond of him and offered him this prophetic word of support in 1892: "You know something of what I feel as to the younger generation in Christ. We who are of the John the Baptist dispensation may have done well in our day, but even the least of you in the new age are greater than those who went before you,

'God having provided something better for you.' "[121] The change of leadership took place in an informal manner and in a spirit of cooperation and support. By the end of the century, the young had stepped forward and taken charge. Many of the older generation had spent years working to their positions of leadership, whereas the younger leaders jumped to the front in a relatively short time. Neither generation remarked about this, likely because they were so committed to the same goal, the evangelization of the world.

CHAPTER 6

Secretary of Presbyterian Foreign Missions

"Ten Thousand Times Ten Thousand"

The major base of Speer's foreign missions work was the Board of Foreign Missions of the Presbyterian Church in the United States of America. He began his career with the board on November 1, 1891. Once he accepted the call to become one of the board secretaries, he stayed the course, even beyond the normal retirement age. The secretarial work was his primary vocation, which he understood as his ministry, and his major economic support. It dominated his daily routine and occupied most of his time. It was also the nerve center of his large missionary network, linking together those he met through the SVM, his board colleagues and missionaries, and his fellow secretaries in the ecumenical organizations he joined or helped create. However much he was identified with the SVM or other student work, and whatever reputation he earned through his efforts with the world missionary organizations, he never saw himself and never encouraged others to view him as a nondenominational or interdenominational leader, in the way people viewed his friend Mott. That said, he placed his denominational work in a larger ecumenical perspective. He saw himself as a denominational leader who worked to achieve denominational goals in the context of larger cooperative and global ecumenical ones.

The General Assembly of the Presbyterian Church, duly constituted in 1789, had at first administered its missionary work directly, but as that work expanded it debated whether or not to create a special agency for missions. During the early years of the new nation, many local and regional independent missionary groups organized, and Presbyterians were very involved in some of them. The Congregationalists created the American Board of Commissioners for Foreign Missions in 1810, and two years later the General Assembly commended it to Presbyterian churches. In 1831 the Synod of Pittsburgh established the Western Foreign Missionary Society as "the first Board of Missions under the direct supervision of the

146

Presbyterian Church."[1] In 1837 the General Assembly adopted it as its Board of Foreign Missions and passed enabling legislation to the end that it would "superintend and conduct . . . the work of Foreign Missions" through the board.[2] This dramatic development came after several years of substantial debate and was in large measure the result of the vision of Elisha P. Swift, the secretary of the Western Society, who argued that it was not appropriate for the Presbyterian Church to funnel its foreign missionary work through any voluntary or independent agency, like the American Board of Commissioners for Foreign Missions. Instead, he succeeded in persuading the General Assembly "to organize itself as a missionary agency; holding that it was the business of the Church as such to conduct the foreign missionary enterprise and to be responsible for the administration of that enterprise."[3]

The Board of Foreign Missions

Over the years the General Assembly varied the size of the Board of Foreign Missions to meet new circumstances. When Speer began his work, there were twenty-one members, most of whom lived in or relatively near New York City, where the offices were located. The only major change in board size during his tenure came in 1922–23 when the assembly merged the Woman's Board of Foreign Missions into it and enlarged it to forty members. Board members were from the very beginning and without exception volunteers, ministers, and laypersons. The board was led by a president, who typically was much more involved in the work than many of its other members.

Speer developed an excellent working relationship with the board and the many persons who rotated on and off during his years of service. Though they were technically his employers, he treated them as his colleagues and basic support group for sustaining and extending the foreign missionary cause. They responded in like manner. Occasional disagreements with individual members over policies or programs never became more than that. He had very good rapport with the board presidents he served and came to know most of them quite well. He started under the Rev. John D. Wells, who was succeeded by the Rev. George Alexander in 1903, the Rev. James C. R. Ewing in 1924, and the Rev. Charles R. Erdman in 1925. He wrote a biography of Ewing, who had served for forty-six years as a missionary to India, and he vacationed with and participated in a prayer group with Erdman.

From the outset the board had worked to formulate a management policy. It employed a secretary to run its daily affairs and function as a director or chief executive officer. But it also created an executive committee, which met weekly to carry on its business. That became a burden for a widely scattered and voluntary board. After the reunion of the Old School and New School Presbyterians in 1870, which increased the number of missions under the board's care, it shifted its management more fully into the hands of its secretaries. They became the focus of administration and control, and the board met only monthly, primarily to review their work and make decisions on their recommendations.[4] That was the policy in place when Speer began with the board and the one it continued to use throughout his career. Elliott was involved in a fund-raising campaign at the Northfield schools in 1929 and asked his father for advice about the role of boards of trustees. Speer replied: "My experience has been that we don't get very much help from our Boards in these matters beyond their official endorsement. In the case of our Board, for example, it is we secretaries who have to do everything. We have a very excellent Board and now and then individual members help, but very little in the matter of raising money."[5]

This policy placed great trust in the secretarial staff and gave them remarkable room to generate and direct programs. Near the end of his career, Speer told Margaret that he had never "felt any constraint" on his thoughts or actions from the board. He had always "said what I thought and shall go on doing so."[6] Many Presbyterians in the Ellinwood-Speer-Brown era could be excused for attributing the great success of their church in foreign missions to one or another of them or their secretarial associates rather than to the board, for they more than any board member, including its president, symbolized it. When the squalls that occasionally surrounded it became a roaring hurricane in the 1930s, the eye of the storm hovered over Speer, at the time the senior secretary.

The first secretary was the Honorable Walter M. Lowrie, former United States senator from Pennsylvania, who gave distinguished leadership from 1837 to 1868. His son John C. Lowrie, one of the board's first missionaries to India, became assistant secretary in 1838 and coordinate secretary in 1850, a post he held until he retired in 1891. Speer came to the board as his replacement. Although he said very little about it at the time, he was very aware that he was a link with the founders, which he later called an "apostolic succession." Walter Lowrie's family had immigrated from Scotland when he was eight years old, and the family had settled on a farm in Huntingdon County, not far from where Speer later grew up. Although the family subsequently moved to another county and Walter's son John and his wife went as missionaries from another presbytery, Huntingdon Presbytery and Speer claimed a "proprietary interest" in him.[7]

Whenever the board brought in a new secretary, it typically treated him as equal with the other secretaries, spurning any hierarchy. Speer was something of an exception to the rule, for it hired him as an assistant secretary. When the Board made him a full secretary less than two years later, Trumbull wrote a note of congratulations on the "well-deserved promotion," not for himself but for the "Missionary cause." Trumbull added, "It was worth more to that cause when you were called to your present place, than the commissioning of fifty missionaries."[8] That friendly opinion may have been shared by the board, but it had not often used special titles for its appointees and may have done so in his case because he was so young and relatively inexperienced. Perhaps this was done also because Speer was the first secretary since Walter Lowrie who was neither ordained nor theologically educated. Those appointed during Speer's tenure were all given full secretarial rank and were all ordained ministers with experience in ministry. They were Arthur J. Brown in 1895, A. Woodruff Halsey in 1899, Stanley White in 1907, and Cleland B. McAfee in 1930. The secretaries at any given time, together with a treasurer, constituted the executive staff.

Under the benign supervision of the board the secretaries worked as a team of managers to accomplish the tasks. They carried out their individual assignments and then met in executive council to discuss and decide all issues and formulate recommendations to the board. Long before he arrived, the board had divided the tasks into two categories, the secretarial and the financial. The secretaries maintained contact with both the missionaries and the home churches and were involved in recruiting and interpreting the work, both at home and abroad. This meant they each shared in all aspects of the work. The treasurer handled financial matters. The substantial growth of the work in the 1890s, much of it traceable to the recruits generated by the SVM, persuaded the board to reorganize the tasks at the end of the decade. It created a foreign department and a home department, assigning Ellinwood, Speer, and Brown to the former and hiring Halsey to organize and run the latter. The major change was that the foreign secretaries could focus their attention on the missionaries and the missions, transferring all correspondence and contacts with local churches to Halsey. All the secretaries continued to share in interpretation at the major meetings, the General Assembly held each May and the synod and presbytery meetings in September and October. Each also continued to have his own speaking and preaching schedule, which involved much informal contact with the local churches.

In the large reorganization in 1923 the board faced a major challenge. The growth of the work since the prior reorganization, combined with the extensive program of the women, required an expanded and altered structure. The board created two new departments, a candidate and a medical one, on the model of the foreign, home base, and treasury ones. Increased activity in the older departments had already necessitated the hiring of what were called executive departmental secretaries, and the merger had added four more. The need for adequate organization and supervision of the enlarged staff led it to partially abandon the coequal status of the secretaries, and to charge two of them "with the general supervision of the entire work of the Board."[9]

The board designated Speer and Brown coequal senior secretaries. Speer's sphere of responsibility became the "general supervision of the correspondence of the executive secretaries with Europe, Syria, Persia, India, Africa, and Latin America, of the Committee on Furloughs, and of the work of the Home Base Department and the Treasury Department, recognizing the proper authority and responsibility of the heads of these departments."[10] Brown supervised the correspondence of the executive secretaries with China, Japan, and the rest of Asia and of the candidate and medical departments. Speaking for himself but reflecting Speer's experience, Brown felt that the change was primarily a rearrangement of duties that enabled him "to devolve some of the routine office work upon the departmental secretaries and to give more time to questions of policies and methods and to the increasing number of interdenominational and international movements to which the missionary enterprise was related."[11] Although the new leadership plan put a hierarchal business model in place of one built on the equality of Christian fellowship, it did not replace Speer and Brown, who had always worked well together and continued to do so. Nor did it affect their staff relationships, partly because both had been with the board for over twenty-five years and already possessed the authority of age and experience, regardless of structure or title. Speer became the senior secretary when Brown retired in 1929, and remained alone in that role until he retired.

The secretarial work was the keystone of Speer's economic life as well as his ministry. Here he was not a volunteer. The first year at the board he earned $2,500. His salary rose periodically, only to remain on plateaus for years. He earned $5,000 annually every year from 1900 to 1910. In 1912 he received $6,500 and continued to receive that amount until 1919. By

1926 he was earning $8,000, and not long thereafter $10,000. Although his salary was determined each year, it also carried a special rider. Whenever the board experienced a decline in contributions or a rise in costs that required budget cuts, the reductions were shared by all employees, beginning with the secretaries. In the Great Depression those cuts reached 20 percent. He never raised a question about his salary nor about the need for cuts. Extremely popular as a speaker and preacher, he kept careful account of those engagements that were directly related to board work, and when he received remuneration for them, he scrupulously turned over to the board whatever he received. Offered several part-time jobs during his secretarial service, as distinct from special lectureships like the Duff or Stone ones, he turned down all of them, on the grounds that the time required would compromise his board commitment.

Frank Ellinwood

The board appointed Speer to its secretarial staff in response to the strong recommendation of secretary Frank Ellinwood. Ellinwood had joined the staff in 1871 after two pastorates and work with the Presbyterian Church on several national projects, including the Reunion Fund. Senior to all but John Lowrie by 1891, he had worked tirelessly to advance the cause, initiating many procedures and programs that his successors continued. He had strong interdenominational interests and spent considerable time working with various youth and student groups, including the SVM.[12] The movement had advanced the idea that each church should support its own missionary. Ellinwood and two of his fellow staff members had written to its leaders: "We have before us a long list of testimonials from pastors who have tried the experiment with most gratifying results; and we are assured that if this method should become general throughout the church, it would mark a new era of progress in foreign missions. . . . We gladly recognize the influence which has been exerted along these lines by the Student Volunteer Movement. . . . The interest which they [the volunteers] create and the funds which they raise are a clear gain."[13] SVM leaders were grateful for the letter, a sign that they had accomplished something, and recognition from one of the largest and most effective denominational boards.

Ellinwood was present at the first SVM quadrennial in the spring of 1891 as a representative of his board, where he heard his letter read into the record and came into contact with Speer. That may not have been their first meeting, but it appears to have been the occasion that aroused his interest in the young leader. Within a few months he was in pursuit of him, with what his wife called his "usual zeal," determined to secure him for his staff.[14] He often said that one of the best things he had done for the board had been his share in persuading Speer to join it.[15] Much attention has been given to the role of the SVM in the general expansion of foreign missions in the 1890s, but not enough has been made of its special impact on Presbyterian missions, a combination of Ellinwood's cultivation of the SVM, his invitation to Speer, and Speer's decision to bring his considerable reputation among students to its staff.

Speer's brief apprenticeship as an SVM executive had given him an introduction to secretarial work, particularly in the areas of recruitment and record keeping, but that had been the minor leagues compared to the Board of Foreign Missions. The scope of his work moved from the United States to the world and from college and seminary campuses to every Presbyterian church, missionary organization, and mission. The board supported 598 missionaries, and there were 28,000 members in Presbyterian churches in the mission fields. The annual income of the board from home churches was over $900,000, and contributions from the foreign field amounted to $38,000. The permanent reserve funds to support the work were $110,000.[16] The kinds of work he supervised, directly or indirectly, included "evangelistic activities, churches, schools of all types from kindergartens to universities, hospitals, dispensaries, orphanages, asylums for lepers and the insane, schools for the blind and deaf, translations of the Bible, books, tracts and periodicals in a score of languages, printing presses annually publishing hundreds of millions of pages." In addition, secretaries supervised the gathering and shipping of supplies to the missionaries and the proper investment of legacies.[17]

Although awed by the immensity of the tasks, he was not overcome by them, largely because of the careful and loving attention he received from Ellinwood, who eased his young charge into the work by focusing his initial assignments on two tasks: recruitment and correspondence. The first was obvious, for it made use of his primary asset: his contacts with the SVM, the Christian Endeavor societies, and the Y associations. And it made it easier for him to continue to attend the meetings of those groups and to volunteer his services. Some recalled that the board had specifically searched for a youth worker, but that was not part of his memory, nor was it his entire assignment.[18]

He worked well with Ellinwood from the start and developed a relationship with him similar to, but also different from, his relationships with Pierson and Moody in the SVM work and with Trumbull in his personal life. Ellinwood was a father figure, as they were, but he was also a colleague. Ellinwood's daughter Mary said Speer and her father had a "twofold" relationship: "that of father and son, and also that of brothers." "My father," she added, "felt an enthusiasm of admiration for the splendid abilities of the younger man, and for his consecrated Christian character."[19] Ellinwood did not retire until 1907 but carried a much diminished work load in his later years. Speer wrote him frequently, most notably on his seventy-sixth birthday in 1902, and said: "I want to write you a note of congratulation and of love. I could not tell you if I tried, all that you have been to me; and how fully I trust and admire you, or how deeply I love you. . . . In kindness, in generosity, in high-mindedness, in charity such as Paul extols, in patience, I have just seen no flaw in you all these years. . . . I count my association with you one of the rarest and best blessings of my life, and I have had many, rare and good."

To this beautiful tribute, one of the strongest he ever wrote, he added a reflection on the senior man's approach to missions and revealed one of the major sources of his own views: "It has been a constant stimulant and delight to see you always open to anything new, that is also good, and trying all things while holding fast only what is worth keeping. You have set before us always an illustration of right liberality and progressiveness of views, and I hope I shall never forget the great lesson you are ever teaching in this regard."[20] In 1904 he dedicated his large two-volume history of missions to him, "with an admiration for his scholarship, sound judgment and unselfish purity of character which the intimacy of years has steadily heightened, and with a truly filial love."[21] Years later he described this particular father-brother as "one of the ablest, finest, most sagacious men I have ever known."[22] Their relationship was obvious to others. Colleague Halsey said in 1903, "Take these two, Robert E. Speer and F. F. Ellinwood, one representing in his intellectual and spiritual capacity the youth of the Church, and the other in his old age, the ripened thought of the Church, his mind and spirit as vigorous as of yore, and they will stand comparison with the best officials in any similar organization in the world."[23]

Work Ethic as Administrator

Speer had not been with the board long before he realized that he needed to develop methods to deal with the large amount of work. His schedule, even with Ellinwood's shepherding, filled up and spilled over almost from his first week at the office. The diaries of his youth and college years became datebooks in his working years, with few words of commentary interrupting the continuous listing of events and their locations. It became common for him to speak in ten or fifteen different places each month, sometimes more than once at a given meeting, while sustaining his office work. Some of the methods for coping he simply adapted from his college and SVM years, for they had helped him succeed and seemed appropriate. But he also faced some new situations, like working closely with others on a collegial basis and helping to manage an office and staff, and he developed procedures for them too. His peers fairly quickly came to see him as a most able administrator. That image grew after Ellinwood retired and left Speer senior secretary, in years of service if not in formal title. But he rarely saw himself in such terms, and never offered any systematic description or analysis of his administrative work.

The key to his administrative success was his work ethic, similar to but more intense than the one he had developed as a student. In those years he had become, especially after his conversion, as frugal with his time as his money. As a secretary he began to watch every minute, and he continued to do so for his entire career. When he was at home, he worked during his trips to and from the office and then in his study in the evenings. On the road he worked continuously, almost always choosing to stay at hotels rather than in private homes, so that he could work before or after a presentation. He even squeezed work into his vacation. He carried books and papers with him virtually everywhere he went so that he could use whatever time might become available to him. At General Assembly meetings, when he was not responsible for a report, he would sit in the back of the hall bent over a book or a document, or he would be in his hotel room writing. Once a blizzard stalled his train for a day in the Allegheny Mountains. While other passengers idled away the time, he spent it studying the titles Paul used for Christ.[24] Will Moody approached him in 1899 to write a piece for the *Record of Christian Work*, and he responded that he had already accepted "twenty or so" writing assignments for the coming year and added a description of his philosophy of work: "It is never a good thing to look ahead and see how much work you are going to do in that year, however. Who knows whether he is going to live a year? It is better to pack in just as much work as one can, and then at the end you find you have done a great deal more than you thought you could do when the year began."[25]

Under the canopy of this general method, he created or adopted from others a number of specific rules. He always tackled the hardest problems first. The correspondence was immense and often required, in the case of missionaries and local church leaders, serious effort to settle sharp differences of opinion at long distance. He began each Monday when he was in his office dictating letters. Not all the letters were about difficult matters. It was in these sessions that he wrote to his daughter after she went to China. He gave careful attention to detail. Whatever issues he dealt with—whether furloughs, medical expenses, or the pros and cons of a particular decision—he always worked with specific and accurate information. He kept many projects going at once. He told Will Moody, "I get so much work done through having a whole lot of things in mind and just taking up whichever one is ripest for me and I am ripest for at the time, instead of trying to force matters."[26] He did much of his work in his head. He dictated letters, reports, and sometimes speeches without resort to notes, wasting no time on drafts. When he did make notes, for a sermon or a talk, he typically used one side of a three-by-five inch piece of notebook paper that fit a small ring binder. He kept his desk clear. He rarely picked up the same piece of paper twice, preferring to complete each task when he faced it, and to keep the uncompleted work in his desk drawers.[27]

Other people produced rules that he found useful. Hanging on a wall of the office for many years were some by Edward White Benson, archbishop of Canterbury. They were part of a larger list, and included: "Not to be dilatory in commencing the day's main work"; "Not to groan when the letters are brought in; not even a murmur"; "To bear blame rather than share or transmit it." Although this was advice for work, he never separated work from faith, and so he understood them to be a way people could ask themselves whether their "lives have been yielded to live under the eye of Christ and under His law of love."[28]

A major feature of his board assignment was the close working arrangement with other secretaries and the office staff. He developed what might be called personnel policies. Ellinwood and Lowrie had some of them in place by the time Speer arrived, and others emerged as he worked with the other secretaries. Whatever the source, he made them also his own. First, he shared leadership with his fellow secretaries. He inherited a democratic structure and perpetuated it, even after the board introduced some new titles in 1923. After one particularly long discussion in the executive council, one of the executive secretaries who worked under him remarked that he had been very patient. He replied, "Well, this is a democracy." That secretary later wrote, "Never did he try to use his prestige and standing to force through a vote against the judgment of his colleagues, but patiently and carefully he would explain why he favored or was opposed to the action being discussed."[29]

Second, he trusted his colleagues and staff to do their jobs. One observer noted that his style was to say to those he supervised: "Here is your desk! Here is your task! Work in your own best way!"[30] Third, and a corollary to the second, he shouldered a full share of the load, working alongside his colleagues, never asking them to do what he was not prepared to do. He had handled all the administrative details of the missions assigned to him since the beginning of his work. Some members of the board began to feel, when he became a senior secretary, that it should relieve him of many of the routine tasks, like dealing with the budgets of missionaries, so he could devote more time to policies. He resisted and remained foreign secretary for the India and Persia missions until he retired. He believed, a colleague reported, that "he could be in closer touch with the work and more truly identified with it if he had intimate and direct personal contact with individual missionaries and individual missions."[31]

The fourth and most important of these personnel policies was that he treated his fellow board employees as members of a Christian community and formed deep and enduring relationships with many of them. Margaret Duncan, who had worked on his staff, wrote in 1908 to thank him for the help she had received from a sermon he had preached and told him she was still with the telephone company, and "while everyone is most kind to me, I think with deep longings of the days (truly blessed days) when I worked for you. Yes, down there amidst the hurry and bustle of the great throbbing business world, I think of those three years as a green oasis."[32] Lucia Towne, in an editorial written on the occasion of his retirement, said: "But we in 'the family' cherish most his personal friendship in the 'Board offices'; his frequent leadership of the fifteen minute noonday prayer meeting held at '156' each weekday; the delightful play of wit and keenest humor which can send a dinner of missionaries or Clerical Staff members into gales of laughter and applause."[33] Edith Dickie was his secretary in the early years, handling his correspondence until she received a call to become a missionary. When she left the staff in 1906, he wrote that they would "go right on with the old relation," and thanked her "for all the help you have been, and the loving friendship with you on the part of all the family."[34] He used "family" broadly, but whether it meant the office family or his home one, it represented his effort to reach out and embrace those he worked with most closely into a family atmosphere, one based on trust, loyalty, and love.

The colleague with whom he worked most closely was Arthur Brown, and they developed a particularly strong relationship. He stopped at

Brown's office to see him the day Brown retired, but missed him and wrote that he found the prospect of him no longer being there impossible. He added: "It will be lonely, beyond words, without you. And I shall go on as in an unreal world without your presence in the office. But love abides and you must come in, if not daily, at least almost daily. We shall need your help constantly, your counsel and your prayer. . . . We have had a great life together in a great time and been part of a great movement at what, thus far, has been its greatest period—may there be even greater ahead, but no one knows what form the next outbursts of Life will take."[35] In 1935, after two difficult years of controversy over board policies, he told Brown that he missed him "from our life long fellowship more than I can say. The Board will never have any servants of the cause who will see more nearly eye to eye on the great issues of Christianity than you and I."[36]

One sign of this intimate sense of community was his willingness to truly open himself up and allow his humorous and playful self to appear at the office and with his colleagues. In short, he was willing to behave with his staff the way he did with his home and camp families. He often livened the annual staff dinner with his humor, sometimes in the form of poetry and other times by acting out a role. The 1916 party was held shortly after Woodrow Wilson defeated Charles Evans Hughes in the presidential election. The toastmaster at the party announced the presence of a distinguished visitor, and out stepped Speer made up like Hughes, "with silk hat, whiskers, cutaway coat, striped trousers, gloves and cane," to regale his office family with a speech titled "Why I Lost the Election." One St. Patrick's Day he stood at the door of the assembly room just before the noonday service and told the staff as they came that "only those who have remembered to wear a bit of green are privileged to occupy the front seats, which have been specifically reserved for the faithful."[37]

This description of his personnel policies, especially the family or community image, runs counter to a widely perceived sense that he was cool toward personal relationships. Unfortunately, biographer Wheeler bore some responsibility for this perception, for he said that Speer's capacity "to keep ahead of his work" was achieved "through a rigid exclusion of social and personal relationships."[38] That phrase contained two misleading terms. What he excluded were the casual relationships. As for social and personal friendships, he had many of them, but he kept their number under control. Wheeler was led in part by comments of several of Speer's close friends, Mackay and Coffin, for example. Coffin and his wife moved to Lakeville in part to be near the Speers, yet Coffin, "in reminding his classes about the importance of personal contacts in life used Speer as an example of what to avoid since no one could meet Speer on a train and engage him in conversation because he was always too involved with a book."[39] But the source of Speer's style was neither, as Charles Forman has suggested, the result of "an extraordinary and even inhuman degree of organization of life," nor was it, as James Patterson has claimed, one of the ways he "came to grips with his introspective nature, sublimating his anxieties and doubts about his spiritual progress by staying busy."[40] Instead, it was the consequence of his spiritual intensity, which placed primary value on his relationship to God and on the duty he felt to fulfill his call.

His methods and policies had spiritual roots, but there was also a practical reason he held to them so firmly throughout his career: the pressure created by the expansion of the work. In his first decade it had grown so much that the board added a secretary and reorganized it. By 1910 he estimated that the work was "double now what it was when I first came to the board. . . . As I compare now and then in the missionary enterprise, there seems to be all the difference between noontide wakefulness and activity and the doze of twilight."[41] New staff never matched the growth, and he became more watchful of his time and more overworked. One constant theme in the correspondence he received from relatives and friends, including fellow staff members, was that he was working too hard, and they either admonished him or tried to lure him away for vacations. Uncle Stewart tried the latter ploy in 1914, only to be told by his nephew that he could not come but that he was "getting to the point of feeling that the seven days a week pace ought not to be kept up, and just as soon as I can get things shaped up and cleared off a bit, I am going to take a little more playtime than I have done in the last twenty-five years."[42] He never did. Occasionally he chafed under his burdens, like the time he told Margaret that he was speaking somewhere every day and commented: "I don't see how the poor political candidates fare with anywhere from two to ten speeches a day. However, it lasts only a few weeks with them while I have to keep it up year in and year out."[43] More typically, however, he enjoyed the activity. He returned from a long trip in 1930 and told Elliott that he was "almost every night on sleeping cars," but everywhere was met "only with friendship and goodwill, and the fruitage of the contacts of the many years."[44]

He served the board for almost five decades. He kept careful records, some of which he retained for his personal files, but most of which were preserved by the board. The volume and quality of these materials could sustain a separate book about his work as a board secretary. At the very least, they make possible a representative outline of it, well beyond the largely anecdotal one Wheeler was able to provide without access to all the materials. His ministry as missionary secretary fell into five general roles: counselor, interpreter, traveler, planner, and defender. The terms were not his, nor were the duties his alone, because of the way the secretaries shared the work. Although the roles were distinct, they were not really separate. He always saw his work as a whole and never divided it into neat compartments. In fact, his responsibilities often flowed together, so that when he traveled he found himself often both interpreter and defender of the board's work and of foreign missions in general. All the roles were part of his work throughout his long career, but they shifted about in importance as new occasions brought new duties.

Counselor

The counselor role was heaviest in his early years, but it never really stopped. To later generations, the term creates images of formal settings and established theories, but it meant neither in the 1890s. It consisted of discussion and advice, offered in person or through the mail, and he and others sometimes called it simply "personal work."[45] It was much of the substance of his assignment as a recruiter of missionaries. In his first two decades with the board, mission counseling was often continuous with his SVM recruiting work, the complement of it. His vision for the volunteer bands had included direct contact with the various mission boards, since they were the sending agencies, and he continued to make the point that the aim of the SVM was not to create "a new organization," but to get men and women "to form the purpose of going, and to lay the responsibility for the manner of their going upon their own hearts and upon the churches."[46] As a board representative, the only one among the SVM leaders, he picked up that responsibility and quickly developed a more comprehensive perspective toward the missionary formation process. His counseling, therefore, covered a wide range of topics, from initial religious feelings to questions about changing assignments once missionaries were on the field.

Evidence of his counseling at meetings and conferences has survived primarily through letters of thanks and the testimonies of others. Although the specific issues he dealt with often remain obscure, people typically felt he helped them along their spiritual journey. A woman wrote from Nashville, Tennessee, to say that since she had spoken with him, she had been able to resolve the question she faced. She concluded: "So with

God to help me I shall give Him possession of my life. May I thank you for the message you brought to me last night and ask for your prayers in my behalf."[47] A Yale student who had trouble adjusting to college thanked him "for the kindly interest you have taken in one individual."[48] Fellow secretary White offered the most impressive summary of Speer's impact. He wrote to Speer in 1922 that in his fourteen years of working with candidates he had come into "contact literally with thousands of young people either in person or correspondence. Very early, I began to see through these contacts how widespread was your influence and what a real inspiration it had been in opening the eyes of young men and women to the glory of a world task and a consecration of the whole of life to that task. Again and again, they referred to conferences with you and influences started by what you had said in public utterances which was an eloquent testimony to the effectiveness of your plea."[49] To these should be added the many tributes from colleagues and friends that were gathered for the various anniversary celebrations held for him.

Much of his counseling was done through the mail. Although he never described his strategy, he always corresponded in the context of personal and friendly advice, transforming an office routine that could have been accomplished by form letters into a special opportunity. Some inquirers wanted to know how to become a candidate for missionary service and he carefully informed them of the requirements set forth in the board *Manual.* After outlining the procedures to one such person, he closed with an offer: "I trust that you may find in this wide world that precise sphere of service in which you can best glorify One who owns all our service, who has bought us ourselves; and I should be glad if, in finding this sphere of service, there is any way in which I can help you."[50] A Princeton Seminary student said that he was uncertain of his call because he seemed to lack both spirituality and enthusiasm. Speer advised him that the knowledge of such needs was an important step along the road to overcoming them, and then gently reminded him that spirituality was more than a missionary need, "for just as much spirituality is required in any Christian man who is called to the trade of a carpenter as is required of one who goes to the heart of China. Every Christian must have the spirit of Christ."[51] On occasion, parents or friends of prospective candidates sought his advice. Woodrow Wilson wrote as a concerned parent in 1909 to say that one of his daughters had developed an interest in the SVM: "We fear that she is in danger of pursuing a mistaken course and would like very much to have a frank talk with you about it."[52] Speer arranged to talk directly with Wilson and his wife.

The board developed a form that people filled out to formalize their candidacy, and the answers often became the basis for further discussions and final decisions. After general biographical questions came questions about religious life, including: "What are your habits of Bible study?" "How have you been used in bringing men to Christ?" "Are you a personal worker?"[53] Speer gave no indication of what he expected to find on these forms when he entered the secretarial work, but he was surprised when he found that those who wanted to be missionaries abroad were not missionaries at home. In his SVM work he had largely been involved in the excitement and idealism generated by those who heard the call, but at the board he had to deal with the reality of what they put down on paper. He had been amazed, he told a gathering of students in 1894—and he believed they would be too—if they "saw those blanks filled out by the men whom you perhaps look upon as the best Christian workers in your colleges or universities, to see what a paltry few there are who can say they know that God is using them to bring other souls one by one into His Kingdom. . . . You may have a theological education, you might pass all the physical tests, have an exceptional character, a good Christian spirit; but you may lack the most essential Christian qualification of all, that is, the faculty of 'soul winning.' "[54]

He did not find it particularly difficult to advise a person who admitted he had never done any evangelistic work, however much formal education he might have, but the problems Speer faced as a counselor were more complex than that. The board, as he told one inquirer, had "no hard and fast requirements in the matter of qualifications for missionary service." But it wanted to be as certain as possible "that those who go should be competent to undertake and successfully carry through the work that will fall to them," and that they are "in their spiritual lives unusually close to the Lord in whose name all our work is done, and from whom alone can be obtained the spirit to do it."[55] Few candidates were without some qualifications in each of the two major areas, and his task was to sort out the various degrees of readiness and to weigh them against the needs in the field.

He had been from the outset of his career a staunch supporter of higher education and a strong advocate of theological preparation for those who sought ordination, and he continued to stress those kinds of preparations for missionary work. But as the years passed, his bias in favor of religious preparation, or what might be called spiritual formation, grew stronger. Some recruiters put major stress on proper training, which usually meant education, and he found himself more and more cautious about that emphasis. He told SVM secretary Fennell P. Turner in 1915, "There have been, and there will continue to be men without all this desirable preparation who are able to do as good work as any body and we must not shut the door too tight for them."[56] He made a number of studies of missionary leadership and found the preparations of former missionaries instructive, sometimes using their ways into the work as examples. Jeremiah Evarts had studied law, but "God had allowed his decision as to his profession because he knew that the discipline Evarts was choosing for himself would fit him for the work God had already chosen for him better than any technical theological courses. The technical theological course is useful and proper, but God's men never have been and are not today to be ground out by any device of uniform discipline. It is good for us to make room in our schemes for the free and surprising operations of God."[57]

Over the years he became very adept at his counseling, able to deal with all kinds of situations and personalities and to say both yes or no with skill and kindness, to applicant and long-term missionary alike. He offered to both the accepted and the rejected words of encouragement and advice. To one whom the board appointed he said: "I am very glad that you are to have the greatest of all privileges that can be given to any one in this world. . . . I trust that these days of further preparation may be sanctified to you by the over-brooding and indwelling presence of Him who has promised to abide with us."[58] To one whom the board rejected he wrote, "Light was sought from every possible source, and much was learned which the Board is confident will justify the hope of your Christian usefulness anywhere." After adding the negative vote, he concluded that the "Board desires to express its fullest wishes for your usefulness in service, and to extend to you its most hearty sympathy in any work to which God may lead you."[59] He gained a reputation among his colleagues for his ability to say no gracefully. On one occasion when Speer wrote a letter inviting a particularly troublesome missionary to resign, department secretary George Scott reported: "His letter was a magical composition which I do not yet understand; in its beginning the man was a friendly missionary apparently in good standing but at its end, without any noticeable intervening change, he seemed not to have the slightest relation to the Mission or Board. I searched that letter for evidence of the transition and could find none. . . . In due time and in fairly amiable spirit, the missionary's resignation arrived."[60]

Candidate correspondence diminished over the years, in part taken over by others and in part displaced by contact with missionaries. He followed those missionaries assigned to him very closely, quite literally shepherding them and treating them as part of his family. They typically responded in like manner. Speaking for himself but reflecting the experience of others, J. J. Lucas, long-term missionary to India, said Speer had "ministered to us and to our children out of a pastor's heart. No sorrow has touched us that has not touched him. No mission problem has perplexed us without his sharing it and helping us solve it." "Is it strange," he asked, "that we missionaries with such a pastor, though ten thousand miles away, ministering to us and our children in ways known often only to us, should carry him in our hearts with a love and reverence ever-deepening?"[61] One of the best examples of this was his relationship with Robert Wilder, his SVM mentor and partner, who went to India under the board and became part of his flock. Able and ambitious, Wilder constantly sought new fields. After one exchange in 1895, he wrote that Speer's letters "were a *great* comfort to my wife and me, for after reading them we had a settled conviction that *you* understood us and that you knew [how] deeply we desired to know His will and follow His leading."[62]

Counseling was a two-way street, and he gained new friends and perspectives from it. One novel idea that emerged from his work with Wilder gradually became very important to him. In 1899, Wilder received an invitation from the international committee of the YMCA to become the traveling college secretary for India. He contacted Speer to find out the attitude of the board and whether or not it would release him for the new mission. Mott wrote in support of the change. Speer sent a long and thoughtful letter to Mott in which he drew some new distinctions. If Wilder were to work among students in a direct way, thereby building up "the institutions of the Christian Church, and doing it in the rich work of a living evangelization," then he would approve. He was not sure, however, about "any general Y.M.C.A. work in a foreign field," and would "be sorry to see Wilder's capacity for vital work and personal impression swallowed up by any work which would absorb his strength in formal organization or the unifying of methods, important as these branches of work may be."[63] What did he mean? He did not elaborate to either Mott or Wilder, and if they responded, the documents have not been found. In the immediate case the board granted Wilder's full release, and Speer offered his own and the board's support for the new work.[64]

In subsequent instances, where he was faced with a choice between Y work and more direct church work like missions or the ordained ministry, he almost always advised the individuals who raised the question to choose the church. A friend and supporter of the Y wrote in 1907, protesting such advice in reference to a particular student, and Speer responded: "I had no hesitation whatever in advising him to go on into the ministry. I have always given this advice to young men, believing that, important as the work of the religious department is, it is not as important and does not offer to young men as large and permanent a field of service as the ministry."[65] This marked an important stage in the distinction he developed between his vision of foreign missions and the one held by Mott and many others associated with the YMCA.

Interpreter

The role of interpreter was as public as the one of counselor was private.[66] In a sense, everything he said or wrote after he became a secretary could be fitted into it. Wherever he went, hosts and hostesses introduced him as secretary or senior secretary, even when he spoke from SVM or Federal Council platforms, and the bylines of a substantial number of his books and articles identified him the same way. By midcareer he was the best known, most persuasive, and most powerful spokesman for foreign missions in his church, and some have argued in the nation. He used the means most readily available to him, his voice and pen, but also tried two new mediums when they emerged, radio and film. After he broadcast for the first time in 1922, the amount of mail his effort generated startled him and alerted him to its possibilities. Although he used it on other occasions, he did not incorporate it into his work and never apparently thought of doing for foreign missions what S. Parkes Cadman and Harry Emerson Fosdick did for their ministries with their National Radio Pulpit and National Vespers. His first and only work with film came during the centennial of Presbyterian foreign missions, at the end of his career.

Fully aware that those in his audiences typically received his words as those of his board, he accepted the broad definition of the interpretative role gladly, seeing it as opportunity and not burden. It was the nature of the job, different from that of a university professor, who could in normal circumstances communicate about a field of knowledge and not worry about his listeners' confusing what he said with the policies of his university. Because of his unbounded enthusiasm for the cause, he was willing to go anywhere at any time, utilizing his method of overbooking himself so as to expose as many people as possible to the urgency of the missionary enterprise and to enlist their personal and financial support. He never complained about the size of this task, but he did recognize that he, and the board, needed help. Concerning the search for a new secretary in 1927 he said: "Where the Board needs reenforcement is in the matter of the ability of its secretaries to represent it and the Mission cause here at the home base. At present, I suppose, I am doing more foreign missionary speaking, and have done so for years, than any other officer of the Board—perhaps as much as any two other officers."[67]

The traditional arenas were the outdoor settings of the summer conferences and the pulpits and assembly halls of churches. Summer assemblies for adults attracted him as frequently as those for students. He returned refreshed from meetings at Montreat, North Carolina, and Massanetta Springs, Virginia, in 1929 because he had experienced anew "the great body of intelligent, living Christians on which our Churches and the missionary enterprise are resting."[68] Often in Presbyterian pulpits, especially those in and around New York City, he welcomed invitations from other churches. One special occasion came in the spring of 1927 when he preached at the First Congregational Church in Washington, D.C. It felt good, he wrote sister Margaret, "to preach the gospel just as simply and directly as one could without paying any attention to the fact that the President was there."[69] He also spoke to a wide variety of groups in other settings. When he went to Baltimore to speak at the Presbyterian Social Union of Maryland in 1933, he was joined by the new president's wife, Eleanor Roosevelt. He found her "a very nice homelike person."[70] During World War I he spoke at "a missionary gathering" in one of Billy Sunday's tabernacles. Definitely in a different sort of setting, he had to stop once or twice because the noise of the rain on the roof drowned him out, and he was also interrupted when "a crazy woman came up an aisle and had to be taken out and a drunken man up another."[71]

Some speaking assignments required a narrower and more precise understanding of the interpretive role. First and foremost among such presentations were the ones he made for the board to the General Assembly, and in a slightly different polity context to synod and presbytery meetings. He functioned in the same mode when he attended the Foreign Missions Conference and the committee on foreign missions of the Federal Council. Although they were consultative and not deliberative bodies, he was nonetheless an official representative of his board.

The more narrowly defined speaking occasions were distinctive in that they were somewhat formal, before elected or representative groups. His first experience with the General Assembly was during his college days, when it had made a day trip to Princeton for a special meeting in the chapel and he had charge of the ushering. When he returned as a board secretary, he had official status. The secretaries shared in preparing the annual reports and then took turns presenting them. They did not read the report but offered an interpretive address, which he described as "speaking to the General Assembly in connection with the Report."[72] His initial opportunity came at the General Assembly in Washington, D.C. in 1893, the first of many similar appearances, and he "felt very keenly the responsibility."[73] At the close of his presentation Moderator Willis Craig rose "and stretching out his hand turned towards that young secretary and said, 'Brethren, the Church is not poor to whom has been given the gift of this young man.' "[74] In an even greater accolade, a reporter at the General Assembly in Buffalo in 1904 described Speer's presentation of the board report as "statesmanlike," "compelling," and "the greatest speech of the assembly thus far," and then called him "the Roosevelt of Presbyterianism."[75]

His presentations to the General Assembly, taken together, constitute a remarkable periodic history of the foreign missionary work of his church for almost fifty years. He invariably included a summary of the statistics in the formal report, noting the changes in the number of missions and missionaries, native workers and communicants, and he included a roll call of those missionaries who had joined the church triumphant in the previous year. Another constant was the financial situation, and the gains or losses and their impact on the work. But no two presentations were the same, for he constructed each one out of the fabric of the events of the previous year, piecing together the different and often disparate developments into a coherent story. The task was never easy, but some years were downright difficult. In Philadelphia in 1901 he had to make sense of the Boxer uprising in China and to create a vision for the future in the midst of the considerable physical destruction and the martyrdom of several missionaries. In Columbus in 1933 he faced questions raised by the Hocking Report and criticisms from within the church. Whatever the trials, he concluded every General Assembly presentation with a review of the successes of the year and an outline of his hopes and dreams for the future.

The printed word was another form of his interpretive role. He wrote on average more than one book and twenty substantial articles a year. The total surpassed seventy books, counting the unpublished ones, and twelve hundred articles. That did not include shorter reports, newspaper articles, book reviews, editorials, Bible study notes, and prayers. The majority of this sea of material related directly to foreign missions, although a substantial body dealt with the Bible and the life and work of Jesus. In general, he wrote as an individual and for the broader missionary movement, but there were occasions, as in his speaking career, when he wrote more directly as a secretary of the board. The board had a "checkered experience" with missionary magazines, and had ceased publishing the *Foreign Missionary Magazine* shortly before he joined the staff.[76] It had no separate periodical for almost two decades before he created *All the World* in 1905. *Five Continents* succeeded it in 1926. When he wrote for these magazines, or for the more general denominational ones like the *Assembly Herald* or the *Presbyterian Magazine*, he did so explicitly as a secretary of the board.

The board put its imprint on eight of his books, two titles on the general topic of missions, five reports of missionary trips, and one missionary biography.[77] In these, as in the official periodicals, he spoke directly as a representative of the board. The first of the general books, *Presbyterian Foreign Missions*, published in 1901, was the board's effort to provide for Presbyterians and others "a brief account of the foreign missionary work of the Presbyterian Church."[78] The second general volume was one of the few truly apologetic books he ever wrote. *Are Foreign Missions Done For?* published in 1928, was "sent by the kindness of a United Presbyterian layman through the Board" as "an attempt to meet fairly and honestly some of the present day questions which are raised with regard to the foreign missionary enterprise."[79] It was also "a campaign document" to raise money for the board.[80] Whatever the particular form of interpretive work, the substance of his message included his conviction that the missionary task was the Christian task, and that no one needed a special call to do it.

Travels for the Board

As a board secretary he was also a traveler. The role had a specific meaning, referring to the trips he and other secretaries took abroad. Such trips to acquaint missionary secretaries with the fields and the people who labored in them had been a standard part of the work of many missionary boards, particularly of the American Board, from their beginnings. The Presbyterian Board under Walter Lowrie had been an exception. It had no visitation of the fields until 1874, when Ellinwood introduced it. When he went to Asia that year, he countered one of the objections to his trip by raising some of the funds for it from outside sources.[81] Speer, in reviewing the visitations, said that since that trip "the Board has followed an enlightened and advanced policy, and provided for a visitation of some of its missions by some of its officers and members at least once every five years."[82]

His duties as traveler for the board (or "visitor" as the board sometimes called it) were substantially different from his duties as traveling secretary for the SVM, although the job titles were similar and both required him to be on the road. The SVM sent him in search of recruits, and he moved from one group of strangers to another, issuing the call. The board sent him to the missions and mission councils where he met with the missionaries and native workers and those who belonged to the newly created churches. He arrived announced and expected, as colleague and friend or, as one of his traveling companions said, as "a missionary to missionaries."[83] He brought word from home and personal interpretations of the most recent actions of the board as they related to particular missions. More important, his presence signaled that the board felt that each missionary was a significant part of a much larger task. He typically tried to see every missionary along his routes and sometimes took long side trips to visit those who were in more isolated locations. On the initial trips in the 1890s he met many people for the first time, although he had corresponded with some of them. Later visits were more like family reunions, for by then many of the missionaries were people he had recruited, counseled, and shared in appointing. Because the trips also involved much informal investigation and formal data collection, they were not really over until he had finished writing his reports.

He realized the importance of the traveling role and shared in it fully, taking his turns. His journeys began with one to Mexico in 1894, and ended with the one to Jerusalem in 1928. The latter visit counted as a missionary trip in a way his trips to Keswick in 1894, London in 1900, and Edinburgh twice in 1910 did not, because he spent time after the Jerusalem meeting visiting missionaries in Syria. In between he visited missions around the world in 1896–97, in South America in 1909, in Asia in 1915, in Latin America in 1916, in India, Persia, and China in 1921–22, in South America in 1925, and in China, Japan, and Korea in 1926. The shortest trips were to Mexico and Latin America, each about a month long; the longest, those that began in 1896, 1915 and 1921, each lasted more than eight months.[84] Altogether he spent about a tenth of his career traveling, not counting the report preparation time. Although it was not his favorite role, because it separated him from his family, he managed to make it more palatable by arranging to take Emma along on the first two and last three trips, before the children were born and after they were grown. In addition, Billy went with them to China in 1926, and Constance was with them in Jerusalem.

The trips were very carefully planned. The board informed the missions about his coming and its expectations, and he made the specific arrangements. The world trip in 1896 was typical. President Wells wrote the

"Brethren of the Missions" that the board was sending Speer "to spend a few months in your several fields, that he may in conference with you and by personal observation become the better acquainted with the conditions which confront you." Wells signaled that the board had a special interest in two problems, the "proper place of education with reference to the other departments of missionary activity, especially with reference to direct evangelism," and "the organization of a self-reliant, self-supporting, self-propagating Native Church, as an essential factor in the redemption of the nations of the earth unto our Lord Jesus Christ."[85]

Speer organized his itinerary and wrote ahead to the missions, setting aside some time to visit missions of other denominations that were along the way. Following Ellinwood's example, he raised special funds to help cover his expenses. He made a list of the books he needed to read, beforehand or along the way, in order to become better acquainted with the lands in which he planned to travel, and he formulated a list of articles he planned to write. Emma discovered on that 1896 trip, and other companions found on later ones, that, as much as he could, he kept to his home schedule of work when he was abroad. That meant few wasted moments, a regular reading and writing schedule, and a constant series of Bible studies, talks, sermons, and formal speeches. All the while he kept detailed financial records, separating out the expenses of the members of his family when one or more of them was along, and filled small notebooks with his impressions, including data about each mission, and responses to the inquiries of the board so that he could prepare the report.[86]

Each trip had its own character and made a distinctive contribution to his work. The world trip was the most important, even though he said the Asian trip that began in 1921 "was the most interesting one I have ever taken."[87] Although he did not visit all the missions, and never visited those in Africa, he gained a strong sense of the global scope of the work. He also accumulated an immense amount of information about the various nations and their cultures, and particularly their indigenous religions. On this trip he had his first real encounter with many of the non-Christian religions outside the classroom and books, and he promptly began to use what he had learned as a basis for further study and in public presentations. He wrote two books about the trip, many articles, some of which were published before he returned home, and a number of speeches.[88] The serious needs of the foreign missionary enterprise so impressed him that he decided to formulate policies responsive to them; hence, the journey established an important part of his agenda for several years.[89]

The world trip was the only one on which he became seriously ill. This was rather surprising, given the conditions of travel and the likely exposure to diseases. He reported that his first thought about the typhoid fever was that it was "a discipline of God for past shortcomings," but shortly he came to see "the divine purpose of our detention in Hamadan." The extended stay made it possible for him to study "the Mohammedan missionary problem" and to "enter into missionary life in its daily routine."[90] Emma wrote home frequently in the midst of the illness, sending cables to the board and letters to her family. She told her mother, shortly after the fever began in November, that she was anxious, but not really afraid. She realized, she said, "that if I had any good stuff in me, now was the time to show it," and "that God would take care of us here just as well as in New York, and that His way was always loving, no matter how hard it might seem."[91] By January she was reading books to Robert, and he was chafing to get on the road. "We have daily battles," she wrote, "but I shall not leave Hamadan one day before Dr. Holmes assures me that it will be perfectly safe for Rob to travel."[92] Surrounded by the love and support of missionary friends, Emma kept her composure, and he recovered.

When he was sufficiently well to think seriously about the rest of the trip, he began to figure ways to get to all the places he felt he needed to see, especially the Central China Mission, "with which I have had the correspondence for so many years, but some of whose members I have never been able as yet, to understand."[93] After they resumed their journey, he received a note from Trumbull affirming the decision to continue and telling him he knew "you are not a man to turn back from the furrow you are set to plow. God leads you and God guards you while he guides."[94] By extending their trip and with some careful reorganization, they were able to visit most of the places he had scheduled. He dedicated his book *Missions and Politics in Asia* "to The Missionaries in Hamadan, Persia," as an expression of his gratitude for their tender care.

Later trips went smoothly. The one to South America in 1909 awakened him to the needs of that continent and led to the formation of the Committee on Cooperation in Latin America. The trip back to Persia and China in 1921 was a grand homecoming, reflecting the depth of the ties he had forged in 1896. And the one to China in 1926 included the China Evaluation Conferences, where the "central point of discussion . . . was the question of the relations of Church and Missions."[95] The latter trip included moments of special personal satisfaction. He was present for the dedication of Yenching University's new campus, and he celebrated his daughter's appointment as a missionary educator in the Western

Languages department. He kept his own notes on all the trips, but beginning with the one in 1909 he invited someone to join him and serve as secretary. Joseph Cook went that year, followed by Guthrie Speers in 1915 and Henry Welles III in 1921. Speers, who had attended the Hill School and had met Speer when he had spoken there, was a little apprehensive about the trip but "soon discovered that he was a prophet with a great sense of humor and the most amazing fund of knowledge. . . . Just being with him was as good as a college education. Nobody could miss his single hearted devotion to Christ."[96] Other board staff joined some of the later trips.

Speer accomplished many things through his role as traveler, but three results were particularly significant. One was the reports he and the secretaries produced, although he did almost all of the writing. Remarkable in scope and content, models of what missionary visitation reports should be, they included histories of the work at each mission, statistical summaries, and reviews of the vital issues at the time of the visits. He added reflections, summing up the way each mission fitted into the larger missionary venture and offering advice for the future. After the 1915 visit to the Philippines, he refuted charges from some, particularly Roman Catholics, that the Presbyterian presence was an intrusion. The Roman Catholic Church had accomplished some good and useful work, but much remained to be done, and the call to work there was "as clear an obedience to duty and the call of God as could be found."[97] Reflecting on China, he told the board that the "absolute unselfishness of the missionary movement needs to be guarded with scrupulous care." Many commercial interests were in China only for their own benefit, whereas "American missionaries are not in China to promote trade or intercourse or better feeling between China and the United States. They are there to advance the cause of human unity, to hasten the day when all men shall be brothers, to bind not two races together in political and commercial relationship, but to bind all men together in Christ."[98]

Although the reports were about Presbyterian missions, their abundance of general information made them useful to others. The Rev. Frank Mason North, secretary of the Board of Foreign Missions of the Methodist Episcopal Church, wrote about the report of the 1915 trip: "I marvel at your power to reproduce impressions and to gather in journeying in the East the materials for so exact and complete a discussion of your observations. This, I believe, is a most valuable record." In acknowledging the kind words, Speer declared he could not have done it without a secretary, but that "taking a secretary really enormously increases the labors of such

a trip because it leads one to feel obligations" to produce a better report.[99]
His response primarily reflected his modesty, since he had produced a very
comparable report of his world trip without a secretary.

Another result of his travels was the new information and ideas he
gained, which made the trips like periodic graduate seminars for him. The
professors were the missionaries and the native workers, as well as those
who believed in the traditional religions of their lands. On many different
occasions he sought out the latter to discover, from those who would talk
with him, what Hindus and Buddhists and others were thinking about
their own faiths and Christianity. Speer used extensively the information
from such encounters, supplemented by what he constantly gathered from
his reading. It was one of the secrets of his success. He remained an effective leader for so many years partly because he combined strong convictions about fundamental principles with the latest information about the
missions and the developments in their lands. "I have learned a great deal
from our visits to the missions thus far," he wrote as he completed his
world trip, "and am sure I shall be able to do my work more intelligently
and more sympathetically when I return."[100] After he returned, he began
to work on his science of missions. The trip to Asia in 1915 made him
realize how virulent racism had become. He reported to the board that it
was "the duty of Christian men and especially of the missionary enterprise
to set an example of just and generous race judgment." To condemn the
governments of the Far East "because they are oriental, to express of them
a distrust which we do not feel toward western governments 'because these
are white men's governments,' is not only un-Christian, it is foolish and
wrong."[101]

The third and the key result of his visits was contact with the missionaries. He traveled primarily to get to know them and their circumstances,
to listen to their concerns and to offer advice, support, and whatever
counsel he felt they needed. They were fulfilling Christ's last command
most directly, and he saw himself as the essential connecting link between
them and the home base of moral and financial support. The trips gave
him an image of "the ordinary foreign mission station, made up of a little
group of men and women in the midst of an enormous mass of population, and oftentimes with a great area of country in which they are the
only representatives of the new ideas and life which they have brought. It
is wonderful to think that men can believe that it is possible, and it is wonderful to know that it really is possible for such a little group to triumph
over all the inertia and the obstacles in their way, and actually to be the

means of working a regeneration in the lives of individuals and in the whole life of communities."[102] After one trip he reported to the board: "The central elemental agency of missions is the body of missionaries. . . . It is because the missionaries represent the standard of character and devotion and ability which they do, that it is such a privilege and inspiration to visit the mission field."[103] William Miller, an SVM recruit, was in a station in Persia hundreds of miles off the beaten path. He reported that not only did Speer take the extra three weeks to reach him, but then "gave himself wholly to us. He seemed to have nothing in the world to do except become acquainted with Meshed and its opportunities and problems, to share our joys and sorrows, to meet our friends; to encourage us to go on with Christ's work. His chief interests were not in our property needs, which were urgent, but in how we were endeavoring to make Christ known to Moslems."[104] Every trip was a series of similar experiences.

Planner and Policy Maker

Whenever he returned from his travels, he resumed his other roles. One that always needed his attention was that of planner and policy maker. A distinct role, it related to every aspect of the board's work, and included specifically the formulation and implementation of policies, the maintenance of the missions and the missionaries, the management of finances, and the development of the secretarial staff. At the policy-making level his specific contributions were, and have remained, largely invisible, a consequence of the board's democratic approach to decision making and staff appointments. Moreover, whenever the board proposed new policies to the General Assembly or launched new programs, it never attached the names of those who originated them. The distinctive contributions of individuals on board and staff remained within the confines of board and executive council meetings and the more informal office discussions. Church members and the general public may have assumed, once Speer and Brown became the senior secretaries, that they were the sources of new policies and directions, but they rarely claimed to be. At the practical level of spelling out the policies, Speer's individual contributions were more visible, but primarily to those most directly involved, which meant the board, the staff, and the missionaries. The members of the Presbyterian Church and the general public, well acquainted with him as interpreter and traveler, rarely saw him as planner. The sources, especially on some of the most important policy questions, describe his contributions primarily by inference and offer, at best, brief glimpses of an effort that required much time and careful thought.

The 1900 General Assembly's landmark decision on Christian unity in foreign missions work was an important example of this. Ever since it had founded the board, it had espoused various degrees of unity in its foreign missions endeavors. In 1887 the General Assembly had specifically supported the formation of "indigenous national churches holding Reformed doctrine and Presbyterian polity" and had agreed to permit presbyteries related to it to withdraw to form such union churches.[105] The board was following such policies when Speer joined it, and he found them a comfortable fit with his own ecumenical inclinations. The first extension of the unity policy he experienced was the board decision in 1893 to participate in the creation of the Interdenominational Conference of Foreign Missionary Boards and Societies. He supported it and became a founding member. This was an exceptional case where the source of the policy was clear. Ellinwood had pioneered the idea, and at least his secretarial colleagues in the several denominations involved knew that. The policy statement announced: "The Board believes that the foreign mission work of the Presbyterian Church should not be a sectarian effort to extend a denomination in other lands, but a broadly Christian enterprise, and the Board wholeheartedly unites with other evangelical bodies in presenting the Gospel of Christ to the peoples of non-Christian lands."[106]

Between 1899 and 1901 Speer was very involved in discussions about comity at the Interdenominational Conference and within his own board. He helped persuade the conference to adopt a very advanced statement on the principles of comity in 1899. In the midst of those debates and decisions, his board proposed to the General Assembly at its St. Louis meeting in 1900 a very forward position on comity, which the Assembly adopted unanimously. The policy began by reaffirming its 1887 statement and added, "The object of the Foreign Missionary enterprise is not to perpetuate on the mission field the denominational distinctions of Christendom, but to build up on Scriptural lines, and according to Scriptural principles and methods, the kingdom of our Lord Jesus Christ." It went on to specify the use of the principles of comity in divisions of territory, in the adjustment of native worker salaries, in recognizing acts of discipline of other missions and churches, in educational work, in the use of printing establishments, and in the judicious use of established medical facilities. It concluded, "Fellowship and union among native Christians of whatever name should be encouraged in every possible way, with a view to

that unity of all disciples for which our Lord prayed, and to which all mission effort should contribute."[107] The ideas and the language of the
Interdenominational Conference and General Assembly statements were
similar, and the consequent policy virtually identical. The fact that Speer
was the common denominator of these two policies invites the conclusion
that he *must* have been the source of both, but the actual source of the
General Assembly policy has remained a mystery. While Speer could have
initiated it, so could Ellinwood or Brown or any one of several other persons, and none of them claimed it.

One policy of the board was to cooperate as much as possible with
other boards. Speer's role in implementing this policy led him into one of
his many contacts with John D. Rockefeller, Jr. After the Edinburgh meeting in 1910, Mott approached the Rockefellers for funds to "establish a
foundation that would unify the worldwide Protestant missionary movement."[108] Although they turned down the proposal, the idea remained
alive, and they reconsidered it in 1913. Jerome D. Greene, secretary of the
Rockefeller Foundation, interviewed secretaries of several foreign missions
boards, beginning with Speer. Greene called on him on September 8 and
wrote a revealing memo of the meeting, putting Speer's sentiments into
his own words. Speer knew something of Mott's general ideas but nothing
of the particular proposal to create a "new board to hold and spend the
moneys contributed and to take the initiative in promoting the various
lines of investigation and co-operation advocated by Dr. Mott," but
he believed that the Presbyterian board would be willing to discuss the
matter.[109]

However, Greene reported, Speer raised two significant qualifications
to the proposal. First, many of the substantial Presbyterian supporters of
foreign missions were from "the reactionary element" that "was actually
out of sympathy, to say the least, with some of the co-operative steps
already taken," and therefore any additional cooperative action would
have to be undertaken slowly. Second, Mott's views did not entirely coincide with his own. Greene described the difference: "Dr. Speer attaches
very great importance to the Church as an historic institution, using the
word 'Church' in no narrow sectarian sense, an institution which feels
bound to regard jealously its prerogative as God's agent on earth for the
accomplishment of His Divine purpose." Dr. Mott, however, "attaches
much less importance to the Church, regarding its historic character as
merely one of a number of influences entering into the religious life of
mankind." As a consequence, Greene said: "Dr. Mott regards himself as a
champion of Christianity rather than as a champion of the Christian

Church. The distinction is one which Dr. Mott would probably not recognize as significant, but to Dr. Speer the distinction seems of vital importance." Speer, Greene concluded, suggested working through the committee on reference and counsel of the Foreign Missions Conference, which represented the boards and agencies of the denominations, and if it decided on a course of action that required substantial financial support, it could approach the foundation.[110]

The other secretaries Greene interviewed shared many of Speer's opinions. On behalf of the foundation, Greene notified Mott in October that it could not take the initiative in the matter, because, in light of the strong role of the denominational boards, "the success, and indeed the justification, of the whole enterprise properly depends upon its being both initiated and controlled by these boards and agencies themselves."[111] Speer's views were obviously important in the foundation decision. They also indicated a much more developed stage of the conviction he had articulated earlier, in the discussions concerning Wilder's mission in India, of the differences between the work of the churches and that of the nondenominational agencies. Although Mott's general proposal failed to find funding, a subordinate part of it to establish "a complete missionary library" succeeded when the Rockefellers provided the basic funds for the Missionary Research Library.[112] Speer subsequently became chairman of the Missionary Research Library board.

One of the main tasks of the secretaries was to help prepare and support the missionaries so they could better accomplish their various missions. That effort required a great deal of planning and interpretation of policy. An instance of the former, which Speer credited to himself and Brown, was the New Missionaries Conference.[113] Until the 1890s the typical missionaries had applied to the board, had been interviewed by someone designated by the board but not always a board member or secretary, and had been approved and received appointment. If they lived in the east and were sailing from New York, they met board members and secretaries before sailing. But if they lived in the midwest or west and were going to Asia, they usually left from their homes, often without ever having met a member of the board. Moreover, many of those trained for medical or educational work "had received no adequate instruction regarding missionary problems or conditions, and some of the ordained men had received little in their theological seminaries."[114]

After Speer and Brown alerted the board to these unsatisfactory conditions, it approved a plan to bring all new missionaries to New York for a conference prior to their sailing. The first of these meetings, in June 1898, helped the new missionaries receive "a better understanding of mission policies and methods and the problems with which they must deal," and it "changed the whole atmosphere in the relations of the Board and the missionary body." Brown reported that "it was such an overwhelming success that no question about its continuance was ever afterward raised, and it became an annual event."[115] Speer often invited those missionaries for whom he was responsible to his home one night for a party, including an informal meal and an evening of games, beginning the family connection.[116] He also addressed the conferences, and one missionary recalled that his message her year was "to keep fresh, to keep abreast of the times and their thought, to keep vital contact with the Lord, and all of this, he said, would require that we read much."[117] True to its policy of seeking unity wherever possible, the board invited other denominations to share in the conferences, since much of the information was not specific to any one group, and a number of denominations were involved in union conferences for new missionaries by the 1920s.[118]

The board sponsored many other meetings with the missionaries for the purpose of enhancing the work, but two, at Princeton in 1920 and at the Hotchkiss School in 1931, were remarkable in design and execution. Called for the purposes of planning, they were innovative in gathering together all the scattered elements of the Presbyterian missionary enterprise. Made possible in part by the dramatic improvements in travel and communication since the turn of the century, the board called the first the Conference on Policy and Methods of the Board of Foreign Missions and the second the Decennial Conference. They were delegated meetings, with great care given to include the missionaries. The one in 1931 attracted over one hundred missionaries representing all twenty-six missions, some fifty officers and members of the board, about the same number of representatives of local churches, and nine representatives of national churches. The board, Brown said, "took the delegates fully into its confidence and frankly discussed with them its policies, methods, expenditures, relationships, and related problems."[119] Speer described the Hotchkiss meeting as a time when the delegates faced "together the whole problem of the missionary enterprise at the present time . . . our policies abroad and the line of advance at home."[120] The meetings were quite successful in ironing out misunderstandings, proposing policy changes, and projecting new directions for the work. He was deeply involved in planning them both. He may also have conceived them, but he never claimed that, nor has anyone else, and their ultimate origin remains veiled.

A substantial part of his work with the missions and missionaries had as its reference point the board *Manual*, its basic policy book. The board had revised the book, first published in 1862, as the work had grown and become more complex. Major changes during Speer's career were made in 1896, 1922, and 1927.[121] Although he had a hand in formulating the policies, he spent a great deal more time implementing and interpreting them. Applying the general guidelines in such handbooks to individual missionaries, serving under diverse conditions in many different nations, was often difficult.

The policy on political activities of missionaries was particularly hard to interpret. The *Manual* said in part, "It is the general duty of missionaries to refrain from direct political activities and not be involved in political movements or disputes."[122] Speer wrote board member and Girard College president Cheesman A. Herrick in 1925 and reflected on the issue, "I noticed in the papers the other day that Dr. Ford of our Mission in Syria was reported to have asked for a government gun boat to be sent to Sidon. There one has in a nut shell the whole problem that we need to consider. It is certainly a difficult matter in which to see perfectly straight." What was a "general duty"? Missions might, he proposed, take the position that they would do all their duties but claim no rights. Then again, it was "not always possible to distinguish between duties and rights. There are rights which perhaps it is a duty not to surrender and there are other rights which perhaps one is not allowed to surrender, even if he would." He closed his letter with his personal solution: "I should be satisfied if we could get a universal acceptance of the principle of religious liberty and toleration. This would involve no preferential policy, no exclusive or party rights, but simply give us a world of freedom in which the Truth would make its way by its own power."[123] That might have resolved the questions, but since it did not happen during his career, they kept appearing on his desk in all their confusion and complexity.

Another problem area was furloughs, initially available after seven or eight years of service. By the mid-1920s the board granted them after only five years. However, the shorter term failed to prevent a constant stream of requests for all kinds of exceptions to the rule. He faced a hard one in 1928. The North China Mission, at the request of the university for which his daughter Margaret worked, proposed granting her a furlough after four years, partly to resolve a staffing problem and partly so that she could return home and earn an advanced degree. The plan upset him. He knew it was not her plan, but he urged her to do all she could to get it changed. He reminded her of the regulations and added: "It is not a good thing for our family to be setting the example of undercutting the regulations.

Personally I do not believe that we should ease up the situation in any particular institution by abbreviating the terms of service, which are already short enough, but rather by lengthening out here and there so as to effect the right adjustments."[124] As father to daughter he told her he wanted to see her, but as board secretary he had two other requests to modify the furlough policy, and others would surely come along. What was he to do? If he advised the board to grant her an exception, others would say to him, "You have nothing to say because this is just what you have been doing in your own family."[125] He regretted the circumstances, but the main issue was the integrity of the regulations. The situation changed, and she was able to serve a full term before she returned home for graduate study in the summer of 1930. Missionaries were colleagues, friends, and family, and because he experienced them that way, he did not always find it easy to implement board policies.

He exercised his planning and policy-making role in two other areas, finances and staffing. He was raising money for the work from his first day on the job. He was quite successful at it, partly because of the many contacts he had already made through the SVM, and partly because he was such an obviously earnest and trustworthy person. Among the generous donors was his Aunt Clara, who contributed funds to build McMurtrie Chapel in Mexico and who supported a number of board projects in other parts of the world. He encouraged her and others who approached him about investments to consider the annuity program of the boards of foreign and national missions, for he believed them to be "as solid and trustworthy as any investments that could be made."[126] On occasion people willed money to him as well as to the board and directed him to use the funds for the advancement of the work.

Financial planning was more than fund-raising. He discovered how much more when the board reorganization made him the supervisor of the treasury department. The full weight of the financial responsibility fell on him in the late 1920s, when Brown's retirement left him alone to deal with the impact of the Great Depression. He filled his letters to family and friends with references to how the declining income affected the work. Board receipts were 10 percent behind in the summer of 1932, a serious situation, but not as disastrous as expected or as experienced by some other boards, including the Methodist one.[127] By February 1933 receipts were off 20 percent, which required some difficult decisions, including a cut in salaries. He told Margaret that such a reduction would fall "very heavily on some of the official staff here, but multitudes of people are thankful for only shelter and raiment and food these days. One hears the most distressing stories from every side, and yet everybody holds on, hoping for the dawn."[128]

When the economic sun did not rise for another two years, he and the board faced the task of reducing the work. They encouraged retirements and did not fill vacancies; when those strategies fell short, they finally cut thirty-three missionaries. It was, he said, "the most painful duty that the Board had ever been compelled to perform."[129] Even so, the careful planning he and the board did made it possible for their work to emerge from the economic night in relatively better condition than the foreign missions work of many other denominations, and better than many other kinds of educational and religious work.[130] Still facing financial constraints in 1936, he told his executive staff, "If we still have faith and believe in God and the gospel, we must not plan for contraction but for expansion, nor for mere perpetuation of the past but for something that will conserve all the good of the past and yet go on to something greater."[131] When Speer retired in 1937, the Presbyterian foreign mission work was in relatively good economic shape, with 1,356 missionaries, more than "any foreign mission agency in North America at that time," a tribute to the Presbyterian Church and his leadership.[132]

Planning for the secretarial staff, like all the other forms of planning, was a shared role. The board called new secretaries, but its management style relied on the continuing secretaries to be very much involved in the process. Ellinwood had exercised considerable individual authority as staff planner, but after he retired, no one secretary picked up the role until Speer was more or less compelled to by Brown's retirement. His first task was to find a replacement for Brown, which turned out to be difficult. He and board president Erdman agreed on the Rev. Hugh T. Kerr, but unfortunately he declined. Speer told Kerr it was "a deep disappointment," for he "had hoped it might be God's will for you to come in for the next ten years that we might together work at this missionary task, at the new apologetic for the Church at home, at the true synthesis of right method old and new in the process of the enterprise abroad."[133] Speer was thrilled when Cleland McAfee, who had been on the board since 1903 and was thoroughly familiar with the work, agreed to join the staff in 1930. The economic turmoil of the years that followed forced him to interface his financial and staff planning roles as he rearranged the work in order to keep it going in the face of continuing reductions.

On occasion, Speer shared his planning skills with the church beyond the field of foreign missions. The most public display of these skills was his work the year he was moderator of the General Assembly. The least visible display came in 1920. The General Assembly that year appointed a Special Committee on the Reorganization and Consolidation of Boards and Agencies. John Timothy Stone, prominent New York City pastor and Speer fishing partner, chaired it. Speer, concerned for the fate of his board in a reorganization, but aware that a proposal from him might seem like undue influence from one of the boards, sent a comprehensive plan for reorganization in a personal memorandum to Stone. Stone responded that the plan was "one of the sanest and strongest papers which could possibly be prepared and will be invaluable to us." The committee liked it, measured all the other plans by it, and finally sent a plan based on it to the General Assembly, which adopted it.[134]

Speer performed well in the role of planner. By most criteria, especially the board's survival of the economic crisis intact and its ability to move forward, he had accomplished a great deal. His success was even more striking when placed in the context of the other crisis in those years. The theological crisis, which had been simmering for some time, finally came to a boil in the 1930s. It required him to perform yet another of his roles: defender. He had exercised this role since the beginning of his work as he responded to challenges to foreign missions from both inside and outside the church. But it took a decidedly new turn in these later years as he found himself defending not only foreign missions, but his vision of the Presbyterian Church and himself. The debate over the Hocking Report and the Independent Board of Foreign Missions took place in the larger church setting and belongs properly in the context of his work as a Presbyterian leader.[135]

Defender of Missions

Although his role as defender was not as prominent in his early years, it was nonetheless a constant part of his work. Of his various roles with the board, it was the one he liked least. He had so many other jobs that seemed more crucial to him that he dealt with criticism and controversy only when it came to him, and then with great reluctance. While criticism could and did on occasion damage the movement, he believed that in general it yielded "great advantages": "If prompted by a bad spirit, it at least shows that the work is conspicuous and sufficiently effective to challenge attention; if by a spirit of religious indifference or of vindictive animosity, the missionary movement benefits by contrast. On the other hand, sincere and honest criticism, intended to correct and improve, is to be welcomed ever."[136] From the outset he adopted a position that he adhered to without exception: he always responded to criticisms at the issue level and refused to allow the disputes to become personal.[137]

The criticisms fell into two broad groups, and his defenses followed definite patterns. On the one hand were those directed to the board, about its policies or the way one or another secretary was or was not enforcing them. These typically came from church members, acting individually or on behalf of a presbytery. Speer's standard response was to assume that the person or persons were right-minded and generally supportive and simply needed to be more fully informed. So he repeated the policy, often with reference to the *Manual*, and included some statement about the reasonableness of it. When the criticism was just, as he sometimes felt it was, he acknowledged it and explained what he or the board proposed to do about the issue. He was less charitable when he regarded the criticism as unjust. In January 1921, Griffith Thomas spoke at the Presbyterian Social Union in Philadelphia and launched a full scale attack on Presbyterian missions in China, declaring there were modernist tendencies among many of the missionaries. Charles Trumbull, editor of the *Sunday School Times*, had traveled with Thomas and used his journal to publicize the accusations. The charges generated a firestorm of protest, to which Speer felt compelled to respond. Speaking to the same Social Union in late March, he denied the charges and defended the missionaries, arguing according to one report, "Dr. Thomas was mistaken in his facts, guilty of misrepresentation and uncharitable in his judgment of the brethren."[138]

He was sometimes troubled by such internal criticisms, even the just ones, and his responses occasionally carried a note of self-righteousness. Why was it, he asked a missionary friend in China in relation to the Thomas incident, that the critics, "instead of seeing the great need as the first thing and the faithfulness and substantial unity of the missionary body as the second thing, and the tendencies of weakness and the elements of mistake and divergence as the third thing," typically put "this third thing first, and have so exalted it and magnified it as to throw everything out of perspective and to stir up at home here a spirit of bad feeling and hostility which shows its effects not against the evils which they criticize only, but against the whole body of missionary work in China."[139]

On the other hand were the attacks on the foreign missionary enterprise as a whole, usually from sources outside any church. His standard response was similar to the one he gave the internal critics, but he rarely presumed that they had any serious interest in the movement. When Tissington Tatlow, secretary of the British SVM, wrote in 1902 to inquire how he handled criticisms of missions, he referred him to his forthcoming book, *Missionary Principles and Practice*, and told him it dealt "in large part with the criticisms which have been made on Missions within the last few years."[140] A number of the chapters in part II, "General Principles Applied," were extended responses to specific critics. He used the debate model, lining up the arguments and responding to each in turn, showing that they were based on false information or faulty perspectives.[141] He could be quite sharp in his judgments. Sydney Brooks, in a *New York Times* article titled "Regulation of Missionaries in China," argued that missionaries had no right to be in the interior of China and that they were responsible for the troubles there. The problem with Brooks' article, Speer wrote, was that "it is not original, it is not intelligent, and it is not true."[142]

He never again published such an extensive collection of essays defending foreign missions, but he occasionally wrote individual articles for the religious press. In "The Bugaboo of Missionary Denominationalism," published by the *Sunday School Times*, he challenged Lord Curzon's argument that foreign missions had extended denominationalism to the mission fields, introducing Western divisions to people for whom they made no sense. He agreed with Curzon's argument "that we ought not to inflict our denominationalism on the mission field," but denied that it had been done to an extent to justify the charge. First, he argued that there were many union churches on the mission field, unlike at home, and where they did not exist, comity kept the denominations apart. Second, he claimed that most of the non-Christian religions had more divisions than Christianity, and therefore, the missionaries who did create separate groups were not introducing a new idea. In Japan alone there were "nine principal Buddhist sects, and forty-two sub-sects, with differences of opinion and characteristics more grave and serious than those which separate Protestant denominations." He concluded that Curzon, however poorly informed, raised some important questions that those who supported missions should ask themselves: "Why are we not one? Do we need so many divisions? Can we not draw closer together? Can we not remove what real grounds do exist for criticism? Why can we not realize now that unity of all believers for which our Lord prayed?"[143]

When he had joined the Board of Foreign Missions as a lowly assistant secretary, he had done so in response to a call, which he had accepted as God's choice of ministry for him. He never lost the sense of urgency of that call and tried to do everything he could to fulfill it. Almost from his first day on the job, his colleagues and others who observed him recognized that he had an extraordinary vision of foreign missions. An able administrator, he worked to humanize office tasks, seeing them as means to ends and never as ends in themselves. One observer commented that he never "allowed himself to become an 'organization man.' "[144] He was skillful enough as a counselor or as a interpreter, or in any of his particular roles, that he could have forged a career in any one of them. In fact, he created one that included them all, and each at a remarkable level of accomplishment. He has been described as "the epitome of an efficient administrator" who was also able to "translate the missionary vision into effective action."[145]

Friends and colleagues were constantly amazed at his high level of performance in all his roles, and they experienced some difficulty characterizing him. SVM partner Eddy called him "a great board secretary."[146] Mackay, who worked with him at the board in the years immediately before his retirement, called him a "Christian missionary statesman."[147] The phrase highlighted the three major features of his life and work. He was first and foremost a disciple of Jesus Christ. He fulfilled his call in the field of missions. And his global vision offered leadership not only to his own board but to the entire missionary enterprise.

CHAPTER 7

Advocate for Ecumenical Missions

"Go therefore and make disciples of all nations"

The explosive growth in foreign missions in the years surrounding the turn of the twentieth century was a surprising new event in American religious life. The chief beneficiaries of this surge of activity were the major sending agencies, denominational and nondenominational foreign missions boards, and of course the many foreign fields to which the new missionaries went. An additional consequence was new enthusiasm for the foreign missionary movement as a whole and the idea of world mission. There soon emerged a number of world missionary organizations, most of them ecumenical on the model of the Student Volunteer Movement. Some of these could trace roots to ecumenical or foreign missionary ventures in the mid-nineteenth century, but all had their real beginnings after 1890. They were all world missionary agencies in terms of their major goals, even though most began and remained based in the United States.

No one has ever tried to measure—and one probably could not do it with any accuracy—the general influence of the SVM in creating these organizations, but one easily identifiable contribution was leadership. In particular, Robert Speer and John Mott were in on the ground floor, as young observers, important participants, or prime movers. Speer was at the founding meeting of the Interdenominational Conference of Foreign Missionary Boards and Societies in the United States and Canada (IC), renamed the Foreign Missions Conference of North America (FMC) in 1911. He helped initiate and actively participated in the Ecumenical Missionary Conference in 1900 and had an important leadership role in the World Missionary Conference in Edinburgh in 1910, which became the basis for the International Missionary Council (IMC) in 1921. He also founded the Committee on Cooperation in Latin America. In every case his roles matched those he played in the SVM: he contributed his ideas and accepted organizational responsibilities, always in a voluntary capacity.

The Growth of Ecumenism in Foreign Missions

These new missionary organizations emerged over a period of three decades, an era of rapid ecumenical evolution. Groups formed, developed goals and achieved some of them, formulated new ones and changed their names, and spun off new groups with different but related goals. The relationships among them were complex even when they appeared simple. The Interdenominational Conference sponsored the Ecumenical Missionary Conference, and that meeting helped lay the foundations for the World Missionary Conference in Edinburgh in 1910. But a host of other factors also led to Edinburgh, not the least of which was the growing sympathy for united national churches in some nations that had received missionaries.

Despite the complexity and the changing goals, the leaders of all of these groups shared, if only in a preliminary way, a common vision. They agreed that the foreign missionary movement showed the way forward from a broken to a healed world and from a divided to a united church. They also agreed that the world and the Christian church needed a fuller measure of ecumenical Christian fellowship, in both geographical and theological terms. They began by embracing the SVM idea of evangelization of the world but then sought to take the next step, which was gathering together those converted in an effort to create a world fellowship of Christians, an international form for the church of Jesus Christ. In the language of a subsequent generation of students of foreign missions, they hoped to fulfill the global mission of the church.

The vision projected well into the future. The leaders of the organizations faced a great deal of preliminary practical work. They believed that any global unity depended upon some kind of national unity, at home and on the mission fields. The realities of the era were far removed from any kind of unity. Foreign missions, since its rebirth in the late eighteenth century, had been largely under the direction of various denominational and nondenominational foreign mission boards and agencies. One count in 1900 found fifty-two such boards in the United States, eight in Canada, and no less that forty-nine "auxiliary organizations."[1] When the missionaries of these boards won converts, they typically entered them onto the rolls of the denominations or mission groups they represented, even though the accepted goal of many foreign missionary boards had long been the Anderson-Venn "formula." Named for missionary pioneers

Rufus Anderson and Henry Venn, the formula sought "the planting and fostering of churches which would be self-governing, self-supporting, and self-propagating."[2] China and India and other mission fields were looking increasingly like the checkered denominational pattern of the United States.

Movement from this reality to the ecumenical vision was a major task, requiring careful thinking and maneuvering. The leaders of the new organizations, Speer included, were almost without exception involved because they were first leaders of denominational boards or other missionary agencies. Few of them wanted to abolish denominations at home, although the idea of an organic church union surfaced in the discussions from time to time. Nor did they particularly desire a federal merger of their mission boards and agencies, although that proposal emerged too. What they hoped for at home, at least as a start, was coordination and cooperation, and what they came to hope for on the field was the emergence of united native churches. While that may not sound threatening, the idea was new. Many people who had given money to foreign missions, assuming new Christians overseas would be Methodist or Baptist or Episcopal or whatever their own variety was, were either unresponsive to the ecumenical vision or more directly opposed it.

The task of the leaders was to move their respective boards and agencies from where they were to where they hoped them to be, and at the same time to sustain a growing movement. Viewed from this perspective, it was a remarkable challenge. Speer accepted it early in his career as one of his duties with the Presbyterian Board. He believed his ecumenical vision fulfilled his denominational commitment, and he maintained that position the rest of his life. Other people representing various boards and agencies shared his viewpoint, but he rather quickly became one of a small handful of spokespersons, on occasion the most visible one, for the ecumenical vision.

The Interdenominational Conference

The first of these new missionary organizations was the Interdenominational Conference of Foreign Missionary Boards and Societies. It met for the first time on January 12, 1893, in the Presbyterian Mission House in New York City, in response to an invitation from the Committee on Missionary Co-operation of the Western Section of the Alliance of the Reformed Churches Holding the Presbyterian System. Missionary board leaders from twenty-one different groups and representatives of the American Bible Society and the YMCA met "for the discussion of practical questions of missionary policy," and to explore the possibilities for "real cooperation in their common work." Strongly encouraged by the experience of sharing, they decided to meet the following year and gradually created the Interdenominational Conference as a formal organization. Evidence exists that they realized they were breaking new ground, for the "Prefatory Note" of the published *Report* of the first conference observed that the gathering "constituted an object-lesson in Christian unity at which all true Christians might well rejoice, and to which all dark prophets of discord and failure might profitably give heed."[3] One historian of church cooperation in America has agreed, and described it as "the first official instrument of cooperation among denominational agencies."[4]

Speer was present at the initial meeting as one of the representatives of his board and likely at the express invitation of his mentor Ellinwood, who had originally suggested the idea and hosted the event.[5] He was a very junior member of the foreign missions staff at that time and offered nothing for the record. Here and at subsequent conferences the representatives exchanged ideas on a variety of missionary topics, including the developments in different fields, the problems of recruitment, and self-support in mission churches. The meetings featured open discussions on announced topics and occasional formal papers on major issues. He made his first contribution at the third conference in 1895, when he responded to a paper on the Japan-China War with some reflections on its impact on missionary work.

Once he broke the ice, he became an increasingly active participant. Appointed to the business committee at the next conference, he gave its lengthy report. At the sixth conference in 1898 he moved into a leadership role. He presented his first major address, and the members elected him to two committees, a newly created one on comity and unoccupied fields and one on arrangements for the following year.

The paper he read was part of a session on reports of visitation of fields and was simply one among several reports by missionary secretaries who had recently returned from tours abroad; however, the straightforward title, "Report of Recent Tour in Asia," belied both the real substance of his presentation and its significance. Beginning in travelogue fashion, he listed the stops he and Emma had made on their long and very arduous fourteen-month trip, but he quickly turned away from description to several "observations." He reported that the discussions at their conferences, however informal and nonbinding, had a major impact on the field.

Discussions four years ago on self-support had "practically transformed sentiment in a great many of our missions," and the more recent ones on length of a missionary term were currently having great effect. This had come as a surprise to him and was perhaps news to them, and so he admonished, "We should remind ourselves of this in these discussions, and be sure that we hold up nothing but the high ideals, and that we encourage no low and sordid views of the missionary spirit or aim."[6]

He shared three important needs he discovered on his trip. First, the missionaries he visited expressed the desire for "some rational *statement of mission principles*," what he thought from the technical point of view might be called "*a science of missions*." In field after field, regardless of the missionary board involved, younger missionaries were reinventing the wheel in terms of missionary practice. The waste of time and talent was immense. True, some missionaries did not want principles or did not believe they could be formulated. But, he urged his fellow secretaries, the deepest conviction of his trip was that "*the time has come for us to attempt to gather these results of missionary experience and to frame them into some kind of missionary judgment and policy*."[7] Second, "*enormous missionary machinery*" existed everywhere he went. The problem was common to every board and revealed the danger of "more body than vitality." He shared a case from his own denomination "where we organized a church before we had a convert and a Presbytery before we had a church." He was forced to wonder, he said, "*whether this work was dependent for its success chiefly upon contributions of American money, or upon the vital presence of the living God*." Given such an option, he chose to stress "*the fundamental conception of the Christian missionary. It is the dispensing of divine life*."[8]

The third need he learned from his trip was that the denominations had much more to do regarding "*questions of comity*." Such questions reached into many areas, like higher education, schools, and medical work, and it seemed unfair to place the burden of dealing with them on the missionaries alone. Even though strong opposition persisted both at home and abroad, from those who believed "that the denominational lines are providential gifts to the children of men," or who wanted to perpetuate their own doctrinal positions, he believed comity held the promise of the future. He closed his report with a personal ecumenical confession and hope for the church on the mission field: "Looking forward to the far distant future, I hope that those of us who are younger may live to see the day . . . when these barriers that separate us here are held of light account in comparison with a genuine unity. I believe in one Christian Church on each mission field. I do not believe in building up in Korea a Methodist

Church, and a Baptist Church. I do not believe in that sort of thing. *I believe in one Church of Christ in these lands.*"[9]

The published *Report* of the sixth conference contained no record of responses to his presentation, nor has any correspondence been found referring to it. Surely some of those who heard it recognized it for what it was, a position paper on the state of foreign missions and a chart for navigating the murky waters that lay ahead. He presented it at the beginning of a year marked by similar thoughtful work, including a speech on the watchword to the third quadrennial of the SVM and preparation of the powerful book *Remember Jesus Christ.* On the one hand, these presentations sustained his reputation for thoughtful reflection on the nature and task of foreign missions. On the other hand, they marked a departure, a search for first principles and a promise to work them out in some systematic way. The task took him four years, finally completed when he published his major theoretical study of foreign missions in 1902 (see chapter 8 for further discussion).

Why had this search begun in 1898? He offered one clue in his speech. The tour had come only after five years in the home office, learning the ropes and becoming acquainted at a distance with the fields and their major issues. So when he went abroad, he knew what questions to ask and was prepared to consider how solutions to specific problems might lead to first principles. But something else happened on that trip: he had a life-threatening experience. Although he rarely mentioned his illness and never connected it with his work, it was surely more than coincidence that he shifted into a higher gear after his return and began his search to discover for himself the fundamental principles of foreign missions.

The Science of Missions

He continued to use the IC as a forum to explore two of his ideas: the science of missions and comity. He presented a major paper on the science of missions at the very next conference, and although it was in the form of a proposal that he later revised, he never changed it substantially, and it remained his essential thought on the topic.[10] The phrase "the science of missions" belonged to the missionary thinker Gustav Warneck of the University of Halle in Germany. Speer argued a science of missions was possible because God had created one world full of souls needing redemption, despite "distinct national peculiarities," and because, as his journeys had revealed, mission problems were pretty much the same in every land. Such a science was needed if the missionary movement, after one hundred years of experience, was going to move forward and evangelize the world.

The substance of his argument turned on definitions of the aim, the means, the methods, and the agents of missions. While he admitted some areas of disagreement, he plunged ahead convinced that there was enough general consent to establish a science of missions. The aim of missions was "to preach the Gospel" and to establish churches on the Anderson-Venn formula, in spite of some continuing differences concerning its precise application. The means were first and foremost spiritual and needed to remain spiritual, regardless of the attractiveness of some of the institutions missionaries had founded and of how much some people were attached to them. He concentrated on what he called the four main methods or departments of mission work: evangelism, education, medicine, and literature. Of these, education presented some of the most complicated problems. He proposed that missionary schools, particularly at the secondary level, should aim "to develop Christian character," and therefore should be "unqualifiedly Christian, bringing and keeping all their pupils under powerful and personal religious influence." One possible rule was for mission boards and missionaries to establish schools in the context of Christian communities, rather than using schools in hopes of creating such communities. Missionaries were the primary agents for initiating all the different kinds of missionary work, and substantial agreement existed about their training and qualifications; but more work needed to be done to develop principles for the preparation of the agents of native churches as those churches emerged. He concluded with an appeal to his fellow secretaries to seize the moment and accept the task of creating a science of missions. "We have," he told them, "been doing this piece by piece, from year to year. We should complete this work so far as we are able. And the voice of the confusionist, of the missionary anti-nomian, of the experimentalist, ought not to deter us."[11]

He left no record to suggest what he anticipated at the end of his presentation. The year before, no one had responded to his position paper. This time his ideas sparked a long and vigorous debate. The chairman of the session, the Rev. Henry N. Cobb, secretary of the Board of Foreign Missions of the Reformed Church in America, began with unqualified praise: "In my judgment we have scarcely had a more important paper presented in any of these conferences."[12] Brown, Speer's colleague on the Presbyterian Board, supported the concept and suggested the conference proceed by referring different parts of the paper to appropriate committees. The Rev. A. B. Leonard of the Missionary Society of the Methodist Episcopal Church and the Rev. M. G. Kyle of the Board of Foreign Missions of the United Presbyterian Church of North America demurred, more or less certain that such a science was impossible. After much give and take, the Rev. Alexander Sutherland, representing the Missionary Society of the Methodist Church in Canada and the first chairman of the IC, rose and offered an opinion and a motion. He did not see, he said, the use of referring the matter to any committee, since he had "never heard of any science being formulated by a committee." Moreover, Speer had a version of the science ready, and they should use it. He thought "a very good beginning would be to put a copy of this admirable paper in the hands of as many of our ministers and laymen as possible," and moved that the IC print it, "not only in the Annual Report, but in a separate edition for general circulation."[13] They voted accordingly, a somewhat surprising outcome to a debate that had involved sharp differences.

The vote signaled general support for the idea and made his proposal a printed document, but did not constitute a policy decision. Presumably to that end, his colleagues elected him chairman of a committee on the science of missions. The Interdenominational Conference folded into the Ecumenical Missionary Conference the next year, and the science committee did not report until the eighth conference in 1901; by then it had changed its name to the committee on general principles. Using his proposal as a guideline, committee members had searched the *Reports* of the IC and the proceedings of a predecessor meeting, the Union Missionary Convention in New York in 1854, looking for principles that had been "adopted" in either a formal or informal way. Their report reflected many of his ideas but featured a different organization, dividing them into home base and foreign field categories. The committee concluded that it had found "general principles of great importance," and even though "they do not furnish us with a science of missions, . . . they cover many of the main points of missionary policy." As for the future of such a science, "it seems to us wise to let it grow."[14] The IC adopted the report and voted to publish it separately, if there were enough subscriptions to pay for it. The committee ceased to exist, but Speer had won his science of missions in substance if not in name. He had been the moving force in helping the main body of Protestant missionary boards and agencies become more self-conscious about the fundamental principles of their task.

"Denominationalism by Geography"

Comity was another concern high on Speer's agenda. Unlike the science of missions, which had little or no American antecedent, comity was a very familiar term. The idea had been in circulation for sixty years and the word had come into popular usage in the 1880s. It meant simply a division of territory, or "denominationalism by geography."[15] It achieved two important goals: the reduction of friction between denominational groups and the cooperation necessary to assure wise use of personnel in the evangelization of large areas. Even though many of the foreign missionary boards used the idea, no formal policy existed to which they all subscribed. The IC met for five years without paying any significant attention to comity, although it could be argued that the IC itself constituted a form of it. But it did not move formally to act on comity until after Speer had laid out his position and issued a call for concentrated thinking and action. In response it created a committee on comity and unoccupied fields "to correspond with Boards and Societies relative to the most economic distribution of the missionary force supported by the American and Canadian Churches" and appointed him to serve on it.[16]

Sutherland, chair of the committee on comity, apologized when he reported to the seventh conference on January 12, 1899, because circumstances had prevented "proper correspondence" with the boards, but his committee had gone ahead and prepared "a general report on the principles that seem to be involved." The committee claimed that whatever missionary executives thought about principles of comity, many missionaries believed they were needed. It defined six aspects of missionary work where the comity already practiced suggested a principle or where the lack of comity required the creation of one. The first topic was church union, and the recommended principle represented by far the most advanced and most dramatic change: *"The aim of the mission movement should be, it appears to us, the establishment of a common Christian Church in each land, and not the extension and perpetuation of those divisions of the Church which owe their origin to historic situations significant to us, but of little or no significance to the young mission churches."* In the case of territorial divisions, it had long been "axiomatic" that *"different missions should work without crossing lines."* In education, publishing, and hospitals, and in the intermarriage of missionaries of different societies, there were opportunities for greater comity, and the committee suggested principles.[17]

Most of the missionary executives who responded to the comity committee's proposals pledged support, but some raised the issue of its relation to their denominational commitments. Sutherland acknowledged that some of the principles "may perhaps seem to some too advanced," but added that progress required someone to step forward: "We have to carry the colors a little beyond where the rank and file has reached as yet, but

every one knows that what seemed years ago to be a very advanced position for the colors is a very remote position now." Persuaded, the IC
"received" the committee's report, ordered it printed, and continued the
committee for further work, noting in particular that it did so in order
"that the Ecumenical Conference might have the advantage of its report."[18]
Although no direct evidence has survived that Speer actually wrote the
comity report, he clearly played a major role in formulating the proposals.
They not only reflected his ideas but contained some of the phrasing he
had used in his position paper. Shortly after the conference he wrote a substantial article for the *Churchman* in which he described the contents of
the committee report, highlighting the proposal on church union. "No
novel positions are advanced here," he said, and then, without claiming
ownership, he added, "excepting, of course, the form of statement and
perhaps some of the implications of the first recommendation."[19]

Part of the charge of the committee was to help prepare for the
Ecumenical Missionary Conference. He took the lead and formulated and
distributed a questionnaire to missionary executives. He solicited suggestions for speakers, sought examples of successful comity agreements and
breaches of them, and inquired about the possibility of union churches in
mission fields. He enclosed a copy of the committee report for review. He
sent his collected material and his own suggestions to Sutherland early in
the summer. The chairman's response contained two very revealing pieces
of information. "I assume," he told him, "that the Report of the Committee on Comity will be chiefly your work." Since he was not referring
to an entirely new report, that could mean Speer had essentially authored
the committee report. Noting that Speer had left his name off the list of
speakers, he wrote, "Your deep interest in the subject and your diligence
in gathering data, are widely known, and I think there will be general disappointment in the Conference if you are not heard at some length."[20]
Speer neither changed his mind nor gave a reason for his omission and did
not speak at the session on comity and division of fields the following
spring.

The committee on comity reported to the eighth conference that discussions, "notably in the Ecumenical Missionary Conference . . . have
placed the importance of Comity in so clear and convincing a light that
any further discussion of the general question seems to be unnecessary."
Moreover, the report continued, many of the principles of comity were
now so widely and practically accepted that the remaining task seemed to
be to communicate formally to the boards and agencies the basic principles, requesting their "concurrence." During the long discussion that

ensued, the sticking point continued to be denominational prerogatives, particularly as they related to organic church unions on the field. Offering a strong positive note, Brown reported that the General Assembly of the Presbyterian Church had voted unanimously to encourage its board "to move in the direction of Comity, co-operation, and organic union with other denominations on the foreign field."[21] The conference finally adopted the report and continued the committee to monitor and report new developments. Speer had been the main driving force behind this issue, not as visible as in his quest for a science of missions, but just as determined to move Protestant foreign missions to adopt policies that would move them toward greater unity.

The Interdenominational Conference remained an annual conference of missionary board and agency executives, important for creating fellowship and a sense of common purpose, but rarely generating much activity between meetings, until 1907. That year it created a committee on reference and counsel to meet on its behalf at any time at the call of a board or agency. This committee provided a continuing group to handle emergencies and to study knotty issues, and "signalized a new development in the functional cooperation of denominational agencies."[22] The next and most important change came in 1911. Inspired by the actions of the World Missionary Conference in 1910, it drew up a constitution that reformed it into a "carefully structured and representative body," and changed its name to the Foreign Missions Conference of North America. The committee on reference and counsel became its administrative arm.[23] The FMC agreed to formalize what had heretofore been its unwritten policy: "No resolution shall be considered which deals with theological or ecclesiastical questions that represent denominational differences."[24] Adapted from the World Missionary Conference and not specifically inspired by Speer, it reflected his concern for the disruptive nature of doctrinal and denominational differences. The FMC in 1921 became the largest of the several component units of the International Missionary Council and in 1950 joined with other groups to form the National Council of the Churches of Christ in the U.S.A.[25]

Speer worked in a variety of IC and FMC administrative capacities over the years, and although he never dominated the organizations, he became widely recognized as one of the primary leaders, especially in the years after World War I. He accepted a range of responsibilities, including service on the committee on arrangements for several of the annual meetings; membership on the Anglo-American communities committee from its inception and chair for many years after 1907; service on the committee

on the Mohammedan problem in 1910; membership on the committee
on reference and counsel for several different terms; and, service as one of
the conference chairs in 1905 and as chair in 1926 and 1937. He faithfully participated in the meetings, except when he was away on a missionary tour, and almost always had some leadership role. This usually
meant leading a devotional period, giving a report, or presenting a major
platform paper. As the Student Volunteer Movement was his major ecumenical channel for recruiting missionaries, the IC and then FMC were
the major organizations through which he worked out his principles and
practices of missions with other missionary leaders.

The Ecumenical Missionary Conference

Participation in the Interdenominational Conference led him directly into
another of the world missionary organizations, the International
Missionary Council, which essentially began with the Ecumenical
Missionary Conference in New York City in 1900. The idea for a missionary conference on a world scale has been traced to William Carey, who
proposed one for 1810, and of course to the actual conferences held in
New York and London in 1854, in Liverpool in 1860, and in London in
1878 and 1888.[26] However, the most important sources for what became
the Ecumenical Missionary Conference were not the meetings of the past
but the needs of the present. The idea surfaced in 1896 at an event overlooked by historians. Speer introduced to his IC board colleagues the Rev.
J. R. Davies, chairman of the committee on foreign missions of the
Presbytery of New York, who reported on "simultaneous missionary meetings" that had been held in his presbytery with the strong assistance of
Speer and the Presbyterian board. The weeklong series of meetings were
climaxed by a great gathering at Carnegie Hall, presided over by Benjamin
Harrison, former president of the United States. The results in support
and excitement for foreign missions had been so remarkable that Davies
hoped, with the help of the IC, to encourage other denominations to
adopt the plan. Although Davies did not refer to a world conference, the
usefulness of exchanging ideas with missionary leaders of other nations
had come up in the discussions of several other conference reports. Speer
made the report of the business committee at the meeting, and two of the
resolutions concerned missionary conferences. One approved the plan for
"a simultaneous missionary campaign" and appointed a committee to
work on it. The other extended the idea to the international level and

appointed another committee, chaired by the Rev. Judson Smith, corresponding secretary of the American Board of Commissioners for Foreign Missions, and charged it "to consider the advisability of calling an ecumenical missionary conference to meet in this country within the next four years, and to make any preliminary preparation therefor, . . . and to report at the meeting next year."[27] This marked the first reference to what became the Ecumenical Missionary Conference and one of the first uses of the adjective "ecumenical" in this era.[28]

The committee on ecumenical missionary conference prepared a tentative proposal and solicited opinions from missionary groups around the world. At the Interdenominational Conference in 1897, this committee reported that the responses, from more than fifty missionary organizations, were unanimous in their support of the plan, and recommended the formal adoption of it. Smith noted that the only real question of substance had come from those who viewed " 'ecumenical' as savoring of ecclesiasticism," but the committee could not think of another word "that so fitly expresses exactly what we mean."[29] The IC adopted the plan and authorized the committee to proceed. Speer did not contribute to the planning in its early stages, perhaps because he was away on his world missionary tour from the summer of 1896 through the fall of 1897. However, as the time for the meeting approached, the committee embraced some other IC committees, like the committee on comity on which he served, and created a large number of new ones. He became part of the executive committee and the committee on students and young people and chaired the committee on devotional services. He made a major presentation at one of the meeting's initial sessions, chaired the mass meeting for men, offered prayer at the session for students and other young people, spoke on behalf of "missions in Persia" at a session on Muslim lands, and shared in discussions on the native church and moral questions and missionary literature for home churches.

The Ecumenical Missionary Conference, which opened on Sunday, April 22, 1900, in Carnegie Hall, closely resembled the Presbyterian missionary gathering Davies had described. Former President Benjamin Harrison was the honorary president and presided at the opening session, where President William McKinley and New York Governor Theodore Roosevelt spoke. (The two shortly paired up again to head the Republican ticket and win the general election in November.) General assemblies met in the hall, and so did some of the smaller meetings, but the organizers had prepared so many sessions that the conference spilled over into nearby churches. Missionary organizations sent representatives, but the meeting was open to all interested parties, and thousands came. Estimates of the total attendance at the ten-day conference exceeded 150,000.[30] Chairperson Smith was overwhelmed by the turnout. Attendance at the initial meeting was "phenomenal, and was fully maintained, and even increased as the days passed; till at the closing session Carnegie Hall was crowded beyond all precedent." Sheer numbers were far from the whole story. "Protestant Christendom has never been so widely represented before," Smith claimed, for there "were present about 3000 accredited delegates from all Protestant lands, of whom 700 were missionaries fresh from those majestic labors on continents and islands all around the globe."[31]

Speer's major presentation came early in the Ecumenical Conference in one of two identically titled sessions, "Authority and Purpose of Foreign Missions." Held the morning after the dramatic opening meeting, they represented the effort of the planners to accomplish two goals: (1) to symbolize the international character of the conference by having speakers from the United States and Great Britain at each session; and (2) to get down to the serious business at hand. Speer spoke in Carnegie Hall on "The Supreme and Determining Aim." He directed his opening remarks to those present who were not part of the foreign missionary enterprise in a technical sense and who should understand that foreign missions was part of the larger Christian task, not all of it. That was an important distinction because he proposed to focus on the particular aim of foreign missions, not on "the aim of the Christian Church in the world, or of the Christian nations of the world." The aim of foreign missions was fundamentally religious. "We cannot state too strongly," he said, "in an age when the thought of men is full of things, and the body has crept up on the throne of the soul, that our work is not immediately and in itself a philanthropic work, a political work, a secular work of any sort whatsoever; it is a spiritual and a religious work." The aim of foreign missions "is to make Jesus Christ known to the world."[32] His full presentation was his most important theoretical statement on the aim of foreign missions and will be explored in depth in chapter 8.

By all reports the Ecumenical Conference was a huge success, a great rally for foreign missions. The large crowds, fresh reports from hundreds of missionaries from foreign fields and even from a few of those they had converted, and thoughtful analyses of mission policy by some of the best missionary minds in the world created great excitement and enthusiasm for foreign missions. But why was it so successful? What accounted for such a large turnout? Some historians have observed that it was one of the beneficiaries of the burgeoning idea of progress, in the particular forms of humanitarianism and nationalism. A few have argued that missionaries and mission executives, including Speer, turned aside from the old and conservative reason for foreign missions, to save souls, and were increasingly advancing what was then a new and liberal reason, to civilize the heathen.[33]

Evidence in general and from Speer in particular fails to support such an argument, either at the time of the Ecumenical Conference or later. A more judicious analysis has placed the success of the meeting in the context of a "blend of piety and progress," which had begun to help sustain the missionary undertaking.[34] Support for this view has been drawn from the work of a committee that put together the presentations for publication and included progress as an important element in assessing its success. It cited the recent expansion of American and European commercial interests and the new contacts with the world resulting from the war with Spain, and claimed that such developments had " 'widened the circle of thought, and resulted in an increased appreciation of the condition of the non-Christian portions of the world, and deepened the conviction that human progress is inseparably bound up with Christian missions.' "[35]

Speer made his personal position on the sources and meaning of the Ecumenical Conference absolutely clear. The published *Report* contained his statement, "The Significance of the Ecumenical Conference." In this document he replicated the role he played at the quadrennial meetings of the SVM, where he typically offered the closing statements, but in this case in written rather than spoken form. Quite conscious of the political and social changes in the world, he chose to see the conference as "a revelation of the unabated power of the missionary spirit," and added specifically, "Its reaffirmation of faith in the fundamental convictions of the gospel startled many who had supposed that the Church had departed from these foundations."[36] From its beginning to its end "the missionary enterprise was set forth as a religious enterprise, aiming at religious ends, and appealing to religious motives. Its purpose was declared to be to proclaim Christ to the world as the Saviour from sin, and the Lord of Life."[37]

The main message of the meeting was, he declared, that the missionary work of the church demonstrated that the Christian faith was alive and well, but there were other important outcomes. First, in terms familiar to those who had heard him give the missionary call, he asserted it "proclaimed that Christ's religion is essentially missionary, that to receive Christ is to receive the obligation of communicating Him, that missionary sympathy is not a matter of praiseworthy and superfluous consecration on the part of a section of Christians, but the solemn and unavoidable responsibility of all." Second, it demonstrated "the essential unity of the evangelical churches. Far above all separating peculiarities the single Spirit of the single Lord lifted the hearts of his servants, and they found themselves to be brethren." Finally, it "revealed the method of ultimate union. It showed that the best way to heal some breaches is to bridge them in higher air. The members of the body are divided for their various functions; but all are united in the Head."[38]

The Ecumenical Missionary Conference took place at the junction of two centuries. For many of those who gathered in New York, senior missionaries and mission executives, it was a fitting postlude to all their labors of the past century. They were fully aware that they had helped spread the Christian message throughout the world and had become part of a great and increasing chorus of voices as the church had become truly worldwide. They agreed with Speer on the identification of the Christian and missionary task. They were part of the reason that Latourette, at the time a young man not yet called to foreign missions, would one day describe their century in the context of the expansion of Christianity as "the Great Century."[39] But for others present, younger missionaries and mission executives, it was a grand prelude to the future. Speer spoke for them too in hoping that the chorus would continue to grow, but the themes were unclear. When he added unity to missions, he reflected his personal hope, not the collective sentiment. Now, at the end of the then-new century, considered by many Christians to be the ecumenical century in the life of the church, he stands as one of the ecumenical pioneers and prophets.[40]

The hope almost died at birth, and ironically his board was very much involved. The day the conference adjourned, "a supplemental meeting" took place in the Central Presbyterian Church, where a large number of conference officers and missionaries contemplated the future. They proposed the creation of an "international committee, who by correspondence or conference or both, shall deal with certain practical questions of co-operative work on mission fields, and shall make known the results of their deliberations to the societies which have been represented in this Conference."[41] The executive committee met the next day to draw the business of the conference to a close and considered this proposal. Deep differences of opinion emerged; finally the committee referred the matter to a subcommittee and charged it to report to the next meeting of the IC. By the time that meeting arrived, Speer's board had joined the debate. Widely recognized for its leadership in matters of Christian unity and comity, the Presbyterian Board issued a formal statement supporting the goals of "a closer fellowship in foreign missionary effort and a more wise, economical, and effective co-operation in the use of men and money," but opposed the creation of "any outside committee or bureau" to achieve that end. Instead, it urged fuller use of the already existing IC.[42] In part because of this weighty objection from one of the largest and most prominent of its members, the IC dropped the idea of an international committee, which might well have served as a continuation committee for another conference.

The Interdenominational Conference did not, however, simply let go of the ideas generated at the Ecumenical Conference. It helped create a General Bureau of Missions, with a focus on missionary research and information.[43] It became a major spin-off of the Ecumenical Conference. Speer made the conclusive motion that commended the bureau "to the co-operation of the several Boards here represented and of all interested in the purposes of such an organization," and added that it was distinctly understood that the denominational boards had no financial responsibility for it.[44] He never separated his views from those of his board. Did he personally favor a continuation committee? Very likely. But he also probably concurred that the proposal before the IC did not accomplish that. The discussion turned not on the possibility of another world conference, but on continued cooperation and greater unity, and he clearly agreed that the IC could and should continue to serve as the vehicle to accomplish that.

"The Birthplace of the Modern Ecumenical Movement"

The idea for another world conference on foreign missions disappeared from public discussion, but when it reappeared, Speer and the Interdenominational Conference were instruments in reviving it. The Rev. J. Fairley Daly, associated with the Livingstonia Mission of the United Free Church of Scotland, wrote Speer in 1906 about some matter and "asked incidentally whether the Mission Boards of America had any plans or views as to the holding of another Conference."[45] When Speer raised the issue at the IC that year, it charged the committee on arrangements for the meeting in 1907 to correspond with the boards and agencies about the matter and report back. He served on that committee and apprized Daly of the process. The committee discovered considerable support for another conference but a difference of opinion on whether it should be in Europe, with Mott and a few others in support of that location, or in the United States. As the committee was formulating its report, Speer received another communication from Daly, inviting the IC to respond to a tentative call for a "Third Ecumenical Missionary Conference" to be held in Scotland in 1910. The committee proposed and the IC voted to accept the call, and thereby set in motion the three-year process that led to the World Missionary Conference at Edinburgh (in ecumenical literature, often simply called Edinburgh).[46] He never spoke publicly about his crucial role, but took quiet satisfaction in "initiating with Fairley Daly the Edinburgh Conf[erence] 1910."[47]

Although "church union" was not on the agenda, the World Missionary Conference has been described as "the birthplace of the modern ecumenical movement," because it made more explicit than ever before the vital connection within the missionary enterprise of the evangelization of the world and the establishment of the church throughout the world.[48] Part of the world missionary conference tradition that included London (1888) and New York (1900), and hence called initially the Third Conference, Edinburgh differed from the former ones in three crucial respects. Those conferences had invited representatives of foreign missionary organizations and other interested parties and were primarily assemblies for sharing information and spreading enthusiasm for missions. Edinburgh was a delegated body. Only boards and agencies that sent missionaries to the field were eligible to send representatives, and then only in proportion to their expenditures. Many of the boards were official denominational ones, and therefore Edinburgh drew closer to truly representing the churches than had the previous meetings, although it was "still a conference of societies and not a council of Churches."[49] Delegates to the previous conferences had heard presentations prepared primarily by individuals. Edinburgh established eight conference topics and set up serious study commissions to prepare extensive reports and distribute them beforehand. Review of these documents and consultations on the issues they raised constituted its essential work. Earlier conferences had ended without careful preparation for a future gathering. Edinburgh set up a continuation committee. The delegates were aware they were moving into uncharted waters when they unanimously passed the resolution to create it and then, in response to the emotion of the moment, rose and sang the Doxology.[50]

On board from the beginning, Speer shared in many phases of the preparation. The IC served as the North American organizational base for the meeting. It appointed a committee on world missionary conference with eleven members, including Speer and Mott. That committee kept in consultation with its European counterpart and gradually added to its membership and became the American executive committee. Speer served on two subcommittees, one on leaflets and another on preconference meetings in the United States and Canada, and chaired one on delegates. Since delegates were limited, he advised the boards and agencies that "men and women are wanted there who are moulding [sic] the thought and leading the action of the Church, and who will be able to carry the influence of the Conference back into their own bodies."[51] As the conference approached, he became vice-chairman of commission IV, working with Professor David S. Cairns of Aberdeen, Scotland, who was the chairman. The responsibility of commission IV was the missionary message in relation to non-Christian religions. This work sparked his close friendship with Cairns.

His role on this commission was linked in part with another significant event in his life in 1910, the Duff Lectures. Named for the pioneer Scottish educational missionary Alexander Duff, who had inspired and presided at the missionary conference in New York in 1854, they offered the appointed lecturers a distinguished and highly visible platform. Speer traced his invitation to the SVM meeting in Nashville in 1906. The Rev. George Robson of the Foreign Mission Committee of the United Free Church of Scotland had been present and had "approved" of his address on "The Inadequacy of the Non-Christian Religions to Meet the Need of the World" and had commended him to the Duff trustees.[52]

The Duff Lectures were scheduled the January and February preceding the World Conference. So prominent were they, and so popular was Speer among students in Scotland because of his SVM work, that his hosts informed him in the fall of 1909 that they had decided "to make use of you in preparation for the World Conference." Robson told him that the lectures were ordinarily given in the cities of Edinburgh, Aberdeen, and Glasgow, but in addition they had planned speaking engagements in other major cities and "the Christian Student Unions are on your track, and I have made one or two promises of your services at a meeting in each of the University towns."[53] Speer told Daly, "I have undertaken the appointment with some misgivings. I know our people over here and am sure of my ground among them, but I have an hesitation about venturing out into another field. One does not have, in a new field, the instinct as to what to take for granted, how to put things, and what things most need putting; but I shall make ready with the earnest prayer to be guided by the higher Wisdom, and so earnestly hope to be able to say something serviceable to the Cause."[54] The lectures were a great success. Mackay, one of the students he inspired during the lecture tour, later recalled: "He was the first American I had ever looked on in the flesh. I thought as I listened to

him speak that he was the greatest man I had ever seen."⁵⁵ By the time the
delegates began to arrive in June, Speer had tilled a great deal of ground
for the cause of foreign missions.

The World Missionary Conference met June 14–23. The 1,200 delegates fulfilled the dream of the planners to create the most truly representative of the world missionary conferences. In their midst was a small but
significant number of leaders from the churches emerging in the mission
fields. Members gathered in the assembly hall of the United Free Church
of Scotland, high on the dramatic ridge that cuts through the city, dominated at its highest point by the great castle and the sacred St. Giles'
Cathedral.

Speer played a very important and highly visible role at Edinburgh
from beginning to end. Indeed, his first part came before the official start
of the meeting, when the University of Edinburgh held a special assembly
in M'Ewan Hall to recognize fourteen of the "distinguished members" of
the conference by awarding them honorary degrees. He received a D.D.
and Mott an LL.D.⁵⁶ One observer reported that the students followed
their custom of "razzing" each of the recipients as he came forward, but
when Speer's name was called, "dead silence fell upon the student group.
Only the sound of traffic on a distant street was heard. It was the eloquent
tribute of the student body of the University of another country, to one
whom they regarded as doing most for the student life of the world."⁵⁷ The
Edinburgh branch of the Student Volunteer Missionary Union sent him a
note of congratulations spelling out the meaning of the silence: "There
can be hardly anything more gratifying to us than that the Senatus
Academicus should grant this well-deserved distinction on you who have
done so much for the cause of Christ. Your unwearied efforts in promoting His Kingdom, your deep researches into the realms of non-Christian
religions by which you have stirred men up to do their duty towards the
Evangelization of the World in This Generation have already caused your
name to be graven on many hearts."⁵⁸ He almost refused to accept the
degree, not wishing to push himself forward, but finally did so at the
urging of Mott and other friends.⁵⁹ At the end of the year, he wrote one
missionary friend that the Edinburgh degree was a "fine thing to have as
a tribute to the missionary enterprise, which it was meant to be," but he
found it a personal "burden" that he hoped to keep out of public view.⁶⁰
That was impossible, and he increasingly came to be called Dr. Speer.

The formal opening took place at the direction of Lord Balfour of
Burleigh, president of the conference. He presented a strong message of

support and encouragement from His Majesty the King. He then gave his opening address, followed by the archbishop of Canterbury and Speer. Conference leaders, in putting such a relatively young American layman alongside such prominent persons, signaled his status as one of the leading spokespersons of the world foreign missionary movement. He spoke on his favorite topic, "Christ the Leader of the Missionary Work of the Church," and set out his thesis in brief but eloquent fashion. They had come, he said, at the call of Jesus Christ, and what more could he say other than to remind them all of the fact, the way, and the meaning of his leadership. Jesus issued a personal call, inviting people to follow him and encouraging them to join in a personal relationship with him. Christians were called to say with Paul, "To me to live is Christ," and to accept Jesus' personal leadership of their lives. "If it were not that Christ had led us," he said, "we should not be here. If it were not that we are sure that we shall be under His leadership during these days, it were better that we should part to-night." Jesus also led his church, most remarkably in its missionary work.

They had journeyed to Edinburgh, he affirmed, to learn new things and to experience a sense of unity, fully aware that the task ahead, the full evangelization of the world, remained as difficult as it had ever been. But, he proposed, they had also gathered because they believed "that He has been moulding [sic] the thoughts of men in the generation to which we belong, and has made ready the hearts and minds of Christian men now, at last, after all these twenty centuries have gone by, to fulfil what we know to have been the great purpose and desire of our Lord." If that were true, if the "time he has waited for may now have come," then how could they permit anything to stand in their way? He invited the throng of missionary leaders to allow a new realization of Christ's leadership to be awakened within them so that their renewed "living faith will make it possible for Him to make use of us for the immediate conquest of the world."[61]

The World Conference proceeded without a hitch. It appointed Mott chair for the work sessions and Oldham secretary. It met daily to hear commission reports and to join in formal discussions of them. Mott served as a superb, if sometimes overbearing, chair and also presented the report of commission I on carrying the gospel to all the non-Christian world. He gave the closing address, and the continuation committee elected him its chair. Speer joined in one of the formal discussions and in the presentation of the report of his commission, where he made the commission's response to the discussion. He also spoke at an afternoon sectional meeting on the responsibility of ministers with regard to the evangelization of the world, and at two evening meetings, one in Edinburgh and one in Glasgow, on the sufficiency of God.

Appointed to a small subcommittee with Cairns and W. H. Frere, he helped draft the messages from the conference to the church. No record of particular authorship has survived, but his sentiments marked each message. To the members of the church in Christian lands, the conference announced that the missionary enterprise had "reached a greater unity of common action than has been attained in the Christian Church for centuries," but to carry it forward, "every member of the Church" and not just missionaries needed to share in the task. To the members of the Christian church in non-Christian lands, the conference offered thanks "for the spirit of evangelistic energy which you are showing," and "for the longing after unity which is so prominent among you," and "for all the inspiration that your example has brought to us in our home-lands." In a version of the Anderson-Venn formula, the conference said: "It is you alone who can ultimately finish this work: the word that under God convinces your own people must be your word; and the life which will win them for Christ must be the life of holiness and moral power, as set forth by you who are men of their own race."[62]

When he later offered his personal evaluation of Edinburgh, he emphasized these very themes. He found the gathering remarkable for "the general unity of view among so many and so divergent minds, the absence of discord even over questions which are threatening to divide communions within themselves, . . . the avoidance of unimportant disagreement which seemed instinctive rather than deliberate." And it was very important, he added, that the delegates "appreciated and recognized in a new way the place of the native Church in the aim of Missions and in the evangelization of the world."[63]

Edinburgh led him into something new and unexpected. He had never been country- or region-specific in his foreign mission work, open to taking the gospel anywhere and everywhere, despite the fact that he had responsibility for several distinct missions with his board. Latin America became the exception to this after 1910. The exact course of events that led him to make this exception remain obscure, but events at Edinburgh were clearly the turning point in his thinking. He had made initial and very brief acquaintance with Latin America in 1894 when he went to Mexico on his first missionary trip. In the years that followed, his administrative work brought him into some contact with Latin American issues. When the Interdenominational Conference reviewed its first decade, he had responded to a question about causes for advances or declines that the situation in Latin American countries was complex, for there was both "an increased realization of their need, coupled with an increased dislike of America, because of our course in the Spanish War, and our shaking the 'big stick' in the Monroe Doctrine."[64]

Latin America

Latin America had entered his life in a major way in the planning for Edinburgh after 1907. As a member of the American committee, he faced the issue of the scope of the meeting. The proposal that succeeded was to invite only those boards and agencies with missions to non-Christians. It had the strong support of the British committee, especially the Anglican members, who opposed missions to persons who were Christian. Some Anglicans argued that their church would not join the conference on any other terms. The decision omitted some Protestant missions in Europe but, more importantly, all Protestant work in Latin America. He led the argument against the exclusion and found many in sympathy with his views, but not enough to change the decision. Oldham said it was the "gravest issue" he faced in preparing for Edinburgh.[65]

Right in the midst of his dissatisfaction with the Edinburgh decision, he left for his second trip to Latin America. Some have inferred, Mackay for one, a connection between these events, but no hard evidence for it has surfaced.[66] Speer left in May 1909 and spent almost half a year visiting a large part of South America. He returned on fire for the cause of "evangelical" foreign missions there. Latin America was technically a Christian region, so Protestants often described their efforts there as "evangelical," an adjective rarely used with their work in other parts of the world.

He began speaking and writing about missions to Latin America as soon as he returned home, and he elicited some quick responses. One correspondent heard him speak and advised him in a friendly spirit to cast his argument more judiciously and broadly to "Romanists and non-Romanists instead of seeming to appeal to non-Romanists against Romanists. Otherwise, the great bulk of your hearers go away with only a dim realization that you have been making an argument for missions to South America but with a very distinct impression that you have poured hot shot into the Roman Catholic Church."[67] Speer concurred and began subsequent talks on the subject with some "preliminary observations." The best example of this came at the sixth quadrennial of the SVM in

Rochester, New York. Meeting just prior to his departure for the Duff Lectures, he used platform time twice to lift up Latin America, once in a brief and statistical way, defining "South America's Appeal," and again in a substantial argumentative speech on "The Spiritual Claims of Latin America upon the United States and Canada." Although his observations were meant to turn aside some criticisms, they were sincere opinions. He was not, he said, opposed to the Roman Catholic Church. While he believed it was in error, he also believed it "held, in part, the saving truth, and we are not willing to be driven into any attitude of hostility or lack of sympathy or prejudice with regard to it." Moreover, his critique did not include the Roman Catholic Church in the United States, Canada, or Europe, for in those places he believed it was "a great religious force; that it holds, with us, the fundamental truth of the deity of our Lord; and that to no other body should the conditions in South America appeal more strongly." There were those who wished to start a war with the Roman Catholic Church in Latin America, but he was not among them. He hoped, instead, for a "cleansing of that great organization," as a preface to the reunion of all Christians into "the one universal Church."[68]

The substance of his argument turned on what he believed to be the great "moral, intellectual, and religious need to be found in Latin American lands." He offered his large student audience a great deal of factual information to establish the "grounds" of the need, and then addressed the major religious issues. There was a severe shortage of priests, joined unfortunately to a substantial lack of respect for the clergy in general. To substantiate such claims, he used data produced by Latin American Catholic officials, but he moved to less secure and more theological ground when he claimed, "The people of South America are a people practically without any real religion." What he meant was that many or most were nominal Christians. They were at fault for not taking their faith seriously; but so was the church, for it was not giving the people access "to the living Christ at all." "We went," he said, "to more than eighty churches in South America. In not one of all those churches was there a symbol or a picture or a suggestion of the resurrection or of the ascension—not one. In every case Christ was either dead upon the cross or He was a ghastly figure, lying in a grave. Where is the living Christ? a man cries out again and again as he travels up and down South America and no voice answers him in reply."

The spiritual need became a spiritual obligation for Protestants who could give what Latin America needed. "We owe them," he argued, "a response to their brotherly call of need. We owe them Christ and spiritual freedom. . . . And we have not paid that debt." He named the handful of Protestant missions at work and appealed for help: "Surely now at last the day has come for us to take up our obligation to these Latin American peoples." He closed with a story. One night their boat had docked on the bank of the Magdalena River to take on fuel. He heard a noise that sounded like someone falling overboard and then a rush of footsteps and a cry from the rushing waters: "Oh Hombre." In the morning he discovered that a man had apparently fallen asleep and the motion of the boat had rolled him overboard, and he was lost. Translating "hombre" as "friend," he said the man's cry was in fact "the cry of many millions of South American peoples making earnest, if silent, appeal for the things that in Christ we have to give. 'O Friend!' That voice calls to you, men and women of Canada and the United States. Will it find in you the heart of a friend, to reply?"[69]

Latin America became a major issue during his stay in Scotland. In April he wrote that it seemed "at last as though the churches were waking up to take some interest in South America, and we certainly have stirred up the Roman Catholic papers in the United States, which are denouncing the documents which we have been quoting from their own authorities as spurious, because they are unprepared to believe the facts as these documents recognize them."[70] Then at Edinburgh he shared leadership of two rump sessions to raise the issue. The first was a lunch meeting with some friends, including "several missionaries from Latin America," one of whom explained that the purpose of the meeting was "to discuss the restoration of Latin America to its rightful place in the missionary program of the Protestant Church." Quite informal, it led to a more formal gathering to which were invited "a number of board secretaries with responsibility for work in Latin America." The officials agreed that proper assessment of Latin American problems required a conference on the Edinburgh model and promised to provide such a meeting.[71]

Speer emerged as the leader. He presented the matter to his colleagues at the Foreign Missions Conference and they appointed him chairman of a committee on Latin American missions. Working with his committee he arranged the Conference on Missions in Latin America, which met March 12–13, 1913, at the office of the Presbyterian Board in New York. Delegates attended from American and Canadian agencies with work in Latin America and represented home as well as foreign mission boards. He chaired the conference and made the opening presentation, "Survey of Present Mission Work." The subject of their meeting, he told the delegates, was all the more important because "of its omission from consideration by other missionary conferences within the last few years." Painful as that had been, he believed that the exclusion, especially from Edinburgh, had drawn more attention to work in Latin America and had helped highlight its urgency.[72] The extended meeting, two days instead of the one devoted to missions in China or Japan, was necessary because this was their first meeting. The subject, he reminded them, was missions in Latin America and not the Roman Catholic Church.

Ground rules established, he surveyed the field in a highly statistical manner, naming the missions and their various kinds of work. The data justified describing Latin America as "a neglected missionary field."[73] At its close the conference adopted a motion: "that Mr. Robert Speer be requested to associate, with himself, two brethren of two other denominations, to deal with his whole subject of the work in Latin America and especially with the question of cooperation, and to make any presentation they may deem desirable to the Boards." That marked the birth of the Committee on Cooperation in Latin America, working with the FMC and reporting annually to it.

The conference was the end of the beginning. In the roughly four years since his trip to South America, Speer had almost single-handedly moved that continent from a mission field largely abandoned by Protestants to a major area of concern. He had also written two books, *Missions in South America* in 1910 and *South American Problems* in 1912, the former his report of his trip and the latter a mission study book published by the SVM. In the three years after this conference he advanced South America to the front and center as a full partner in the foreign missionary enterprise. As a first step he enlarged the Committee on Cooperation by inviting each interested board to name its official representative. His committee began to discuss the possibility of a missionary conference in the region and to that end sent letters of inquiry to missionaries serving there. And he hired the Rev. Samuel Guy Inman, a Disciples of Christ missionary to Mexico, to work as committee secretary.

Inman began February 12, 1915, in an office next to Speer at the Presbyterian board and tackled his first assignment, organizing the Congress on Christian Work in Latin America, scheduled to be held in Panama in February 1916. Speer helped raise funds, often from the same persons who gave generously to his own board, and shared in designing the program.[74] Following the suggestion made at Edinburgh, the plan for the congress was virtually identical to the plan used at Edinburgh. Eight commissions studied various aspects of the Latin American situation and sent preliminary reports to the delegates. As he prepared to depart for

Panama, he confided to a close friend: "It has been pretty severely criticized from both extremes. From the High Church Episcopalians because it is anti-Roman, and by the ultra-Protestants because it is not anti-Roman enough. From this you can gather that it is probably pretty close to the true attitude."[75]

Professor Eduardo Monteverde of the University of Uruguay convened and presided over the congress, with Speer chairing the working sessions and Mott the business ones. Roman Catholics were invited to attend, but none did; instead, the Roman Catholic archbishop chose to denounce it. Compared to Edinburgh it marked "a definite advance," in the sense that "it was a conference of nationals and missionaries in Latin America," rather than of home base secretaries and executives.[76] Despite outside opposition and some inner differences, the congress worked to a successful conclusion. Before adjournment the delegates decided to continue cooperative work and unanimously named the Committee on Cooperation as the agent to achieve it.

Speer immediately set about making certain the congress would bear fruit. He gave talks, wrote positive evaluations for a variety of religious periodicals, and prepared a book, *The Unity of the Americas*, which the Educational Committee of the Missionary Education Movement published as a mission study textbook.[77] He told readers in the introduction that he proposed to offer them new information about South America and to "quicken the desire" for more unity among the Americas than currently existed. He based his exposition heavily on the materials prepared by the Panama commissions, especially when he dealt with the religious issues, where he simply reproduced large sections of the reports of commission I, on survey and occupation, and commission II, on message and method. He was not trying to be original but to spread the word and introduce as many people as possible to the work of the congress. At the end of the book he returned to his own words, recalling the sense of obligation he had placed before the students at Rochester six years earlier at the beginning of his crusade for Protestant missions in Latin America, but also announcing a hope for future successes, now possible because of what he had helped accomplish. He concluded, "In the light of all the facts it is declared, and surely with justice, that the evangelical churches have a fundamental obligation to extend their help to Latin America and that evangelical Christianity need not hesitate to declare that through acceptance and application of the gospel of Christ, the highest hopes of the earnest leaders of Latin America can be fulfilled wherein they are right, and transcended wherein they are imperfect; and that the true welfare of

212   ROBERT E. SPEER

the republics can be realized in the establishment of what Jesus meant by the kingdom of God."[78]

The years following the congress were full of growth for Protestantism in South America. Committees on cooperation emerged in Brazil and Mexico and eventually led to national councils of evangelicals in both nations. He and Inman remained very much involved but in a secondary role, a fact clearly highlighted at the second Congress on Christian Work in Latin America, held in Montevideo, Uruguay, in March and April 1925. Speer chaired the business committee and led in organizing the congress, but there his responsibilities ended. The presiding officer was Erasmo Braga, former moderator of the Presbyterian Church in Brazil. The sessions, held in Spanish, were run by Latin Americans or missionaries. The North Americans said little, and Speer never mounted the platform. After all was said and done, he edited the official report.[79] It had been good to meet Braga, he told Cairns, and "to see how solid they have their feet on the ground. It was clear that these Churches in South America are just as indigenous as the Roman Catholic Church; some much more so."[80] That was another way of saying that evangelical missions had fulfilled the Anderson-Venn vision very quickly. Although historians have noted the "striking advance in Evangelical Christianity" in the years between Panama and Montevideo, and have credited the missionaries and the Latin American leaders, they have rarely properly acknowledged Speer's leadership.[81] His vision and determination not only offered rebirth to Protestant missions in South America, but also prefigured the Good Neighbor policy subsequently developed by his nation.[82]

The International Missionary Council

Growth of evangelical missions in Latin America was one of the unexpected consequences of Edinburgh. The expected result was the emergence of some kind of permanent international missionary agency. The prospects for that looked bright in the afterglow of Edinburgh. Mott and Oldham steered the continuation committee through a series of meetings, including the one that turned out to be the last at The Hague in the Netherlands in 1913. Speer served in relatively minor roles on a number of special committees on topics such as missionary survey and occupation, and Christian education in the mission field. All these efforts came to a crashing halt with the eruption of World War I. Speaking for himself, but undoubtedly reflecting the views of many in the missionary establishment, a few months after war began Speer noted: "One of the most dreadful consequences of the war has been the rupture of the international fellowships which have been so laboriously built up, and to which the Edinburgh Conference made so great a contribution. . . . The unification of the Protestant missionary forces of the world has been halted, and greater difficulty has been developed in the Roman Catholic Church, whose bishops are arrayed across the gulf of racial hate and war."[83]

Deterred but not defeated, Mott, Oldham, and others created in London an emergency committee that functioned to hold the tenuous international fellowship together until after the war. A group of missionary leaders, including Mott and Oldham, met in Crans, Switzerland, in the summer of 1920, informally but practically as the extension of the continuation and emergency committees.[84] They laid plans for the creation of a new and permanent international missionary organization. In October 1921 delegates gathered at Lake Mohonk in New York and formed the International Missionary Council (IMC), fulfilling a dream of many missionary leaders dating back to the London gathering in 1888. They chose Mott chairman, a position he held until 1941.

The IMC began to meet periodically, in different locations around the world, working to be ever more inclusive of different branches of the Christian church and striving always to achieve greater cooperation in the missionary task. Speer fully agreed with its goals but was not often involved in the meetings. The Oxford Conference in 1923 invited him to prepare a paper on the question "Is Identity of Doctrinal Opinion Necessary to Continued Missionary Co-operation?" Unable to attend, he sent the paper, which made a powerful impression on the delegates, and opened the issue for discussion in "a penetrating and suggestive way."[85] He acknowledged that doctrinal differences among missionaries had prevented cooperation at times in the past and continued to keep some individuals and groups apart, but missionary experience showed much cooperation in spite of doctrinal differences. Ever in search of principles of missions, he offered what he called on this occasion some "generalized conclusions." Cooperation in the form of "organic church unity" required "a clear measure of agreement" both in matters of doctrine and church polity. This had happened in the Church of Christ in Japan and in the United Church of Southern India and in some other cases, but in these unions the uniting groups had "kindred" backgrounds.

Although he believed the future for organic unions between groups with similar traditions looked good, there were also useful principles for those groups that had major differences. Cooperation short of such organic union "has been found possible wherever the members involved trusted one another as fellow-Christians and possessed the agreement of view essential to the co-operative conduct of the particular work involved." There existed cooperatively run hospitals, theological schools, and presses, and although none of the tasks those institutions performed technically required doctrinal agreement, they worked to the degree that the parties involved truly trusted one another.

Of course, some believed that doctrine was important to running a hospital or a theological school. In those cases the rule of trust gave way, and he offered in its place his personal opinion, which was his proposal for the fundamental basis of all cooperative action. He did not believe, he said, identity of opinion on the "whole body of Christian doctrine" was essential to cooperation. The Bushnell terms he used were likely lost on that largely European audience, but his argument struck home when he claimed that "in many matters a diversity of view which assures a fuller apprehension and presentation of the truth than any one individual or group of individuals can achieve is desirable, is indeed the very *raison d'etre* both of our individualism and of our fellowships, but that one thing only is essential, and that is that we should hold a fundamentally unitary faith in and about our Lord Jesus Christ as He is set forth in the New Testament." Any genuine cooperation required a new and broader level of tolerance. Missionaries had survived in some measure due to the tolerance between themselves and the non-Christian religions wherever they went. If Christians had tolerated non-Christians until they won them over by friendship and love, should not "a spirit of love and tolerance similar in principle . . . prevail within the Christian fellowship among people who call themselves Christians?" "One wonders," he mused in closing, "whether it would not be well for us to try to live yet more fully by these normal and regulative ideals of comprehension before we venture too far on the difficult path of judgment and excommunication where our human frailties have ever too free a play."[86]

The Jerusalem Meeting, 1928

The climax of Speer's participation in IMC ventures came at the important Jerusalem meeting in 1928, during his term as moderator of the Presbyterian Church. It became his last large missionary gathering, since he retired before the next one met in Madras in 1938. Planning for Jerusalem had begun in 1925, with hopes for a wide representation from the emerging churches on the mission field, what had come to be called the younger churches. Mott played the major role in inviting the delegates and shaping the agenda. Jerusalem attracted representatives from fifty nations. Continental European churches were heavily represented, as were the younger churches, which supplied fully one-fourth of the delegates.[87]

In preparation and structure, Jerusalem bore some resemblances to Edinburgh. Planners chose a series of topics and invited preliminary papers, which were distributed to the delegates prior to the meeting for study. Mott presided at the plenary sessions, where delegates heard one or more presentations on each topic and had the opportunity to discuss them in turn. But Jerusalem had a much more complex organization and more difficult task than the Edinburgh meeting almost two decades earlier or any of the other prior international meetings. The organizers had chosen a principal subject, the Christian Life and Message in Relation to Non-Christian Systems of Life and Thought, shortened in the discussions to the "Message," and modified in its final published form to "the Christian Message." This received almost twice the plenary session time of the other topics. Delegates were divided into small groups to consider the several topics in greater detail and regrouped in even smaller groups to work as "drafting committees" to prepare statements for council consideration and adoption. The IMC meeting became, therefore, a deliberative body, structured in such a way "that each subject was brought effectively before each member of the Council, and so far as possible the experience and knowledge of each country was brought to bear upon each subject."[88] Jerusalem issued a series of declarative statements as well as the traditional message.

The Jerusalem meeting opened on schedule on March 24 and met through the Easter season, closing on Easter Sunday. Costs had reduced the number of delegates to about 240 but did not affect their representative character. A recent earthquake did not create any delays, although it did change the housing arrangements, forcing the men to live in a barracks and tents and the women in a Russian Orthodox convent. Mott launched the conference in an exuberant mood, thrilled with the truly ecumenical character of the delegates seated before him: "We, of so many races and communions coming from all continents, doubtless represent more truly than any other gathering in the history of the Church the vast world field which Jesus Christ had in view when, near the spot where we are now gathered, He gave His disciples the Great Commission."[89] A historian of the ecumenical movement has agreed, calling it "the first truly representative, global assembly of Christians in the long history of the church."[90] Mott outlined his expectations in each of the topic areas, and then in general. Hopefully, he said, Jerusalem would be the place for "nothing less than the rebirth of the world Christian mission."[91]

Speer played a central role at the meeting, a more important role than in any of the previous international meetings he attended, and an absolutely crucial one in helping to determine its outcome. The focus of his contribution was the principal topic, and his work fell into four distinct stages. At the entry level the conference planners invited him to direct the American preparations for the message. William Temple, then bishop of Manchester and subsequently archbishop of York and then Canterbury, directed preparations in Great Britain. This involved soliciting, gathering, and distributing preconference reports. Once the conference convened, a new stage appeared as the two men became cochairs of the committee on the message. They shared leadership of the morning sessions devoted to it. Assuming that the delegates had taken the preconference materials seriously, they decided to dispense with public presentations and moved directly to the discussion. Speer initiated it with an opening statement, and Temple drew it to a conclusion.

Regrettably, the exact words of these sessions have not survived, but only abstracts prepared by the secretaries. Speer offered some distinctions between past conferences, Edinburgh in particular, and the present one. At Edinburgh the message had taken a back seat to "carrying the Gospel to the world," and the focus had been on "a survey of the fields yet to be occupied." Here, he said, the focus was on the message, "the Christian message," in its relation to "non-Christian systems." He did not note that he had helped chair the sessions at Edinburgh that had moved the issue front and center at Jerusalem. The issue before them, he said, was the question "Is there a Christian message which is distinctive?" He believed the answer was yes, but that it needed to be stated in the context of their time, in response not only to the non-Christian religions, but to the "new secularistic and naturalistic view that has spread across the world." And the message needed to be stated in personal terms, rather than in academic or theoretical ones, directed to real men and women, for real people espoused the various systems. He stressed the need to speak more directly to women, too often and too long neglected by the church. Their business together, as the secretaries recorded Speer's words, "was first to discern and to proclaim those elements in Christianity which were essential and universal and which were held in trust for all mankind; secondly, to disentangle Christ from all that confused and obscured Him, from all that perplexed men needlessly; and thirdly, to implicate Christ in realms in which He had not yet been implicated and which belonged to His

Lordship and through which He could be known by the evidence of His healing and redeeming power."[92]

The discussion that ensued attracted a number of the most active and thoughtful leaders in Christendom, many of them Speer's old friends and one of them his wife. Hendrik Kraemer of the Netherlands Bible Society spoke, as did A. K. Reischauer of the Japan Mission of the Presbyterian Church in the U.S.A., Karl Heim of the University of Tübingen, E. Stanley Jones, a missionary to India of the Methodist Episcopal Church, Francis Wei of the Central China Christian University, K. T. Paul of the YMCAs of India, Burma, and Ceylon, Zwemer of the American Christian Literature Society for Moslems, W. E. Hocking of Harvard University, McConnell of the Board of Foreign Missions of the Methodist Episcopal Church, and Erasmo Braga of the Committee on Cooperation in Brazil. Emma, representing the National Board of the YWCA, declared, "If there was one thing to which the Church was summoned it was to face the implications of our Lord's teaching about women."[93] Speer found Kraemer's presentation "impressive" and Hocking's "helpful."[94] Temple presented a careful and balanced summary, suggesting that the apparent differences of opinion were not serious, but reflected a deeper unity. No one disputed Kraemer's call for a "really Christian world-view," or challenged Emma's emphasis on women. The delegates, Temple urged, "must insist that the universality of the claims of Christ applies to all of these regions of life," by which he meant all the various non-Christian systems they had discussed. The message, he declared, had not changed. It remained "Jesus as Saviour of the whole world, Jesus as the King of all life in every conceivable activity."[95]

As the meeting moved forward from discussion to deliberation, Speer's involvement moved to another stage. He and Temple led a small committee through the process of formulating and preparing the message for presentation. Their challenge was to create one whole out of the myriad pieces that had emerged from the various discussions. Although the manuscripts from which they worked do not appear to have survived, clues about their method have. Both men said they worked from drafts. Temple described the work as "quite easy. We got the various sections so to state their own views that they were compatible with one another; and then it was only a matter of putting the bits together in the right order."[96] Speer reported that in one of their meetings "two of the men from Asia raised the question whether we other men from the West were not falling altogether too much into Western modes of thought and Western forms of expression." The Westerners replied that they thought what they had writ-

ten   was
generally universal but invited the Asians to go off and draw up a draft.
When the committee next met and the Westerners asked to see the draft,
the two men refused to show it. When asked why, they said, "We find that
what we have written is more Western than what you have written." Speer
recounted this story to make the point that "the great historic statements
of the Christian church had universalized themselves already. . . . They
were not racial; they were not sectional; they were just reaching out after
the great truth of the whole body of mankind." He also revealed that the
message had been the result of a truly cooperative effort.[97]

Apparently Temple put the document in its finished form, what one
historian has called "the final summary."[98] As he presented the committee
report to the delegates for their consideration and vote, a hush fell over the
audience. "Our Message is Jesus Christ," he read. "He is the revelation of
what God is and of what man through Him may become." The document
embraced the statement of the World Conference on Faith and Order that
had met the previous year at Lausanne, thereby linking two of the world
ecumenical movements that had grown out of Edinburgh. It affirmed that
the motive for sharing this message was that it "is the answer to the world's
greatest need. It is not our discovery or achievement; it rests on what we
recognize as an act of God." The call went out to Christians to give evidence that they testified to Christ's message "in their own lives and in the
social institutions which they uphold." But it went also to non-Christians
and secularists, made in full awareness that God's light was also revealed
in their religious traditions and systems, in their scientific or intellectual
visions of the world. Echoing Speer, the call, finally, was "not to systems
of opinion only, but to human beings, to men and women for whom
Christ died. . . . The Gospel must be expressed also in simplicity and love,
and offered to men's hearts and minds by word and deed and life, by righteousness and loving-kindness, by justice, sympathy, and compassion, by
ministry to human needs and to the deep want of the world."[99] Given a
day to reflect on the proposed message, the delegates adopted it by a
unanimous standing vote.

Historians have been at odds about the authorship of this stirring document, forming two schools of thought. Some have claimed it was
"chiefly" Temple's work, doubtless influenced by his role in presenting it
to the conference.[100] Others have argued more accurately for shared
authorship. One historian approached Emma Speer several years after her
husband's death and asked her to check his files for his draft. She could
not find one and told him: "As a matter of fact, the authorship of the

Jerusalem message is not really important and my husband would be the last to claim or to want credit. The only thing that matters is the value of the message which I hope is still ringing down the years."[101] Without a draft, there was insufficient evidence to identify individual contributions, and the historian concluded, "I think that the best that can be said is that it was the product of their joint authorship."[102] In describing the formulation of the message to his wife, Temple carefully called it "our report" and "our Message."[103] Some years after Jerusalem, Speer wrote that one of the special events of his life had been "drafting with Temple as Co-chairman the Jerusalem Message."[104]

When the meeting adjourned Easter Sunday afternoon, its work was not done. There remained the task of communicating the message to the world, a task that moved him onto the fourth and final, and doubtless the most time-consuming, stage of his work. At the close of the meeting, members of the IMC met to discuss how to disseminate the reports, particularly the message. He proposed a volume be printed on it, and they accepted his plan, naming him its editor. In addition, Mott, speaking for them, agreed that Speer "should prepare the interpretive report of the discussions of the plenary meetings on the Message" and concurred with his proposal to solicit several papers prepared just for the volume on topics that would highlight aspects of the message, including one by Kraemer. Mott thanked his old friend and told him, "I do not think we can easily exaggerate the importance of having such a volume and of making it absolutely first-class in every respect."[105]

The fruit of his labor appeared as *The Christian Message*, volume one in the eight-volume set on Jerusalem. The superb editing work deviated from his plan in only one major instance. Because Kraemer's health prevented him from preparing a paper, Speer wrote on the topic assigned to Kraemer: "What Is the Value of the Religious Values of the Non-Christian Religions?" This had emerged as a key question in the preconference gatherings, especially one held for many of the continental European delegates. They feared that many of the preliminary papers reflected a syncretism, an effort to merge those things that were "good" in other religions into Christianity, which some believed would make it an entirely different religion. The same anxiety had appeared in post meeting critiques. He developed his argument about the "values of the religious values" carefully. His theory will be discussed in depth in chapter 8.

In explanation and defense of the message, he pointed out that the problem for some of the delegates and some distant observers lay in Jerusalem's methodology. The IMC had decided to confine its attention only to the "values" and deliberately omitted "the faults, shortcomings, and defects." The purpose was "to find the most effective and persuasive approach for the Christian message," and he hoped "the actual presentation of Christianity to the non-Christian peoples may prove ultimately to be a full vindication of the method."[106] Offering his view of the message, Speer said it declared that Christianity was both unique and universal. "In so far as the Council could speak for the missionary enterprise and for the Christian Church both in the older branches of it and on the mission field," he concluded, "there is to be no attempt at an amalgamated religion. The missionary enterprise will not be a search for a more adequate and satisfactory religion than Christianity. It will be the offer of the only Lord and Saviour Jesus Christ to the whole world and the common effort of Christian men of all lands and races to explore and experience His unsearchable riches, infinite and inexhaustible."[107]

From Speer's earliest days with the Student Volunteer Movement and the predecessors of the International Missionary Council, those who planned the larger meetings had typically offered him a platform for a spiritual address, whatever his other assignments. The organizers at Jerusalem did the same, inviting him to give the sermon at the closing Easter Sunday service. Many aspects of the meeting stirred him, from the serious discussions to the remarkable and truly ecumenical fellowship. Just as important was the land, the environment, the opportunity to walk where Jesus had walked and to experience, centuries apart in time, what the first disciples had experienced. When he had decided to attend the meeting, he had written his Aunt Clara that he had "longed all my life to get to Syria and Palestine," and he was not disappointed.[108]

He joined those attending the conference Maundy Thursday for a communion service by the Jaffa Gate, where they sat down, "men and women of all lands and races and branches of the one Christian Church." They walked to the Mount of Olives and sat in the Garden of Gethsemane and prayed together. And they went early Easter morning to the tomb, where they read the Easter story and then made their way up the mount "to the German Hospice" where they sat in memory and expectation of Christ.[109] There, on the Mount of Olives, in sight of both Calvary and the empty tomb, he preached on "The Resurrection." It was, he affirmed, the "controlling principle of our Christian life," and the "foundation of the Christian faith." He quoted Paul, "the boldest and most massive mind in the early Church," on the centrality of the resurrection and reminded them that it was his experience of the resurrection, of the presence of the living Christ, that had transformed him. The resurrection was also the "assurance of the Christian hope," a hope they needed. "Often," he continued, "during these days when we have been discussing, perhaps light-heartedly, the question of the security of missionaries and the establishment of the Church my mind has turned to the cost and method of all real spiritual and creative achievements," to what he called the "law of the grain," which must die in order to bring forth new life. "The morning is ever breaking," he concluded, "for those who know the meaning of Easter Day."[110]

Many of the leaders of the Jerusalem meeting declared that it fulfilled the hopes and dreams of Edinburgh. In particular, it was the most truly ecumenical of all the great missionary conferences, in both theological and geographical terms. Speer took special pleasure in the participation of a small but important group of representatives who helped make that true: delegates from Latin America. Although present not so much because of Edinburgh but in spite of it, they were full participants and brought the voices of a previously silent continent to the ecumenical discussion.

Speer began his venture in the largely undeveloped realm of ecumenical foreign missionary organizations in the 1890s, with the Interdenominational Conference, a very small group of missionary executives hesitantly probing the future. Much of the ecumenical life of the twentieth century in the United States and the world flowed directly from that source, more of it inspired by him than anyone has recognized. There was no prime mover, but there were key leaders in Europe and the United States, and he was one of those. He stepped forward at crucial times to offer ideas and inspiration, like the opening ceremony at Edinburgh and the closing service at Jerusalem. And he helped launch a new phase in the ecumenical (in the Protestant context) missionary work in Latin America. He shared in these ventures because he believed in them, and because he saw them as part of his ministry.

CHAPTER 8

The History and Theory of Missions

"O Zion, Haste"

Robert Speer had a lifetime interest in the history and theory of foreign missions. As deeply involved as he was in his board and the ecumenical foreign missionary organizations, he never permitted administrative duties to crowd out his historical and theoretical studies. He believed they contributed to his work as much as, if not more than, anything else he did. Books, articles, and speeches in these areas flowed from his pen, creating a virtual flood. They were greater in number than those about Jesus or the Bible or the more practical aspects of foreign missions. History provided a glimpse of the way that had led to the present, with all the turns and detours as well as stretches of open road, and, more important, contact with those who had served as guides. Theory meant reflection and analysis of the nature and purpose of foreign missions, and it brought into clearer focus basic principles and those who had first enunciated them. He published his first major historical study in 1898 and his first theoretical one in 1902, early in his career. While he was recognized as an emerging leader in foreign missions before he wrote them, the books enhanced his position and set him apart as a person of unusual perspective and thoughtfulness. By the end of his career he had achieved a wide reputation as both a historian and a theoretician of foreign missions.

Although he based his historical and theoretical studies on the same data base, carefully gathered from his extensive reading program and his interviews with missionaries and others, he used distinct methodologies in preparing them. For most of the historical ones, he chose a straightforward narrative to describe the development of foreign missions in an era or a region of the world. More than half of his histories were biographies of missionaries. For the theoretical ones, he restated a theory from the past or formulated a new one and then developed a series of supporting arguments and illustrations. The resulting volumes were quite different in subject and form, but they had a deeper thematic unity. They were a significant part of his effort to share one of his most profound convictions about the Christian faith: its universality. He used his histories to demonstrate how foreign missions had begun to meet the needs of the world everywhere, which revealed that the Christian faith was geographically universal. He used his theoretical works to demonstrate that the Christian faith was a universal religion. Even though he never stated a preference for history over theory, perhaps because he believed they both worked to the same end, he nevertheless had a greater interest in history.

Ideas About History

History had attracted his attention when he was quite young, and he had the good fortune to have a series of teachers who nurtured his interest. He stood first in his class in history at both Phillips and Princeton. It was not only his best subject in college but his favorite one, despite the efforts of "our old physics professor" to persuade him to study medicine and "old Dr. McCosh" to lure him to teach in the philosophy department.[1] Many of his school and college papers were on historical topics, and some of them revealed an interest in the nature and purpose of history.[2] His valedictory had been an affirmation of the uses of the past in the context of a growing liberalism that proposed cutting away from it. By the time he left college, he was reading history on a regular basis and storing away the stories of events and people that would one day appear in his books and speeches. In *A Young Man's Questions*, he advised readers, "Next to the joy of doing good to those whom he can help, a young man will get his greatest pleasure in life from reading." "History and Politics" was the number one category of books he recommended.[3]

The end of his formal education did not interrupt his inquiry into the larger historical questions. In the process of writing history, he formulated a set of convictions about its nature, incorporating his earlier views and extending them. They constituted, in very general terms, his philosophy of history, although he never described them as such. His fundamental conviction was the reality of history. Simply put, facts were facts. Jesus of Nazareth lived, died, and rose from the dead. He disagreed with those who adopted the "whole Ritschlian view," named for the German theologian Albrecht Ritschl, "who think that our new scientific forms make the old historic forms of Christianity untenable and who still desire to hold as much as possible of the moral and spiritual values which the old forms enshrine." He believed that the values of the past were inextricably bound to the data of the past and that to separate them, to remove the values from their historical context, was as impossible as trying "to carry a pint of milk in anything but a receptacle."[4]

A related but distinct idea was that there was a vital connection between the past and the present. Some acknowledged that the past had been real, but argued that it was dead and of no use in the present and that the only way forward was to reject it. He regarded that as "silly talk" and in response echoed the theme he had used in his valedictory: "that time is not mechanical but organic; that the present is only the projected and continuing past, and that the past, so far from being closed and complete, is all open and contingent, waiting for the full determination of its character upon the loyalty or disloyalty of the present and the future."[5] Time and again he cited two of his mentors on this point. Trumbull had addressed a Fourth of July celebration at Northfield on "Our Duty to Make the Past a Success," using as his text the passage in Hebrews: "And these all, having obtained a good report through faith, received not the promise; God having provided some better thing for us, that they without us should not be made perfect."[6] Bushnell, in his speech "Our Obligations to the Dead," had proposed that the living owed the dead thanks for what they had created and passed on and the completion of those things they had begun but had not lived to finish. "So often," Speer said, "we think of the past as though it were something finished and laid away, not realizing that it is all unfinished and incomplete, and depending on those who follow to carry to its fulfillment the work the past began."[7]

He modified this slightly on occasion, making the past an active force. Speaking on the occasion of Mackay's installation as president of Princeton Theological Seminary in 1937, he reminded his younger colleague, "The very nature of the past is something to build upon, something to go on with. It is not something to be left behind. It is something to carry forward. The past is the source of momentum for advance. . . . It is too often we who are hesitant and slow, while the Past chides us and presses on us and seeks to urge us to move forward in our day as the Past moved in its day. This movement of life is the essential note of authentic Christianity, the Christianity of the New Testament. The Gospel itself was a new covenant. Its inner principle was growth."[8]

He expanded on his earlier views about the lessons history taught. They were both individual and collective, positive and negative, but he usually emphasized the individual and positive ones. He typically began a history of foreign missions in a region by listing the challenges the missionaries faced and invariably concluded it by describing the successes of their missions, even if they had been quite modest. The lessons varied but, as often as not, turned on the willingness of the missionaries to sacrifice their own interests to meet the needs of the people they served, in short, to behave as true disciples of Jesus.

A final idea, visible in his earliest thinking but more prominent as he began to write for publication, was the importance of persons in history. Jesus was by far the most important person, with Paul a close second. His view was not a version of what some historians have called "the great man theory of history." Although he wrote about the great missionary leaders, like Carey and Livingstone, he also traced the lives of many relatively unknown people who believed themselves to be "in Christ" and with that faith worked changes, however small. His choices reflected his belief that most of history was made by inconspicuous men and women who faithfully went about their callings. "The great work of the world," he argued, "was done by mothers in the homes, teaching little children; by school teachers in obscure country districts, shaping the ideals of honor and truth of little boys and girls; the great work of the world was that done by the moral forces content to work in silence and obscurity."[9] Consider, he proposed, the years just before the Protestant Reformation. The "real event" that was happening took place "in an obscure German village" where "a miner's wife was bringing forth her firstborn son," and later "taught him to despise lies with all his will, and to love purity and honor and justice."[10] Publishers refused some of his biographies, particularly those of Louise Andrews, Charles Lewis, and George Bowen, because the subjects were not well enough known to attract buyers. Undeterred and fully convinced of the worthiness of the message of their lives, market or no market, he either solicited financial support from friends or published them himself.

Historical and Biographical Work

These several convictions constituted the premises of his historical and biographical work. He could have used them to forge a career that included a wide range of historical study, following some of the interests awakened in school and college, like the Civil War. He never did. His missionary call controlled this part of his life just as it did all other parts of it, and he almost never wrote a history or a full biography that was unrelated to foreign missionary work. Near the end of his life he became intrigued with the history of the early church and wrote *When Christianity Was New*.

This was church history as distinct from missionary history, but he never separated them, since he believed that the church was, or should understand itself to be, a missionary society. Alice Jackson and John J. Eagan were subjects of full biographies, and although neither was a missionary, each fulfilled a vision of mission. His board turned Jackson down for health reasons, and she redirected her efforts to industrial missions at home. Eagan was a businessman who saw his life in the context of mission. Both were part of what he understood to be the social gospel.[11]

Almost as soon as he began writing history, he received strong, positive endorsements of his work. Trumbull, Ellinwood, and others close to him were enthusiastic. Ellinwood wrote a rave review of *Missions and Modern History* and told him, "The research you have given to this work is simply marvelous. Nothing seems to have escaped your eye, or your pen."[12]

No evidence has been found that Speer ever had either a short- or long-term plan for his historical work. He followed his interests and accepted invitations from publishers of periodicals or from college and university lecture committees as they came. He gave his first lecture series on the history of missions during his senior year at college, when he traveled to New York City to speak to the men employed in a banking firm on the topic "American Missionary History."[13] In addition, his work with the missions and his trips directed his attention to particular areas. His historical work can be grouped in such a way that it encompasses the history of missions, first in the early church, with a focus on Jesus and Paul, and second in the modern church since the late eighteenth century, with greatest emphasis on the nineteenth century. In his one general history of foreign missions, *The Church and Missions*, published in 1926, he gave only ten pages to the era from Constantine in the fourth century to the beginning of modern missions in the late eighteenth.[14] However, in *The Finality of Jesus Christ* he devoted a lengthy chapter to the otherwise missing era.[15] The missionary biographies were almost entirely from the period since 1800 and included some persons who had been members of his missionary flock. The only figure in the long era between the early and modern church to whom he paid serious individual attention was Raymond Lull, the thirteenth-century missionary to the Moslems.

The work was heavily ecumenical. He chose to focus it on Christian missions in general, rather than on the work of any one denomination, including his own. This aspect of his work particularly excited Ellinwood, since he had pioneered such a "comprehensive view" many years earlier in articles in the *Foreign Missionary Magazine*.[16] Speer did, of course, write a good deal about Presbyterian work, including one book in which he surveyed all of it and a large number of shorter pieces in which he described it in one or another mission field. He was also very interested in the missionary work of seminaries and their graduates and directed his attention almost entirely to Presbyterian ones. His interests were primarily in the work overseas, which meant that he never wrote a history of his own board, an important task skillfully completed by his colleague Brown.

He used rich and varied sources for his work. He studied the major histories that were available and began very early to develop his own foreign missions library, which eventually grew to remarkable proportions. Shortly after his conversion, he began to study and store away copies of the *Missionary Review of the World*, and he continued to read it and many other missionary periodicals. A few of his books and articles were based almost entirely on such secondary sources, but most of them also reflected the use of different kinds of primary ones. He gathered considerable first-hand data on his trips, including those to Edinburgh, Jerusalem, and Latin America, from direct observation, interviews, reports, and the inevitable consultations and meetings. He had available to him the board files, those he generated and those from the past. He used them where he could to fill in pieces of a story, but he did so judiciously, careful to omit anything that might identify individuals. And he used his very extensive personal correspondence with a wide variety of people involved in foreign missions work in the same way. He wrote in clear and well-organized fashion, following a chronological outline in most cases, and he included personal testimonies and examples whenever he could, to bring as much life to his story as possible. The resulting narratives had a sense of immediacy and freshness.

While he used various combinations of these sources for all his historical studies, he sought additional ones for his larger biographies. He collected the publications of his subjects and solicited their letters and personal papers from families and friends when it was possible, creating for each one a personal archive. The resulting biographies, based largely on primary sources, broke new ground. When he could, he returned the materials to the people who had loaned them to him, but in some cases no one claimed them, and they have remained part of his own papers. One recent evaluation of his historical studies described them as "synthesized and popularized from good secondary sources."[17] That assessment, accurate to a point, is too sweeping and fails to acknowledge the substantial body of creative and original work he produced, especially the biographies.

He rarely published a longer historical study without explaining his purpose. He wrote about all the regions of the world, including those he believed were neglected, like South America, and those he had never visited, in order to convey the truly universal character of the foreign missionary effort. His first published history, *Missions and Politics in Asia*, originated as a series of lectures at Princeton Theological Seminary based on his world trip. He told his readers the object of his work "was to sketch in broad outline the spirit of the Eastern peoples, the present making of history in Asia and the part therein of Christian Missions. They are at once the fruit and the ground of the conviction, vindicated by the obvious facts of history and of life, that Christ is the present Lord and King of all life and history and their certain goal."[18] He opened his book *The Church and Missions* with the question "How soon did the universal note come into Christianity?" Some scholars argued that it came later, well after Jesus' life and ministry, but Speer claimed that "even if we eliminate the Fourth Gospel and accept the critical results as to the Synoptics, we cannot fail to see that the Gospel held from the beginning in the thought of Jesus the principle of universality. The opening words of the Gospel of Mark set forth the conception of the Kingdom, and the Gospel forbids an exclusively nationalistic interpretation of the conception. . . . The idea of God's fatherhood and of a Kingdom not of Israel but of God, the God Who was behind all things and Who made rains to fall and the sun to shine was an idea wider than any one race or nation."[19] He concluded that book by claiming that the "enterprise of foreign missions" had taken that note seriously and "however inadequately and ineffectively . . . made Him known all over and through the non-Christian world."[20]

Although each of his historical studies had its own character, the one on *Presbyterian Foreign Missions* had many features common to the others. He began with his statement of purpose, hopeful that his effort would give "proof of the power and extent of the missionary enterprise."[21] Using a chronological outline, he traced the development of the Presbyterian missionary movement around the world. He described the early efforts in each region, named the first and honored leaders, and summed up the results of the work. The mission to India, for example, began when two couples, the John Lowries and the William Reeds, sailed from Philadelphia on May 30, 1833. Only John Lowrie survived the ravages of disease to reach his destination, Lodiana in North India, where he established the first American Presbyterian mission station. The Wilsons and the Newtons arrived in 1835 and were followed by many others who opened new stations in surrounding areas. The first convert and native minister, Mr. Goloknath, opened the first station in the Punjab at Jullundar in 1847. Persecution and disease took their toll, but by the end of the nineteenth century, there were five presbyteries of the American church in India, with nearly 150 missionaries, using "every missionary method for bringing the gospel to bear on the lives and wills of the people."[22] He included a brief outline of Indian history and a characterization of the variety and complexity of Indian religious life.

The book contained many and sometimes long quotations from histories of a particular area or from the reports and published diaries of missionaries. Ellinwood told him, in reviewing another of his books, that although that technique of using long quotations diminished somewhat the literary quality of his work, it also helpfully provided "the testimony of scores and hundreds of witnesses who supply us with their first-hand knowledge."[23] In a brief conclusion Speer reiterated his purpose and invited his readers to action. The survey demonstrated: "The missions of our Church thus girdle the world. There is never an hour when our missionaries are not telling to some hearts the glad tidings of the Saviour. On every continent, save Europe, and among the adherents of every religion our representatives are at work; in North America, South America, Asia, Africa, and the Islands of the Seas; among Hindus, Mohammedans, Buddhists, Confucianists, Shintoists, Shamanists, Fetich worshipers, and degraded forms of Christianity." "Is not," he asked, "our Saviour the Saviour of the world? That is his desire and his prayer. And his will for us is that we should carry him to the world, should lift him up before the world, that, being lifted up, he may draw all men unto himself."[24]

The longer historical studies were readily available to the general public, but they were the tip of the iceberg of his historical writing. Short histories were buried in his five travel reports and General Assembly presentations for the board, and a multitude of others appeared as articles in a variety of periodicals. He based some of them on communications from missionaries and used them as a way of keeping the readers of the various periodicals for which he wrote up to date on the developments in particular missions. Many others were speeches or essays prepared for special celebrations, and he usually adopted one or the other of two methods for these. He used one method in "Two Hundred and Fifty Years of Foreign Missions," a speech in 1933 for the anniversary of the arrival in America of Francis Makemie, a major founder of the Presbyterian Church in America and its first moderator. He offered his listeners a brief chronological outline of the beginnings and then used a thematic approach to describe the early workers. We can be thankful, he said, "for the clear discernment and definite affirmation by the founders of the inherent missionary character of the Church," for "the courage of the founders and the faith with which they launched out on the missionary undertaking," for their "clear understanding" of the "aims of missions" and its "methods," and for "the tradition of unswerving evangelical loyalty, which has come down to us unbroken . . . and which, please God, is to continue unbroken in our time and to go on unbroken by our children's children."[25]

At the centennial celebration of Princeton Theological Seminary in 1912, he chose a different method to tell his story: minibiographies of those who had gone from the seminary into foreign missions. Although he packed this essay with statistics (for instance, in its first century Princeton had sent 410 men to the foreign field), he attached to each piece of data the name or names of some of those who had served and stories about what they had accomplished.[26] Two of them had been part of his own history, Ellinwood of the class of 1853 and Forman of the class of 1885. He estimated that "the years of foreign missionary life given by the sons of this institution would be equivalent to the time of two men preaching the gospel from the hour of our Lord's birth down to this present day." These men had passed on a most priceless possession, "the conception of the whole Church as a missionary society," what he called on this occasion "the church theory of missions."[27] He saw them as part of an apostolic succession, dating from Paul and continuing to his own day.

The histories that were biographies occupied an important place in his effort to communicate the universality of the Christian faith. The Bible drew him to biography, he said, for it was "in the main, simply a book of biographies," featuring Jesus' story as the "most wonderful" one.[28] The missionaries he studied were those he believed had followed Jesus in such a way that they had incarnated him and his principles to others in all the regions of the world, living proof that Jesus was still at work inviting everyone to believe.

He wrote one of his frequent correspondents, Florence Smith, a missionary to Chile, that he believed the key to such model missionaries was their ability to keep word and work together: "They knew the Gospel of the New Testament and believed in it; were convinced that it was the power of God unto salvation, and while they were very large-minded in their use of every available method of school and press and hospital they never for one moment lost sight of the primary aim and they preached Christ by word and deed, by day and night."[29] "In the missionary propaganda, especially," he told his audience at the Cole Lectures at Vanderbilt University in 1911, "the supreme element is personality. It is not linguistic skill, or intellectual superiority, or fertility of method, or masterfulness of organization, or physical endurance. All these are valuable and desirable, but the one vital and indispensable thing is holy personality, the presence in the human agent of the divine life, and the unwearied attempt to impart that life through the exposure of personality, so to speak,—its living contact with other living spirits, lacking as yet the divine indwelling."[30] He titled one collection of his short biographies *Men Who Were Found Faithful* and another *Servants of the King*.

Although he wanted to preserve the stories of such faithful servants of God, he wrote primarily to encourage his readers to catch their enthusiasm and vision. If such persons had served God, sometimes with relatively few talents and in the remotest areas under extremely difficult circumstances, could not others do the same? "And surely we will serve him better," he wrote, "as we see what a fine, great thing their service was."[31] When clergymen and others claimed they could not arouse interest or support for foreign missions, he asked, "Do you use the rich and ever richer stories of missionary biography?"[32] In order to make the witness of his subjects as real and live as possible, he carried to extreme lengths his method of quoting sources, especially diaries, letters, and other primary materials. In the preface of one of his longer studies he wrote, "I conceive that the true business of a biographer is not to set forth his interpretation of the life with which he is dealing, whether it be in the way of approval or disapproval, but to present the material in such form and fulness as will enable each one who reads to form his own judgment for himself."[33]

His first short biography was of David Livingstone, which he completed as part of his work with the Princeton Band. Most of his subjects were men. Eleanor Chesnut was an important exception. She was born in Waterloo, Iowa, in 1868. Her father had early abandoned the family, and shortly afterward her mother died. Although she was adopted and raised in a loving environment, she experienced difficulty accepting her new home and poured her energies into her schooling. She worked her way through Park College and while there joined the church and decided to become a foreign missionary. She subsequently completed work at the Woman's Medical College and the Illinois Training School for Nurses, both in Chicago, and became a physician and a nurse. When she applied to the Presbyterian board in 1893, she wrote that she was interested in Siam, but had not set "my heart on any one place, but rather pray that wherever it may be it will be the appointed one, that what powers I possess may be used to the best advantage."[34] The board assigned her to South China, and she sailed in the fall of 1894. As soon as she arrived at her station, Sam-kong, she began to learn the language and opened a hospital for women. She was especially drawn to them. She moved to Lien-chou in 1898 and worked in a men's hospital until one for women could be built. After a furlough home, she returned to China in 1903, enthusiastic for her work. On the evening of October 28, 1905, a group described as "rabble" attacked the station and murdered Eleanor and several other missionaries. Speer concluded: "All the hardness of the early years was gone, and she was perfected in love at last. The peculiarity and desolation of her girlhood had been transformed into sympathy with all who were in need and complete and Christlike ministry to all suffering."[35]

In all his biographies he expressed some personal affinity for his sub-jects beyond their exemplary character. Although he never chose any one over all the others, he was strongly drawn to the social witness of John Eagan and the spiritual witness of George Bowen.[36] He first learned of Bowen while he was in college, very likely by reading his obituary in 1888. He immediately began collecting materials for a biography, which he called a "memoir," and eventually published a short essay on him in 1911. But he could not get Bowen out of his system and took up the task of a longer biography late in his career, finally completing it the year he retired.

Bowen was the son of a successful wholesale merchant. After working in the family business during his teenage years—educating himself by reading from his father's library rather than attending school—he left at age eighteen to live the life of a rich man's son. He fell in love, but his fiancee died in January 1844; she bequeathed him her Bible with instruc-tions to read it. He followed her advice and some three months later had a conversion experience; almost immediately he decided to join the church and become a foreign missionary. He lacked a formal education and had no specialized training; so his pastor advised him to enroll in Union Theological Seminary in New York City.

Seminary experience marked the beginning of Bowen's ministry, for he immediately began to win others to Christ and his fellow students to a richer spiritual life. "He realized," Speer said, "that the only possible preparation for many kinds of work is to do them, and to be a winner of souls in India ten years in the future he knew that he must be a winner of souls where he was. There is no spiritual alchemy in a sea voyage that will make a missionary out of a man who is not already one before he goes."[37] During his seminary time he had his initial deeper "spiritual experience." Bowen reported the event in the third person: "Nothing in heaven and earth astonished him more than the discovery made on that day that Jesus was his sanctification, and that all he had to do was to abide in Him as the branch in the vine, and the goodness of Christ would sway him moment by moment, and it would always be Christ's goodness, and not his own, for there is none good save one, that is God."[38]

The American Board of Commissioners for Foreign Missions assigned Bowen to Bombay, India, and he sailed in 1847. He never returned. He immediately faced two questions: "the mode of life of the missionary and his spiritual example and influence."[39] He answered the first when he decided two years later to surrender his missionary salary and to move from the mission house to a small room in a poor section of the community. He supported himself by tutoring and later by editing the Bombay *Guardian*. He answered the second question by choosing to live an ascetic life, as much like that of the people he served as he could manage. His ministry was writing and preaching and living the Christian life. Speer summarized: "No faintest shadow of uncandour, of hypocrisy, of professionalism, darkened George Bowen's life. He was what he appeared. He appeared what he was. . . . But Bowen believed that the only reality of life is the right adjustment of itself to God and goodness and he strove thereto. And men were influenced by him through his reality."[40]

Why was Speer so attracted to this person he called "the Christian Mystic"? Although he never said so, he may have found in Bowen the image of himself in another generation, a person absolutely riveted by his call, literally bending everything he did to it. But there was likely something deeper. After Elliott's death, Speer began to have very personal, mystical experiences of Christ. The deep spiritual life Bowen experienced and wrote about may have spoken directly to Speer.

Theoretical Studies

He wrote fewer theoretical than historical studies and never strictly separated the two. His histories often included theoretical components, sometimes as separate chapters. The best example was his longest and most ambitious history, the two-volume *Missions and Modern History*, published in 1904. He wrote a dozen chapters on the social and political upheavals in the nineteenth century in those nations around the world where the foreign missionary movement was at work, chapters with titles such as "The Tai-ping Rebellion," "The Indian Mutiny," and "The Tong Hak Insurrection." He capped it with an important theoretical chapter on "Missions and the World Movement." Many of his theoretical works included substantial historical material. His first and most important early one, *Missionary Principles and Practice*, contained an entire section of historically-oriented chapters based on his world trip.

His theoretical studies typically began as speeches or short articles, which he expanded into longer essays and then gathered into books. The resulting volumes were "collections of wide-ranging ideas rather than complete systems of understanding," although he approached truly systematic theoretical studies on two occasions—in the Duff Lectures, *Christianity and the Nations*, in 1910, and in the Gay and Stone Lectures, *The Finality of Jesus Christ*, in 1932–33.[41] Two other books that contained significant theoretical materials were *The Gospel and the New World*, published in 1919, and *The Unfinished Task of Foreign Missions*, the James Sprunt Lectures at Union Theological Seminary in Richmond, Virginia, published in 1926. He offered reflections on missionary theory in a number of other books, including his travel reports, and in many individually published essays and speeches.

Even though he never created a fully systematic theory of foreign missions, he dealt in a careful systematic way with a number of important issues. He chose to study those topics that attracted him, not unlike the way he approached the study of the life and ministry of Jesus or Paul; first and foremost among these issues were those that had practical implications. He often called his formulations principles rather than theories. They fell into two broad categories, specific and general, although he never used those terms and they were not mutually exclusive since the specific ones had general implications and the general ones had specific applications. He acknowledged his debts to his missionary forebears for the rich resources they provided. A historian of missionary theory has claimed that he was and has remained an exception in that regard, for every other "author has given the impression that he was starting from the beginning and the same ideas have recurred from time to time as if they were fresh discoveries."[42] That judgment may help explain why Speer has remained in a virtual time capsule in terms of his contributions to missionary theory.

Many of the specific principles emerged early in his career with the Student Volunteer Movement and the Interdenominational Conference and he gave them their final form by the end of his first decade in the secretarial work. They included his ideas about the missionary call, the watchword, comity, and the science of missions and have already been described in some detail in the contexts in which he developed them. The missionary call was universal, synonymous with the call to become a Christian. It was issued to laity and clergy alike and to persons of every nationality. The key thrust of the watchword was the evangelization of the entire world. Comity helped divide the fields so that every person in the world could be reached in the most efficient manner and with the least confusion over denominational differences or conflict between missionaries. The goal was united churches on the fields, which would become part of the one church of Jesus Christ. The science of missions was an effort to formulate a holistic missionary policy with principles that could be applied everywhere in the world.

He reflected on the general principles while developing the more specific ones, but he did most of his hard thinking about them between his world trip and the Duff Lectures. He shaped them in the context of his work and by careful study of both the Bible and the history and practice of foreign missions. Once he reached conclusions about them, he regarded them as settled, fundamentals from which he never deviated. They were like precious gems; from time to time he looked at different facets and altered the terms he used to describe what he saw, but he never thought of changing or discarding the gems themselves. That explains why he sometimes republished statements of a major principle virtually unchanged some years after it had first appeared. He had a prodigious memory and had not forgotten; rather, he believed the new generation needed to become acquainted with one or another of his general principles. His main principles concerned (1) the aim of foreign missions, (2) the superiority of the Christian religion, and (3) the unity of the Christian church. Stated separately for purposes of clarification and discussion, he believed they were closely related and together defined not just foreign missions but Christianity. Each had other issues attached to it. The aim of foreign missions opened the issue of the relation of the entire missionary enterprise to the process of extending Western civilization to other cultures. The superiority of the Christian religion raised questions about the relationship of Christianity to other religions. The unity of the Christian church more often than not challenged those who were strongly attached to denominational structures or to any group less encompassing than the universal church.

The Aim of Foreign Missions

In his effort to define the aim of foreign missions for himself and his generation, he never claimed that he had discovered a new idea or that he broke new ground. After all, the topic was as old as the missionary movement and had been worked through by Anderson in the previous generation. His own board *Manual* contained a carefully worded definition. But his world trip had alerted him to the issue in the context of what he believed to be a serious need in all the missionary fields for a science of missions. At the same time he had begun to deal with various critics of the missionary movement at home, who in their arguments often confused the aim of foreign missions with other things. His first try at restating the aim was to his colleagues at the IC in 1898, and he chose to describe it as "*the dispensing of divine life.*"[43] Before the same group the following year, in his report on the science of missions, he claimed, "Everything else" depended on the aim, which was "to preach the gospel."[44] At the great Ecumenical Missionary Conference in 1900, before a large public audience in one of the most prominent lecture settings of the conference, he set out his definition of the aim and spelled out his general principle of it. The conference published the speech, "The Supreme and Determining Aim," in its *Report* and he republished it two years later as "The Aim of Christian Missions," in *Missionary Principles and Practice*. It was his definitive statement on the topic.

He offered his listeners in this short and carefully crafted speech some important preliminary considerations, a definition, and a challenge. Foreign missions was not, he declared, the entire Christian church, and Christians in general and missionaries in particular needed to remember that there were "many good and Christian things which it is not the duty of the foreign missionary enterprise to do."[45] At the very least, the aim needed to be stated in such a way that it did not preempt the duties of the "new Christians," or "the native Christian churches that shall arise."

People made two common mistakes when they tried to define the aim. One was to confuse it with the results. Because they could readily see political and social changes in the lands where the missionaries went, they concluded that was what the missionaries aimed to accomplish. He noted that there was "no force in the world so powerful to accomplish accessory results as the work of missions. Wherever it goes it plants in the hearts of men forces that produce new lives; it plants among communities of men forces that create new social combinations." But the idea that the aim was "the total reorganization of the whole social fabric" was "mischievous doctrine." There was nothing, either in the experience of the Christian church or "from the example of our Lord and His apostles to justify it. . . . They were content to aim at implanting the life of Christ in the hearts of men, and were willing to leave the consequences to the care of God." In a ringing affirmation of the spiritual character of foreign missions he announced, "I had rather plant one seed of the life of Christ under the crust of heathen life, than cover that whole crust over with the veneer of our social habits, or the vestiture of Western civilization. We go as the trustees of His life."

Another frequent error people made was to confuse the aim with the methods. This was especially apparent in connection with the "philanthropic" work of missions. "It is a pleasant thing," he noted, "to feed the hungry, it is a Christian thing to heal the sick; and many times have we not, with a view to attaining our direct missionary aim, launched these philanthropic agencies, only to see them in due time absorb our aim itself, and demand our support for their own sakes, irrespective of the relation which they bear to the supreme aim?" While it was easy to understand how this happened, it misled people into thinking that the fundamental aim was social or educational or medical rather than spiritual. Results and methods were obviously important and had their place but were poor substitutes for the true aim.

The heart of the matter, the true aim of foreign missions, was "to make Jesus Christ known to the world, with a view to the full salvation of men, and their gathering into true and living churches in the fields to which we go." Some people preferred other phrases, like "the evangelization of the world," or "to preach the gospel to the world." He had used both at times, and "if we understand these terms in their scriptural sense," then they could carry the meaning of his definition. But he liked his new phrase with its dual emphasis. "The salvation of men" came first and highlighted the missionary call to offer Jesus Christ to individuals. God converted them, but men and women were called to place themselves "between His life and their death, channels of the grace and salvation of God." However, foreign missions was not charged with "a purely individualistic gospel." "Their gathering into true and living churches" reminded missionaries that they were "bound also to make known to the world that there is a body of Christ, which is His Church, and to gather up these saved men into visible churches, which shall be outward evidence of the body of Christ, and shall secure to the gospel an influence and perpetuity which institutions and not individuals must supply." Invoking the names of Venn, Warneck, and Anderson, he declared that the missionary aim embraced the duty "to establish and foster native churches, self-extending, self-maintaining, self-directing, which shall carry to their own people, whom we may not reach, the message that has come to them, and shall carry down into the generations that are to come after them, the blessings which we have given them as their own."

The aim presented all Christians, not just missionaries, with a challenge to make the aim supreme and determining in their lives. The adjectives reminded them of the importance of keeping the aim first and foremost. Dramatic results often attracted greater support, but the supreme aim was "neither to establish republics or limited monarchies throughout the world, nor to lead Chinese or Hindu people to wear our dress, nor to remodel their social institutions where these are already wholesome and clean." Missionaries all too often succumbed to the temptation to lose sight of the determining aim and "to drift into methods of work that presuppose a quite contrary aim," or "to slip into indirect conceptions of our duty, to do what God can do through other agencies." The supreme and determining aim offered a clear, direct path to the future. "Has not the time now come at last," he asked his listeners, "for action, for great action, for a serious attempt by the whole Church to attain our aim?"

Some ten years later he devoted one of his Duff Lectures to this same topic, under the title "The Missionary Aim and Methods." He used the basic outline and much of the wording from his earlier presentation and added extensive supportive documentation. He retained the same three-fold aim but stated it in slightly different terms: "first, the proclamation of Christ; second, the salvation of men; and third, the naturalisation [sic] of Christianity."[46] The final phrase was the equivalent of "their gathering into true and living churches" in the earlier version. "Naturalisation" made clear the intent to establish "indigenous organizations which will take their own forms and come to their own statements of the truth of Christianity, as wrought out in their own study of the Bible and their own Christian experience."

He believed that indigenous churches would grow to the degree that missionaries were able to communicate the truly "universal elements" of Christianity and to draw people to the "one Saviour." But he recognized in 1910, in a way he had not a decade earlier, that identifying and sticking to the universals had become an almost intransigent problem. There seemed to be no real agreement on universals at the home bases, much less on the mission fields. One missionary's statement of faith might seem to another to be nothing more than some aspect of Western civilization. This was a significant problem, and Speer suggested three responses to it. First, he advised the missionary movement to acknowledge it. Churches and their agents, like other agencies, carried "their treasures in earthen vessels" and therefore should understand that the "introduction of Western elements in our intercourse with the non-Christian people was inevitable."[47] While those elements were not all bad, missionaries sometimes confused them with the Christian faith, and that had left some people unclear about the faith. Missionaries were not perfect and had done some things that would have to be undone. Second, he believed awareness of the aim of foreign missions could alert the movement to deviations from it and therefore help prevent them. He provided specific descriptions of the kinds of things that violated his theory. The aim was "not to impose our Western systems of theology or our Western forms of Church government upon the converts who may be gathered upon the mission field," nor was it "to denationalise those who become Christian disciples, to interfere with styles of dress or modes of life, to give Occidental institutions to them or to Westernise their minds or hearts."[48] Third, he thought that clarity about the aim, which he felt was both "simple and coherent," could keep the movement, despite the real dangers, on the true course.[49]

Although disagreement about the universals continued, many things improved. The formation of the IMC in 1921 helped bring the missionary agencies closer together, and the Jerusalem meeting revealed a substantial agreement on the basic premise of foreign missions. The small handful of Christians at Edinburgh who represented the indigenous churches increased to fully one-fourth of the delegates at Jerusalem. By then united churches were emerging in quite different settings around the world. In 1922 his board changed the wording of its aim, formally adding to its emphasis on preaching and conversion a third component, the creation and sustaining of indigenous churches. The wording of the past had been this: "The great aim of missionary life and service is the preaching of Christ crucified. All forms of work must be subordinate to this end, and all methods of missionary effort, medical, educational, industrial, etc., will be sanctioned and supported by the Board only as they contribute to a wider and more effective proclamation of the Gospel and give promise of vital missionary results." The new wording clearly reflected his emphases, particularly his meaning of naturalisation: "The supreme and controlling aim of Foreign Missions is to make the Lord Jesus Christ known to all men as their Divine Saviour and to persuade them to become His disciples; to gather these disciples into Christian churches which shall be self-propagating, self-supporting and self-governing; to cooperate, so long as necessary, with these churches in the evangelizing of their countrymen and in bringing to bear on all human life the spirit and principles of Christ."[50]

He played some direct role in many of these developments. In addition, he never tired of reminding audiences of his version of the true aim of foreign missions. He often used his original wording, and, even when he altered the terms, he sought to convey the same ideas he had articulated at the turn of the century. To those gathered for the Sprunt Lectures in

1926 he said, "The supreme and determining aim of missions in any country, India for example, is to get Jesus Christ made known and accepted. Elemental to this aim is the establishment of a Christian Church in India, but the establishment of the Church in any land is not a matter of terminology. It is a matter of fact. And a Church that is a Church in fact and not merely in term will be self-dependent, self-governed, and most of all a force of living and spontaneous propaganda."[51] In 1937, at his last Foreign Missions Conference, he told his secretarial colleagues that the "fundamental aim and central method" of Christian missions remained unchanged. "Our business," he concluded, "is to live and work in and to bring the life and work of the world into conformity with and obedience to the pure and righteous and loving will of God revealed in the mind of Christ."[52]

His reflections on the aim of foreign missions led him to consider the consequences of the work of the missionaries of his generation. While he openly acknowledged their failures, he paid a great deal more attention to their successes. Part of his interpretive role was to present the movement so that the churches, his own and others, would support it. When he focused on the achievements, he usually differentiated between what he called the fruitages, or the consequences, of the movement and the accessory results, or simply the results. Although he was not absolutely consistent in this usage, the distinction was significant.[53] The fruitages represented those achievements that were primary and direct outgrowths of the aim. They included converts, native pastors and churches, and ultimately united churches that were moving toward true autonomy in accord with the Anderson-Venn vision.

He collected examples of fruitages from his correspondence and trips and used them frequently. In Nakon, Siam, he attended a worship service in a "neat building, spotlessly clean," and listened as the "congregation sang, in their own tongue, some of the great old hymns of the Church and read all in unison the last chapter of the Gospel of Matthew." As he looked out from the platform, he could see the decaying ruins of an old pagoda and mused that there was "Siamese Buddhism, indolent, torpid, ineffective, living on only as a sedative and opiate. . . . And across the street, was Christianity, alert, living, serving mankind in the ministry of an active love, filled with the spirit of Him who said, 'I came to minister,' and 'I must work.' "[54] He attended a native Chinese church in Tientsin, China. The pastor had gone to America to study, and one of the elders led the service. He noticed on the wall above the preacher "three great characters in gold, faith on his right hand, hope on his left hand, and between the two in larger outline and against a background of red like crimson stood the great bold character for love. There it was, the one central and essential thing, the only thing that has ever redeemed any man, the only thing that can redeem China to-day, love on a groundwork of sacrifice, sheer goodness dipped in blood and faithful even to the cross of death."[55]

The results were less important than the fruitages, and he presented them as the secondary effects of the movement. They typically involved the extension of some aspect of Western civilization into the lands that were mission fields. Speer reflected the sentiments of most Westerners that these achievements in social or educational or medical services marked clear improvements in the lives of the people and their nations. But he realized he had a difficult interpretive problem, a version of one familiar to many missionaries. They sometimes confused the aim and its fruitages with the results, because the results were easier to measure. In presenting the results, he had to be very careful to define them in the context of the aim, despite the fact that his audiences were often primarily attracted to the results. Their interest was quite natural. Even though they were often made up of churchgoers or students who had at least a nominal interest in Christianity, they were not typically composed of people who had intimate knowledge about the missionary enterprise or who understood mission theory. Moreover, their Christian orientation did not prevent them from sharing some of the more gross enthusiasms of their generation. Their times, roughly the years between the emergence of the SVM and World War I, were the heyday not only of foreign missions, but also of Western imperial expansion, featuring the conquest and carving up of Africa, commercial developments in Asia, and flurries of jingoism at home. Whether or not the missionary explosion was inspired by the political one, it certainly was enhanced by it. He, along with most other missionary leaders, frankly acknowledged that. But in what ways and to what degree? To use terms more familiar to a later generation, he constantly faced the challenge of defining the line between Christ and culture; in Speer's own terminology, the struggle was to find the line between the aim and the results of foreign missions.

In some specific instances he found it relatively easy to draw the line. He had no difficulty responding to negative opinions of the watchword or the Ecumenical Missionary Conference, when critics charged that they had either secular motivations or consequences (see chapters 5 and 7 for further discussion of this). But for every opportunity to respond to a particular issue, there were hundreds to offer general interpretations of the results of missions. Those who listened to or read his presentations carefully knew that he kept his eye on the line. "The Civilizing Influence of Missions" appeared in 1902. Religion was a vital part of the lives of the peoples of Africa and Asia, he pointed out, effecting their governments and all aspects of their social and economic lives. People should not be surprised to learn, therefore, of the "immense influence exerted by missions in other directions than that of the direct evangelization *which is their chief concern.*"[56]

He followed that very important qualification with one of his earliest lists of the secular results of foreign missions. It had helped governments establish and maintain order; introduced the "agencies of civilization" among the "savage races," opened the world and brought "the knowledge of it to the civilized nations," and helped allay "hostility which diplomats and traders" had aroused."[57] Consider, he concluded, the testimony of James A. Dennis, who in his *Christian Missions and Social Progress* demonstrated in the following *"subordinate and secondary spheres"* that foreign missions had "promoted temperance, opposed the liquor and opium traffics which are fatal to wise commerce, checked gambling, established higher standards of personal purity, cultivated industry and frugality, elevated woman, restrained anti-social customs such as polygamy, concubinage, adultery and child-marriage and infanticide, fostered the suppression of the slave trade and slave traffic, abolished cannibalism and human sacrifice and cruelty, organized famine relief, improved husbandry and agriculture, introduced Western medicines and medical science, founded leper asylums and colonies, promoted cleanliness and sanitation, and checked war."[58]

Unreservedly enthusiastic for foreign missions, he worked to build and refine the list of things missionaries had done for the world, using as his base the one he generated in 1902 and the items suggested by Dennis. He presented it in its more or less final form in a speech he gave to the Canadian National Missionary Congress in 1909, which appeared as a pamphlet and, ten years later with a slightly revised title, as a chapter in a book.[59] He developed the list around the theme "The World's Debt to the Missionary" and defined no less than nine major items. Although he repeated a number of the items in his earlier list, like opening up the world to Western civilization and Western civilization to the world, this was a much more sophisticated effort with some important new ideas. "We owe the missionary a great debt," he said, "for having done something to atone for the moral shame of our Western contact with the East." In addition, the missionary had transformed the entire Western attitude "to the heathen nations." It had not been many years since Westerners simply took whatever land they wanted; now, at least, because of the missionary, they needed some good reason.[60] The final and in some ways most important debt was the missionary contribution to unity, in the church and the world. It was the missionary who was showing the church "how much the things in which we agree outweigh the things in which we disagree," and who was "the greatest agency in binding the dissevered fragments of our human race into one." "Other people," he added, "are talking brotherhood; the missionary is actualizing it; other people are saying what a beautiful dream it is; the missionary is realizing it."[61] Careful to make clear the context of all these results, he prefaced his list with the affirmation that the missionary enterprise achieved them without aiming at them. Its aim, he declared, was "to make Jesus Christ known throughout the world."[62]

In the 1930s he quoted Dennis' list again. The results, he claimed, continued to be as remarkable as they had been at the turn of the century. But he reminded his readers that "we have to go right down to the central need and heart of things, and with all our other doings do the thing without which all of them will be vain, make Jesus Christ our Lord known to all the rest of the world. . . . We need to go back to the old motto, 'The Evangelization of the World in this Generation.' The new generation requires it just as the old generation."[63]

While the distinction between the aim and the results was both real and important, he believed they were related in complex ways. On the one hand, expansion was part of the very nature of Western civilization. Some of the political and economic means it had used had been ruthless and exploitive and could not be condoned by right-thinking persons. In general, the only "justification of the Western movement is moral." This meant, he hastened to add, that "the only grounds on which it can defend its extension over unwilling people is the ground of its moral superiority, and its purpose to uplift the people over whom it acquires influence into a higher life and, after all, to larger freedom."[64] The only agency available to help moralize the Western advance was the missionary movement, and therefore the "Western movement needs the Christian mission for its own sake."[65] On the other hand, the missionary movement had its own clear aim and did "not wish to be entangled with forces which too often act in divergence from Christian principle."[66] But, short of entanglement, it sought "as free an opportunity as possible to do its own work of planting in individual character and in family life the new life of the Gospel," and hoped to work in harmony with social and economic agencies involved to the end that they "should recognize the principle of an unselfish service as the law of all intercourse of nations and races, and of men."[67]

His views on the nexus of issues surrounding the aim of foreign missions elicited strong support and some criticism. The latter was confined largely to his correspondence. This aspect of the debate between Christ and culture never generated serious negative public discussion, much less the kind of heated controversy that erupted over his views on war during World War I (see chapter 9). What contemporaries largely accepted, some historians have chosen to question. Patterson, for example, has found in Speer's work what he called an "unresolved ambivalence concerning the cultural dimension of foreign missions." Patterson discovered that he used "patronizing language," which he attributed to his "role as a missionary administrator." "In his mind," he continued, "any attack on the evils of imperialism in the early 1900s would have alienated the business community at a time when its support was essential."[68] Speer may have crossed the line between aim and results occasionally, but no evidence supports the concept of "ambivalence," and none even hints at the calculus suggested by the judgment that he was reluctant to offend businessmen. Hutchison, in a more careful and thoughtful analysis, has portrayed him as the student of Anderson who lived in a more difficult time, and who managed to keep separate the claims of his faith and those of his culture.[69]

The Superiority of the Christian Religion

The aim of foreign missions implied the superiority of the Christian religion. The latter could be considered a corollary of the former, but he developed it as another of his general principles. If Christians fully achieved the aim, then Christianity would replace all other religions and become superior, the one universal religion, in fact as well as in theory. Speer believed in Christianity's superiority and frequently articulated his theoretical basis for it, locating it in what the incarnation revealed about God and how the early Christians responded to it. He saw the incarnation as the key moment in all history, when God had intervened personally on behalf of his creation (see chapter 3). That moment had revealed the depth of all humanity's need and the breadth of the true and one God's searching love to meet it. In the language of missions it meant, "We cannot think of God, I say it reverently, without thinking of Him as a missionary God."[70] Those who believed in the God who had sent his Son had to believe in foreign missions, for it was "in the very being and character of God that the deepest ground of the missionary enterprise is to be found."[71] Christ shared that character. Some Christians were satisfied to base the missionary task on Christ's last command, but "what was the last command of His lips must have been one of the nearest desires of His heart," and "the work of missions is our duty, not chiefly because of the command of Christ's lips, but because of the desire of His heart."[72]

In missionary concepts more familiar to a later generation of mission theorists, he told his audiences that the members of the early church had understood this, for they had created no missionary organizations but instead had conceived the church to be a missionary society. They had been "drawn together spontaneously by the uniting power of a common life, and they felt as spontaneously the outward pressure of a world mission. The triumphant prosecution of that mission and the moral fruits of this new and uniting life were their apologetics. They did not sit down within the walls of a formalised and stiffened institution to compose reasoned arguments for Christianity. The new religion would have rotted out from heresy and anaemia in two generations if they had done so."[73]

The first Christians had received two signals from Christ that they had picked up and made central to their mission. They had believed him to be "indispensable." He had said, "I am the way, the truth, and the life," and "No man cometh unto the Father but by Me." Christ was the key figure, the unique and final Savior. "Christ," Speer wrote, "is not only the centre. He is also the beginning and the end. He is all in all. The Christian faith is a conviction and an experience, and Christ is the object of each."[74] As important as Christ's teachings were, it was not possible to share them without sharing his historic personality.[75] They had also understood that he "thought and wrought in universals," and they adopted his universal claims. The child of one of "the most centripetal of all races," he nonetheless "looked forward over all ages and outward over all nations. The bread which He would give was His flesh, which He would give for the life of the world. He was the light of the whole world. If He should be lifted up He would draw all men unto Himself. His disciples were to go into all the world and make disciples of all nations. . . . It was not of a race but of a world that the Father had sent Him to be the Saviour." Whenever, he added, the church "shrinks into a mere racial cult, it separates itself from its Founder and life, and utterly abandons its essential character."[76]

He usually stated his general theory about Christianity's superiority in the context of presentations about the non-Christian religions. He rarely called them inferior, but chose instead to describe them as inadequate or insufficient to meet the religious needs of humanity. While he acknowledged that other religions claimed to be "authoritative," "sufficient," or even "universal," he argued that "Christianity contests all these claims

when it sets forth on the foreign missionary enterprise, offering itself as
better than all other religions for all men and for every man."[77] His study
of the non-Christian religions occupied a good deal of his time, especially
in the years between his world trip and Edinburgh, and his views about
them and their relationship to Christianity became one of the important
themes of his career. A speech on that relationship at the Student
Volunteer quadrennial in 1906 earned him the invitation to give the Duff
Lectures, and he devoted one of them to the topic. At Edinburgh and
Jerusalem he worked on the commissions that dealt with the missionary
message in relation to the non-Christian religions or systems, a sign not
only of his interest but of the way his colleagues understood his work and
the place where he could make the most significant contributions. In addition to the numerous articles and reports that he produced throughout his
life, he wrote two books on various aspects of this issue, one in comparative religion and the other about the way the church had from its founding
understood and related to other religions. This brief survey can do little
more than provide an outline and delineate some of his major views.

   Although he may have begun to study the non-Christian religions
before he joined the board, his work there definitely encouraged him to
investigate them more deeply. By the time he arrived, Ellinwood had
established himself as a pioneer in the field of comparative religion.
Ellinwood's early work with the board had persuaded him that "a missionary secretary could very poorly perform his duty as a missionary advocate at home or a missionary administrator abroad, if he did not know the
non-Christian religions."[78] In 1887 Ellinwood had accepted a call from
New York University to become a professor of comparative religion, as an
addition to his secretarial work. In his course "The Relations of Oriental
Religions to Christianity and the Work of Missions," he approached the
non-Christian religions sympathetically. He subsequently founded the
American Society for the Study of Oriental Religions. Speer never indicated that he actually took Ellinwood's course but applauded him as "the
great leader of the thoughts of Christians in this land to a new study of
the religions of the non-Christian peoples, and to a surer missionary
apologetic."[79]

   The world trip beginning in 1896 marked a major step forward in
Speer's knowledge about non-Christian religions and encouraged him to
intensify his study of them. He encountered most of them on their home
grounds, both in the persons of some of their believers and in their institutions. A number of the things he witnessed startled him, like the rituals
along the Ganges and in the Hindu holy city of Benares. After visits to the

Golden Temple and the nearby Cow Temple, he and his companions were "dazed" with a "sense of unreality, which we agreed, when we tried to analyze it, was the sense of having been near the grotesqueness, the sulfurous wretchedness of Dante's hell."[80]

Shortly after he returned home, the *Churchman* published his first thoughts on the topic "The Need of the Non-Christian World For Christ." He opened the article with an apparently autobiographical note. Imagine, he invited the reader, what your life would be like if God had withheld his Son from the world and therefore the possibility of the Christian life from you. How would you live "without the Son of God as the light and the Lord" of your life? If one "shudders at the thought of such a gloom and poverty for himself," then one should "remember that the vast majority of his fellow-creatures are thus dark and poor." He reported that in his study of "the non-Christian religions during the past year in the different lands of Asia, I have wanted to think well of them, to see the best that is in them." But his search had discovered "no best" in them, for their "elements of truth have been counteracted and distorted by their error," and their "original simplicity and fervor have died away into gross superstition and fanaticism." "Even at their best," he asked, "their highest appraisement, what are the religions of the world? If they be lights at all, they are but broken." The "spiritual insufficiency of the non-Christian religions" meant that a majority of the people of the world were not receiving the spiritual food they needed, but it also opened a way for the Christian faith to offer true spiritual sustenance. He closed his essay with an invitation to his readers to accept the challenge and join the foreign missionary movement.[81]

In some respects this was a very preliminary statement. Five years later he wrote his first truly substantial article on the topic "Christianity and Other Religions." He had become somewhat more irenic in his presentation of the subject. He began advising Christians, when they investigated the non-Christian religions, to avoid the attitudes of scorn or contempt, on the one hand, and those of "silly and ignorant sentimentalism," on the other. Other religions needed to be treated as Christians would want their faith to be treated, "with absolute justice," in order to discern the truth about them.[82] He also began to distinguish between the attitudes appropriate for missionaries and others in their personal encounters with those who believed in other religions and the attitudes useful when dealing with other religions as systems of thought. In the former case, the purpose of the meeting for the Christian was "to commend his religion to his brother, to persuade him of its truth, to lead him to accept it." That meant the

willingness to acknowledge some common element or truth, and he
affirmed some good or truth in all the world's religions, from which the
Christian could then proceed to such points of difference as might lead to
conversion.[83] He was not as positive in the latter case, which involved the
coming together of representatives of different religions for the purpose of
conference and consultation. The World's Parliament of Religions, which
had been held in Chicago in 1893, had been such a meeting. One of its
purposes had been "to inquire what light each religion has offered or may
afford to the other religions of the world."[84] He had objected to that conference and others like it because they suggested that Christianity lacked
something and was less than the final and complete religion he believed it
to be, and they encouraged the representatives of the non-Christians religions to see themselves as equal with Christianity and as having some
special truth to offer, which he did not believe to be true.[85]

The approach he adopted in studying non-Christian religions was to
work through their history and beliefs, with special emphasis on their theology and its impact on the life of the believers. He concentrated on the
main groups in each religion rather than on the smaller or splinter groups,
looking, as he told many of his audiences, for what was best and most representative in them. He read their holy scriptures and writings, in translation of course, and sought to discover their meaning for himself. A keen
observer and good listener, he learned a great deal from his conversations
with members of other religions during his trips. In his research he said he
used "the most fair and competent authorities," and his citations appear
to substantiate the claim.[86] But he was never truly an unbiased student. He
bent his study of the non-Christian religions the way he did everything
else in his life, in the direction of his call to be a Christian missionary.

The technique he selected in his study of the relation of Christianity to
the non-Christian religions was that of comparison and contrast. He chose
topics or themes, often theological ones, and lifted up and evaluated the
differences, always in favor of Christianity. Sometimes he used the ideas or
practices of a particular religion, but more often he treated non-Christian
religions as a group. His used this technique in "Christianity and Other
Religions" in 1902 and republished it immediately under the title
"Christianity the Solitary and Sufficient Religion." In 1906 he presented
many of the same ideas, but in a much reorganized and longer form, to
the delegates at the Nashville meeting of the SVM under the title "The
Non-Christian Religions Inadequate to Meet the Needs of Men." This
essay contained the basic substance of his position, despite the fact that he
reshaped it from time to time, adding new elements as they emerged from

his continued study. There were others who were working along the same lines. Speer had attended and spoken at the International Student Missionary Conference in London in 1900 and may have heard the Rev. J. A. Campbell speak on "The Inadequacy of Non-Christian Religions to Meet the Need of the World."[87] Although he may have borrowed from Campbell's title and fully agreed with his emphasis on the superiority of Christianity, he created his own arguments and supported them with his own data.

He opened his Nashville speech with two brief caveats that served, like the preliminary remarks he subsequently used in his presentations on Roman Catholicism in Latin America, to turn aside certain kinds of challenges. He acknowledged that he held "unswervingly to the Evangelical faith," and consequently had certain biases. An intellectual bias was a "deep sympathy with the religious needs of mankind."[88] Every student of non-Christian religions began with some kind of intellectual commitment. Surely, he argued, it was better to evaluate them from a position that understood what the religious needs were than from some mental stance which questioned or denied the existence of such needs. A sentimental bias "was a love for the non-Christian nations" and for their peoples that had grown out of the efforts of missionaries "to live among them and lay down their lives for them." The understanding wrought by such love offered a better base for judging the relative adequacy of the non-Christian religions to meet their needs. Christians, therefore, despite their aggressive missionary campaign "to displace and transcend" the non-Christian religions, could make fair judgments about them.

The argument he developed fell into two parts, roughly equal in length: (1) the considerations that were not the basis of his argument; (2) the needs of people that the non-Christian religions failed to meet but that Christianity met. He used the considerations as ways to separate out what he believed to be the nonessential issues. It was not important to reflect, for example, on the great numbers of people who had abandoned the non-Christian religions. Many had fallen away from them, but the same could be said of Christianity. Defections, however numerous, were not the issue. Neither was the quality of civilizations they had inspired. Most Westerners shared the conviction that their civilization was the best, but his argument focused on the relative merits of the religions. Comparing civilizations missed the point and clouded the issue, just as it did in discussions of the aim of foreign missions. He argued that another unfruitful line of reasoning attributed the non-Christian religions to the "evil one." While there was biblical precedent for such a view, from the Hebrew prophets through

Paul, he refused to press it because many believed that, pushed to its logical conclusion, such a perspective foreclosed any reasoned judgment about them.

Another consideration that missed the point but deserved substantial attention was the claim that there was "no good" in non-Christian religions. "Of course," he responded, "there is good and truth in the non-Christian religions. It is the good and the truth that is in the non-Christian religions that has enabled them to survive, that gives them their great power"; however, their good, "which we joyfully admit," he set in the context of what he called "several great facts." One was that there was "no great truth in the non-Christian religions which is not found in a purer and richer form in the Christian religion."

He followed this affirmation with what became a set piece, repeated in the Duff Lectures, in the Gay and Stone Lectures, and many other times: "It is true that Hinduism teaches the immanence of God; it is true that Mohammedanism teaches the sovereignty of God; it is true that Buddhism teaches the transitoriness of our present life; it is true that Confucianism teaches the solemn dignity of our earthly relationships and our human society." Christianity not only taught these truths, but balanced them with other, equally important ones that Speer felt were missing from the other religions: "Hinduism teaches that God is near, but it forgets that He is holy. Mohammedanism teaches that God is great, but it forgets that He is loving. Buddhism teaches that this earthly life of ours is fleeting, but it forgets that we must therefore work the works of God before the night comes. Confucianism teaches that we live in the midst of a great framework of holy relationships, but it forgets that in the midst of all these we have a living help and personal fellowship with the eternal God, in whose lasting presence is our home." The presence of some truth in each of the non-Christian religions presented a very real problem, especially for missionaries. People who believed they possessed truth, however partial it might be, often clung to it tenaciously and successfully resisted the claims of what Speer called the "larger truth" of Christianity.

Even though he dismissed, for the purposes of his argument, the charge that there was no good in the non-Christian religions, he found some truth to it. Each was "seamed through and through with great and positive and hideous evils." The problem with Hinduism was its "immorality," and the absence of any tie between religious faith and moral life. Buddhism denied "the reality of our present life," and advised those who would finally "attain Nirvana" to break away from some of "our holiest relationships," like those between husband and wife, parent and child.

"Mohammedanism" had been "sterile intellectually" for 1,200 years, and had failed to challenge people to a true moral life. Joseph Cochran, whom he had met on his world trip and of whom he later wrote a biography, told him toward the end of his long life as a medical missionary to Persia that "he had never met one pure-hearted or pure-lived adult man among the Mohammedans of Persia." Speer found these things to be very unpleasant and did not relish talking about them. "I can honestly say that for myself," he confessed, "I should like to believe that the non-Christian religions are adequate to the needs of men. I should like to believe that God is finding the hearts of His sons and that His sons are finding the heart of their Father in all of these great non-Christian religions." Unfortunately, he believed, the facts told another story.

Important as these considerations were, they were the preliminaries to the main attraction—the needs of humanity and the ways the non-Christian religions failed to meet them. He divided human needs into four general categories and dealt with each in turn. Intellectual needs were first. Interested in theology but disinclined to theological discourse, he offered only the simple assertion that those who sought answers to the great religious-philosophical questions about human origin, duty and destiny, found little in the non-Christian religions to satisfy them, especially in light of the scientific revolution.

Moral needs were not necessarily more important but were more interesting to him. He believed that non-Christian religions fell short at every turn. Each failed to offer its members a moral ideal, someone or something to live up to. Jesus offered himself as such an ideal, which Speer said neither Confucius nor Buddha dreamed of doing, and as for "the Hindu gods, we are better gods ourselves than they are." One serious problem in all non-Christian religions was the absence of a sense of sin. That was not surprising, he believed, because the sense of a "sinful man" depended on the presence of a "holy God," a vision not present in the non-Christian religions. And so, people in search of moral direction found instead chaos. Without a sense of sin, there was no call for forgiveness and deliverance and movement to a better life. Christianity was not pure, but, unlike the non-Christian religions, Christianity had built into its very nature a "self-purifying power," which pressed its followers to seek to improve their lives. One important example of this was the way non-Christian religions, two of them at least, treated truth. He was dumbfounded that both Mohammed and Krishna taught that lying was permitted in certain cases and agreed believers could lie to women. "Any religion or religious teacher proclaiming the possibility, the allowability of lies," he concluded, "excavates the foundations under human confidence, under all living faith in a real God, and makes impossible an answer to the moral needs of men."

When he moved from the moral to the social needs of humanity, he despaired at the ability of the non-Christian religions to meet them, describing them as "utterly" inadequate. Socially, people needed a sense of worth, the possibility of progress, and a vision of human unity, and in every case the ideals of non-Christian religions were inimical to those ends. Women were one-half of society, fundamental to the family and the home, and yet those religions, with few exceptions, not only limited women's access to religious truth but in some cases denied their self-worth and condemned them "in principle or legal right to the place of chattel or of slave. The very chapter in the Mohammedan Bible which deals with the legal status of women, and which provides that every Mohammedan may have four legal wives, . . . goes by the title in the Koran itself of 'The Cow.' One could get no better title to describe the status of woman throughout the non-Christian world." Indeed, Buddhism proclaimed that woman, as woman, could not be saved. Nor did any of these religions encourage social progress. Islam, for example, remained tied to "the Arabian institutions of the seventh century," and wherever it is in control "progress will be inconsistent with that faith."

The roles non-Christian religions assigned to women betrayed their views of human unity. Every one of them, he argued, denied it: "Hinduism with its caste, Confucianism with its conceit, Islam with its fanatical bigotry, and Buddhism with its damnation of all women." He noted that some representatives of these religions were using the phrases "the fatherhood of God" and "the brotherhood of man," but such ideals were "alien to all the non-Christian religions," and the conceptions "sheer plagiarisms from the Christian revelation." "Every one of the non-Christian religions cuts humanity up into sections," he concluded, "and bars from privilege great bodies of mankind."

Finally, humanity had spiritual needs, satisfied by a relationship with God. Speer affirmed that the non-Christian religions fell far short in this area and opened his presentation on this point by claiming that all of them were "practically atheistic." Hinduism, he said, had so many gods it had none, and Buddhism denied "any absolute being." But he recognized this charge was extreme and settled for an argument that he repeated on a number of subsequent occasions. The best that could be said, what he called "the most charitable view" of the non-Christian religions, was that they represented "the groping search of man after light. They show us the non-Christian peoples stumbling blindly around the great altar-stairs of

God, the more pitiably because they do not know that they are blind." The great comparison with Christianity was that it represented "the loving quest of God after man, the full, rich revealing of His light and life, the unfolding of His love toward His children, whom He has come forth to seek in a way of which none of the non-Christian religions have ever conceived."

Satisfied that he had demonstrated the various kinds of inadequacies of the non-Christian religions and the corresponding superiority of Christianity, he drew his speech to a close with two final reflections. Considerable evidence from around the world indicated that people were discovering these shortcomings for themselves. In his own relatively short life, he had witnessed "Confucianism slain in Korea," "Shintoism publicly degraded from the status of a religion to a mere code of court etiquette in Japan," and "one of the greatest religious transformations that ever took place in the non-Christian world passing over Hinduism." Even monolithic Islam had experienced "schism upon schism." It seemed to him that, one after another, the religions were seeking to transform themselves, thereby "confessing" their "inadequacy to meet the needs of men."

The concept of the inadequacy of religions other than Christianity was nothing new, and those who thought it was he reminded of its biblical basis. After all, Jesus had come "to the best of all the non-Christian religions—the religion between which and all the other non-Christian religions a great gulf is fixed—Judaism, . . . and that, the best of all religions, He declared to be outworn and inadequate." Jesus had announced that the time had come "to supplant it with the full and perfect truth that was in Him." In a sense, Calvary had closed the question of adequacy, for there God answered it. The cross was the final word, and for those who believed "no other word needs to be spoken regarding the absoluteness of His faith and the inadequacy of the half-teachers who have gone before Him, or who were to come after Him." Speer rarely ended a speech without a missionary appeal, and this one was no exception, and so he asked the members of his audience: "As the owners and the bearers of that name, how can we withhold from the hearts of men the sufficient message of their Father's life, their Father's love, made known alone in our only Lord and Saviour, Jesus Christ?"[89]

He worked through his ideas on this topic again in connection with Edinburgh and the Duff Lectures. He titled one of his Duff Lectures "Christianity and the Non-Christian Religions." He used the language of adequacy and inadequacy less, but he retained many of the arguments he had used at Nashville, some of them without altering a word. He included in the lecture two topics he had only hinted at in the earlier presentation. First, he reviewed several different ways of looking at the religions of the world. For example, many of the leaders of the non-Christian religions had taken the position that "all religions are fundamentally the same." He vigorously disagreed and argued that the only thing they really had in common was that they were responding to "the same deep human need."[90] Second, he formulated a nine-point list in which he identified what he thought the attitude of Christianity ought to be toward the non-Christian religions. A thoughtful and carefully drawn list, it included the following suggestions: "Christianity should joyfully recognize all the good that is in the non-Christian religions and build upon it"; "Christianity should not slur or ignore the points of difference"; "Christianity should welcome all transformations of the thought of the non-Christian peoples which bring that thought nearer to Christianity"; and "Christianity should perceive and unswervingly hold to the truth of its own absolute uniqueness." Last and most important of all, he reminded his listeners that all the discussion about the non-Christian religions and the proper attitudes toward them was neither the Gospel nor the message to non-Christians. It was something Christians said to one another when they examined "the grounds of our enterprise and state its warrant to the Christian Church." The message to non-Christians was "the one simple, positive yet infinite and inexhaustible message of Christ."[91]

One year after the Duff Lecture, he wrote his only book in the field that then was called comparative religion. It included reasonably objective presentations of Hinduism, Buddhism, Animism, Confucianism, Taoism, and Islam, but it was a mission study book. The Central Committee on the United Study of Missions, which had originated in connection with the Ecumenical Missionary Conference, commissioned and published it and distributed it through the Women's Boards of Missions. He titled it *The Light of the World* and proclaimed in the introduction, "Christ is the Light of the World." Two of his main reasons for the study were "First, to discover where the points of contact and of separation are found, in order that Christianity may be the more effectively presented to the non-Christian peoples; Second, to bring clearly into view those fundamental differences between Christianity and all other religions which justify and require the effort of missions to make Christianity the religion of all men."[92] The title of the final chapter announced his conclusion: "Christ, The Only Light of the World."

Almost two decades later he returned to this topic in the context of the IMC meeting at Jerusalem. His important work at that meeting has been defined in an earlier chapter, but he also authored a substantial post-conference essay on the value of the religious values of the non-Christian religions. While he had always affirmed that there was some good and truth in the non-Christian religions, this essay was his most forthright discussion of the topic, in terms of values. The values were "real" ones when: (1) they bear witness "to great spiritual needs and to some elemental religious ideas"; (2) "they testify to the spiritual view of life and the world and provide in their measure a resistance to the secular and mechanical conceptions which are threatening to dominate human thought"; (3) "they remind us of forgotten or overlooked values in Christianity"; (4) "they provide a meeting place of common accord"; and (5) "they are the truth."[93] For the third value he chose language that suggested human frailty rather than divine omission, for he believed that "all good is in Christ." The fourth value was primarily about the meeting of persons, not systems of thought, so, for example, he suggested a point of contact between the Christian and the Confucianist "in the truth of the moral law as the will of Heaven." The final value meant that truth was truth and came from God wherever it was found. The message of Jerusalem had recognized "as part of the one Truth that sense of the Majesty of God and the consequent reverence in worship, which are conspicuous in Islam; the deep sympathy for the world's sorrow and unselfish search for the way of escape, which are at the heart of Buddhism; the desire for contact with Ultimate Reality conceived as spiritual, which is prominent in Hinduism; the belief in a moral order of the universe and consequent insistence upon moral conduct, which are inculcated by Confucianism; the disinterested pursuit of truth and of human welfare which are often found in those who stand for secular civilization but do not accept Christ as their Lord and Saviour."[94]

The values, of course, did not stand alone. They needed to be "honestly qualified" and measured in relation to the Christian faith and its values. When he turned to this part of his argument, he repeated many of the things he had said in similar contexts earlier in his life. These values were "not a supplement to Christianity," as if something were missing from it. Christianity not only contained all the values in other religions but balanced and corrected them in order to form one complete religion. Christianity was both unique and superior to all other religions in "its ethical essence" and "its idea of God." He interrupted the flow of his discussion in order to acknowledge that the rising tide of nationalism in the 1920s had increased the difficulty of making the case for superiority. Whole peoples had been swept up by the tide and with its power had developed a "tenacity to glory in all that has entered into the national or racial past." In light of this, Paul's attitude toward values seemed the best one for the believer: "But what things were gain to me those I counted loss for Christ. Yea doubtless, and I count all things but loss for the excellency of the knowledge of Christ Jesus my Lord."[95]

The values of what he called in this instance the "old religions" were not only real but should be salvaged, and the only way to accomplish that was to redeem or convert them. Evidence indicated to him that the non-Christian religions were waning, despite nationalism. Reflecting his increasing interest in church history, he noted that "Christianity enshrines in its present forms a great deal that it took over from the thought and life which it met in the world." The present task, he concluded, was to wash the values of the non-Christian religions "in the blood of the lamb," so that they could survive, and become "as material for Him that the works of God may be manifested in the world."[96] Although he continued to believe as much as ever in the superiority of Christianity, his position on redeeming the values demonstrated that he had moved away from his earliest view that there was "no best" in the non-Christian religions. The shift was subtle, one of emphasis, inspired perhaps by the constant pressure of the missionary imperative to seek points of contact in order to create a basis for sharing God's love in Christ.

When Princeton Theological Seminary invited him to give the Stone Lectures, he decided to focus them on missionary theory, in particular on his understanding of the superiority of the Christian religion in relation to the non-Christian ones, centering his discussion on Jesus Christ. They were formal academic lectures, like the Duff ones, so he approached them academically. By late 1931 he had created an outline around theme sentences and had started his research. He asked the Rev. Wilbur M. Smith, pastor of the Presbyterian Church of Coatesville, Pennsylvania, to help him with bibliographical suggestions for his study of the early church. Smith replied that he thought Speer knew at least as much as anyone in the country about the topic, but agreed to help and by early 1932 produced "A Suggested Bibliography for the Study of the First Three Centuries of the Christian Church. With Particular Reference to the Conflict of Christianity With Paganism."[97]

Speer spent every spare minute in the spring and summer of 1932 working on the lectures. He loved the study, especially in the fathers of the early church, an area he had never explored in detail.[98] One discovery he made was that the "later generations present no more thorough-going presentation of the finality and absoluteness and the universality of Christ than one finds in St. Paul."[99] He worked through the biographies of the major missionaries from St. Patrick to his own day, with two questions in mind, first, their views of Christ and the gospel, and second, their attitudes toward other religions. "The story," he found, was "an unvarying one until one gets to the end of the nineteenth century with the influence of the new theology and studies in comparative religion and the radical changes which then began to take place in the non-Christian religions."[100] He finished his work in early August, happy but a little concerned about its length. He had written for publication and faced the task of cutting the material down to lecture size, which meant omitting about two-thirds of each chapter.[101] The title concerned him a little, and he toyed with *The Uniqueness and the Finality of Christ* before settling on *The Finality of Jesus Christ.*[102]

The lectures at Princeton in mid-December, five in number, went well. At the same time he presented two of them at nearby New Brunswick Theological Seminary, and the following March all of them at the Southern Baptist Theological Seminary at Louisville. Almost as soon as Revell issued the book based on them in 1933, he began to receive personal letters of congratulation. The published reviews were more mixed, with some readers very unhappy with one or another of his interpretations. The criticisms were no real surprise, for as he was completing the manuscript he thought he would "get into trouble with the 'Christian Century' and all that group as a result of these lectures."[103]

The book appeared a few months after the publication of the Hocking Report and doubtless received more attention than it otherwise might have, because it seemed to be an answer to the report. However, the fact that the two books showed up in bookstores about the same time was entirely coincidental, since he had actually finished his work well before the report was published. Although he quickly realized the relationship between his book and the report, he also saw the need for a direct and separate response to the report, and so he wrote a substantial one, significant enough to set him apart as the chief protagonist in the ensuing debate over it (see chapter 13). Whether in its own right or because of the Hocking Report, *The Finality of Jesus Christ* attracted such a large audience that the publisher brought out a second printing by the end of the year.

Mackay later described this book as Speer's magnum opus and noted that it demonstrated "the vast range of the author's interests and his unexcelled knowledge of church history, Christian biography, the missionary movement, and comparative religion."[104] But Speer wrote other "great" works, including *Remember Jesus Christ, Missionary Principles and Practice, Christianity and the Nations,* and *Five Minutes A Day.* The term that Mackay might better have used, the one that matched his definition more closely, was *summa.* He produced no other book quite like it. The initial two chapters were a combination of his early studies on Jesus and Paul and his later studies on the life of the early church. The third was missionary history and biography. The fourth raised the question of the contemporary validity of the primitive view of Christ and contained a number of theological reflections. The fifth moved the focus to the central theme, "to which all our investigation has been leading us," and asked those who continued to believe in the primitive view of Christ, "What View, Then, Shall We Take Today Of Non-Christian Religions?"[105] A sign of the importance others attached to this chapter was that it appeared in abbreviated form in the *Missionary Review of the World* as "The True Christian Attitude Toward Non-Christian Religions" and as a pamphlet under the title: *The Christian Attitude Toward Non-Christian Religions.*[106]

He opened the final chapter with several arguments, all of which he had made before in one context or another, but which he believed were important to this topic. Religion and race were not the same thing, and Christianity was not a racial religion in any sense of the word. It was, on the contrary, "above race," a way of "uniting races," and "the bridge of the races."[107] Religion and culture or civilization were different. The missionary was not an agent of Western civilization but of the Christian religion. There was also a clear difference between a non-Christian religion and those who believed in it. A Christian might soundly condemn a non-Christian religious system "yet think only with good will and kindness and love of the men and women who adhere to this system."[108] A related issue was how missionaries communicated with non-Christians. Echoing a point he had first defined in his Duff Lectures, he said that the missionary's message, whatever his judgment might be about a particular non-Christian religion, was not that judgment but Jesus Christ.[109] A final distinction he drew was between "fundamental" or "essential" or "primitive" Christianity and "the explications and accretions which have gathered around it."[110] He was convinced that such primitive Christianity existed, with Jesus Christ at its center. That was the kind of Christianity that had generated the missionary movement and had called forth new Christians in mission fields. The debate was not between one or another form of culture Christianity and the non-Christian religions, but between essential Christianity and those religions. Moreover, the issue between them was more than theoretical, not only for the missionaries but also for those who belonged to the "indigenous or national Christian Churches." For them it was a "matter of life and death, of the validity or invalidity of their very existence."[111]

As he shifted from these distinctions to his main question, he introduced a new issue into his argument, one he had not dealt with in previous discussions of this topic: How had the missionaries of the recent past responded to the non-Christian religions and their adherents? Some claimed that missionaries in more recent times had moved away from the methods of Carey and Duff and "regarded the non-Christian religions as unqualifiedly evil and that their preaching was destructive and controversial."[112] He argued that was untrue and demonstrated what he believed to be the truth by tracing the attitudes of missionaries and their leaders through a series of national and international conferences, beginning with the Punjab Missionary Conference, held in Lahore, India, in 1862–63 and concluding with the Jerusalem conference. He was in a unique position to make such a survey, since he more than any other person had participated in and helped write the messages of many of those conferences, particularly the international ones after 1900.

While some individuals attacked and denigrated the non-Christian religions, "the corporate mind of Christianity" from India to China to Latin America and then in the great world conferences since New York in 1900 took a different view. The true mood had been expressed, for example, at the All-India General Conference at Allahabad in 1872–73. Delegates there gave "not a syllable of support for the idea" that the religions of India "were adequate or were to be syncretized in any way whatsoever with Christianity"; but, they also set a "pure, true, positive, evangelical Christian tone" for their approach to those who believed in those religions.[113] Some fifty years later, he continued, those who attended the Jerusalem conference espoused similar views. They declared Jesus Christ to be "the final yet ever-unfolding revelation of the God in whom we live and move and have our being," and also said to non-Christians: "We welcome every noble quality in non-Christian persons or systems as further proof that the Father, who sent his Son into the world, has nowhere left Himself without witness."[114]

Speer gathered together the corporate missionary mind to formulate his answer to the central question. In his Nashville speech and Duff lecture he had relied heavily on his study of comparative religions. In this Princeton lecture, his last, most extensive, and mature word on the topic, he integrated that information with what the missionaries of the immediate preceding generations had thought and done in relation to the non-Christian religions. Many of the ideas and some of the phrases from his earlier efforts survived in this last one, but in it he achieved a degree of organization and clarity he had not reached in the past.

His study of the missionary experience revealed that the question was really twofold: first, what view should the Christian hold of the non-Christian religions; second, what attitude and action should the Christian take toward them, both at home and abroad? As answers to the first inquiry, essentially the ways Christians should *think* about non-Christian religions, he proposed four ideas. The non-Christian religions revealed the "religious nature of man" and demonstrated that "men everywhere feel the need of help from without."[115] That was different from the Christian vision, which included God seeking man, but it was nonetheless an important idea. They all had "good and truth" in them, which had "enabled them to survive and given them their power." The good and truth they had was found more fully in Christianity, but at least they had both good and truth in them, despite the fact that they were "seamed with evils from which Christianity is free."

He cautioned that the religions were flawed, not necessarily those who believed in them. But he also spelled out one of his more pointed lists of the evils: "in Confucianism and Taoism, polytheism, idolatry and concubinage; in Hinduism, pantheism, polytheism, idolatry, caste and the moral fruitage of pantheism in the confusion of ethical distinctions; in Buddhism, pessimism and atheism; in Islam, fatalism, polygamy,—and back of all these are false and inadequate conceptions of God." Finally, taking the non-Christian religions "as they are, good and evil together, as represented not in any immoral practices or in any unfair distortion, but in their founders or heroes, their ideas of God, their sacred books and their essential principles, they are not classifiable with Christ and the authentic Christian faith." This final thought left the Christian faith where he believed it belonged, above all the other religions, supreme and universal, not one among equals but the one above all others. They were genuine religions, but not comparable with Christianity.

The second inquiry focused on the ways Christians should *act* toward non-Christian religions and their adherents. They should definitely pay attention to them.[116] Some Christians, he claimed, Karl Barth for one, seemed to suggest that Christians ought to go their own way, more or less ignoring other religions. He argued that was inappropriate. The proper Christian attitude, which he credited to Ellinwood, must be one "of intelligent understanding and appreciative recognition of every possible point of human contact in the realm of ideal and in the friendly and helpful relationship of common life and neighbourliness." But understanding and appreciation had its limits. If it ruled out attacking and destroying them, it also excluded any effort to preserve or merge with them. While the church should seek out and stress what was good and true in the non-Christian religions, it did so not to find its own fulfillment in them, but to discover the points of contact where it could offer redemption to those who believed in them.

The mission of Christianity, he concluded, "may be described in terms of salvation for individuals and salvage for their religions." Some Christians used the language of conquest, and he found nothing wrong with it. What was true in the non-Christian religions should be conserved, and what was untrue "conquered, driven out, destroyed." It was, after all, Christ who did the conquering, and "we rejoice to be His disciples as our Master, and His subjects as our King. This is the true relationship of men to Him, whether it be men of Asia or men of Europe, men of Hinduism or men of Christianity." And when Christ won, which he assuredly would one day, he and his religion would be, in fact as well as theory, the one universal faith.

The Unity of the Christian Church

The third of Speer's general missionary theories was that the movement of all peoples to Jesus Christ and Christianity would lead to the goal of one universal Christian church. That was the ultimate aim of foreign missions and of the work with those who were not yet Christians. This theory was somewhat different from the other two theories, since he had experienced it very early in his religious life and in his work with the SVM, before he actually studied and articulated it. Although he later attributed some of his views to Duff, he owed his convictions more to his own reflections and experiences than to any particular ideas of his predecessors. This theory had several components, in particular his views on comity, which tied this general theory to a specific proposal for action (see chapter 7). Moreover, his vision of unity extended beyond the arena of foreign missions and included what he hoped for the church in America and ultimately the world (see chapters 9 and 10). The driving force behind this theory, like the other ones, was his determination to affirm the universal character of Christianity.

One of the most dramatic and advanced positions he took on Christian unity in the mission fields was also one of the first. It appeared in the conclusion of his "Report of Recent Tour in Asia," at the Interdenominational Conference in 1898, summed up in one sentence: "I believe in one Christian Church on each mission field" (see chapter 7). He proceeded to spell out what he meant by this in such bold terms that he quickly became recognized as one of the leaders for the idea in his generation. And he defined it in such a way that opponents who favored some denominational prerogatives had little room to maneuver, a situation revealed in the IC debates. Although he spoke to the issue on a number of occasions, by far his most complete and systematic statement came at the organizational meeting of the Federal Council of Churches in 1908: "Christian Unity on the Foreign Field: Possible, Desirable, Practicable and Actual." He expanded it for his Duff Lectures and changed the title to "The Relation of Missions to the Unity of the Church and the Unity of the World." It was one of the definitive expositions in his era on Christian unity in the context of foreign missions.[117]

Christian unity was one of the major goals of the missionary effort, and Speer believed that a number of conditions made it both "desirable and necessary." First on his list was the "magnitude" and "urgency" of the task, which demanded an end to all waste, inefficiency, and duplication and the immediate unification of effort to reach everyone in the current generation. "Even if," he said, "one Christian body might hope to accomplish the work in many generations, were we to wait for it, we cannot wait, for these multitudes are passing away, and before they pass are entitled to know of the Lord who died for them and Who would be their Way and Light, and no one denomination of Christians has a right to claim the whole world as its preserve, the generations to wait until it can compass them all in its denominational name."[118] What people needed, after all, was what was most fundamental and essential in Christianity, "the character of God, and the love of God, and the life of God," and on those things many Christians, regardless of denominational affiliation, agreed.[119]

There was also widespread agreement that the missionary aim was to create strong national churches in accord with the Anderson-Venn three-self formula. If the missionary movement accomplished that, those indigenous churches would be united ones. He summed up this argument with an extended version of the statement he had made some dozen years earlier to his missionary executive colleagues: "For we are not trying to spread over the world any particular view of Christian truth or any particular form of Christian organization. I belong to the Presbyterian Church, but I have not the slightest zeal in seeking to have the Presbyterian Church extended over the non-Christian world. I believe in one Church of Christ in each land, and that it is far more important that the Presbyterians of Japan should be related to the Methodists of Japan than that either of these bodies should possess any connection whatever with any ecclesiastical organization in the United States."[120]

The final condition, and one of the most important conditions that pointed toward unity in the field, was the "Occidental character of our divisions." They made some sense in the context of American or European history, but they should not be exported, because they held no meaning at all for the "Chinese and Indians." He included doctrine as well as polity in his argument and proposed something that many disputed: "The things that have kept us apart here do not root down to what is fundamental or universal or eternal or really transportable." If missionaries focused on the essential things, then unity would have an opportunity to emerge. Those who possessed what he called the "universal mind" would "not be responsible for the perpetuation of these divisions."[121] He retained this mind the rest of his life, despite considerable opposition and persistent denominationalism at home and abroad.

The kind of unity he hoped for had external and internal components. It was not enough to avoid friction, to achieve a negative comity in which groups said to one another "Hands off." One form of the goal was "positive co-operation," in which groups put their "hands together." The evangelization of the world, he urged, could "not be done by companies of Christian men who agree to differ," but could only be achieved by those "who relate themselves for common and united action." Useful as this external unity was, the true goal lay beyond it in "spiritual unity," the kind for which Jesus prayed. Some claimed that what was needed in the mission fields was "fraternal relations." Speer would have none of it. Jesus had not prayed "that they all may be one as John and James are one, or as brothers are one," but "that they all may be one as Thou and I are one." The ideal was that kind of organic unity, in the case of the churches on the mission fields, a "corporate oneness." "We must," he said, "give Christ a body in which He can express Himself to the one humanity that He came to save."[122]

He devoted a substantial portion of his presentation to the considerable degree of unity that had been achieved despite obstacles to it. Missionaries and their sponsoring churches had resisted importing some things into some fields. He found it a happy circumstance that some words, including "Presbyterian," "Methodist," and "Protestant Episcopal," could not be translated into many languages. Protestant missionaries to the Philippines had agreed in the early days to use a common name for the evangelical churches. In many of the fields, churches had agreed to recognize "the ordinances and acts of discipline of other Christian organizations." An "advanced union" had been achieved "in the spirit of prayer," and the Week of Prayer originated in the field. Many mission fields, while not yet at the point of the ideal, had created various kinds of committees and organizations to advance cooperative work or to settle difficulties. In China it was called the Advisory Board of Reference and Co-operation and in India the Court of Arbitration and Appeal, and there were many others. Steps toward greater unity were being taken in some fields, particularly in India, China, and Japan. The future looked promising.[123]

Movements toward unity overseas had become so pervasive that he believed they were beginning to have an impact on the church at home, by demonstrating the possibility, the duty, and the method of unity. Some believed that the "sectarian phenomena of the last three or four centuries are to be the permanent characteristics of Christendom," but the unity already achieved in the mission fields revealed the possibility of a new age of unity in every land, like the one that had existed in New Testament times. Missionaries had discovered that unity was part of their duty, not just a useful tool. The home churches needed to make the same discovery because continued separation at home was, in some cases, preventing unity in the fields. There was evidence that some of them were. He found it ironic that the new churches had so subscribed to the gospel and its call for unity that they had begun to show the home churches the way. As a consequence, some of those churches were beginning to realize that it was their duty to participate in the movement toward unity because it was "essential to the fulfillment of the task of Christianity in the world, to bring the Gospel home to each man and each nation, and to unify mankind."[124]

The methods missionaries used were also applicable at home. He found four of them important enough to share with his listeners and subsequent readers. First, unity was often the result of working at a "common task." People who worked together toward a goal often ignored or forgot the things that divided them, in particular the theological issues. Second, "the power of fellowship" was so great that it could "dissolve" the differences between men and "purify" the errors on each side, making unity possible.[125] He quoted Bishop Charles H. Brent, then bishop of the American Episcopal Church in the Philippine Islands, who advised, "Actual sharing with one another of our good things as far as conscience permits will do more than anything else to advance God's truth and unite us according to His purpose."[126] Third, unity came when men and women relied on God, who alone could show them how to transcend their differences. The different theologies, especially, would be "reconciled at last, not by a restatement which will balance them afresh and establish a universal compromise and equipoise. They are to be reconciled in God. The living God will unify them and supplant them."[127] Fourth, nationalism worked as the principle of unity abroad and could serve the same function at home. It was the direction in which the Christians of Japan and India and Canada were moving. Should it not be, he asked, the goal in Scotland and the United States? He did not mean a federation or a council of churches, despite the fact that he was already involved in the Federal Council of Churches, but an organic union. What he had in mind emerged in the United Church of Canada in 1925 and the Church of South India in 1947.

As he drew his argument to a close, he shifted his emphasis from the role of the missionary movement in the unification of the church to ways it could help unify humanity, nationally and internationally. The "missionary construction of Christianity alone" preached and practiced racial inclusiveness and repudiated segregation. It affirmed "the dignity of each national genius and destiny, and the necessity of its contribution to the perfected family of God."[128] It was one of the few agencies at work that encouraged "peace," "good-will," and "friendship" among the different peoples and regions of the world, and it shared with the entire world the principles crucial to its unity, including "truth," "freedom," and the "equality of man and woman, of man and man."[129] Beyond this, it had carried everywhere the one "supreme uniting power," the Christian religion.

Throwing caution to the wind, he set out a grand vision of national and international unity: "The task which St. Paul performed for the Roman Empire we have now to perform for the world, and in a more complicated form, but a form for which Christianity is entirely adequate. We have to locate Christianity in the life of each separate nation for the perfection of its national character and the accomplishment of its national destiny, and we have to set it in the whole life of the world so as to bind into one each perfected nationality and to cement and complete with its unity the whole varied life of mankind. This is the work that must now be done, and which Christianity alone can do."[130]

This expansive vision was the logical conclusion of all his historical and theoretical studies, for, different though they were, they all ended up affirming his conviction that Jesus Christ was the one Savior through whom not just the church but the world would become one. He found it very significant that the religion of the Christ was the only one "which is trying to make good its claim to universalism." Christianity was "moving out over all the earth with steadily increasing power, with ever multiplying agencies, with ever enlarged devotion, and with open and undiscourageable purpose to prepare for Christ's kingship over the world."[131] As a missionary administrator and activist he was also a great missionary statesman. As historian and theoretician he was "the most influential American teacher of missionary principles after Rufus Anderson," and the Anderson of his era.[132]

PART III
American Churchman

Special Commission of 1925 (Robert E. Speer, top row, 1st on left)
Presbyterian Historical Society
Presbyterian Church (U.S.A.) (Philadelphia)

CHAPTER 9

Prophet of Christian Unity

"Looking Through the War Clouds"

The career Speer forged as an American churchman paralleled in many ways the one he created as a missionary statesman. They were closely related, because his status as a churchman began with his missionary successes, especially with the Student Volunteer Movement, and that work led him through ecumenical foreign missions to ecumenical and denominational work at home apart from foreign missions. But his careers as a statesman and a churchman were also distinct. As a churchman he served in key national leadership positions on three occasions, twice with the Federal Council of Churches, as chair of the General War-Time Commission of the Churches beginning in 1917 and as president of the council beginning in 1920, and once with the Presbyterian Church in the United States of America, as moderator in 1927. The only comparable office he held in foreign missions was chairman of the Committee on Cooperation in Latin America, and he did so primarily because he organized that committee.

The common denominator of the national offices, and that which encouraged him to accept positions that he ordinarily declined, was that in each case his peers approached him in what they perceived to be a crisis situation and persuaded him to accept the task. His life as an American churchman was considerably more crisis-centered than his one as a foreign missions executive. He entered the work on behalf of the American church through the same gate as the missionary work, the one marked ecumenical, and led the Federal Council before his own church called on him.

He did not seek out these crises, and was not a person who liked being at the center of controversy. One of the ironies of his life was that he preferred to work behind the scenes in private ways or to share leadership as he did at Edinburgh and Jerusalem. Yet his reputation as an American churchmen turns very heavily on the way he exercised leadership in the midst of crises and the way he dealt with very controversial issues.

Why did people approach him? The crises were times of potential division, when things seemed on the verge of coming apart. That was particularly true when the churches faced World War I and as his church confronted the theological issues of the late 1920s. The people who approached him knew that he believed passionately in Christian unity and would do everything anyone could do to hold things together. He had the ability, to an unusual degree, to discern the main issues in a given dispute and formulate an acceptable settlement. In short, he practiced reconciliation. Moreover, he had a high public profile as a person of genuine spiritual experience. People trusted him not only to lead, but to be led by the Spirit.

And why did he accept? That question has both a simple, straightforward answer and a much more complicated one. In each case where he responded positively, those presenting the challenge made him see it as a Christian duty. He never turned aside from an appeal once he saw it that way. But there were other, more subtle and not so clearly stated, reasons. By the time he began to be called on to serve in positions apart from foreign missions, he had concluded that it was his turn. Most of his mentors had joined the church triumphant, including Ellinwood, Trumbull, Pierson, and Moody. The leadership torch had been passed and was now in the hands of his generation. Another consideration was his many appeals to Christian unity. In those appeals he had hoped people would practice what he preached. When church leaders urged him to step forward and try his hand at reconciling the different parties in the ecumenical ministry or in his own denomination, he agreed.

Vision of Christian Unity

His vision of Christian unity embraced all aspects of his work. He fully integrated what he hoped for in foreign missions with what he projected for the church in America. He believed in one standard of Christian unity, and the effort to achieve it abroad required one at home. This was a crucial linkage. It was one of the major reasons he joined the American ecumenical movement as soon as it emerged. He was entirely devoted to his call to foreign missions, but when he realized that the fulfilment of the call depended in significant measure on the success of the church unity movement at home, he directed some of his energies to it.

There were at least three sources for his ideas about Christian unity. They were like separate streams which gradually flowed together to form one larger one without any order of priority or distinct point of junction. The first and obvious source was his work as a missionary secretary. There he came face to face with the ways some missionaries and their societies were transplanting American church divisions overseas. That led to his efforts for comity and united churches in the mission fields and also, particularly after his return from his world trip, to increasing references to the need for unity at home.

The most extensive argument he developed concerning the relationship between unity abroad and at home was in an article in the *American Journal of Theology* in 1907 titled "Should the Denominational Distinctions of Christian Lands be Perpetuated on Mission Fields?" He answered a resounding no and offered no support for perpetuation of the distinctions and many arguments against it. Distinctions at home had no meaning in other cultural settings, and also ran counter to the aim of a "rational missionary policy," which was to establish "strong national churches." Those mission societies that were trying to found American churches in other lands should beware, he believed, because those churches would ultimately break down "under the proper spirit of nationalism which education and contact with modern political ideas will inevitably produce," which meant that nationalism in China would one day lead to a Chinese church. On less certain ground, he proposed that the "majority" of those who supported the missionary enterprise did not want more denominations but simply hoped "to spread the simple knowledge of Christ" and would support those missionaries who worked for unity and who were "abandoning western denominationalism in the interest of national church organizations." In the context of this presentation he made the following succinct statement of his position:

> I believe that the denominational distinctions of Christian lands should not be perpetuated on the mission fields, for the simple reason that they ought not to be perpetuated at home. I believe there is no adequate excuse for the continued existence of the scores of ecclesiastical bodies now existing in America. The Presbyterian and Reformed churches should be united in one body, all the churches of the Congregational polity in another, the Methodist churches in another. Further than this, there is no sufficient reason for the separation of Presbyterian and Congregational churches, nor of Calvinistic and Arminian Christians, nor of Christians who baptize by one mode and Christians who baptize by another. There are, perhaps, certain general temperamental types now divided among the various churches, and it may be well, until we reach a riper stage of Christian character, to retain

provision for the separation of the types; but such diversities will tend to disappear, and they furnish no adequate basis for a permanent division of Protestant Christendom. The doctrinal differences of truly evangelical Christians and their differences of polity, are not, to my mind, sufficient reason for an indefinite perpetuation of denominationalism. Not believing in it at home, except as a temporary necessity, I do not believe in its extension abroad.[1]

Another source of his vision of Christian unity was his Bible study, especially of Jesus and Paul. He believed that Jesus had embodied the concept of unity, proposed it as the rule for his followers and passed it to Paul, who developed it. Speer began his study of Jesus' message of unity with his relationship with God as his father, because that relationship defined the "ruling principles of His life." One of them was fellowship: "To know God as Father is to know and to do His will and be close to Him."[2] Jesus had explained it to his disciples as loving one another, and, Speer claimed, his vision had been that "the Christian Church should be a body of men and women who had learned to love God and His Spirit and His Son with all their hearts and minds and souls and strength, and one another better than they loved themselves."[3] Jesus had described what he hoped for when he used the organic image of the vine with himself as the trunk and the disciples the branches "springing out from Him, all of them bound together because they were common branches of one vine, while there flowed through them all, whether upper branches or lower branches, large branches or small branches, the one common tide of the single life."[4] A distinctive feature of the early church and one of its major reasons for success had been that it said "to a world filled with people who knew no such fellowship: 'Come, join our brotherhood; we will love you; we will take you into friendship; you too may belong to this unique society of men and women who are all truly lovers one of another.' "[5] Moreover, this fellowship had been both inclusive and universal, more open to different kinds of people and broader geographically than any other of its day, particularly Judaism.[6]

Paul had caught Jesus' vision and had the opportunity to translate it into life. Speer called 1 Corinthians 12 "one of the most splendid passages in his letters."[7] There Paul had used the body as a metaphor for the church and had declared that the many parts, of whatever apparent value, were interrelated and that all were affected by all, and worked best in a condition of peace and harmony. Paul not only "could not endure the idea of schism or partisan division," but he had worked hard to achieve unity, among both the Corinthians and Philippians. Speer proposed that a "marvelous transformation would pass over our Christian life if our conception of our relationship to one another fulfilled this great ideal of Paul."[8] Jesus and Paul had taught him that "if we are Christ's we are one another's also, and all of us are one body in Him."[9]

The final sources of his conviction of unity were his personal experiences of it. They had begun in his childhood and continued essentially uninterrupted throughout his life. He never really experienced a denominational ghetto and refused to be drawn into debates that focused on denominational prerogatives. He told sister Margaret in 1930 that he was "glad of our contacts with the various denominations in Huntingdon in the old days. It is very helpful in meeting men of the other denominations in the conferences of today."[10] The strongest influences in his college and early postgraduate years were the SVM and YMCA, both ecumenical in structure and spirit. Speaking to those assembled for the thirty-fifth international convention of the YMCA, he called to mind the divisions within Christianity and offered the following opinion: "It has been one of the glories of this brotherhood that here all those things disappear. Looking into your faces this morning, I cannot distinguish to which churches you belong. What a great thing it would be if only this spirit of perfect union and trust could pervade the entire Christian Church."[11]

Such experiences, repeated in many settings, persuaded him that Christian unity was a real possibility, if Christians permitted it to evolve from their faith experiences. He developed several perspectives on this and articulated all of them, well before he became more formally involved in ecumenical work. First, his era was full of movements in the churches that were "sweeping to convergence." When he announced this in 1899, at the end of a decade full of religious turmoil, few people understood it, but the events in church federation at home and in national churches abroad in the following decades confirmed it.[12] Second, the way to unity was through common action and service. The more Christians from different denominations worked together, the more they were likely to understand one another and to look toward greater unity. Third, ordinary Christians were not interested in doctrine, but in life, particularly life in Jesus Christ. He ventured to say in 1901, "The great mass of church members of all Christian bodies in this country have substantially the same doctrinal convictions." Doctrinal differences were most prevalent among "theological instructors and the ministers who have been taught theology." Even among them, he thought, "the tides of development are sweeping them to a catholic doctrinal view. Practically, as has been often said, all Arminians are Calvinists when they pray, and all the Calvinists are Arminians when they preach."[13] He never changed his mind, not even in the disruptive fundamentalist controversy some thirty years later. That debate made his point, for it was led in his denomination by a seminary professor and ministers, and, although they had a following in the churches, they were not pushed to the front by a popular uprising of the laity. The way toward unity was through simpler doctrinal statements and focus on living the Christian life, as in his immensely popular "What Jesus Does for Me," which he wrote in 1930 in the midst of that struggle (see chapter 3).

Inter-Church Conference on Federation

The sources of his ideas about Christian unity had been flowing together for some years when in 1905 he received an invitation to a special ecumenical occasion. The meeting was the Inter-Church Conference on Federation, which opened on November 15 in New York City and continued for a week. The planners included in their agenda a meeting for young people. They asked Mott to serve as chair and invited five people to make presentations at a session titled "Interdenominational Gathering in the Interest of Young People's Organizations." The speakers were not what a later generation would consider young people, but represented the leadership of various youth organizations, including persons in higher education. Mott was forty, Speer had just turned thirty-eight, and Woodrow Wilson, then president of Princeton University, was forty-eight.

Speer decided to use this opportunity to draw together his thoughts on Christian unity, especially as they related to the church at home. Although he chose to title his remarks "The Bases of Unity Among Young People and Steps Toward Achievement" and acknowledged that he had been invited as the "mouthpiece" of the younger generation, he offered the large audience gathered in Carnegie Hall an analysis not limited to a particular age group. It was his personal ecumenical agenda for the future. It was one of the era's most forthright and future-looking definitions of Christian unity relating to the domestic scene and, paired with his subsequent statement to the Federal Council and the Duff Lecture on unity in foreign missions, constituted his thinking on Christian unity at home and abroad (see chapter 8 for a more thorough discussion of this).

He opened his presentation with an important distinction and a startling affirmation. The current generation was different from the one which preceded it when it came to the question of Christian unity. Young men and women had been meeting in large assemblies, reading "common books" and writing "common papers," and had discovered "a common heart and a common sympathy," whereas their parents all too often had experienced the limitations of denominational boundaries and viewpoints. Without naming Bushnell, who was never far from his thought when he reflected on Christian unity, he said his generation had reached its view "by a process of *comprehension* that has lifted us up above those subjects of division which have harassed those who went before us, and made us feel that we have already grounds for fellowship sufficient to warrant the closest possible union among us." But how close? His generation shared the "ideals of federation." He paused, and then declared, "and—I will say with perfect frankness—of Church union."[14]

The younger generation, he claimed, were already at the point of union in many ways. They were one in the belief that the true substance of Christian character was the willingness to give of oneself in self-sacrificial service. The proof of their conviction lay in their willingness to offer themselves in missionary service despite the costs. Evoking the memory of the Boxer martyrs in China, he proposed, "You might wipe off the face of the earth the whole missionary body to-day, and we would replace it within a few years." His generation had begun to dream, "as Christ dreamed, of the saving of a world, and their ideals of service are ideals that run with the ambition of the missionary spirit which Christ fired when he set the Church's eye upon the uttermost parts of the earth." They shared a "consciousness" and a "conviction" of human need and a sense that it was their duty to help meet it. They agreed above all on the centrality of Jesus Christ. His generation did not believe it was possible to "state His Gospel except in Christological terms." The "great organizations" of the young people, by which he doubtless meant at least the SVM, Christian Endeavor, and the Ys, had "grown up on this one central fact. They believe in Christ, they love Christ, they want to serve Christ, they want to make Jesus Christ the Lord of all mankind; they call Him first Lord and Saviour, and Teacher afterwards; and it is because they are united in these great convictions that the degree of unity that we have attained to-day is a possible thing."[15]

He cautioned that the unity his generation had achieved was far from complete, and could only be made so when everyone, all generations and all distinct groups, joined together. The "apprehensions of truth" revealed "larger comprehensions of truth" toward which all must work. As well as they knew Christ, there was more to be known, which would only be known "as we draw together for those social visions of Him that are only possible to all the saints, the realizations of that love that is to be revealed to us never alone but with all the saints, that unity of the faith that we are to attain never separately but only when we all come to it."[16] As fine as their sacrificial service was, the "magnitude of the task" that remained required a greater degree of unity. "We are appealing for Christian union," he declared, "not because Christians are quarreling with one another, for they are not; we are appealing for Christian union because there is waste where there should not be waste, because the army should be one army, because brother should now clasp the hand of brother, that alike through the daylight and the night the whole army may step forward to its mighty world-wide task." As strong as their prayers were, fully united prayers would be more powerful. It was that "power in prayer" the world needed, and it depended "entirely upon that unity among Christians which brings them all together in the right relationship to God."[17]

He had promised "Steps Toward Achievement" of a more perfect unity, and he concluded his speech by pointing out four of them. The steps were individual ones, but he believed that, despite the naysayers, they were "converging." His suggestions broke no new ground, and he turned them in typical fashion toward the practical and experiential and away from the doctrinal and theological. First and foremost, Christians would be brought closer to one another if they simply practiced the Christian faith, for the things that had kept them apart "are not points of Christian principle but defects of Christian practice. Once Christian men and women begin to practice the Christian faith of love and tenderness and kindness and self-repression and humility, they will find that the very practice of the Christian faith is itself a unifying power."[18] Second, Christians should continue to work together, especially toward the goal that had been drawing them toward unity, "the evangelization of the whole world." Their era had at long last recovered that "great apostolic conception," and he speculated "whether the Mohammedan missionary problem has not been reserved for this day in order that it might constitute the wall against which as the Christian churches hurled themselves they should discover that only as they fused together into one and then smote would they be able at last to penetrate that wall and to conquer for Christ the two hundred millions who have known His name and exalted above it another name."[19] Third, Christians needed to continue to move nearer to Christ, for the closer they came, the more one they would become. Finally, whatever steps Christians took, God's Spirit was also at work. As Christians moved toward unity, the Holy Spirit knitted them into a more perfect union. He concluded with what amounted to a prayer: "Oh, that it might be in our day that at last the expectant Christ should see of the desire of His soul and be satisfied, that in our day at last, for the conviction of the world, for the full setting forth of the divine unity of the Son with His Father, those who call Him their Master might in Him be one."[20]

His prayer articulated, as well as anything said at the conference, the dreams of those who planned it and may have exceeded those of many who were not yet ready for the degree of unity he projected. The Rev. Elias B. Sanford was primarily responsible for preparations, and he for one hoped the conference would mark the beginning of an era of fuller Christian unity. The new beginning he and others hoped for would be a form of church unity constituted by the churches as official bodies, so that the Protestant denominations could meet and think and act as one. The conference did not disappoint the leaders who held such a vision, for it recommended to the denominations, those that acknowledged "Jesus Christ as their Divine Lord and Saviour," the creation of a federation to be called the Federal Council of the Churches of Christ in America.[21] Three years later, in 1908, after most of the denominations represented at the conference had officially ratified the proposed constitution, delegates met in Philadelphia at what came to be known as the first quadrennial, and formally created the Federal Council.[22] The city where the nation had come together became the one where the Protestant churches found a common voice.

Reviewing the span of ecumenical history in the United States from the beginning of the twenty-first century, the Inter-Church Conference stands as a major turning point of the twentieth century. The conference was also a turning point in his life as an ecumenical leader. Before the conference, the primary contributions he had made on behalf of Christian unity were in foreign missions. After it, he developed contacts and a context for his ecumenical ideas and work at home and became one of the key figures in the effort to make unity a practical reality. Although he did not become an ecumenical officeholder immediately, the Inter-Church Conference marked the beginning of his relationship to the Federal Council. He served domestic ecumenism the same way he served missionary ecumenism, as a volunteer.

Work for the Federal Council

Over the following two decades Speer gave time and energy to the Federal Council in a variety of ways and at increasing levels of responsibility. He attended the first quadrennial as a representative of foreign missions and presented his remarkable statement on ecumenism in foreign missions (see chapter 8 for discussion of this). Not everyone was pleased with the degree of unity he espoused, especially with his claim to have little interest in extending the Presbyterian Church around the world. The editor of the *Presbyterian Standard* chastised him for playing down what he considered to be important and biblically based differences that existed between groups in both church polity and doctrine.[23]

The Federal Council worked through committees and commissions, the latter considered more permanent and perhaps more important than the former, and he worked on both in the early years. It organized a Committee on Foreign Missions at the Philadelphia meeting, and he was one of several missionary executives invited to serve. It was a natural appointment, given his prominence in foreign mission circles. This was his first formal council work. When this committee became a commission for the quadrennium 1912–16, he became its chair.

This committee/commission turned out to be a source of concern to Federal Council leaders. Circumstantial evidence leads to the conclusion that council officials chose him to be chair because they believed he could resolve it.[24] The issue was primarily over turf. This was a novel situation, for unlike previous eras, when there were very few unitive movements, this period seemed to have a surfeit of them. When the council had organized, it had taken the position that it represented all the work of the churches and had decided to include foreign missions. However, the Inter-denominational Conference, by 1912 the Foreign Missions Conference, had for some years occupied that ground, and many of its members considered the Committee/Commission on Foreign Missions a duplication of its efforts. They had opposed any kind of separate continuation committee of the Ecumenical Missionary Conference in 1901 on those grounds, and they did not appreciate what the council was doing. A simple solution would have been for the FMC to become the council's agent in foreign missions work, but the FMC had developed a strong identity, and its members were reluctant to make a change that had any potential to weaken it. Moreover, although FMC and council sponsors overlapped, they were not identical. There seemed to be space for each group, since the FMC dealt more with foreign missions in the international arena and the council in the national one, but the key was working out the relationship and defining the spaces.

Speer contacted the members of his commission and told them it seemed desirable to simplify "as greatly as possible the machinery of our interdenominational missionary relationships." To that end he enclosed a proposed resolution of the problem and invited them to a meeting on

November 13, 1913, to debate the issues.[25] They decided to accept his settlement. The first and crucial point was that the commission agreed to
avoid duplicating FMC programs and to work toward a time "when the
foreign mission function of the Federal Council may be discharged
through the Annual Conference of the Foreign Mission Boards." This
essentially placed the program initiative in the hands of the FMC and left
the Federal Council commission in a supporting role in which it would be
free to advance "those movements of co-operation and unity which the
Foreign Mission Boards are promoting," publish occasional pamphlets
that would encourage greater unity in foreign missions, and keep "before
the Churches the attainments already made in foreign missionary work in
federation, co-operation and unity, as a help to the Church at home in its
consideration of the methods and possibilities of unity in the work of the
church in the United States."[26] The settlement meant that he had decided
that the first step toward resolution of the problem was strategic withdrawal. He called the next meeting of the commission to coincide with the
annual meeting of the FMC.

When the commission presented these arrangements to the FMC in
January 1914, its members received them well, as they should have. After
all, he had already alerted his missionary colleagues in the role of inter-
mediary and negotiator that "some mutual adjustment should be made to
prevent overlapping and confusion."[27] Moreover, the settlement essentially
left the FMC in charge of its turf. The administrative committee of the
Federal Council subsequently approved the plan.[28] The rest of the quadrennium the commission functioned, with its much reduced portfolio,
through an executive committee of seven, led by him. Five of the seven
members were also active in the FMC. Council secretary Charles S.
Macfarland reported to his executive committee on developments in
1914, "With Dr. Speer as the Chairman of the Commission, the Federal
Council is always sure of a representative in all co-operative missionary
movements, and in due time, under his wise direction, a more satisfactory
adjustment between the Federal Council and co-operative movements
among the existing foreign mission agencies is sure to be brought about."[29]

The commission made no reports to the council in 1914 or 1915. Its
report to the third quadrennial in 1916 proved to be its last. The council
had organized a committee of fifteen in 1915 to "survey" all of its work
and "to interpret in some measure its present status."[30] He had served on
this committee and offered his advice on a number of matters, including
in particular those relating to foreign missions. He had informed
Macfarland that he believed the commission should become once again a

committee made up largely of persons who were also members of the FMC. This fell short of his long-term solution to the problem, but even if it failed to establish "an official relationship" between the council and the FMC, it would "set up a relationship in fact." In addition, "the beginning of an official relationship would be made if it were now formally agreed" that the FMC would submit reports to the council on its work for foreign missions, either directly or through the commission/committee. The committee of fifteen's final proposals for foreign missions followed his advice to the letter.[31] When the Federal Council adopted them, the commission became a committee once again, with a very modest assignment.[32] His actions had reduced the council's bureaucracy and had resolved, temporarily at least, an important problem and advanced its goal of unity. He continued to serve on the committee until the council abolished it in 1920, in response to the FMC decision to formalize its relationship with the council and become a consultative body. That action was exactly his long-term solution to the problem.

General War-Time Commission

One of the more challenging assignments of his life was the one he accepted with the Federal Council after the United States entered World War I. It was as unexpected as his work with the Committee/Commission on Foreign Missions was expected. He was strongly sympathetic to the efforts undertaken by some government officials, leaders of the Federal Council, and other citizens in the fall of 1916 and the early months of 1917 to find a way to bring about peace and to keep the United States out of the war. As much as he favored peace, he did not linger over failed initiatives. After President Wilson and Congress made the decision to enter the war in April 1917, he supported the new policy. When the leaders of the Federal Council, concerned about the impact of the war on the people and their churches and particularly interested in providing an adequate number of chaplains for the military, called a special meeting for Washington for May, he readily agreed to attend and give one of the major addresses.

Joined on the platform by old friend Mott and recently elected council president Frank Mason North, he helped set the tone for the assembly. In his speech, "The War and the Nation's Larger Call to World Evangelism," he urged the churches to greater cooperation and an enlarged ministry. He noted that some church leaders advocated altering the programs of their churches and turning most of their energies and resources to war-related tasks. While he recognized the need for wartime ministries, he believed the churches should retain their regular programs and even extend them, particularly in foreign missions. The missionary movement was "an expression in flesh of our conviction that humanity is one."[33] Through the missionary enterprise people had seen the great possibilities of interdenominational, international, and interracial service. Now was the time, he declared, to advance cooperation on all those fronts.[34] Moreover, unity of action was not enough. The churches must also speak out clearly on the issue of internationalism. Too often the churches simply sanctioned the existing order without exercising their prophetic imperative to look beyond that order to other possibilities. He believed that nothing should be permitted to limit their policy: "We betray our mission and fail God if we shrink into a nationalistic sect that can conceive only of our own national functions, unless those national functions include for us the whole human brotherhood and the duty of speaking and thinking and living by the law of a world love."[35]

The delegates at the special meeting adopted the "Message to the Churches," which was the council's statement of the relationship between the churches and the war and served as the basis for its wartime ministry. Although it was a collective effort, formulated by the ecumenical Protestant leadership, Speer had a large influence in it and found it fully congruent with his own views. It said in part, "We are Christians as well as citizens. Upon us therefore rests a double responsibility. We owe it to our country to maintain intact and to transmit unimpaired to our descendants our heritage of freedom and democracy. Above and beyond this, we must be loyal to our divine Lord, who gave his life that the world might be redeemed, and whose loving purpose embraces every man and every nation."[36] The message invited Christians and churches to make a number of pledges, including these: "to purge our own hearts clean of arrogance and selfishness"; "to hold our own nation true to its professed aims of justice, liberty, and brotherhood"; "to testify to our fellow Christians in every land, most of all to those from whom for the time we are estranged, our consciousness of unbroken unity in Christ"; "to unite in the fellowship of service multitudes who love their enemies and are ready to join with them in rebuilding the waste places as soon as peace shall come"; and "above all, to call men everywhere to new obedience to the will of our Father God, who in Christ has given himself in supreme self-sacrifice for the redemption of the world, and who invites us to share with him his ministry of reconciliation."[37]

Willing as he was to share in shaping the council's wartime message, he was not enthusiastic about taking a leadership role in the churches' war effort. North approached him several times in July in an attempt to convince him to chair a proposed wartime commission. He demurred each time, arguing that others like Harry Emerson Fosdick or William Adams Brown were more suited and that his personal wish was to be a "private in the ranks."[38] North was not to be denied. He wrote Speer a long epistle in which he said that the proffered job was a question of duty and shared his growing feeling that the times ahead were critical ones for the church as well as for the nation. He mentioned his apprehension "that unless men like yourself come out into the larger leadership which existing conditions seem to require, and which seem to be planned in the mind of the Master, days of regret, if not disaster, are before the church."[39] North thought that the primary function of the proposed commission should be to keep the various denominational and interdenominational programs going in one general direction, motivated as much as possible by a common set of purposes. It should uphold all genuine attempts to minister to the needs of men and nations, rather than abrogate programs already begun. However, North felt that few if any of the already organized programs and only a minority of Christians had an inkling of "the whole task." He sought to persuade Speer that the proposed commission, led by a man of his "foresight and insight," could so interpret the policy of the Federal Council as to comprehend that task.[40]

North's argument convinced him, and within two weeks he was busily at work as chair of the newly named General War-Time Commission of the Churches, selecting members for it and inviting them to the organizational meeting. The key to his acceptance most likely lay in North's appeal to duty and his concern for "larger leadership." Shortly after the declaration of war, many denominations established war commissions and special wartime programs. The conflicts between these spheres of interest were already becoming manifest, to the detriment of the total ministry of the churches and the nation's war effort. In addition, the warmongering, judged by many later historians to be almost the sole word of the churches during the war, was beginning to appear in various prominent pulpits and religious periodicals.[41] "Larger leadership" was needed to bring unity and coherence to a fractured ministry and to raise a voice of moderation and restraint in the message the churches spoke to a nation at war. It was also needed if postwar reconstruction plans were to measure up to the Kingdom of God.

His initial charge from North defined the two major aspects of his work, administration and interpretation. He accomplished both without taking a leave from his board, a tribute to his ability to do several things at once and to his supporting cast. The administrative work proved to be very time-consuming, but relatively straightforward. The war crisis and the need to expand ministry during the war were obvious to almost everyone, and most of those whom he approached for help responded and followed his lead. He shared in planning the four general meetings of the commission, the first in September in the offices of the council in New York and the last in April 1919. He directed the executive committee, which met twice a month, also in New York, and which drew a faithful group of about twenty-one. William Lawrence, the Protestant Episcopal bishop of Massachusetts, became vice-chair, and William Adams Brown, on the faculty at Union Theological Seminary in New York, served as secretary. Speer and Brown, along with North, Macfarland, and several assistant secretaries, carried much of the load. Brown wrote him after the war, "You and I have had the rare experience of learning to know each other as we have tried to think our way together through a difficult and inspiring trial. There may be a better way to make friends. I have not found it. There may be a better friend to make, I have not found him."[42]

Speer used his many organizational and reconciling talents to good advantage. The agenda for the initial meeting included time to consider a statement of purpose, and he prepared a draft to get the discussion started and offer it some direction. The version the commission adopted reflected his priorities, and included the following purposes: "to coordinate existing and proposed activities and to bring them into intelligent and sympathetic relationship so as to avoid all waste and friction and to promote efficiency"; "to suggest to the proper agency or agencies any further work called for and not being done"; "to provide a body which would be prepared to deal in a spirit of cooperation with any new problems of reconstruction which may grow out of the war."[43] The commission focused on the first purpose and filled in the gaps as they appeared.

When difficult issues emerged, as they did with the YMCA and the War Department, in both cases over ministry to the armed forces, he became a key figure in the negotiated resolution. Because of his role as commission chair, he served on the committee of six, created at the suggestion of the War Department and chaired by Father John J. Burke of the National Catholic War Council, to advise it on matters relating to the chaplaincy. He told Cairns that there were some real problems: "On the one hand, to work whole-heartedly with other religious forces and yet at the same time not to compromise our own freedom of action and our own distinctive conviction; on the other hand to carry fully our share of the national burden, and yet to keep the Church's true position, and not to let it be merely an echo of political leaders or a mere agent for government policies."[44]

The commission ran smoothly under his leadership, quickly adopting several working principles. It maintained a small working staff. He called its members "liaison officers" because they worked to bring the churches and agencies together to exchange ideas and operate programs.[45] It had a cooperative budget, modeled after that of the council. It carried on much of its work in committees. The procedure was commonplace, but not in the ecumenical context. By the time the commission dissolved, it had created no less than twenty-nine committees of four discernible types. Standing committees dealt with long-term issues and included those on finance, camp neighborhoods, and the welfare of African American troops. Special committees focused on short-term concerns, like interned aliens and a church flag. Joint committees were quite numerous and featured cooperation with other groups, like the home missions council. Among them were those for war production communities and cooperation with the American Red Cross. Committees of conference ironed out difficulties with other agencies.[46]

He managed all of this the way he did his board work. He chose, or shared in choosing, committee chairs and then turned them loose to accomplish their assigned tasks, expecting action and appropriate reports. Six months into the work he told those gathered for the second commission meeting that things were going well: "We have zeal here, but most of it has risen from a feeling of pastoral responsibility and has been animated by no sectarian spirit and no desire on the part of the different churches 'to run their own show' for their own glory, but to make sure that the Church of Christ is doing its work and making its impact on the lives of the young men and the nation."[47] Macfarland summed up the work of the commission: "It would be hard to think of any agency or area of service which was overlooked. Thus, by the time the war was well under way an administrative agency was developed which reduced duplication of effort and unified the Protestant bodies, both denominational and interdenominational, to a degree hitherto deemed impossible."[48]

The interpretive role was as difficult as the administrative one was easy. He had definite convictions about the war and its meaning for the church and had expressed them many times after the guns of August had shattered the peace in Europe, usually in the context of missionary publications and gatherings.[49] America's entry into the war did not change his mind, for the views he presented at the special meeting were identical to those he had expressed since 1914. The one thing that changed after he became commission chair was how other people regarded his views. No one spoke ex cathedra for the commission or the council, and when he spoke, he made it absolutely clear that he did so for himself; but after he assumed office, the public began to accept what he said on issues, particularly war and peace, as the positions of the commission and council. Like it or not, once in the leadership role, he was also in an interpretive one. This was a version of what he had long experienced as a secretary with the Board of Foreign Missions. However, in that context his interpretive role was confined largely to foreign missions and to those in the Presbyterian Church, although after Edinburgh he had a more general audience. When he acted as an officer of the council, the topics expanded greatly, and the audience extended to the constituencies of most of the large Protestant churches and the general public. His views on war and peace, and in this sense those of the council, were tested in a public confrontation. He later refined and clarified them in a number of speeches, articles, and books.

Public Controversy

The public confrontation came rather unexpectedly. Speer was a popular writer and speaker, much in demand to reflect on foreign missions. After his new council assignment in the summer of 1917, he had given many speeches and written several articles on the ministry of the churches in the war and had received no critical response.[50] Therefore, when he spoke at a mass meeting held under the auspices of the Intercollegiate YMCA of New York City in the gymnasium of Columbia University on February 18, 1918, he had no reason to expect that his words would arouse a furor. He had agreed to speak on behalf of an innocent cause. His task was to interest students in enrolling in a study course sponsored by the YMCA on the Christian program of reconstruction, and his host had charged him to emphasize the religious and democratic elements of that program. He had been warned by the general secretary of the Intercollegiate Association that the audience would include members of a radical group, evidently so designated because of their non-Christian orientation, and he had been told that he should speak so as to interest and challenge them too.[51]

He organized his address around the title "World Democracy and America's Obligation to Her Neighbors." In the initial part of his presentation, he analyzed five main factors in the world that had helped to precipitate the war and had to be changed if the future was to be different from the past. These were (1) "the imperfect development of democracy," (2) "the contested claim of nationalism to be above the moral law," (3) "the retarding or the breaking down of the process of social evolution and human progress for the want of adequate agents to carry them forward," (4) "the persistence of race prejudice and suspicion," and (5) "the resistance of national individualism to the spirit of world brotherhood and to common human interests."[52] He illustrated each of these with examples from all belligerent nations, including the United States. To make his point on race prejudice, for example, he cited not only German racial attitudes but also American attitudes toward the Japanese and the Native Americans. In reference to the fifth factor, he pointed to American movements in the interest of "pure national individualism" and argued that they could easily destroy the nation's ability to hold onto "universal ideals and the universal spirit."[53]

In the second half of his speech he showed how these problems had their solution in the Christian ideals and spirit as they were expressed in the missionary movement.[54] The main thrust of the entire speech was against those things, including a narrow patriotism, that abrogated worldwide democracy and the international spirit, however dear such things were to the hearts of most Americans.

At first it seemed that the speech would go all but unnoticed. The *New York Times* carried a brief report but offered no editorial comment.[55] The anticipated reaction from the radicals did not materialize. Then, on February 22, the same newspaper published a letter from Henry B. Mitchell, professor of mathematics at Columbia University, under the title "Weakening Patriotism." Mitchell had attended the YMCA meeting, and he turned out to be a much more dangerous kind of radical than those about whom Speer had been warned. Speer was a man of reputation, reported Mitchell, a man who held important posts in the Presbyterian Board of Foreign Missions and in the General War-Time Commission of the Churches; but his speech at the university was "insidiously corrupting, both to the will and the intelligence, because it breathed throughout the spirit of pacifism and minimized the infamies that Germany has perpetrated." Mitchell continued, "His argument was the stock one of pro-German agitators in this country—that Germany had only done what all other nations had done, or would do if they had the power." He was disturbed because Speer had made no "appeal for aid in the prosecution of the war." Were men such as this, he asked, making similar speeches on behalf of the YMCA all over the nation?[56]

This single letter brought a storm of criticism raining down on Speer and the YMCA. Within two weeks the *Times* printed no fewer than ten letters and three editorials commenting on Mitchell's version of the speech. The authors of most of the letters followed Mitchell in soundly chastising Speer for his pacifism and denying the right of anyone to speak words that might detract from the nation's glory in time of war. The temper of the times was captured by two of the correspondents. The chaplain at Dartmouth College wrote, "The war with Germany is the whole thing now, and none of our other problems will suffer, while we bend every energy to secure the right conclusion. Surely on this point there should be no wavering."[57] More damning publicly was the opinion of Professor Charles Fagnani of Union Theological Seminary. He substantiated the pro-German label Mitchell had pinned on the speech and said he recognized many Germans and those with "Teutonic susceptibilities" at the meeting. He concluded, "The German-American Alliance would have found absolutely nothing to object to in Mr. Speer's address, on the contrary."[58]

The editorial remarks in the *Times* were all pro-Mitchell. The editor accepted without question the accuracy of his reporting and declared that Mitchell had performed a patriotic duty that should receive the praise of all sane Americans.[59] The editor added that those accused would likely scold him, but that was a small thing compared to the service he rendered, for pacifism was "no less harmful, no less despicable, when done under Y.M.C.A. auspices than when it is the work of the Kaiser's secret agents."[60] Fletcher S. Brockman, associate general secretary of the National War Work Council of the association, quickly responded to the jibes and incriminating remarks of Mitchell and the newspaper with a staunch defense of the association's purposes. Brockman pointed to the many services the YMCA was rendering the nation as proof of its devotion to winning the war. While he denied that Speer had made any pacifist utterance, he did not unequivocally approve of his speech. In fact, Brockman's statement was somewhat less than generous to him.[61]

Several days after Mitchell's attack, Speer spoke for himself. He said he was amazed and indignant at the response made to his address. There never was any uncertainty in his own mind about the rightness and necessity of the war and that it should be continued until "everything has been done that can be done by the war to establish an order of justice in the earth." "I hate war," he continued, "but I believe that this is a war against war and that it must be waged in order that war may be destroyed."[62] He explained to the readers of the *Times* that the speech was not on the war, but on world problems related to the war. However, he was not prepared to retract his attitudes toward loyalty and patriotism, despite the attacks made on them. He did not feel it was necessary for the patriot to affirm the "impeccability" of the nation's past or the "perfection" of its present. He added that "whoever takes any other view and requires of the man who would be loyal that he must deny facts or tolerate in America what he is warring against elsewhere comes perilously near to the 'insidious disloy-alty' of whom one of your correspondents speaks." The task before the nation was "to replace an order of selfishness and wrong and division with an order of brotherhood and righteousness and unity." He believed that the war with Germany was only a part of this task.

The editor of the *Times* was far from satisfied with either of these defenses. He approved of the speed with which the association denied pacifism, but wrote that its statement should have contained some public repudiation of Speer.[63] As for his defense, it simply revealed the reason for the controversy, for he really was a kind of pacifist.[64] The editor, recalling Speer's statement that the war was only part of the problem, argued that this was not the point. There were other problems in the world, but the war was the only important one at the moment. To divert attention from it was to risk the label "pacifist." Speer took the risk and deserved the label.

During the entire controversy the *Times* published only one pro-Speer letter. It affirmed that the Columbia meeting had been held to probe the deeper issues of the war, not to arouse patriotism. The militant spirit of the times dictated the letter writer's anonymity.[65] The mood of the people was so much against utterances that sounded pacifist that the New York *Evening Post* could seriously propose that every speaker, whatever the topic, be obligated to state a position on the war as a preface to the remarks. Such a "patriotic grace" would enable speakers to show their patriotism without dwelling on it at length.[66] Speer clipped out a response to this suggestion that the same newspaper published in early March. It was a letter from "True-Blue," who had been accused of being soft on Germany when he failed to make a patriotic appeal at the opening of a speech on "Plumbing." He suggested—perhaps seriously, but evidently Speer took it in a different humor—that it should be the rule "that every public speaker and preacher during the war should begin his remarks with the words, 'God Damn the Kaiser,' and that the audience should stand during the repetition of this prayer."[67]

Other newspapers picked up the story and extended the controversy to other towns. Most of these stories were reprints of parts of the *Times'* cov-erage, but his hometown paper, the Englewood *Press*, ran a more extensive exchange on the matter. Feelings evidently ran high in Englewood for he gave notice to its churches that he would make a public statement in reply to the charges made against him, which he did in the chapel of the First Presbyterian Church on March 3. He told those who assembled that he had given the Columbia speech four times previously in different parts of the country without arousing any criticism, and that he definitely was not a pacifist. He then explained his attitude toward the war.

When the pastor of the church reported the meeting to the *Press* he said that there did not seem to be grounds for the accusations made against Speer, and that most of those accusing him did so either from misapprehension of what he said, or from second hand reports which were inaccurate.[68] But the mayor of Englewood was not satisfied and scolded Speer for his attitudes. The mayor said what many of the critics had said and what the majority of the populace, not only of Englewood but of the United States, likely believed: "What the American people and their President and their Congress need and expect from every one of us is an uncompromising and undistracted attention to the immediate task of defeating German propaganda and German arms, and then and when that shall have been definitely accomplished—but not before—of establishing a peace which shall be based upon no principle of surrender and upon no principle of compromise."[69]

As a result of this extensive publicity, he received a number of letters from friends and acquaintances, some challenging his point of view and others approving of it.[70] Many of the supportive ones came from commission members. The letters reveal not only the scope of Speer's friendships, but also the attitudes of representative Protestant leaders in relation to the war. The Rev. Henry A. Atkinson, Congregationalist, wrote, "I have been very much interested in following the attacks that are being made on you through the *New York Times*, and am amazed at this attitude. In my mind it simply indicates one thing, and that is there is a determined effort being made throughout the country to put over a harsh militaristic regime for America. . . . You and I and the rest of us are agreed that we must win the war. There is nothing else to be done. But that does not commit us, soul and body, to the military party, junkers and profiteers, who are trying to make the cloak of patriotism long enough to hide their forked tales and cloven hooves."[71] The Rev. Frederick H. Knubel, Lutheran, wrote, "Very, very many thoughtful men stand with you in your true patriotism and abiding devotion to the best interests of our country. It would be a strange and weak loyalty and patriotism which could sustain itself only by remaining blind to facts of the past and present. If we cannot stand the truth then there is something false in our present position."[72] Close friend Coffin said, "You have my genuine sympathy, for not a week has passed, I think, without some objection or criticism coming to me, on account of an expression or phrase in prayer or sermon. I would gladly relapse into total silence, if God would make that possible for me. One is misunderstood in the most amazing fashion, and men simply will not look at the situation we face from the Christian point of view."[73]

One letter sent to him revealed very precisely the relation of his position to the point of view of the pacifists. He thought of himself as neither a pacifist nor a militarist, but he believed that the greatest danger to the nation in the long run lay in the militant mentality. His position, therefore, could sound, as it did to Mitchell and others, like that of the pacifists. Pacifist leader Norman Thomas was quick to pick this up.

> Christianity suffers by the abject tone apparently adopted by the Y.M.C.A. authorities in expressing their stand and yours. Surely your patriotism is above reproach. Surely it is possible to call upon men and women to repent of their own sins without being accused of apologizing for others. I know you do not at all share the views of some of us with regard to the absolute incompatibility of war and Christianity, but however we may differ on this, it seems to me that we must be united in believing that it is the high function of Christianity to call for a national penitence and a new effort for the kingdom of God. Neither the Y.M.C.A. nor the Church can be true to their mission if they have no other conception of their duty that [sic] that of auxiliaries of the Security League in promoting patriotic ardor. Christianity will lose her distinctive message to the world unless she speaks with a prophetic voice now. . . . Your address stuck the right note and needs praise and not apology.[74]

A Christian View of War

Sometime before he spoke at Columbia, he had written a book setting forth his basic views on the war. Once the crisis passed, he was able to devote time to getting this volume ready for publication. He was working on galley proofs of it in April when he wrote Elliott that he did not know whether it was substantial enough to win anyone to his perspective. His recent experience exposing to the public his views on war led him to expect it to be "criticized both by the ultra-militarists and by ultra-pacifists."[75] He shared with his brother Will another reason for his uncertainty when he told him that the "third chapter of this book contains substantially the address which I made a Columbia University last February and over which there was such a foolish little fluster."[76] The volume, however, inspired no public uproar and was important primarily as a forthright and extensive statement of his position.

His analysis of the relation of the Christian and the church to the war hinged on the reality of a world already at war. Some Christians spent their energies decrying the involvement of the United States, while others ignored wartime dilemmas in the name of planning for the postwar peace. He repudiated both perspectives, because the war was real and required a clear commitment to grasp its meaning and to develop ministries to meet the needs it created. He urged the Christian to "take Paul's counsel and seek to behave as a citizen in a manner worthy of the Gospel, believing that his present duty is to be a Christian not in some other world but in this one, and that this duty can be done in the highest loyalty both to humanity and to Christ."[77] Peace was far better than war, but there was no peace. It was all right to think about a future day of peace, but "we shall never bring that other and better day in if we do not do our duty now."[78]

Accepting the war did not mean embracing it. He was not a crusader. War in general was evil; but, when he judged that a particular engagement was a lesser evil in a given social and political context, he did not hesitate to call it, in relative terms, good.[79] The World War was right when it was understood as a "war in defense of human rights, of weak nations, of innocent and inoffensive peoples, an unselfish war in which the nation seeks absolutely nothing for itself and is willing to spend everything in order that all men, including its enemies, may be free."[80] He turned to this familiar Wilsonian terminology of the defensive war whenever he wrote of the war in a favorable light. Although his words conveyed the values of the traditional just war theory, he expended very little effort in the task of intellectualizing them. Instead, convinced that there was a rationale for the war that the Christian could adopt, he devoted himself to delineating acceptable ministries for the individual and the church.

Of the several possible stances the Christian could take, he found those labeled either pacifist or militarist unacceptable. He rejected the pacifist dogma that "in our present state of social and political development all war is in principle wrong," because he believed it was based on an unreal estimate of the world's progress.[81] He regarded as foolish the argument that the way to stop the war was simply to stop fighting. That kind of behavior would constitute a clear surrender to the militaristic powers of the world. An aggressor nation would not hesitate to attack a pacifist one that possessed valuable land and resources. America's failure to arm for three years did not prevent attacks on her property. The worst evil that could grow out of abject surrender to a warring nation could be the tyranny of injustice, and in the present case it could have led to a worldwide tyranny. He believed that life in such a world would be intolerable, and if war were the only possible way to prevent the loss of justice and righteousness, then war must be accepted. "There are days in human history," he had written in an article published in the fall of 1917, "when war is the lesser evil and when its necessary work must be done."[82] Ten years later, in the pacifist era and while he was serving as moderator of his church, he refused to endorse a statement in behalf of the pacifist position and was reported to have said, "There are occasions in history when criminal nations emerge and these nations must be restrained."[83]

Christian pacifists repudiated war for other, more specifically religious reasons. One of these was that it was wrong to kill. He quarreled only with the application of this point of view to the present war. It was a war against war. The remedy was dreadful, but "if it is the only remedy, the greater wrong is in flinching from its use."[84] A more central reason was that war was "contrary to the teaching and spirit of Jesus."[85] He concurred but added that the real problem arose when another nation started a war and involved the Christian in it. In that case he did not believe that it was required of the Christian that he stand aside and let those who used war for selfish gain win without opposition. The error involved in the total rejection of war on the basis of Jesus' teaching was in seeing him and his words in terms of love and compassion alone, and not also in terms of justice and truth, "He taught the duty of pity and unselfishness and forgiveness, but He never abrogated or compromised the principles of righteousness. Neither in His example nor in His teaching is there any warrant for the surrender by society of the political order of human life to the power of evil and wrong-doing."[86] The pacifist arguments were relevant to a war of aggression, but they could not be applied to the present, primarily defensive conflict.

The militarist stance received no support at all. He defined this position as the belief that war in itself was good and even creative.[87] He saw any argument for the war based on national glory or pride, racial superiority, or territorial acquisition as essentially militaristic. Germany was the chief proponent of these views, but they were not absent from the British and American scene, and he cited examples from all three nations. He did not perceive the extent to which selfish nationalistic forces dictated his own nation's policies, but he was aware of numerous instances of overt racism and jingoistic nationalism, and he quoted many of them. He cited one newspaper that appealed to its readers to help stop the war between the white races and to unite to fight the real enemies, the yellow races, and he noted a pamphlet that enjoined hatred for the German nation and argued that after the war it should be ostracized for a thousand years.[88] Repudiation of similar views at Columbia had turned out to be extremely unpopular with the militant nationalists. Reaction had not forced a retraction then, nor did it change his mind when he published his views.

The true Christian wartime lifestyle, neither pacifist nor militarist, was a middle way. He was not dogmatic on this point, and he had no label for his perspective. He believed Paul's advice was sound. The Christian ministers to others in all circumstances, including war. This ministry should bring Christian principles to bear on the present situation insofar as possible.

> It bids us be rid of our prejudice and passion, to chant no hymns of hate, to keep our aims and our principles free from selfishness and from any national interest which is not also the interest of all nations, to refrain from doing in retaliation and in war the very things we condemn in others, to avoid Prussianism in our national life in the effort to crush Prussianism, to guard against the moral uncleanness which has characterized past wars as against pestilence, to magnify the great constructive and humane services for which humanity calls in every such time of tragedy, to love and pray for our enemies, to realize that the task set for us is not to be discharged in a year or five years, nor by money and ships and guns, but by life, that it is a war to the death against all that makes war possible.[89]

The terms belonged to World War I, but the argument and mood were akin to those explored in greater depth by the Christian realists led by Reinhold Niebuhr in World War II.[90] He was one of the forerunners of that group, in search of a viable middle ground between pacifists and militarists, and he associated himself with them when they emerged in the days prior to that war.

An important component of his view was the obligation of the church to minister to the needs of the people and the nation, in war or peace—if necessary, regardless of the wishes of the state. He believed the church constituted the one group in American society that could adequately handle the task of bringing social realities into conformity with social ideals. It could do that in part because it maintained an independent role in relation to the state and had its own voice and distinct resources. If it should ever become an appendage of the state, it would quickly be reduced to a "nullity."[91] He considered this a major issue and restated it on a number of occasions. Just after the war he said, "The Church is not a mere agency of government, nor a convenient channel of publicity, nor an echo of the state, nor a political judge or divider. It is a ministry of service, a fountain of moral life and duty and a witness to enduring and universal principles."[92]

During his service with the commission, he had a number of opportunities to put his version of Christian realism to work. Even though the church had judged this war to be right, indeed because it had made that judgment, it faced some difficult challenges. The denominations as well as the commission were called to serve as the moral conscience of the nation and to bear witness to the basic principles of justice and righteousness. He outlined this responsibility in an address to the Congress on Purpose and Methods of Inter-Church Federations, which met in Pittsburgh in October 1917: "Every influence which Christianity can bring to bear upon America today is necessary to keep us from destroying for ourselves what we are fighting to keep others from destroying for us. As we war against injustice and wrong, are we preserving only justice and right among ourselves? As we fight the spirit of racial self-aggrandizement and ill will, are we cherishing only the spirit of brotherhood and equal judgment toward other nations? Are our own hearts pure of hatred and passion and our hands so clean that we can hold the sword of God? The Christian faith must make us ask these questions. It alone can help us to answer them right."[93] The churches were also called to render unselfish service. It should be as united as possible and should include definite elements, such as providing the young men in the army and navy with a sacramental ministry appropriate to their tradition, Protestant or Roman Catholic. And it had to be as broad as possible, hence the multiplication of commission committees and the effort to reach out to groups often slighted by the larger society, like the African American troops.

An aspect of the moral conscience of the churches was the concern for the humanity of the enemy and readiness to repent for doing violence to it. One of the clearest and most forthright expressions of that came in the fall of 1917, when Speer signed *A Call to Prayer*, which the commission issued for use at Thanksgiving. This pamphlet carried a strong note of national penitence, and one part of it called for prayer "for all men, for the suffering and the destitute, for our allies and for our enemies, . . . for all mankind and for the coming of its one hope and deliverance in the reign of Jesus Christ our Lord as the King of all the earth."[94] The Lutherans felt more deeply than most Protestants in America the errors expounded by irresponsible patriots. The editor of the *Lutheran* praised Speer and the commission for "calling attention to the fact that we must not give ourselves so exclusively to confessing other nations' sins; America has a few of her own." National penitence was "a new note in our war literature, and we shall watch with interest its effect on those among whom Robert E. Speer is a name to conjure with."[95]

In the postwar period he recollected that the theme of repentance encountered resistance during the war. Doubtless referring in part to the Columbia episode, he said, "Any reminder that we had motes or beams in our own eyes, that the hands that held the chalice in the name of God must be clean, . . . was denounced as the seditious talk of a pacifist, forgetting that the battle is in God's hands and that we have Him to deal with as well as the enemy."[96] He acknowledged that these were not easy tasks and was certain that the church, functioning through the commission or any other instrument, would never accomplish them except "by the power of God living in the Risen Lord."[97] The need of the world and the capacity of the church to meet it was in the final analysis beyond human power. The new life required of people and nations was available "in one place alone, that is in God in Christ. To believe this and to try to live by this belief is the highest loyalty."[98] His appeal to the "power of God" was no pious platitude, but an essential part of his character as an evangelical Christian.

As leader of the united Protestant wartime work, he held a unique position and faced issues and decisions in a way no one else did. But as a citizen and parent of a teenage son, he had to deal with the war like the vast majority of Americans, on a personal and family level. Shortly after the nation joined the war, he decided that he would not take a leave from his post at the Board of Foreign Missions, and he held to his decision despite attractive invitations to render various kinds of service abroad. He was not able, he told Cairns, to see any work anywhere that had "a stronger call than the maintenance of the foreign missionary work. . . . We need every agent and instrumentality of international brotherhood and service that we possess and ought not to surrender any of them, least of all the one activity of Christianity which still preserves, in part at least, the principle of super-nationalism."[99] When Mott, Eddy, and other friends went abroad on special assignments, he felt the urge to follow them but resisted. The moderator of the Presbyterian Church proffered an "urgent invitation" to be part of a commission visiting Presbyterian churches in Great Britain, and Archbishop Nathan Söderblom of Sweden invited him to attend a conference of representatives of churches from "various neutral and belligerent countries," but he declined both offers.[100] Too old to be covered by the Selective Service Act—he was forty-nine when the United States joined the war—he joined Company I of the Home Guard. He belonged to the "old men's section" and described it as made up of those "not called on for patrol duty" but who "may be needed in times of emergency," and he found it a good way to lend moral support.[101]

The Speer family became much more personally involved in the war through Elliott. When it began, he was at Princeton and eighteen and caught the war fever that swept the country. Many of the colleges, especially those like Princeton that enrolled only men, faced the prospect of losing a large number of their students and turned into virtual training camps. Emma, with her Quaker background, felt her son needed "an application of Quaker principles." She told her husband that she believed guiding "him patiently thro this militaristic whirlpool," would be "the hardest thing we have had to face with this youth" and advised her husband "to give him some very constructive counsel."[102] Family discussions revealed that "his heart was set on rendering service somewhere," and he very shortly accompanied Eddy to Europe as a volunteer with the British Army YMCA.[103] He was in France for a time and then in England, stationed at a camp on the coast in Kent. By November he was writing home with news that he might be going to India. The Speers were frustrated by the difficulty of counseling their son at such a great distance, but Robert tried and offered the following advice: "If there is work to be done directly in connection with the war that you can and ought to do, well and good, but as between Y.M.C.A. work in India, and the completion of your training here for whatever your life-work may be, I think the latter is far and away the more important."[104] Elliott decided to accept this advice, returning in the summer of 1918 and going back to Princeton in the fall.

Reconstruction

One of the reasons Speer had accepted leadership of the commission was his concern for peace and reconstruction. The churches had not been able to prevent the war, but he believed they should work to make a peace that might prevent another one. The commission adopted as one of its purposes his proposal to deal with reconstruction problems in a cooperative spirit. "Reconstruction," in both Protestant and Roman Catholic circles, meant three things. First, it involved replacing brick and mortar in war-ravaged nations and rebuilding community among the many dislocated peoples. Second, it required development of proposals for a new community of nations and a new order in industrial relations. Third, it called for an openness to the coming of the kingdom of God. Many of the Protestant leaders tied their practical efforts to their theological understanding of the kingdom of God, following Walter Rauschenbusch's thought that "the Kingdom is for each of us the supreme task and the supreme gift of God. By accepting it as a task, we experience it as a gift."[105]

By late fall 1917, the commission and the council were flooded with reconstruction proposals. So great was the pressure that Macfarland went before the annual meeting of the executive committee in December and with commission support called for the creation of a separate committee for reconstruction work. In February 1918, Speer became part of a small group to draw up a plan for this new committee. His deep involvement was neither accidental nor incidental. He was a recognized advocate for reconstruction. Moreover, he was in constant correspondence with Cairns in Scotland, who had already helped create such a committee in Great Britain.[106] The council formed the Committee on the War and the Religious Outlook to focus on reconstruction problems and proposals and charged it, using the words of the report probably written by Speer, "to consider the state of religion as affected by the war, with special reference to the duty and opportunity of the churches."[107] Henry Churchill King, president of Oberlin College, chaired the committee, succeeded by William Adams Brown. Samuel Cavert, already working with the commission, also became the secretary of the committee. Speer was a member from the outset.

The committee decided to focus on research and publication, rather than on action programs. That decision reflected the active involvement of many other council committees and commissions in a great variety of programs, as well as the absence of a group engaged in serious study. It was also the model the British committee had used. The committee published a series of small pamphlets, really tracts for the times, lifting up many different reconstruction needs. It also published several larger and more comprehensive studies in what it considered to be the most important areas. He wrote the first of the pamphlets, published in May 1919, and chaired subcommittees that prepared two of the larger volumes, which meant that he essentially edited them both. They were on two of his favorite themes, *The Missionary Outlook in the Light of the War* and *Christian Unity: Its Principles and Possibilities.*[108]

In the tract *The War and the Religious Outlook*, he opened up the general theme of the affect of the war on religion and introduced most of the topics explored in later publications. He claimed that the early days of reconstruction had already revealed some of the negative influences the war had on religion. Many of the men who had served overseas were returning to America with European moral standards, and that often meant a distinct lowering of moral tone in the life of the men and of their home communities. Those who had remained at home had begun to show the effects of the emotional tensions built up by the war. The nation's idealism had served it well but had been and was still being weakened by constant appeals to the passions of hatred and revenge. Many people were also criticizing the churches, first for failing to prevent the war and second for being too much a part of it. Favorable influences more than balanced these unfavorable ones.

If the war had shaken the personal moral life of many men, it had also magnified the moral values of discipline and righteousness and lifted up for widespread examination such basic themes of Christianity as service and vicarious sacrifice. The fact that criticisms leveled at the churches were, for the most part, coming from within told Speer that critics were trying to fulfil their ministries rather than destroy them. The war had also demonstrated a new spirit of Christian cooperation.

When he turned away from analysis and toward peace, he projected two key tasks for the churches. In the first place, they must help build a Christian social order at home, in practical and concrete ways, especially in the areas of industrial life and race relations. They must seek to democratize and Christianize industry, and they must also solve the race problem. Racial harmony went beyond toleration to respect, and the Christian principle of "brotherhood" provided the only stable foundation for it.[109] One historian has claimed that this emphasis revealed "that the war had conveyed a new message to Speer," a social gospel one. To the contrary, it was simply another occasion for him to lift up one of his lifetime concerns: the unity of the human family.[110] In the second place, the churches must help reconstruct international relations. He favored a league of nations, but did not in this pamphlet advocate a particular plan, since the point he wanted to make was that the important thing about reconstruction was the spirit of cooperation and goodwill that had to replace the spirit of selfishness.

These two tasks lay beyond the reach of the churches, he argued, unless they agreed to a substantial reorganization. If they were to fulfill their ministry in peacetime, they needed a more progressive program of Christian education; a fuller and richer experience of life, by which he meant a more effective program of evangelism; and, above all, a greater degree of Christian unity. Unity was the key. They could not preach it for the world, in some kind of league of nations, without practicing it themselves. It was the great lesson of the war, for its accomplishments through the War-Time Commission had only begun to reveal its possibilities. The churches, he concluded, "have actually found themselves working together in great common tasks in a way which they had not realized to be possible before. But the tasks that now confront the church are no less challenging than those that faced it during the war. The church cannot hope to deal with them adequately unless it approaches them in a spirit of common purpose and united endeavor."[111]

He emphasized this point time after time in the months after the end of the war. He told the executive committee of the council in December 1918, in a speech carefully titled "The Call to a Larger Christian Coopera-tion," "We have been taught clearly this last year the absolute indispens-ableness of an adequate, unselfish instrumentality for cooperation in the name of the Church and with the consciousness of the Church in its rich-est historic and spiritual significance."[112] The council held a special meeting in Cleveland, Ohio, in early May 1919, to complement the one held two years earlier. That one had developed a wartime ministry; this one pro-posed a peacetime one. In one of the major platform speeches Speer declared, "Nobody can live in the Gospels without realizing that the fundamental message of Christianity must be a united message of a united humanity."[113]

Reconstruction weighed so heavily on his conscience that he not only prepared speeches and essays on it in relation to his council responsibili-ties, but also wrote two books about it. They gave him a more diverse audience, beyond those interested primarily in ecumenical or even reli-gious matters. Their titles, *The New Opportunity of the Church* and *The Gospel and the New World*, revealed that he saw the postwar era as a time of potential renewal, a time not just for the reestablishment of peace, but for a broadening and deepening of it. In *The New Opportunity* he intro-duced his vision with a word of caution. Now that peace had come, its tasks had to be confronted directly, for if they were not, the peace could be lost. This striking concept was hardly self-evident in a nation that remained mesmerized by mobilization for total victory many months after the war was over. Some things, peace among them, were more difficult to live for than to die for.

> It is easy to draw misleading inferences from the war analogies. We think that because war beheld such unity of national purposes and readiness of national sacrifice we shall now see the same in peace. War has always been able to draw out what peace commands in vain. War is a transient interest. Peace is an unending task. War appeals to all that is worst in men as well as to all that is best. Peace can only call upon the highest and truest self. War

> can use the unifying energy of a common hate. Peace knows that it is the
> hater who is hurt by his own hate. . . . The task and summons, and the test
> and entreaty of peace remain. Can men meet these as they met the challenge
> of death? Can the man do this harder thing?[114]

These strong words measured his realism and alerted his readers that
the trials of peace could be as difficult as the agonies of war. He never
wavered, however, from the conviction that the peace could be won and
claimed, "I firmly believe that what is known as the after-the-war sentiment will direct the destinies of all classes for generations to come."[115] The
analogies of war could be misleading, he claimed, but they should not be
ignored, for they could also point the way to a greater sense of the "brotherhood of man" and ultimately to world unity. The challenge to show the
world the right use of the spirit of unity aroused by the war fell to the
churches. Their peacetime task was to assert the "possibility here and now
of a new and better world, the kind of world for which Christ lived and
died, and lives again." After all, "Christians have known from the very
beginning, that any generation might have the Kingdom of God if it
would open itself to the full inpouring of the will and the power of God."[116]

The contribution of the churches to the kingdom was a greater commitment to unity. In *The Gospel and the New World* Speer reiterated the
appeals he had made in his various presentations to, and on behalf of, the
council. His speech to the executive committee appeared under the title
"The Duty of a Larger Christian Cooperation." In it he claimed that the
way for the nations to share in the kingdom was to adopt the plan for and
become part of the League of Nations. He had pointed out during the war
that one of the great world problems was the exultant claims of nationalism to be above the moral law and superior to any international authority.
These claims were a special problem for the Christian, since his faith was
innately internationalistic. Indeed, Christianity's worldview, manifested
most sharply in the foreign missionary efforts of the churches, helped
mold the consciousness of unity now seeking expression in the "political
instrumentality" of the League.[117]

He had little to say about the specific content of the League Covenant,
apparently accepting the decisions of its formulators, but he had a great
deal to say in favor of its adoption by the nations of the world. Of the
many arguments he adduced in support of the League, the central one was
the need for a political "institute of humanity" that could deal with the
obvious international relationships and at the same time realize the basic
fact of the unity of the human race.[118] Humanity had always been one, but
its oneness had been obscured by poor communication and strong nation-

states. "God," he said, "has thrown the whole of humanity together in an actual experience of the unity of man and out of that unity we are compelled to think today the plans of organization that shall deal with this actual constitution of mankind."[119]

When he turned from these general considerations to the more specific conditions in the United States, he spoke directly to the isolationists and others who worked to keep his country out of the League. "Men who tell us," he said, "that we should draw off from the rest of the world simply preach against the irresistible tides. We are enmeshed in all the life of the world today. We cannot unmesh ourselves. Every day that passes entangles us more inextricably with all the rest of mankind and we are simply imbecile if in face of the fact we shut our eyes to it and do not try to devise the agencies by which that fact should be dealt with."[120] Unwilling to confine his work for the League to words alone, he joined the Pro-League Independents in the fall of 1920. His name appeared on the letterhead of this group, which issued appeals for the election of the Democrat and pro-League James Cox over his Republican opponent, Warren Harding. This was one of the rare times in his life when he publicly supported a political candidate, and he made the exception only because of his conviction about the importance of the League.

He entered the ecumenical movement in the United States at a critical time, when it was moving from a collection of individuals interested in Christian unity to a national organization, the Federal Council of Churches, which represented the cooperative ideals and work of many of the major Protestant denominations. He brought his ideas of unity and his vast energy to this new organization and played an important, although not central, role in it until 1917. The work the new council did in defining and organizing the wartime ministry of the Protestant churches in World War I and its postwar efforts on behalf of reconstruction were the most important successes in cooperative Christian action in its brief existence. He was at the center of these efforts. He also was one of a very small number of ecumenical leaders who projected a vision of greater cooperation in the future. In this work he was a prophet of Christian unity for the Protestant churches. His efforts complemented his work for and vision of Christian unity in foreign missionary work.

CHAPTER 10

President of the Federal Council

"That they may all be one"

The armistice that ended World War I touched off one of the more remarkable periods in American history. After the euphoria of victory and the conviction that the goals of the war had been achieved came the reality of victory and the weight of the responsibility for the peace. The vision of a reconstructed world guided by a League of Nations became the fact of extended negotiations and national lobbying for and against joining the League. People paraded in the streets and welcomed "Johnny" home, and then some of them turned on their neighbors with a frenzy that set a record for racial confrontation in America. Others revived the prewar campaign to restrict immigration and by 1924 had effectively put a "Closed" sign in front of the Statue of Liberty. The nation seemed to be riding an emotional roller coaster, reaching great heights of excitement and sudden depths of despair. The nation included its churches and their members. The experience of Christian cooperation and unity during the war created a vision of greater unity and a reconstructed social order when it was over. The reality never reached the vision. Speer was one of a relatively small number of church leaders who struggled to hold fast to the vision, even as reality clouded it.

His greatest contribution to Christian unity in the postwar era was his decision to remain with the Federal Council as the vehicle for his national, as distinct from foreign missions, ecumenical work. Joined to that decision was his willingness to accept new levels of responsibility for the organization. A man of many words, he continued to advocate Christian unity from the wide variety of platforms offered him, but he never limited himself to words alone. As the General War-Time Commission closed out its work, he accepted another assignment with the council. He had been a formal advisor of the administrative committee since 1914, and in the spring of 1919 he agreed to be one of its two vice-chairs. The move was a

major step upward in the council bureaucracy, for the administrative committee met monthly and made many of the council's routine decisions.
The primary motivation for his continued service was his vision of a full
Christian unity and his conviction that it would come primarily through
a sustained program of cooperation. Another motivation for this decision
was the opportunity for continued general oversight of War-Time
Commission matters that had been left unfinished and that had been
parceled out to other council groups. He also remained on the Committee
on the War and the Religious Outlook, and sustained his commitment
until its work was done in the early 1920s.

New Proposals for Uniting the Churches

His decision to continue his council service came at time in American
Protestant life when other ecumenical options appeared on the scene.
Arising in part because of the remarkable success of the council and the
degree of Christian cooperation it achieved during the war, they were
products of the effervescent optimism that greeted peace. Two of the more
interesting experiments, and in many ways the most important ones,
emerged from meetings held in December 1918. He was aware of both
from their beginnings and became involved in them, in varying degrees,
until they began to fade from the scene in the spring of 1920. He wrote a
careful review and analysis of both in the fall of 1920 and subsequently
played a surprising and unexpected role in their ultimate outcome.

One of these ventures was the proposal, originating in his own denomination, for what came to be called the "United Churches of Christ in
America." Overtures from thirty-five presbyteries to the General Assembly
of 1918, encouraging it to propose to other denominations an organic
union, led the assembly to authorize its Committee on Church Cooperation and Union to issue a call for a meeting. Seventeen denominations
sent delegates to the Conference on Organic Union held in Philadelphia
the first week in December 1918. The conference formed an ad interim
committee, led by William H. Roberts, a Presbyterian and one of the men
who had helped lead the way to the formation of the Federal Council.
Representatives of eighteen denominations met in Philadelphia in
February 1920 as the American Council on Organic Union of the
Churches of Christ, agreed on what came to be known as the Philadelphia
Plan, and sent it to the churches.[1] The original proposal had contained the
phrase "the Evangelical Churches" in its preamble, but the representatives

changed it to read "the Christian Church." The union was to become operational when any six denominations voted to join.

Three months later the plan ran into serious difficulties when the General Assembly of the United Presbyterian Church in North America, the first denomination to consider it, voted it down and decided to "continue its relations with the Federal Council of the Churches of Christ in America." Its reasoning proved to be influential with other denominations: "The Council of the Churches of Christ in America proposes at the present time a little further advance toward real organic union, but has as yet not accomplished anything practical in the field of Christian activities; the Federal Council has made less progress toward organic union, but, through its many organizations, has already accomplished much practically for Christian activities throughout the United States."[2]

When Speer reflected on the proposal, he was torn. He had been in favor of organic church union for many years and continued to raise the issue, pointing to such a union as the goal of the Christian church at home and abroad. From that perspective, he felt the Philadelphia Plan "springs from an earnest desire to deal with the root of our present difficulty, namely, the divided consciousness of the different churches themselves. It springs from a feeling that this state of things should cease." It proposed an admirable thing, which would enable "each of its constituent members" to say, "I belong to the one Church of Christ."

Supportive as he was of this scheme, he felt it had two serious problems. First, he did not think it was really practical, given the degree of power it called on the "larger Christian churches" to surrender. He believed this, fully aware of the action of the United Presbyterians, but before the plan failed to gain the support of a sufficient number of the presbyteries of his own denomination. Some of the presbyteries objected specifically to the deletion of the term "evangelical," an early warning of theological difficulties to come.[3] Second, he believed it was unwise. Its relationship to the existing Federal Council was unclear. The council included denominations and a number of associated groups. "Unless," he argued, "all the bodies represented in the Federal Council accept the new proposal, there will still remain for the churches that form the new and more compact organization the problem of relating themselves to the bodies that lie without, and for this some agency like the existing Federal Council will be necessary."[4] In that all too likely case, given the action of the United Presbyterians, the result of adopting the plan would be greater disunity. The plan died for lack of sufficient official denominational support. Although not persuaded by the plan, he had been working and continued to work for organic and well as federal Christian unity, especially among the churches in the Reformed tradition (see chapter 12 for further discussion of this).

The other venture that began in December 1918 was the Interchurch World Movement of North America. It emerged "on the horizon as suddenly as a meteor" from a meeting of the denominational executives of missionary, educational, and other benevolent agencies which met on December 17 at the headquarters of the Foreign Missions Conference in New York City.[5] Stimulated by the remarkable success of a financial campaign at the end of the war, the United War Work Campaign, and by the spirit of cooperation generated by the war effort, these leaders proposed to extend the accumulated positive energy and spirit into the postwar era to ensure a better peace. Quickly expanded from the interests of those who attended the first meeting, the leaders hoped to bring all the agencies of the Protestant churches under one great umbrella. They developed a plan for a massive survey of postwar needs, a major publicity campaign to share the facts discovered in the survey with all Protestants in America, and a giant financial campaign, all to take place in little more than a year. He was present at the initial meeting and led the devotional exercises. He also served on the executive committee. Many of his missionary executive colleagues and a number of those who had been part of the War-Time Commission were involved. Mott served as chair of the executive committee.

The Interchurch Movement generated a tremendous amount of activity. It grew from an idea to an agency employing more than 2,000 people in less than a year. The initial organizers were members of various denominational boards, but not delegated representatives of the denominations. It took some six months for the leaders of the movement to recognize the need for official denominational recognition and to move to secure it. It also initially bypassed the major interdenominational agencies, but many of them soon came on board, especially the Foreign Missions Conference, the Home Missions Council, and the Missionary Education Movement. The Federal Council was an exceptional case. It endorsed the movement at its special meeting in 1919, but did so in "a carefully worded statement clarifying the differences in nature and function between the two organizations."[6]

As the movement grew and reached out to the denominations, council leaders became more concerned and finally realized that it constituted a serious challenge. In the spring of 1920, when the movement's financial campaign began to move forward, the council offered the following distinction between the two organizations: "The Interchurch World Movement is only carrying forward, in an aggressive way, the interests of the missionary agencies of the churches whose normal activities of a more general sort have been so successfully provided by the Federal Council."[7]

Speer was at most a cautious participant in the movement, troubled by what he called its pell-mell character. He told its executive committee in May 1919 that he had "heard objection on the ground that we were launching an indefinite undertaking, that once launched it would be beyond our control, that it might grow to what no one now is prepared to commit himself to."[8] When a review of the finances in the spring of 1920 indicated less support for the central budget than initially proposed, he moved to reduce it "to bring it within the limits of the underwriting which is assured."[9] Rockefeller, who had recently joined the executive committee, blocked this move, and "won approval of the full budget by secretly offering to underwrite further bank borrowing should that prove necessary."[10]

There were echoes in this debate of his reaction to Mott's plan in 1913 for a worldwide missionary agency (see chapter 7 for more information). An intense study of the relationship among Speer, Rockefeller, and Mott has praised Speer for his "insistence upon genuine consensus and faithful representation" in cooperative religious and social projects and has portrayed Rockefeller and Mott as representatives of "centralized administrative power derived from financial control" and "unrepresentative financial administration."[11] Although differences of opinion and approach existed between Speer and Rockefeller, and the churchman could on occasion be described as the businessman's "critic," they maintained a warm personal relationship.[12]

The financial campaign appealed to the denominations through their various organizations, such as the New Era Movement of the Presbyterian Church in the U.S.A. and the New World Movement of the Northern Baptist Convention, and to "friendly citizens" directly, hoping for $40,000,000 from the latter, much of it earmarked for the Interchurch Movement's central budget. Wondrously, the denominations eventually raised around $200,000,000, the most that had ever been raised by an interdenominational effort, and their leaders considered the campaign a tremendous success. Alas, "friendly citizens" did not contribute as expected, and, more damaging, pledges to the central budget fell far short of the almost $8,000,000 already spent. A brief second campaign raised almost nothing. The Interchurch Movement faced bankruptcy.

Several denominations held their national meetings in the spring of

1920 and responded to the movement's bad news by deciding to diminish radically their commitments to it. The General Assembly of Speer's church debated a motion for total withdrawal. Supporters of the movement encouraged him to speak for it, and he did, with great reluctance, because he was not a commissioner at the assembly and had no official status. Wheeler took notes and recorded that he said, "*I do not believe in the Inter-Church World Movement as it is at present organized.* Its emphasis has been on the organization instead of upon Christ. . . . Its expense has been extravagant and impossible. The campaign for funds has been carried on like that of a secular organization, a company trying to sell its stock to possible buyers." However, he opposed the motion to withdraw, since that would "demonstrate the fact that Protestant organizations, and especially those interested in foreign missions, cannot co-operate successfully." He proposed continued participation contingent on a dramatic reduction of its overhead expenses.[13] The assembly adopted a version of his proposal and conditioned its continued support upon a major restructuring of the movement.[14] At the same time it agreed to pay its obligation of one million dollars toward the indebtedness, which he subsequently called his church's "debt of honor."[15] The general committee of the Interchurch Movement voted in July to reorganize completely, set a modest budget of $75,000 for the coming year, and selected a committee of fifteen, which was to consult with its various constituent groups and propose its ultimate fate.[16]

The evaluation he made of the movement, which he described as an effort at "Administrative Union on an Inclusive Scale," did not carry the same positive sentiments he expressed in his review of the Philadelphia Plan.[17] The movement had been inspired by a genuine spirit of cooperation and unity and by the concern of its originators to face the "whole duty" of the churches in the postwar world. And it had provided for the "coordination of a score of denominational forward movements, which were seeking by common methods to accomplish common aims and which needed to use each other's experience and to amass a common momentum."[18] These were good and useful things, but they had not been enough to enable it to succeed.

He identified a number of problems with the movement and he believed each of them taught a lesson that might prove useful in future cooperative endeavors. Among the most important were concerns about its ambitions and its lack of clarity of purpose. The "generally accepted" view had been that it was to be a temporary agency, but some church leaders came to feel it was on the verge of becoming a superchurch movement and to believe that "under the guise of cooperation in an enterprise of a

modest and legitimate nature, pressure was being brought to bear upon
them to surrender the autonomy they had hitherto enjoyed and to commit the charge of the most important enterprises of the Church to men
not responsible to its authority or represented in its counsels."[19] Moreover,
its leaders had never fully thought through its basic principles, and therefore had failed to reconcile important differences. He summed up those
differences: "Some joined the Movement with the understanding that it
was temporary; others with the view that it was a beginning which must
be carried forward into a new, permanent form. Some joined on condition
that it would be promotive only and not administrative; others saw in it a
chance to displace old and, as they deemed them, slow and inadequate
administrative agencies. Some based their cooperation on the assurance
that denominational interests and prerogatives would not be disturbed,
and that the Movement could operate through denominational grooves;
others deemed this an opportunity to transcend these." The result of these
"contrasted tendencies" was that sooner or later there would be "difficulty
and misunderstanding."[20]

The lessons of the movement's demise, as he saw them, were that
greater Christian unity could only come from the properly delegated
leaders of the churches, and when they moved forward, they needed to do
so on the basis of clearly articulated principles. Although he did not draw
the comparison, he had a model of what he thought would work in the
Foreign Missions Conference, which had been created by the official
foreign mission executives and had forged, at his urging, a set of basic
principles.

As the movement wound down, Rockefeller was at work to salvage
something from the wreckage. He had become interested in creating a
fund "for the advancement of cooperative religions." He passed the idea
by Speer in the summer during an informal discussion at Seal Harbor,
Maine, and again in written and more formal form in September. Speer
responded at length and defined his ecumenical thinking at the time. He
said, "To set up an independent self-contained endowment is a thing well
worth doing in many fields of action, but I am not sure it would be well
in the field of cooperation. I should fear that it might result in that field
in merely setting up a new undenominational agency." Getting the
churches to cooperate required "the development and the support of
actual interdenominational cooperation." He acknowledged that some
individuals were restive and wished to move quickly to Christian unity,
perhaps an allusion to Rockefeller, but that was not the best way. He concluded, "I believe myself in complete Christian unity in the most com-

prehensive and organic sense, and I sympathize with all who are working for it and will work with them. But that goal is far ahead of us and if those who believe in it insist on obtaining it at once, the result would be not church unity, but only another denomination advocating the reduction of the number of denominations at the same time that it has added to them. The wise and necessary course is to get the different bodies to cooperate themselves and to support every means of cooperation for which they are ready."[21]

Federal Council President

By the fall of 1920 there were plenty of signs that the country and its churches were in the midst of a major crisis, particularly from the perspective of the initial postwar euphoria and the conviction that cooperation was about to replace competition in all aspects of life. In the two years since the Armistice the good feelings had eroded. They were eaten away by such events as the steel strike in 1919 and the Red Scare, and they took a serious loss in the spring of 1920 when the U.S. Senate failed, again and finally, to muster support for the Treaty of Versailles and rejected with it the League of Nations. Things in general seemed to be coming apart, but at least as bad, from the point of view of ecumenical church leaders, was what was happening to the churches, especially their involvement in movements for unity. Two experiments in church cooperation and unity had failed and were on the verge of disappearing. Unfortunately, both had entangled the Federal Council, which already had its hands full with its own administrative and economic problems. Officials at the council believed they needed a new and vigorous leader, one who could pull things back together again, not just for them, but for the ecumenical movement as a whole. They turned to Speer and nominated him to be their president for the quadrennium 1920–24.

This was not the first time that council leaders had considered him for the major leadership position. Secretary Macfarland had raised the question in the fall of 1916.[22] Speer had set the stage for the renewed invitation when he had demonstrated his abilities to lead during the war and then accepted one of the major positions on the administrative committee. Ironically, the leaders of the Interchurch World Movement were interested in him too. James M. Speers, Mott's successor as chairman of its executive committee, proposed to other leaders, including Rockefeller, that they invite Speer to be their new chief executive. In Speers's thinking,

"Dr. Speer will command the confidence and respect of all the denominations." Rockefeller concurred and added, "Your suggestion strikes me most favorably."[23] That thought apparently never became an offer. The proposal from the council arrived on Speer's desk in November.

The invitation did not surprise him, but he was far from ready to accept it. His initial response was negative, and he wrote President North and others at the council and asked them to withdraw his name. He believed he could render greater service outside the council presidency in unofficial ways and declared that his position was "definite and clear."[24] He shortly softened his stance and decided to examine the offer as a call, and began his usual procedure in such situations, a combination of personal reflection and consultation with others. There were problems and possibilities, and he weighed them both. The War-Time Commission work had been successful, but he had learned from it that the ideal of Christian cooperation was not shared by everyone, especially in the churches. He had found practical cooperative work often "thankless and discouraging" and had told Cairns that he planned to do his best "to stay away from any similar undertakings when the war is over."[25] His experiences with the Interchurch Movement had confirmed that feeling. The precipitous decline of idealism had affected the foreign mission work as well as everything else. He would not leave the board, but could he spread his time even thinner? And he was aware that the council had its share of spots and wrinkles.

The friends he consulted reminded him of some of these issues but generally focused on the possibilities and favored a positive decision. Edwin Bulkley, Uncle Ned to the Speer children, told him he would be the last person to advise him to take on something new, since he was "the most overtaxed man I know," but supported the view that it was "a critical time for a movement working for Christian unity with the crisis suffered by the Inter-Church, and it is easily to be understood that the Federal Council may now serve a far greater purpose than at any time heretofore."[26] A member of the Board of Foreign Missions, Bulkley said he thought the board might offer him some relief if he chose to accept the job but added, "I do not think you would be contented to divert your energies in any considerable degree from the Board to the Federal Council." Close friend William P. Merrill, a Presbyterian pastor and also a board member, shared his "absolutely clear" belief "that it would in the long run mean more for the church and for the Kingdom of God to have you lead the Federal Council movement into the right way than to have you serve our Board on full time," and added that he would have "the chance here to come nearer to a working out of the problem of uniting our Protestant forces than anyone else can come in any other way."[27]

As he searched for more insight, he wrote Brown, his partner in wartime work, and told him he was in agony over the situation, "trying to see just what the path of duty is." Brown responded immediately in a long and powerful letter and put the issue in the persuasive terms of "duty" and "call." In a reference to some of the personality problems in the council, he argued that the only way to change that is to "introduce a personality big enough to command the support and allegiance of other big personalities. Your friends believe you to be such a man. I think they are right. . . . If it is right for you to do this thing," he concluded, "then God will make the way plain for you, and the inner peace that always comes from doing His will with complete surrender will give you the power to overcome whatever obstacles may be in the way, and do the service to which God calls you."[28]

The exchange with Brown was decisive, for the day after it, despite some continued "reluctance and misgiving," he notified the council that he would accept.[29] He explained to Rockefeller that he had come to realize "that I had no right to avoid this difficult task . . . having in mind the things that it may be possible to achieve and the things that it may be possible to prevent."[30] Although he held onto the ideal of organic unity, he cast his lot with federal unity and determined it was his duty to see it continue to live and grow.

The fourth quadrennial of the council convened in Boston the first week of December. The delegates elected him president for the coming four years and he assumed leadership of the proceedings. He was the fourth president of the council and the first layperson. If he had any remaining doubts about his decision, the outpouring of support in the following weeks surely resolved them. Individuals, churches, and the editors of religious periodicals wrote letters and editorials of congratulation and encouragement. They greeted him as a person with a "prophet's vision," and as a man who had "the confidence of all parts of the Church."[31] Rockefeller agreed and told him that he had not been fully supportive of the council because he did not have a very good opinion of some of its leaders, but "your coming into the leadership of the movement will go far toward removing that obstacle and will inspire general confidence and bring about increased support of the enterprise throughout the country."[32] The *Christian Advocate*, a Methodist journal, described him as "perhaps the best known and most trusted leader of evangelical Christianity in America" and said the churches could "look to him to hold the Federal

Council true to the best inheritance of the evangelical faith, and to be a forceful leader in the direction of its policies."[33] Those who wrote struck a common chord: he inspired confidence. His election alone promised a better future.

The four years of his leadership marked a dramatic surge forward in the life of the council and of ecumenical Protestantism in America. The failure of the Interchurch Movement had led to discouragement and despair among many Protestant leaders. He helped them recover a positive attitude. He had a strongly optimistic personality and a contagious enthusiasm for the causes he decided to serve. Although he was hardly solely responsible for this recovery, he was the key leader, the person at the center initiating, directing, and especially reconciling differences of opinion and spirit. He made three significant contributions that were important to the forward movement of the council, and all of them became permanent features of it and hence of American ecumenical life. First, he led the council administratively, through a process of reorganization, to adopt a revised and much clearer set of cooperative principles. Second, he encouraged the council programmatically to extend its ministry into new areas, particularly racial justice. Third, he challenged the council idealistically to become the most vocal advocate for and the center of ecumenical Protestantism in America.

Administrative matters were not his first love. He did not see himself as primarily a board administrator and did not relish the administrative role with the council. But he had been more than a casual student of the council and its needs. He had made a modest effort along the lines he believed to be needed when he had served as chair of the Commission on Foreign Missions. At the end of the war, as he was about to join the administrative committee, he had told Brown it was time to define the functions of the council and the principles that should govern its work.[34] When he had reviewed the various movements for unity, in his essay "The Present Situation in the Church as a Whole," he had measured the council. He had found it generally effective, but also wanting in several distinct areas. Among them were the needs for a broader range of programs, a stronger base of financial support from constituent churches, and a better working relationship with other interdenominational agencies.[35] On October 22, not long before he received word that he was going to be nominated for the presidency, he had agreed to chair a new council group, the Committee on Methods of Cooperation. Created by the administrative committee, it developed a report for the quadrennial. By the time the council elected him president, he not only knew that he needed to focus on administration, but he had helped shape a plan of action. Curiously, the various printed copies of this report fail to mention that he served as chair. It is altogether possible that he employed the democratic procedure he used with his board so that the report might make the greatest possible impact as the work of the entire committee.

The report of the Committee on Methods of Cooperation, described as "easily the most important matter" to come before the quadrennial, pointed out the painfully obvious.[36] The denominations had given every indication that they wanted and needed the council, but despite the fact that it was "apparently adapted in form to serve the churches in conducting or coordinating their cooperative work, the situation has been too complicated and confused to allow the adequate cooperative service required." The committee then offered an interpretation that made room for change. What had gone before had been "pioneer work." The "present situation and our war experience" suggested that the time had come to take "another step forward." The committee made seven recommendations, which the council adopted after a few minor revisions. In sum, the agenda for the coming quadrennium was (1) the maintenance of "the closest possible relationships" with the denominations; (2) the enlargement of cooperative work; (3) the provision of adequate financial support from the constituent bodies, in the amount of $300,000 per year for the coming two years; (4) the creation of a greater understanding with the interboard agencies; (5) the adjustment of the council's structure to better serve the denominations; (6) the reorganization of the council commissions if necessary; and (7) "the achievement of a richer form of expression of that 'spirit of fellowship, service, and cooperation' in which the Federal Council began and which it is its duty and its joy to promote."[37] The key themes were the first, clearer attachment to the denominations, and the fourth, more definite relationships with the interboard and interdenominational agencies.

Important Changes for the Federal Council

Speer took the lead. Between the close of the Boston meeting and the distribution of a formal letter to council constituents in May 1921, he worked at a feverish pace. Pressed forward by the need to resolve important issues as quickly as possible and hemmed in by a sailing date for another of his missionary journeys (he left for India, Persia, and China on July 21 and was gone for almost ten months), he approached both themes in the same way: conferences featuring open discussion and concluding with consensus around basic principles. He tackled the issues in their reverse order, largely because relations with the interdenominational agencies, particularly the Interchurch Movement, required immediate attention. He had been present in an advisory capacity at a three-day meeting the movement had held in early November and was aware of its urgent call for a conference of interdenominational groups to deal with serious questions.[38]

The Conference of Interdenominational Agencies met at the Central Branch of the YWCA in New York on December 13, 1920. He called it to order and explained the purpose of the gathering in terms of defining more clearly the relationships between the agencies. The representatives elected him chair and Cavert secretary. Methodist Bishop Thomas Nicholson spoke for the Interchurch Movement and asked those assembled if they believed there was "need for any more closer and more mutually supporting relationships between the agencies represented in this conference?" They agreed there was. Speer proposed they continue their discussion by focusing on three possible ways to achieve greater mutuality, including the creation of a consultative committee to explore and coordinate future plans. Nicholson let it be known that if those gathered did not think the movement was needed, the committee left in charge of it would likely vote to end it.

After an afternoon of discussion, the representatives reached consensus on a number of issues and announced what might be called principles of future cooperation. They agreed that "the churches possess in the existing agencies sufficient organizations for the needs of their cooperative work at the present time," which ended any thought of creating a revised version of the Interchurch Movement. They concurred that the movement "might wisely adjust and conclude its activities" and recommended it distribute its vast survey materials, which had been one of its genuine successes, to the appropriate agencies, including the Foreign Missions Conference, the Home Missions Council, and the Federal Council. They encouraged all the agencies to "maintain and cultivate the relations of consultation and affiliation through the Federal Council which have been established." And they created a committee on consultation, to convene at Speer's call, "to consider matters of common interest" and "study the problems of cooperation" among the agencies.[39] The press release Speer issued highlighted the consensus, but he kept his thoughts about the importance of what had transpired to himself. However, the conference accomplished two things necessary to the council's forward movement.[40] A group of influential leaders representing a wide variety of ministries had agreed, first, that the

Federal Council was to be their agent for cooperation and, second, that the Interchurch Movement should cease to exist.

The process of shoring up relationships with external groups underway, he turned to the other theme, the council itself. The evening the Boston meeting adjourned, he convened the executive committee, which directed the administrative committee "to prepare a program of the Council's plan of organization" for presentation at its next meeting, scheduled for January 21, 1921. A flurry of activity followed, and he was involved at every turn. Christmas vacation was short, sandwiched between two meetings of the executive council. He led them both. The principles set forth in the report of the Committee on Methods of Cooperation served as a point of departure for proposing specific changes. By the end of the year he had drafted a tentative plan to revise the organization of the council.[41] Early in the new year he wrote Cairns with the news of the demise of the Interchurch Movement, which had "left a heavy legacy of liabilities behind it," but offered optimistic news of the council. It had problems, but "I think we are seeing some way to progress in all of these."[42]

The meeting of the executive committee on January 21 of the new year was crucial to the future of the council. It adopted the administrative committee's "plan of organization." First, the denominations had created the council and should be more involved in its activities. To that end, formal policy statements should be shared in advance so that they represented the views of the constituency. Semiannual reports and minutes of the administrative committee should be distributed to all members. Second, the administrative committee had functioned as the major operating committee since 1919. It should become truly representative, with a member from each denomination, each of the interdenominational agencies, and each of the council commissions. Third, the commissions and committees should be better integrated into the council structure. They were agents of the council for "cooperative service in some field where the denominations are not acting or where they need some supplemental instrumentality to their activity." The proposal defined ten commissions and abolished the committees concerned with foreign and home missions. Representatives of the Foreign Missions Conference and the Home Missions Council joined the administrative committee.

The acceptance of this plan signaled no radical departure from the way the council had been operating, but marked a clarification of principles and procedures and charted the course for the quadrennium and beyond. It clarified, finally, the meaning of "federal" in Federal Council, and guaranteed denominations and cooperative agencies equal representation in all major council decisions. In a closing statement, which came from Speer's mind if not his pen, the proposers of the plan said, "Amid all perplexities, however, our course is plain. It is to seek the path of duty, of the right and necessary cooperative action, never more demanded than now, and quietly, without the publication of programs or the advertisement of proposed effort, to render service as means for it are provided."[43] Mott wrote Speer a few days after the meeting, "It has been much in my thought, and, I am glad to say, even more in my prayers." He responded that it had been a "good meeting," which had ended in a profitable resolution of some of the fundamental questions.[44]

With principles established to the satisfaction of all interested parties in the key areas of external and internal relations, he set himself and the council on course to follow up the agreements and work out specific relationships. He called the committee on consultation together in March and they decided on a second Conference of Interdenominational Agencies. He called it to order on April 28, 1921, and presented the first paper, "The Present Status of the Movement for Interdenominational Cooperation and Unity." The forces of cooperation and division were openly clashing in the churches, he told the delegates, but he was certain the tendency toward unity was more powerful because it was "inseparable from our Christian faith." Since the "ideal of organic unity has suffered a temporary set-back," it was "important that we recognize this and concentrate our effort upon present practicable steps." Moreover, he believed they should "carefully conserve all the gains that we have won and exercise great care lest we imperil anything which has been thus far built up." The conference voted to continue the committee on consultation and to look for ways for the agencies to cooperate in their recruiting policies and publicity. The delegates also agreed to search for "a common approach to the racial question."[45] He also presided at a Conference of Representatives of Denominational Forward Movements in March, where he set the agenda and was an important part of two racial conferences that met to consider the role of the council in the field of race relations.[46]

One conference he called may have been the first of its kind in America. At his invitation the moderators, presidents, or other official representatives of seventeen major denominations met at the offices of the council in New York on April 13, 1921. He explained that he had called the conference because "various denominational bodies are confronted with such similar responsibilities," and in light of the coming annual meetings their leaders might welcome a chance to take counsel with one another. Cavert took notes and recorded the "substance" of the remarks made at the meeting.

Speer opened the conference with a statement of his personal commitment to unity: "The influence of the churches upon the life of the whole people would be far more powerful if we could make it more unmistakable that we are all animated by the same spirit and are seeking the same ends." He offered a suggested agenda for their meetings, beginning with the need for continued focus on "the perennial emphasis on winning men to personal discipleship to Christ." His list included traditional topics like the churches and education and the concern for ministerial recruits, but he also proposed discussion of "the true function of the Church in relation to social, industrial and economic conditions" and "the relation of the Church to the nation and to other nations and races." He asked, "While guarding the principle of the freedom of church and state, have we failed to work out such true relationships as will bring the influence of the Church to bear most effectively upon national policies? Has the church, for example, a present duty with relation to the question of disarmament?" After a lively discussion and the presentation of many different points of view, the leaders unanimously concurred with two suggestions he made for their coming meetings: (1) they would encourage their churches to "bring in recommendations concerning the cooperation of the denomination with other bodies," and (2) they would use their influence to "create a spirit of brotherliness" throughout their own denominations. "A real ministry of goodwill and brotherhood to the world" depended upon unity within and among the many branches of the Christian church.[47]

The council had sent "A Message to the Churches of America" immediately after the Boston quadrennial, but had addressed it "to all who love and would follow our Lord Jesus Christ," rather than to its member denominations.[48] The council did not officially communicate with the latter until May 1, when it issued a formal letter, "To the Constituent Bodies of the Federal Council," under the signatures of Speer and the other general officers and the members of the administrative committee. The letter described the Boston meeting as "the most representative and significant meeting of the Council that has ever been held," and invited careful review of the attached report of the Committee on Methods of Cooperation. It assured the denominations that changes in accord with the report were underway and that the council was moving forward. Reflecting Speer's concerns, the letter called attention to the problems confronting the churches in terms of their need to lead people into a fuller personal discipleship of Jesus Christ and added that such discipleship "must include every area of human life. The Gospel must be brought to bear upon all our social and industrial order, upon all our inter-racial and international relations. All these great tasks call the churches to the most effective cooperation with one another that can possibly be secured."[49]

Leadership of the Federal Council

His administrative involvement in the years 1920–24 was not limited to conferences and consultations, nor was it over in his first six months of service. Except for the time he was overseas, he was constantly active in council affairs. His work covered a wide spectrum, from formulating draft statements on public occasions and issues to writing letters to potential donors, consultations with Council executives about appointments and procedures, responses to critics, and attendance at a wide range of national and state conferences as the representative voice of the council. He lobbied long and hard with the leaders of the Protestant Episcopal Church and the newly created United Lutheran Church to encourage them to lead their denominations into the council.[50] He visited the annual meetings of many denominations, with reports of council activities and proposed budget figures. The clerk of the General Assembly of the United Presbyterian Church told him, in reference to a council request for $4,000, "Our people have confidence in you, and if anyone can persuade them, you are the man."[51]

Niebuhr wrote him in the spring of 1921 asking him to encourage the council to send a letter to the churches of Germany, offering reconciliation. The Boston meeting had not agreed to send such a letter, and he hoped that Speer would take up the matter. He added that as a young man he had "often sat at your feet while in college (I often heard you at Yale in 1913–1915)," and had "absolute confidence in your Christian spirit and sincerity of purpose." The council subsequently sent such a letter.[52]

Speer's missionary trip in 1921–22 included the Near East. After his return he chaired a conference of organizations interested in the need to end the struggle between the Turks and the Armenians and provide relief funds. The council subsequently arranged a mass meeting on the topic, which took place September 24, 1922, in the Synod Hall of the Cathedral of St. John the Divine and drew an unexpectedly large turnout of over 3,000. The *Times* reported that he called for just and reasonable proposals to end the bloodshed and quoted him as follows: "There are many whose hearts are heavy because of what the Turk has done. We are not to speak one word of wrath or anger against the Turk. . . . We seek not vengeance. . . . We can plan our part and do our simple duty to all, including the Turk. What is right and Christian must be done."[53]

One of his least pleasant tasks with the council, as with his board, was response to criticism. He considered it a toll on his time with few positive consequences. Most critics did not link their criticisms of the council to him personally. An exception was those who were Presbyterian. They typically regretted that he had decided to lend his good name to what some of them regarded to be an unworthy organization. David S. Kennedy, editor of the *Presbyterian*, said that he could not "refrain from expressing regret, directly and personally, to you, that you are henceforth to stand before the Church as one divided in your energies between the great work of foreign missions . . . and the Federal Council; which is an indefinite proposition in the minds of many devout and faithful members of the Church."[54]

The criticism fell into two broad categories, theological and social, although it was not always easy to distinguish between them. Critics of the first kind typically claimed that the council was usurping the proper roles of the denominations and had produced a complex organization where a simple one would do. Unity was fine, Kennedy said, but it could be achieved without "the machinery of an elaborate organization with a secretarial body."[55] Joseph T. Gibson, editor of the *Presbyterian Banner*, essentially agreed and said the search for a "super church organization" had brought down the Interchurch Movement and would eventually destroy the council.[56] Critics of the second kind argued that the churches should not, either cooperatively or individually, be involved in social issues, and their criticism attacked the social witness of the council.

The line between administration and program was not always distinct. Some administrative decisions, like those which involved the secretarial staff, had little to do with programs, but others did. He tended to leave the programming to the council staff, particularly to the two secretaries, Macfarland and Cavert, and to the commissions. He made an exception in the general area of the social witness of the council and particularly in the area of race relations, in which he became so active and involved that it became a significant part of his work (see chapter 11).

The main reason he volunteered his time to the council was his commitment to cooperative Christianity. The administrative and programmatic tasks were simply means to an end. In his presidential role he never chaired a conference or wrote a letter or engaged in a debate without making some definite reference to the ecumenical ideal which drove him. The message was not new. His foreign missionary colleagues, those who attended the SVM quadrennials, and members of his denomination had heard versions of it before. The context was new because it embraced all aspects of the ministry of the church, not just foreign missions. The audience was new, literally as broad as Protestantism. In his four years as council president he became the most outspoken advocate for unity on the American scene, a prophet for unity. He used his office as a pulpit to press forward the claims of Christian unity.

A number of his most distinctive statements were made initially to various council groups, and then either he or the council distributed them to a larger audience. He spoke to the annual meeting of the executive committee in December 1923 on the subject "The Federal Council and the Churches." He affirmed that the council was "nothing but the servant of the denominations" and that it had been "created to minister to their collective wants, to serve their common needs." Although he presented the address to the council, he really spoke to the churches and their need for a common mind. They would be "vastly stronger and more effective in their own distinctive denominational character and action, and could use far more fruitfully and powerfully their common agency in this Council," if they could discover a truer unity within themselves. The unity was present, just unrealized. Reflecting his foreign missionary experience, he claimed that from the point of view of "the non-Christian religions" and other outsiders, "the evangelical churches seem to be marked by a unity so thorough that it is difficult to authenticate its divisions."

One of the most serious problems was "partisanship," and he spoke directly to it in his conclusion. This was the occasion when he dramatically announced that every Christian ought to be a liberal and a conservative, a fundamentalist and a modernist. For his part he wanted no label but "Christian." The council published this as a pamphlet and gave it wide circulation.[57] While his position received general applause, it failed to please everyone. The editor of the *Watchman-Examiner* argued that his effort to walk the middle of the road involved too many risks. Such a position might be expected from "the ordinary promoter of great 'get-together' movements, but it is hardly what the Christian churches have a right to expect from Dr. Speer." Speer typically saw the middle of an argument as the point to seek to comprehend differences; his critics usually saw the middle as the point of compromise with error or what they believed was just as bad, a place of indecision.[58]

He made his farewell address to the council at the fifth quadrennial in Atlanta in December 1924. He put his fundamental conviction in the short and pithy title: "The Indivisibility of the Church's Life." The overwhelming impression he had gained from his service with the council was that there was "nothing in Christ that any one communion can monopolize." The things the denominations held in common far outweighed those they held separately. They held sin in common. There was no such thing as a "Presbyterian type of sin." They had a common task, to overcome sin "through the power of their one Saviour and Lord." They also agreed remarkably on moral issues. If, he said, you "erased the denominational names" from the various recent resolutions about war and peace, "no one could possibly tell which declaration came from which body."

There were difficulties to be sure. The first concerned the relation of the churches to the world. Some would silence the churches. But Christians must ask themselves, "Are there areas of life of which He is not meant to be Lord? If so, then He is not the Lord of all, as we had supposed." He affirmed, "The whole of human life belongs to Him and must be brought under His mastery." The second difficulty was the relationship of the churches to one another. They had to find a common mind. He closed with a stirring appeal to unity: "We must grapple ourselves with these momentous tasks, and in order to do so with power we must develop a will to unity that will relegate to a secondary place all details of polity and organization and draw the Churches together in a growing oneness of spirit and purpose."[59]

When his term as president ended, he received many words of personal and public congratulations. Cavert told him that his "personal friendship is one of the deepest treasures of my life" and added that he was happy they could call on him, for "we simply cannot do without you."[60] The council passed a formal resolution: "With prophetic vision and a high courage, but also with sympathetic understanding and patient consideration, he has brought the Council to that place where more nearly than ever before, it is able to throw the total impact of our American Protestantism upon the vital issues of our own country and of the world."[61] Heady credits, which he modestly and steadfastly declined. But the council had taken remarkable steps forward since 1920. The *Christian Century* reviewed the Atlanta quadrennial and found it wanting in exciting dialogue, but praised the council for making progress while holding the often fractious denominations together.[62] Cavert, late in what was a distinguished ecumenical career, described the years 1920–24 as "among the most creative" in the council's history.[63]

The curtain came down on his presidency, but not on his council service. He continued to hold membership on a number of council groups, including the executive committee, the Commission on the Church and Race Relations, and a number of other committees. In 1930 council leaders invited him to become the general secretary, but he declined. It was a road he could have taken, a suitable climax to his career. Instead, he recommitted himself to foreign missions. "I cannot see," he said in response to the invitation, "that it would be right for me to leave the distinctive foreign missionary service. It was to this work that it seemed to me more than forty years ago I ought to give my life and my sense of duty today is just what it was then. I have always been eager and am eager now to do all that I can in every way to help forward the Christian Cause in all its forms, but I still think that my primary and special responsibility is in this field and that in it and from it I can still render my best service to the general cause, and especially to the cause of Christian cooperation and unity."[64] The council was the context for his most prophetic domestic ecumenical statements and actions. He served the cause of ecumenism, in and out of the council, the rest of his life.

CHAPTER 11

Social Gospel Witness

"Of One Blood"

One of Speer's earliest and firmest convictions was that the gospel had a social as well as an individual meaning. He was an important, although hitherto unheralded, witness to the social gospel. His understanding of it was quite broad and embraced all aspects of society, for he believed that one goal of the gospel was a redeemed social order, a true Christian community. His specific contribution was in race relations, in the development and articulation of ideas concerning racial cooperation and justice and in the creation of a program to achieve those ends. It was a significant part of his work as an American churchman.

Members of his generation recovered the social gospel and named a movement after it, which was in many respects a religious version of political and social progressivism. Washington Gladden and Walter Rauschenbusch focused their attention primarily on urban and industrial problems and on related economic issues. Rauschenbusch published his landmark analysis of the relationship between religion and American life in 1912 and announced that business life remained the only unredeemed part of society.[1] Students of the social gospel have for many years focused on economic issues and claimed that it generally ignored race, more specifically that its leaders "neglected the Negro's plight."[2] Recent studies of the social gospel, however, have discovered that the movement was much more extensive than the standard interpretation has claimed and that it included a search for racial justice as fervent as the search for economic justice.[3] Speer was part of that larger movement.

Sources of His Social Gospel Vision

He derived his social gospel vision from his study of the Bible, from the founders of the missionary movement, and from his mentors, particularly

323

Moody. When Speer turned to the Bible on this topic, he looked to Jesus and his teachings. There was no question in his mind that "Jesus taught personal religion," but one that had two components, "a new life with God, and a new life with men."[4] When Jesus had spoken about the latter, he had often done so in terms of the kingdom of God. He had announced it early in his ministry, as reported by Mark and Luke, and then had traveled as spokesperson for it, encouraging people to believe in it and join it.[5]

He believed Jesus had spent his time establishing "the principles which should govern men under all forms of social organization," rather than reorganizing the society of his time, because if he had defined the principles in terms of a particular social form, then "men in other lands and times would have evaded the weight of obligation His teaching imposed" by arguing that his ideals did not fit their circumstances.[6] Instead, Speer argued, Jesus had advanced a bold and original plan, remarkable for its scope, including all persons in all nations over the centuries. It excluded no one. At its heart was "a new spiritual relationship centered in Himself, a brotherhood of lovers, each loving as He had loved."[7] Jesus had declared that the new relationship took precedence over "all human ties, even the closest. His statements are unhumanly uncompromising on this."[8] He found this idea a truly revolutionary one, for it meant "the renovation of the world and the readjustment of social relations," and although it had not yet been realized, it remained the most remarkable proposal for a new human and social order ever conceived.[9]

In his study of the careers of the founders of modern missions, he discovered that they had both understood and used the social aspects of Jesus' message. He put his version of their thoughts together in an essay on "The Social Ideals of the Founders of Modern Missions." Writing in 1926 and using the terms "social ideal" and "social conscience" rather than "social gospel," he noted the widespread perception that the founders of the modern missionary movement "were destitute of the social ideal," and that their aims were "purely individualistic and other worldly." Beginning with William Carey, and reviewing the lives of Alexander Duff, Henry Venn, David Brainerd, Samuel Mills, the early Moravian missionaries, and others, he demonstrated how they all had joined their message of individual salvation with efforts to transform the social or political or economic life of the societies they served. Carey had worked in agriculture and Duff in education, both in India, and Brainerd had worked to preserve the traditional lands for the Native Americans. "If," he said, "we could have asked those early missionaries whether their motive was to save the people to whom they went from future death or for a present life, and whether their ideal was to reach a few individuals or to set free redemptive forces in human society which would help to bring in the Kingdom of God, they would have answered, 'You talk in terms of 'either—or,' with us it is 'both—and.' Why do you see as mutually exclusive that which with us is combined in one?' "[10] He concluded, "The social ideal is implicit in the missionary purpose. The man who sets out to save another man is acting socially. His theory may be called individualistic but his act is social. The relationship which he takes up is cellular to the Kingdom of God."[11]

He believed his mentors, particularly Moody, had held the same theory. When he defined the great evangelist in such terms, his listeners were inclined to be surprised, because Moody had been so strongly identified as part of the movement to save individuals. However, he pointed out that Moody had also called "for redeemed life here and now, and wherever he went institutions and movements of philanthropy, of social service, of moral reform flowed directly from his influence."[12] Moreover, Moody had personally founded schools. Moody was like the fathers of modern missions, who had conceived their work "not only in terms of individual conversion but also in terms of human service and brotherhood."[13]

The Kingdom of God

In Speer's view the kingdom of God was a radically new social order, embracing all aspects of social life. Although he and Rauschenbusch worked at different tasks, their thinking on the nature of the kingdom had remarkable parallels. He sounded like Rauschenbusch when he called for the church to deal with social and industrial issues and when he declared that the "commercial and materialistic solution of the world's problem has been fully tried," and it was time to turn to the gospel solution.[14] Surely, he urged, "Our modern world is not made up of individual persons alone, but is made up of collective persons like Labor Unions, Corporations, aggregations of power of many kinds which men have created, but which are themselves each a sort of gigantic and collective man. Is the Gospel not to be preached to these creatures as well as to others? . . . [Jesus'] words clearly mean that the principles of Christianity are to be applied to nations and to all other institutions and agencies created by men which determine the well-being of the bodies and souls of God's children." If these things were true, then the church was called "to seek first the Kingdom of God and His righteousness and to have the law of God and of his Son Jesus Christ obeyed in all the individual and corporate life of men."[15] He agreed with Rauschenbusch in calling for kingdom men and women. He quoted one of his prayers in a meditation titled "Peace on Earth": "O Christ, Thou hast bidden us pray for the coming of Thy Father's Kingdom, in which righteousness shall be done on earth. . . . As we have mastered nature that we might gain wealth, help us now to master the social relations of mankind that we may gain justice and a world of brothers."[16]

He frequently used Jesus' social ideal to challenge individuals and groups. To students in the 1890s he said, "And do not narrowly think that the kingdom of God is national, or sectional, or racial; but believe that it is what Christ said it was and the early Church believed it to be. Men who have learned the lessons of those early days are needed in these days."[17] To those gathered in May 1919 to reflect on and sum up the work of the Protestant churches in World War I, he claimed that their united ministry had demonstrated "the possibility here and now of a new and a better world, the kind of world for which Christ lived and died and lives again." In the euphoria of that moment he created a hymn to the possibility of the coming of the Kingdom:

> It will be a new world in which the principle of competition shall have given way to the principle of association and fellowship. It will be a new world in which the principle of unity shall have replaced the principle of division, or in which at least the principle of division will see itself only as the servant of the principle of a larger synthesis. It will be a new world in which the sacredness of property will find its sanction only in the greater sanctity and dignity of personality and human life. It will be a new world in which the social and individual ideals and services will be reciprocal and complementary. It will be a new world in which brotherliness and friendship will have displaced antagonisms except the war against evil. It will be a new world in which obedience to truth and duty will find its ground in the Will of a transcendent, sovereign God. It will be a new world in which Jesus Christ will be the head of humanity and His life and spirit will do for men what no injunctions or ordinances can ever avail to do. That new world, held before men's eyes, will be worth as many sacrifices as men were willing to make for what was held before their eyes in the four years that have gone by.[18]

Quite often he claimed that one of the significant motives of the missionary movement was "the building here on earth of the Kingdom of God," and argued that missionaries were "agents to bring into reality here an order of human society regenerated and remade by Jesus Christ."[19] Indeed, he believed the missionary enterprise was the most likely way God's kingdom would be realized, even though he understood that ultimately God would usher it in. He never equated the kingdom with the carrying of Western civilization to other lands and peoples, a confusion made by some who advocated the social gospel in the missionary context.[20]

What he meant he described when he invited those gathered at the SVM convention in Buffalo in 1932 to dream about God's kingdom in terms of a "Christlike world." It was obvious to all, he said, that the world was far from Christlike, for if it were, there would be "no navies or armies," "no armaments or military preparedness," "no speculative wealth," "no injustice or inequality, or hate," and "no lust or crime." In such a world these negative things, the kind that seemed to dominate life, would be replaced by positive ones. Lifting his language to match his vision, he exclaimed, "What beauty there might be, what glory and love, what equality and justice, what peace and joy in a world that was Christlike, where the mind of Christ had come to prevail and where everything had been brought under His government as living King and Lord." He acknowledged that living the Christlike life in a world that was not yet transformed was risky, but he challenged his listeners to accept the risk and "to live to bring in the mind of Christ upon our earth."[21]

Although historians have, in general, missed his social gospel emphasis, many of his contemporaries recognized it, and some strongly opposed it. The challenges to his views were most frequent in the 1920s and often came from individuals who took a very conservative, if not fundamentalist, line in their arguments, charging him with becoming involved in "politics." To one such correspondent in 1923 he responded by quoting from the Lord's Prayer: "Thy kingdom come, Thy will be done on earth as it is in heaven." "Does this not mean," he asked, "that we must work for these ends as well as pray for them, and does it not mean that the Church must do so as well as individual Christians?" He recognized that there were differences of opinion about "the boundary line within which the Church should confine its work." Over the years there had been people "who thought it ought not to say anything about slavery, and others that it ought not to say anything about prohibition, and others that it should say nothing about divorce or sex relationships, and others that it should say nothing about social or industrial questions. Many real problems no doubt arise in this field, but I am sure you would not want to say that the Church had nothing to do with earth but only with heaven. How could one take that view and continue to pray the Lord's Prayer?"[22]

He greatly admired and occasionally wrote about those who served in social gospel ministries. Alice Jackson, a fellow resident of Englewood, gave her life to social service and attracted him so strongly that he wrote her biography, one of his most moving life stories. She graduated from Smith College in 1898 and that summer attended Northfield and received a call to be a foreign missionary. The Presbyterian Board refused her because of a serious diabetic condition. Undaunted, she took up social work, beginning at a settlement house, the Christodora House, in New York City. There and at several other locations she ministered to working women and young girls, most of whom were recent immigrants, until the disease took her life in her thirtieth year. He pointed out that, even though she had died young, she had achieved a full ministry. He described her life in the same terms he used for the missionaries about whom he wrote, as a sacrificial offering, and presented her as a true witness for Christ in some of the most difficult social and economic conditions.[23] In the 1920s Elliott spent two years in a similar ministry at Bethlehem Chapel.

Focus on Race

In a general sense Speer witnessed to the social gospel throughout his life in his role as missionary leader. He believed it was, as the missionary founders had said and shown, an integral part of the missionary enterprise. But even before he began his missionary work, and then in the course of it, he developed a distinct and quite specific area of social gospel witness, in his concern for race relations and racism.

His choice of race as a primary concern was his own. No one in his family heritage appears to have had an interest in persons of other races in general or in African Americans. The Western world literally oozed racism during his lifetime, and his career completely overlapped what could be described as America's "Racial Era" (1875–1925). Only eight years after Congress passed the dramatic Civil Rights Act of 1875, the Supreme Court struck it down. A little more than a decade later the Court sanctioned segregation in its decision in *Plessy v. Ferguson*. Jim Crow laws solidified into rigid segregation codes in many southern states by 1910, and lynching persuaded African Americans to obey those laws. The Ku Klux Klan was a power in the 1920s, symbolized by its massive march on Washington in 1925, the largest such march in American history, not eclipsed until the civil rights march of 1963. The Chinese Exclusion Act (1882), the Gentlemen's Agreement with Japan (1907), and the Johnson Act (1924) kept America relatively racially pure, even though they fell short of the goals of the immigration restrictionists. Racism and nationalism burst forth in Social Darwinist imagery, Anglo-Saxon fantasy, and outright racist tracts for the times as early as the 1880s. Social gospel advocates sometimes joined this effort, as did Josiah Strong in *Our Country* in 1885, when he appealed for Anglo-Saxon supremacy.[24] Later tracts, not in the social gospel mode, were simply viciously racist, like Madison Grant's *The Passing of the Great Race* (1916), and Lothrop Stoddard's *The Rising Tide of Color Against White World Supremacy* (1920).[25] The racial views of Speer's era were tidal waves, rolling in one after another, engulfing virtually all opposition. The remarkable thing was not that he was drawn to the issue, but that he developed and then consistently advocated views that went against this tide, and finally helped generate a counterforce.

His experience with people of other races began in his hometown with African Americans, where a familiar and friendly figure in his youth was Henry Lott, "who cared for our furnace and did our chores."[26] In Speer's freshman year at Princeton he became involved in teaching the "colored class at Prof. Smith's school on Witherspoon Street."[27] He taught there regularly and in his junior year became superintendent of what he called the "Colored School".[28] When he referred to this experience, he did so in the context of the difficulty of teaching growing boys, telling one group of Sunday school teachers, "I used to teach the main school for negro boys in Princeton. They 'worked off' on me as an ignorant freshman. There were boys coming to the age when they had eyes to see—girls! And they were very hard to handle. It was one of the hardest things in the world to teach these boys and keep them interested with spiritual things."[29]

While still in college he demonstrated that he fully grasped the American version of racism. His senior year he won the Baird Prize, an oratorical award, for his speech "The National Antipathy to the Negro." It was a brief but ringing declaration of the devastating results of slavery and the immorality of segregation. What had slavery wrought? he asked. "The negro was possessed of reason: slavery made him a craven beast of burden. He might have been a prince among his people: slavery made him an outcast in social life. He had laws and hopes: slavery deprived him of the right to cherish them, shackled him with the restraints of civil inequality, made justice blind before him in the courts of law, and barred in his face the gates of the house of God." In the aftermath of the Civil War and reconstruction and the bitterness of both experiences, the south, "the New South," finally "left the negro his liberty and his equality on the statutes, but has proclaimed openly . . . that the white race must dominate in a land consecrated by their father's blood." It accomplished this by guaranteeing his rights only when he agreed to exercise them "distinctly separate from the white race and to surrender them when their maintenance might mean encroachment upon the inherited privileges of the dominant people."

These decisions had created a grinding caste system, which he claimed "denies that his nation was ever made in the image of God, denies that he is of one blood with all nations of men, denies all duty and responsibility in regard to him." He proposed, somewhat naively, that political reforms would correct the political inequalities. Social equality would also be forthcoming, despite the thousands of southern voices that opposed it, because "the great moral truths of revelation and of humanity" required it, and he added, "when he is worthy of it, his color shall be no barrier." His conclusion, which he labeled "radical," may have seemed so in the largely white and privileged environment of Princeton, but it placed on African Americans yet one more burden, achieving worthiness, that could hardly be justified. However, the body of his speech, with its clear understanding of the history of American racism, revealed a person ready to learn about the global dimensions of the problem.[30]

Those more advanced lessons came in his early years with the SVM and during his missionary journeys. He began to interpret his conversion and SVM work as experiences of "brotherhood" in the general rather than specific racial sense of that term. "Brothers" Forman, Wilder, and his prayer partners among his classmates had mediated Jesus to him and had helped spark the call to go to his "brothers" in other lands. "It is absolutely essential to men," he said, "that if they ever find Christ or the fullness of His life they should find it through their brothers." Christ was and remained the true brother, "showing to every man of us what a brother a man ought to be to his brother, and being Himself but the representative to the world of the real bond of unity between all men who call Him their brother and their friend. . . . No man can know Jesus Christ all to himself."[31]

His visits to other lands made him particularly critical of the popular emphasis on the glories of the Anglo-Saxons. Speaking on foreign missions at Mount Hermon in the summer of 1895, he said that "no one race is peculiarly dear to God nor peculiarly essential to his plans." "We talk," he continued, "as if God had a larger place for America in his heart than for the other nations and that therefore we are entitled to something which the other nations are not entitled to. You never heard a missionary coming home from the missionary field with his head full of this Anglo-Saxon conceit."[32] Shortly after he returned from his first world trip, he offered this assessment of his experience:

> On the surface the different parts of this world differ greatly from one another: the colors of the complexions of distinct races of men differ. They live in different kinds of houses; they speak different languages; they eat different sorts of food. In all superficial and external ways the human race is torn apart into diverse sections. But when one pierces beneath the superficial, differentiating characteristics, one understands how closely akin all

peoples of this world are; how that though our reasoned intellectual judgments may differ from one another, our fundamental moral instincts are
pretty much the same; how true it is that God has made of one blood all
the races of men, and looks down upon them as the Father of them all, His
children![33]

He began to tell audiences as early as 1901 that it was "not possible for any
one of us any longer to be a citizen of one small community." God was acting to open the eyes of Americans to the world and to show them that "they
belong to the brotherhood of mankind. . . . Every one who is a citizen of
this land has other fellow citizens, and we are bound up as we never were
before to a sympathy of the whole world and the people of the world."[34]

Important as his experiences were, they were not the sole basis of his
views on race. He was a person of faith, constantly engaged in Bible study.
He found the Bible an excellent source book on race and turned to one of
two passages whenever he wanted to explain its teachings on the subject.
The text that he used in his college essay and much later in the title of one
of his books was Acts 17:26: "God hath made of one blood all nations of
men for to dwell on all the face of the earth." "Of one blood" symbolized
the unity of humanity: "The negro's Father and God is mine; the China-
man's Father and God is mine; the Persian's Father and God is mine. . . .
The same kind of blood and color of blood runs in every man's veins, the
same ambitions, and the same hopes and the same sorrows and the same
sympathies."[35] Humanity was one in blood and need; humanity was saved
by the shedding of one blood.

His other favorite "race" passage was John 10:16, where Jesus said, "I
have other sheep not of this fold." He argued that although Jesus belonged
to a race that had intense racial and national feelings, he did not share "in
its narrowness and exclusivism."[36] In fact, Speer said, Jesus' racial views
were an important basis of his problems with his fellow Jews, especially
over the issue of the treatment of Samaritans. If Jesus would admit "no
narrower field of work and salvation for Himself than the world," how
could his focus on the salvation of the "house of Israel" be understood? He
responded that Jesus "had to make a beginning" and used his mission to
the Jews as a springboard for his universal message.[37] In one of his most
explicit essays on race he linked the "other sheep" passage to words of Paul
in Ephesians 2:14, which he said helped explain it: "For Christ is our
peace, who made all one, and broke down the wall of division, that He
might reconcile all in one body." Speer concluded:

Humanity is a unity. It is one flock. The sheep may be of different strains.
The hues of their wool may vary. But there is one Shepherd, and all the

sheep are His sheep and one flock as they follow him. Humanity is an organism with many members but one body. Each member is a race. All the members differ, but all are one. A common life pervades the whole. If one member suffers, all suffer with it. Each feeds the tissues of all the rest. . . . In the light of the city whose lamp is the Lamb all the races are to walk, and men shall bring the honor of all the races into it; but nothing unclean shall be there, no race prejudice. . . . This is Christ's view of the race problem. Woe unto us and our children if it is not ours.[38]

By the turn of the century he had a clear vision of the complexity of racism and the Christian response to it. He chose to express his social ministry two ways, as an advocate calling for what he understood to be the Christian resolution of the racial problem, which he did for the rest of his life, and as the molder of an institutional response, which he accomplished during his presidency of the Federal Council. A strong and forceful opponent of racism, he often raised the issue at student missionary conferences and in missionary and other meetings and challenged audiences to join in helping resolve it. He spent a great deal of time on the issue, especially in the context of his council work. In the years after he left the council presidency in 1924, he became heavily occupied with denominational and missionary matters that occasionally included racism, but not as the primary issue.

Speaking Out Against Racism

When he spoke on the race problem, he typically set it in its largest context, as a problem for all races and all nations. Even though his first essay on racism was about African Americans, he never singled out black-white relationships as *the* race problem. He continued, of course, to reflect on racism as it related to African Americans, and when he did he often turned his attention to the evils of slavery and lynching. His references to slavery were to the social and economic compromises people had made in America and elsewhere, which in turn had allowed that evil system to emerge and persist.[39] On his first world trip he encountered an instance of modern slavery when he met a man who had rescued eighteen African boys from an Arab slaver. Each of the children had a brand burned into his cheek. As he looked at those boys, he said he understood what made abolitionists like John Brown "endure any ignominy or persecution, even death, that they might strike the shackles from the wrists of the last slave and reinstate him again with his rights as a man."[40]

Racial injustice at home, particularly lynching, not only destroyed life in the most illegal and heart-wrenching ways, but also created major difficulties for missionaries, especially those who worked among other races. He reminded the members of the Laymen's Missionary Movement who attended the Men's National Missionary Congress in Chicago in 1910 that they needed to put their own house in order.

> It is futile to hope that a little band of men, however much they may attempt to isolate themselves from the national and racial life out of which they came, can preach to the world the gospel of love, if in our corporate and national life we are preaching the gospel of selfishness and distrust. It is futile to hope that we can send to all the world the message of love of God in Christ, by those who go out to represent our Christian churches, if we are preaching to the world by other tongues, tongues so loud that they almost drown the still small voice of the missionary enterprise, a message of hate and discord and the waste of life.[41]

Racism in relation to Asians, both in Asia and in America, also attracted his attention. He told the men at the congress that there were all too many "instances of the domineering assertion of the sense of racial superiority, and of the way in which Western men by the thousands have gone out over the Eastern world and have affronted the fundamental principles of human brotherhood and equality. Again and again our personal touch with the non-Christian world has been radically un-Christian."[42]

In the spring of 1913 he became deeply involved, through the Federal Council, in an issue involving Japanese living in America. Proposed land legislation in California would discriminate against Japanese there, and Christians in Japan had asked missionaries to appeal to the Christians of America to intervene. The American Board of Commissioners for Foreign Missions sent a special Japan mission to the United States, which included Sidney L. Gulick, who had been a missionary in Japan for twenty-six years. The council heard his appeal and created a preliminary joint committee on Eastern race relationships. Speer cochaired this group and helped arrange a national speaking tour for Gulick. By 1914 council leaders were convinced they were dealing with a serious long-term problem and created a Commission on Relations with Japan. Speer served on it and signed the petition it sent to Congress, "An Appeal to Congress and the People of the United States for an Adequate Oriental Policy." The petitioners urged Congress to adopt an "Oriental policy based upon a just and equitable regard for the interests of all the nations concerned."[43]

It soon became obvious that not all persons in Congress shared the council's vision. In debates on Japanese immigration, some representatives not only argued for total exclusion, but also predicted an inevitable race war between "whites and yellows."[44] Why, Speer asked, should anyone, let alone someone in Congress, talk in such fashion; why should he so "brutalize his interracial relationships?"[45] Mankind was one, and it was "as irrational that Japan and the United States should be set in hostility as that a body should take its fingers and tear out its eyes."[46] In 1916 the council broadened the charge of its commission and changed its name to the Commission on Relations With the Orient.

Appeals to "brotherhood," his and those of like-minded persons, did not dissipate the deep national opposition to Japanese and Chinese immigration, nor did they resolve the problems of Japanese-Americans and Japanese aliens in California and other western states. He pressed his case again in 1917, this time in a pamphlet directed specifically to the issue: *How to Preserve Fellowship and Right Understanding Between Japan and the United States.* He outlined a number of steps for improving relations, beginning with "keeping our heads," and concluding with "showing kindness and courtesy to Japanese in America." In the midst of these generalities he offered the following specific opinions: "What is right is a question to be considered calmly and without prejudice, but the problem of the rights of Japanese in California to own property, their right to acquire citizenship, their right of justly regulated admission to the United States, is a problem to be considered without racial prejudice or bigotry and on the basis of moral and economic justice to both Japanese and Americans."[47]

By the time he had expressed these views, the World War had come to America. As leader of the General War-Time Commission he had many opportunities to speak about the causes and nature of the war and about war in general. He began to argue that war and race were interrelated. In reflecting on the war, he said it was but a temporary conflict, the overt sign of much deeper and more permanent problems, which he identified as "the imperfect development of democracy," "the claim of national trusteeship to be above the moral law," "a breakdown of the processes of social evolution," "racial suspicion and inequality," and "the resistance of national individualism to the spirit of world brotherhood and to the common interest of humanity."[48]

After the war he began to see that the end of racism was crucial to a new world order and claimed that race had become one of the two "unsolved problems" of the world—the other one was "the problem of church and state"—that had to be resolved if a world of peace and justice were to emerge and survive.[49] Racial prejudice had become such an important factor to him that he described it as the source of more "woe and wrong and desolation" than anything else except "sin and selfishness in human hearts."[50] In the tract he wrote for the Committee on the War and the Religious Outlook, he appealed to the churches to work together to solve the race problem. Several years later he elevated the race problem to an ultimate level when he opened his book on race with the assertion: "The questions of race and race relationships are the most insistent questions of the modern world."[51]

Immediately after the war, the Federal Council issued two incisive position statements on racism. No evidence has surfaced to indicate that Speer was primarily responsible for these statements. The council, interracial since its founding, had organized a Committee on Negro Churches before the war. However, the treatment of African-American soldiers at home and abroad during the war and the twenty race riots that erupted in 1919 awakened it to action. In the first of these declarations, "The Church and Social Reconstruction," it defined as just the demand of "the colored people of the nation" for "equal economic and professional opportunities." Moreover, it argued that the "barbarism of lynching" should be both "condemned by public opinion and abolished by rigorous measures and penalties."[52] In the second document, "Statement and Recommendations on the Present Racial Crisis," it offered its most unequivocal expression of the depth of the racial problems and one of the most remarkable statements to appear in the entire Racial Era. It confessed that the churches had been "too little inspired by the fundamental principles and ideals of Jesus Christ. Communities that have expressed horror over atrocities abroad, have seen, almost unmoved and silent, men beaten, hanged and burned by the mob." The challenge to the churches was to preach and promote "brotherhood." In closing it touched the heart of the entire racial question in words simple, clear, and powerful: "The root of the matter is the failure to recognize the Negro as a man. . . . Respect for Negro manhood and womanhood is the only basis for amicable race adjustment, for race integrity and for permanent racial peace."[53]

The Federal Council and Race

When the Federal Council elected Speer its leader in 1920, it matched a person who had determined that racism was one of the two most important issues facing society with its own need to act on its recent declarations.

It joined two parts of an unseen puzzle, each needing the other to make a clear picture. He recognized the possibilities at once. Council organization dictated to some degree the course he should follow. It had commissions, led by chairs and run by executive secretaries, to carry out its important tasks, and committees, made up entirely of volunteers, to deal with lower priority matters. It worked through cooperation, consultation, and persuasion, because its federal character required it. The task, as he saw it, was to move race from committee to commission status, from volunteer to professional leadership, which would enable the council to move its policy forward and extend it into new courses of action. This policy was exactly the opposite of what he thought the council needed to do in foreign missions. He believed the council should turn its foreign mission work over to other, more prepared and effective groups, like the Foreign Mission Conference. However, his wartime ministry had taught him that there were no existing, much less effective, national church groups facing the racial crisis. In short, he decided to make race a major council priority.

He began by conferring informally with various denominational leaders. The council, together with the Home Missions Council, held a "racial conference" on January 24, 1921, to consider the general racial climate and what could be done to improve it. Those who attended shared their feelings that the churches were at a crisis stage in their ministries regarding racial issues. As the discussion wound down, he proposed a larger and more representative gathering. The conferees concurred, asked him to work with a few others to call it, and directed that the meeting "include others than those of the Anglo-Saxon race."[54]

Leaders of several African American denominations were present at the second conference, which met February 3. The plan that evolved from these meetings was to create a new commission within the Federal Council. When the executive committee of the council voted to do this it signaled more than the simple transfer of race from committee to commission status; it marked the arrival of race as a major priority of the churches united. The editor of the *Federal Council Bulletin* described the situation precisely in the title of the article that announced the formation of the Commission on Negro Churches and Race Relations: "*New* Interest in Inter-Racial Problems."[55] The council charged its new commission "to find practical ways of giving concrete expression to the growing spirit of brotherhood between the negro and white races in this country and to develop that spirit further."[56]

During this consultation process he contacted a number of his friends, in and out of council work, asking for suggestions. Dr. George E. Haynes was one of his correspondents. A former professor at Fisk University and a cofounder of the National Urban League, Haynes had also been director of the Bureau of Negro Economics with the U.S. Department of Labor. He had also worked with the Interchurch World Movement, where he had made a survey of the involvement of African American churches in racial affairs.[57] Speer proposed to him some of the issues a new commission might deal with and the name of a possible leader. Haynes responded, saying he agreed on the issues of the education of African American leadership and the development of better race attitudes among southern whites but added that the new commission should work to improve racial attitudes of northern whites as well, "in view of the many evidences of race friction we have had in the North during the past two years." He also endorsed "unqualifiedly the suggestion of the name of Mr. John J. Eagan of Atlanta to lead such a commission."[58]

Eagan had already given his native south a full measure of his talents in dealing with the problem of race. Most notably, he had helped found in 1919 the Southern Commission on Inter-Racial Cooperation, a grass roots organization to promote cooperation and better relations between African Americans and whites. It had a director in each southern state and committees in most counties and larger cities. Eagan was a fellow Presbyterian, a member of the Presbyterian Church in the U.S. He had a remarkable vision, given the surging emotions of the Racial Era, of a society at racial peace. That vision attracted Speer, who persuaded him to serve as chair of the new council commission. Eagan worked to organize the new commission and chose its membership, with advice from Speer and other council leaders. Some years after Eagan's untimely death in 1924, Speer wrote a biography of him with the subtitle "A Memoir of An Adventurer for the Kingdom of God on Earth."[59]

The Commission on Negro Churches and Race Relations met for the first time on July 12, 1921, in the Washington office of the Federal Council, with about twenty-five representatives of various denominations and church groups present. Speer called them to order and shared with them three of his most deeply held convictions. First, in accord with his theory of race, he told them that the problem of race was the most "difficult of mankind" and presented the "most searching test of our Christian ideals and convictions." Yet Christians believe that God is "the common Father of all," humanity is "an organ," and humanity is "all bound together in one bundle of life." Second, in terms of his ecumenical commitment, he said that a united Christian approach was the best possible one. "The Federal Council," he argued, "representing the life of the churches as a whole, both colored and white, ought to afford a central meeting place for all the agencies dealing with various phases of race relations, ought to reinforce all that is now being done and see to it that no important phase of the task is overlooked." Finally, in light of his view of the solution to the racial crisis, he affirmed that the "mere existence" of the commission testified to the fact that "in Christianity there is a real solution for our inter-racial problem and that the churches are going to deal courageously with their responsibility of seeing that the Christian solution is achieved."[60]

The commission responded well to Eagan's leadership. It developed a set of purposes and initiated several specific programs. By November it was exploring hiring an executive secretary to give full attention to its work. Some of its members were already unhappy with its name, for the phrase "Negro Churches" seemed to suggest race was a problem only for some churches. On January 6, 1922, commission members took two crucial forward steps in the churches' racial ministry. They hired George Haynes to be their first executive secretary and voted to change their name to the Commission on the Church and Race Relations.[61] Speer was on one of his periodic missionary trips when the commission made these decisions, but he endorsed them after he returned. He told Rockefeller, for example, that "the Commission which is dealing with the relation of the churches to the Race question has also . . . been working with real wisdom and efficiency," and he added words of special commendation for Eagan and Haynes.[62]

The Way of Christ in Race Relations
Of One Blood

During the second meeting of the commission, discussion turned to the need for an educational project and the issue of how best to bring the Christian perspective of the race problem to church members and the public in general. William Adams Brown suggested the publication of a book, possibly including the views of leading white and African American Christians. The commission directed him to see if his Committee on the War and the Religious Outlook might not produce such a study.[63] Brown's idea moved along routes not yet discovered and reached its destination with the Council of Women for Home Missions, the Missionary Education Movement of the United States and Canada, and Speer. The two groups agreed to publish a joint home missions study under the theme "The Way of Christ in Race Relations."[64] They chose Speer to write the book.

He agreed to do the study and had an outline together by the end of 1922. He decided to be sole author of the volume, but both he and the groups publishing it sought advice and information from a wide circle of friends and associates. He turned to academicians, missionary friends, and Federal Council colleagues. A variety of college professors offered him information, from biological definitions of race to historical data about Indian and Chinese history. His letters of inquiry included a substantial list of questions: "What is the origin and what do you conceive to be the divine purpose of race and racial differences?" "What is your definition of race?" "What is the cause of racial prejudice?" The response from Sir Narayan Chandavarkar of India was so long and well organized that Speer used it as a separate chapter.[65]

Council personnel who were already at work on the problem provided him with some of his most useful information. Haynes gave substantial help and encouragement, from the outline stage to final review and correction of the galley proofs. He had counseled Speer during the organization of the commission to be careful to see the race problem in national perspective; he now advised him to cast his book in the broadest of international terms. He was particularly concerned with the views of the non-white peoples of the world and said: "I can conceive of no greater service that a book might render than to bring the white world short up against the folly of the proposition laid down by Lothrop Stoddard and the jingoism which goes on believing that generation after generation the 'reeking tube and iron shard' will enable the white world to dominate the balance of mankind. For if this doctrine of force continues, as sure as darkness follows daylight, when the darker peoples of Asia and Africa have learned the methods of militarism they will turn the tables, and then God alone will be able to keep the human family from suicide."[66] Haynes was enthusiastic when he read the galley proofs and told Speer he was "delighted with your whole approach and treatment, as well as your point of view indicated by the title [Of One Blood] and the broad way you have treated it."[67] Speer incorporated many of Haynes's suggestions before he sent the book off to the printer.

Leaders in the Council of Women and the Missionary Education Movement solicited advice from others about the project. Ideas and information poured in from correspondents around the nation, and they forwarded them to Speer. Their suggestions about the nature and outline of the proposed volume varied, but they were of one mind about its author: he was the best man for the job. Cavert, for example, said he had "no wisdom on the subject which justifies me in making any suggestions to a person like Dr. Speer."[68] Another writer said he believed Speer knew more about the problem than anyone in the entire nation.[69] Haynes summed up the consensus: "I know of no one better able than Dr. Speer to bring out the fact that the only hope is in the application of the ideals of the Lowly Nazarene."[70]

The data from the people who responded was valuable, but Speer had been working on the topic his entire life and had well-developed convictions and files of material. When he finished his manuscript in the summer of 1923, he found he had a very long document. Because his goal was a study guide suitable for individual and small group use, he condensed the manuscript, cutting out one chapter and many long quotes, and it appeared in the spring of 1924 as *Of One Blood*. The unabridged version appeared later that year as *Race and Race Relations*. He believed the longer volume with its substantial quotations would be a valuable source book for the shorter one.

Those persons who picked up *Of One Blood* when it became available and who were familiar with his views would have found little new in it, even though they may have been, as one was, overwhelmed with the scope of the study and his "gift of synthesis."[71] Speer took the ideas of his lifetime of Bible study, mission work, and ministry, and he poured them into this effort. In some sections he quoted himself without saying so, but most of the time he put his ideas into new prose. He opened the book with a discussion of the origin of race and closed it with a review of specific racial problems. Grant, Stoddard, and others who held racist views received particular attention and refutation. "One would like to ask Mr. Grant," he wrote, "what race has produced more 'bastardized population' than the superior white race, and also why the principle of the inherent right of worth and merit and of the 'right of merit to rule' is not valid in behalf of those men of colored races who exceed in worth and merit the vast majority of the white race."[72]

His goal, however, was to put race in Christian perspective, not to attack the racists, and his book was primarily a systematic presentation of his own views, rather than a rebuttal of those of others. The heart of his message was in chapter 6, "The Solution of the Race Problem."[73] He presented six solutions then in circulation in the intellectual market place, beginning with those he found least acceptable and moving toward what he believed to be the true solution. The first three proposals were conflict, segregation, and subjection, none of which offered the slightest chance of real success. He said of conflict what he felt about all three, "We cannot feel very greatly indebted to those who offer us this as the only solution of the problem of race relationships."[74] Eugenics was a fourth idea. He believed the effort to breed better persons was difficult enough from the biological point of view alone to offer much of positive value. The only way he thought eugenics might be of some help would be in the possible creation of persons with better character who might in turn hold improved moral ideals.[75]

Amalgamation or intermarriage was the fifth solution, and he spent more time exploring it than any of the others, including the final one. Anthropologists, he noted, agreed that it had taken place in the past and would continue to do so, and historians had turned up numerous instances of it on a grand scale, including Chinese amalgamation in the Malay Peninsula and widespread intermarriage of members of various races in Latin America. He felt the proposal had some merit but also serious drawbacks. First, the race problem was at a crisis stage, and amalgamation would take a long time to effect change, and in the meantime "the friction and prejudice and mal-relationships which constitute the problem would remain." Second, intermarriage "imperils race personality and autonomy and self-development." Until the races fulfilled what he called their "missions," it was better to choose racial integrity. Third, amalgamation was a subversion of racial equality, since it was usually forced on one race by another. Even when it was not, it worked against what he called the full development of race personality. Finally, he claimed that amalgamation ran counter to the historical processes of racial differentiation, which seemed unfinished. "The races," he said, "appear still to be necessary to accomplish the tasks for which they came into being." In conclusion, amalgamation hindered the full development of "race personality, integrity, and mission."[76]

His views on amalgamation or intermarriage may appear equivocal. He did not think so. He argued that his position against intermarriage was not based on any sense of racial inequality but on the conviction that full race development and full peace between persons of different races could be achieved better in another way. He was also chastened by the behavior of members of his own race. It was the white race which had forced itself on the African American: "the violation of racial integrity all over the world is the offense of the white race." He confessed he found it curious "that the race which has most highly exalted the theory of race integrity should have done most to destroy it." As he drew his consideration of intermarriage to a close, he asked, as he surely had to ask, given his views of human unity, an obvious question, "If the human race is one and its ultimate goal is a unified humanity, why are not those men and women of various races to be praised who pioneer the road by intermarriage?"[77] Because, he answered, there was a better way.

Christianity was the final and only genuine solution of the race problem. It was the "only reasonable and right answer." It alone helped people see that "All the races are in the world to help one another, to work together for their common good, to build unitedly on the earth a human commonwealth." The "right solution" was "the simple solution of justice and righteousness, of brotherhood and good-will." The Christian answer turned on three key ideals of the faith. In the first place, faith taught the true equality of human beings, their "equal rights to justice and to life, to happiness and to work, to self-development and to liberty.... Christianity asserts this right for every man of every race." In the second place, faith preached an ideal of service and love. "The race problem," he urged, "will not be solved by men who are driven to the philosophic conclusion that only brotherhood will solve it. . . . It is to be found only where men look upon other men with a brother's love." In the third place, the Christian faith shared a unique vision of human unity. Humanity was one body; all races were part of one living organism, of which Christ was the Head and Savior. He concluded: "If looking out over humanity, torn with race feuds and embittered with race hatred, we ask with Paul, 'Who can deliver us from the body of this death?' The answer is simple and clear: 'Christ is the Savior of this body.' "[78] The "ultimate truth about the races," was "they are one body, of one blood."[79]

The issues of racism and race relations were on Speer's mind for much of his life. Once convinced of the biblical imperative of one humanity of one blood, he held to it and proclaimed it throughout his ministry. Without question, the focus of his career was in the fields of ecumenical and denominational foreign missions. But it was also true, if less obvious, that he was one of his generation's important witnesses to the social gospel, both in his general appeal for the fulfillment of the kingdom of God and in his particular call for action to achieve racial justice. The ideas and ideals he advocated were not new, but his reputation gave them considerable weight, and he had the courage to stay with them over a long period during which the popular trends ran another way. One of his major contributions was his work to establish the Commission on the Church and Race Relations. It gave the goal of racial justice a new status within the Federal Council and encouraged important new personalities to join the effort to achieve it through the churches. The commission became a leading force for racial reconciliation in the following decades. The churches united have long been identified by historians as prophetic on various industrial and economic issues; they were also prophetic, and he was partly responsible, on racial issues.

CHAPTER 12

Moderator of the Presbyterian Church

"He Who Would Valiant Be"

The Presbyterian Church in the United States of America nurtured Speer in his early years. Once he formally joined it through the First Presbyterian Church of Princeton, he remained in it, moving his local church membership when he moved his family. In their retirement years he and Emma participated in the Congregational Church in Lakeville. He accepted his Presbyterian identity as an important part of his life, although he never engaged in debates about its merits in relation to other kinds of Protestantism. He believed that Protestant denominations were important in the historical development of the Christian church and that they would continue until the day a united church emerged. His vision of Christian unity was real, but it did not affect his commitment to his denominational work, either in foreign missions or other areas. When his church called on him for general work, meaning work unrelated to foreign missions, he responded to its call.

The most important denominational request for his leadership, after his call to be a secretary of the Board of Foreign Missions, came in 1927 when the General Assembly elected him moderator. That election began a period of roughly ten years when various forms of denominational service, including his board responsibilities, dominated his life. He shared in a variety of ecumenical ventures during those years, including the Jerusalem meeting in 1928, the annual meetings of the Foreign Missions Conference, and the work on behalf of missions in Latin America, but all ecumenical activities combined consumed a small portion of his life compared to the period before 1927. His election moved him from what turned out to be the relatively low profile areas of foreign missions and ecumenical service to a position as representative of the Presbyterian Church. He was never again simply Secretary Speer.

Much of his service after 1927 required that he assume two familiar roles, that of defender, which he had often practiced on behalf of foreign missions, and that of reconciler, which he had often faced in his various ecumenical efforts. But his experiences in those settings did not fully prepare him for his new responsibilities. His denomination faced issues that threatened to tear it apart, and he struggled courageously to hold it together. He was never alone in that work, of course, but he was on several occasions the person out front leading the way. The ten years beginning in 1927 became the most crisis-filled of his life. He felt the stress associated with crisis most heavily twice, during his year as moderator and during the debate in 1932–34 that joined the controversy over the Hocking Report to one over the integrity of the Board of Foreign Missions. Shortly after the second of these crises, Elliott was murdered, adding his most profound personal crisis to those of his career. Emma referred to Robert on occasion as Mr. Valiant, an allusion to a character in John Bunyan's *Pilgrim's Progress*. A line from a Bunyan hymn characterizes these years: "He who would valiant be 'gainst all disaster, let him in constancy follow the Master."[1]

His pilgrimage as an American churchman followed the pattern established in his role as a missionary statesman: he was president of the Federal Council of Churches before he was the moderator of the Presbyterian Church. That may seem like a curious reversal of events, but it is not really puzzling. Prominent as he was in the fields of missions and ecumenism, he was a layperson, and denominational leadership, in and out of Presbyterianism, ordinarily fell to clergy in prominent places of service, ministers of major churches, or presidents of church-related colleges or theological seminaries. He had been the first layperson to lead the Federal Council in its short existence and became only the second to lead the Presbyterian Church in its much longer history. Moreover, his most visible nonmission position was as president of a fledgling ecumenical venture. The office of Federal Council president was a position of service not status, an indication of individual commitment to church unity, not a recognition given for denominational leadership. The council did not fully command the respect of the denominations until after 1924, and the degree of respect given then was due in good measure to his leadership. He defined himself as a person in mission for foreign missions, and through missions as an advocate for Christian unity. He set the order of his life, and never indicated he either desired or expected to lead his denomination.

The Presbyterians elected a moderator at the beginning of each General Assembly, and that person presided during that assembly. After the meeting the moderator typically traveled widely, visiting presbytery and synod meetings, other major church gatherings, and local churches. The office of moderator had great prestige and symbolic authority, and the person elected to the office served as the titular head of the Presbyterian Church. This person, however, did not have real ecclesiastical power, nothing to match, for example, that exercised by a Methodist bishop. The moderator represented, in a general but not technical sense, the Presbyterian Church. His tools were those of the mediator and reconciler, sweet reason and an appeal to spiritual sensibilities. Speer had those tools and a large reputation as a person with great persuasive powers, both in public gatherings and interpersonal relations.

He was well acquainted with the primary setting of the moderator's work. He attended approximately two-thirds of the assemblies held between 1891 and 1927, usually to speak in relation to the report of the Board of Foreign Missions, but sometimes in other roles, as a member of one or another assembly committee or commission, or as a commissioner from his presbytery. He was chosen a commissioner by the Jersey City Presbytery in 1927, and that made him eligible to be elected moderator. Family and close friends learned, sometime near the middle of his career, that he did not like attending General Assemblies. On the plus side, they were great occasions for renewing friendships and for promoting the cause of foreign missions. Those important opportunities were countered by what he considered to be long and often tiresome debates about matters of little interest to him, and the meetings took time away from the always-pressing needs of foreign missions. He had such negative feelings as the time for the assembly of 1927 approached. A secretary in the board office wrote Elliott, "Your father left yesterday for the General Assembly. . . . You know how he dislikes going to the Assembly meetings and this year I fear it will be more distasteful than ever!"[2]

Divisions Among the Presbyterians

Many Presbyterians doubtless shared the same "fear" that year, especially those who followed the life of their church and were concerned for its continued unity. The source of their anxiety was the fundamentalist controversy, which had ebbed and flowed in and out of several denominations, especially after World War I. The controversy surged for the Presbyterians beginning in 1922, when Baptist clergyman Harry Emerson Fosdick, then serving First Presbyterian Church in New York City, preached one of his most dramatic sermons, "Shall the Fundamentalists Win?"[3] Published and distributed widely, it evoked a furor. In the spring of 1923, J. Gresham Machen, a Presbyterian on the faculty of Princeton Theological Seminary, published *Christianity and Liberalism*, defining the argument from the fundamentalist perspective and establishing himself as one of the key representatives of that position.[4] The issues that Fosdick raised and Machen challenged sharply divided the assembly of 1923. Each succeeding assembly faced at least one theological or constitutional issue that revealed the existence of different and competing groups in the Presbyterian Church.

Nothing about the fundamentalist controversy was simple, beginning with the basic definition of terms. Fundamentalism was a movement that emerged within several denominations in the late nineteenth century. It was not a church or a clearly defined organization, although it did generate a World's Christian Fundamentals Association in 1919.[5] Fundamentalism grew dramatically after 1909 when *The Fundamentals*, a series of small books, twelve in number, began to be published setting forth fundamentalist positions.[6]

The movement was conservative, a reaffirmation of what its adherents considered to be the great biblical traditions of Christianity, quite literally, the "faith of the fathers." Fundamentalists often summarized their views in the "five points," which Machen and others often called the "Standards." These were the inerrancy of the Bible, the virgin birth of Christ, the vicarious atonement, the bodily resurrection, and the miracles of Jesus. The movement developed in the context of perceived threats to the faith from biblical criticism, the study of other religions, and new scientific theories that offered explanations of many aspects of life without reference to the Bible or the Christian tradition.

While fundamentalists perceived these developments as threats, other Christians accepted them as offering new insights for the faith and on the basis of them had begun to liberalize or modernize the faith. Some of these liberals, as they often named themselves, or modernists, as fundamentalists often called them, worked to bring the Christian faith into conversation with the modern world, but others among them sought to reshape the faith to the modern world. The labels often created confusion. Fundamentalists typically saw themselves as the true evangelical Christians, but many of those who saw themselves, or who were seen by fundamentalists, as liberals and/or modernists also defined themselves as evangelical Christians, and believed themselves to be firmly rooted in the traditions of the faith.

The controversy came to the Presbyterian Church in the 1920s as the fundamentalist-modernist controversy, or simply "the Presbyterian controversy."[7] Loetscher, in a study of these theological controversies, and using terms that some parties to the dispute used, characterized the issue among Presbyterians as a dispute between those who saw the church, its profession of faith, and its relationship to the world in exclusive terms— the fundamentalist position—and those who saw them in inclusive terms—the modernist position.[8] The "exclusive-inclusive" language helps clarify the controversy, because it suggests flexibility and the possibility of movement between the poles of absolute exclusion and absolute inclusion. The reality among Presbyterians in the 1920s was that there were more than two sides to the dispute, more than two groups involved in the discussion. Relatively few people were at the extreme ends of the exclusive-inclusive spectrum. Most of the key leaders and many members of the assemblies in those years sought some middle ground on specific issues as they emerged. Loetscher said they were "moderate conservatives" and Longfield called them "moderates." William Westin has named them "loyalists."[9] When faced with particular issues, those in the middle often shifted toward the exclusive side to declare the purity or accuracy of their faith, or to the inclusive side to demonstrate their interest in the continued unity of their church. Sometimes the issues did not appear to have a middle ground, and no compromise or alternative seemed possible.

The most obvious time of clear decision came with the opening business of each assembly, when commissioners selected a moderator. The signature of the debate in the Presbyterian Church, and arguably the most divisive moments of the assemblies beginning with the one in 1923, was the election of the moderator. The final choice that year was between William Jennings Bryan, frequent candidate for president of the United States, a true evangelical Christian in full accord with the exclusive position and one of the leading Presbyterian laypersons of his day, and the Rev. Charles F. Wishart, president of the College of Wooster, where the new science was part of the curriculum.[10] Bryan, the pre-assembly favorite, lost by 24 votes out of a total of 878 cast. Despite Wishart's victory the General Assembly directed the New York Presbytery to deal with Fosdick in light of his inclusive views and reaffirmed the five points of the fundamentalists, previously affirmed by the assemblies of 1910 and 1916.

The division continued at the assembly of 1924, when the candidates were the Rev. Clarence E. Macartney, pastor of Arch Street Presbyterian Church in Philadelphia and one of the acknowledged leaders of the exclusive group, and the Rev. Dr. Charles R. Erdman, a professor at Princeton Theological Seminary. Macartney emerged the winner by 18 votes out of the 910 cast. Reports circulated proposing Speer as a possible candidate that year, and he was elected a commissioner, but he declined the election, which made him ineligible to stand for moderator.[11] He had a definite opinion about Macartney's successful election: "The Fundamentalists, though they would disavow the word, have the chairmanships of all the committees in their hands. They bear now a very heavy responsibility and seem disposed to move very carefully. I hope and pray that division may be avoided and that constructive and peaceful counsels may prevail."[12]

The moderator elections in 1925 and 1926 continued to reveal the division in the church. The Presbytery of New Brunswick endorsed Erdman in 1925, giving him a second opportunity. In pre-assembly campaigning, Erdman opponents, led by Machen, characterized him as a modernist, and described his program as "a policy of palliation and of compromise."[13] He responded with pledges of the orthodoxy of his faith and promises to work for peace in the church.[14] The assembly elected Erdman by a margin of 50 votes. At a point of near division in a debate over constitutional and theological issues involving the New York Presbytery, he surrendered his moderator's chair and moved that the assembly create a Commission of Fifteen "to study the present spiritual condition of our Church and the causes making for unrest, and to report to the next General Assembly, to the end that the purity, peace, unity and progress of the Church may be assured."[15]

The General Assembly of 1926 met in great anticipation of the report of this commission. It elected as moderator Dr. W. O. Thompson, former president of Ohio State University and a person committed to Erdman's program, by a margin of 153 votes out of 917 cast. It was the largest margin of victory in four years. The assembly received the report of the Commission of Fifteen and adopted it with only one dissenting vote. It was, however, a preliminary report, with the final one due at the assembly in 1927. The assembly also voted to create a committee to investigate problems at Princeton Theological Seminary.

Moderator

A number of Presbyterian leaders believed the 1927 assembly would be crucial to the outcome of the debate and would perhaps determine the future of their church. It would receive reports from both the Commission of Fifteen and the Princeton committee. Some of the leaders, representing a variety of perspectives in the controversy, went in search of a candidate for moderator who could bring the assembly together and perhaps, in the best possible case, resolve the issues before the church. They found Speer. Erdman, an inclusivist and a partner in one of his prayer groups, pressed him to become a candidate, and so did the exclusivist Mark Matthews.[16]

In a highly confidential memoir Speer wrote some ten years after the event, he recalled that various individuals and a committee approached him and asked permission to submit his name as a candidate for moderator. He told them he "would do nothing to promote such an idea and all I could to prevent and suppress it." One way to prevent it was to decline appointment as a commissioner. However, when Jersey City Presbytery elected him a commissioner, he found no way to refuse the commission without creating "bad feeling in the Presbytery." At the assembly, he "refused to enter any conference or to discuss the matter and I stated that I would not be a candidate and would refuse to allow the Assembly to consider my name if I were nominated *with others* and be subject to a vote of the Assembly." In retrospect, he observed: "When wholly without my connivance and against my protestations I was nominated and elected by acclamation it seemed to me to be my duty to serve and to do what I could to hold the Church together in unity."[17]

His account of the events surrounding his election raises three questions. Why did fellow Presbyterians think he could bring their church together? Why did he require no opposition as a condition of his candidacy? Why did he finally change his mind and agree to stand for election?

He attracted the attention of those who desired the continued unity of the church because he had established himself throughout his career as an advocate for and instrument of unity. Any gathering of Presbyterian leaders, or leaders of other denominations for that matter, after 1910 was virtually certain to include individuals who had received their calls to ministry at the sound of his voice at a Student Volunteer Movement meeting, a college lecture, or any of literally hundreds of other settings. Those occasions were typically ecumenical. His focus had been, throughout his life and without exception, on the universal call of Jesus Christ to ministry in a universal church. Moreover, he had never been identified with those who occupied the grounds at the ends of the exclusive-inclusive spectrum. As a representative of the Board of Foreign Missions he avoided party politics, not wanting to entangle foreign missions in the debate. But he was also constitutionally opposed to the "party spirit." In his well-reported speech to the Federal Council in 1923, he had announced his opposition to all parties in the Christian church and had declared that Christians ought to hold the best ideas of all groups, including both the fundamentalists and the modernists (see chapter 3 for further discussion of this). In terms of the Presbyterian dispute, he had serious credentials to be counted in both the defined groups. He had written two articles for *The Fundamentals*, and he had actively engaged in social ministries during World War I and during his term as president of the Federal Council. In fact, he stood between the groups and was therefore seen by people in each group, like Mark Matthews and Charles Erdman, as a natural point of contact, a potential reconciler.

His decision to permit others to nominate him only if he could be certain there would be no opposition suggests that he was afraid of the possibility of losing the election. The decision was well enough remembered ten years later for him to underline the phrase "with others." But this had nothing to do with what a lost election might do to him personally. Among the letters he received prior to the assembly, the one from Dr. Robert R. Littell of the Tioga Presbyterian Church in Philadelphia carried a warning. Littell, writing from the conservative perspective, said that rumors were in circulation that he was being promoted for the moderatorship by the "liberal party." If true, it would likely spark a renewal of the controversy, and "there would be a contest to the bitter end, and that defeat seemed more than a possibility." The bitter feelings generated by such an event would be hard on him, "and the Board which you represent, which belongs to the entire Church." If he were to wait one more year, he would doubtless be elected by "acclamation."[18] Littell understood his primary concern about a contested election. Speer believed that a division over his candidacy, especially one that drew a sharp line, like the elections of 1923 and 1924, could seriously damage the foreign missions work. His reluctant willingness to stand alone or not at all could be interpreted as pride. It was, rather, based on his determination to do nothing that might bring harm to foreign missions.

The 139th General Assembly convened the last week of May 1927 in the Exposition Auditorium in San Francisco, completely upstaged by the trans-Atlantic flight of Charles Lindbergh. But the assembly had its own surprise when the list of potential nominees for moderator evaporated. As many as three laypersons and five clergy had been mentioned, but only Speer received a nomination. J. Williston Smith, a conservative and a layman from Philadelphia, himself a candidate, nominated him, seconded by the Rev. Dr. Hugh K. Walker of Los Angeles, also a candidate. Walker said Speer was "the most outstanding Protestant on the American continent" and claimed that with "his leadership the church would be united as it had not been for years and would go forward to the greatest constructive year in its history." Dr. Walter B. Greenway of Philadelphia moved to close the nominations and called for a unanimous vote of the assembly.[19] Speer did not interrupt this process and accepted the acclamation that followed. He did so for the same reason he had accepted the position as chair of the wartime ministry of the churches and the presidency of the Federal Council: he saw it as his duty. Ever since his father charged him to "march to duty," he expressed moments of crisis in the language of duty. On those occasions he suppressed his strong natural inclination to step back from the front line and agreed to accept the challenge before him.

He revealed his attitude in his communications to Emma, who had not accompanied him to San Francisco. On the Saturday before the assembly he wrote, "I still hope and pray against the moderator matter." The following day he told her, "The moderator business keeps me in ceaseless misery. I still hope and pray for a way of escape." The day of his election he sent the following message by telegram: "Alas but it was unanimous and full of goodwill."[20]

Friends gathered around him and ushered him quickly to the platform as the prolonged applause signaled wide support. It may also have represented a collective sigh of relief that for the first time in five years the assembly began with something other than a note of division. Outgoing moderator Thompson, in a relaxed mood, welcomed his friend as "the first Christian statesman in the United States today" and offered him a copy of the book of rules of the assembly, which he confessed he had not read, and the gavel, which he said he had rarely used.[21]

Speer responded, setting the stage for his leadership and announcing his vision for the assembly. "I have earnestly hoped and prayed that this might not be done," he said, and that the assembly might have selected someone else. "More and more as the years go by," he continued, "one comes to see that the strength of every church lies in its pastors. No church can do too much to glorify and dignify the task of the pastor. I had hoped that you might have chosen a pastor, the leader of a definite flock. He ought to be an old pastor, if possible an old country pastor who had toiled in some quiet place. It would be a job to lift such a one into this highest honor, an accomplishment of our belated obligations." He then turned to his vision of the task before him, and before them, and to the reason he accepted this duty: "I feel by your choice of me that this Assembly wants to bear a sure and clear testimony, to assert to the whole world in these days of unrest and upheaval and of questioning, in clear and unequivocal terms, that deathless tenacity by which we intend to hold to our missionary obligation and purpose. We want also to show the indissoluble unity of our fellowship. We are not divided. We mean to find the way through our difficulties in loyalty to our convictions and our Lord. I ask you to pray that the Holy Spirit may come upon us and guide us in this first hour until the last."[22]

Moderator Speer led the assembly through a full agenda. At his side stood the Rev. Dr. Lewis S. Mudge, stated clerk and chief permanent official of the assembly, and also Speer's college classmate, seminary roommate, and lifelong friend. In his hands were dozens of supportive telegrams, including one from his friend and former moderator Wishart, who said simply, "This is the day I long have sought and mourned because I found it not."[23] The various reports elicited differences of opinion and, on occasion, heated discussion, but no division. In the days immediately preceding the assembly, the *New York Times* published two articles with very different projections. On May 22, the first heralded, "Presbyterians See Peaceful Sessions," and on May 25, the second predicted, "Sharp Fight Awaits the Presbyterians."[24] Peace prevailed, partly a result of Speer's leadership, and partly doubtless as a result of the determination of the commissioners who had elected him to represent peace and to do their part to sustain it.

Three of the major reports before the assembly involved Speer. He had a hand in preparing two of them, the report of the Board of Foreign Missions and the report of the Commission of Fifteen, and he was a vitally interested party in the report of the Princeton committee. Although he did not present any of these reports, his role as presiding officer put him in a delicate and potentially compromising situation. In a pre-assembly letter written to warn him away from the moderatorship, a "Princeton man" pointed out the possibilities in relation to the Princeton matter: "The report of the Committee, as it now stands, will bring a stiff fight on the floor of the Assembly. Would it not put you in an embarrassing position if you were Moderator and an Official of Princeton, agreeing with what seems to be the Committee's report?"[25] To his credit he managed to steer a clear course through these reports, without charges of favoritism.

Foreign Missions Report

Of the three reports, the one on foreign missions was the easiest for him to deal with, the one with the least potential for division. In fact, the members of the assembly used the occasion to confirm the foreign missions program and to affirm him as *the* missionary leader of their church, if not of their generation. The Rev. Dr. Stuart Nye Hutchison, a member of the Board of Foreign Missions, presented the report in a highly charged atmosphere. During the year there had been uprisings in China, especially in Nanking, and a devoted missionary, Dr. John E. Williams, had become another in a long line of missionary martyrs. At the close of Hutchison's presentation, missionaries from all parts of the world, using a symposium format, shared firsthand views of conditions on the mission fields.

Speer concluded the session with a stirring presentation on foreign missions. His focus in "The Old, Ever New Call of Christ" was the entire foreign missionary program of the Presbyterian Church, not just the events of the previous year. He challenged his listeners to hear the call of missionary achievements of the past and to celebrate the many who had become Christians through the ministries of missionaries. But the past was prelude to the present and future, and the assembly needed to learn about and respond to the work that still needed to be done. There were many "new opportunities," in Latin America, in Africa, in Islamic lands, and, he added, in China. He spoke with great conviction about China, since he had just spent three months attending a series of evaluation conferences there. Skeptics argued that China was too full of "anti-foreign and anti-Christian feeling" to make it possible to sustain a mission, but he responded, were not the same feelings present in the United States? "Fundamentally," he said, "the heart of China is just as sound and true as the heart of any other people," and that land would one day again be fully open to the Christian message. The martyrs of China, he declared, called out to the commissioners to hear and heed the "call of the dead," who "do not grieve at what they experienced," but who "would grieve at our disloyalty. If we fail them now, how can they rest?"

In the closing section of his speech he did one of the things he did best: he transformed his message into a personal challenge. Under the heading "The Joyous Call of New Difficulties," he presented foreign missions as someone who always believed in the possibilities of the future, whatever the difficulties. He acknowledged that the problems were real, but no more so than those which had faced the first Christians. They had been ordered to surrender their mission and be silent, and had they not said, "We cannot but speak the things which we have seen and heard"? There were those, he told the assembly, who argued that missionaries should not go where they were not wanted. "As for wanting us," he replied, "why the world is today just as it was in Christ's day. Some men wanted Him and some did not. His sheep know His voice and they follow Him today." And then he asked his listeners, "And will not His Church follow him, too, to bring in to the one fold the sheep who are scattered abroad in every land and of every race?" In the final analysis, "The missionary enterprise never has been built on human applause or the world's wealth, or on any foundations whatsoever save the one Foundation of Jesus Christ. He began the missionary enterprise with no great organization, with no human supports, with no financial resources." Jesus, he said, showed the way, and John Williams walked it. Will you, he challenged the members of the assembly, hear again and respond to "the old, ever new call of Christ, 'If any man will come after Me let him deny himself and take up his cross and follow Me'?"[26]

The assembly received his speech with great enthusiasm and voted that it be distributed as widely as possible. The Office of the General Assembly subsequently printed it as a pamphlet and sent it "To the Officers and Members of the Presbyterian Church in the U.S.A.," which meant that every member of the General Assembly and every minister of every local church received a copy. Mudge wrote a brief letter to accompany it. He said in part, "It is to be earnestly hoped that these printed pages will bring to every reader something of the devotion to, and the enthusiasm for the bringing of the Gospel of our Lord and Saviour to the whole World, which have been for more than a generation the inspiration of Dr. Speer. Few men in any generation have been permitted to exercise as wide and as beneficent an influence in the affairs of the Church Universal, as the beloved Moderator of the General Assembly."[27] Mudge's highly personal tribute may or may not have made more of Speer and his speech than the assembly intended, but it appears to have made more of the event than he did. In one of his regular letters to Margaret, he lifted up seven "notable incidents" at the assembly, including the Celebration of 125 years work in home missions and the completion of the $15 million pension fund, but said not a word about his presentation on foreign missions.[28]

Commission of Fifteen

The other two reports that involved him had their roots in the long debate between the disputing groups in the Presbyterian Church. The Commission of Fifteen had met for the first time in the fall of 1925. Moderator Erdman had selected eight ministers and seven laypersons reflecting a variety of theological positions, but most of them the broad middle or moderate point of view.[29] Speer was in that group, as was the commission chairman, the Rev. Henry C. Swearingen of St. Paul. Despite the presence of two pastors of the exclusive persuasion, Matthews and Lapsley McAffee, Machen expressed concern over the "partisan character" of the commission.[30] The commission decided to create five committees. Speer chaired the one on causes of unrest, described as one of the two most important ones.[31] The commission announced that it would receive written statements and that it would hold an open meeting when it would accept verbal testimony from anyone who wished to make a presentation. The written materials included position papers from individuals and petitions. Personal testimonies were given by most of the key representatives of the different parties, especially those near the ends of the spectrum. Henry Sloane Coffin and William Adams Brown spoke for those in favor of inclusion and Machen and Macartney spoke for those who favored exclusion.[32]

Speer was a very active member of this commission. He approached this work with "no doubt that the overwhelming mass of both ministers and people want peace but that they do not want it at the cost of things that they believe to be indispensable to the maintenance of the life and truth of the New Testament."[33] He led a committee of three, the other two of whom were clergy: Thompson, who would be elected moderator in 1926, and Edgar W. Work of New York City. In November, in preparation of a draft of his committee report, Speer wrote Cheesman A. Herrick, a member of another committee, "I think our committee, however, was given the toughest end of the job." Herrick confirmed that: "I quite agree that your Committee was given the 'tough end of the job' for the Commission of Fifteen. That's why you were given it."[34]

As the assembly of 1926 approached, the commission worked hard to bring the report together. It met for two days in Chicago in March and then again in Baltimore just before the assembly convened. After the last meeting he wrote Margaret: "We were able to reach a unanimous report which was a miracle."[35] Loetscher did a very careful study of the work of the commission and struck a different note about the final report: "There were differences within the commission—on occasion, some sharp differences—but these were overcome partly through Dr. Speer's wisdom and leadership."[36] Westin, in a more recent study, concurred and claimed, "Speer's vision shines through the commission report."[37]

The commission report had been the most important event of the 1926 assembly. Swearingen had read it, beginning with the definition of the commission's goal. In the section of the report on causes of unrest, in Speer's mood and perhaps his words, the commission denied the idea advanced by some fundamentalists, particularly Machen, that two religions existed within the church, a liberal one and Christianity, and argued that Presbyterians were united and evangelical. In the section of the report on historical precedents, the commission affirmed that "the Presbyterian system admits of diversity of view where the core of truth is identical" and claimed that "the Church has flourished best and showed most clearly the good hand of God upon it, when it laid aside its tendencies to stress these differences, and put the emphasis on its unity of spirit."[38] The commission had recommended that the assembly accept the report and extend the commission for a year for further study. The assembly had received the report with prolonged applause and rejected all proposed amendments. "Why," Speer wondered, "will not our ultra-fundamentalist friends realize that the whole church is sound in its conviction and that the real enemy to be fought is not inside the Church but outside?"[39] He wrote Cairns and told him, "We had a real deliverance and the Church has got back at least for the time being and I hope for a long time, to its old traditional feeling and spirit."[40] Machen held the opposite view. In a telegram to Macartney during the debate he said, "If the evangelical party votes for this report its witness bearing is gone and all the sacrifices of the past few years will go for nothing."[41]

By the time the report of the Commission of Fifteen reached the assembly of 1927, it had passed its most difficult test, but there remained the potential for controversy. The final report of the commission turned on questions of polity, many of which had theological implications. The commission proposed, first, that presbyteries had primary responsibility for licensing and ordaining candidates for ministry. General Assemblies could review such procedures "in extraordinary cases" but could not as a rule interfere with decisions of the presbyteries. This was essentially the position that the New York Presbytery had argued before the assembly in 1925, which had been the occasion for the creation of the commission. The commission proposed, second, that a review of the Adopting Act of 1789 indicated that no judicatory of the church, presbytery, synod, or general assembly, could determine which doctrines of the church were "essential and necessary." Those doctrines had been established in the basic law of the church and could be changed only by an extensive legal process, not by a simple vote of any judicatory, even the General Assembly.[42]

The assembly adopted this report, as Speer noted, "without a word of debate."[43] Its action voided the decisions of the three recent assemblies, which had adopted the five points of the fundamentalists and had made them, in the eyes of many, "essential and necessary" articles of faith. He commented after the vote that the work of the commission had been "very interesting," but it was much more.[44] Westin has argued that in the long struggle for pluralism in the Presbyterian Church, "the most successful competitors of all . . . were the loyalists of the Special Commission of 1925."[45] The commission report provoked a major decision and helped bring to a close part of the controversy in the Presbyterian Church. But it did not end the dispute, for that had moved to another stage while the Commission of Fifteen had been putting the finishing touches on its report.

Controversy Over Princeton Theological Seminary

Princeton Theological Seminary had emerged at the assembly of 1926 as the next focus of the dispute. Speer had been a member of the board of directors of the seminary since 1914 and was very interested in the controversy, but he played little or no direct role in it at the assembly level. The seminary, from a time well before he attended in the early 1890s until the 1920s, had been the center of Old School Presbyterian thinking. It was conservative and evangelical, and remained that way despite the new theological and ecumenical trends that unfolded in the first two decades of the twentieth century. When President Francis L. Patton resigned in 1913, the seminary directors chose Dr. J. Ross Stevenson to be his successor, in large measure because many of them hoped that "the seminary might, under his leadership, be brought into closer relationship with the Church as a whole."[46]

When Stevenson arrived, he found a division of the faculty over the curriculum. One group, led by Benjamin B. Warfield, opposed virtually any proposed change. Machen, who came to the faculty in 1906 to teach Greek, became part of this group. The other group, which included Erdman, who had joined the faculty in 1905 as professor of English Bible and practical theology, desired to open the curriculum to new theological ideas. Stevenson aligned himself with this group. He also brought his own ideas and interests. In particular, he had been involved in several interdenominational ventures and continued to follow his ecumenical instincts, eventually becoming involved in the Philadelphia Plan. At the assembly of 1920, he presented and supported the plan in his role of vice-president of the Assembly's Committee on Church Cooperation and Union. The assembly sent the plan to the presbyteries, which returned a negative vote.

Faculty at the seminary split on this issue, which has been described as a debate over "the nature of the church," with a majority opposing it.[47]

The division, along the lines created by the arguments over the curriculum, continued through the early 1920s. It became increasingly acrimonious as first one issue and then another polarized the two sides. Stevenson and Erdman emerged as the leaders of those in favor of opening the seminary to new ideas, and Machen became the leader of a majority of the faculty that "was committed to defending and propagating Old School Calvinism alone."[48] The seminary had two governing boards, a board of directors and a board of trustees. They were likewise divided, the majority of the directors in sympathy with the Machen-led majority of the faculty, the majority of the trustees supporting the Stevenson-led minority of the faculty. Speer was in the minority of the board of directors.

The issue that moved the division at Princeton Seminary to the floor of the assembly began in 1925. A member of the Machen majority faced retirement. The board of directors offered the position to Macartney, who declined it, despite Machen's pleas. The board then elected Machen to the chair. He accepted it, fully aware that the General Assembly would have to approve it, and pretty certain it would.[49] Speer had been present at the board meeting that made the appointment and reported that it had made him "sick."[50] Aware that the "Machen matter" was a divisive issue, he had been part of a group on the board that had tried "to persuade the majority to withhold the matter and repeated the attempt at the Assembly but in vain."[51] In response to the board majority's action, some of the directors and trustees had asked the assembly of 1926, through its Standing Committee on Theological Seminaries, to investigate the seminary, to discover the reasons for the differences of opinion, and to seek a peaceful resolution of them. In support of this request, President Stevenson had said, "We are the agency of the combined old school and new school, and my ambition as President of the seminary is to have it represent the whole Presbyterian Church and not any particular faction of it."[52] The assembly had created a Committee of Five to visit the seminary and make inquiries, and had deferred action on Machen's appointment until the committee reported at the assembly of 1927.

The Committee of Five held hearings at the seminary in November 1926 and released the substance of its report before the 1927 assembly convened. Speer privately longed for "some kind of agreement or settlement which will save anymore bitterness."[53] The committee had heard a great deal of testimony and had accepted the point of view of President Stevenson and those who agreed with him.[54] The committee, however, cast its recommendations to the assembly in organizational rather than theological terms. The key problem seemed "to be in the plan of government by two boards." Dual control amounted to no control. In addition, the relation of the seminary to the assembly was not very clear. The committee recommended the assembly enlarge the committee to nine members and charge it to reorganize the seminary under a single board and to define in specific terms the relationship of the seminary to the assembly.[55] The exclusivists were distraught.[56] They generated an extended and heated debate over the report, which Speer described as "intense but also restrained," and managed to change the size of the continuing committee to eleven and its charge to the development of a plan for reorganization that would be reported to the next assembly for action. Machen's promotion was held over until the reorganization issue reached a settlement.[57] A *Times* correspondent, in an article titled "Liberals Win Again on Princeton Issue," reported that "So-called ultra-Fundamentalism in the Presbyterian Church of the United States made its final stand in the General Assembly today on the Princeton Theological Seminary issue and was defeated by the liberal group."[58] Perhaps not final, but Machen did tell a friend that the assembly was " 'probably the most disastrous meeting, from the point of view of evangelical Christianity, that has been held in the whole history of our Church.' "[59] A Machen apologist held Speer partly responsible and later claimed that he "had contributed by his moderatorship to the creation of an atmosphere of evasion of the doctrinal issues of the hour."[60]

In reflecting on the assembly, Speer noted, "All went well until the last Tuesday afternoon when we nearly went on the racks."[61] At that time the assembly received Judicial Case No. 1 from the Permanent Judicial Commission. The case involved the Presbytery of New York and the degree to which those ordained and licensed in the presbytery should be required to affirm their belief in the major elements of the traditional creeds, and in addition the five points of the fundamentalists. It was another stage of the case that had been before the assembly in 1925. The Judicial Commission proposed that presbyteries had primary control of licensing procedures, which meant those ordained in New York Presbytery, or elsewhere for that matter, might not be required to affirm belief in the virgin birth or any of the other points. As the discussion developed, there occurred in rapid succession a series of parliamentary errors in which persons spoke who did not have legal standing to speak, and persons voted who did not have the technical right to vote. The assembly adopted the Judicial Commission's recommendation.

The next day, when the assembly considered the minutes of the previous day, questions were raised about the procedures. Speer explained that there had been errors in procedure, apologized for making them or permitting them to happen, and said he believed they had been made innocently. He asked the assembly to approve the actions of the previous day, despite the errors, and not reopen the case. The assembly concurred despite some disagreement, which left some commissioners unhappy. After the vote a commissioner, described by a *Times* reporter as an "elderly, snowy-haired fundamentalist," rose and asked "if the ruling was to be interpreted that the Church did not accept the doctrine of the virgin birth." Before anyone realized what was happening, Speer began to recite the Apostles' Creed, and by the time he reached the phrase referring to the virgin birth the entire assembly had risen and joined him. The commissioner said: "I am satisfied. . . . The assembly has spoken."[62] Speer's deft use of the Apostles' Creed turned what could have been the occasion for a dispute into a ringing affirmation of unity. Criticism of the parliamentary errors lingered until the next assembly.[63]

The General Assembly of 1927 largely fulfilled the vision of those who elected Speer to be moderator in the hope that he would be able to keep the peace, do the work of reconciliation, and achieve unity in the church. The commissioners could not see the future; nonetheless there was a widespread feeling, as the assembly approached its final hour, that their acceptance of the report of the Commission of Fifteen had closed a major phase of the often harsh and divisive debate. Historians, with the benefit of hindsight, have declared that this was the assembly that settled the controversy at the general church level, in constitutional and confessional terms. Loetscher said it was one of the important turning points "in the theological history of the church since the reunion of 1869."[64] It was a clear, if not absolutely final, victory for the moderates and all those determined to hold the church together. It benefitted most those at the inclusive end of the spectrum, for it established a place for them under the umbrella of toleration.[65]

As he approached the platform for his final words to the commissioners, Speer did not think in terms of winning and losing. He was not a prize-fighter and did not see anyone as his opponent. In his mind the Presbyterian Church was a fellowship of brothers and sisters in the faith of Jesus Christ. Without reference to the vigorous and sometimes divisive debates that had taken place the previous days, he sent the commissioners to their homes with a series of friendly admonitions about useful spiritual goals for the coming year. He told them what he most deeply believed: "Our first great obligation this coming year is to be in our lives loyal disciples of Jesus Christ." He then challenged them to preserve "our great Presbyterian home inheritance in the midst of the challenging conditions

of the modern world," by raising their children in the context of a
Christian home. In conclusion, he urged, the church must put evangelism
in its rightful place, in the forefront of its work.[66]

When he assessed the assembly and his role in it, he decided, "It was
really a very happy experience and though there were some anxious times
I thoroughly enjoyed trying to help the Assembly through and, certainly,
we did get through in the most wonderful way."[67] Ever hopeful, he told
North, "We certainly had God's evident and abundant blessing at the
Assembly and I trust and pray that it may be the beginning of far better
and rich things for our Church in the days to come."[68]

Leadership as Moderator

His leadership during his year as moderator took two official forms, one
more informal than the other. Informally, and in accord with the practice
of former moderators, he moved about the Presbyterian Church from one
meeting to another, bringing greetings, preaching, and doing pretty much
whatever he was asked to do. He had visited many places by October and
reported, "I have met no division or friction anywhere, and am hoping
that the year will prove a really good and useful year in binding the
Church together and in confirming its confidence in its own evangelical
loyalties, and in kindling a little brighter fires of true evangelistic purpose
and action."[69] Emma accompanied him on many of these trips, as she did
when he went to Huntingdon in early November. His home church held
a celebration, and he then itinerated around the presbytery. He was the
first person from his home presbytery to be elected moderator.[70]

In January 1928 he took a seventeen-day trip through the south, visiting Louisville, Nashville, Knoxville, Birmingham, Memphis, Little Rock,
Dallas, Houston, and then back to Kansas City and St. Louis. He spoke
two or three times a day and spent the nights in sleeping cars. Everywhere
he went, he found a welcome and open reception, with no sign of the
dispute. One thing he found that he did not expect was the number of
new churches under construction. Commentators were claiming that
Protestantism was dying out, yet everywhere he went he found new
churches, so many that he figured it was "literally true that more new
churches are going up in America this year than there are new temple or
mosques building in all the non-Christian world."[71] Ever on the watch for
signs of united Christian fellowship, he took special pleasure from an
experience in Ohio. A state pastors conference there held "a communion

service in which all the denominations including Baptists, Lutherans, and Episcopalians participated."[72]

The formal part of his leadership of his church included presiding at meetings of the General Council. It carried on the administrative work of the church between meetings of the assembly. As the moderator he became chair of the administrative committee. Mudge served as its secretary. He chaired meetings in June and November 1927 and February 1928. He wrote a number of formal letters to various groups in the church, such as those involved in home missions and Christian education. These duties took time, and the Board of Foreign Missions had to add an administrative secretary to maintain its work. He knew mission work might suffer when he accepted the moderatorship, but he felt that "what is let down will be far more than made up by what ought to be done in connection with the general work of the Church this year."[73]

As soon as the assembly adjourned, he set about organizing the General Council and formulated a long letter with the agenda for the November meeting. Mudge wrote him a note of thanks on this occasion, suggesting that not all moderators had been so helpful: "It is simply wonderful to have associated with me not only a dear old friend but one who takes the work of the General Council so seriously."[74] He wrote the members of the General Council that it was "clear from the overtures which came to the General Assembly and from the spirit and action of the Assembly itself that the Church desires a year of deepened devotion and service. Will not those of you who are ministers," he continued, "do all you can to strengthen and support such a movement as the Church desires by doing everything possible to strengthen the preaching of the Church in its apologetic and evangelistic power . . . and will not all the lay members of the Council make this a new year in the way of personal conversational effort to win men to Christ and in discussing with individuals and groups the ways of reviving family religion."[75]

He shared these sentiments in his first formal letter, sent "To the Ministers and Members of the Presbyterian Church in the U.S.A" at the end of June.[76] He sent a copy of this letter to the missionaries, attached to a separate, more personal note to them. He reminded them of their close relationship with one another and that he had interpreted his election as moderator to be the assembly's confirmation of its total support of foreign missions. And he asked them to increase their evangelistic efforts, reminding them, "This is our elementary and fundamental business, to make Christ known—the facts of the Gospel and the everlasting power of Christ to forgive sin and renew life." He signed it "your sincere friend."[77]

The General Council, at its meeting in November 1927, directed Speer and Mudge to send another general letter to the church, highlighting financial and spiritual matters. This letter, dated at the beginning of the new year, reported that giving to benevolent causes was down compared to the previous year. That was difficult to understand in a booming economy, when "an ever rapidly increasing portion should be given to the Saviour's service in the work which our Church is doing through its Boards." The council, recipients learned, had issued "a call to the moderators of Presbyteries urging that at the earliest possible moment, the Presbyteries be called together for a day of special prayer, humiliation and conference, earnestly seeking the direction of the Holy Spirit in planning for more effective evangelistic effort, and for the deepening of the spiritual life of the churches of the Presbyteries." In words that Speer surely penned, the letter concluded, "We need to recognize and proclaim the power of God in the Gospel of Christ. We are meeting in our modern age a purely naturalistic interpretation of the world and of life which leave no place for true religion, and this temper of mind may easily creep into our own hearts. Our answer must be the answer of the New Testament faith and also of the New Testament life; the answer of a reasoned conviction about Christ and the answer of a living experience through which Christ confronts men and assures them of His love and power."[78]

The next meeting of the General Council was on February 22, 1928. It was a hurried time for him, because he and Emma were getting ready to leave for the Jerusalem meeting. He had made clear when he became moderator that he needed to arrange his schedule to be away much of the spring of 1928. At the close of the council session, he had taken a few minutes to review the year. He had written "credits" and "debits" on a scrap of paper and used them to create what he called "A Present-Day Balance Sheet of the Church's Life." He was unprepared for the enthusiastic response to his presentation. One council member recommended it be shared with "important pastors and laymen throughout the Church," and another told him he wanted him to share it with the leaders of the General Assembly.[79]

Surprised by the interest, he wrote Mudge asking about the stenographer's copy of his comments. He told Mudge that if he planned to distribute the list to members of the council, he should remember that the remarks were extemporaneous and needed to be cleaned up. He had special reference to number 16 on the debit side, "A few centers of contentiousness and strife," where he had used the phrase "lie or lies." Mudge followed directions, and the final document did not contain those words.

He began the credits with his most startling discovery, "the church buildings," and ended it with "the persistent refusal of our spiritual life and
idealism to be killed out by secularism and materialism." The list included
references to the "great Body" of noble laymen and laywomen in the
church, the "growth of comity and the sense of interchurch unity," and the
true "brotherhood of our ministry." The debits began with "very little
attention to our future ministerial supply" and concluded with "the need
of rich moral and spiritual influences, intellectually convincing and emotionally persuasive." He was concerned about the "total neglect of Church
discipline," "the lack of Bible study and Bible reading and family prayer,"
and "the feebleness and ineffectiveness of all the church organic union
movements." Although the list contained an equal number of credits and
debits, he created it as a challenge, not just a summary, and even the credits could be seen as opportunities for future action.[80]

The Speers embarked for the Middle East on the ship *Adriatic*. He left
denominational matters behind and turned his attention to international
and ecumenical missionary issues. The trip was hardly relaxing, since he
was deeply involved in the Jerusalem meeting, writing reports and preparing the final sermon, which he preached on Easter. But it was a change
and turned out to be an inspirational time and, as it happened, the last of
his international conferences.

Almost immediately after he returned home, the General Assembly
convened in Tulsa, Oklahoma. His formal role at the assembly was to wel-
come the new moderator and to preach the opening sermon. Fresh from
Jerusalem, he chose as his text Luke 2:45 and used the words as his title,
"And They Turned Again to Jerusalem Seeking Jesus." A celebration of
Christ, he described it as both a "very simple sermon" and as setting forth
"as high a Christology as it is possible for Christian thought to project."[81]
Shortly after the assembly he wrote Cairns, "It is good to have the
Assembly over and my term as Moderator past. The Moderatorship leaves
behind it here no such dignity as remains with you in Scotland."[82] It had
been a year of considerable stress—although he never indicated this—a
time when he was in front, in full public view, representing the
Presbyterian Church and working for reconciliation and peace.

The dispute over Princeton Seminary remained unresolved during his
term. After his duties at the assembly in Tulsa were over, he sat as an
observer and listened as the Committee of Eleven, the enlarged Princeton
committee, reported a plan for reorganizing the seminary. The proposal
was to create a single board of trustees with full power to act, including

the removal of a president or professors without consultation with the assembly, and to give the president of the seminary much greater power. Conservative Mark Matthews moved to delay action for one year to give time for the board of directors to bring the problems at the seminary to a peaceful resolution. The assembly voted for Matthews's motion, but Speer voted against it, arguing, "It seemed to me that probably every other recourse had been exhausted and there was nothing to do but pursue the radical course proposed by the General Assembly's Special Committee."[83] Machen withdrew his acceptance of the nomination to a chair at Princeton Seminary.

The assembly of 1929 reviewed several proposals for settling the Princeton matter and finally adopted the committee's plan of reorganization, despite an impassioned appeal by Machen, who argued that reorganization would mean the end of the "old Princeton."[84] The assembly created a new board of trustees, taking members from each of the former boards and adding a number of others to bring the total to thirty-three. Speer reluctantly agreed to serve on the new board. He commented that the "seminary matter was decided by an overwhelming majority adverse to Dr. Machen and the attitude which he represents. . . . a new Board has been appointed which I hope will manage the Seminary wisely and effectively, and with fidelity to the true tradition of the institution."[85]

Machen, convinced that he could not work under such a board, resigned from the faculty. Joined by three other former Princeton faculty members and a number of supporters, Machen worked through the summer of 1929 to formulate plans for a new institution, which opened in Philadelphia in September 1929 as Westminster Theological Seminary. The Presbyterian Church had not divided, but its oldest and most distinguished seminary had.

The initial year of crisis past, Speer enjoyed several years of relative calm, at least in the context of the theological controversy. It seemed over. He wrote Erdman in the fall of 1929, "These have been difficult times these past years and one hopes and prays that they may be over now and that the years ahead may be calm and bright and years of peace and rest."[86] In the spring of 1930 he told Cairns that he had just been on the west coast raising funds for foreign missions and that the churches there were "much united and almost unanimously disinclined to any revival of the fundamentalist-liberal theological issues." He added his assessment of the nature of the Presbyterian Church on theological questions: "Our Church is tempermentally [sic] a progressive conservative. We have some reckless liberalism and also some reckless fundamentalism and we have altogether too many men who are not thinking adequately over the theological issues at all. In general things are going fairly well."[87]

Role of Women in the Presbyterian Church

He dealt with stress well and seemed able to work effectively on several things at the same time. During his year as moderator, he managed to give attention to many other matters, some continuing responsibilities, like negotiations concerning possible union with other churches in the Reformed tradition, and some emerging ones. The most important new issue was the role of women in the Presbyterian Church. The issue had a theoretical and a practical—which is to say political—component. The theoretical one was the equality of the sexes, on which he had taken an unequivocal position from the outset of his career. The practical one was the degree to which women should share in the leadership of the church at all levels, including the ministry, and he became a vital part of an effort to answer that question, beginning in 1926.

His views of the equality of the sexes, like those on the equality of the races, emerged in his college years in the context of debates and Bible study. When he began to publish Bible studies in the 1890s, he asserted that the gospel "had a joyful *emancipation for woman*. It made her free from servitude, that she might the more freely serve."[88] He argued that Jesus established the new pattern, breaking the "conventional limitations" in all his dealings with women. Jesus "admitted women to the circle of His disciples," constantly helped "women who were in need," and "took some women into the closest circle of His friends." Some of those women had "followed His steps to the cross, and chanted after him their dirge of lamentation, recognizing, many of them, in Him the Friend and Redeemer of Woman." Jesus, he declared, "had treated them as equals and given them a foremost place in his kingdom."[89] Christ set women free, despite widespread opinion to the contrary, and full practical equality would come only "with His help through the wider acceptance among men of His teaching and will."[90]

He was absolutely convinced that his view of the gospel on this issue was correct; he was also aware that he held a minority opinion. Opponents represented the cultural tradition of patriarchy and often supported it with Bible passages, typically two written by Paul, one in 1 Corinthians and another in 1 Timothy. He responded that these were but two passages, when there were "scores" of others that argued the other way. Indeed, if the two passages were taken to their logical conclusion, women would have to stop doing virtually everything, including teaching Sunday school and serving as missionaries. Whatever Paul may have meant in those passages, Speer concluded, he wrote in Galatians 3:28 "the charter of human equality" when he declared, "There is neither Jew nor Greek, there is neither slave nor free, there is neither male nor female; for you are all one in Christ Jesus."[91]

This teaching of Jesus, then Paul, he claimed, had no comparison in the world of religion, in the past or the present. He repeated this point over and over in his mission talks when he compared Christianity to other religions. He put it this way in 1902: "If anybody should ask me to risk Christianity on one single cast, to stake everything on one argument, I sometimes think I should almost be willing to select, of all the positions of Christian apologetics, the attitude of Christianity towards women and children as over against the attitude of every other religion of the world towards woman and the little child."[92]

The practical experiences he had of such equality before 1926 came primarily in the contexts of his home life and his missionary contacts. His wife Emma was a true partner in his ministry and had her own ministry with the YWCA. She was never ordained, of course, and always served as a volunteer. Their extensive correspondence reveals that they shared with one another the issues that emerged in their respective ministries. He had a remarkable correspondence with his daughter in China, one that evoked the image of partners in mission, not father and daughter. Women had demonstrated, since the outset of his career with the SVM, that they were very interested in missions, and many had become volunteers. True, he had said in the 1890s, more men than women had volunteered, but not because "the young women in our colleges are not susceptible to the missionary appeal." The recruiters, most of them men, had spent almost their entire time at the men's colleges.[93] Fund-raising was an important part of his work, and he typically found the women of the church more effective than the men in meeting their financial goals.[94] He also had strong, positive working relationships with the women who worked for the Board of Foreign Missions, either on the staff or in the mission field.[95]

The search for status for women in the Presbyterian Church was not an entirely new theme, but it received tremendous impetus from the roles women played in World War I, the success of the movement for women's suffrage in 1919, and the actions of some other denominations. Speer approved of better status for women in the church, but he had no record of working for it. He was not linked, in any visible way, either to the unsuccessful overture of 1920 in favor of the election of women to the office of ruling elder or to the successful effort in 1923 to make women eligible for the office of deacon. His first serious brush with the issue came during his service on the Commission of Fifteen in 1925. During his work on its committee on causes of unrest, testimony indicated that one contributing cause was the status of women in the church. The preliminary report of the commission, adopted by the assembly of 1926, contained the following paragraph, perhaps in Speer's words: "And lastly, there are many women in the Church who are not satisfied with present administrative conditions. Some of them fear the loss of the organizations through which they have worked so long. Some regard as unjust the lack of representation of women in the church."[96] "Lastly" meant at the end of the list, not least important. The wording was quite general, likely on purpose, and did not suggest any particular course of action.

The General Assembly referred the issue of women to the General Council, which in turn appointed two prominent, highly respected women, Margaret Hodge and Katharine Bennett, to study the issue. Hodge, with the Board of Foreign Missions, and Bennett, with the Board of National Missions, undertook an extensive study of the concerns of women in the church. In July 1927, Hodge wrote her fellow board executive and current moderator Speer that she and Bennett were "well on the way with our paper on the 'Causes of Unrest among Women.' "[97] He responded with strong words of encouragement for them "to continue unimpaired in your distinct work."[98] The "distinct work" arrived at the November 1927 meeting of the General Council, which he chaired. Titled *Causes of Unrest Among Women of the Church*, it has been described as "the first such analysis written by women rather than by clergymen."[99] *Causes* received a full hearing, which it doubtless would have under any circumstance, but the influence of Speer as moderator and chair, with his strong interest in gender equality, helped propel forward the issues it raised.

The women used questionnaires, a survey, and extensive consultation in formulating their report. They found that women were unhappy that they had "no part in determining the policy or defining the faith of the Presbyterian Church" and believed that they were excluded, simply because of their sex, "from a seat in the General Assembly and the other courts of the Church." What women wished for was "the removal of inhibitions which constantly remind them that they are not considered intellectually or spiritually equal to responsibilities within the Church. Most ask for no one thing, only, that artificial inhibitions that savour of another century having been removed, they may take their place wherever and however their abilities and the need of the Church may call." He summarized the report at a later date: "The report . . . came clearly to the view that one fundamental cause of unrest was the failure of the Church to recognize and welcome the equal participation and responsibility of women in all the life and work of the Church."[100]

Causes presented no demands from women and proposed no program. The General Council faced a dilemma. It needed to act on the report, given the time and energy spent on it by two highly respected women and the obvious seriousness of the issues it raised, but the report offered no clear program on which to act. Simple acceptance did not seem enough, but generating proposals for the next General Assembly seemed too much.[101] The council resorted to a study committee and charged it to prepare recommendations. This committee of four included Hodge, Bennett, Stated Clerk Mudge, and Moderator Speer.

Committee of Four

Speer was a major player on the committee of four, but so were each of the other members. He was the most highly visible because he was the moderator and his colleagues often pushed him to the forefront, but he was not its leader. The committee could best be described as a group of coworkers and close friends, major executives in the church, who had worked together before and slipped easily into this task. Not every decision awaited a formal meeting time. A very careful and thorough study of the committee has discovered gaps in the written record, often at times of major decisions. He described one of those times to daughter Margaret: "After a great deal of discussion *behind the scenes* we were able to secure a happy and harmonious understanding with regard to the presentation of the overtures for the full ecclesiastical equality of women in the Church."[102] Although the issue they faced, sexism in the church and how to deal with it, was very serious, it was not in itself a threat to the unity of the church. *Causes* reported that those women who were unhappy in the Presbyterian fold often took their leadership abilities elsewhere, into the secular world, rather than raise a protest in the church. This was not, in his mind or in the collective consciousness of the committee, a crisis. He had long advocated the equality of women and looked forward to the work of this committee as an opportunity to achieve it.

The committee began its work by calling a unique conference. With the permission of the General Council, it invited fifteen leading Presbyterian women to meet with the council in November 1928. Emma was among them. When the meeting convened in Chicago, it became "the first time in the history of the Presbyterian Church in the U.S.A. or of any other American Reformed denomination that male and ordained church leaders met together with women specifically to discuss questions relating to sexual equality in the functioning of church government."[103] Speer offered some opening remarks, followed by much frank discussion that settled on the issue of the need for sexual equality. As the meeting neared its conclusion, he called for recommendations. Further discussion produced many different opinions but no consensus. He suggested the General Council assign the committee of four the task of preparing proposals for action, and the council made the assignment.[104]

The target date for a report was the General Council meeting scheduled for March 6, 1929. In early January he sent a proposed outline of the report to the other three members of the committee. The first four sections would contain background information for the fifth section, which was a "definite proposition." He suggested the committee recommend that the General Council resubmit to the presbyteries the "question of the admission of women to the eldership." He asked his friends whether this proposal was "either too far, or not far enough."[105] Hodge and Bennett responded that they did not think it was far enough. Bennett, in a carefully worded letter, told him she thought that now that the question of full equality was a possibility, "I am not willing to have an overture asking that women be admitted to the eldership: I ask that expediency be set aside and the principle be faced by the church."[106] Mudge took a more cautious view, arguing that Speer's proposal was about as far as the church might be willing to go.[107]

Speer agreed with the women and in early February shared a revised list of proposals with his friends. If the others agreed, he proposed that the committee present the General Council with several alternatives: (1) an overture supporting women as ruling elders; (2) an overture supporting women as ruling elders and evangelists; (3) an overture removing from the Form of Government all language that "implied or acknowledged sexual inequality."[108] The committee met to debate his proposals and reached agreement that it would stand on the principle of full equality. Although it sent all the alternatives forward, it added to the third one a notation that it favored an overture that would accomplish it, namely, full equality for women in the church.[109] Speer presented the report to the General Council in March. Much discussion followed at the meeting and in a series of letters afterward. The council voted 13–6 to accept the third recommendation and directed Mudge, as stated clerk, to draw up overtures for the General Assembly.

Mudge busied himself with the overtures. Concerned to be as careful and precise in his language as possible and to define the issues as clearly as possible, he prepared two: Overture A, "On Admission of Women to Full Ecclesiastical Standing," and Overture B, "On the Amendment of Constitutional Rule No. 1." The first would remove all sex-oriented language from the Form of Government; the second would change the *Constitution* of the church to permit anyone to become a local evangelist.[110]

The General Council's decision to send overtures to the assembly generated a vigorous discussion in the denomination. Members of the council who did not concur had already begun their debate, several of them with Speer. Matthews, his colleague on the Commission of Fifteen, was one of the first to write him and raised the issue all the others raised: the timing was wrong. Matthews told him, "I sincerely love you," but "I was so grieved when you brought forth the proposal to send down the overture regarding the women. . . . The real womanhood of the church does not want it. . . . Will you consent to postpone sending this overture down until we can pray over it another year?"[111] Suspecting that timing was not the entire issue, Speer offered two responses. First, he felt the primary decision was whether or not the issue was "right in principle and in the light of the teaching of the Scripture[.] If this is clear must we not stand on it and act accordingly?" Second, was there any reason to believe that a year's delay would bring about unanimity on the issue? If not, then the best thing to do was to send the overtures forward and let the church decide.[112] The committee of four met in mid-April to consider the course of action and decided to proceed.

Two meetings were held in St. Paul just prior to the General Assembly. The Conference on Women's Status and Service in the Church met on May 20–21. Hodge presided at a session to consider two questions proposed by the council: (1) Should the overtures be sent forward immediately or postponed? (2) should the issue be full legal status for women, or status by degree, ruling elder first, with other steps to follow? Speer and Mudge spoke and then left the meeting. The women decided to tell the council they wished to proceed immediately for full equality.[113] The council met on May 22. The result was a surprise, a compromise apparently proposed by the committee of four. The two overtures became three, with a new one giving the presbyteries the right to choose to elect women as ruling elders. The new one inserted between A and B, became the new overture B.[114]

Historians have claimed that the new overtures "undercut" the principle of equality, and gave the church the opportunity to give some ground to women without deciding the basic issue.[115] That judgment appears fair, although the change seems to have been the decision of the committee of four. Speer interpreted the shift to three overtures somewhat differently. The fundamental principle remained in Overture A, and he noted, "If the first is adopted it will carry with it the other two and will open the ministry, the eldership, as well as the office of lay evangelist to women on equal terms with men." What the church had with three choices was an open rather than a closed option. He personally hoped that all three would be accepted by the presbyteries.[116]

The General Council chose Speer to present the overtures to the General Assembly. They were received and sent forward with virtually no objection and none concerning their substance. They generated substantial debate during the following year. Some traditional conservatives, members of the exclusive group like Macartney and Matthews, urged defeat of the overtures, but the debate never polarized along exclusive-inclusive lines. Speer joined the debate in a highly public way. He titled a chapter of *Some Living Issues*, published in 1930, "The Equality of Women in the Church." In it he stated the case for the adoption of the overtures as forcefully and as frankly as anyone did during the debate:

> The Church needs today all that women can bring into it. If there are women who, as elders, evangelists, or as ordained ministers, can serve the Church better than the men to whom otherwise the Church would be confined, the Church ought to be free to command their service. There will be such women. . . . The door will be fully open to all that women can give and do. And the reproach of the past, that the Church alone denies to women the principle of Christianity which has gone out from the Church over all the rest of life, will be once and for all removed. We shall have done right, and that is all that we need to do. But some will say that it is inexpedient or premature. It is not inexpedient to do what is right. And it is scarcely premature to do late what through the influence of Christ has been already done in realm after realm of life, and that only now we are coming so tardily to do in Christ's own Body, the Church. [117]

He followed the progress of the overtures through the presbyteries. Things looked bad for Overture A from the start, and it failed. The overture concerning lay evangelists passed but not with enough votes to become church law. He told Matthews that he would "not hear the sweet voices of any authorized woman minister in the Presbyterian pulpit." Hopefully he added, "Some day our Church will get into accord with the teaching of the Scriptures in this matter."[118] The church passed the overture enabling women to become ruling elders. His personal view was that it "was the important one inasmuch as it will give women an equal place with men as far as constitutional right is concerned in all the courts of the Church and in determining the policy and practice of the Church."[119] Although he did not find the outcome fully satisfactory, he felt the effort was "an honest attempt to do what I think is right and what some day, if it is right, will certainly be done. It would not mean I think that there would be many women preachers or women elders, but it would remove the barrier from the way of any whom God was calling to either form of service."[120]

By the time the theological issues involved in the Princeton Seminary debate and the vote on the status of women in the church were off his agenda, financial concerns had taken their place. Theological issues aside, the years from 1929 to 1932 were hardly tranquil for any American. The stock market crash in the fall of 1929 triggered the deepest and longest economic depression in American history. Foreign missions ran on faith and dollars, and the dollars began to run out as the depression persisted. Mission boards cut back, at home and abroad. Some denominations were hit harder than others. The Presbyterians began the cutback by reducing salaries across the board and by increasing their appeals for support. In the spring of 1932 Speer's board met to decide "how we can keep first things first in missionary apologetic and appeal and also in missionary administration and expenditure."[121] He saw the economic situation as a challenge, not a danger, and believed that "the fundamental cause of the present situation in the Church at home and abroad is not economic and that the great need is for a clear and tenacious grasp of the simple fundamental things of the primitive and abiding faith."[122] The financial picture was still grim in 1932, but he was looking ahead to what he believed would be better days.

CHAPTER 13

Defender of Christian Missions

"The Finality of Jesus Christ"

There were few quiet periods in Speer's life, times without schedules and specific responsibilities. One of those came in the summer and early fall of 1932. Life was almost idyllic for those few months. He managed to get away from the city and up to Rockledge frequently, planting the flower garden in the late spring and then tending it during the summer. He took great pride when son Billy, a member of the crew at Princeton, helped win a sweep in a competition with Massachusetts Institute of Technology. Invited to preach for a series of Sundays at Fifth Avenue Presbyterian Church as a summer replacement, he noted that there were fewer students in the congregation than in the past, and conjectured it was due to the completion of Riverside Church, near the Columbia University and Union Seminary campuses. He spent considerable time working on the Stone Lectures for Princeton Theological Seminary, which he was scheduled to give the following winter. They became "The Finality of Jesus Christ." The news of the day included hints of the coming political campaign between Herbert Hoover and Franklin D. Roosevelt, with reports of very different views on prohibition. He strongly opposed Roosevelt's promise to end it.

By the end of the summer he was doing what he usually did at the end of his summers, visiting church conferences and speaking on foreign missions or preaching. In late August he attended the Southern Methodist Summer Conference at Lake Junaluska, North Carolina, where he spoke and renewed his acquaintance with Josephus Daniels, who had been Secretary of the Navy in World War I. He then worked his way east in North Carolina, speaking first to "a great crowd of people in a big beautiful auditorium" at the Presbyterian grounds at Montreat, then to YMCA and YWCA groups at Blue Ridge, and finally to the Southern Baptist Conference at Ridgecrest. It was, all in all, a pleasant and comfortable summer.[1]

Events those months offered no advance warning that it would be his last truly peaceful time for several years. The crises that loomed were beyond any prophet. They were like the one in 1927 in that they were very public, but they were also different from it. When he had stepped forward to become moderator, he had entered a large, national controversy that was beyond any one personality. Contending groups had been snapping at one another for years, like competing wolf packs, and his role was to stand between them and invite them to seek common ground. He was personally involved, but the issue was not personal. People in both groups knew where he stood, and they chose him precisely because they also knew that he was absolutely fair and above reducing the debate to personalities. He had given them what they had asked of him: calm, courteous, fair mediation, which helped create a settlement that a more contentious personality could not have achieved.

A Time of Crisis

The crises which arrived in late 1932 and lasted through 1934 each had a strong personal element. The first was a professional crisis, which turned on the character of Christian foreign missions, the integrity of the Board of Foreign Missions, and his leadership of it. The second, which was a family crisis, was the murder of his son. Although it is possible to examine these crises separately, it is important to remember that they happened to the same person as a continuous sequence of events. Rarely before in his life had public crises been so personal, and never had they followed one another so closely. The professional one recalled his World War I experience when he stood virtually alone under attack for his views on the wartime ministry of the churches. The family one drew him back to the deaths of his father and his daughter, feelings long buried but quickly uncovered. The professional crisis had two things in common with the crisis the year he was moderator. It was intensely public, and its resolution turned fully on the character of his leadership. He was again out front, where he longed not to be.

The professional crisis was really a combination of two quite different but related events. The first was the publication in the early fall of 1932 of *Re-Thinking Missions: A Laymen's Inquiry After One Hundred Years*, described almost immediately as the Hocking Report or simply the Report, named for Dr. William E. Hocking of Harvard, chairman of the commission of appraisal which produced it. The second was the decision by Machen in the spring of 1933 to renew the exclusive-inclusive contro-versy, this time aiming his attack at the Board of Foreign Missions, and more directly at Speer.

He saw these two events as one larger crisis, a challenge to the entire foreign missionary enterprise, both in his denomination and in American Christianity. He understood his task to be more than defending foreign missions from its critics, although it included that. More important, he felt, was the task of guaranteeing as best he could that foreign missions would continue to have a distinctly Christian voice and would continue in that voice as a major part of the work of the Presbyterian Church, in constitutional as well as programmatic terms. No one elected him leader, but he took the lead, voluntarily in response to *Re-Thinking Missions*, and with little choice when challenged by Machen. The proof that he saw the crisis correctly came when it was settled, not by any action of the Board of Foreign Missions, but by a series of decisions by General Assemblies over a four-year period. Those decisions affirmed the central role of Christian foreign missions in the Presbyterian Church and denied the constitutionality of separate boards or agencies, and the right of ministers to support them. Ecclesiastical trials followed that led to the end of the controversy in the church.[2]

The Laymen's Report

Although he did not see the crisis coming, he was fully aware of the appraisal of missions and even lent it a helping hand. In a sense, he was in on the ground floor, and that made the final report all the more difficult to oppose. He lunched with Rockefeller on April 29, 1930, to thank him for inviting son Billy to go with them on their summer vacation to the Rocky Mountains. Rockefeller used the occasion to share his interest in "a plan for a fresh study of missions." Speer responded, with some caution, that he thought it was a good idea, "if the right men can be found to do it," and added that it would not be too useful if it were simply a "techni-cal survey."[3]

Rockefeller moved his idea forward and funded the Laymen's Foreign Missions Inquiry. Initially it was planned as an inquiry conducted by laity, appointed by and representative of the various denominational boards of foreign missions. Not all the boards expressed enthusiasm, although many offered moral support, and the laypersons directing the project decided to move it forward on their own. The inquiry had no formal ties to any denomination. One of the leaders was, however, James M. Speers, vice-president of the Presbyterian Board of Foreign Missions. The laypersons hired the Institute for Social and Religious Research, which Rockefeller had founded in 1921 and continued to fund, to carry out the study. They selected Hocking to chair the appraisal commission and then chose the other members of the commission, fifteen in all.

The commissioners visited a number of the missions in 1931 to make their own inquiries and wrote the report based on their findings and the extensive survey data.[4] The areas surveyed included missions in Japan, China, Burma, and India. Margaret was at one of the Presbyterian stations in China visited by the appraisers, and he encouraged her to meet with any of them who might visit her mission.[5] Family friends were on the commission, including the Hockings; Dr. Clarence Barbour, president of Brown University; Dr. William Merrill, pastor of Brick Church in New York City; and Mrs. Harper Sibley, chair of the Woman's Auxiliary to the National Council of the Protestant Episcopal Church. Margaret managed to see and spend time with almost all of them.[6]

The Hocking Report appeared on Speer's desk in late September 1932. It was a prerelease copy, shared by the inquiry with its own members and the denominational boards. It arrived with a condition, that the boards would treat it as confidential until the public release scheduled for November 18. The inquiry promptly violated its own rules and began a series of highly sensational press releases, quoting some of the most provocative passages. Speer objected: first, it was unfair for the inquiry to violate its own agreement without releasing the boards from that agreement; second, the time between the first release of information and possible board response created widespread negative feelings toward all concerned, the inquiry, the boards, and, most unfortunately, the foreign mission enterprise.[7] Margaret shared her father's reaction: "It seems odd to tell the whole world what you consider your friend's faults, before you discuss them with your friend himself. Those of the Commission that I met when they were here didn't at all give the critical impression that this Report itself does."[8] Not surprisingly, the foreign mission boards, including the Presbyterian one, reacted quickly and not always positively.

Speer dutifully attended the meeting at the Roosevelt Hotel in New York City for the formal release of the report and noted that there was "no opportunity for any discussion or there would no doubt have been some very discordant views expressed."[9] By then his board had met once on the topic, and the General Council had heard his views on it. A few days after the inquiry's public unveiling, the Presbyterian Board met to make its decision. He had prepared the draft of a possible statement, and with his guidance the board adopted a version of it. It took an irenic approach to the report. The position paper defined six fundamental theological points with which the board could not agree; it acknowledged that many of the recommendations, once separated from the objectionable positions, were good and useful. In the section on the six fundamental points the board chose to affirm its own position, what it called "the Evangelical Basis" of the foreign missionary work of the Presbyterian Church, rather than attack directly those positions outlined in the report.[10] The decision of the board not to reject the report outright helped fuel the debate.

Re-Thinking Missions hit him very hard. Although he had been cautious about the inquiry and his board had not joined it, he had hoped that it might be useful to the cause of foreign missions. When he read the report, he recognized immediately that it would precipitate a crisis. There is no indication that he knew how much of a crisis it would become, but, at the very least, the theoretical part of the document represented the extreme inclusive end of the theological spectrum, the most modernist or liberal point of view. Attacking the report meant wading into the muck of the controversy once again. He also faced a serious personal dilemma. Good friends had participated in the inquiry. He was reluctant to risk spoiling those friendships.[11] They were difficult, painful days. Emma told Billy that the report "spoiled" his father's holiday and that she had "never seen him so tired."[12]

Appraisal of the Report

He decided to take public issue with the report immediately after its release. The day after its unveiling, he wrote Hocking that he would have to take a position "at variance" with him and that he did not want that to "interfere with the warmth and continuance of our friendship."[13] He formulated his response over the Thanksgiving holiday and titled it an "appraisal of the Report."[14] It appeared in the January issue of the Missionary Review of the World as "An Appraisal of the Appraisal," and then in both hard and soft cover as "Re-Thinking Missions" Examined. His extensive analysis and critique immediately set him at the forefront of the debate over the report.[15]

The inquiry, he said at the beginning of his critique, had been "undertaken and has been carried through with the highest motives and with the earnest intent of advancing the missionary cause." He made clear that his criticism of the report was not an attack on the appraisers or their motives.[16] Nor was he writing to defend foreign missions from criticism, since truthful criticism was always welcome and often useful. His concern was the degree to which the issues raised in the report were "just and true."[17] He moved immediately to a series of preliminary issues, important but hardly crucial to his argument, such as the degree to which the report was truly the work of laity, the relatively short time the appraisers were in the field, and the rather small number of missions and missionaries they had visited. The last and most serious of these introductory matters, what he called a "grave error," was the idea conveyed by the report that readers had to take it or leave it and could not accept any particular part of it without accepting it all.[18] He reported that the commission leaders repudiated that idea at the public meeting releasing the report and that some members of the commission had disagreed with the theological arguments, but few people who read the report attended that meeting. It was vitally important, then, to understand the definitive sections of the report, the two major proposals and the recommendations, in order to see what taking it all meant.

Now at the heart of his argument, he said that taking it all meant accepting its two major proposals, which was "impossible." The first of these was theological. Whatever readers may think about theology, he said, Hocking was right in putting it up front where it belonged, in the first four chapters of the report. But the theology was wrong. It made the following claims:

> Christianity and the other religions must join in a common quest for truth and experience which are not offered in any final and absolute way in Christianity. The missionary "will look forward not to the destruction of these religions, but to their continued co-existence with Christianity, each stimulating the other in growth toward the ultimate goal, unity in the completest truth." "It would be difficult to point out any one general principle [in Christianity] which could not surely be found nowhere else." "The relation between religions must take increasingly hereafter the form of a common search for truth." And the aim of missions is defined thus, "To seek with people of other lands a true knowledge and love of God, expressing in life and word what we have learned through Jesus Christ and endeavoring to give effect to His spirit in the life of the world."[19]

This was, Speer said, "the old Protestant liberalism," and he declared it totally unacceptable.[20] Neither religious pluralism nor religious syncretism was good theology. The simple confession of the Christian was and remained "Jesus, the Son of God, is Lord." Speaking in the plural but

offering his personal confession, he said: "Christianity is not for us the life
and teaching of Jesus only, or man's thought of God, or man's search for
God. For us, Christ is still *the* Way, not *a* way, and there is no goal beyond
Him, or apart from Him, nor any search for truth that is to be found outside of Him, nor any final truth to be sought by a universal religious quest,
except it be sought in Him who is the Way, the Truth, and the Life."[21]

The general theology defined in the report was wrong, he said, and
completely missed the mark when proposed as the basis for foreign mission work among non-Christian peoples. He had just concluded his lectures at Princeton on "The Finality of Jesus Christ" when his critique of
the report appeared. One of their major themes was the relation of
Christianity to the non-Christian religions, so he was fully prepared to
challenge the report on this issue. The missionary movement agrees, he
declared, on the principles fundamental to any true Christian approach to
non-Christian religions, and they were quite different from those set forward in the report. The true principles were:

> Christianity should be proclaimed in a simple positive message by words
> and deeds transfused with love. It should recognize joyfully all the good in
> the non-Christian religions and build upon it. It should not attack or deride
> the non-Christian religions, nor should it slur over or ignore their points of
> difference from Christianity. It should make no compromises, but antici-
> pate the absolute triumph of Christ as acknowledged Lord and Saviour. It
> should welcome all transformations of the thought of non-Christian peoples
> which bring it nearer to Christianity. It should perceive and hold fast the
> truth of its own uniqueness. It should welcome any contribution to a fuller
> understanding of its own character.[22]

Most readers of the report could probably make sense of its theology
and his critique of it; however, they were likely lost when they read his
response to its second proposal. The report proposed that foreign missions
needed a new administrative system, a "centralized autonomous body"
that would include representatives from the denominations but would be
separate from them. The denominational mission boards would continue,
but entirely as "promotional agencies." He found this idea "impracticable"
and gave his reasons, perhaps fully understood only by his fellow missionary administrators. "It is a mistake," he said, "to think that in Christian
missions or anywhere else centralized monopoly is a good thing. All life is
cellular, and it is far better to have freedom and experimentation and often
individual failures than to trust everything to a group of such super-men
as really have no existence."[23] Such a scheme would increase the power and
authority of the senders, whereas the goal of foreign missions was in the

opposite direction, to increase the church in each nation where it emerges.[24]

The ultimate source of the report's second proposal was Rockefeller, with his vision of a united and cooperative Protestantism, another version of the vision that had inspired the Interchurch World Movement. Speer had always been skeptical of such nondenominational ventures and did not like this one, tied to a vague corporate entity. He was thoroughly ecumenical, but he believed from the outset of his career that a fully united church could only emerge from the context of uniting denominations. The SVM never sent a missionary but referred recruits to denominational boards, and he had worked hard to make the Federal Council more fully the collective work of the churches. He was not prepared to surrender foreign missions work to some super-agency independent of the churches, even it if was fully funded by a friend who happened to be one of the wealthiest men in the world.

The Hocking Report married its two proposals to an extensive list of recommendations. Speer was troubled by the hard knot the commission used to tie its report together, but he was willing to give the commission its fair due on the recommendations. If, he said—and it was a large "if"—the recommendations could be untied from the theological argument, as the Presbyterian Board had already suggested in its statement, then many of the recommendations were "excellent." He cited a dozen, most of them about long-recognized concerns in foreign missions dealing with issues that crossed his desk as mission administrator every day. They included "its emphasis upon the need for the ablest and most devoted men and women as missionaries," "its discernment of the special importance and beneficent influence of the work done by missionary women," "its insistence on the principle of self-support and genuine independence in the indigenous churches," and "its discernment of the duty of Christian missions toward the great masses of men dissatisfied with their old religions."[25]

He concluded his critique with his most profound concern. "The central and gravest issue" was that the report had already created serious division of opinion. Mission boards and missionaries, which had been moving forward in a variety of cooperative programs, were once again in the midst of divisive debates. In short, the report threatened Christian unity, at home and abroad. He hoped his analysis would diminish the threat. His final word was one of his favorite themes, duty. The only proper way to deal with the report was to get "all the good and as little as possible of evil out of this situation." The duty before every missionary board was to "settle itself anew on the Rock that is Christ, the one and only basis and foundation, never to be altered, the true motive and message and aim, and standing there, consider this criticism and appraisal honestly, fully and fearlessly, with complete readiness for any and every wise change."[26]

The public debate that ensued took place from the pulpits of America, in the religious and sometimes in the secular periodicals, in lecture halls, and at the official meetings of Protestant denominations at every level. Speer was far from alone in this debate, but he was the key opponent of the report, not only in the Presbyterian Church. The report had generated a sizable volume of correspondence in the board office before he went public, and the publication of his argument dramatically increased it. By late March he noted, "Not a day passes that we do not have to write letters explaining or complaining or dissenting or protesting. It would be a glorious thing if all the energies that have to be used in these ways could be concentrated on positive and constructive tasks."[27]

North wrote to thank him for his critique and added that he felt the situation was very dangerous because "the Hocking statement lacks the heart of the Gospel."[28] In response, he noted, "One of our missionaries in India writes that when the Report came up for discussion at the meeting of the National Christian Council of India, the British missionaries dealt with it with derision."[29] Some of his friends were effusive in their praise of his critique. One said it was all he could wish for "in substance, manner, and spirit. Why should not all the Boards concerned subscribe to it with one consent? Even the Pope should be ready to subscribe to it."[30] Wilder told him it was "one of the best pieces of work that you have done during the nearly 50 years we have known each other. It must have taken much study and prayer."[31]

Pearl Buck

Those who took exception to his views came from both the exclusive and the inclusive sides of the controversy, but the fundamentalists were by far the more vocal and hostile. From the opening of the debate they challenged the board's response to the report and Speer's views. They also strongly repudiated the ideas and attitudes of Pearl Buck. Buck, the successful novelist and author of *The Good Earth*, reviewed the report at the time of its release for the *Christian Century*. She took a totally uncritical position, exclaiming, "I think this is the only book I have ever read which seems to me literally true in its every observation and right in its every conclusion."[32] In early November she spoke to a large gathering of

Presbyterian men and women on the topic "Is There a Case for Foreign Missions?" She called for changes in foreign missions.[33]

Buck became embroiled in the Presbyterian controversy, and an issue for the board and Speer, because she was a Presbyterian missionary to China. Some letters the board received praised it for having such an exemplary and forward-thinking missionary, but the more typical correspondent denounced her position, and by inference the position of the board, and demanded her dismissal. Once the Buck issue emerged, it did not go away, primarily because she continued to present her point of view in a variety of public forums, including lectures to women's groups and in magazine articles.[34] She offered little of substance to the discussion, but she was a lightening rod, a symbol to the exclusive party of what was wrong with the board.

Despite mounting pressure, the board, at the advice of Speer, refused to rush to judgment on Buck. Board secretary McAfee met with her, Speer told one correspondent, in the hope that she "might be brought back to her old evangelical position."[35] She responded to entreaties that her mind had, in fact, changed. She had not accepted a salary from the board for some time and finally decided in late April to ask the board to release her, since it had become evident to her, "from the recent publicity, that the presence of my name on its list of missionaries is proving embarrassing to the Board."[36] The board accepted her resignation "with regret." Speer noted that she parted from the board with "nothing but satisfaction and praise" for its spirit. The Buck issue persisted even after her resignation, as complaints poured in, some from those who claimed that the board should not have accepted it, and others from those who said the board should not have expressed regret.[37]

While the board was dealing with Buck, the fundamentalists continued to attack. The most prominent Presbyterian among the early challengers was former moderator Macartney, who denounced the report in a sermon in early January.[38] The session of his First Presbyterian Church in Pittsburgh wrote the board in March, objecting to the theology of the report and to the views of Buck. Why, the leading members of First Presbyterian inquired, had not the board simply denounced the report in its November 1932 statement? What, they asked, was the board going to do about Pearl Buck?

The board took all letters and requests seriously, but it took special interest in this letter and care to respond quickly and fully.[39] Erdman, as board president, sent an extensive letter, one that Speer helped compose, responding to the questions in their order. The board, Erdman said, had

decided to use the occasion of the report to reaffirm its traditional position on foreign missions and to set forth "its position and the position of
the Church at variance with the main positions of the Report." He made
clear that the board absolutely rejected the theological section of the
report. He directed the session's attention to the many statements board
leaders had made opposing the report, and he highlighted Speer's critique,
noting that the board had sent out 30,000 copies of it. The case of Mrs.
Buck, he concluded, was "exceedingly difficult and perplexing."
Describing his information as confidential, he explained a number of personal aspects of the Buck case and asked for patience as the board tried to
work toward a conclusion which "would be in closest accord with the
mind of our Church and the mind of Christ."[40]

Machen Attacks the Board
of Foreign Missions and Speer

The fundamentalist attacks on the board as a consequence of Buck's position, even the challenge from Macartney, turned out to be mild compared
to the missile Machen launched at a meeting of the Presbytery of New
Brunswick on January 24, 1933. Buck was, after all, her own person and
not the board, and Macartney's church had assured the board of "its loyalty to the Presbyterian Church, and to the work of our Board of Foreign
Missions."[41] Machen proposed an overture to the General Assembly
directly challenging the board and its management. He saw his proposal
as a program of reform, to maintain what he considered to be the integrity
of the Presbyterian Church and its foreign missionary program.[42]

The overture had four parts, the first by far the most important.
Machen proposed that the General Assembly "take care to elect to positions
on the Board of Foreign Missions only persons who are fully aware of the
danger in which the Church stands and who are determined to insist upon
such verities as the full truthfulness of Scripture, the virgin birth of our
Lord, His substitutionary death as a sacrifice to satisfy Divine justice, His
bodily resurrection and His miracles, as being essential to the Word of
God and our Standards and as being necessary to the message which every
missionary under our Church shall proclaim." Presumably the General
Assembly had not elected the right board, persons who could affirm the
five points of the fundamentalists, and needed to elect another one as soon
as possible.

The other three parts were management issues, strongly suggesting that

Secretary Speer had not been doing his job. The board needed to select a candidate secretary who met the "Standards," to rewrite the application blank so that candidates were asked the proper questions and given an accurate understanding of true and faithful missionary work, and "to warn the Board of the great danger that lurks in union enterprises at home as well as abroad, in view of the widespread error in our day."[43] William Hanzsche, editor of the *Presbyterian Magazine* and a member of the presbytery, wrote Speer a friendly note and told him about the overture. He added that he had made a motion, adopted by the presbytery, which "officially invited" him to be present at the meeting of the presbytery on April 11 to "hear and answer those charges made by Dr. Machen."[44]

Speer was not surprised that Machen joined the debate, but he was startled at the boldness of the overture. Machen had decided to challenge the board and Speer in public, something he had up to this point done only in private. Speer was well acquainted with the opinions Machen held of the board and of himself, because he had been raising various questions about the board and its procedures since 1926. In 1928, for example, he wrote the candidate secretary of the board, the Rev. Lindsay Hadley, about a concern he had regarding a question on the candidate reference blank. He said he was motivated by the response one of his Princeton students received when he sought a summer appointment with the board. He quickly turned the correspondence from the questions on the blank to the board's attitude toward other Christian groups. He was concerned that the board looked for candidates who would say they would work cooperatively with other missionaries. Such a cooperative attitude was fine, he said, if the other missionaries were doctrinally sound.

The correspondence lasted into the spring of 1929, when Hadley, realizing he was out of his league, referred Machen to one of the "older men, such as Dr. Speer or Dr. Brown, who could give you a much more satisfactory answer."[45] Machen promptly wrote Speer, reminding him of their extensive correspondence over the years, telling him that his "objections to the policy of the Foreign Board have not become less but rather greater than in 1926," and warning him that he was moving toward bringing his concerns "to the attention of persons of evangelical conviction in the Presbyterian Church." He enclosed a paper he had written, titled "Can Evangelical Christians Support our Foreign Board?" Would Speer offer criticisms and suggestions?[46]

The exchange of letters, really documents, that took place in April 1929 remained private until the two men met for public exchange at the Presbytery of New Brunswick. Machen's twenty-four-page epistle was a frontal assault on the board and Speer. He said the board's humanitarian work was "valuable," but there were many serious questions about its evangelical work, which was the most crucial part of its work. Other problems were pervasive, and the candidate reference blank, and the way it was used, was just one of them. He argued that the questions on the blank encouraged perspective missionaries to be "tolerant" of other positions, when the board should demand that they "*not* tolerate the point of view of those who are opposed to the gospel of Christ as it is set forth in Holy Scripture." The board tolerated opinions like those expressed in the Auburn Affirmation, but refused to be intolerant of views hostile to Christian truth. No evangelical Christian, he concluded, could contribute to such a missionary program "without disloyalty to his Saviour and Lord."

He raised equally serious questions about Speer and his "utterances." In particular, he took exception to his argument in *Are Foreign Missions Done For?* He found the book "evasive and vague." Speer claimed that the "definite and comprehensive" aim of foreign missions was "to make the Lord Jesus Christ known to all men as their Divine Saviour and to persuade them to become his disciples." Machen argued that the statement was not definite at all, but vague, and could be believed by a modernist. And that was true for most of the other arguments in the book. In fact, Machen exclaimed, Speer made no mention of the virgin birth at all, or of other key features—meaning the five points of the fundamentalists—of the traditional Christian faith.

Machen concluded that despite the attitude of the board and the vagueness of its leader, many faithful missionaries were serving "under the Board who are proclaiming the full gospel as it is set forth in the whole Word of God. These faithful missionaries of the Cross should not be allowed to suffer because of the faults of the administrative agency under which they stand." Perhaps, he conjectured, the time had come "for the establishment of a truly evangelical missionary agency in the Presbyterian Church—an agency to which evangelical Christians can contribute . . . an agency which shall keep clear of entangling alliances and shall proclaim the full glories of the Reformed Faith as they are found in the Word of God?" This letter demonstrates that in the spring of 1929, before his separation from Princeton, Machen considered the establishment of a separate board of foreign missions. Was this simply a threat to persuade Speer to come around to his way of thinking, or did he have the outlines of a plan for separation well before he had the opportunity for it?[47]

The letter Speer crafted (he prepared at least two drafts of his twenty-page response) was as direct and confrontational as anything he ever wrote, private or public. Machen had asked him to offer correction for anything in his paper that was "untrue or unjust," and Speer responded that in his opinion, "the paper, as a whole, is as 'untrue and unjust' as it is in detail." He challenged virtually every point of Machen, using historical and biblical resources to support his arguments. It was false, he claimed, to try to divide the humanitarian work of the gospel from the evangelical one. "The Gospel," he said, "includes human service. The New Testament is full of that principle. It insists on such service as one of the evidences of fidelity to the Gospel." He defended the candidate department of the board and said he did not know of a single instance of the board turning down a candidate from Princeton Seminary. He told him that he had reread the Auburn Affirmation and discovered that the signers included in their statement a declaration of full acceptance of the Westminister Confession of Faith and the doctrines of evangelical Christianity. He declared, "In their positive affirmation surely these men are as much entitled to be trusted and believed as you and I think we are."

He then turned to Machen's challenges of his "utterances." The aim of foreign missions was not his alone, but the one the board had adopted in 1920. The aim was scriptural, he insisted, and had been taken from Jesus' command to his disciples. "Your views," Speer added, "explain away and even attack the clear meaning and the very words of the Great Commission as Matthew records it." It was not reasonable, he continued, to make the virgin birth the touchstone of every statement of faith. He pointed out that Machen, in two of his most important books on faith, mentioned the virgin birth only once and then in an aside. That omission did not diminish the importance of those books, so why should it diminish the usefulness of any book? His own book was a "poor little thing," but it was "not the vague and evasive and unevangelical thing you allege."

He closed his argument by taking Machen head on: "I find myself in deep and thankful accord with almost all of your great convictions. . . . Where I differ from you is at the points where, it seems to me, you differ from the Scriptures. Some great Scripture truths you ignore or qualify. You twist or interpret some passages out of their plain and obvious statement. . . . The New Testament teaching is far richer and freer than your view appears to be. It teaches not that the Cross saves us or that we are saved by the Cross. It teaches that Christ saves us, and that He saves us by Himself, by His death and by His life." He invited Machen to "put away all this bitterness and railing and suspicion" and spare one another "a controversy like this between you and me." If, he concluded, he wished to go forward and publish his paper, he proposed they publish their papers together: "But, my dear friend, there is a more excellent way."[48]

Machen responded immediately and definitively, although he took no action until four years later, when he presented his overture. He told Speer that his letter had only confirmed his objections to the policy of the board. Moreover, "the appeal for peace in the Church and between us, with which your letter closes, seems rather strange at a time when you are actively engaged in the attack upon the conservative control of Princeton Seminary and in the effort to substitute the policy favored by the President for the policy which the institution is bound by the most solemn trust obligations to maintain. The policy of tolerance hardly seems to work both ways. The conservatives are not only to tolerate in the Church but also to give active support [to] the message that you proclaim; while you, on the other hand, are engaged in destroying almost the last remaining powerful agency which the conservatives possess for the propagation of their Faith in the Presbyterian Church."[49]

The Debate at Trenton

The people of the United States were unsettled in the spring of 1933. They had elected Franklin Roosevelt their next president, and they awaited his arrival, with hopes for some solution to their national crisis. On March 4 he informed them that they had nothing to fear but fear itself, and in the 100 days that followed he launched one of the most remarkable legislative periods in American history. It was the birth of the New Deal. One month into this social experiment and far removed from its concerns, Speer and Machen confronted one another at the meeting of the New Brunswick Presbytery in the Fourth Presbyterian Church in Trenton.

The protagonists had prepared for the event quite differently. Speer worked behind the scenes with his friend Erdman, a member of the presbytery, and proposed a procedure for the meeting. Erdman reported to Speer the week before the event that he agreed with the plan, had spoken with other members of his presbytery, and that they hoped to put it in place. Machen would speak and then Speer would speak, and then, without discussion, someone would move the previous question on the overture. If the overture was defeated, the presbytery would move immediately to a vote of confidence in the board.[50] The agenda arranged, Speer made two crucial decisions. First, he wrote out his statement, something he rarely did. His motive was to avoid, if he could, being "led into contro-versy."[51] Second, he adhered closely to the four sections of the overture in order to focus the presbytery's attention on the central issue before them, not on other themes, especially theological ones.

Machen decided to take his issue to his public. Very shortly before the meeting (Speer received it the day before) he issued a 110-page pamphlet that he titled "Modernism and the Board of Foreign Missions of the Presbyterian Church in the U.S.A." It was a revised and considerably expanded version of his private paper to Speer four years earlier.[52]

The debate was set for 2:30 P.M. A staff correspondent for *Christianity Today*, the recently founded journal of the conservatives, reported that Fourth Church filled up quickly with ministers and laity from within and without the presbytery, and with students from both Princeton and Westminster seminaries. There was a "sense of suppressed excitement," because "for the first time the outstanding militant conservative scholar stood on the same platform with the foremost representative of religious pacifism to discuss the missionary policies of the church."[53] The presbytery adopted an agenda similar to the one Speer had privately proposed, but with two ten-minute periods for discussion. Each speaker had a hour.

Machen spoke first. He acknowledged Speer as one of the "outstanding figures of the Christian world," and one of the most "eloquent." He said he, Machen, had little to offer in speaking ability, but a great deal to offer that was true. The board was on trial, and the issue was whether its "course is right or wrong, true or false? What is the standard of judgment?" He proposed the Bible and proceeded to challenge Speer's use of it in his most recent book, *The Finality of Jesus Christ*. He questioned the board's proce-dures and the phrasing of some of the questions on its official forms. Why had the board not, he asked, fully and clearly denounced the "Laymen's Report"? And then there was Mrs. Buck, whom the board retained despite her "plain repudiations of the Gospel." He offered no new arguments. His presentation was more a sermon than a debate. The correspondent of *Christianity Today*, in portraying the event to its readers, said Machen seemed at times to be like one of the great figures from the past, "a Knox, a Luther or an Edwards."[54]

Speer was neither eloquent nor combative. He read from a prepared typescript, as planned. He said he had come "to be of whatever help I can to the Presbytery as it seeks to deal wisely and justly with the proposed overture." He added that he intended to deal with statements "of fact and constitutional principle" first, and then with the "the general attitude and method of procedure" that the overture represented. He responded to the sections of the overture one at a time, offering nothing new. The challenge to the membership of the board was unfair and discriminatory, since there were three other boards of the church and they were not being challenged. The overture offered no evidence of "danger" to the church, and even if some danger existed, the board was widely recognized as "a bulwark of the gospel." The candidate secretary was a minister in good standing. He had been a devoted missionary to China, forced home by illness. The overture was not the legal way to handle the issue, if there was an issue. The various forms the board used could be improved, but there was no evidence that they had in any way prevented the church from selecting and sending excellent persons as missionaries.

He acknowledged that there were dangers in joining church unions, but added that there were also dangers in remaining out of them. He asserted that the part of the overture that spoke to the union issue was too general to be useful. He offered historical reflections on some parts of the overture and made references to the legal and constitutional issues involved in them. As he drew his argument to a close, he said he had tried to be fair in his response, but he believed that the overture "both in form and in content . . . contravenes the Constitution and traditions of our Church, and that the Presbytery of New Brunswick should not transmit it to the General Assembly." Using a strategy common to the formal debater, he concluded with a quotation from one of Machen's own books, in which the scholar had "expressed a deep desire . . . to live and work in a Church free from turmoil and dissension as a place of refuge from the unbelieving world."[55]

Almost as soon as Machen and Speer were finished, with time for only a very brief direct exchange between the two men, a member of the presbytery moved the previous question, which, if passed, would close debate. Machen objected that they, the presbytery, needed time for serious discussion, but the presbytery voted to end the debate and then moved immediately to a vote on the overture. It lost by a substantial margin. The presbytery promptly passed a vote of confidence in the board, with but three dissenters, one of them Machen.[56] Although Machen lost in his own presbytery, the issue was not dead. A member of the Philadelphia Presbytery introduced the overture there, and it passed. The General Assembly received no less than seven overtures relating to the Board of Foreign Missions, three of them calling for change.[57]

The confrontation at Trenton promised real drama. Although it did not deliver in terms of a highly charged debate and did little if anything to settle the controversy, it was a time of great personal tension for the parties involved. It was also a most important moment. It merged, in a highly public way, the debate over the Hocking Report with the continuing controversy between the exclusive and inclusive parties within the Presbyterian Church. It brought together the key elements of the crisis and set the stage for continued debate at the coming General Assembly and beyond.

Speer had his typical constant round of speaking engagements that spring. In late March he was at Grace Episcopal Church, the fifth speaker in a series that had already heard Hocking and Merrill. He launched into a discussion of the Hocking Report, only to find that his audience "knew nothing whatever of the issues involved," so he dropped that topic and turned to a more direct and simple description of foreign missions.[58] In early May he spoke in Providence, Rhode Island, to an interdenominational group about the report. He was getting "a little weary" of the issue, "and yet the money behind the movement is launching a new set of publicity releases." Seven volumes of the survey were about to be issued, along with a Chinese translation of the report. He conjectured, "Mr. Rockefeller intends to keep the matter alive if money can do it."[59]

"Weary" did not do justice to his mood as he spent time in May preparing for the coming General Assembly, to be held in Columbus, Ohio. He had been convinced before Machen entered the discussion that the issues raised by the Hocking Report would come up at the General Assembly, and now, with the overtures on the table, he knew they would, complicated by the theological faction led by Machen. He shared his innermost thoughts in a confidential letter to the Rev. W. Reginald Wheeler, a missionary in China and the person who eventually wrote a memoir about him. "I may say to you frankly," he told Wheeler, "that I cannot remember a time of as much anxiety and trouble as this year has been,—with the Report of the Appraisal Commission, and Mrs. Buck and Dr. Machen. The Laymen's Report and Mrs. Buck have just played into the hands of the extremists of both wings and there have been many injudicious things said and done." He had never expressed such feelings during the crisis of 1927, but he had more to say, indicating the degree to which this crisis was much more personal that the earlier one:

> There have been times in the midst of all this strain when I wished that I
> had taken advantage of the option of retiring at the age of 65. I hate this
> kind of controversy and contention and I don't see how God's blessing can
> rest upon it. I believe in standing immovably for the truth but I believe in

gentleness and kindliness and love toward persons whether they agree with us or not. All this bitterness and feeling and judgment seems to me to be just unChristian. Of course there are limits to cooperation and fellowship and I think we should observe those limits but that we ought to do so with Christian courtesy and loyalty to the true tradition of our Church. I think there have been grave mistakes and errors on both sides and that the extremists—both fundamentalists and modernists are both to blame. I would stand as firm and immovably as granite on the rock that is Christ Jesus but I don't believe that one can truly stand on that rock except in the gentleness of the love of Christ.[60]

The General Assembly of 1933

The two major items he prepared for the General Assembly were quite different. One document he directed to the assembly's standing committee on foreign missions. This committee would receive and give initial consideration to the overtures on foreign missions. His document was the board's response to the Machen overture and, incidentally, to the other negative overtures. He created a substantial package of materials that he broke down into five chapters. The first contained a copy of the overture and other materials Machen had published about it. In his communication to the committee explaining the materials in this chapter, he said, "It is a mistake to suppose, however, that Dr. Machen's attitude is due to the arguments set forth in his pamphlet and address or is likely to be modified by any answers to these arguments. For some years, and antecedent to most of his present allegations, he has felt and expressed his distrust, and opposition to the Foreign Board." The other four chapters contained various responses to Machen's arguments and included his own New Brunswick statement.[61] The second document was his formal "Address" to the assembly about the work of the board.

Parties to the controversy exhibited different moods as the assembly drew near. The Machen supporters looked forward to it with great anticipation. *Christianity Today* editorialized that now that the "oldest Presbytery in the Church" had adopted the Machen overture, "the issue" was alive and well and would likely "overshadow all other issues at the approaching Assembly." The future looked bright for "a great evangelical reaction."[62] While the exclusive party geared for battle and victory, Speer had "no heart for it at all." The contending groups, including the Westminster Seminary people and "the entirely opposite extreme, . . . have stirred up all the bitterness that they could and we shall have to meet a great body of criticism." Perhaps, he mused, the "opposite attitudes will neutralize one another," but whatever happened, he believed God would "bring the Church through once again without an open schism."[63]

The assembly sent the exclusive group a sharply negative message. It elected a moderate as moderator by a 7–1 vote over the exclusive candidate. The standing committee on foreign missions held open meetings to discuss the overtures and other matters before it. To the surprise of some and doubtless the chagrin of the exclusive group, only Machen and three others appeared on behalf of his position.[64] The standing committee sent two reports to the assembly, a majority one representing forty-three members of the committee, including its chair, in full support of the board and its actions, and a minority one from two of its members, urging the adoption of the Machen position. The assembly adopted the majority report by such an overwhelming vote that it did not count the negative vote. The assembly, in direct opposition to the first point of Machen's overture, expressed "its thorough confidence in the members of the Board of Foreign Missions and its belief that they have steadfastly endeavored and are endeavoring, by every means within their power, to support the secretaries and the missionaries of the Board in the Gospel enterprise." The assembly also spoke to the Hocking Report. It decided to leave any useful application of the recommendations of the report in the hands of the board; however, it "definitely repudiates any and all theological statements and implications in that volume which are not in essential agreement with the doctrinal position of the Church."[65] And it added, in terms Speer had used if not written, "The Assembly cannot see its way clear to approve a complete centralized administration of Protestant Foreign Mission work."[66]

The commissioners greeted Speer with a standing ovation as he made his way forward to present his report on the board's work.[67] One commentator reported that the audience spontaneously sang "Blest Be the Tie that Binds."[68] Charged by Machen with modernism, or as a commissioner noted, with being "a dishonest man," he appeared calm and self-possessed: "His speech was a great moment and the supreme climax of the Assembly and left it hushed into profound quiet and reverence."[69] In a strong and unwavering voice he told the assembly that this was the fortieth anniversary of his first report to an assembly. Only about six missionaries in a total body of almost fifteen hundred were active when he began his work. He saluted the members of the board and described them as "men and women who without reward, have patiently and fearlessly followed in the path of duty and done what they believed to be right and in accord with the law of the Church."

He admitted to the assembly that it had been "a difficult year through which God has brought us; the most difficult, I think, that I can remember in the forty-two years and more that I have been connected to the Board." Difficult because of the deaths of faithful missionaries and financial shortfalls. But really a hard year, he was frank to say, because of other matters, including the report of the appraisal commission and the criticisms directed at the board "from two diametrically opposite positions." He defined those positions very generally, and did not mention a single name, not Machen or Buck. Instead, he challenged their style and attitude by appealing to the "great leaders of our Church in the past." He asserted that no one could read what those leaders had said "without feeling the largeness of their spirit, their faithfulness to truth and at the same time their kindliness of temper and their charity of mind and speech, without desiring to preserve this great tradition and to maintain it in these troubled and irritated days and to bequeath it to our children."

The rest of the speech was quintessential Speer. In spite of these difficulties, he said, "it has yet been a bright and glorious year." Yes, there had been financial cutbacks, but less than feared and far less than experienced by some other denominations, which has made it possible to maintain "the work of the missions with very little curtailment." We can thank God, he said, for the faithfulness of the missionaries. He also thanked God for signs of his presence "day by day in the offices of the Board as we have sought, turning neither to the left hand nor to the right, to work with Him in His rightful place in the midst." Missionaries in distant and lonely places relied on God, and then, in what came across as a personal note, he added, "And I do not know what we would have done at many an hour if we could not have laid our problems and perplexities at His feet and have asked Him to have only His way and His will with us and with all the missionary work of our Church." There were many signs, he told the commissioners, of positive and constructive social and religious change around the world, much of it inspired by the missionary enterprise. He concluded by posing a question he understood people were beginning to ask: "Will Foreign Missions go on?" "Yes," he answered, "they will go on." Always looking forward, he affirmed, "We welcome all the signs of the times and the evidence of the progress of the Church but our trust is in God and His promises and His invincible will that his Son is to be Lord of all and that every knee in heaven and on earth and under the earth is to bow to Him."[70]

The year had been difficult. The issues had become both more confrontational and more personal than at any time since the beginning of the controversy in the Presbyterian Church. In recognition of the fact that the

primary burden of leadership during the year had fallen on the senior secretary, the assembly adopted a personal tribute to him on the recommendation of its standing committee: "The General Assembly is convinced
that the work of Dr. Robert E. Speer, our Senior Secretary and his associates, and also the work of the missionaries in the various foreign fields as
a whole, deserves the whole-hearted, unequivocal, enthusiastic and affectionate commendation of the church at large. We know that Dr. Speer
stands absolutely true to the historic doctrinal position of the Presbyterian
Church, and we would be remiss if we did not testify to our recognition
that his entire life bears testimony to his supreme effort to extend the
Gospel to humanity across the world."[71]

The assembly was a victory, for the position of the board on the issues
raised and for its temperate and Christian spirit, and for Speer. However,
he did not see it that way. He believed in reconciliation, not victory and
defeat. One astute commentator has described these events as a "bittersweet victory," and there is no better way to characterize his true feelings.[72]
He said little in public about the assembly actions. In his most private correspondence, he said some version of the following comment he sent to
Elliott: "The Assembly overwhelmingly sustained the Board . . . but I am
afraid the group which Dr. Machen leads is absolutely implacable and
inaccessible so that we cannot hope for peace or trust for many a day. It is
too bad that Christ is wounded in this way in His own house!"[73] His
correspondence contained not a single reference to the General Assembly's
affirmation of his work. Years later John Mackay, himself a figure in the
controversy, described the events of the year as the "saddest and bitterest
moment" in Speer's career.[74] He agreed, for after all the debating was over,
his church remained divided.

Speer's assessment was more dramatic than the situation warranted.
The division was different from what it had been in 1927. Then it threatened the entire Presbyterian Church; now it turned on the personality of
one man and a rapidly shrinking number of his followers. But the division
did continue to exist. Almost as soon as the assembly voted on the foreign
mission issues, H. McAllister Griffiths, managing editor of *Christianity
Today* and a member of the exclusive group, announced "a new Board will
be organized by Bible-believing Christians to promote truly Biblical and
truly Presbyterian mission work."[75]

Machen and his supporters organized the Independent Board for
Presbyterian Foreign Missions in June, and in October that board elected
him its president. Speer was concerned, but hardly surprised. When he
had read about a separate, evangelical mission board in Machen's 1929

letter, he had responded that the idea was a "grave" proposal, and could not understand how it might work, since it would be "a rival foreign missionary agency in our Church, independent of the General Assembly and supported by members of our Church who proclaim their fellow members to be unevangelical."[76] Things did not go entirely well for the Independent Board. Clarence Macartney, one of the most visible and respected of the conservatives, refused to join it.[77] Speer decided that the best response was no response and paid relatively little public attention to it. His view was that the issue had become constitutional and that the church would in due time do the right thing and challenge the Independent Board on legal grounds.

Speer and Machen came from very similar evangelical and conservative backgrounds, but their differences were substantial, more profound than the claim made by one student of their conflict that they represented "two different brands of conservatism."[78] Nor can their differences be traced to the fact that one of them was an ordained minister and a scholar and the other a layperson who considered himself to be a simple believer. Machen met his match in Speer when he challenged him, and on virtually any ground, biblical, historical, or theological. The heart of the matter was that at the outset of his career Speer had adopted a version of Horace Bushnell's vision of the comprehension of Christian truth into one grand unity. Speer was a moderate, in the middle, but for him the middle extended as close to the ends of any argument as possible, and his goal was always to embrace those persons at the extremes. Machen became an increasing frustration for him, because they agreed on many theological points, and they recognized the great need for the evangelization of the world. But Machen was an exclusivist and refused to be embraced by anyone who did not pass the litmus test of extreme exclusion.

Reflecting on the results of the assembly, Speer reached the conclusion that Machen had made a "tactical mistake" in attacking him. He came to believe that if Machen had "kept his movement impersonal," the assembly might well have been less emphatic in its actions.[79] Historians have agreed. Patterson wrote, "It would appear that Machen committed a strategic blunder in attacking Speer." With the benefit of hindsight, but with considerable insight, historian William Hutchison, son of a missionary mentored by Speer, depicted Machen as "fighting a rearguard action." The attack on the board in general and Speer in particular revealed, Hutchison said, "the extremity to which fundamentalism, at least for the time being, had been driven, . . . reduced to endless chronicles of guilt-by-association and heresy-by-omission."[80]

For his part, Speer maintained his usual active schedule, pleased that virtually everywhere he went, audiences received him well and showed enthusiasm for foreign missions. He found the members of a synod held shortly after the assembly "warm-hearted and responsive," and some "men whose minds had been poisoned by the campaign which has been going on were completely won over."[81] Later that summer he spoke to a Southern Baptist convention in Norfolk, Virginia, and found it "rather amusing to have Dr. Machen calling my orthodoxy in question on one side, and to have the Southern Baptists, who are the most conservative body theologically, open their arms on the other side."[82] To conservative friend Matthews, he reported late in the summer that all synods he had attended, including "Illinois, Indiana, Ohio, Pennsylvania, Kentucky, and others, have endorsed the General Assembly's action, and have affirmed their confidence in the Board and their intention to support it," and presbyteries were following that lead.[83] In October he received a warm reception in the Chester Presbytery, a "stronghold of fundamentalist support."[84] As he made his rounds of churches and meetings, he discovered more and more support for the board and less and less for Machen, and relatively little discussion of the Hocking Report.

The major issue before him and his board from the fall of 1933 through the spring of 1934 was financial. Receipts were down, at first seriously, but then the losses tapered off. There was some turnaround by spring, not sufficient to escape further reductions in the board's budget, but enough to prevent deep cuts. He conjectured that "the campaign of misrepresentation and falsehoods which has been carried on" may have misled some but that others, angered by it, increased their gifts.[85] In many ways, he found the decisions about where to cut the budget more painful than the debates the previous year, since they affected missions and their staffs.

He happily reported to Mudge in late March that he was not planning to attend the coming General Assembly. He was not a commissioner or a member of the General Council, and his board had not appointed him to attend. Mudge told him to rethink his decision, because they needed his help, for it was "certain, humanly speaking, that difficult situations will emerge, in which the Board of Foreign Missions has a vital interest." The board subsequently appointed him to attend, but he told his friend he would go without enthusiasm, because he despaired "of getting anywhere with men who can so conscientiously shut their minds to what is true."[86] As the assembly approached, he described the Independent Board as a movement for "schism and rebellion in the church."[87]

End of the Presbyterian Controversy

By the time the General Assembly of 1934 convened in Cleveland, the stage was set for the beginning of the end of the Presbyterian controversy. It also marked the end of his active involvement in the debate, with two relatively small but irritating exceptions, one an encounter with the Rev. Carl McIntire and the other an acidic exchange with Charles G. Trumbull. The exclusive party had declined from the previous year; its candidate for moderator received only one vote in ten. Speer had argued from the outset of this crisis in 1932 that the deeper issue was constitutional, not personal or theological. The General Council had sent every commissioner a lengthy legal study that defined the powers of the assembly over its boards and agencies and "denied the right of Presbyterian ministers or members to form any sort of combination to resist or subvert this authority."[88] The assembly acted in accord with this conclusion. The commissioners voted by a majority so large that "no division was called for" that the Independent Board should cease to function within the Presbyterian Church, those ministers and laymen who were related to it should sever their relationship with it, and presbyteries should begin legal action against any ministers who did not conform to this decision.[89]

After the General Assembly, the General Council sent a letter to all ministers and church sessions spelling out its actions in relation to the Independent Board and directing all Presbyterian ministers and laity to end any relationship they might have with it.[90] Speer noted that there were some who were "absolutely irreconcilable," and that it remained to be seen if they would remain in the church. "It is now," he told Margaret, "a matter of fidelity to the constitution of the church. That was precisely where the General Assembly insisted that it was standing. It is, I am inclined to think, just an extension of the Princeton controversy and permeated by the same personal elements."[91]

Machen and several of his closest associates remained irreconcilable. The Presbytery of New Brunswick asked Machen for his response to the action of the General Assembly, and he replied that he considered it to be unconstitutional. The presbytery subsequently brought charges against him because he continued to lead the Independent Board. It held a trial in the spring of 1935, found him guilty, and suspended him from the ministry.

Speer was not party to any of these actions. In the several months after the murder of Elliott in September 1934, he spent the vast majority of this time on family matters. Almost immediately after his return to the office in the spring of 1935, he faced another overture hostile to the board. This one came from the pen of McIntire, one of Machen's former students and a minister in the Presbytery of West Jersey. The overture was largely a rehash of Machen's effort two years earlier. Speer prepared a carefully worded and detailed brief against it, and the board published it. The presbytery subsequently rescinded the overture, so it never reached the General Assembly.[92]

In late March Speer received another jolt, this one from Charles Trumbull, editor of the *Sunday School Times*. Under the title "Foreign Missionary Betrayals of the Faith," Trumbull accused the board of modernism, and in a series of asides printed in smaller type he challenged Speer and his leadership of the board. The article did not carry the weight of the overtures, and the arguments were not new, but Speer was very troubled by the publication. Trumbull's father had been one of his mentors and had performed his wedding, and he had known Charles virtually all his life. He had wrestled with him before, in the early 1920s, over criticisms of the board's work in China, but he refused to tangle with him now. Trumbull sent him a long letter to tell him the article had been published, but he had already seen it. He responded that he found Trumbull's views "a sad, sad mingling of right and wrong, with the wrong predominant" and referred him to one of his own father's books. He refused to argue with him and signed the letter, "Ever affectionately yours."[93]

He attended the General Assembly of 1935, which confirmed the actions of the previous assembly in relation to the Independent Board and those clergy associated with it, but he was not involved in the discussions or debate. One pleasant experience occurred on May 29. The General Assembly presented him with a lovely embossed folder and resolution in recognition of his forty-five years as secretary of the board. The assembly extended to him "renewed expressions of its affectionate CONFIDENCE and ESTEEM." The resolution concluded: "His unfailing loyalty to the saving gospel of CHRIST and his unbroken zeal for its propagation throughout the world have cheered and strengthened the Church and its missionary forces, and the Assembly desires him to know that he carries the full confidence of the Church and its heartfelt love."[94] Several times between the assemblies of 1935 and 1936 he expressed the hope that the controversy, now contained by the legal mechanisms of the church, would come to an end. He observed, along with the rest of his church, dispute and then division in Machen's ranks. Speer saw such dissension "inevitable where the principle of the infallibility of every man's conscience is set up and then a particular individual demands that his conscience shall be recognized as the authoritative one."[95] Westminister Seminary went its separate way in January 1936.

Speer left for the 1936 assembly in Syracuse hoping for the end "of this period of contention and strife which has been such a grief in our Church these last 10 years and more."[96] Some ministers had persisted in supporting the Independent Board, and their presbyteries had tried and then suspended them from the ministry. Several appeals of these decisions, including one from Machen, reached the General Assembly and were denied. Machen had already moved to schism. In June 1935 he had participated in the creation of the Presbyterian Constitutional Covenant Union, dedicated to maintaining "the Constitution of the Presbyterian Church in the U.S.A."[97] Just two weeks after the assembly of 1936 adjourned, the Covenant Union became the basis for a new church, led by Machen: the Presbyterian Church of America.[98]

The departure of Machen and his followers marked the end of the Presbyterian controversy. Speer hated division. It had been a long struggle, perhaps not "epic" as one commentator has claimed for his confrontation with Machen, but of crisis proportions on two occasions.[99] He welcomed the peace in his church. It arrived as he prepared to retire. He felt settled, hopeful that he had done all that he could to secure the place of Christian foreign missions as a vital part of the continuing ministry of the Presbyterian Church.

There was no single, defining moment in the ten-year period of his denominational leadership. He moved in and out of the times of crisis, drawn in each time by a sense of duty. He had lofty goals in the midst of each crisis, to achieve reconciliation and create peace in his church. Those goals were never fully achieved. He disliked settling for less than the best, but he accepted the realities of life. He somehow succeeded in maintaining his composure in the most difficult of the debates, those with Machen in 1933, and he managed to avoid personalizing the issues. On the fortieth anniversary of his service to the Board of Foreign Missions, the editor of the *Presbyterian Banner* described him as "a living gospel, the kind that the church lives by and that keeps the gospel alive and saves the world."[100] He doubtless blanched when he read it. He did not live to read what his good friend Mackay said of him, in reference to his entire career, but truly appropriate to his years as a Presbyterian leader, that he was "the most truly Pauline figure of his generation."[101]

PART IV

Iona

Robert E. Speer and John Mackay, 1943

Bryn Mawr College

CHAPTER 14

New Ministries

"We Who Are Children of Time"

The conclusion of Speer's formal missionary career came in the fall of 1937, when he retired from the Board of Foreign Missions. By then he had said good-bye to his associates in the Student Volunteer Movement and his missionary executive colleagues in the Foreign Missions Conference of North American and the Committee on Cooperation in Latin America. The order in which he left these several posts was a function of when they scheduled their annual or quadrennial meetings, but it coincided with the way he entered foreign missions work, first the ecumenical organizations and then the denominational one. The SVM had been his springboard into foreign missions, but it had been his collective efforts through all of the organizations that established him as the premier missionary leader of his era.

When he stepped down from these various foreign missionary commitments, he put them behind him in two important but different ways. He separated himself from the organizations, retaining only sporadic correspondence with some of his fellow missionary executives. He did not look over the shoulders of his successors, nor did he interfere with their work in any way, almost always declining to become involved when asked. More remarkably, he also shifted the primary focus of his ministry. From the outset of his career he had understood himself to be called to ministry, a lay ministry but nonetheless real, and he had practiced it primarily in the context of foreign missions. Along the way he had entered other work, prominently that associated with the Federal Council of Churches and his own denomination at the General Assembly level, and had also forged a career as one of the key church leaders of his day. In retirement he lowered his foreign missionary profile dramatically and raised his profile as a church leader. The primary areas of his ministry in his remaining years were ministerial education and spiritual leadership. He wrote five books in the ten years of his retirement, only one, a memoir of a missionary who attracted him because he was also a Christian mystic, on foreign missions.

Retirement

Retirement had been on his horizon for some time. His fortieth year with the board slipped by in 1931, and his sixty-fifth birthday came and went in 1932. Friends recognized both occasions with celebrations. However, those were difficult years for the board and his church, and he responded to requests from colleagues and his own best instincts that he needed to keep his hand on the plough. If he had retired in 1932, his day of departure would have come just about the same day the Hocking Report arrived on his desk. There were times in the following years when he murmured that he should have retired on time, but, modest as he was about his own importance, he knew within days of the arrival of the report that he was more needed as spokesperson for foreign missions than he could have imagined when he had made the decision to extend his retirement to the mandatory age of seventy.

Circumstances of various kinds made retirement attractive. One very strong push was the pressure from some members of the younger generation that it was their turn to lead. This had been particularly true in the SVM in the 1920s. It had not involved him personally, but he had helped create a compromise between the old and new leadership. There was no visible push in his board, but there was a generational shift. Colleague Brown had retired in 1929 after thirty-four years of service, all of it at Speer's side. By the time Speer stepped down, new and younger secretaries were in position to take charge. One very strong pull was his belief that retirement was a fitting reward for long, hard work. He occasionally spoke of it as an "entitlement," a time free of "the shackles of organization relationships," when one could "reap the harvest of the years."[1] The issue was not rest but freedom, so that he could have "the years that remain for a number of pieces of work that I should like to do."[2]

One primary loyalty created the largest attraction for his retirement: Emma. Since her retirement from the National Board of the YWCA in 1932, she had spent more and more time at Rockledge. She supervised house repairs, barn construction and renovations, and the several gardens for flowers and vegetables. She planned her stays to coincide with his trips, except for the summers, when she was there most of the time and he came whenever he could and then for his full vacation at the end of each summer.

By 1937 it had become their mutual vision of paradise. One month before retirement he wrote a friend that he had just returned from Rockledge to the "sultry city" and was relieved that in about a month "I will be back with Mrs. Speer in our little home to stay."³ Emma wrote him just at summer's end to say that the past few months had seemed to her nothing but "waiting, waiting" for "our new life together."⁴ One year after retirement he told a close friend, "We are the two happiest young married people in the world, living in a perpetual honeymoon—the last of life for which the first was made—Rabbi Ben Ezra."⁵

The path from New York City to Rockledge, from organizational obligations to a personal agenda, lay through a series of farewells to those groups with which he had worked over the years. There was a seemingly endless number of them, boards and societies he had served in one way or another, but there were three major ones, and each marked an important step away from his life work. The twelfth quadrennial of the Student Volunteer Movement met in Indianapolis during the college Christmas break in 1935. Luminaries filled the platform, since the meeting marked the fiftieth anniversary of the movement. Major speakers included William Temple, archbishop of York; Reinhold Niebuhr of Union Theological Seminary in New York; and John Mackay of Princeton Theological Seminary. Mott, Sailer, Speer, and Wilder were the old-timers; the first three had never missed a quadrennial. Speer and Mott gave paired presentations, as they had often done over the years. They spoke on New Year's Eve, just prior to the watchnight service, Speer on "The Achievements of Yesterday," and Mott on "The Tasks of Tomorrow."

Speer opened his address with a confession that his memory was "very full tonight" and shared the story of the founding years. Things were "simple" then, similar in many ways "to that Movement 1900 years ago which some young men joined by the waters of Galilee."⁶ The SVM had recruited almost thirteen thousand volunteers who had dramatically raised the profile of the missionary movement, not just because of their number, but more as a result of the intensity of their faith. The primary achievement of the SVM was "the creation of persons, of Christlike men and women, who, across this generation, have done their best faithfully to follow in the footsteps of their Master and their Lord." He called a partial roll of them, telling the stories of several and naming those who had been martyred for their faith.

Another of the movement's major achievements was the way it had enhanced unity in and out of the church. First, he claimed, "in the history of the Christian Church there has never been anything surpassing the spirit of unity, of community, of good will, brotherhood, and fellowship that has characterized the whole body of the modern missionary enterprise, whatever the distinctive name was of the group that went out as a part of the great undertaking."[7] Second, he proposed, missionaries had helped create a new and more unified world. Because of them, in large measure, "we are facing a world where we have to live as members of one common household." Across and around the world, missionaries had "thrown the shuttles of a common intellectual life" and "the shuttles of love," and both were drawing the different parts of the world closer and closer together.[8]

When he reached the end of his list of achievements, he arrived at the moment when he typically offered the invitation to service. On this occasion he paused and put the offer in dramatic and quite personal terms, as if the men and women before him were his own sons and daughters. The future was theirs, he told the students, but it would be more difficult than at any time in recent memory. Gathering in Europe, even as they met, were "the forces of darkness and of death and of wrong," the very kind that "slew Jesus upon the cross." The only way to stand before that evil was to have clean hands, pure hearts, and God in their lives. And he pleaded, perhaps prayed: "Please God you may come to it here tonight. Not the pure heart and the clean hand only, but the surrendered will that is surrendered not that we may never have it again but that we may get it back again, clean and strong and resolute and invincible because indwelt with the will of God." As he closed his speech, he reflected, accurately as it turned out, that his words "may be the last word one will ever have a chance to speak in a convention of the Student Volunteer Movement, and I don't know how to put it, as I would like." The message that they needed had been "cut on the stone over Mr. Moody's grave on that little green hill where he lies buried in Northfield, until the resurrection day. I pray God that they may be graved in the heart and life and character and purpose of every one of you: 'He that doeth the will of God abideth forever.' "[9]

His last meeting as a member of the Foreign Missions Conference of North America was the annual meeting, which convened in Asbury Park, New Jersey, in early January 1937. Unlike the SVM quadrennial, where he did not know for certain about his future involvement, he knew absolutely this would be his last conference, because, once retired, he would not be eligible to be a delegate. Emma accompanied him, as she did on a number of his trips, especially those in and around the city. His missionary executive colleagues honored him by making him chairman of the conference, their forty-fourth. His valedictory in the long school of ecumenical foreign missions was "Some of the Changing and Unchanging Things in Foreign Missions."

He spoke from a rare position and with unusual authority. Very few were alive who had been at the initial conference, and he was the only one present to represent them. Many of those who listened to him had joined the missionary secretary fellowship in response to his call. He accentuated the change of leadership by calling a partial roll of missionaries and mission secretaries who had joined the church triumphant, but he did not linger over this list as he had done at the SVM meeting the year before, since those in this audience were very familiar with those persons and their work. Attitudes toward foreign missions had also changed, and he confessed that he had "seen so many issues rise and disappear that I can view with a calm mind many of the eddies and drifts of the present day." He rejoiced at the remarkable changes he had witnessed in the Christian church. The worldwide expansion of Christianity had begun to be truly realized. There were, he pointed out, more Christians in Chosen [Korea] than in the Roman Empire at the end of the first century and more in India than in the entire world at the end of the third century.[10]

Some things had not changed, and most of the ones he enumerated were theological. God had not changed, nor had Jesus Christ. Ever concerned to raise the issue of unity, he claimed that the greater unity of the present simply revealed a greater realization of the "unchanging inheritance . . . of our common catholic faith." "It was a significant thing," he pointed out, "that at the first 'Faith and Order' Conference at Lausanne the only commission's report which could be adopted was the report on the common faith, a report which was embodied in the message of the Jerusalem Missionary Council." The "spiritual principles and issues" of foreign missions had not changed. "Go back and read the resolutions adopted by the early Foreign Missions Conferences," he challenged, and they would discover those principles still applicable. He did not add that he had been instrumental in formulating many of them.

He invited his listeners, the leading missionary executives of the present and future, to do what he had been encouraging his colleagues to do all his life: "We need to do our thinking deeper down in the organic unity of the enterprise." He told his friends, his tone one of warning, a version of what he had told the students a year earlier, that in Europe a threat to the Christian faith was emerging that could challenge it as it had been challenged in its earliest years, and he hoped they would "be spared those deep tragedies through which others of us have had to pass." Finally, the "unchanged and unchanging" summons was the one issued by Jesus

Christ: "If any man will come after me, let him deny himself and take up his cross and follow me."[11]

Final Words to the Board of Foreign Missions and the General Assembly

His most important farewell was the one from the Board of Foreign Missions. It was his final step away from foreign missions work. Ecumenical foreign missions was important, but his Presbyterian work had been his full-time career. His last year with the board was unusually full, the work load increased by another coincidental alignment similar to the one with the SVM: the year of his retirement was also the one hundredth anniversary of the board. He was deeply involved in preparing for the centennial, forming plans for celebrations across the nation and participating in a first for himself and his board: the production of a film. He was the featured speaker in "Our Century of Progress." It was "the first foreign missions motion picture in sound to be made in the country."[12] Centennial meetings began in early 1937 and occupied a great deal of his time. The first of a series of informal retirement events occurred at the February meeting of the board, where he was tried in good fun before "a court called to determine" whether he was "entitled to be honorably retired or not."[13] The main events were at the General Assembly in late May and early June in Columbus, Ohio. He did not formally retire until his seventieth birthday, September 10.

The Foreign Missions centennial held an honored place at the Assembly. The celebration included missionaries representing many of the missions of the church and leaders of a number of the national churches. Margaret Hodge, vice-president of the Board of Foreign Missions, present, she said, "as the representative of the organized women and children of the whole world," introduced Speer. She was selected for the honor because of her own outstanding work, but also as a recognition of his efforts on behalf of women. He built his speech, subsequently published by the board, around the theme "One Century Past, Another to Come."[14]

When he rose to speak, he represented in a unique way the history of the board. He knew from personal acquaintance all but three secretaries. He had joined the work in 1891 to take the place of John C. Lowrie, the first missionary and the second secretary. Their careers encompassed the entire one hundred years of its work. The board had sent some five thousand missionaries abroad and he had known four-fifths of them. He opened his remarks with typical and sincere modesty. The assembly and Miss Hodge were too kind, he said, and although grateful for their praises, he felt "regret that the service has not been better." The thanks they had given him should be shared, and he devoted much of his speech giving thanks for and to those who had made the missionary program what it was. God came first on any of his lists of thanksgiving, and he thanked God for the men and women, missionaries and home secretaries alike, who "had their joy in being lost in the missionary undertaking." Many were not, unfortunately, well remembered, especially those from the earliest days, even though they had sacrificed much and had typically left for service "never expecting to return." The Presbyterian Church had begun its work with two missions in India and now had more than 5,000 churches scattered around the world. The truly great accomplishment of the work, worthy of great thanksgiving, was "the National Churches all over the world, these great living, autonomous, indigenous, National Churches; ecclesiastically independent of us, but our children."[15]

The assembly had a great deal to celebrate in its foreign missions work, and his list offered many obvious reasons for thanksgiving. But he never ended a speech without moving beyond the past to the present and the future, without offering a challenge. He did not fail his listeners this time, many of whom knew him well and waited for the turn of his speech. But they could hardly have been ready for what he said: sharp, jarring thoughts, clear and unequivocal words of warning. The efforts of the past were preparations for the present, and his listeners needed to realize that the world, with a focus on Europe, was demonstrating "on every side the reality of that titanic struggle which is going on in human life and history between darkness and light." There was a tragedy in the making, a challenge to God best described in biblical terms as "against the principalities, against the powers, against the world rulers of this darkness." These were echoes of similar thoughts spoken in softer words to the students and missionary executives. "Is there one man here in this meeting," Speer challenged, "who has not in his own experience come to grips with this tragedy, convincing him that life and history are no easy unfolding of latent benignant possibilities in human nature?" "We are not," he concluded, "moving out smoothly into any experience of a Golden Age today."[16]

If not an age of gold, at least an age with some new resources, adequate, he felt certain, to meet the difficulties that lay ahead. Women were the "new force" that had been released in the world in the past twenty years. Men may think they "represent the dynamic of human progress," but they do not, for behind them "is the great force that is the real compelling influence in the world—the mothers, the wives, the sisters, who shape the generations as they come and pass. . . . One of the greatest veils that has ever been across human society has been rent in our time, the veil that has hung over the face, and across the force of womanhood. And the sooner we awake, the sooner we realize that this colossal energy is to be linked to the progress of the Gospel as it was that morning when women first saw the Resurrection, and bore first witness to it, the sooner will the new century tell a different story from the past."

Another resource, not new but renewed, was democracy. Those who feared for the future of democracy because of the "iron hand" in Europe needed to think globally, to recognize the rising force of democracy in India and China. "We are not" he affirmed, "at the end of the day that our Lord made possible when He came, common Man among men, and founded His Church on the foundation stones of the Apostles and prophets and martyrs—a brotherhood of free common men." The missionary enterprise had a future, he exclaimed. Paul had seen it, even when chained in a prison long ago. The present age has its darkness too, but also "the Voice of One Who walked with our fathers the bright road of the 100 years that are gone, and Who is calling us today to walk with Him the more glorious road of the 100 years that lie ahead."[17]

The memory of the applause of the throng at the assembly lingered long after he returned home, sustained by a massive volume of letters of thanks and farewell. He had a copy of the most recent issue of the *Presbyterian Banner*, full of tributes to him and his work.[18] And he had an editorial from his hometown newspaper, the *Times*, which described him as "A Dominant Leader." The editor, writing with a degree of familiarity, said, "But it is the hope of all who know him that he will live on, though unofficially, ministering to a world that needs more than ever his counsel and his pervading influence. He has enriched humanity by what he is, by what he has said (and how he has said it) and by what he has done in pursuing and achieving the chief end of man."[19]

Speere set about immediately to make final preparations for the move to Rockledge. They had surrendered their lease at Gramercy Park, effective September 30. He spent the summer packing carton after carton of files and books, from home and office. Every trip north was a partial move against the September deadlines. He gradually completed his office tasks and passed his voluminous board correspondence to his successor. At one point in the spring he realized that they would be leaving the city for good, after many years of life and work there; but if he had any regrets, he kept them to himself.[20]

Sometime during the summer he made the momentous decision to leave foreign missions work. Of course, he continued to speak about it and support it, and on occasion to write an article about it. But in the months leading to his retirement he had been formally invited to continue in the field. The first offer came from his own board, which wanted him to accept the Joseph Cook Lectureship, a speaking tour to the major cities of Asia, explaining and defending the Christian faith. Among the other offers was appointment to the chair of missions at San Francisco Theological Seminary. He accepted neither offer, nor any others related to foreign missions.

Rockledge and Iona

He joined Emma at Rockledge in September, and they began what became the rest of their life together. They created a small card with a picture of their house on the front and the following message inside: "This is where we live, winter and summer. The latchstring is always out to you, and we send you our warmest greetings."[21] The house was gracious, with space for a study and guest rooms for family and friends. Some of the children and grandchildren lived there for periods, Billy during summers in college, Holly and the girls for a time, Margaret home on furloughs, and Pat and her daughters during the early stages of World War II. Emma had fallen in love with it the first moment she saw it; he quickly came to love it too, and often described it as "heavenly" and as "a glorious place for tramping around."[22] He had used the study as his work room away from the city for years, but as he contemplated retirement, he realized he would need more space.

Iona solved their space problem. It was really a barn they had constructed in 1935. They located it some distance from the house, in sight but partially hidden by trees. The first floor was a garage. The second floor included a very large room, with some windows but with extensive walls lined with shelves for books and files. As it neared completion, Emma wrote that the "room is beautiful . . . and when you come you can just get your books and papers in order, so that the room will have a missionary atmosphere for your confreres." Emma chose the name, informing him that "Iona is both a place and a state of mind."[23] It was a wise and telling choice.

The real Iona is a small and beautiful island on the west coast of Scotland, still accessible only by sea. Saint Columba arrived in the year

563, a missionary from Ireland, and built a monastery. The one that survives was built by the Benedictines in the thirteenth century. The nearby graveyard contains the resting place of Macbeth and many other kings and three remarkable tall stone crosses. Speer's Iona, in its relative isolation, became his retreat, a place as totally apart as he could reasonably make it. Pat said when her father was at Iona, he was "unreachable."[24] It matched, as Emma well knew, his monastic instincts, spartan in appointments and with opportunities for silence to match his need. He began working in Iona in the summer of 1936, finishing *The Meaning of Christ to Me* and beginning *George Bowen of Bombay*. He found the new space an "endless comfort," "a quiet place where the books are all easily arranged. One can work all day long undisturbed."[25] By the time he reached retirement, he on occasion referred to his Iona as "a sacred place."[26]

Retirement brought many changes. He and Emma spent much more time together than at any other period of their lives. They spent some of it on joint house or garden projects or reading. They read aloud to one another, and he typically read to her. They took one overseas trip, in 1939 to visit Pat and her family in England. This trip thrilled Emma, for herself, but more for him: "The whole experience will be to him like a little foretaste of heaven. This is the first journey out of the thousands of miles he has traveled, without definite and very heavy responsibilities."[27] He continued to be away a great deal on a variety of speaking engagements. There was a significant number of them, more than two hundred a year from 1939 to 1943, a greater number than in either of his last two years of work. Despite the number, or perhaps because of them, he scheduled carefully to confine them to the spring and fall months and tried to be home from May through September and in the deep winter. This created a rhythm to the year that he sustained throughout retirement.[28] He told his classmates on the occasion of their fiftieth reunion in 1939: "Mrs. Speer and I are busier and happier than we ever were and have plans of work and play for many years to come."[29]

A dramatic consequence of retirement was loss of the normal amenities of an office, including a secretary and a stenographer. He never learned to type. His official correspondence, of course, came to an abrupt halt. That included, unfortunately, his bimonthly letters to Margaret, a virtual diary for more than a dozen years. Evidence suggests that he and Emma began to use the telephone to keep in contact. He continued to get a substantial volume of mail, from organizations and individuals. Emma described him as swimming "hard against the current of correspondence."[30] He was loathe to spend time writing, and his letters became brief compared with those of his working years. Correspondents were likely grateful for the brevity, because his handwriting became increasingly tiny and difficult to decipher. Even close friends had problems, frequently replying to his notes with the hope that they had understood what he had written.[31] When friends inquired about his activities, he replied with some version of the following, which he wrote to Mudge in 1940: "We are still settled happily in our country home. . . . I can commend gardening, book binding and carpentry as good occupations."[32] He did not recommend correspondence.

The first task he faced when he finally settled in at Iona was to organize his books and papers. The books were relatively easy, once unpacked and arranged by topic. He had been moving them for at least two years and had a substantial portion of them in place by 1936. It was still a major effort, because he was a bibliophile and his library—and it was in truth a library of over 10,000 volumes—represented a lifetime of collecting. The papers were another matter. Emma reported that he had them "in perfect order" by the fall of 1939.[33] He may have finished the project before that, but it could well have taken him that long, given his active speaking and writing schedule and the size of the task. He sorted the printed materials by organization and the correspondence by topic or author.

He had collected a large number of pamphlets over the years, and he gathered them by organization if published by one group and by topic if published by different groups. He purchased a small binding machine, and he stitched the pamphlets together into booklets. He used the same binding process for letters where there was a substantial number on one topic or relating to one occasion, like his retirement. He used scrapbooks to organize his very large file of journal articles, newspaper clippings, and the small notices that had appeared in a wide variety of publications. The scrapbooks numbered sixteen and contained more than 1,240 articles and a countless number of smaller items. He had forty-six years of accumulated material from his board service, plus all the gathered papers from other groups, and the papers of his family, including those of his childhood and his father. He retained the papers of some of the subjects of his biographies, and he organized those materials too.

The immense effort expended on this project and the carefully planned filing system he devised demand a definite purpose, an intended use. He never wasted time and surely had a reason for this task, but whatever it was has not been discovered. The files rested on his shelves in Iona for eight years, ready to become the basis of a historical study, or of a thematic essay on missions or ecumenism, or of an autobiography, but he never used

them. One possible explanation was his compulsion to collect and organize things. As a good administrator he rarely picked up the same piece of
paper twice, but as a collector he saved virtually every piece of paper he
touched, and then some. With time on his hands in retirement, he organized what he had collected. This is not a very helpful explanation, since
he did not really have time on his hands.

A more probable explanation can be traced to his sense of history. The
system he created was primarily chronological, and the cross filing he did
with letters and reports would be received as a gracious invitation by
almost any historian. He wrote many histories, and although he did not
want to write one involving his own life, he put the documents he had in
order for the future. This reason makes sense but fails to give appropriate
weight to one important element; the materials he created had a heavy
autobiographical content. By the end of his career, he had created a long
and consistent record of modesty. He never publicly claimed credit for any
particular achievement and never accepted acclaim without passing credit
on to others. He expressed no interest in writing an autobiography,
although he could easily have written one, and he left a directive for his
wife and family that they authorize no biography once he was gone.[34] He
believed he had good reasons for this, concerned that readers would think
he was making too much of his role and not enough of Jesus Christ or of
others who worked with him. But the best explanation for the vast expenditure of time putting together his files is that he was preparing them to
be used to tell his story.

Family and friends knew he was at work on his papers, and several
former colleagues wrote asking what he intended to do with them or inviting him to donate them to one place or another. Although he never shared
his intentions concerning their use, he did establish the order of distribution in a letter to Mudge in December 1938. "Marnie and Billy" were to
have first choice, and "then the Board's Foreign Missions Library, then the
Historical Department of the Genl. Assembly, then the Foreign Missions
Research Library, then Princeton Theological Sem. Library."[35] When in
the 1950s Emma and the family decided to find a final location for these
materials, they did not follow his plans very closely. "Marnie and Billy"
chose first and took what they wanted, including the most personal family papers and the brief family histories their father had written. After this
initial selection, the family adopted its own scheme. It shared many of his
books with missionary libraries in Europe that had suffered serious damage in the war. As for the main materials, the very extensive pamphlet collection went to the Missionary Research Library (the Foreign Missions

Research Library) at Union Seminary in New York, and the remaining books and all the papers ended up at Princeton Seminary.

The work on his collected things was a joyous duty, part of setting up Iona as a proper place to work. But it was only preparation for his ministry in retirement. He had projected, as early as 1926, that he had "enough work in mind to last, I imagine, 20 or 30 years."[36] He had never specified what he intended to do during those years, other than occasional references to finishing his memoir on Bowen. Now, settled in Iona, he continued to work without a specific plan. Instead, he accepted what came to him, what seemed needed to be done. It was a little strange for the consummate administrator, driven for almost half a century by the needs of several different organizations, to sit back and be led. He believed God would unfold his plan, call him to his tasks.

He continued to be associated with a number of organizations, as many as thirty of them, some remnants of his years as missionary secretary. They included the board of the American Colleges in Teheran, the Joint Committee on United Missions in Mesopotamia, the trustees of the Church Peace Union, the board of the American Bible Society, the Joint Committee on Christian Education in India, and the trustees of Near East Relief. He went to meetings when he could, but there is no indication that he spent significant time on any of these groups. He attended two general assemblies, the one in Philadelphia in 1938 and the one in Milwaukee in 1942, and spoke at both. He made a presentation at the New Missionary Conference sponsored by his board in 1941. One of his favorite projects, the *Missionary Review of the World*, claimed some of his time. It had been a very important journal in his early years, especially supportive of the SVM. Edited by Arthur Pierson, and by his son Delavan after 1911, it had floundered in 1916. Speer had come to the rescue, raised funds, and chaired its board of directors. By the fall of 1939 it had run out of funds, and after an effort to save it again, he had to notify stockholders and readers that it would fold.[37]

World War II

Much of the time he gave these organizations and some new ones turned on their involvement in the issue that dominated all of American life in his retirement years: war. He was keenly aware of the growth of national socialism in Germany in the 1930s and became convinced very early in its development that it posed a major threat to Christianity. His views on

Germany were a distinct feature of his parting thoughts to all of the missionary organizations he served. When war erupted in Europe in August
1939, it came directly to their household in the form of their English
grandchildren, who arrived to escape German bombs. He attended a
meeting of the Church Peace Union in 1939 and agreed to speak at their
goodwill service later in the year. He also assisted the union in 1941 in the
preparation of a "study course on basic issues confronting the churches in
this crisis of international affairs."[38]

He committed time to at least one project of the American Bible
Society when he agreed to be chairman of the National Sponsors
Committee for the Emergency Fund Campaign in 1940. He wrote a
letter soliciting funds that said in part, "During the critical days through
which our world is now passing there must be no blackout of the Bible
anywhere. It is the one Book that brings an eternally valid message of
comfort, hope, and both national and personal guidance. But it cannot
bring its message unless it is in men's hands." This was a necessary appeal
because the other major Bible societies were in war-ravaged lands, and
the American Bible Society was "the *only one* unfettered by the bonds
of war."[39] Speer solicited Rockefeller on this occasion but did not get a
contribution.[40]

He joined several new groups, many organized to maintain the peace,
like the American Committee for Non-Participation in Japanese
Aggression. He always considered himself a peacemaker, but as Nazi
aggression increased, he moved to the interventionist position. He was a
member of the sponsoring committee of *Christianity and Crisis* in the
spring of 1941. He signed a statement issued by that journal in the fall of
1941 that read in part, "The undersigned heartily welcome the Roosevelt-
Churchill declaration and find in it a long desired statement of peace aims
by the responsible leaders of the democratic world. It calls for a new order-
ing of national and international relationships which is, unlike the plans
for Hitler's 'new order,' congenial to the Christian conscience and compatible with Christian ideals. We agree that the destruction of Nazi
tyranny is a prerequisite to any just and durable peace. But we are also
convinced that the defeat of Nazism will not of itself create a new world.
Peace is a positive achievement and rests upon a harmony of cooperating
wills."[41] After war came to America, he became part of a Committee for
the Defense of our Defenders, with a purpose to provide positive envi-
ronments in and near the military training camps.

The ministry he had performed in World War I had been a major
source of his reputation as a leader of the churches. No similar opportunity

for wartime ministry came his way during World War II, and there is every reason to believe that he would have rejected it if it had. His role was that of elder, lending his name and influence. His position on war remained what it had been in World War I. He had not found it easy to get listeners to really hear what he was saying then, and he continued to have that difficulty. A report in the *Presbyterian* in the winter of 1940 quoted him as saying that "Christianity must fight for the defeat of the totalitarian states."[42] He wrote one correspondent, who questioned his views on the basis of this report, that he had been misquoted. What he believed about Christianity and war was that: "the Christian Church . . . never as a Church has been called to go to war. . . . While believing, however, that Christianity and the Church are not to wage war I am not and never have been a pacifist. I believe that resistance to wrong may be a duty of government and that this may involve the use of military force. And I believe that when this is the case as at present in the case of Chinese resistance to Japan and British resistance to Nazism, the individual citizens Christian faith does not debar him from doing his civil duty but makes him all the more determined in it."[43]

He participated in a "Japan War Meeting" shortly after Pearl Harbor. That attack had a double edge to it for his family, since it not only brought the United States to the war, but also brought the war to Margaret in China. She was initially forced to live with other missionaries in one compound and then moved to an internment camp in the spring of 1943. He shared in a symposium of eleven former moderators of the Presbyterian Church in the pages of the *Presbyterian Tribune* in January 1942 on the theme "The Duty of the Church in the Present Crisis." His list of duties was similar to the collective list he had helped prepare during World War I.[44]

1. To proclaim the law of righteousness and justice as binding on nations as well as individuals.
2. To discountenance all compromise with evil and all appeasement of wrong doers.
3. To discourage all vain boasting and foolish predictions.
4. To continue to proclaim human unity and to denounce all denial of it, by false nationalism and racialism.
5. To bind our own people together in unity and concord, to condemn all selfish exploitation in the interest of any class or group, to continue to call for the substitution of cooperation for conflict in industry and all of life.
6. To foster indomitable resolution in the nation to find an end to the evil forces which are destroying peace and brotherhood and to secure and guarantee a just and enduring settlement of the present issue for all mankind.

7. To keep the spirit of our people clean and true, free of all vindictiveness and hate except against falsehood and cruelty.
8. To lead the nation to put its trust in God, to seek to know and to do right as His will, and to preach Christ faithfully as first the King of Righteousness and after that King of Peace.

Race, he believed, was one of the important issues of the war. Racial justice had always been one of his concerns, and he restated his views in the context of the special racial issues raised by this war. The Japanese, he noted, matched Hitler's claims of racial superiority. "Authoritative spokesmen assert," he said, "the unique and decisive origin and right of the present dynasty, the superiority of the Japanese race and its mission to dominate the Far East. And in accordance with such a doctrine it seeks to subjugate China as it has already subjugated Chosen." Sad as Japan's racial views were, he noted that the idea of racial superiority continued to survive in the United States. Against those racial views, wherever they existed, he argued, "Christianity affirms the truth of human unity." "The Christian conception," he affirmed, "is the vision of a world of peace, a world of good will and brotherhood, where each race serves all and all races serve each."[45]

He published *When Christianity Was New* in 1939, and declared in a chapter on the race problem in the early church, "Of all the characteristics of primitive Christianity which we need to recover today, none is more essential and more vitally indispensable than its doctrine of race. The nationalistic and racial ideologies of today deny the fundamental Christian postulates. They give us a world of strife and division and hate. Primitive Christianity proclaims a world of unity and brotherhood and love."[46] He chose the unity of humanity as the central theme of what turned out to be his last major public address, the baccalaureate sermon at the Hill School in the summer of 1947. The title was his message: "Not Against One Another But Together." He told the young men seated before him, "There will be no peace in a world which clings to the notion of racial struggle and rejects the law of love and unity."[47]

Ministerial Education

War and race were important issues, but they did not, relatively speaking, occupy much of his time. Rather, his ministry in retirement focused in two areas. The first of these was ministerial education. In shedding his organizational commitments, he retained a major one. He continued to serve as an officer of the board of trustees of Princeton Theological Seminary. Ministerial education had been one of his interests from the start of his career. He had visited theological seminaries in search of missionary candidates beginning with his very first days as a recruiter. He had lived through the turmoil at Princeton Seminary in the 1920s as a member of the board and then accepted appointment to become a member of the reorganized board. Closely associated with President Stevenson and Professor Erdman, the key survivors of the seminary dispute, he emerged as one of the leaders of the new board. He was vice-president in 1935 and deeply involved in board discussions about the next president of the seminary, helping to identify two possible candidates.[48] One of them was John Mackay, who became the president. He spoke at Mackay's installation in the Princeton Chapel on February 2, 1937, giving the "charge in behalf of the Trustees."[49] He celebrated the occasion, for he had helped inspire Mackay at the time of the Duff Lectures and more recently had drawn him to the Board of Foreign Missions as one of its secretaries. It was a "happy day," he said, but the assembled friends of the seminary should not forget those times when it had "been tried as by fire, and no doubt such times will come again." While those fires had helped "try and refine" it, he reminded his listeners that no one could do anything to them "if our walls are built on the foundations of the apostles and prophets, Jesus Christ Himself being the chief corner-stone."[50]

Someone, likely Mackay, not only persuaded him to remain on the seminary board, but also prevailed on him to become its president in 1937.[51] He served in that capacity until his death ten years later. It was not a position he sought nor particularly wanted to keep. The chairman of the nominating committee wrote him in 1939 and told him that he had shared his letter, without question a request to step down, with members of the committee. They were aware, he said, that things were going quite well at the seminary. However, that was not a sufficient reason to leave the presidency, because "there are some matters which have caused discussion by those who are always seeking to find some reason to question the conduct of the affairs at Princeton, and we believe that any changes in the leadership of our Board at this time would be a mistake."[52] The service he performed consumed some time and thought but was not onerous. The seminary was in excellent hands. The board reviewed faculty appointments and discussed a variety of issues as they rose. He took special interest in plans for a new library. The official board minutes were limited to formal actions and contain no record of the opinions of individual board members.

His involvement in Princeton Seminary was predictable, given his long tenure on its board and his sense of duty. The Faith and Life Seminars were something new. They were two-day meetings with a focus on theology and ministry, at first for clergy only, and offered some ministerial education after seminary. Mackay accurately described them as "the precursors of 'continuing education.'"[53] Hugh T. Kerr, president of the Board of Christian Education, generated the idea for them. They began as seminars on modern theology held at the noon hour at General Assembly. Interest in those seminars dwindled over the years, but the idea lived on and emerged under the leadership of the Rev. George Irving. His plan was to create longer and more intensive seminars, apart from the General Assembly, held specifically for the purpose of providing "for Presbyterian pastors those opportunities for fellowship in the understanding and living of the whole Christian gospel, inseparably personal and social, which the times demand."[54] His idea was for small groups of clergy to gather for serious theological discussion, meditation, and prayer at a time and place apart from their ministry settings. Each seminar would be led by a theologian and a minister. Church administration and program matters were not on his agenda. The Board of Christian Education named this plan the Faith and Life Seminars, invited Irving to join its staff, and directed him to launch the seminars in 1937.

The seminars attracted Speer's attention as a creative and valuable ministry. He was without portfolio, free to choose where he spent his time and energy, and he decided to join the seminars. It was an important decision and led to his most extensive ministry in his retirement years. The seminars were a complement to his seminary work, and together they formed a unique commitment to ministerial education. Irving had begun slowly, completing only six seminars his first year and eleven his second. When Speer joined him in 1939, the program was still in its infancy. There is no clear indication of the way he joined this program. He may have been invited by Irving, or he may have simply volunteered. Shortly after they began to work together, Irving wrote him, revealing their relationship and his hopes for the seminars: "It was an unceasing joy being with you on the trip in Ohio. At every point your service was greatly appreciated. Since we met in 1900 at Northfield, when I was still a student at McGill, I have heard you under many circumstances but never more effectively and with greater blessing to the group. I feel that God has something very definite for us in these Pastor Seminars and am praying that we may have clear leading as to how to develop them more effectively."[55]

The two men worked together for four years. They were tremendously successful as a team. Irving had held an average of eight Seminars the first two years; the program averaged twenty-two in their years together. Although Speer was not at every seminar, his enthusiasm helped propel the program forward. He was officially neither theologian nor minister, but he was in some senses both, and he was as well known as anyone in his church. He kept a small notebook of his seminar activities, which indicates that he sometimes preached, sometimes lectured, sometimes led a Bible study, and in general offered words of encouragement and inspiration.

Letters poured in from participants, almost uniformly thankful and full of praise for the spiritual quality of the gatherings. They also revealed Speer's role, as father in the faith, a singular source of inspiration. A minister from Charlotte, North Carolina, said it was good to have Speer present: "This veteran of the Cross carried us to great heights." A minister from Lytton, Iowa, wrote, "It was a tremendous joy to hear Dr. Robert E. Speer. One young in the ministry gains for himself a picture of the stability of the church. Seeing him and hearing him brought to me a sensation which comes to one who looks up from the lowlands upon some majestic mountain peak which has stood the testings of eternity. Thank God for such a man." The dean at Dubuque University testified, "It has been a long time since I have seen men moved as deeply as these men were following the closing address of Dr. Speer. He really got into their hearts in a marvelous way and led many of them to make some resolutions for the days that are before them." From Montana came the following confession, shared with both Speer and Irving: "I have been raised in a so-called Fundamental circle and taught that men of your group are modernists. Never have I attended a Fundamental conference where the power of the Spirit was more manifest. I have never been more deeply moved in my life. It was borne in the most convincing way that men really filled with the Spirit are ecumenical in the strict sense of the word, they belong to the Church as a whole. It was a great revelation to me."[56]

Suddenly, in the early summer of 1943, Irving became ill and died. Speer had just told a friend that the seminars had "been one of the best things in the life of our Church."[57] He was shocked and deeply saddened. He and Irving had given fifty Seminars together in twenty-three states and had been constant companions during the months they worked together. They had begun as father in the faith and son, and had become brothers. He told those who attended the memorial service, "We traveled together, and no brothers could have been closer or dearer. There was never a shadow on our friendship, nor a note of discord in our work together."[58] He described Irving's death as one of his "gravest sorrows."[59] After the memorial service a member of the Board of Christian Education wrote advising him that the board wished to continue the seminars and asked him if he was willing to keep the schedule Irving had planned.[60] He participated in the seminars that fall but admitted, "I missed and miss him sorely. He was a close spirit and friend, with a great many of D. L. Moody's qualities."[61]

He was still giving seminars in 1946, working his way back and forth across the country. He introduced at least one major innovation, or assented to it, when the wives of ministers participated in the seminar at Winona Lake in Indiana. Irving had wanted to keep the meetings for men only, but Speer told Emma, "I think we ought to count the wives in. I wish mine was here that they might all see what the right ideal and standard is."[62] Emma was never ready to see him leave Rockledge on the lengthy seminar trips, but she reluctantly let him go. The "Ministers' Seminars" were, she believed, in some ways "the most fruitful ministry of his life."[63] Others agreed with that assessment. The Rev. Peter Emmons, a member of the seminary board, and Speer's successor as president, said: "I have heard repeated testimony that his ministry of the Word and spiritual leadership have meant even more to the rank and file in the Churches during these past few years, since he has been released from his administrative responsibilities, than ever before. What a glorious life he has lived and what *hosts* of individuals young and old of all races and classes have come to know God better through knowing him."[64]

Spiritual Leadership

Emmons lifted up the theme of "spiritual leadership" as one of Speer's special gifts. This became his second ministry in retirement. Associates had remarked about it from the very beginning of his career, younger partners like Mott and mentors like Trumbull. It had been a defining characteristic then, a gift for such a young man. As he grew older, to the age when those mature in the faith are more typically defined by such a gift, his seemed to increase in intensity. He recognized the gift and accepted it but never became introspective about it. He was inclined to periods of silence, to thinking things out, praying about them, but his retreats were always relatively brief, not those of the monk or mystic. The quiet days with his two prayer groups suited him and provided him spiritual refreshment, but they were annual events.

Spiritual leadership was for him religious experience. It was the ability to communicate to others in such a way that they could "feel" the experience, be moved by God, and believe it was God and not some emotion that moved them. He rarely tried to explain it. One exception was the following reflection: "With reference to the 'Quiet Hour,' I think there is always a risk of our losing sight of the fact that solitude is not so much a matter of time and place, as of spirit; and that a man can have a quiet season walking up Broadway when it is crowded with people, just as truly as if he were out in the Sahara Desert at midnight. Perhaps he could be more quiet in the former than in the latter situation. I do believe in the hidden life, the life that knows so familiarly the ways of access to the secret of His presence, that such times and places being taken for granted, the whole day can well be made a secret fellowship with the ever-present, inseparable Lord."[65]

The way his peers, and elders when he was younger, responded to the depth of his spiritual leadership was to invite him to pray when occasions called for it, to select him to give the opening and closing addresses at their meetings, and to make certain he issued the calls or invitations, as circumstances arose. He did these things year in and year out at all kinds of meetings, and virtually always with telling affect. It became one of his roles at the Faith and Life Seminars. Peers thanked him and individuals wrote him to share their religious experiences and changed lives.

Prayer was a particularly important part of Speer's life. He had quiet times at the beginning and close of each day. The Board of Foreign Missions set aside a time of prayer each day, frequently led by him. He wrote about prayer often and throughout his life, frequently in separate articles and as parts of books. His SVM pamphlet *Prayer and Missions* remained in use thirty years after it first appeared in 1893. It had the longest usage of the many pamphlets the SVM published.[66] His Bible studies of Jesus and Paul included chapters on prayer, and so did *The Principles of Jesus*, published in 1902 and *Some Living Issues*, published in 1930. He had signed *A Call to Prayer*, issued by the General War-Time Commission in the fall of 1917. In 1939 he prepared a small pamphlet, issued by the Department of Evangelism of the Federal Council of Churches, for the nationwide Week of Prayer for the Churches, January 8–14, 1940. In contained Bible readings and prayer topics for each day of the week.[67] His last book, *Jesus and Our Human Problems*, published in 1946, included the chapter "The Good News of the Son of God about Prayer."

From the earliest days of his conversion he had collected prayers of others and written many of his own. He also collected poems that spoke to his spirit. He had put part of his collection together in a little book that he had prepared for his personal use. Sometime in the early years of his retirement, the Westminster Press "learned of it and wanted to make it available for the help of other common Christian folk—lay people, men and women, in our Churches—in the pressure of our daily life and work." The book, *Five Minutes A Day*, appeared in 1943. He told readers that it included Bible readings, a poem, and a prayer for each day, but no meditation. They could reflect on the readings and prayers as they wished. It was a guide for spiritual nourishment. The book contained no calendar; instead, each day had a title, a topic, or a theme. Readers could create any number of calendars, by beginning at the first page and proceeding to the last, or by putting together themes as they fit their daily or weekly spiritual moods. He explained, "It is a simple, homely affair for busy people who can find, because they must, a little time at the beginning or ending of the day for a bit of quiet thought and prayer."[68]

Five Minutes quickly became one of his most popular books. The size of the sales, more than 35,000 copies in the first two months, startled him, and so did the many thoughtful letters he received. It was one of his most personal books, but it had few obvious autobiographical notes. Only the people who knew him best could pick out the favorite Bible passages from the large number he suggested reading. Only such persons could see him in the multitude of poems and hymns he chose. The only obvious personal part was the prayers. He signed nineteen of them and Emma believed that he wrote the thirty-two that were unsigned.[69] That would account for roughly one-seventh of the prayers in the book. The others were chosen from traditional sources, like *The Book of Common Prayer*, and from more contemporary collections, like John Baillie's *A Diary of Private Prayer*. He also used the prayers of the fathers and saints of the church, including Chrysostom, Anselm, and Francis of Assisi. Two of his favorite contemporary prayer writers were William Adams Brown and Walter Rauschenbusch.

By the time this devotional book appeared, he had very definite views about prayer. He had summed them up in an article in 1936, "Our Need to Pray." Simply put, he said, Christians are to pray because "Jesus prayed, and he was far busier that we can ever be." Christians need in their lives "what prayer did in Jesus' life. It kept his vision clear to duty, and to the moral distinctions which so often become blurred to religious leaders. It nourished his strength to bear and to achieve. It was the spring and glory in his transfiguration."[70] Speer had concluded quite early in his ministry that "prayer should be one of two things. Either it should be just such careful, reverent prayer as one finds in the Prayer Book, or it should be the genuine, reverent loving outpouring of heart and mind toward God."[71] He followed his guidelines and chose for his book prayers of each kind. His own and those of his contemporaries fell into the second category.

He typically began his prayers "O Lord Jesus Christ" or "O God, our Father." In a prayer on the theme "Christ at Home with Us," he prayed, "We hear Thee gladly and we have room for Thee in our homes and in our hearts. Thou needest not now to wander homeless. There is warm and waiting room in our hearts for Thee. Be pleased to enter, Lord." He wrote *Five Minutes* in the midst of World War II and prayed, "O God . . . who hath made of one blood all the nations and hath appointed unto them the bounds of their habitation, forgive us that we have so shamefully marred our human unity and have made of the earth which Thou didst create a field of conflict and war. . . . do Thou intervene and do through us and for us what we have been found unable to do for ourselves. Make peace, O God, who madest man, make peace."[72] Emma told their children that the following prayer in the book was a perfect expression of their father's faith:[73]

> O God our Father, we who are children of time come to Thee who art above time. For us the days that are past are past beyond recall and what we have written on life's page we may not erase. But our past is still present to Thee and Thou canst undo what is beyond our power to change. Thou canst restore the wasted years. And we bring them to Thee—all the time past of our lives. Take it into Thy moulding hands. What was amiss, do Thou amend. What was faulty do Thou fulfill. We bless Thee for forgiveness but we ask for more, even that Thou shouldst annul the evil that we have done and accomplish the good in which we failed. We thank Thee that Thou art ever open to our cry, that none can come to Thee too late, that the door of the Father's house is never closed to any child who would come home. Father, we come bringing our marred lives for Thy remaking, our stained hands for Thy cleansing, our tired feet for Thy rest, our wearied hearts for Thy peace.

In the fall of 1946 he prepared a devotional guide, *The Fellowship of the Spirit*, at the suggestion of the Department of Evangelism of the Federal Council. It was for use from Easter to Pentecost 1947. This guide was more directive than those he had prepared in the past. Each day had a topic, a meditation, and a very short prayer. The topics were all about the Holy Spirit, and the obvious purpose of the guide was to encourage people to think about the Spirit. The topics included such things as "The Love of the Spirit," "The Mind of the Spirit," and "The Marks of the Spirit."[74]

His ministries went well. They were sustained by his peaceful home life. He enjoyed having the grandchildren around, and he retreated to Iona when he wanted to work. He typically spent his mornings there. When he was away, he and Emma continued the correspondence they had maintained throughout his working career. Their letters became somewhat more personal than those in the earlier days. His contained recollections and memories of events of the past, often evoked when he visited a place they had been together. Traveling through Harrisburg, he "crossed the bridge over the river which replaced the old wooden bridge of dearest memory to you and me."[75] She followed his work closely, offering supportive comments, "Early this morning I read II Timothy through, to be near you in your lecture at eight."[76] They rejoiced when Margaret returned safely from internment in China in early December 1943. He expressed surprise in 1946 that people were still asking him to sign copies of *Five Minutes*. The years passed as quietly as any could in the midst of a world war, but with no public controversy. He was not, of course, in any formal administrative position, and so he was unlikely to face anything like what he had faced in World War I or during the dispute over missions in the years after 1932. However, he remained a public figure and had taken a highly visible position on the war. Emma had told him, some years before the war actually broke out, that if he were in Germany, he would be "in prison."[77]

The only interruption to their life came in the fall of 1944, when he became seriously ill and spent some weeks in a New York City hospital. Emma stayed with the Coffins. He was back at work the following spring, but the time off had forced him to curtail his speaking engagements, from the typical two hundred a year to a little more than a hundred. This was only his second serious illness; the first had been typhoid fever that he had caught in Persia. He and Emma had both contracted malaria on their world trip.

Family and friends constantly expressed amazement at his good health, given his work schedule. He traveled extensively in all kinds of weather and, more often than not, slept on trains to and from appointments. His Huntingdon family, early in his career, advised him to take more time off. Emma knew him better and simply encouraged him to monitor his health. He did that on a regular basis by visits to Clifton Springs in western New York, a sanitarium and spa used by the Board of Foreign Missions for its missionaries and other personnel. She also knew that she could not stop him, especially, as she said on a number of occasions, if he thought of any particular trip as a duty. She described him to their children in many ways, but the one that most fit her vision of him and was closest to reality was "energetic atom."[78]

Honors and Tributes

Honors came his way in retirement. He had tried to avoid them all his life. He had a philosophy about them, formed early in his career and most clearly stated in his book *Seeking the Mind of Christ*. He described the book as "some devotional papers on different aspects of the mind of Christ." Jesus, he told his readers, was "meek and lowly" and did not seek praise. Why then, he asked, should his followers? He argued, "To become subjects of praise is to run the risk of obscuring Christ, of usurping glory which belongs to Him. For what good is there in us or our doings which is not from Him and to His praise?" The Christian, far from seeking praise, should "cultivate instead a positive distaste for it."[79] Despite his philosophy, the honors came, the first in 1938 when the Board of Foreign Missions named him secretary emeritus. Princeton University followed with a doctor of letters degree in 1939, the fiftieth anniversary of his graduation. It was the eighth and last of his honorary degrees and, in the mind of some, very belated. A close friend wrote, "The honor at the hands of Princeton, too long deferred, is most richly deserved. To those who know, Princeton has honored itself."[80] In 1941 the Ulster-Irish Society of New York honored him as one of its own with its Medal for Notable Service. He matched the typical hyperbole of such an occasion with some untypical and good-humored hyperbole of his own, claiming he was 125 percent Scotch-Irish: 50 percent on his father's side, 50 percent on his mother's side, and 25 percent from his wife.[81]

In addition to these honors from organizations, he received many letters of thanks, encouragement, and support. The personal tributes were not always attached to a particular occasion, although many of them were from persons who had taken part in the Faith and Life Seminars. The exception to this was the scheme developed by Carlyle Adams, editor of the *Presbyterian Tribune*, in the fall of 1947 for the double celebration of Speer's eightieth birthday and the twentieth anniversary of his election as moderator. Adams created this tribute at the suggestion of a former member of the Board of Foreign Missions who, in a world tour of Presbyterian missions, had asked the missionaries at many different places how they had made their career decisions. Time after time, she reported, they said, "When I was a student I heard an address by Robert E. Speer."[82]

Adams, impressed that he had been elected moderator as a layperson, asked the Presbyterian Churchmen's League to solicit tributes, and devoted a part of the September issue of his journal to Speer. In an editorial Adams said, "Thousands can still hear the echo of his remarkable voice as it rang out in college halls many years ago, calling upon Christian youth to follow the example of St. Francis of Assisi and to walk courageously in the footsteps of the Master. There always has been a compelling urgency about his message. One either decided to follow it wholeheartedly, or else one spent some sleepless nights resisting his appeal."[83]

The tributes included poems and prose, brief and somewhat longer testimonies, all with the same theme: Speer had helped make God real in their lives. Most of the letters were from persons who had been students before World War I. They had heard him at Northfield, or Yale, or Lake Geneva, or Occidental College, or at a General Assembly, or Princeton, or at a SVM quadrennial, or at a variety of other places. Some, like William McCall, could not remember what he had said but could still "see him today as he stood on the platform with Bible in hand speaking to us."[84] Others, like Arthur Limouze, said he was "the best illustration of John Wesley's advice to his preachers, which was never to speak without presenting Christ."[85]

A poem by Howard Bement was on the cover of the issue. He turned the focus inward, as did many of the writers, when he said, "Your ringing word / Breaks through the barrier and assails the heart; / And even he who fain would not have heard / Has heard, despite; nor can there e'er depart / From that young heart the cleanness that you preach, / Nor from his soul the honesty you teach." Editor Adams generated this tribute without consulting Speer, because he was sure his "innate modesty would impel you to discourage me from going ahead with the project." Speer thanked Adams and told him the tributes were "altogether over generous judgements. . . . I do heartily appreciate your good will and the good will of the friends who have written those letters, though I know only too well what an unprofitable servant I have really been."[86]

Final Illness and Memorial Services

Not long after this unexpected birthday celebration, he became ill. He continued to keep some engagements, including leadership of the annual retreat of the Presbytery of Philadelphia in late September, but he began to lose strength. He was very weak when he went to Poughkeepsie, New

York, on November 5, 1947, to hold the last of a series of Bible classes on the Gospel of John. He always lectured standing up, but this time he spoke sitting down. This was his last public appearance.[87] The next day he wrote George Innes that he was laid up with a "bad case of bronchitis and physical exhaustion from having undertaken a little too much this fall in travel and speaking."[88] There is no indication that he had a premonition of the future, but he also wrote the chairman of the seminary board nominating committee asking to be relieved of the presidency. The committee, after consulting with Mackay, agreed and sent him a letter to that effect dated November 22.[89] By then he had been in Bryn Mawr Hospital for a week under treatment for leukemia. He joined the church triumphant on November 23.

Emma and her family sent out word to the larger family and friends that he had "entered into Life."[90] The phrase was characteristic of their belief about the relationship of life and death, one Emma and he had shared many times over the years in their loses of Eleanor and Elliott. It was rooted in the Christian tradition and its teaching about the resurrection. Robert spoke for both himself and Emma when he said, "We think of death as a great mystery, but it is not death that is the great mystery, it is life. If we understood life we would have no trouble understanding death. Death is only an incident in life. Our mystery is life. And yet of life and death alike the meaning is also clear and plain. Christ tells us of it, 'I am the resurrection and the life. He that believeth in me though he were dead yet shall he live again, and whosoever liveth and believeth in me shall never die.' "[91] Several of the daily devotions in *Five Minutes* were on the theme of death, one of which he titled "Death Not Sundown But Dawn."[92]

The first memorial service took place immediately in the Bryn Mawr Presbyterian Church. It was a family service, conducted by Coffin and the pastor, the Rev. Rex S. Clements. Emma must have been prepared for her husband's death, for she had available a prayer he had written on the occasion of her brother's death in 1938. Coffin prayed it at her request: "And now we ask Thee for Thy grace for our present need. Bless those to whom this sorrow and loss come most closely home. Be Thou their rest and peace. Fill up all the loneliness with Thine own presence. Strengthen those who must carry on the tasks that have been laid down. Make them faithful to their so great inheritance. Help us all to live less bound to earth and earthly things and with our spirits set at larger liberty to range with Christ the boundless joy and freedom of God."[93] Coffin conducted the service of burial in Brookside Cemetery in Englewood, where Speer was laid to rest beside his daughter and not far from his son.

In the weeks that followed, there were other memorial services, some large and planned in order that Emma and other members of the family could attend, others at local churches and as parts of regularly scheduled meetings, few of which any family member attended. The Board of Foreign Missions sponsored the largest of these services. The board consulted Emma about the service, including her choice of hymns, and invited the cooperation of three other organizations: the Federal Council of Churches, the Foreign Missions Conference of North America, and Princeton Theological Seminary. This service took place in First Presbyterian Church, their former church in New York City, on the afternoon of December 15. Mackay was one of the speakers, and Coffin led the prayers. The bulletin, at Emma's suggestion, contained a copy of his prayer "We who are children of time" and of a favorite poem by Christina Rossetti, which he had used in his final lecture at Poughkeepsie. The last stanza proclaims, "Lord, Thou art Life, though I be dead; / Love's Fire Thou art, however cold I be; / Nor heaven have I, nor place to lay my head, / Nor home, but Thee."[94]

Two other notable memorial services were held, one in his hometown church and the other at Princeton Seminary. The Huntingdon service in January 1948 featured one of his favorite Bible passages, 2 Timothy 2, and an address by his good friend Hugh Kerr. Alumni and friends of Princeton Seminary gathered at Miller Chapel on June 7, 1948. Emma had again been consulted and selected the hymns and likely the scripture, which was another favorite passage, Philippians 2. The major meditations were by Erdman, who described his good friend as an "interpreter of Christ," and Mackay, who called him a "missionary statesman."[95]

The family drew together after his death, very much as it had in former situations of loss. Emma took the lead, as might be expected. To the hundreds upon hundreds of people who sent her cards and letters she sent a small acknowledgment card that contained her husband's birth and death dates, the Rossetti poem, her husband's prayer "We who are people of time," and short readings from *Pilgrim's Progress* and *The Wisdom of Solomon*.[96] On the first anniversary of his death she sent a small leaflet, "A Message to his Missionary Friends," to all Presbyterian missionaries. She reviewed her husband's life and some of his key beliefs, including his view of the true status of women in church and society, the role of the Bible and prayer in the Christian faith, and the place of Jesus as the Redeemer of the world. She told them her husband's one purpose had been to "bring every thought into captivity to Christ." With each letter she sent a copy of *Five Minutes*, in the hope and prayer that it would inspire them.[97]

Memorial minutes and formal resolutions arrived from all kinds of groups within and outside of the Presbyterian Church, both in the United States and around the world. They contained words of celebration, and she responded to them with little difficulty. Emma was harder pressed by the many requests from individuals and groups who wanted to create a memorial to her husband.

The idea was not new. As early as 1927, the president of Juniata College had written Speer inquiring about the possibility of naming a building after his father or him. Speer had told him no, absolutely not and never.[98] The East Liberty Presbyterian Church in Pittsburgh, Pennsylvania, had included him in their "American Presbyterian History Window" in 1935. He had attended the dedication ceremony but left no record of his feelings.

Speer Library

Lloyd Ruland, on behalf of the Board of Foreign Missions, raised the issue of a memorial with Emma shortly after her husband's death, in a gentle and informal manner, fully aware of her husband's feelings about a memorial of any kind, to determine her feelings about "some fitting memorial to the life and service of Dr. Speer."[99] That thought hit a dead end, but another that arrived from Mackay about the same time did not. He had in mind "a little project which has been taking shape in my mind to perpetuate Dr. Speer's memory in a worthy way on our Seminary Campus. He was a lover of books. I would like to see our new library called by his name."[100]

The possibility of a memorial library at Princeton Seminary became a major issue for Emma. The proposal from Mackay created a conflict. On the one hand she knew her husband's wishes all too well, and by and large she agreed with them. On the other hand she knew he had been vitally interested in the new library project. Moreover, Mackay was more than a close friend. She had already sent him her husband's lovely robe, a very personal gift, a sign of the deep relationship between the two men. And she had received a letter from Mackay's wife about that robe: "You cannot imagine how moved my husband was as he put it on. I think he felt almost as Elisha must have felt when Elijah's mantle became his."[101] Mackay pushed her cautiously but steadily for a decision. In July he was in Huntingdon for the dedication of a memorial tablet in Speer's home church, donated by Aunt Clara. He told Emma that the Huntingdon family thought naming the library for her husband was a good idea. He reported that he had spoken with some members of the Board of Foreign Missions and of the office staff, and they agreed. After all, her husband's "missionary devotion began to burn" at the seminary, and he left the seminary to join the Foreign Missions Board. "Could anything be more appropriate," he concluded, "than that the new library should bear his name."[102] By the end of the summer she had decided, despite Mackay's arguments, that she would not consent.

Mackay refused to quit, but he decided to step back and pass to someone else the task of approaching Emma. He encouraged John Buchanan, an old friend of the Speer family, who had made a presentation at the memorial service at Princeton, to make another appeal. Buchanan wrote Emma a long, thoughtful letter. He told her that he had contributed to a memorial fund at Princeton in her husband's name without thinking of any specific use for it, but once the library idea emerged, he realized it was a perfect fit. It would not be the Speer Memorial Library, but the Robert E. Speer Library. The seminary had three named buildings, Alexander Hall, Miller Chapel, and Hodge Hall, and one proposed building, Warfield Hall. These were all men "to whom the institution and the Church owe a great deal. . . . With these four names there is no other which may be so appropriately selected to preserve in tangible form the Princeton tradition for future generations as that of Robert E. Speer." It was also true, he said, that more funds could be raised if the seminary could associate her husband's name with the plan for it. He made a distinction that he believed to be important, which was that the funds would be raised for a Speer library but not solicited in Speer's name.[103]

Emma wavered, perhaps persuaded by the thought that it could be the Speer Library and not the Speer Memorial Library, so she wrote Ruland asking for advice. He politely declined, telling her that he believed "this is a very personal matter which you and the members of your immediate family will have to decide," and added that, as he saw it, the problem was to make a decision that both observed her husband's "personal wish," and furthered "the work of the interests most near to his heart."[104] Within a week of receiving these letters, she changed her mind. She did not say precisely what led her to reverse herself, but she told James Quay, vice-president of the seminary, that she found Buchanan's point very strong and would allow the use of her husband's name "with the understanding that the name is to be used only as a *fact* not a *lever*, in raising the money." She added, almost casually, "The family will contribute much of Mr. Speer's theological library to this Princeton project."[105] Quay told her he was thrilled and said he hoped that when the building was in place "you will

find abundant and lasting satisfaction in the knowledge that it will keep
green in the memory and thought of generations of students yet to come
the great ministry of Dr. Speer throughout the Christian world."[106]

Princeton Seminary put much effort into moving Emma to a decision
to name the new library but then experienced delay after delay in getting
the building under way. Buchanan wrote her in 1951 to report on the
relative lack of progress. Finally, construction began in 1956. The corner-
stone ceremony took place in the fall of that year and the dedication of the
new library in the autumn of 1957. The *New York Times* reported that the
seminary described it as "the largest and best-designed theological library
in the country."[107] Margaret and William, but not Emma, were able to be
present on October 8, 1957, for the special event. Buchanan, Emmons,
and Mackay were part of the ceremony, with Buchanan offering remarks
about Speer. Nathan Pusey, the president of Harvard University, presented
the address and spoke on the need for an educated ministry and somehow
managed to do it without a single reference to Speer. Mackay wrote the
inscription for the bronze plaque set in place to the right of the main
entrance to the library: "This Building Which Bears the Name of a
Christian Statesman Scholar and Saint Robert E. Speer Lover of Books
and of the Kingdom of Christ is Dedicated to the Hope that Within
These Walls the Light of Learning May Illumine the Life of Piety in the
Service of Jesus Christ the Truth."[108]

From the very early stages of his career to the moment when the Speer
Library received his name and its inscription, his peers and mentors,
including the closest members of his family, showered him with praise.
People wrote him to thank him and then offered some word to describe
what he had meant to them, or created some metaphor to try to explain
how he had influenced them or remained the central model or hero of
their lives. The words, when strung together across the years, exhaust the
vocabulary of praise. On the fortieth anniversary of his work as a missionary secretary in 1931, one of his secretary colleagues said, "In order to
tell the truth about Robert Speer one would have to draw upon all the
superlatives at his command."[109] Drawn to metaphor, Kerr described him
to the congregation gathered at the memorial service in Huntingdon: "He
was like a tower rising among the ramparts of the City of God. He was
like a planet among the constellations of the sky. He was like a rock,
unmoved amid the cross-currents of the world's conflicts and the Church's
uncertainties."[110] Four themes emerge from all of these praises: spiritual
leader and saintly person; Christian or missionary statesman; apostle of
Christian unity; and Christian, Christ like, or Christ's man. These themes

were not exclusive categories, and there were some, Mackay for one, who believed all of them were appropriate.

Four Themes

At the beginning of Speer's career Trumbull had picked him out of the crowd of young missionary leaders and identified him as a person of precocious spirituality. Trumbull's words remained his own, but many others caught their meaning and used it in describing him. The faithful elder had told his junior friend, "My wonder is that *you* can be so tender, and considerate, and sympathetic, and helpful in your loving ways to one like me, without long years of training. And that will continue to be a wonder, but it is a blessed wonder."[111] Trumbull had also referred to him as Great Heart—the first person, apparently, to compare Speer to one of Bunyan's characters, but far from the last.[112] Emma used those characters to refer to her husband, at times in letters to him but more often to their children. She also on occasion described him as her angel or archangel, her hero in all things. When she met him at Northfield, he was already a recognized leader and she the follower. Although they led a remarkably shared life, in which they related to each other as equals, she retained a sense that she was always learning, taking, receiving more from him than he from her.[113] He did not agree with her and told her often in his letters that she was the most spiritual or Spirit-filled person he knew.

Many others shared the view that he was a spiritual person, especially those who worked most closely with him. They revealed their opinion of him when they constantly chose him to make the invitation at a meeting of students or to pray. SVM partner Sherwood Eddy testified that at the meetings Speer "struck the deepest spiritual note" and helped him personally "more than any other in the deepening of my spiritual life."[114] The term "saint" entered the letters to him in the later stages of his career. His son and brother in the faith, Mackay, used it on occasion and then set it in bronze, for future generations to read and ponder.

The theme Christian or missionary statesman appeared in his honorary degree from Juniata College in 1920, which described him as a "champion and exemplar of true Christian statesmanship."[115] It may not have been the first usage of this theme, but it was one of the earliest. Variations of the phrase multiplied in the 1930s as he neared retirement and people and groups reflected on his role in the missionary movement. Kerr used it, describing him variously as "the far-seeing statesman" and "the great ecclesiastical statesman."[116] The Board of Foreign Missions lifted up the theme in 1937, on the occasion of his retirement, declaring that his work had "won for him a recognition as one of the leading missionary statesmen of the age."[117] Mackay cast this theme in bronze too. Early in his career Speer had disapproved of the connection between the terms "missionary" and "statesman." Wheeler had heard him speak on the topic in China in 1915, when he had said the true missionary duty was to be "found faithful." Missionary work relied on "love and patience," and "not brilliance or conspicuous qualities of minds and hearts that the world so often applauds."[118] Virtually no one tried to explain the theme, but fellow missionary secretary James Franklin of the American Baptist Foreign Mission Society expressed an opinion shared by many when he said that Speer had risen above denominationalism and represented all Christendom.[119]

Some persons who used this theme did so in a quite specific historical way, in an effort to place him in a much larger historical context. Frank Fitt said, "If he had lived in the first, second, or third century he would be known today as one of the Fathers of the Christian church."[120] Others with a bent to history described him as the Rufus Anderson of their day, and those inclined to theology called him the Horace Bushnell of their era. Kerr put his tribute in historical terms. "In the course of Presbyterian history in America," he said, "a few figures have emerged who dominate: Francis Makemie—colonial era; John Witherspoon—revolutionary era; Charles Hodge—19th century," and when "the next generation comes to survey and evaluate the influence and significance of our great Church in national and world affairs during the closing days of the nineteenth century and the first half of the twentieth century, the towering position occupied by Dr. Robert E. Speer in practically all of the great evangelical Christian movements of this period will, we believe, be recognized."[121] The "American Presbyterian Window" in East Liberty Church placed him with Makemie, William Tennent, Samuel Davies, Witherspoon, David Brainerd, John Lowrie, Charles Hodge, and several others. He is pictured standing with his hand on a globe. He was the only living person chosen for the window.[122]

Many admirers were attracted to Speer's vision of Christian unity. Cavert, his colleague in Federal Council work, described him as an "Apostle of Christian Unity." Some Christians, Cavert said, thought of unity in terms of efficiency, whereas Speer "thought of unity in a more fundamental sense; for him it was not something we achieve so much as something that we receive. For Dr. Speer unity was something *given*,—

given in what God has done for us through Christ. His basic position was not that the Churches *ought* to be one but that they *are* one by virtue of their common relation to Christ and that they should make this oneness *manifest* to the world."[123]

Those who praised his ecumenical vision did so from a variety of different angles. Joseph Sizoo said his greatness was that "somehow he holds together and unifies the whole fellowship of the Presbyterian Church and all who represent the Calvinistic faith."[124] Walter Lingle said he "was not content to think only in terms of his own denomination. His mind and heart included all denominations that believe in Jesus Christ as Saviour and Lord." Lingle added that in that respect Speer resembled Calvin.[125] Emmons prepared the "Robert E. Speer Memorial Minute" which the seminary trustees adopted. Speer's fellow trustees characterized his career as "World Evangelism and Kingdom Statesmanship," and him as "a global Christian."[126] Many people rang the global bell, including two who knew him best, A. J. Brown and Mott. Brown said he had "the international mind in religion," and Mott celebrated his "world program of Christ."[127]

Without question the most common theme in the tributes over the years and at his death was the one that lifted up his vision of Jesus Christ, his commitment to Jesus Christ, or his Christian character. People referred to him as "a *strong* representative of the Master," as the "servant of Christ," and declared that he set forth "the mind of Christ" and possessed a "vivid consciousness of the Living Christ."[128] More frequently people said simply that he was the greatest or most remarkable Christian they knew or, as Buchanan told Emma right after his death, that her husband was "our ideal of what a Christian should be."[129] One version of this theme was popular with those who worked closely with him: the interpreter of Christ. Erdman and Inman, his colleague in South American missions, both focused on this idea. Erdman used this theme in his meditation at the seminary memorial service and proposed that everything Speer wrote, whatever the title, was about Jesus Christ and that everything he did, in or out of the church, was done to make Jesus better known. He added, "His interpretation was not theoretical; it was experimental."[130]

There were those persons, typically those who had come to Christ through Speer's ministry, who pushed this theme further, deeper, and who argued that he was Christ like or Christ's man. That would not be unusual for persons who dated their religious lives from an encounter with him. Mackay sometimes spoke in such terms. He perceived that Speer "understood that a Christian must be a "Christ man" in the timeless New Testament tradition."[131] Kerr described him as "fettered to Christ."[132] Eddy called him the "most Christlike character among the student leaders of the last generation," and said "his life was wholly Christocentric."[133] Speer had recruited William Miller for foreign missions, and the board sent him to Persia. Miller called him "Christ's Man," and explained, "Christ was everything to Robert Speer, and since he ever lived in Christ, it is not strange that many who knew him intimately said he was the most Christlike man they had ever met."[134] A generation after his death, two of his children, Margaret and William, acknowledged that people had responded to their father in these terms but said they were not part of the family image of him.[135]

The life and ministry of Robert Elliott Speer eludes simple definition. Led by his father in his early years to believe in God and to experience God as real and personal, he surrendered himself to God in the personality of Jesus Christ. From that moment until his death, he understood his life to be directed by the Spirit of God, and he followed the path set before him as his duty. He accepted tasks as they arrived, but he was not in any sense a passive personality. As soon as he decided on a responsibility, he put every ounce of his energy and ability into it, typically startling his colleagues with the quantity and quality of his work, and often developing new work. It was not part of his character to calculate his moves, to figure out the way to financial security or status, so the tasks he accepted truly arrived; he did not seek them out. Such ambition had appeared in his life in college until his call; then it disappeared, never to return. Every task he accepted seemed to him to complement every other task. Observers often marveled that he could do, and do so well, so many different things. His secret was that he did not see them as different, as separate from one another. However many different organizations he served, he saw them all working to one end, and so he experienced all his energies merging into one. Weary and often overworked, he was rarely discouraged. The only time he expressed pessimism was during the difficult debates over the Hocking Report and the challenges to his board. Even then, he was certain God would see him and the organizations he served through to a good conclusion.

He had made it clear to family and friends that he did not want anyone exploring his life, so he offered no suggestions for the task. He collected a mass of material and organized it, but he left no interpretative plan, no trail. He did offer some occasional reflections. In 1933, in response to Elliott's request that he write a family history for the grandchildren, he wrote some reminiscences about his childhood. In retirement he wrote "Random Personal Recollections." These were undated and truly random, except for one page he titled "Some Activities which give Special Satisfaction in looking back."[136] If the twenty items he listed can be considered a trail, then he thought of himself in terms of his missionary and ecumenical work. He claimed relatively little for himself, since eight of the activities were his work "with" someone else, including Daly in planning for Edinburgh, Cairns in the work at Edinburgh, Temple in writing the Jerusalem message, and Inman in the Latin American work. Only four events related directly to his denomination outside of missions, and first among them was helping secure the "admission of women to the eldership." He did not include his service as moderator, but did remember his work on the Commission of Fifteen. (After one particularly flowery introduction at a Faith and Life Seminar, he responded, "When we come to face God . . . no one will be thinking about who was Moderator of the General Assembly.")[137]

No one key unlocks this life, but two perspectives bring it into clearer focus. Margaret, taking her cue from her father's conviction that everything he said and did came together, claimed that he was the most "Whole" person she had ever known. She believed that no title could truly describe him because it would reflect one or another aspect of his life and work, and it was not possible to separate anything out as the most important, because everything was related to everything else. What he "was, believed, said, did," were "all one piece—inseparable."[138] Describing him as a whole person makes sense of the way people in his life were constantly in search of new and more dramatic terms of praise. For it is probable that they, like her, had never encountered anyone who managed to live as full an integrated life and sustain it year after year. It was not a life in some remote village, marked by little change. He lived in one of the largest cities of the world and worked on a national and international stage, in the midst of the large economic, political, and religious movements that shook and sometimes changed the world. His life featured debates about the future of a major denomination, the largest national ecumenical organization, and the entire foreign missionary effort. Along the way he faced the deep grief of the death of two children, one of them murdered. When he held together in the midst of such events, people were amazed; when he moved forward, they often expressed wonder and awe.

The other perspective derives from a phrase that Brown, his colleague on the board, used to describe him: "prophet of God."[139] A "prophet" can be a person who sees the future. Many believed he did that, in his vision of the role of women in the church, the need for the churches to confront and help resolve racism, and the centrality of the ecumenical movement in the life of the church. A prophet can also be one who has a gift of spiritual insight. His gift was insight into the life and ministry of Jesus Christ. Those things he foresaw most clearly he claimed to find in the Bible, in the teachings of Jesus. He discovered the way to the future by remembering Jesus Christ. He spent his life inviting and challenging others to do the same.

NOTES

Chapter 1: Roots

1. The documents are in the Speer Family Papers, Bryn Mawr College Archives, Mariam Coffin Canaday Library, Bryn Mawr, Pennsylvania. Hereafter cited as Speer Family Papers.
2. Roberts D. Royer, "The Speer Family," typed manuscript, Speer Family Papers, 1.
3. Ibid., 2.
4. Robert E. Speer, "Elliott," typed manuscript, Speer Family Papers, 3.
5. Royer, 3.
6. Robert E. Speer, "Address By Dr. Robert E. Speer." *Ulster Irish Society and Ulster Club* (Year Book, 1941), 13.
7. Robert E. Speer, "Recollections of My Father, Robert Milton Speer," typed manuscript, Speer Family Papers, 1.
8. Robert E. Speer, "Genealogical and Statistical Notes," typed manuscript, Speer Family Papers.
9. Robert E. Speer, "Random Personal Recollections," manuscript, Speer Family Papers, 1.
10. Huntingdon *Monitor*, 23 January 1890, Robert E. Speer Papers, Department of Archives and Special Collections, Princeton Theological Seminary Libraries, Princeton, N.J. Hereafter cited as Speer Papers.
11. Robert E. Speer, "Some Personal Reminiscences and Memories," typed manuscript, Speer Family Papers, 4.
12. Ibid.
13. Huntingdon *Monitor,* 23 January 1890, Speer Papers.
14. Robert M. Speer to "My dear wife," 10 March 1871, Speer Family Papers.
15. Martha Ellen Speer to Robert M. Speer, 11 March 1871, Speer Family Papers.
16. Speer, "Recollections," 3.
17. Speer, "Random," 2.
18. Brown Notebook, Speer Family Papers.
19. Robert E. Speer (Robbie) to "Dear Mamma," 28 June 1876, Speer Family Papers.
20. Speer, "Recollections," 6.
21. Ibid. See also Robert E. Speer, *Remember Jesus Christ* (New York: Fleming H. Revell Co., [1899]), 194.
22. Robert E. Speer to John R. Mott, 17 October 1909, John R. Mott Papers, Yale Divinity School Library, Archives and Manuscripts, New Haven, Conn. Hereafter cited as Mott Papers.

441

23. Speer, *Remember Jesus Christ*, 53–54.
24. Brown Notebook, Speer Family Papers.
25. "Diaries of Robert Milton Speer," 12 and 16 November 1876, Speer Family Papers.
26. Speer, "Recollections," 6.
27. Speer, "Some Personal Reminiscences," 13–15.
28. Robert E. Speer, "Address by Robert E. Speer, LL.D.," *Lord's Day Leader*, January–March 1931, Speer Papers. See Robert E. Speer, *A Young Man's Questions* (New York: Fleming H. Revell Co., 1903), 70–71.
29. Speer, "Some Personal Reminiscences," 16.
30. Speer, "Address by Robert E. Speer, LL.D."
31. Speer, "Some Personal Reminiscences," 15–16.
32. Ibid., 15. See Robert E. Speer to Mrs. Charles E. Reed (sister Margaret), 17 November 1919, Speer Papers.
33. "Diaries of Robert E. Speer," 25 February 1883, Speer Papers. Hereafter cited as "Diaries."
34. Speer, "Some Personal Reminiscences," 3.
35. "Diaries."
36. Speer, "Some Personal Reminiscences," 4.
37. "Diaries," 18 April 1883.
38. Speer, "Some Personal Reminiscences," 4.
39. Robert E. Speer, "Tottering Thrones," manuscript, Speer Papers.
40. "Diaries," 26 January 1883.
41. Speer, "Some Personal Reminiscences," 3.
42. See chapter 2.
43. Speer, "Some Personal Reminiscences," 12.
44. Ibid., 2.
45. Ibid., 7.
46. Ibid., 5. See Robert E. Speer to Mrs. Charles L. Reed, 4 March 1927, Speer Papers.
47. Speer, "Some Personal Reminiscences," 12; Postcards of the trip, "Childhood-Boyhood," Speer Family Papers. See Robert E. Speer, *Christian Realities* (New York: Fleming H. Revell Co., 1935), 179.
48. Speer, "Some Personal Reminiscences," 12. See "Childhood-Boyhood."
49. Speer, "Some Personal Reminiscences," 12–13.
50. Robert E. Speer, *A Memorial of a True Life: A Biography of Hugh McAllister Beaver* (New York: Fleming H. Revell Co., [1898]), 36ff.
51. Robert E. Speer, "Dell Ross, My Dell," *Nassau Literary Magazine* 43, no. 8 (March 1888): 453–54.
52. Speer, "Some Personal Reminiscences," 11.
53. Speer, "Random," 11.
54. Robert E. Speer to Robert M. Speer, 9 September 1883; Robert E. Speer to Will Speer, 9 September 1883, Speer Family Papers.
55. "Diaries," 9 September 1883.
56. "Diaries," 18 September 1883; 29 January 1884.
57. "Childhood-Boyhood."
58. Robert E. Speer to Robert M. Speer, 14 December 1884, Speer Family Papers.
59. Robert E. Speer to Robert M. Speer, 12 April 1885, Speer Family Papers.

60. Robert E. Speer to Robert M. Speer, 22 March 1885, Speer Family Papers.
61. Robert E. Speer to Robert M. Speer, 1 March 1885, Speer Family Papers.
62. Robert E. Speer to Robert M. Speer, 17 May 1885, Speer Family Papers.
63. Robert E. Speer to Robert M. Speer, 17 November 1884, Speer Family Papers.
64. Will of Robert Milton Speer, Speer Family Papers.
65. "Diaries," 17 January 1884.
66. Robert E. Speer to Robert M. Speer, 15 March 1885, Speer Family Papers.
67. Robert E. Speer to Robert M. Speer, 9 October 1884, Speer Family Papers.
68. C. F. P. Bancroft to Robert E. Speer, 29 July 1885; C. P. F. Bancroft, Principal, to Rev. James McCosh, D.D., 29 July 1885. See "Childhood-Boyhood."
69. Robert E. Speer to Robert M. Speer, 21 June 1885, Speer Family Papers.
70. Robert E. Speer to Robert M. Speer, 22 September, 1885, Speer Papers.
71. Robert M. Speer to Robert E. Speer, 18 November 1885, Speer Family Papers.
72. Robert M. Speer to Robert E. Speer, 16 January 1885, Speer Family Papers.
73. Robert M. Speer to Robert E. Speer, 20 February 1886, Speer Family Papers.
74. Robert M. Speer to Robert E. Speer, 14 June 1886, Speer Family Papers.
75. "Diaries," 2 January 1887.
76. Ibid., 13 December 1887. See "Diaries," 1888–89.
77. Harry Bowlby to Robert E. Speer, 9 January 1946, Speer Family Papers.
78. Robert E. Speer to Robert M. Speer, 20 April 1889, Speer Papers.
79. "School and College Papers and Essays," Speer Papers.
80. Speer, "Random," 26.
81. "Diaries," 14 January 1886. Speer created a list of activities for his four years and entered it under this date.
82. Ibid., 31 October and 9 November 1887.
83. "Clippings," Speer Papers.
84. "Diaries," 30 October 1886. See W. Reginald Wheeler, *A Man Sent From God: A Biography of Robert E. Speer* (Westwood, N.J.: Fleming H. Revell Co., 1956), 45.
85. Brown Notebook, Speer Family Papers. See Wheeler, *A Man Sent From God*, 44.
86. Robert M. Speer to Robert E. Speer, 6 March 1886, Speer Family Papers.
87. Robert E. Speer to Robert M. Speer, 13 March 1886, Speer Papers. See Robert E. Speer, *How to Speak Effectively Without Notes* (New York: Fleming H. Revell Co., [1928]), published as a pamphlet as early as c. 1909.
88. Speer, "Random," 7.
89. "Diaries," 24 February 1887.
90. Robert E. Speer to Robert M. Speer, 6 March 1887, Speer Papers.
91. "Diaries," 3 May 1889.
92. James Stebbins, "Prophecy," *Nassau Herald* 25 (1889): 50–51.
93. Robert E. Speer to Robert M. Speer, 31 January 1886, Speer Papers.
94. "Diaries," 4, 6, 7 February 1887.
95. Ibid., 27 January 1887.
96. Ibid., 29 March 1888.
97. Robert E. Speer to Robert M. Speer, 22 October 1885, Speer Papers.
98. Robert E. Speer to Robert M. Speer, 14 May 1889, Speer Papers.
99. Robert E. Speer, *The Liberalistic Temper: Valedictory Oration, June 19, 1889* (Zaph Press, 1889), published as a pamphlet, Speer Papers.
100. Robert M. Speer to Robert E. Speer, 2 July 1889, Speer Family Papers.

Chapter 2: Call to Ministry

1. "The Shorter Catechism," in *The Book of Confessions* (Louisville, Ky.: Office of the General Assembly of the Presbyterian Church (U.S.A.), 1996), 7.031. This chapter is a reworked version of John F. Piper, Jr., "Robert E. Speer: His Call and the Missionary Impulse, 1890–1900," *American Presbyterians* 65, no. 2 (Summer 1987): 97–108.
2. Robert E. Speer to Robert M. Speer, 27 September 1885, Speer Papers.
3. "Diaries," 10 January 1886.
4. Ibid., 28 January 1886.
5. Quoted in Delavan L. Pierson, *Arthur T. Pierson* (New York: Fleming H. Revell Co., 1912), 189.
6. Arthur T. Pierson to Robert E. Speer, 16 September 1910, Speer Papers.
7. Robert M. Speer to Robert E. Speer, 6 February 1886, Speer Family Papers.
8. For specific citations see "Diaries," January–May 1887.
9. Robert E. Speer, "What This Movement Means," in *The Student Missionary Appeal, Addresses at the Third International Convention of the Student Volunteer Movement for Foreign Missions, 23–27 February 1898,* (New York: Student Volunteer Movement for Foreign Missions, 1898), 141.
10. Robert E. Speer, "What This Movement Means" in *Students and the Missionary Problem, Addresses Delivered at the International Student Missionary Conference* (London: Student Volunteer Missionary Union, 1900), 187.
11. Robert E. Speer to Robert M. Speer, 7 May 1887, Speer Papers.
12. "Diaries," 8 May 1887. The quotation is from David L. Livingstone, English explorer and missionary.
13. Robert E. Speer to Robert M. Speer, 13 February and 6 March 1887, Speer Papers.
14. Robert E. Speer to Robert M. Speer, 27 March 1887, "Sabbath Evening," Speer Papers.
15. William M. Miller, "God's Mighty Men: Samuel Zwemer and Robert E. Speer," *Presbyterian Journal* 26, no. 5 (31 May 1967): 7.
16. "Diaries," 31 March 1887.
17. Robert M. Speer to Robert E. Speer, 3 April 1887, Speer Family Papers.
18. Robert E. Speer to Robert M. Speer, 5 April 1887, Speer Family Papers.
19. "Diaries," 1888. See Robert E. Speer, *A Christian's Habits* (Philadelphia: Westminster Press, 1911), 40–41.
20. Correspondence between Robert E. Speer and various members of his family, April 1887, Speer Family Papers.
21. Speer, "What This Movement Means," *The Student Missionary Appeal,* 141.
22. Robert E. Speer to L. W. Gosnell, 20 May 1907, Speer Papers.
23. Robert E. Speer, *"Lead On, O King Eternal,"* in Robert E. Speer, *Collection of Pamphlets,* vol. 2, Speer Papers.
24. "To the Student Volunteers for Foreign Missions: From the Princeton Volunteers," March 1888, Speer Papers, 5.
25. "Diaries," 29 April, 14 May, 6 June 1887.
26. Robert E. Speer to Robert M. Speer, 23 May 1887, Speer Papers.

27. "Diaries," 16 May 1887.
28. Ibid., 28 May 1887.
29. Robert E. Speer, "A Religious Retrospect," *Philadelphian* (June 1887), 336.
30. Speer, "Some Personal Reminiscences," 5.
31. Speer, "Dell Ross, My Dell," 453–63.
32. Sherwood Eddy, *Pathfinders of the World Missionary Crusade* (New York: Abingdon-Cokesbury Press, 1945), 261f.
33. "Diaries," 22 January 1888.
34. Ibid., 10 April 1888. See also Robert E. Speer to Robert M. Speer, 16 April 1888, Speer Papers.
35. "Diaries," 15 February 1889.
36. For specific citations, see "Diaries," January–December, 1888.
37. Clarence P. Shedd, *Two Centuries of Student Christian Movements* (New York: Association Press, 1934), 307. Emphasis Mott's.
38. Robert E. Speer to John R. Mott, 7 March 1890, Mott Papers.
39. Robert E. Speer to Merrill, 17 June 1891, Speer Papers.
40. Speer, "Random," 18. For a slightly different version of this event, see Wheeler, *A Man Sent From God,* 52.
41. Speer, "Random," 18.
42. Eddy, *Pathfinders,* 262f.
43. Robert E. Speer to Miss Dickie, no date but likely 1900. Two-page typed manuscript with notation "Revised Version, by Dr. Ellinwood," Speer Papers.
44. H. Clay Trumbull to Robert E. Speer, 19 October 1891, Speer Papers. Emphasis Trumbull's.
45. Robert E. Speer to John R. Mott, 21 July 1890, Mott Papers.
46. Inquiries and invitations came from Westminster and Macalester. See also Edwin M. Bulkley to Robert E. Speer, 5 June 1911, Speer Papers.
47. Robert E. Speer to Emma Bailey Speer, 22 March 1892, Speer Family Papers.
48. *Fourteenth Conference of the Foreign Mission Boards in the United States and Canada* (New York: Foreign Missions Library, [1907]), 98.
49. Robert E. Speer, "The Call to Christian Service," n.d., Speer Papers.
50. Robert E. Speer to Rev. W. A. Edwards, 25 November 1902, Speer Papers.
51. Lucius Hopkins Miller to Robert E. Speer, 30 September 1910, Speer Papers.
52. Robert E. Speer to Rev. James H. Ross, 26 February 1900, Speer Papers.
53. Robert E. Speer, undated, untitled speech, Speer Papers.
54. Robert E. Speer to J. M. Buckley, 16 June 1902, Speer Papers.
55. H. Clay Trumbull, *Old Time Student Volunteers* (New York: Fleming H. Revell Co., 1902), 231.

Chapter 3: The Christian Faith

1. Robert E. Speer, *Men Who Were Found Faithful* (New York: Fleming H. Revell Co., [1912]), 156.
2. Robert E. Speer, *The Master of the Heart* (New York: Fleming H. Revell Co., [1908]), 111–12.
3. Robert E. Speer to Margaret B. Speer, 5 July 1929, Speer Family Papers. See Robert E. Speer, *Some Changing and Unchanging Things in Foreign Missions,* 7,

published as a pamphlet, 1937, Speer Family Papers. Hutchison has pointed out that "neo-orthodoxy and the Speer position were well within the same universe of discourse." William R. Hutchison, "Modernism and Missions: The Liberal Search for an Exportable Christianity, 1875–1935," in John K. Fairbank, ed., *The Missionary Enterprise in China and America* (Cambridge: Harvard University Press, 1974), 129.

4. Robert E. Speer to Florence Smith, 9 February 1933, Speer Papers.
5. Ray Anger to Robert E. Speer, 10 April 1940, Speer Papers.
6. Robert E. Speer to J. Gresham Machen, 30 April 1929, Speer Papers.
7. Speer, *Christian Realities*, 44–45.
8. Robert E. Speer, "The Presbyterian Churches and Foreign Missions," in William H. Roberts, ed., *Addresses*, at the Celebration of the Two Hundred and Fiftieth Anniversary of the Westminster Assembly of the Presbyterian Church in the U.S.A. (Philadelphia: Presbyterian Board of Publication and Sabbath-School Work, 1898), 321.
9. This appears on an end page in his Bible, dated 28 May 1887, Speer Family Papers.
10. Robert E. Speer, "Is Identity of Doctrinal Opinion Necessary to Continued Missionary Cooperation?" *International Review of Missions* 12 (October 1923): 498. See Robert E. Speer, *Some Living Issues* (New York: Fleming H. Revell Co., 1930), 136; Robert E. Speer to John Fox, 27 February 1922, Speer Papers.
11. Robert E. Speer, *The Gospel and the New World* (New York: Fleming H. Revell Co., 1919), 220–24.
12. Speer, *Remember Jesus Christ*, 9.
13. Ibid., 75f.
14. Ibid., 77–78.
15. Ibid., 78.
16. Ibid., 74.
17. Ibid.
18. Ibid., 93.
19. Robert E. Speer to Katherine M. Frazier, 24 August 1899, Speer Papers.
20. Robert E. Speer, *Studies in the Gospel of Luke* (New York: International Committee of Young Men's Christian Associations, [1892]); Robert E. Speer, *Studies in the Book of Acts* (New York: International Committee of Young Men's Christian Associations, [1892]).
21. Robert E. Speer, *Studies of the Man Christ Jesus* (New York: Fleming H. Revell Co., 1896); Speer, *Remember Jesus Christ*.
22. Robert E. Speer, *Jesus and Our Human Problems* (New York: Fleming H. Revell Co., 1946).
23. Speer, *Remember Jesus Christ*, 11.
24. H. Clay Trumbull to Robert E. Speer, 24 June 1892, Speer papers.
25. Robert E. Speer, "How to Study the Bible," (1895); "Practical Suggestions for Home Bible Study," (1901), "Scrap-Books," I, Speer Papers. See Robert E. Speer, *Christ and Life* (New York: Fleming H. Revell Co., 1901), 44–45.
26. Speer, *Christ and Life*, 47.
27. Speer, *Studies in the Book of Acts*, 6–7; *Studies in the Gospel of Luke*, 5–6.
28. Speer, *Christ and Life*, 48.

29. Ibid., 49–50.
30. Speer, *Studies in the Book of Acts*, 7; *Studies in the Gospel of Luke*, 5.
31. Robert E. Speer, *The Principles of Jesus Applied to Some Questions of Today* (New York: Fleming H. Revell Co., 1902), 12.
32. Speer, *Christ and Life*, 40–41.
33. Speer, *The Principles of Jesus Applied to Some Questions of Today*, 12.
34. Robert E. Speer to Charles A. Haff, 10 July 1900, Speer Papers.
35. Robert E. Speer to Roswell C. Tripp, 3 June 1902, Speer Papers.
36. Robert E. Speer to Margaret B. Speer, 30 September 1918, Speer Family Papers.
37. Speer, *Christ and Life*, 96.
38. Quoted in Sherwood Eddy, *Maker of Men: The Secret of Character Building* (New York and London: Harper & Brothers Publishers, 1941), 61.
39. See Speer's Bible; Speer, *The Master of the Heart*, 112.
40. See Speer's Bible.
41. Robert E. Speer, *John's Gospel, the Greatest Book in the World* (New York: Fleming H. Revell Co., [1915]), 6.
42. Robert E. Speer, "Lists of Sermons and Index of Books," manuscript, Speer Papers.
43. See Speer's Bible.
44. Robert E. Speer to A.H. Barr, 17 August 1899, Speer Papers.
45. Robert E. Speer to Miss Dickie, 23 July 1925, Speer Papers.
46. Robert E. Speer, "Miscellaneous Note Books," manuscripts, Speer Papers.
47. Nathan O. Hatch and Mark A. Noll, eds., *The Bible in America* (New York: Oxford University Press, 1982).
48. Robert E. Speer, *Paul, the All-Round Man* (New York: Fleming H. Revell Co., 1909), 9.
49. Robert E. Speer, *Some Changing and Unchanging Things in Foreign Missions*, 13.
50. Robert E. Speer to Margaret B. Speer, 20 February 1933, Speer Papers.
51. Quoted in Eddy, *Maker of Men*, 61.
52. Robert E. Speer to D. P. McGeachy, 25 April 1939, Speer Papers.
53. Robert E. Speer, "The Consciousness of Christ," *Union Seminary Review* 55, no. 2 (February 1944): 116, 120.
54. Robert E. Speer, "The Minister, The Man of One Book," *Princeton Seminary Bulletin* 41, no. 3 (Winter 1948): 22.
55. Speer, "The Consciousness of Christ," 120.
56. Quoted in Speer's Bible.
57. John A. Mackay, "Robert Elliott Speer: A Man of Yesterday Today," *Princeton Seminary Bulletin* 60, no. 3 (June 1967): 14. For a brief, perceptive summary of Speer's views on Christ, see Richard V. Pierard, "Evangelical and Ecumenical: Missionary Leaders in Mainline Protestantism, 1900–1950," in Douglas Jacobsen and William Vance Trollinger, Jr., eds., *Re-Forming the Center: American Protestantism, 1900 to the Present* (Grand Rapids, Mich., and Cambridge, U.K.: Wm. B. Eerdmans Publishing Co., 1998), 153–54.
58. "Discovering America's Greatest Preachers," *Christian Century* 41, no. 41 (9 October 1924): 1291; Martin E. Marty, *The Noise of Conflict, 1919–1941*, vol. 2 of *Modern American Religion* (Chicago and London: University of Chicago Press, 1991), 48–50.

59. "The Best Mind of the Church," *Christian Century* 41, no. 52 (25 December 1924): 1673.

60. "Greatness in Preachers," *Christian Century* 42, no. 2 (8 January 1925): 44–45.

61. Robert E. Speer, "The Christ Who Lives in Men," *Christian Century* 42, no. 4 (22 January 1925): 117–120.

62. Speer, *Christian Realities*, 34–35. See Robert E. Speer, *The Meaning of Christ to Me* (New York: Fleming H. Revell Co., 1936); Robert E. Speer, "What Jesus Does for Me," Buffalo YMCA, *Triangle Topics*, December 1931, Speer Papers.

63. Speer, *Remember Jesus Christ*, 12–13.

64. Ibid., 13.

65. Ibid., 13–14.

66. Ibid., 22.

67. Ibid., 15–20. Emphasis Speer's.

68. Frank H. Leavell, "Dr. Robert Elliott Speer," *Baptist Student* 11, no. 9 (June 1933): 2.

69. Speer, *Paul, the All-Round Man*, 29.

70. Ibid., 30. The passage is Galatians 2:20. See Robert E. Speer, *Studies of the Man Paul* (New York: Fleming H. Revell Co., [1900]), 121–24.

71. Speer, *Paul, the All-Round Man*, 31.

72. Ibid., 32–33. See Speer, *Studies of the Man Paul*, 240.

73. Robert E. Speer, *The Finality of Jesus Christ* (New York: Fleming H. Revell Co., 1933), 50. Speer's reference was to Schweitzer's book *The Mysticism of St. Paul*.

74. Speer, *Paul, the All-Round Man*, 33.

75. Ibid., 46.

76. Frederic W. H. Myers, *Saint Paul* (London: Macmillan and Co., 1928), 1, 53. William M. Miller, "Christ's Man," *Sunday Times* 108, no. 53 (31 December 1966): 10. See also Margaret B. Speer, "RES," manuscript, Speer Family Papers.

77. Speer, *The Finality of Jesus Christ*, 5.

78. John G. Buchanan, "Robert E. Speer: The Man," *Princeton Seminary Bulletin* 42 no. 1 (Summer 1948): 6.

79. Robert E. Speer to John D. Wells, 9 October 1902, Speer Papers.

80. Speer, "The Consciousness of Christ," 93–94. Emphasis added.

81. Speer, *Studies of the Man Christ Jesus*, 7. He used Bushnell's argument on other occasions. See Robert E. Speer, *The Deity of Christ* (New York: Fleming H. Revell Co., [1909]), published as a pamphlet, Speer Papers, 13.

82. Speer, *Studies of the Man Christ Jesus*, 7.

83. Ibid., 8. See Robert E. Speer to Eloise Holton, 25 January 1908, Speer Papers.

84. Speer, *Studies of the Man Christ Jesus*, 34–35.

85. Ibid., 161f.

86. Ibid., 244. See Speer, *The Deity of Christ*, 38–39.

87. Speer, *The Finality of Jesus Christ*, 195.

88. Ibid., 269. See Speer, *Some Living Issues*, 30–46.

89. Speer, *Some Living Issues*, 5.

90. Ibid., 64.

91. Ibid., 67, 69f.

92. Emma B. Speer, "Two Deep Convictions," in Wheeler, *A Man Sent From God*, 157.

93. Robert E. Speer, *Five Minutes A Day* (Philadelphia: Westminster Press, 1943), 324.

94. Robert E. Speer, *The Second Coming of Christ* (Chicago: Winona Publishing Co., 1903), 14–15.

95. Speer, *Christ and Life*, 97.

96. Speer, *The Second Coming of Christ*, 9

97. Ibid., 11.

98. Ibid., 13.

99. Ibid., 21–22. The reference is 1 Thessalonians 4:14.

100. Ibid., 26–27. The reference is Romans 8:19–21.

101. Robert E. Speer to Charles E. Robinson (uncle Charles), 23 August 1899, Speer Papers. See Speer, *The Second Coming of Christ*.

102. Speer, *The Second Coming of Christ*, 29–30. The passages are Matthew 24:36 and 24:44.

103. Speer to Robinson.

104. Speer, *Five Minutes A Day*, 96.

105. Lefferts A. Loetscher, *The Broadening Church: A Study of Theological Issues in the Presbyterian Church Since 1869* (Philadelphia: University of Pennsylvania Press, 1954), 105; Eddy, *Pathfinders of the World Missionary Crusade*, 259–60.

106. Walter L. Lingle, "Robert E. Speer," *Christian Observer* 136, no. 1 (7 January 1948): 2–3.

107. Speer, *Some Changing and Unchanging Things in Foreign Missions*, 3.

108. Ernest Sandeen, "*The Fundamentals*: The Last Flowering of the Millenarian-Conservative Alliance," *Journal of Presbyterian History* 47, no. 1 (March 1969): 68.

109. George M. Marsden, *Fundamentalism and American Culture, The Shaping of Twentieth-Century Evangelicalism: 1870–1925* (New York: Oxford University Press, 1980), 122, 168; Norman F. Furniss, *The Fundamentalist Controversy, 1918–1931* (Hamden, Conn.: Archon Books, 1963), 12.

110. Lefferts A. Loetscher, "Robert Elliott Speer," *Dictionary of American Biography* (New York: Charles Scribner's Sons, 1974), Supplement Four, 1946–50, 763–64.

111. James Alan Patterson, "Robert E. Speer and the Crisis of the American Protestant Missionary Movement, 1920–1937," Ph.D. diss., Princeton Theological Seminary, 1980, 34; James A. Patterson, "Robert E. Speer, J. Gresham Machen and the Presbyterian Board of Foreign Missions," *American Presbyterians* 64:1 (Spring 1986): 58–59.

112. Bradley J. Longfield, *The Presbyterian Controversy: Fundamentalists, Modernists, and Moderates* (New York: Oxford University Press, 1991), 189.

113. Robert T. Handy, *A Christian America: Protestant Hopes and Historical Realities* (New York: Oxford University Press, 1971), 135; Hutchison, *Errand to the World*, 107.

114. Hutchison, "Modernism and Missions," 128.

115. Robert E. Speer, *The Federal Council and the Churches*, 10, published as a pamphlet, 1923, Speer Papers.

116. Ibid., 11–14.

117. Ibid., 15. See Longfield, *The Presbyterian Controversy*, 189.

Chapter 4: Family Life

1. "Diaries," 7 October 1888.
2. "Diaries," 6 December 1888.
3. "Diaries," 25 December 1888.
4. Speer, "Recollections," 7.
5. Ibid.; Robert E. Speer to Elliott Speer, 5 January 1931, Speer Family Papers; Speer, "Genealogical and Statistical Notes."
6. Margaret B. Speer, "Marriage and Family," in Wheeler, *A Man Sent From God*, 57.
7. Emma D. Bailey to Robert E. Speer, undated [Spring 1892], Speer Family Papers.
8. Robert E. Speer to Emma D. Bailey, 4 December 1891, Speer Family Papers.
9. Emma D. Bailey to Robert E. Speer, 31 December 1891, Speer Family Papers.
10. Robert E. Speer to Emma D. Bailey, 12 January 1892, Speer Family Papers.
11. Henry Clay Trumbull, *Friendship the Master-Passion* (Philadelphia: John D. Wattles, 1892), 19, 385–87.
12. Robert E. Speer to Emma D. Bailey, 17 February 1892, Speer Family Papers.
13. Emma D. Bailey to Robert E. Speer, undated [mid-February 1892], Speer Family Papers.
14. Robert E. Speer to Emma D. Bailey, 29 February 1892, Speer Family Papers.
15. "Diaries" of Emma Doll Bailey/Speer, Speer Family Papers, 1; Emma Doll Bailey to Robert E. Speer, 11 March 1892, Speer Family Papers.
16. Robert E. Speer to Emma Doll Bailey, 10 March 1892, Speer Family Papers.
17. Emma D. Bailey to Robert E. Speer, 11 March 1892, Speer Family Papers.
18. Robert E. Speer to Emma D. Bailey, 15 March 1892, Speer Family Papers.
19. Robert E. Speer to Emma D. Bailey, 22 March 1892, Speer Family Papers.
20. Emma D. Bailey to Robert E. Speer, 16 March 1892; [March 1892], Speer Family Papers.
21. Robert E. Speer to Emma D. Bailey, 15 March 1892, Speer Family Papers.
22. Robert E. Speer to Emma D. Bailey, 22 March 1892, Speer Family Papers.
23. Eddy, *Pathfinders of the World Missionary Crusade*, 263.
24. Emma D. Bailey to Robert E. Speer, 16 March 1892, Speer Family Papers.
25. Emma H. Bailey to Emma D. Bailey, 28 December 1890, Speer Family Papers.
26. Emma D. Bailey to Robert E. Speer, [Spring 1892], Speer Family Papers.
27. Robert E. Speer to Emma H. Bailey, 21 March 1892, Speer Family Papers.
28. Buchanan, "Robert E. Speer: The Man," 8.
29. Lewis S. Mudge to Emma D. Bailey, 21 March 1892, Speer Family Papers.
30. See letters between Robert E. Speer and Emma H. Bailey, [March 1892–April 1993], Speer Family Papers.
31. Henry C. Trumbull to Robert E. Speer, 10 August 1892, Speer Papers.
32. Henry C. Trumbull to "My very dear Children-in-love," 9 September 1892, Speer Family Papers.
33. Henry C. Trumbull to Robert E. Speer, 26 July 1892, Speer Papers.
34. Robert E. Speer to Mr. Bailey, 13 March 1892, Speer Family Papers.

35. Scrapbook, Speer Family Papers.
36. Emma B. Speer to William Speer, [mid-1930s], Speer Family Papers.
37. Quoted in Margaret B. Speer, "Marriage and Family," 59.
38. Ibid., 57. See Eddy, *Pathfinders of the World Missionary Crusade*, 264; C. G. Gunn to Emma B. Speer, 2 December 1947, Speer Papers; Marion E. Mercer to Emma B. Speer, 28 November 1947, Speer Papers.
39. Interview by the author with Margaret B. Speer and William Speer, 27 March 1984. Emma B. Speer to Elliott Speer, 28 April [1929]; Emma B. Speer to Robert E. Speer, 28 April [1929]; Speer Family Papers.
40. Margaret B. Speer, "Marriage and Family," 61.
41. Robert E. Speer to Margaret B. Speer, 6 January 1927, Speer Papers.
42. Margaret B. Speer, "Marriage and Family," 61.
43. Ibid., 57.
44. Interview with Margaret B. Speer and William Speer.
45. Robert E. Speer to Emma B. Speer, 14 October 1894, Speer Papers.
46. Emma B. Speer to Robert E. Speer, [before 1900], Speer Family Papers.
47. Emma B. Speer to Robert E. Speer, [early 1900], Speer Family Papers.
48. *The Speer Family Papers*, A Guide to the Collection, Bryn Mawr College, 1983.
49. Speer, *Remember Jesus Christ*, 33–34.
50. Charles D. Bailey to Emma D. Bailey, 29 March 1892, Speer Family Papers.
51. Emma B. Speer to Mr. Porter, 22 March 1922, Speer Papers.
52. Emma B. Speer to Robert E. Speer, 21 January 1941, Speer Family Papers.
53. A. H., "The Flowering Years," Lakeville *Journal*, 15 May 1952, Speer Family Papers.
54. Robert E. Speer to J. R. Mott, 1 November 1898, Mott Papers.
55. Robert E. Speer to "Dear Mother" [Emma D. Bailey], [November 1898], Speer Family Papers.
56. Robert E. Speer to J. W. Dawson, 4 June 1902, Speer Papers.
57. Brown Notebook, Speer Family Papers.
58. Robert E. Speer to George Merrill, 9 August 1906, Speer Papers.
59. "Eleanor," 1903–1906, manuscript, Speer Family Papers.
60. Ibid.
61. Ibid.
62. Emma B. Speer to Robert E. Speer, 22 October [1906], Speer Family Papers.
63. Quoted in W. F. Hereford to Mrs. Robert E. Speer, 9 December 1947, Speer Papers.
64. Margaret B. Speer, "Marriage and Family," 67.
65. Robert E. Speer to Elliott Speer, 17 June 1907, Speer Family Papers.
66. Robert E. Speer to Elliott Speer, 8 August 1915, Speer Family Papers.
67. Robert E. Speer to Margaret B. Speer, 1 December 1917, Speer Family Papers.
68. Robert E. Speer to Miss Edith C. Dickie, 14 December 1907, Speer Papers.
69. Robert E. Speer to Miss Edith C. Dickie, 27 July 1911, Speer Papers.
70. Robert E. Speer to Margaret B. Speer, 13 November 1925, Speer Papers.
71. Robert E. Speer to Miss Edith C. Dickie, 10 February 1911, Speer Papers.
72. Robert E. Speer to Miss Mary Speer (sister Mary), 21 February, 10 July 1917, Speer Papers.

73. Robert E. Speer to Elliott Speer, 20 January 1926, Speer Papers.
74. Interview with Margaret B. Speer and William Speer; Interview with Constance (Pat) Speer Barbour, 19 May 1987.
75. Robert E. Speer to Mrs. Charles E. Reed (sister Margaret), 14 September 1914, Speer Papers.
76. Interview with Margaret B. Speer and William Speer. See Speer, "Marriage and Family," 67–68.
77. Margaret B. Speer, "Marriage and Family," 65.
78. Wheeler, *A Man Sent From God*, 274–75.
79. Robert E. Speer to D. S. Cairns, 29 November 1912, Speer Papers.
80. Speer, *A Young Man's Questions*, 180.
81. Quoted in Robert E. Speer, "Draft of *Memorial of Elliott Speer*," typed manuscript, Speer Family Papers, 31.
82. Helen Waite Turnbull Coleman, *Camp Diamond Story* (Privately printed, 1941), 19.
83. Robert E. Speer to Miss Edith C. Dickie, 15 August 1901, Speer Papers.
84. Margaret B. Speer, "Marriage and Family," 69.
85. Ibid., 68.
86. Robert E. Speer, *Owen Crimmins: Tales From the Magalloway Country* (New York: Fleming H. Revell Co., [1931]).
87. Margaret B. Speer, "The YWCA Then and Now," 3 June 1977, manuscript, Speer Family Papers.
88. Henry C. Trumbull to Emma D. Bailey, 12 September 1892, Speer Family Papers.
89. Quoted in Marion O. Robinson, *Eight Women of the YWCA* (New York: National Board of the Young Women's Christian Association of the U.S.A., 1966), 47–48.
90. Quoted in ibid., 48.
91. Quoted in ibid., 49.
92. Quoted in ibid., 50–52. See Speer, "The YWCA Then and Now," 4–5.
93. Quoted in Marilyn E. Weigold, "Emma Bailey Speer," in *Dictionary of American Biography*, Supplement Seven, 1961–65, ed. John A. Garraty (New York: Charles Scribner's Sons, 1981), 708.
94. Robert E. Speer to Clara McMurtrie (aunt Clara), 4 March 1929. Speer Family Papers.
95. Robert E. Speer to Margaret B. Speer, 23 October 1928, Speer Family Papers.
96. Robert E. Speer to Clara McMurtrie, 16 April 1932, Speer Family Papers.
97. Robert E. Speer to Margaret B. Speer, 16 April 1932, Speer Family Papers.
98. Robert E. Speer, *Christian Tithing, A Privilege* (Philadelphia: Board of Christian Education, Presbyterian Church in the U.S.A., [undated]), published as a pamphlet, Speer Papers.
99. Account Books, Speer Family Papers. See Book 1.
100. Emma B. Speer, "A Letter To My Children—All," 2 September 1951, Speer Family Papers. See Interview with Margaret B. Speer and William Speer.
101. William Speer to Miss Ruby H. J. Lee, 8 December 1964, Speer Family Papers.
102. Robert E. Speer to Elliott Speer, 25 November 1930, Speer Family Papers.

103. Robert E. Speer to Marnie and Patty and Bob, 16 September 1934, Speer Family Papers. See Burnham Carter, *So Much to Learn* (Northfield, Mass.: Mount Hermon School, 1976), 156.
104. *New York Times*, 16 September 1934, 1.
105. Carter, *So Much to Learn*, 157.
106. Quoted in ibid., 158.
107. Quoted in ibid., 147.
108. See chapter 5.
109. *New York Times*, 11 February 1929.
110. Carter, *So Much to Learn*, 147.
111. *New York Times*, 16 September 1934.
112. William H. Morrow, "Elliott Speer 1898–1934: The Man," *News*, Northfield Mount Hermon School 24, no. 1 (Winter 1985): 2, 4. See Lynn Stowe Tomb, "Elliott Speer 1898–1934: The Mystery," *News*, Northfield Mount Hermon School 24, no. 1 (Winter 1985): 3, 5.
113. Robert E. Speer to Margaret B. Speer, 19 October 1934, Speer Family Papers.
114. Henry Rankin to Robert E. Speer, 20 December 1934, Speer Papers.
115. Tomb, "Elliott Speer 1898–1934: The Mystery."
116. "Elliott Speer," Speer Family Papers.
117. Cleland B. McAfee, The Board of Foreign Missions, To All Our Fellow-Workers in the Field, 20 September 1934, Speer Papers.
118. Robert E. Speer to Cleland B. McAfee, 25 September 1934, Speer Papers. See Robert E. Speer to Cleland B. McAfee, 19 and 23 September, 1934, Speer Papers.
119. Speer to Marnie and Patty and Bob.
120. "In Memoriam: Elliott Speer, 1898–1934," 33, Speer Papers.
121. Holly W. Speer to "Dearest Father Speer," Christmas Evening, [25 December 1935], Speer Family Papers.
122. Emma B. Speer to Robert E. Speer, 25 March 1935, Speer Family Papers.

Chapter 5: A Student Volunteer

1. Frank Mason North was an important leader in Methodist foreign missions and in ecumenical work. See Creighton Lacy, *Frank Mason North: His Social and Ecumenical Mission* (Nashville: Abingdon Press, 1967).
2. James F. Findlay, Jr., *Dwight L. Moody: American Evangelist, 1837–1899* (Chicago and London: University of Chicago Press, 1969), 348.
3. Martha Lund Smalley, "Historical Sketch of the Student Volunteer Movement for Foreign Missions," 6 October 1980, typed manuscript, Archives of the Student Volunteer Movement for Foreign Missions, Yale Divinity School Library, Archives and Manuscripts, New Haven, Conn. Hereafter cited as SVM Archives.
4. Robert P. Wilder, *The Student Volunteer Movement for Foreign Missions: Some Personal Reminiscences of its Origin and Early History* (New York: Student Volunteer Movement, 1935), 14. See Robert P. Wilder, *The Great Commission. The Missionary Response: The Student Volunteer Movements in North America and*

Europe. Some Personal Reminiscences (London and Edinburgh: Oliphants, [1936]). For other accounts, see Ruth Wilder Braisted, *In This Generation: The Story of Robert P. Wilder* (New York: Friendship Press, 1941), and Timothy C. Wallstrom, *The Creation of a Student Movement to Evangelize the World* (Pasadena, Calif.: William Carey International University Press, 1980), 41–45.

5. Wilder, *The Student Volunteer Movement*, 16. Speer considered Wilder "the real founder of the Movement." See Robert E. Speer to Jesse R. Wilson, 3 November 1934, SVM Archives.

6. Wallstrom, *The Creation of a Student Movement*, 45–46. See James A. Patterson, "The Legacy of Robert P. Wilder," *International Bulletin of Missionary Research* 15, no. 1 (January 1991): 26–32.

7. Wilder, *The Student Volunteer Movement*, 21.

8. Robert E. Speer, "The Achievements of Yesterday," 173, in *Students and the Christian World Mission,* ed. Jesse R. Wilson (New York: Student Volunteer Movement for Foreign Missions, 1936). See John R. Mott, *The American Student Missionary Uprising* or *The History and Organization of the Student Volunteer Movement for Foreign Missions,* August 1889, published as a pamphlet. Robert E. Speer, "The Student Volunteer Movement for Foreign Missions," typed manuscript, SVM Archives. Published in *Sunday School Times,* 27 February 1892.

9. Robert E. Speer to Robert P. Wilder, 3 January 1889, SVM Archives.

10. Wilder, *The Student Volunteer Movement*, 39–40. See Robert P. Wilder to Robert E. Speer, 2 May 1922, Speer Papers.

11. Speer, "The Achievements of Yesterday," 174.

12. Robert E. Speer to Robert M. Speer, 10 October 1889, Speer Papers.

13. Robert E. Speer to Robert P. Wilder, 25 September 1889, SVM Archives.

14. Robert E. Speer to John R. Mott, 31 May 1890, Mott Papers.

15. See Speer's Bible. The other outlines were "The Reflex Influence," "Work at Home," "The Progress," "The Supernatural in Missions," "Medical Missions," "Responsibility," "Call for Money," "The Volunteer Plan for Support," " The Association & the Work," "Miscellaneous."

16. See Speer's Bible.

17. Ben Harder, "The Student Volunteer Movement for Foreign Missions and Its Contribution to 20th Century Missions," *Missiology: An International Review* 8, no. 2 (April 1980): 142.

18. *Report of the Executive Committee of the Student Volunteer Movement for Foreign Missions,* 28 February–4 March 1894 (Detroit: John Bornman & Son, [1894]), 9.

19. Robert E. Speer, "The Volunteer Movement's Possible Perils," *Student Volunteer* 1, no. 2 (March 1893): 22. This is also a typed manuscript, SVM Archives.

20. *Report of the Executive Committee,* 7.

21. Ibid., 7–8.

22. Speer, "The Volunteer Movement's Possible Perils," 22. See R. Pierce Beaver, *Ecumenical Beginnings in Protestant World Mission: A History of Comity* (New York: Thomas Nelson & Sons, 1962), 17, 76–77.

23. Speer, "The Volunteer Movement's Possible Perils," 22–23.

24. Robert E. Speer to John R. Mott, 2 August 1890, Mott Papers.

25. C. Howard Hopkins, *John R. Mott 1865–1955: A Biography* (Grand Rapids: Wm. B. Eerdmans Publishing Co., 1979), 681. For the twin tower concept, see Sherwood Eddy, *Eighty Adventurous Years: An Autobiography* (New York: Harper & Brothers Publishers, 1955), 96–97.

26. Robert E. Speer, "The Volunteer Mission Band," undated manuscript, Speer Papers.

27. This quotation and those in the following paragraphs are from Speer, "The Volunteer Mission Band."

28. Hopkins, *John R. Mott*, 214–15.

29. John R. Mott, *The Young Men's Christian Association*, vol. 4 in *Addresses and Papers of John R. Mott* (New York: Association Press, 1947), 1028.

30. Quoted in Wheeler, *A Man Sent From God*, 270. See Kenneth Scott Latourette, *Beyond the Ranges* (Grand Rapids: Wm. B. Eerdmans Publishing Co., 1967), 108.

31. Wheeler, *A Man Sent From God*, 269. See "Letters Concerning Quiet Day Circle," Charles Rosenbury Erdman Manuscript Collection, Department of Archives and Special Collections, Princeton Theological Seminary Libraries, Princeton, N.J. Hereafter cited as Erdman Collection.

32. Robert E. Speer, *Studies of Missionary Leadership* (Philadelphia: Westminster Press, 1914), 237. See R. Pierce Beaver, "Missionary Motivation Through the Centuries," in *Reinterpretation in American Church History*, ed. Jerald C. Brauer (Chicago and London: University of Chicago Press, 1968), 149.

33. Contrary to Winburn T. Thomas, "Book Review of *The Review of the Gospel* by Rufus Anderson," *Journal of Presbyterian History* 46, no. 2 (June 1968): 155.

34. Robert E. Speer, *What Constitutes a Missionary Call?* published as a pamphlet on many occasions. See Robert E. Speer, *Collection of Pamphlets*, vol. 3, Speer Papers.

35. See the newspaper report attached to: Robert E. Speer to Robert M. Speer, 19 September 1889, Speer Papers.

36. Robert E. Speer, "Men's Question Meeting," *Students and the Missionary Problem*, 256–59.

37. Speer, *What Constitutes a Missionary Call?* 3.

38. Robert E. Speer to John R. Mott, 21 July 1890, Mott Papers.

39. Latourette, *Beyond the Ranges*, 23.

40. This quotation and those in the following paragraphs are from Speer, *What Constitutes a Missionary Call?*

41. Wilder, *The Great Commission*, 84.

42. Hopkins, *John R. Mott*, 231.

43. Wilder, *The Great Commission*, 84. See Dana L. Robert, "The Origin of the Student Volunteer Watchword: 'The Evangelization of the World in This Generation,'" *International Bulletin of Missionary Research* 10 (October 1986): 146–47; Hopkins, *John R. Mott*, 231–33; Beaver, "Missionary Motivation Through the Centuries," 147–51; Wallstrom, *The Creation of a Student Movement to Evangelize the World*, 65–71.

44. For the speeches of Speer and Pierson, see *Report of the First International Convention of the Student Volunteer Movement for Foreign Missions, 26 February–1 March 1891* (Boston, Mass.: T. O. Metcalf & Co., [1891]), 73ff,

81ff.; Max Wood Moorhead, ed., *The Student Missionary Enterprise, Addresses and Discussions of the Second International Convention of the Student Volunteer Movement for Foreign Missions*, 28 February–4 March 1894 (New York: Fleming H. Revell Co., [1894]), 105–15; Robert E. Speer, "The Evangelization of the World in This Generation," in *The Student Missionary Appeal*, 201–16. Speer republished this speech some years later as chapter 44 in Robert E. Speer, *Missionary Principles and Practice: A Discussion of Christian Missions and some Criticisms upon them* (New York: Fleming H. Revell Co., 1902).

45. Robert E. Speer to John R. Mott, 21 May 1900, Speer Papers. See John R. Mott, *The Evangelization of the World in This Generation* (New York: Student Volunteer Movement for Foreign Missions, 1904).

46. Denton Lotz, "The Watchword for World Evangelization," *International Review of Missions* 68 (April 1979): 179–81.

47. Hopkins, *John R. Mott*, 231; Robert, "The Origin of the Student Volunteer Watchword," 146–47; 148–49.

48. Speer, *Missionary Principles and Practice*, 510–26. He spoke on the topic again at the SVM quadrennial in 1914. See Robert E. Speer, "The Evangelization of the World in This Generation," in Fennell P. Turner, ed., *Students and the World-Wide Expansion of Christianity, Addresses Delivered Before the Seventh International Convention of the Student Volunteer Movement for Foreign Missions*, 31 December 1913–4 January 1914 (New York: Student Volunteer Movement for Foreign Missions, 1914), 101–11. See also Patterson, "Robert E. Speer and the Crisis," 18.

49. Speer, *Missionary Principles and Practice*, 510–11.

50. Ibid., 511–12.

51. Ibid., 513–16.

52. Ibid., 516–18.

53. Ibid., 520–23.

54. Ibid., 523–24.

55. See chapter 8 for a discussion of Christianity and non-Christian religions.

56. Speer, *Missionary Principles and Practice*, 524–26.

57. Smalley, "Historical Sketch of the Student Volunteer Movement for Foreign Missions," chart A, 18f. See also Wallstrom, *The Creation of a Student Movement to Evangelize the World*, 86.

58. Nathan D. Showalter, *The End of a Crusade: The Student Volunteer Movement for Foreign Missions and the Great War* (Latham, Md., and London: Scarecrow Press, 1998), 161.

59. Handy, *A Christian America*, 193.

60. Ibid.

61. Robert E. Speer to Margaret B. Speer, 9 January 1932, Speer Papers.

62. Smalley, "Historical Sketch of the Student Volunteer Movement for Foreign Missions," 21–22. See chapter 13 for his role in the debate over the Hocking Report.

63. Robert E. Speer to Milton T. Stauffer, 28 December 1923, SVM Archives.

64. Robert E. Speer to Jesse Wilson, 2 November 1927, SVM Archives.

65. Robert E. Speer to Jesse Wilson, 19 May 1930, SVM Archives.

66. Robert E. Speer to Jesse Wilson, 4 February 1933, SVM Archives.

67. J. Lovell Murray to Robert E. Speer, 2 November 1925, SVM Archives.

68. Robert E. Speer to Margaret B. Speer, 15 December 1925, Speer Papers. See Michael Parker, *The Kingdom of Character: The Student Volunteer Movement for Foreign Missions* (Lanham, Md., New York, Oxford: American Society of Missiology and University Press of America, 1998), 176–79.

69. Robert E. Speer to R. H. Edwin Espy, 22 April 1941, SVM Archives.

70. Beaver, "Missionary Motivation Through the Centuries," 149.

71. John R. Mott, "Robert Elliott Speer," *Woman's Press* 42, no. 1 (January 1948): 9; Eddy, *Eighty Adventurous Years*, 97.

72. John A. Mackay, "The President's Page," *Princeton Seminary Bulletin* 41, no. 3 (Winter 1948): 26.

73. Aunt Mim to Aunt Clara, 24 October 1905, Speer Papers.

74. Robert Moats Miller, *Harry Emerson Fosdick: Preacher, Pastor, Prophet* (New York: Oxford University Press, 1985), 67.

75. Richard C. Morse, *My Life With Young Men: Fifty Years in the Young Men's Christian Association* (New York: Association Press, 1918), 302.

76. Robert E. Speer, "The closing remarks of the Convention," *Report of the First International Convention*, 185–88.

77. Robert E. Speer, "The closing address of the Convention," *The Student Missionary Enterprise*, 162–67.

78. Handy, *A Christian America*, 137.

79. Miller, Robert Moats, *How Shall They Hear Without a Preacher? The Life of Ernest Fremont Tittle* (Chapel Hill: University of North Carolina Press, 1971), 24.

80. Robert E. Speer, "The Fulness of the Living Presence of Christ," in *Students and the Modern Missionary Crusade* (Nashville: Student Volunteer Movement, 1906), 9.

81. Robert E. Speer, "The Uplifted Eye and the Life Laid Down," in *Students and the Modern Missionary Crusade*, 281–82.

82. Ibid., 283–84.

83. "Diaries." See also Robert E. Speer to Mrs. W. R. Moody, [Summer 1903], Speer Papers.

84. May Moody to Robert E. Speer, May–June, 1903, Speer Papers.

85. Robert E. Speer to Robert P. Wilder, 9 September 1919, and Robert P. Wilder to Robert E. Speer, 12 September 1919, SVM Archives.

86. "Collection of Miscellaneous Articles," Speer Papers.

87. Speer, *A Memorial of a True Life*, 92.

88. Robert E. Speer, "Fourth of July Letters—Northfield, 1908," Speer Family Papers.

89. Wilder, *The Great Commission*, 65.

90. Constance E. Padwick, *Temple Gairdner of Cairo* (London: Society for Promoting Christian Knowledge, 1929), 49. See Eddy, *Pathfinders of the World Missionary Crusade*, 268–69; Ruth Rouse, *The World's Student Christian Federation: A History of the First Thirty Years* (London: SCM Press, 1948), 96.

91. Eddy, *Pathfinders of the World Missionary Crusade*, 268. See Ruth Rouse to "My dearest Emma," 14 December 1947, Speer Papers; Agnes R. Fraser, *Donald Fraser of Livingstonia* (London: Hodder & Stoughton, 1934), 26–27.

92. Speer, "Random," 41.
93. Wheeler, *A Man Sent From God*, 143; Mott, "Robert Elliott Speer," 9.
94. Henry Sloane Coffin to Robert E. Speer, 25 May 1922, Speer Papers.
95. John D. Rockefeller, Jr., to Robert E. Speer, 3 May 1922, Speer Papers.
96. Kenneth S. Latourette to Robert E. Speer, 4 May 1922, Speer Papers.
97. Henry B. Wright, *A Life With a Purpose, A Memorial of John Lawrence Thurston: First Missionary of the Yale Mission* (New York: Fleming H. Revell Co., 1908), 179–80.
98. Walter L. Whallon to Robert E. Speer, 24 October 1941, Speer Papers.
99. Frank N. Freeman to Robert E. Speer, 14 January 1906, Speer Papers.
100. Fred Mudge to Robert E. Speer, 18 February 1936, Speer Family Papers.
101. Carter, *So Much to Learn*, 146.
102. Wheeler, *A Man Sent From God*, 309–11.
103. Robert E. Speer to F. Ernest Johnson, 31 October 1931, Speer Papers.
104. Mott, "Robert Elliott Speer," 9.
105. Copy in the Speer Papers.
106. Wheeler, *A Man Sent From God*, 134–45.
107. Robert E. Speer, *Young Men Who Overcame* (New York: Fleming H. Revell Co., [1905]). The other books have already been cited. See "Ideals for Boys," Speer Family Papers.
108. Robert E. Speer, "D. L. Moody," On Founder's Day, 5 February 1931, Speer Papers, 14.
109. Speer, "Random," 5.
110. Speer, "D. L. Moody," 15–17. See Robert E. Speer, "A Torrent of Love and Power," Scrap-Books, D. L. Moody, 1894–1937, Speer Papers.
111. Robert E. Speer, "Christ and the Bible in the Life of Tomorrow," D. L. Moody Centenary, Northfield General Conference, 1937, typed manuscript, Speer Papers, 2.
112. See chapter 11.
113. Speer, "Christ and the Bible in the Life of Tomorrow," 4.
114. Patterson, "Robert E. Speer and the Crisis," 12–15.
115. Richard K. Curtis, *They Called Him Mister Moody* (Garden City, N.J.: Doubleday & Company, 1962), 322; Findlay, *Dwight L. Moody*, 352–55.
116. Speer, "Random," 5.
117. See chapter 4.
118. Robert E. Speer, *A Memorial of Horace Tracy Pitkin* (New York: Fleming H. Revell Co., [1903]), 75–76.
119. Findlay, *Dwight L. Moody*, 354.
120. Speer, "The Achievements of Yesterday," 176.
121. Henry C. Trumbull to Robert E. Speer, 26 July 1892, Speer Family Papers.

Chapter 6: Secretary of Presbyterian Foreign Missions

1. Samuel Hugh Moffett, "The Relation of the Board of Foreign Missions of the Presbyterian Church in the United States of America to the Missions and Church Connected with it in China," Ph.D. diss., Yale University , 1945, 20. See Arthur Judson Brown, *One Hundred Years. A History of the Foreign*

Missionary Work of the Presbyterian Church in the U.S.A. With Some Account of Countries, Peoples and the Policies and Problems of Modern Missions, Book 1 (New York: Fleming H. Revell Co., 1936), 13–37; Robert E. Speer, "The Founders and The Foundations," *Centennial of the Western Foreign Missionary Society, 1831–1931* (Pittsburgh Presbytery, [1931]), 138–62; Gerald H. Anderson, "American Protestants in Pursuit of Mission: 1886–1986, *International Bulletin of Missionary Research* 12, no. 3 (July 1988): 98–118.

2. Brown, *One Hundred Years*, 38; Moffett, "The Relation of the Board of Foreign Missions," 23.

3. Robert E. Speer, "Elisha B. Swift," *Centennial*, 176.

4. Moffett, "The Relation of the Board of Foreign Missions," 24; Brown, *One Hundred Years*, 51.

5. Robert E. Speer to Elliott Speer, 6 June 1929, Speer Family Papers.

6. Robert E. Speer to Margaret B. Speer, 11 April 1932, Speer Papers.

7. Robert E. Speer, "The Presbyterian Church and the Evangelization of the World," *Journal of the Department of History* 15, no. 1 (March 1932): 59–61.

8. Henry C. Trumbull to Robert E. Speer, 8 June 1893, Speer Papers.

9. Brown, *One Hundred Years*, 73.

10. Ibid.

11. Arthur Judson Brown, *Memoirs of a Centenarian*, ed. William N. Wysham (New York: World Horizons, 1957), 32. R. Park Johnson, "The Legacy of Arthur Judson Brown," *International Bulletin of Missionary Research* 10, no. 2 (April 1986): 71–75; Pierard, "Evangelical and Ecumenical," 156–59.

12. Mary G. Ellinwood, *Frank Field Ellinwood: His Life and Work* (New York: Fleming H. Revell Co., 1911).

13. Quoted in *Report of the First International Convention*, 26–27.

14. Laura Ellinwood to Robert E. Speer, 29 October 1908, Speer Papers.

15. Ibid.

16. Robert E. Speer, *One Century Past, Another to Come* (New York: Board of Foreign Missions of the Presbyterian Church in the U.S.A., 1937), 11, published as a pamphlet. See Wheeler, *A Man Sent From God*, 70.

17. This is Brown's description of the work both he and Speer did. See *Memoirs of a Centenarian*, 24.

18. C. W. Douglass to Mrs. R. E. Speer, 13 January 1949, Speer Family Papers.

19. Ellinwood, *Frank Field Ellinwood*, 123.

20. Quoted in ibid., 122.

21. Robert E. Speer, *Missions and Modern History: A Study of the Missionary Aspects of Some Great Movements of the Nineteenth Century* (New York: Fleming H. Revell Co., 1904), 1:5.

22. Speer, "Random," 19.

23. Quoted in Ellinwood, *Frank Field Ellinwood*, 123.

24. Wheeler, *A Man Sent From God*, 166–67.

25. Robert E. Speer to W. R. Moody, 2 November 1899, Speer Papers.

26. Robert E. Speer to W. R. Moody, 9 November 1899, Speer Papers.

27. Wheeler, *A Man Sent From God*, 167–72. See Margaret B. Speer, *"RES,"* 16 November 1967, manuscript, Speer Family Papers.

28. Quoted in Wheeler, *A Man Sent From God*, 171.
29. Ibid., 81.
30. William Hiram Foulkes, "A Tribute to Robert E. Speer," *Presbyterian Tribune* 52, no. 27 (30 September 1937): 6.
31. Wheeler, *A Man Sent From God*, 79.
32. Margaret E. Duncan to Robert E. Speer, 22 January 1908, Speer Papers.
33. Lucia P. Towne, "Robert E. Speer," *Women and Missions* 14, no. 7 (October 1937): 240.
34. Robert E. Speer to Miss Edith C. Dickie, 16 July 1906, Speer Papers.
35. Robert E. Speer to A. J. Brown, 30 June 1929, in the Arthur Judson Brown Papers, Yale Divinity School Library, Archives and Manuscripts, New Haven, Conn. Hereafter cited as Brown Papers.
36. Robert E. Speer to A. J. Brown. 22 December 1935, Brown Papers.
37. Wheeler, *A Man Sent From God*, 84–85; Foulkes, "A Tribute to Robert E. Speer," 6.
38. W. Reginald Wheeler, "The Methods of a Master," *Presbyterian Banner* 123, no. 48 (27 May 1937): 11.
39. Charles W. Forman, "A History of Foreign Mission Theory in America," in R. Pierce Beaver, ed., *American Missions in Bicentennial Perspective* (South Pasadena, Calif.: William Carey Library, 1977), 92.
40. Ibid. See Patterson, "Robert E. Speer and the Crisis," 33.
41. Robert E. Speer to Miss Edith C. Dickie, 27 December 1910, Speer Papers.
42. Robert E. Speer to E. S. McMurtrie, 4 March 1914, Speer Family Papers.
43. Robert E. Speer to Margaret B. Speer, 28 October 1929, Speer Family Papers.
44. Robert E. Speer to Elliott Speer, 21 October 1930, Speer Family Papers.
45. Robert E. Speer, "Paul, The Great Missionary Example," in Moorhead, *The Student Missionary Enterprise*, 11.
46. Speer, "The Student Volunteer Movement for Foreign Missions."
47. Katharine Morris to Robert E. Speer, n.d., Speer Papers.
48. Raymond F. Sarett to Robert E. Speer, 13 April 1908, Speer Papers.
49. Stanley White to Robert E. Speer, 12 April 1922, Speer Papers.
50. Robert E. Speer to Miss Clara L. Porter, 26 July 1892, in the Records of the Board of Foreign Missions, 1829–1895, Presbyterian Historical Society, Philadelphia, Penn. Hereafter cited as Board Records to 1895.
51. Robert E. Speer to Dean R. Leland, 14 December 1902, Speer Family Papers.
52. Woodrow Wilson to Robert E. Speer, 27 March and 5 April 1909, Speer Papers.
53. Speer, "Paul, The Great Missionary Example," 10.
54. Ibid., 10–11. For Speer's idea of a model missionary, see "A Princeton Martyr," *Young Men Who Overcame*, 190–208.
55. Robert E. Speer to Miss Sarah Grace Street, 26 July 1892, Board Records to 1895.
56. Robert E. Speer to Fennell P. Turner, 2 February 1915, SVM Archives.
57. Speer, *Studies of Missionary Leadership*, 56–57.
58. Robert E. Speer to Miss Mary Annie Ricketts, 24 March 1893, Board Records to 1895.
59. Robert E. Speer to Dr. F. M. Gardner, 20 July 1892, Board Records to 1895.

60. Quoted in Wheeler, *A Man Sent From God*, 82.
61. J. J. Lucas, "A Letter and An Appreciation," *Presbyterian Banner* 124, no. 6 (9 September 1937): 15.
62. Robert P. Wilder to Robert E. Speer, 29 March 1895, Speer Papers.
63. Robert E. Speer to John R. Mott, 3 June 1899, Speer Papers.
64. Robert E. Speer to Robert P. Wilder, 26 September 1899, in the Robert Parmelee Wilder Papers, Yale Divinity School Library, Archives and Manuscripts, New Haven, Conn. Hereafter cited as Wilder Papers.
65. Robert E. Speer to Fred B. Smith, 3 June 1907, Speer Papers.
66. James Smylie used the term "communicator" to describe this role. James H. Smylie, "Robert E. Speer: Mission Executive and Visionary," in James H. Smylie, Dean K. Thompson, and Cary Patrick, *Go Therefore: 150 Years of Presbyterians in Global Mission* (Atlanta: Presbyterian Publishing House, 1987), 47.
67. Robert E. Speer to H. C. Velte, 21 September 1927, Speer Papers.
68. Robert E. Speer to Margaret B. Speer, 29 August 1929, Speer Family Papers.
69. Robert E. Speer to Mrs. Charles L. Reed, 4 March 1927, Speer Papers.
70. Robert E. Speer to Margaret B. Speer, 19 October 1933, Speer Papers.
71. Robert E. Speer to Elliott Speer, 1 June 1917, Speer Papers.
72. Robert E. Speer, "Address at General Assembly," Columbus, 1933, typed manuscript, Speer Papers, 1.
73. Ibid.
74. Lucas, "A Letter and An Appreciation," 15.
75. An item from a Buffalo newspaper, [1904], "Scrapbook," Speer Family Papers.
76. Brown, *One Hundred Years*, 61f.
77. Robert E. Speer: *Report on Missions in Asia, Persia, China, Japan, Korea* (New York: Board of Foreign Missions of the Presbyterian Church in the U.S.A., 1897); *Presbyterian Foreign Missions* (New York: Board of Foreign Missions of the Presbyterian Church in the U.S.A., 1901); *Missions in South America* (New York: Board of Foreign Missions of the Presbyterian Church in the U.S.A., 1910); *Report on Siam, the Philippines, Japan, Chosen and China* (New York: Board of Foreign Missions of the Presbyterian Church in the U.S.A., 1916); *Report on India and Persia* (New York: Board of Foreign Missions of the Presbyterian Church in the U.S.A., 1922); *Report on China and Japan* (New York: Board of Foreign Missions of the Presbyterian Church in the U.S.A., 1926); *Are Foreign Missions Done For?* (New York: Board of Foreign Missions of the Presbyterian Church in the U.S.A., 1928); *"Lu Taifu": Charles Lewis, M.D., A Pioneer Surgeon in China* (New York: Board of Foreign Missions, Presbyterian Church in the U.S.A., 1930).
78. Speer, *Presbyterian Foreign Missions*, 3.
79. See "A Note to Those Receiving This Book."
80. Robert E. Speer to Margaret B. Speer, 26 March 1929, Speer Family Papers.
81. Ellinwood, *Frank Field Ellinwood*, 63–64.
82. Speer, *Studies of Missionary Leadership*, 61. See Moffett, "The Relation of the Board of Foreign Missions," 68–75.
83. Hugh T. Kerr, "Robert E. Speer: A Question for the Presbyterian Church to Answer," *Presbyterian Banner* 121, no. 45 (9 May 1935): Inside front cover.

84. Robert E. Speer, "Voyages" in *Chronological Record*, manuscript, Speer Family Papers.
85. John D. Wells and William R. Richards, "To the Brethren of the Missions of the Presbyterian Church in Persia, India, Siam, China, Japan and Korea," 3 August 1896, form letter, Speer Papers.
86. See *Mission Tour, 1896–97*, and related *Account Book Mission Trip* 1896–97, manuscript, Speer Papers. See Stanley A. Hunter, "Minister Appraises Moderator," in *Robert E. Speer, Missionary Statesman* (Philadelphia: General Assembly, 1927), 5–9, published as a pamphlet, Speer Papers.
87. Robert E. Speer to E. S. McMurtrie, 21 July 1922, Speer Family Papers; Robert E. Speer to D. S. Cairns, 21 July 1922, Speer Papers.
88. The books were Robert E. Speer, *Report on Missions in Asia, Persia, China, Japan, Korea*, and *Missions and Politics in Asia: Studies of the Spirit of the Eastern Peoples, the Present Making of History in Asia, and the Part Therein of Christian Missions* (New York: Fleming H. Revell Co., 1898). The articles appeared in many different religious periodicals of the day.
89. See chapter 7.
90. *Report of Robert E. Speer, Secretary to the Presbyterian Board of Foreign Missions, on his visit to the Missions of West and East Persia* (New York: Board of Foreign Missions of the Presbyterian Church in the U.S.A., 1897) [Printed for use of the board], 3.
91. Emma B. Speer to Dearest Mother, 27 November 1896, Speer Papers. The Speer Papers contain other letters from Emma to her family during this trip. See Wheeler, *A Man Sent From God*, 103ff.
92. New Year's Day, 1897, quoted in Wheeler, *A Man Sent From God*, 112.
93. Robert E. Speer to My dear Dr. Larabee, Christmas Day, 1896, Speer Family Papers.
94. Henry C. Trumbull to Robert E. Speer, 26 February 1897, Speer Papers.
95. Moffett, "The Relation of the Board of Foreign Missions," 236f.
96. Quoted in Eddy, *Pathfinders of the World Missionary Crusade*, 266.
97. Speer, *Report on Siam, the Philippines, Japan, Chosen and China*, 235.
98. Ibid., 511.
99. Frank Mason North to Robert E. Speer, 27 August, 1916, and Robert E. Speer to Frank Mason North, 11 September 1916, Speer Papers.
100. Robert E. Speer to Dr. Thomas, 8 May 1897, Speer Papers.
101. Speer, *Report on Siam, the Philippines, Japan, Chosen and China*, 491.
102. Robert E. Speer to J. J. Lucas, 27 May 1914, Speer Papers.
103. Speer, *Report on Siam, the Philippines, Japan, Chosen and China*, 494.
104. Miller, "Christ's Man," 12. See also William McElwee Miller, "Robert E. Speer: Recruiter with a World Plan," *World Vision Magazine* 11, no. 8 (September 1967): 14–15, 29.
105. Andrew T. Roy, "Overseas Mission Policies—an Historical Overview," *Journal of Presbyterian History* 57, no. 3 (Fall 1979): 200.
106. Ibid., 201.
107. Brown, *One Hundred Years*, 88–89; Roy, "Overseas Mission Policies—an Historical Overview," 206. *Minutes of the General Assembly of the Presbyterian Church in the United States of America* (Philadelphia: MacCalla and Company, Printers, 1900), 96.

108. Charles E. Harvey, "Speer Versus Rockefeller and Mott, 1910–1935," *Journal of Presbyterian History* 60, no. 4 (Winter 1982): 284.
109. Memo of 8 September 1913 in "Religious Interests," Rockefeller Family Archives, Rockefeller Archive Center, Pocantico Hills, North Tarrytown, N.Y. Hereafter cited as Rockefeller Archives.
110. Ibid.
111. Jerome D. Greene to John R. Mott, 3 October 1913, Rockefeller Archives.
112. Harvey, "Speer Versus Rockefeller and Mott," 286. See Hopkins, *John R. Mott*, 425.
113. Speer, "Random." See list titled "Some Activities which give Special Satisfaction on looking back."
114. Brown, *One Hundred Years*, 68.
115. Ibid., 68–69.
116. Margaret B. Speer, "Marriage and Family," 66.
117. Dorothy Ferris to Mrs. Speer, 17 January 1949, Speer Family Papers.
118. Brown, *One Hundred Years*, 69.
119. Ibid., 84.
120. Robert E. Speer to D. S. Cairns, 6 July 1931, Speer Papers.
121. For major revisions during Speer's career, see Roy, "Overseas Mission Policies—an Historical Overview."
122. Ibid., 210.
123. Robert E. Speer to President Cheesman A. Herrick, 21 November 1925, Speer Papers.
124. Robert E. Speer to Margaret B. Speer, 28 December 1928, Speer Family Papers.
125. Robert E. Speer to Margaret B. Speer, 19 February 1929, Speer Family Papers. See letters from Speer to Margaret dated: 10 December 1928, 21 January, 26 March, 23 April 1929, Speer Family Papers.
126. Robert E. Speer to Aunt Clara, 14 November 1933, Speer Family Papers.
127. Robert E. Speer to Margaret B. Speer, 21 June and 1 July 1932, Speer Papers.
128. Robert E. Speer to Margaret B. Speer, 20 February 1933, Speer Papers.
129. Brown, *One Hundred Years*, 108.
130. Ibid., 105–12.
131. Charles T. Leber, "Board Policy During the Crisis Decade," in W. Reginald Wheeler, ed., *The Crisis Decade*, A History of the Foreign Missionary Work of the Presbyterian Church in the U.S.A., 1937–1947 (New York: Board of Foreign Missions of the Presbyterian Church in the U.S.A., 1950), 12.
132. Patterson, "Robert E. Speer and the Crisis," 185–86.
133. Robert E. Speer to Hugh T. Kerr, 26 March 1929, Speer Papers.
134. Richard W. Reifsnyder, "Managing the Mission: Church Restructuring in the Twentieth Century," in Milton J. Coalter, John M. Mulder, Louis B. Weeks, eds., *The Organizational Revolution: Presbyterians and American Denominationalism* (Louisville, Ky.: Westminster/John Knox Press, 1992), 57–60.
135. Chapters 12 and 13.
136. Speer, *Missionary Principles and Practice*, 87.
137. Interview with Margaret B. Speer and William Speer.
138. Quoted in Loetscher, *The Broadening Church*, 105. See "Dr. Speer Defends China Missionaries," *Continent* 52, no. 14 (7 April 1921): 415.

139. Robert E. Speer to J. Walter Lowrie, 22 April 1921, Speer Papers.
140. Robert E. Speer to Tissington Tatlow, 14 May 1902, Speer Papers.
141. Speer, *Missionary Principles and Practice*, 130–276.
142. Ibid., 130–31.
143. Robert E. Speer, "The Bugaboo of Missionary Denominationalism," typed manuscript, Speer Papers.
144. Dr. J. V. Moldenhawer in Hugh T. Kerr et al., "Dr. Robert E. Speer," *Presbyterian Banner* 123, no. 48 (27 May 1937): 9.
145. Reifsnyder, "Managing the Mission," 58.
146. Eddy, *Pathfinders of the World Missionary Crusade*, 264.
147. John A. Mackay, "Tribute," in *Robert Elliott Speer*, a memorial pamphlet, n.d., Speer Papers, 13.

Chapter 7 : Advocate for Ecumenical Missions

1. Beaver, "Missionary Motivation Through the Centuries," 115.
2. Ibid., 116.
3. *Interdenominational Conference of Foreign Missionary Boards and Societies in the United States and Canada* (New York: E. O. Jenkins' Sons Printing House, 1893), 4. See Samuel McCrea Cavert, *The American Churches in the Ecumenical Movement: 1900–1968* (New York: Association Press, 1968), 38.
4. Samuel McCrea Cavert, *Church Cooperation and Unity in America. A Historical Review: 1900–1970* (New York: Association Press, 1970), 34.
5. John T. McNeill and James Hastings Nichols, *Ecumenical Testimony: The Concern for Christian Unity Within the Reformed and Presbyterian Churches* (Philadelphia: Westminister Press, 1974), 210.
6. *Report of the Sixth Conference of the Officers and Representatives of the Foreign Missions Boards and Societies in the United States and Canada* (New York: Foreign Missions Library, [1898]), 116–17.
7. Ibid., 117–18.
8. Ibid., 119–20.
9. Ibid., 124–25.
10. *Report of the Seventh Conference of the Officers and Representatives of the Foreign Missions Boards and Societies in the United States and Canada* (New York: Foreign Missions Library, [1899]), 41–49. Reprinted as Robert E. Speer, "The Science of Missions," *Missionary Review of the World*, New Series 12, no. 1 (January 1899): 27–37. The final and somewhat revised version, used for this analysis, appeared in Speer, *Missionary Principles and Practice*, 43–68.
11. *Report of the Seventh Conference*, 48–49.
12. Ibid., 49.
13. Ibid., 53–54.
14. "Report of the Committee on General Principles," *Eighth Conference of the Officers and Representatives of the Foreign Missions Boards and Societies in the United States and Canada* (New York: Foreign Missions Library, [1901]), 59–60.
15. R. Pierce Beaver, *Ecumenical Beginnings*, 15f.
16. *Report of the Sixth Conference*, 4.
17. *Report of the Seventh Conference*, 106–12.

18. Ibid., 117, 4.
19. Robert E. Speer, "Mission Comity," *Churchman* 79, no. 14 (8 April 1899): 511.
20. A. Sutherland to Robert E. Speer, 19 July 1899, Speer Papers.
21. *Eighth Conference*, 24.
22. Cavert, *The American Churches in the Ecumenical Movement*, 39.
23. Cavert, *Church Cooperation and Unity in America*, 36. See chapter 9.
24. *Foreign Missions Conference of North America: Report of Eighteenth Conference of Foreign Missions Boards in the United States and Canada, 1911* (New York: Foreign Missions Library, [1911]), 5.
25. Cavert, *The American Churches in the Ecumenical Movement*, 120, 203–5.
26. Ruth Rouse and Stephen Charles Neill, eds., *A History of the Ecumenical Movement, 1517–1948*. 2d ed. with rev. bibliog. (Philadelphia: Westminster Press, 1967), 355.
27. *Report of the Fourth Conference of the Officers and Representatives of the Foreign Missions Boards and Societies in the United States and Canada* (New York: Foreign Missions Library, [1896]), 117–18.
28. Cavert, *The American Churches in the Ecumenical Movement*, 38.
29. Cavert, *The American Churches in the Ecumenical Movement*, 38; see note 13. See also *Report of the Fifth Conference of the Officers and Representatives of the Foreign Missions Boards and Societies in the United States and Canada* (New York: Foreign Missions Library, [1897]), 100.
30. Cavert, *The American Churches in the Ecumenical Movement*, 39.
31. *Eighth Conference*, 14–15.
32. Robert E. Speer, "The Supreme and Determining Aim," *Ecumenical Missionary Conference,* Report of the Ecumenical Missionary Conference on Foreign Missions, Held in Carnegie Hall and Neighboring Churches, 21 April–1 May 1900 (New York: American Tract Society, 1900), 1:74–75.
33. Paul A. Varg, "Motives in Protestant Missions, 1890–1917," *Church History* 23 (March 1954): 68–82. See Paul A. Varg, *Missionaries, Chinese, and Diplomats: The American Protestant Missionary Movement in China, 1890–1952* (Princeton: Princeton University Press, 1958), chapter 5.
34. Handy, *A Christian America*, 133f.
35. Quoted in ibid., 133–34. See *Ecumenical Missionary Conference*, 1:9–10.
36. Robert E. Speer, "The Significance of the Ecumenical Missionary Conference," *Ecumenical Missionary Conference,* 1:59.
37. Ibid., 1:62.
38. Ibid., 1:59, 63.
39. Kenneth Scott Latourette, *A History of Christianity* (New York: Harper & Brothers Publishers, 1953), ix. See Patterson, "Robert E. Speer and the Crisis," 39.
40. H. McKennie Goodpasture, "Robert E. Speer's Legacy," *Occasional Bulletin of Missionary Research* 2, no. 2 (April 1978): 40–41.
41. *Eighth Conference*, 25–26.
42. Ibid., 28.
43. Ibid., 42.
44. *Ninth Conference of the Officers and Representatives of the Foreign Mission Boards and Societies in the United States and Canada* (New York: Foreign Missions Library, [1902]), 103.

45. *World Missionary Conference* (New York: Fleming H. Revell Co., [1910]), vol. 9, "The History and Records of the Conference," 5–6.
46. *Fourteenth Conference,* 101–6; Rouse and Neill, *A History of the Ecumenical Movement,* 355ff.; Hopkins, *John R. Mott,* chapter 7.
47. Speer, "Random." See list titled "Some Activities which give Special Satisfaction on looking back."
48. Rouse and Neill, *A History of the Ecumenical Movement,* 361f.; Beaver, *Ecumenical Beginnings in Protestant World Mission,* 79.
49. Rouse and Neill, *A History of the Ecumenical Movement,* 357.
50. *World Missionary Conference,* 9:98.
51. Robert E. Speer to H. P. Andersen, 21 October 1908, Speer Papers.
52. Speer, "Random." See page that begins, "My going to Scotland for the Duff Missionary Lectures."
53. George Robson to Robert E. Speer, 28 September 1909, Speer Papers.
54. Robert E. Speer to J. Fairley Daly, 6 January 1908, Speer Papers.
55. Mackay, "Tribute," 11.
56. *World Missionary Conference,* 9:22.
57. Quoted in "Deaths" Robert E. Speer, D.D., *Baltimore Presbyterian* 21, no. 4 (January 1948): 4, Speer Papers.
58. Colin J. S. Mackenzie and S. E. Jones to Robert E. Speer, 14 June 1910, Speer Papers.
59. Hunter, "Minister Appraises Moderator," 7.
60. Robert E. Speer to Miss Edith C. Dickie, 27 December 1910, Speer Papers.
61. *World Missionary Conference,* 9:151–55.
62. Ibid., 108–110.
63. Robert E. Speer, "The Edinburgh Conference—II," in *The East and the West* (October 1910), 369, 374–75, Speer Papers; Robert E. Speer, "The World Missionary Conference, Impressions and Lessons," *Missionary Record of the United Free Church of Scotland,* no. 116 (August 1910), Speer Papers.
64. *Twelfth Conference of the Foreign Missions Boards in the United States and Canada* (New York: Foreign Missions Library, [1905]), 101–2.
65. Rouse and Neill, *A History of the Ecumenical Movement,* 357; William R. Hogg, *Ecumenical Foundations: A History of the International Missionary Council* (New York: Harper & Brothers Publishers, 1952), 131–32.
66. Wheeler, *A Man Sent From God,* 189–90. Mackay infers that Speer took the trip because of his dissatisfaction with the Edinburgh decision. See John H. Sinclair and Arturo Piedra Solano, "The Dawn of Ecumenism in Latin America: Robert E. Speer, Presbyterians, and the Panama Conference of 1916," *Journal of Presbyterian History* 77, no. 1 (Spring 1999): 2–3.
67. George Wharton Pepper to Robert E. Speer, 27 November 1909, Speer Papers.
68. Robert E. Speer, "The Spiritual Claims of Latin America Upon the United States and Canada," in *Students and the Present Missionary Crisis* (New York: SVM, 1910), 92–94.
69. Ibid., 94–108.
70. Robert E. Speer to Miss Edith C. Dickie, 19 April 1910, Speer Papers.
71. Wheeler, *A Man Sent From God,* 190; Hogg, *Ecumenical Foundations,* 132. See W. Stanley Rycroft, *Memoirs of Life in Three Worlds* (Cranbury, N.J.: J. B. Business Services, 1976), 70–71.

NOTES TO PAGES 207–215   467

72. *Conference on Missions in Latin America*, 12 and 13 March 1913 (Lebanon, Pa.: Sowers Printing Co., 1913), 9.
73. Ibid., 17.
74. Wheeler, *A Man Sent From God.*, 193.
75. Robert E. Speer to J. J. Lucas, 26 January 1916, Speer Papers.
76. Hogg, *Ecumenical Foundations*, 174; Sinclair and Solano, "The Dawn of Ecumenism in Latin America: Robert E. Speer, Presbyterians, and the Panama Conference of 1916," 7–8.
77. See *Missionary Review of the World* (April 1916); *Sunday School Times* (18 March 1916); *East and West* (October 1916).
78. Robert E. Speer, *The Unity of the Americas* (New York: Laymen's Missionary Movement, 1916), 113. See chapter 4: "Religious."
79. Hogg, *Ecumenical Foundations*, 235–36; Wheeler, *A Man Sent From God*, 197–203.
80. Robert E. Speer to D. S. Cairns, 14 July 1925, Speer Papers; Rycroft, *Memoirs of Life in Three Worlds*, 72–73.
81. Rouse and Neill, *A History of the Ecumenical Movement*, 396.
82. J. Carter Swaim wrote the citation the Ulster Irish Society gave Speer, and described him as a "far-seeing statesman whose vision for South America antedated by two decades the Good Neighbor policy of his nation." Speer Family Papers. See also Juan Orts Gonzales to Robert E. Speer, 22 May 1941, Speer Papers.
83. Robert E. Speer, "Some Missionary Aspects of the Year 1914," *Missionary Review of the World* 38, no. 1 (January 1915): 16.
84. Hopkins, *John R. Mott*, 581–85.
85. Basil Mathews, "The Agenda of Co-operation," A Sketch of the Meeting of the International Missionary Council, Oxford, 9–16 July 1923, *The International Review of Missions* 12 (October 1923): 482.
86. Speer, "Is Identity of Doctrinal Opinion Necessary to Continued Missionary Cooperation?," 497–504. See Speer, "The Limits of Tolerance," *Some Living Issues*, 135–52.
87. Hopkins, *John R. Mott*, 659–61.
88. *Addresses on General Subjects.* The Jerusalem Meeting of the International Missionary Council, 24 March–8 April 1928 (New York and London: International Missionary Council, 1928), 8:8.
89. Ibid., 9
90. Hogg, *Ecumenical Foundations*, 244.
91. *Addresses on General Subjects*, 8:17.
92. *The Christian Life and Message in Relation to Non-Christian Systems of Thought and Life.* The Jerusalem Meeting of the International Missionary Council, 24 March–8 April 1928 (New York and London: International Missionary Council, 1928), 1:278–82.
93. Ibid., 282–308. For the response by Emma, see 305.
94. Ibid., 282, 301.
95. Ibid., 308–11.
96. F. A. Iremonger, *William Temple.* Archbishop of Canterbury, His Life and Letters (London: Oxford University Press, 1948), 396.
97. Robert E. Speer, "The Missionary Message to the World," in *The Foreign Missions Conference of North America*, 1929, 36th Annual Conference, Leslie B.

Moss, ed. (New York: Foreign Missions Conference of North America, [1929]), 201.
98. Hogg, *Ecumenical Foundations*, 248.
99. *The Christian Life and Message*, 1:402–4, 408–13.
100. Rouse and Neill, *A History of the Ecumenical Movement*, 369.
101. Emma B. Speer to Dr. Beaver, 29 October 1953, Speer Papers.
102. R. Pierce Beaver to Mrs. Speer, 4 November 1953, Speer Papers.
103. Iremonger, *William Temple*, 396–97.
104. Speer, "Random." See list titled "Some Activities which give Special Satisfaction on looking back."
105. John R. Mott to Robert E. Speer, 11 April 1928, Mott Papers.
106. *The Christian Life and Message*, 1:349.
107. Ibid., 348.
108. Robert E. Speer to Clara McMurtrie, 24 May 1927, Speer Family Papers. See Speer, *Christian Realities*, 15–16.
109. Speer, *The Meaning of Christ to Me*, 118–20. See Speer, "The Missionary Message to the World," 202.
110. Robert E. Speer, "The Resurrection," *Addresses on General Subjects*, 1:135–43.

Chapter 8: The History and Theory of Missions

1. Robert E. Speer to Margaret B. Speer, 9 May 1927, Speer Family Papers.
2. Speer, "Random," 20.
3. Speer, *A Young Man's Questions*, 196, 202f.
4. Robert E. Speer to Margaret B. Speer, 12 March 1926, Speer Papers.
5. Speer, *Some Changing and Unchanging Things in Foreign Missions*, 4–5.
6. Ibid., 5. The passage is Hebrews 11:39–40.
7. "Edward Stewart McMurtrie," (1925), Brown Notebook, Speer Family Papers.
8. Robert E. Speer, "Charge to the President," Charge at Inauguration of Dr. John A. Mackay as President of Princeton Theological Seminary, *Princeton Seminary Bulletin* 31, no. 1 (April 1937): 3.
9. Robert E. Speer, *The Marks of a Man* (New York: Hodder & Stoughton, 1907), 94.
10. Ibid., 94–95.
11. See chapter 11.
12. F. F. Ellinwood to Robert E. Speer, 12 December 1904, Speer Papers.
13. Speer, "Random," 20.
14. Robert E. Speer, *The Church and Missions* (New York: George H. Doran Co., 1926), 32–41.
15. See chapter III.
16. Ellinwood to Speer, 12 December 1904.
17. Goodpasture, "Robert E. Speer's Legacy," 40.
18. Speer, *Missions and Politics in Asia*, 7.
19. Speer, *The Church and Missions*, 11–12.
20. Ibid., 222.
21. Speer, *Presbyterian Foreign Missions*, 3.
22. Ibid., 66.

23. Ellinwood to Speer, 12 December 1904.
24. Speer, *Presbyterian Foreign Missions*, 295.
25. Robert E. Speer, "Two Hundred and Fifty Years of Foreign Missions," *Journal of the Department of History* 15, nos. 7 and 8 (September–December 1933): 386–89.
26. Robert E. Speer, "Princeton on the Mission Field," *Journal of the Presbyterian Historical Society* 24, no. 2 (June 1946): 100.
27. Ibid., 103–04.
28. Robert E. Speer, *Servants of the King* (New York: Young People's Missionary Movement of the United States and Canada, 1910), vii.
29. Robert E. Speer to Florence Smith, 23 July 1934, Speer Papers.
30. Speer, *Some Great Leaders in the World Movement*, 17.
31. Speer, *Servants of the King*, viii. See Robert E. Speer to Miss Edith C. Dickie, 28 March 1907, Speer Papers.
32. Speer, *Missionary Principles and Practice*, 393.
33. Robert E. Speer, *George Bowen of Bombay: Missionary; Scholar; Mystic; Saint: A Memoir* (Printed privately, 1938), viii.
34. Speer, *Servants of the King*, 96. See Robert E. Speer, *Eleanor Chestnut: A Servant of the King* (New York: Women's Board of Foreign Missions of the Presbyterian Church, 1909), published as a pamphlet.
35. Speer, *Servants of the King*, 110.
36. See chapter 11 for Eagan.
37. Speer, *Some Great Leaders in the World Movement*, 166.
38. Ibid., 168.
39. Ibid., 173.
40. Ibid., 188–89.
41. Forman, "A History of Foreign Mission Theory in America," 94. See Anderson, "American Protestants in Pursuit of Mission: 1886–1986," 104. Anderson described *Missions and Modern History* and *Missionary Principles and Practice* as two of the "standard texts for the study of missions" in the first decades of the twentieth century.
42. Forman, "A History of Foreign Mission Theory in America," 114.
43. *Report of the Sixth Conference*, 121.
44. *Report of the Seventh Conference*, 44.
45. This quotation and those in the following paragraphs are from Speer, "The Aim of Foreign Missions," *Missionary Principles and Practice*, 34–42.
46. Robert E. Speer, *Christianity and the Nations* (New York: Fleming H. Revell Co., 1910), 60.
47. Ibid., 71.
48. Ibid., 66.
49. Ibid., 75.
50. Roy, "Overseas Mission Policies," 210–11.
51. Robert E. Speer, *The Unfinished Task of Foreign Missions* (New York: Fleming H. Revell Co., 1926), 320–21. See Speer, *The Church and Missions*, chapter 2.
52. Speer, *Some Changing and Unchanging Things in Foreign Missions*, 15.
53. Speer, "The Rich Fruitage of Foreign Missions," *The Church and Missions*, 187–222.

54. Speer, *The Unfinished Task of Foreign Missions*, 23.
55. Ibid., 26.
56. Speer, "The Civilizing Influence of Missions," *Missionary Principles and Practice*, 412. Emphasis added.
57. Ibid., 412–17.
58. Ibid., 419. Emphasis added.
59. Robert E. Speer, *The World's Debt to the Missionary*, published as a pamphlet, [1909], Speer Papers. See Speer, "The World's Abiding Debt to the Missionary," *The Gospel and the New World*, chapter 5.
60. Speer, "The World's Abiding Debt to the Missionary," 127–28.
61. Ibid., 134–35.
62. Ibid., 122.
63. Speer, *Christian Realities*, 254.
64. Speer, *Missions and Modern History*, 2:667.
65. Ibid., 671.
66. Ibid., 689.
67. Ibid.
68. Patterson, "Robert E. Speer and the Crisis," 171–72.
69. William R. Hutchison, *Errand to the World: American Protestant Thought and Foreign Missions* (Chicago: University of Chicago Press, 1987), 121–24.
70. Robert E. Speer, "Foreign Missions or World-Wide Evangelism," in *The Fundamentals* (Chicago: Testimony Publishing Company, n.d.), 12:65.
71. Ibid., 64.
72. Speer, "Missions—Primary and Essential in Christianity," *Missionary Principles and Practice*, 9.
73. Speer, "Foreign Missions or World-Wide Evangelism," 68.
74. Speer, *The Finality of Jesus Christ*, 5.
75. Speer, "Missions—Primary and Essential in Christianity," 11–12.
76. Speer, "Foreign Missions or World-Wide Evangelism," 67. See chapter 11.
77. Speer, *Christianity and the Nations*, 239.
78. Ellinwood, *Frank Field Ellinwood*, 215.
79. Ibid., 156.
80. Robert E. Speer, "Hinduism in Its Holy City," *Independent* 49, no. 2548 (30 September 1897): 16–17.
81. Robert E. Speer, "The Need of the Non-Christian World for Christ," *Churchman* 76, no. 25 (18 December 1897): 819–20. Reprinted in Speer, *Missionary Principles and Practice*, chapter 3.
82. Robert E. Speer, "Christianity and Other Religions," *Missionary Review of the World* 25, no. 7 (July 1902): 509. Republished as "Christianity the Solitary and Sufficient Religion," *Missionary Principles and Practice*, chapter 12.
83. Speer, "Christianity and Other Religions," 510–11.
84. Ibid., 509.
85. Ibid., 509–12. Ellinwood also objected to the Parliament. See Speer, *The Finality of Jesus Christ*, 244.
86. Robert E. Speer, *The Light of the World. A Brief Comparative Study of Christianity and non-Christian Religions* (West Medford, Mass.: Central Committee on the United Study of Missions, [1911]), ix.

87. J. A. Campbell, "The Inadequacy of Non-Christian Religions to meet the need of the World," *Students and the Missionary Problem*, 26–35.
88. This quotation and those in the following paragraphs are from Robert E. Speer, *The non-Christian Religions Inadequate to Meet the Needs of Men* (New York: Board of Foreign Missions of the Presbyterian Church in the U.S.A., 1906), published as a pamphlet, Speer Papers.
89. Speer presented a similar argument in "Foreign Missions or World-Wide Evangelism," 75–83.
90. Speer, *Christianity and the Nations*, 252–54.
91. Ibid., 299–323.
92. Speer, *The Light of the World*, vii.
93. *The Christian Life and Message*, 1:352–54.
94. Ibid., 354.
95. Ibid., 362. The passage is Philippians 3:7–8.
96. Ibid., 366–67.
97. Wilbur M. Smith to Robert E. Speer, 3 December 1931 and 19 January 1932, Speer Papers.
98. Robert E. Speer to Margaret B. Speer, 28 March and 11 April 1932, Speer Papers.
99. Robert E. Speer to Margaret B. Speer, 11 April 1932, Speer Papers.
100. Robert E. Speer to Margaret B. Speer, 1 July 1932, Speer Papers.
101. Robert E. Speer to Elliott Speer, 11 August 1932, Speer Family Papers.
102. Robert E. Speer to Margaret B. Speer, 28 March 1932, Speer Papers.
103. Robert E. Speer to Margaret B. Speer, 5 August 1932, Speer Papers.
104. Quoted in Wheeler, *A Man Sent From God*, 285–86. See Elmer G. Homrighausen, "The Finality of Jesus Christ: Robert E. Speer Memorial Lecture," *Princeton Seminary Bulletin* 67, no. 2 (Spring 1975): 1.
105. Speer, *The Finality of Jesus Christ*, 275.
106. Robert E. Speer, "The Finality of Jesus Christ," *Missionary Review of the World* 56, no. 4 (April 1933): 175–84. The pamphlet edition is in the Speer Papers.
107. Speer, *The Finality of Jesus Christ*, 281.
108. Ibid., 284.
109. Ibid., 290–91.
110. Ibid., 285–86.
111. Ibid., 286.
112. Ibid., 290.
113. Ibid., 292–93.
114. Ibid., 317–18. Quoted from *The Christian Life and Message*, 1:402, 410.
115. Speer, *The Finality of Jesus Christ*, 320–27. For an excellent summary, see 334.
116. Ibid., 348–77.
117. Elias B. Sanford, ed., *Federal Council of the Churches of Christ in America*. Report of the First Meeting of the Federal Council, Philadelphia, 1908 (New York: Revell Press, 1909). The Duff Lecture version is used in the following analysis.
118. Speer, *Christianity and the Nations*, 327.
119. Ibid., 330. See also 333–36.
120. Ibid., 331–32.
121. Ibid., 337f.

122. Ibid., 338–39.
123. Ibid., 341–42.
124. Ibid., 353.
125. Ibid., 354–55.
126. Ibid., 357–58.
127. Ibid., 358. On the issue of theological statements, see Speer, "The Relation of Western Theological Statements and Forms of Religious Experience to Other Races," in *The Gospel and the New World*, 203–24.
128. Speer, *Christianity and the Nations*, 374–75.
129. Ibid., 375–87.
130. Ibid., 393–94. See also Speer, "An Adequate Gospel for the Need of the World," in *Christian Realities*, 197f.
131. Speer, *The Unfinished Task of Foreign Missions*, 43–44.
132. Beaver, "Missionary Motivation Through the Centuries," 144. See Forman, "A History of Foreign Mission Theory in America," 92; Hutchison, *Errand to the World*, 121–24.

Chapter 9: Prophet of Christian Unity

1. Robert E. Speer, "Should the Denominational Distinctions of Christian Lands be Perpetuated on Mission Fields," *American Journal of Theology* 11, no. 2 (April 1907): 212.
2. Speer, *The Principles of Jesus Applied to Some Questions of Today*, 15.
3. Speer, *The Master of the Heart*, 132. See "The Unity of Hearts in Christ," chapter 7.
4. Ibid., 136.
5. Ibid., 132–33.
6. Speer, *Studies of the Man Christ Jesus*, 2, "His Plans and Methods of Work," chapters 1–6.
7. Speer, *Studies of the Man Paul*, 198.
8. Speer, *The Master of the Heart*, 136–37.
9. Ibid., 150.
10. Robert E. Speer to Mrs. Charles L. Reed, 14 June 1930, Speer Papers.
11. Robert E. Speer, "Address by Robert E. Speer at the 35th International Convention of the YMCA," 1904, Speer Papers.
12. Robert E. Speer, "The Trend to Christian Unity," *Churchman* 79, no. 4 (28 January 1899): 125.
13. Robert E. Speer, "A Presbyterian View of Catholicity," *Churchman* 83, no. 50 (15 June 1901): 741.
14. Robert E. Speer, "The Bases of Unity Among Young People and Steps Toward Achievement," in Elias B. Sanford, ed., *Church Federation, Inter-Church Conference on Federation.* New York, 15–21 November 1905 (New York: Fleming H. Revell Co., 1906), 444. Emphasis added.
15. Ibid., 445–48. For a list of the youth organizations, see 80–81.
16. Ibid., 448.
17. Ibid., 449–50.
18. Ibid., 450.

19. Ibid., 451.

20. Ibid., 452.

21. Elias B. Sanford, *Origin and History of the Federal Council of the Churches of Christ in America* (Hartford, Conn.: S. S. Scranton Co., 1916), xiii.

22. Sanford, *Federal Council of the Churches of Christ in America.*

23. "Denominationalism and Foreign Missions," *Presbyterian Standard* 49, no. 2 (13 January 1909): 2.

24. James L. Barton, "Co-operation Among Christian Forces on the Mission Field," in Charles S. Macfarland, ed., *Christian Unity at Work. The Federal Council of the Churches of Christ in America in Quadrennial Sessions at Chicago, Illinois, 1912* (New York: Federal Council of the Churches of Christ in America, 1913), 107.

25. Robert E. Speer to the Commission on Foreign Missions of the Federal Council of the Churches of Christ in America, 1 October 1913, Speer Papers. See Robert E. Speer to Charles S. Macfarland, 25 July 1913, Speer Papers.

26. Robert E. Speer to the Commission on Foreign Missions of the Federal Council of the Churches of Christ in America, 1 October 1913, Speer Papers. See *Annual Reports of the Federal Council of the Churches of Christ in America*, 1913 (New York: National Offices, 1913), 87–88. See also Cavert, *Church Cooperation and Unity in America*, 39.

27. *Foreign Missions Conference of North America. Being the Report of the Twenty-First Conference of Foreign Missions Boards in the United States and Canada* (New York: Foreign Missions Conference, [1914]), 145, 258–59.

28. *Annual Reports of the Federal Council*, 1913, 89.

29. *Annual Reports of the Federal Council of the Churches of Christ in America*, 1914 (New York: National Offices, 1914), 55.

30. Charles S. Macfarland, ed., *The Churches of Christ in Council*, vol. I, *Library of Christian Cooperation* (New York: Missionary Education Movement, 1917), 69.

31. See Robert E. Speer to Charles S. Macfarland, 6 October 1916; Charles S. Macfarland to Robert E. Speer, 14 October 1916, and attached "Report of the Committee of Fifteen"; Robert E. Speer to Charles S. Macfarland, 23 October 1916, Speer Papers.

32. Macfarland, *The Churches of Christ in Council*, 74–75.

33. Charles S. Macfarland, ed., *The Churches of Christ in Time of War* (New York: Missionary Education Movement of the United States and Canada, 1917), 102.

34. Ibid., 103.

35. Ibid., 106.

36. Ibid., 129.

37. Ibid., 133. See John F. Piper, Jr., *The American Churches in World War I* (Athens, Ohio: Ohio University Press, 1985), 14–18. See also John F. Piper, Jr., "Robert E. Speer: Christian Statesman in War and Peace," *Journal of Presbyterian History* 47, no. 3 (September 1969): 201–25.

38. Robert E. Speer to Frank Mason North, 30 July 1917, Speer Papers.

39. Frank Mason North to Robert E. Speer, 6 August 1917, Speer Papers.

40. Ibid.

41. See Ray H. Abrams, *Preachers Present Arms* (New York: Round Table Press, 1933), 244–47; See also Sydney E. Ahlstrom, *A Religious History of the American*

People (New York: Charles Scribner's Sons, 1965). For a contrary view, see Piper, *The American Churches in World War I.*

42. William Adams Brown to Robert E. Speer, 12 April 1922, Speer Papers.

43. *Minutes of the Meetings of the General War-Time Commission of the Churches and Its Executive Committee,* 20 September 1917, Records of the Federal Council of the Churches of Christ in America, 1894–1952, Records of the National Council of the Churches of Christ in America, Presbyterian Historical Society, Philadelphia, Pa. Hereafter cited as FC Records.

44. Robert E. Speer to David S. Cairns, 11 February 1918, Speer Papers.

45. The Committee on the War and the Religious Outlook, *Christian Unity: Its Principles and Possibilities* (New York: Association Press, 1921), 31.

46. Piper, *The American Churches in World War I,* 41–44.

47. "Opening Address: Meeting of the General War-Time Commission," Speer Papers.

48. Charles S. Macfarland, *Christian Unity in the Making* (New York: Federal Council of the Churches of Christ in America, 1948), 137.

49. See, for example, Robert E. Speer, "What is to be Done with the Foreign Missions Deficit," *"All the World"* (October 1914): 114–19, Speer Papers; Joint Letter from the Board of Foreign Missions of the Presbyterian Church in the U.S.A. "To the Missions," 1 October 1914, Speer Papers; Robert E. Speer, "The War's Challenge to Foreign Missions," *Sunday School Times* 56, no. 42 (17 October 1914): 629.

50. The speeches and articles were very numerous. He kept meticulous records of his work and responses to it, and his papers show no critical responses to his activities in 1917. Further search in the periodical literature failed to turn up anything he might have missed.

51. Harry E. Edmonds to Robert E. Speer, 14 February 1918, Speer Papers.

52. *New York Times,* 28 February 1918.

53. Robert E. Speer to John Greene, 8 March 1918, Speer Papers.

54. The Speer Papers contained no copy of this speech. It has been reconstructed from the *Times* article and the letter to Greene, cited above. He later published a version of the speech as chapter 3 in Robert E. Speer, *The Christian Man, the Church and the War* (New York: Macmillan Co., 1918).

55. *New York Times,* 19 February 1918.

56. Ibid., 22 February 1918.

57. Ibid., 1 March 1918.

58. Ibid., 26 February 1918. For the other letters, see the following issues: 23, 25, 27 February; 1, 3, 7, 13 March. An unsigned article in the *Congregationalist and Advance* also agreed with Mitchell and called Speer's address "an ill-proportioned speech and not the full-orbed presentation of the matter which that particular occasion called for." "An Unfortunate Start in New York," 103 (7 March 1918): 293.

59. *New York Times,* 22 and 26 February 1918.

60. Ibid., 22 February 1918.

61. Ibid., 24 February 1918. If Speer received any letters from YMCA officials that supported his decision, he did not save them. John R. Mott sent him a copy of a letter he wrote to George W. Pepper, dated 2 July 1918, in which he wrote, "I consider that a grave injustice has been done to him [Speer] and that there will

be a few things more pleasing to our enemies than to have any doubt associated with his name and attitude with reference to the war." Speer Papers.

62. *New York Times*, 26 February 1918. See "Robert E. Speer a True Patriot," *Presbyterian* 88 (14 March 1918): 4.

63. *New York Times*, 26 February 1918.

64. Ibid., 27 February 1918.

65. Ibid., 7 March 1918. For another pro-Speer letter, see "Dr. Speer Defended," *Congregationalist and Advance*, 103 (4 April 1918): 434.

66. New York *Evening Post*, 28 February 1918.

67. Speer Papers.

68. Englewood *Press*, 9 March 1918.

69. Ibid.

70. Raymond C. Knox, chaplain of Columbia University, wrote "in a spirit of sincere friendship," to say that Mitchell's report was correct, 26 February 1918. Eugene Thwing, president of Western Reserve University, sent Speer a note that contained simply the following quotation: "When men persecute you and say all manner of evil against you falsely, for my sake, Rejoice and be exceeding glad, for so persecuted they the prophets which were before you." Speer Papers.

71. Henry A. Atkinson to Robert E. Speer, 28 February 1918, Speer Papers.

72. Frederick H. Knubel to Robert E. Speer, 27 February 1918, Speer Papers.

73. Henry Sloane Coffin to Robert E. Speer, 25 February 1918, Speer Papers.

74. Norman Thomas to Robert E. Speer, 25 February 1918, Speer Papers.

75. Robert E. Speer to Elliott Speer, 9 April 1918. Quoted in Wheeler, *A Man Sent From God*, 147.

76. Robert E. Speer to William McMurtrie Speer, 24 May 1918, Speer Papers.

77. Speer, *The Christian Man, the Church and the War*, iii.

78. Ibid., 29.

79. Robert E. Speer, "Why and How to Abolish War," *Sunday School Times* 56, no. 33 (15 August 1914): 504.

80. Speer, *The Christian Man, the Church and the War*, 15.

81. Ibid., 8.

82. Robert E. Speer, "Looking Through the War Clouds," *Missionary Review of the World* 41 (January 1918): 14

83. Quoted in Wheeler, *A Man Sent From God*, 150.

84. Speer, *The Christian Man, the Church and the War*, 17.

85. Ibid., 19.

86. Ibid., 21.

87. Ibid., 12.

88. Ibid., 86–87; 58.

89. Ibid., 30–31.

90. See chapter 14. For some typical comparisons of the two world wars, see Roland H. Bainton, *Christian Attitudes toward War and Peace* (New York: Abingdon Press, 1960), 221; James Hastings Nichols, *Democracy and the Churches* (Philadelphia: Westminster Press, 1951), 220; Ray H. Abrams, "The Churches and the Clergy in World War II," *Annals of the American Academy of Political and Social Science* 256 (March 1948): 112, 116; and Ralph L. Moellering, *Modern War and the American Churches* (New York: American Press, 1956), 83.

91. Speer, *The Christian Man, the Church and the War*, 38.

92. Robert E. Speer, *The New Opportunity of the Church* (New York: Macmillan Co., 1919), 22.

93. "Address by Dr. Robert E. Speer, Thursday Afternoon, 4 October 1917," Speer Papers.

94. *A Call to Prayer*, Thanksgiving 1917, The General War-Time Commission, issued as a pamphlet, Speer Papers.

95. "Robert E. Speer's Call to Prayer," *Lutheran* 22 (6 December 1917): 3.

96. Speer, *The New Opportunity of the Church*, 25.

97. Speer, *The Christian Man, the Church and the War*, 38.

98. Ibid., 62.

99. Robert E. Speer to David S. Cairns, 25 May 1917, Speer Papers.

100. See Robert E. Speer to Elliott Speer, 31 December 1917 and 2 February 1918, Speer Papers.

101. See Robert E. Speer to Elliott Speer, 12 November and 23 November, 1917, Speer Papers.

102. Emma B. Speer to Robert E. Speer, [April–May 1917], Speer Family Papers.

103. Robert E. Speer to David S. Cairns, 25 May 1917.

104. Robert E. Speer to Elliott Speer, 18 January 1918, Speer Papers.

105. Walter Rauschenbusch, *A Theology for the Social Gospel* (New York: Macmillan Co., 1917), 141.

106. *Annual Reports of the Federal Council of the Churches of Christ in America*, 1919 (New York: Federal Council of the Churches of Christ in America, [1919]), 166ff.

107. See *Annual Reports of the Federal Council of the Churches of Christ in America*, 1917 (New York: Missionary Education Movement of the United States and Canada, 1917), 59; *Annual Reports of the Federal Council of the Churches of Christ in America*, 1918 (New York: Missionary Education Movement of the United States and Canada, 1918), 38–40.

108. The Committee on the War and the Religious Outlook, *Missionary Outlook in Light of the War* (New York: Association Press, 1920). For a list of the pamphlets, reports and books produced by this committee, see Piper, *The American Churches in World War I*, 198, n. 14; 199, n. 15.

109. Robert E. Speer, *The War and the Religious Outlook* (Boston: Pilgrim Press, [1919]), 24, issued as a pamphlet, Speer Papers.

110. See chapter 11. See also Showalter, *The End of a Crusade*, 47.

111. Speer, *The War and the Religious Outlook*, 27. See Robert E. Speer, "The Work of the Church Today," in Roy B. Guild, ed., *The Church—After the War—What?* (New York: Association Press, 1919), 15–30.

112. Robert E. Speer, "The Call to a Larger Christian Cooperation," Address of Dr. Robert E. Speer at the Meeting of the Executive Committee in Atlantic City, N.J., 10–12 December 1918, in *Annual Reports of the Federal Council*, 1918, 175–93.

113. Robert E. Speer, *The Witness Bearing of the Church to the Nations*, Special Meeting of the Federal Council of the Churches of Christ in America, Cleveland, Ohio, 6 May 1919, issued as a pamphlet, 7. See Piper, *The American Churches in World War I*, 184–86.

114. Speer, *The New Opportunity of the Church*, 60–61.

115. Ibid., 6.
116. Speer, *The Gospel and the New World*, 25.
117. Ibid., 41.
118. Ibid., 29–30. Speer called the church the "institute of humanity" in *The New Opportunity of the Church*, 27.
119. Speer, *The Gospel and the New World*, 30. See "The League of Nations," [1919], Speer Papers.
120. Ibid.

Chapter 10: President of the Federal Council

1. "The Committee on the War and the Religious Outlook," *Christian Unity*, 355–58. See "Plans for Organic Union Adopted," *Christian Century* 37, no. 7 (12 February 1920): 16–20.
2. Quoted in "The Committee on the War and the Religious Outlook," *Christian Unity*, 159. See Cavert, *Church Cooperation and Unity in America*, 325–29; Loetscher, *The Broadening Church*, 100–102.
3. Loetscher, *The Broadening Church*, 101.
4. "The Committee on the War and the Religious Outlook," *Christian Unity*, 158.
5. Cavert, *The American Churches in the Ecumenical Movement*, 108.
6. Eldon G. Ernst, *Moment of Truth for Protestant America: Interchurch Campaigns Following World War One* (Missoula, Mont.: Scholars' Press, 1974), 80. See *Annual Reports of the Federal Council*, 1919, 21–24.
7. *Federal Council Bulletin*, 3 (April 1920): 63–64. Quoted in Ernst, *Moment of Truth*, 81–82.
8. Quoted in Ernst, *Moment of Truth*, 160–61.
9. Interchurch World Movement, in "Religious Interests," Rockefeller Archives.
10. Ibid. See Harvey, "Speer Versus Rockefeller and Mott," 288.
11. Harvey, "Speer Versus Rockefeller and Mott," 296, 283–84. See Charles E. Harvey, "Religion and Industrial Relations: John D. Rockefeller, Jr., and the Interchurch World Movement of 1919–1920," *Research in Political Economy* 4 (1981): 199–227. For Mott, see Hopkins, *John R. Mott*, 569–74.
12. On the use of the term "critic," see Charles E. Harvey, "John D. Rockefeller, Jr., and the Interchurch World Movement of 1919–1920: A Different Angle on the Ecumenical Movement," *Church History* 51, no. 2 (June 1982): 198–209.
13. Wheeler, *A Man Sent From God*, 175.
14. Ibid. See Ernst, *Moment of Truth*, 148–49.
15. Robert E. Speer, "The Church's Debt of Honor," *New Era Magazine*, December 1920, Speer Papers.
16. Ernst, *Moment of Truth*, 150–51.
17. Robert E. Speer, "The Present Situation in the Church as a Whole," in the Committee on the War and the Religious Outlook, *Christian Unity*, 140–50.
18. Ibid., 146.
19. Ibid., 150.
20. Ibid., 146–47. Ernst said that Speer offered "one of the most judicious appraisals of the Interchurch World Movement made by an insider." *Moment of Truth*, 160.

21. Robert E. Speer to John D. Rockefeller, Jr., 5 October 1920, "Religious Interests," Rockefeller Archives.

22. John R. Mott to Dr. Macfarland, 17 November 1916; Charles S. Macfarland to Robert E. Speer, 20 November 1916, Speer Papers.

23. James M. Speers to John D. Rockefeller, Jr., 17 August 1920, and John D. Rockefeller, Jr., to James M. Speers, 21 August 1920, "Religious Interests," Rockefeller Archives. See James M. Speers to William Adams Brown, 18 August 1920, and William Adams Brown to James M. Speers, 21 August 1920, Speer Papers.

24. Robert E. Speer to Frank Mason North, Albert G. Lawson, and Charles S. Macfarland, 16 November 1920, Speer Papers.

25. Robert E. Speer to David S. Cairns, 29 July 1918, Speer Papers.

26. Ned Bulkley to Robert E. Speer, 22 November 1920, Speer Family Papers.

27. William P. Merrill to Robert E. Speer, 19 November 1920, Speer Family Papers.

28. Robert E. Speer to William Adams Brown, 26 November 1920, Speer Papers; William Adams Brown to Robert E. Speer, 26 November 1920, Speer Family Papers.

29. Robert E. Speer to Charles S. Macfarland, 12 November 1930, Speer Papers.

30. Robert E. Speer to John D. Rockefeller, Jr., 1 December 1920, Speer Papers.

31. Peter Ainslie, "American Protestants Getting Together," *Christian Herald* 44 (8 January 1921): 29; "The Essential Oneness of the Evangelical Churches," *Christian Observer* 108, no. 50 (15 December 1920): 2.

32. John D. Rockefeller, Jr., to Robert E. Speer, 4 December 1920, Speer Family Papers.

33. "The New President of the Federal Council," *Christian Advocate* 95, no. 50 (9 December 1920): 1635.

34. Robert E. Speer to William Adams Brown, 25 January 1919, Speer Papers.

35. Speer, "The Present Situation in the Church as a Whole," 150–55.

36. "The Essential Oneness of the Evangelical Churches."

37. Samuel McCrea Cavert, ed., *The Churches Allied for Common Tasks*. Report of the Third Quadrennium of The Federal Council of the Churches of Christ in America, 1916–1920 (New York: Federal Council of the Churches of Christ in America, 1921), 19–28; 330.

38. "Minutes of the Reorganization Committee, Interchurch World Movement," and "Appendix," 3–5 November 1920, Speer Papers.

39. "Report of Progress Made By the Reorganization Committee of the Interchurch World Movement," attached to Abram E. Cory to John D. Rockefeller, Jr., 17 September 1920, "Religious Interests," Rockefeller Archives. See "Minutes of the Meeting of the Executive Committee," 21 January 1921, in Cavert, *The Churches Allied*, 353–54.

40. "Protestant Bodies Hold Meeting Here," *New York Times*, 14 December 1920.

41. "Minutes of the Meeting of the Executive Council," 16 December 1920, Speer Papers; Samuel McCrea Cavert to Robert E. Speer, 4 January 1921, and the attached "Reorganization of the Federal Council," Speer Papers.

42. Robert E. Speer to David S. Cairns, 6 January 1921, Speer Papers.

43. Cavert, *The Churches Allied*, 353–63; 29–34. See "Minutes of the Meeting of the Executive Committee of the Federal Council of the Churches of Christ in America," 21 January 1921, Speer Papers.

44. John R. Mott to Robert E. Speer, 25 January 1921, and Robert E. Speer to John R. Mott, 7 February 1921, Speer Papers.

45. "Minutes of Meeting of Consultation Committee of Interdenominational Agencies," 2 March 1921 and 13 June 1921; "Conference of Interdenominational Agencies," 28 April 1921, Speer Papers.

46. "Minutes of a Conference of Representatives of Denominational Forward Movements," 29 March 1921, Speer Papers.

47. "Minutes of a Conference of Moderators and Presidents of Ecclesiastical Bodies," 13 April 1921, Speer Papers.

48. Cavert, *The Churches Allied*, 310–14.

49. "To the Constituent Bodies of the Federal Council of the Churches of Christ in America," May 1921, Speer Papers.

50. See for example the correspondence between Speer and Frederick Knubel (Lutheran), 7, 16 February, 8 March, 14 May 1921. Robert E. Speer to Bishop William Lawrence, 5 October 1922; Robert E. Speer to Bishop Charles P. Anderson, 27 July 1922, Speer Papers.

51. D. F. McGill to Robert E. Speer, 11 April 1921, Speer Papers.

52. Reinhold Niebuhr to Robert E. Speer, 7 March 1921, Speer Papers. See Richard Wightman Fox, *Reinhold Niebuhr, A Biography* (New York: Pantheon Books, 1985), 71.

53. Conference on Near East Situation, 21 September 1922, Speer Papers. "3000 at Cathedral Protest Atrocities," *New York Times*, 25 September 1922.

54. David S. Kennedy to Robert E. Speer, 28 December 1920, Speer Papers.

55. "Robert E. Speer on the Federal Council," *Presbyterian* 91, no. 2 (13 January 1921): 4. For other Speer-Kennedy exchanges on this topic see Robert E. Speer to David S. Kennedy, 4 January 1921, and David S. Kennedy to Robert E. Speer, 6 January 1921, Speer Papers.

56. Joseph T. Gibson to Robert E. Speer, 14 January 1921, Speer Papers.

57. Robert E. Speer, "The Federal Council and the Churches," *Federal Council of the Churches of Christ in America Annual Report*, 1923 (New York: Federal Council of Churches, 1923), 7–13. Portions of this speech appeared in many religious periodicals, including a Federal Council press release, the *Western Christian Advocate*, the *Federal Council Bulletin*, the *Christian Work*, the *Presbyterian Advance*, and the *Christian Union Quarterly*. The Federal Council issued it as a pamphlet. Speer Papers.

58. "Dr. Speer Pleads for Unity," *Watchman-Examiner*, 31 January 1924, Speer Papers.

59. Samuel McCrea Cavert, ed., *United in Service*. Report of the Federal Council of the Churches of Christ in America, 1920–1924 (New York: Federal Council of the Churches of Christ in America, 1925), 14–15. Several religious periodicals published all or parts of this speech. See *Record of Christian Work* (June 1925) and *Federal Council Bulletin* (March-April 1925). A much revised version appeared as "Our Existing Unity," *Homiletic Review* 89, no. 3 (March 1925): 175–77, 207.

60. Samuel McCrea Cavert to Robert E. Speer, 11 December 1924, Speer Papers.

61. Cavert, *United in Service*, 270.

62. "The Federal Council—Four More Years," *Christian Century* 41, no. 52 (25 December 1924): 1659–60.
63. Cavert, *The American Churches in the Ecumenical Movement*, 114.
64. Robert E. Speer to Charles S. Macfarland, 12 November 1930, Speer Papers. See Robert E. Speer to Rev. John W. Langdale, 25 November 1930, Speer Papers.

Chapter 11: Social Gospel Witness

1. Walter Rauschenbusch, *Christianizing the Social Order* (New York: Macmillan Co., 1921); see part 3.
2. David M. Reimers, *White Protestantism and the Negro* (New York: Oxford University Press, 1965), 53. See also Robert Moats Miller, *American Protestantism and Social Issues, 1919–1939* (Chapel Hill, N.C.: University of North Carolina Press, 1958), 9; Ronald C. White, Jr., *Liberty and Justice for All: Racial Reform and the Social Gospel (1877–1925)* (San Francisco: Harper & Row Publishers, 1990), xiii.
3. See White, *Liberty*. See also John F. Piper, Jr., "Robert E. Speer on Christianity and Race," *Journal of Presbyterian History* 61, no. 2 (Summer 1987): 97–108.
4. Speer, *The Principles of Jesus Applied to Some Questions of Today*, 117.
5. Speer, *Studies of the Man Christ Jesus*, 28. The passages are Mark 1:28 and Luke 9:11.
6. Speer, *The Principles*, 114.
7. Speer, *Studies of the Man Christ Jesus*, 28–29.
8. Ibid., 30.
9. Ibid., 33.
10. Speer, *The Church and Missions*, 115.
11. Ibid., 117. Some students of foreign missions have recognized this social gospel interest. Roy wrote, "While not accepting all the theology that accompanied the movement [social gospel], Robert E. Speer and other missionary leaders often stressed the social results of the world mission." Roy, "Overseas Mission Policies—An Historical Overview," 197.
12. Robert E. Speer, *D. L. Moody* (E. Northfield, Mass.: Northfield Schools, 1931), 20–21.
13. Speer, *The Church and Missions*, 95.
14. Robert E. Speer, *The Stuff of Manhood: Some Needed Notes in American Character* (New York: Fleming H. Revell Co., 1917), 184.
15. Robert E. Speer to Joseph T. Alling, 8 August 1921, Speer Papers.
16. Quoted in Speer, *Five Minutes A Day*, 237.
17. Speer, *Studies in the Book of Acts*, 158.
18. Speer, *The Witness Bearing of the Church to the Nation*.
19. Robert E. Speer, "The War and the Missionary Motive and Message," "All the World," July 1918, Speer Papers.
20. Hutchison, *Errand to the World*, 122–23. See chapter 8 for Speer's understanding of the aim of foreign missions.
21. Robert E. Speer, "The Living Christ," *The Christian Mission in the World Today. Report of the Eleventh Quadrennial Convention of the Student Volunteer Movement*

(New York: Student Volunteer Movement for Foreign Missions, 1932), 175–77.

22. Robert E. Speer to Rev. George Burns, 7 November 1923, Speer Papers.

23. Robert E. Speer, *A Memorial of Alice Jackson* (New York: Fleming H. Revell Co., [1908])

24. Josiah Strong, *Our Country* (New York: Baker and Taylor Co., 1885). Strong began to change his thinking in his later years. See White, *Liberty*, 211–14.

25. Madison Grant, *The Passing of the Great Race* (New York: Charles Scribner's Sons, 1916); Lothrop Stoddard, *The Rising Tide of Color Against White World Supremacy* (New York: Charles Scribner's Sons, 1920). For a variety of perspectives on the racial views of this era, see George W. Cable, *The Negro Question* (Garden City, N.Y.: Doubleday Anchor Books, 1958); George M. Frederickson, *The Black Image in the White Mind* (New York: Harper & Row, Publishers, 1971); I. A. Newby, *Jim Crow's Defense: Anti-Negro Thought in America, 1900–1930* (Baton Rouge, La.: Louisiana University Press, 1965); I. A. Newby, ed., *The Development of Segregationist Thought* (Homewood, Ill.: Dorsey Press, 1968); Ray Stannard Baker, *Following the Color Line* (New York: Harper & Row, Publishers, 1964).

26. Speer, "Some Personal Reminiscences and Memories," 6.

27. "*Diaries*," 14 February 1886.

28. Ibid., 18 September 1887.

29. Robert E. Speer, "Address by Mr. Robert E. Speer, of Englewood, Delivered before the Triennial State Convention and Forty-Third Anniversary of the New Jersey Sunday-School Association," 21 November 1901, Speer Papers.

30. Robert E. Speer, "The National Antipathy to the Negro," *Nassau Literary Magazine* 44, no. 6 (January 1889): 363–67.

31. Robert E. Speer, "Address by Robert E. Speer at the 35th International Convention of the YMCA."

32. Robert E. Speer, "The Call to Foreign Missions," Northfield talk, 7 July 1895, Speer Papers.

33. Robert E. Speer, "Missionary Convictions," Northfield talk, 3 July 1898, Speer Papers. See also chapter 23 in Speer, *Missionary Principles and Practice*.

34. Speer, "Address by Mr. Robert E. Speer, of Englewood."

35. Robert E. Speer, "Address on International Peace," Lake Geneva Student Conference, 18 June 1914, Speer Papers. See also Speer, *The World's Debt to the Missionary*, Speer Papers.

36. Speer, *The Principles of Jesus*, 228.

37. Ibid., 230f. See also Robert E. Speer, *The Place of Missions in the Thought of God* (Board of Foreign Missions of the United Presbyterian Church of North America, 1905), 4, issued as a pamphlet; Speer, *Studies of the Man Christ Jesus*, 137–38.

38. Robert E. Speer, "The Race Problem and Its Solution," *Christian Endeavor World* 29 (26 January 1915): 18. For a version of this article, see chapter 3, "Christianity and the Race Problem," in Speer, *The Gospel and the New World*, 65–88. In 1924 he said 1 Corinthians 12:4–27 was "the greatest utterance in all literature on the race problem." See Robert E. Speer, *Of One Blood: A Short Study of the Race Problem* (New York: Council of Women for Home Missions

and Missionary Education Movement of the United States and Canada, 1924), 68.

39. Speer, *The Stuff of Manhood*, 134.
40. Speer, "Address by Mr. Robert E. Speer, of Englewood," 15.
41. Robert E. Speer, *The Impact of the West Upon the East Must Be Christianized* (Laymen's Missionary Movement, 1910), issued as a pamphlet, Speer Papers.
42. Ibid.
43. *Annual Reports of the Federal Council*, 1914, 18–19.
44. Speer, "The Race Problem and Its Solution," 343.
45. Speer, "Some Missionary Aspects of the Year 1914," 9f.
46. Speer, "The Race Problem and Its Solution," 344.
47. Robert E. Speer, *How to Preserve Fellowship and Right Understanding Between Japan and the United States* (Philadelphia, 1917), issued as a pamphlet, Speer Papers.
48. Robert E. Speer, *The Christian Man, the Church and the War*, 68ff.
49. He first mentioned this in his 1915 essay, "The Race Problem and Its Solution." See also Speer, *The Gospel and the New World*.
50. Speer, *The Gospel and the New World*, 65.
51. Speer, *Of One Blood*, 1.
52. Cavert, *The Churches Allied*, 111.
53. "Report of the Committee on Negro Churches," *The Churches Allied*, 143ff. See John A. Hutchison, *We Are Not Divided* (New York: Round Table Press, 1941), 1333.
54. "Digest of Remarks at Racial Conference," 24 January 1921, Speer Papers.
55. *Federal Council Bulletin*, 4 (April–May 1921): 60. Emphasis added.
56. Ibid.
57. Daniel Perlman, "Stirring the White Conscience: The Life of George Edmund Haynes," Ph.D. diss., New York University, 1972, 15.
58. George E. Haynes to Robert E. Speer, 21 February 1921, Speer Papers. See also Samuel Kelton Roberts, "Crucible For A Vision: The Work of George Edmund Haynes and the Commission on Race Relations, 1922–1947," Ph.D. diss., Columbia University, 1974.
59. Robert E. Speer, *John J. Eagan: A Memoir of an Adventurer for the Kingdom of God on Earth* (Birmingham, Ala.: American Cast Iron Pipe Co., 1939). See White, *Liberty*, 239–44.
60. *Minutes of the First Meeting of the Commission on Negro Churches and Race Relations of the Federal Council of the Churches of Christ in America*, 12 July 1921, FC Records. See "Churches to Consider Race Relations," *Federal Council Bulletin* 4 (June–July, 1921): 73.
61. *Minutes of a Meeting of the Commission on Negro Churches and Race Relations*, 6 January 1922, FC Records.
62. Robert E. Speer to John D. Rockefeller, Jr., 27 July 1922, Speer Papers.
63. *Minutes of the Meeting of the Executive Committee of the Commission on Negro Churches and Race Relations*, 4 November 1921, FC Records.
64. Robert T. Handy, *We Witness Together: A History of Cooperative Home Missions* (New York: Friendship Press, 1956), 86f.
65. Robert E. Speer, *Race and Race Relations: A Christian View of Human Contacts* (New York: Fleming H. Revell Co., [1924]), chapter 6.

66. George E. Haynes to Franklin D. Cogswell, 15 June 1922, Speer Papers.
67. George E. Haynes to Robert E. Speer, 11 February 1924, Speer Papers.
68. Samuel McCrea Cavert to John Bailey Kelly, 14 June 1922, Speer Papers.
69. Robert N. McLean to John Bailey Kelly, 30 June 1922, Speer Papers.
70. Haynes to Cogswell.
71. J. M. G. Darms to Robert E. Speer, 7 July 1924, Speer Papers.
72. Speer, *Of One Blood*, 44. See also 6–8, 10, 21f., 80, 137f., 166f.
73. For earlier version of this chapter, see, "The Race Problem and Its Solution," and *The Gospel and the New World*, chapter 3.
74. Speer, *Of One Blood*, 166.
75. Ibid., 173.
76. Ibid., 176–88.
77. Ibid., 188.
78. Ibid., 189–99.
79. Ibid., 236.

Chapter 12: Moderator of the Presbyterian Church

1. John Bunyan, *The Methodist Hymnal* (Nashville: Methodist Publishing House, 1939), 265.
2. To Elliott Speer, 18 May 1927, Speer Family Papers.
3. Longfield, *The Presbyterian Controversy*, 4.
4. On Machen, see George M. Marsden, *Understanding Fundamentalism and Evangelicalism* (Grand Rapids: Wm. B. Eerdmans Publishing Co., 1991), chapter 7, "Understanding J. Gresham Machen." See also D. G. Hart, *Defending the Faith: J. Gresham Machen and the Crisis of Conservatism in Modern America* (Baltimore and London: John Hopkins University Press, 1994); Ned Stonehouse, *J. Gresham Machen: A Biographical Memoir* (Grand Rapids: Wm. B. Eerdmans Publishing Co., 1954).
5. Loetscher, *The Broadening Church*, 90f.; Marty, *The Noise of Conflict*, 159–64.
6. Ernest R. Sandeen, "*The Fundamentals*: The Last Flowering of the Millenarian-Conservative Alliance," 55–73. *The Fundamentals* (Chicago: Testimony Publishing Company, 1910–15).
7. Longfield, *The Presbyterian Controversy*, 4–8. See also Miller, *Harry Emerson Fosdick*, chapter 7; Edwin H. Rian, *The Presbyterian Conflict* (Grand Rapids: Wm. B. Eerdmans Publishing Co., 1940), chapters 1 and 2.
8. Loetscher, *The Broadening Church*, 94–95
9. Ibid., 128; Longfield, *The Presbyterian Controversy*, 238, n. 11. See Delwin G. Nykamp, "A Presbyterian Power Struggle: A Critical History of Communication Strategies Employed in the Struggle for Control of the Presbyterian Church, USA, 1922–26," Ph.D. diss., Northwestern University, 1974, chapter 7. See also Charles Evans Quirk, " 'The Auburn Affirmation': A Critical Narrative of the Document Designed to Safeguard the Unity and Liberty of the Presbyterian Church in the United States of America in 1924," Ph.D. diss., University of Iowa, 1967. Quirk identifies three groups, the exclusivists or militant conservatives, the moderates or conservatives, and the inclusivists or liberal evangelicals. See "Parties Within the Presbyterian Church," 53–59. See William J. Westin,

Presbyterian Pluralism: Competition in a Protestant House (Knoxville, Tenn.: University of Tennessee Press, 1997), xiii.

10. Longfield, *The Presbyterian Controversy*, 72f.

11. Quirk, " 'The Auburn Affirmation': A Critical Narrative," 242–43. Miller, *Harry Emerson Fosdick*, 131. See *Time* 3, no. 9 (3 March 1924): 18. "Dr. Speer Will Not Be Moderator," *Christian Century* 41, no. 19 (8 May 1924): 607.

12. Robert E. Speer to Margaret B. Speer, 25 May 1924, Speer Family Papers.

13. Longfield, *The Presbyterian Controversy*, 149.

14. Ibid., 149–51.

15. Loetscher, *The Broadening Church*, 127–28. See *Minutes of the General Assembly of the Presbyterian Church in the U.S.A.* Third Series, vol. 4, 1925 (Philadelphia: Office of the General Assembly, 1925), 88. See also Quirk, " 'The Auburn Affirmation': A Critical Narrative," 283ff.

16. Charles R. Erdman to Robert E. Speer, 2 May and 14 May 1927; Samuel C. Hodge to Robert E. Speer, 11 May 1927; Robert E. Speer to Samuel C. Hodge, 13 May 1927; Speer Papers.

17. Untitled manuscript that begins "Various proposals . . ." Rockledge, 13 December 1937, Speer Papers.

18. Robert R. Littell to Robert E. Speer, 28 April 1927, Speer Papers. For a letter with similar sentiments, see W. B. Greenway to Robert E. Speer, 5 May 1927, Speer Papers.

19. Quoted in Walter Irving Clarke, "Moderator Speer in Action at the General Assembly," 13–14, in *Robert E. Speer. Missionary Statesman.* See "Selection of N.Y. Man Wins Acclamation of Assembly," San Francisco *Chronicle*, 27 May 1927, Speer Papers. See also "Dr. Speer Elected Presbyterian Head," *New York Times*, 27 May 1927.

20. Robert E. Speer to Emma B. Speer, 21 and 22 May, 1927, Speer Family Papers. He sent the telegram on 26 May.

21. Clarke, "Moderator Speer in Action at the General Assembly," 14–15.

22. Quoted in Hunter, "Minister Appraises Moderator," 5–6.

23. Telegram, Wishart to Robert E. Speer, 27 May 1927, Speer Papers.

24. *New York Times*, 22 and 25 May 1927.

25. Greenway to Speer, 5 May 1927.

26. Robert E. Speer, *The Old, Ever New, Call of Christ.* Address delivered at the General Assembly of the Presbyterian Church in the U.S.A., San Francisco, California, 1 June 1927 (Philadelphia: Office of the General Assembly of the Presbyterian Church in the U.S.A., [1927]), issued as a pamphlet, Speer Papers. The report of his trip to China and Japan was already published: *Report on China and Japan.* See Shirley Stone Garrett, "Why They Stayed: American Church Politics and Chinese Nationalism in the Twenties," 304–10, in Fairbank, *The Missionary Enterprise.* The quotations are from Acts 4:20 and Matthew 16:24.

27. *The Old, Ever New, Call of Christ*, introduction.

28. Robert E. Speer to Margaret B. Speer, 10 June 1927, Speer Family Papers.

29. Quirk, " 'The Auburn Affirmation': A Critical Narrative," 283–90; Westin, *Presbyterian Pluralism*, 73.

30. Nykamp, "A Presbyterian Power Struggle," 410. See Longfield, *The Presbyterian Controversy*, 156. See also Stonehose, *J. Gresham Machen*, 382; Westin, *Presbyterian Pluralism*, 72ff.

31. Westin, *Presbyterian Pluralism*, 77.
32. Quirk, " 'The Auburn Affirmation': A Critical Narrative," 290–94.
33. Robert E. Speer to Edwin M. Bulkley, 11 September 1925, Speer Papers.
34. Robert E. Speer to Cheesman A. Herrick, 23 November 1925, and Cheesman A. Herrick to Robert E. Speer, 25 November 1925, Speer Papers.
35. Robert E. Speer to Margaret B. Speer, 8 June 1926, Speer Papers.
36. Loetscher, *The Broadening Church*, 130.
37. Westin, *Presbyterian Pluralism*, 81. See also William Westin, "The Presbyterian Controversy: The Triumph of the Loyalist Center," in Jacobsen and Trollinger, *Re-Forming the Center*, 119–21.
38. *Minutes of the General Assembly of the Presbyterian Church in the U.S.A.* Third Series, vol. 5, 1926 (Philadelphia: Office of the General Assembly, 1926), 78. See Longfield, *The Presbyterian Controversy*, 156ff; Loetscher, *The Broadening Church*, 132f.; Westin, *Presbyterian Pluralism*, 79–80.
39. Robert E. Speer to Mrs. Charles L. Reed, 12 June 1926, Speer Family Papers.
40. Robert E. Speer to David S. Cairns, 30 July 1926, Speer Papers.
41. Quoted in Loetscher, *The Broadening Church*, 132–33.
42. "Special Commission of 1925," *Minutes of the General Assembly of the Presbyterian Church in the U.S.A.* Third Series, vol. 6, 1927 (Philadelphia: Office of the General Assembly, 1927), 58–86. See Longfield, *The Presbyterian Controversy*, 161; Loetscher, *The Broadening Church*, 133–34.
43. Robert E. Speer to Emma B. Speer, 31 May 1927, Speer Family Papers.
44. Robert E. Speer to Margaret B. Speer, 10 June 1927, Speer Family Papers.
45. Westin, *Presbyterian Pluralism*, 138.
46. Loetscher, *The Broadening Church*, 138.
47. Ronald T. Clutter, "The Reorganization of Princeton Theological Seminary Reconsidered," *Grace Theological Journal* 7 (1986): 179–201.
48. Longfield, *The Presbyterian Controversy*, 162.
49. Stonehouse, *J. Gresham Machen*, 385–86.
50. Robert E. Speer to Margaret B. Speer, 24 May 1926, Speer Papers.
51. Robert E. Speer to Margaret B. Speer, 8 June 1926, Speer Papers.
52. Loetscher, *The Broadening Church*, 141. See *New York Times*, 3 June 1926.
53. Robert E. Speer to Emma B. Speer, 25 May 1927, Speer Family Papers.
54. Longfield, *The Presbyterian Controversy*, 167; Stonehouse, *J. Gresham Machen*, 471.
55. Loetscher, *The Broadening Church*, 144–45; *Minutes of the General Assembly*, 1927, 87–134. The committee recommendations are on 133–34.
56. Nykamp, "A Presbyterian Power Struggle," 454.
57. Robert E. Speer to Emma B. Speer, 29 May 1927, Speer Family Papers.
58. 31 May 1927.
59. Quoted in Longfield, *The Presbyterian Controversy*, 168.
60. Stonehouse, *J. Gresham Machen*, 471.
61. Untitled manuscript that begins "Various proposals . . ." Rockledge, 13 December 1937.
62. 2 June 1927.
63. "An Illuminating Letter," *Presbyterian* 98, no. 19 (10 May 1928): 19f.
64. Loetscher, *The Broadening Church*, 135.
65. Westin, *Presbyterian Pluralism*, 29–30.

66. Hunter, "Minister Appraises Moderator," 9.
67. Robert E. Speer to Mrs. James Bailey, 28 June 1927, Speer Papers.
68. Robert E. Speer to Frank Mason North, 23 June 1927, Speer Papers.
69. Robert E. Speer to Margaret B. Speer, 31 October 1927, Speer Family Papers.
70. Ibid. See Robert E. Speer to Elliott Speer, 27 October 1927, Speer Family Papers.
71. Robert E. Speer to Margaret B. Speer, 31 January 1928, Speer Family Papers.
72. Ibid.
73. Robert E. Speer to Margaret B. Speer, 23 June 1927, Speer Papers.
74. Lewis S. Mudge to Robert E. Speer, 21 June 1927, Speer Papers.
75. Robert E. Speer and Lewis S. Mudge, "To The Members of the General Council," 21 June 1927, Speer Papers.
76. See copy, dated 30 June 1927 in Speer Papers.
77. Robert E. Speer, "To the Foreign Missionaries of the Presbyterian Church in the U.S.A.," 27 July 1927, Speer Papers.
78. Robert E. Speer and Lewis S. Mudge, "To the Ministers and Members of the Presbyterian Church in the U.S.A.," 12 January 1928, Speer Papers. See Robert E. Speer and Lewis S. Mudge, "To the Moderators of the Synods and Presbyteries," 4 January 1928, Speer Papers.
79. George G. Barber to Robert E. Speer, 23 February 1928, Speer Papers. See William C. Covert to Robert E. Speer, 24 February 1928, Speer Family Papers.
80. "A Present Day Balance Sheet of the Church's Life," [February 1928], manuscript, Speer Papers.
81. Robert E. Speer to David S. Cairns, 1 August 1928, Speer Papers; Robert E. Speer to Margaret B. Speer, 6 June 1928, Speer Family Papers.
82. Robert E. Speer to David S. Cairns, 1 August 1928. See "June 1927–February 1928," in *Chronological Record*, Speer Family Papers.
83. Robert E. Speer to Margaret B. Speer, 6 June 1928.
84. Longfield. *The Presbyterian Controversy*, 173.
85. Robert E. Speer to Margaret B. Speer, 3 June 1929, Speer Family Papers.
86. Robert E. Speer to Charles R. Erdman, 29 August 1929, Erdman Collection.
87. Robert E. Speer to David S. Cairns, 2 April 1930, Speer Papers.
88. Speer, *Studies in the Book of Acts*, 155.
89. Speer, *Studies of the Man Christ Jesus*, 135–36.
90. Ibid., 137.
91. Speer, *Some Living Issues*, 195–99. The quotations are from 1 Corinthians 14:34–35 and 1 Timothy 2:11–12.
92. Speer, *Missionary Principles and Practice*, 458.
93. Speer, "The Student Volunteer Movement for Foreign Missions."
94. Speer, *Some Living Issues*, 183–84.
95. Margaret E. Hodge, "Introduction of Dr. Speer," in Speer, *One Century Past, Another to Come*, 4.
96. *Minutes of the General Assembly*, 1926, 70. For the full report, see 62–87. See Katharine Bennett to Robert E. Speer, 29 January 1929, Speer Papers.
97. Margaret E. Hodge to Robert E. Speer, 7 July 1927, Speer Papers.
98. Robert E. Speer to Margaret E. Hodge, 20 July 1927, Speer Papers.
99. Lois A. Boyd and R. Douglas Brackenridge, *Presbyterian Women in America, Two Centuries of a Quest for Status*. A Publication of the Presbyterian

Historical Society, no. 9 (Westport, Conn.: Greenwood Press, 1983), 125. See *Causes of Unrest Among the Women of the Church*, Report of Special Committee to the General Council of the Presbyterian Church in the U.S.A., 1927, published as a pamphlet, Speer Papers.

100. Speer, *Some Living Issues*, 183.
101. Boyd and Brackenridge, *Presbyterian Women in America*, 127.
102. Ibid., 127–38. See Robert E. Speer to Margaret B. Speer, 3 June 1929, Speer Family Papers. Emphasis added.
103. Boyd and Brackenridge, *Presbyterian Women in America*, 127–28.
104. Ibid., 129. See "Conference of the General Council with Fifteen Representative Women at the Fourth Presbyterian Church, Chicago, Ill., 22 November 1928," mimeographed minutes, Speer Papers.
105. Robert E. Speer to Lewis S. Mudge, Miss Margaret E. Hodge, Mrs. F. S. Bennett, 11 January 1929, Speer Papers.
106. Bennett to Speer, 29 January 1929.
107. Boyd and Brackenridge, *Presbyterian Women in America*, 131.
108. Ibid.
109. Ibid., 131–32.
110. Ibid., 132–33.
111. Mark A. Matthews to Robert E. Speer, 12 March 1929, in the Records of the Stated Clerk of the General Assembly, Correspondence and Files, 1921–38, Presbyterian Historical Society, Philadelphia. Hereafter cited as Stated Clerk Records.
112. Robert E. Speer to Mark A. Matthews, 25 March 1929. See also letters from Matthews to Speer, 29 March 1929 and Speer to Matthews, 17 April 1929, Stated Clerk Records.
113. Boyd and Brackenridge, *Presbyterian Women in America*, 135.
114. "Special Committee on Status of Women in the Church," in *Minutes of the General Assembly of the Presbyterian Church in the U.S.A.* Third Series, vol. 8, 1929 (Philadelphia: Office of the General Assembly, 1929), 186–91. For the overtures, see 189–91.
115. Boyd and Brackenridge, *Presbyterian Women in America*, 135.
116. Robert E. Speer to Margaret B. Speer, 3 June 1929, Speer Family Papers.
117. Speer, *Some Living Issues*, 202–3.
118. Robert E. Speer to Mark A. Matthews, 12 May 1930, Stated Clerk Records.
119. Robert E. Speer to Margaret B. Speer, 17 May 1930, Speer Family Papers.
120. Robert E. Speer to Margaret B. Speer, 30 April 1930, Speer Family Papers.
121. Robert E. Speer to Margaret B. Speer, 18 February 1932, Speer Family Papers.
122. Robert E. Speer to Margaret B. Speer, 16 April 1932, Speer Family Papers.

Chapter 13: Defender of Christian Missions

1. See letters to Margaret B. Speer, 11 May, 13 July, 20 July, 15 August, 29 August 1932, Speer Family Papers.
2. See Hutchison, *Errand to the World*, chapter 6; Patterson, "Robert E. Speer and the Crisis"; and Patterson, "Robert E. Speer, J. Gresham Machen and the Presbyterian Board of Foreign Missions."
3. Robert E. Speer to Margaret B. Speer, 30 April 1930, Speer Family Papers.

4. Harvey, "Speer Versus Rockefeller and Mott," 294–95; Robert E. Speer, "Address at General Assembly," Columbus, 1933, manuscript, Speer Papers; Robert E. Speer, *Re-Thinking Missions" Examined* (New York: Fleming H. Revell Co., 1933), 7–15; Longfield, *The Presbyterian Controversy*, 199ff.
5. See letters to Margaret B. Speer, 5 February, 11 March, 8 June 1932, Speer Papers.
6. Margaret B. Speer to "Dearest Mother and Father and Holly and Elliott," 11 April 1932, Speer Family Papers.
7. Robert E. Speer to Margaret B. Speer, 11 October 1932, Speer Papers; Speer, *"Re-Thinking Missions" Examined*, 11–13.
8. Margaret B. Speer to "Dearest Mother and Father," 13 November 1932, Speer Family Papers.
9. Robert E. Speer to Margaret B. Speer, 22 November 1932, Speer Papers.
10. Robert E. Speer to Margaret B. Speer, 7 November 1932, Speer Papers; *Action of the Board of Foreign Missions Regarding the Report of the Appraisal Commission of the Laymen's Foreign Missions Inquiry*, pamphlet issued by the Board of Foreign Missions, Speer Papers; "Board Speaks on Report," *Presbyterian Banner* 119, no. 22 (1 December 1932): 14–15.
11. Interview by the author with Margaret B. Speer and William Speer.
12. Emma B. Speer to William Speer, 14 November, 4 December [1932], Speer Family Papers.
13. Robert E. Speer to Margaret B. Speer, 19 December 1932, Speer Papers.
14. Robert E. Speer to Margaret B. Speer, 10 December 1932, Speer Papers.
15. Robert E. Speer, "An Appraisal of the Appraisal," *Missionary Review of the World* 56, no. 1 (January 1933): 7–27. On Speer as leader, see Hutchison, *Errand to the World*, 166ff.
16. Speer, *"Re-Thinking Missions" Examined*, 7–8.
17. Ibid, 8.
18. Ibid., 25–26.
19. Ibid., 28–29.
20. Ibid., 29.
21. Ibid., 31.
22. Ibid., 33–34. See chapter 8. For the Duff Lecture version of this, see *Christianity and the Nations*, 299ff.
23. Speer, *"Rethinking Missions" Examined*, 36–37. Quoted in Harvey, "Speer Versus Rockefeller and Mott," 294–96.
24. Ibid., 37f.
25. Ibid., 47–48.
26. Ibid., 63, 64.
27. Robert E. Speer to Margaret B. Speer, 27 March 1933, Speer Papers.
28. Frank Mason North to Robert E. Speer, 15 January 1933, Speer Papers.
29. Robert E. Speer to Frank Mason North, 3 February 1933, Speer Papers.
30. Henry W. Rankin to Robert E. Speer, 23 January 1933, Speer Papers.
31. Robert Wilder to Robert E. Speer, 16 January 1933, Wilder Papers.
32. Pearl S. Buck, "The Laymen's Mission Report," *Christian Century* 49, no. 47 (23 November 1932): 1434. Longfield, *The Presbyterian Controversy*, 201. He described Buck as "Gushing with enthusiasm" over the report.

33. Peter J. Conn, *Pearl S. Buck: A Cultural Biography* (Cambridge and New York: Cambridge University Press, 1996), 148. The *New York Times* titled its report of this meeting "Better Missionaries Urged By Mrs. Buck," 3 November 1932.

34. Paul A. Doyle, *Pearl S. Buck* (New York: Twayne Publishers, [1965]), 54–57; Conn, *Pearl S. Buck*, 148–55. See Pearl S. Buck, "Is There a Case for Foreign Missions?" *Harper's Magazine*, 166 (January 1933): 143–55.

35. Robert E. Speer to W. Reginald Wheeler, 16 May 1933, Speer Papers.

36. Pearl S. Buck to Cleland B. McAfee, 28 April 1933, Speer Papers.

37. Speer to Wheeler, 16 May 1933.

38. Longfield, *The Presbyterian Controversy*, 203–4.

39. "To The Board of Foreign Missions of the Presbyterian Church in the United States of America," in the Papers of Clarence Edward Macartney, The McCartney Library, Geneva College, Beaver Falls, Pa. Hereafter cited as Macartney Papers.

40. Charles R. Erdman. "To the Session of the First Presbyterian Church, Pittsburgh, Pa.," 23 March 1933, Speer Papers. Evidence suggests Speer had a hand in writing this. See "Machen-Speer Debate Historic Event in Presbyterian Church," *Christianity Today* 3, no. 12 (Mid-April 1933), 19.

41. "To The Board of Foreign Missions."

42. Rian, *The Presbyterian Conflict*, 145ff.

43. The overtures are in "Machen-Speer Debate," 20.

44. William T. Hanzsche to Robert E. Speer, 26 January 1933, Speer Papers.

45. The correspondence is in the Speer Papers. See letters between Hadley and Machen, 27 February; 7 and 8 March; 7 and 13 April 1928; 5 and 28 March 1929.

46. J. Gresham Machen to Robert E. Speer, 12 April 1929, Speer Papers.

47. J. Gresham Machen, "Can Evangelical Christians Support Our Foreign Board?" April 1929, Speer Papers. For a perceptive analysis, see Patterson, "Robert E. Speer and the Crisis," 140–41. Patterson says Machen "strained a good deal to malign Speer's book, giving the impression that he formed his judgments before he read it."

48. Robert E. Speer to J. Gresham Machen, 30 April 1929, Speer Papers. See Patterson, "Robert E. Speer and the Crisis," 141–43.

49. J. Gresham Machen to Robert E. Speer, 4 May 1929, Speer Papers.

50. Charles R. Erdman to Robert E. Speer, 7 April 1933, Speer Papers.

51. Robert E. Speer to Margaret B. Speer, 15 April 1933, Speer Papers.

52. Patterson, "Robert E. Speer and the Crisis," 149.

53. "Machen-Speer Debate," 19; See Stonehouse, *J. Gresham Machen*, 478.

54. Ibid., 19–21. Machen subsequently published his review of Speer's *The Finality of Jesus Christ* as "Dr. Robert E. Speer and His Latest Book," *Christianity Today* 4, no. 1 (Mid-May 1933): 15–16, 22–26.

55. "A Statement by Mr. Robert E. Speer to the Presbytery of New Brunswick at Its Meeting in Trenton, N.J., 11 April 1933," Speer Papers. See "Machen-Speer Debate," 21–22.

56. Ibid., 22–23.

57. *Minutes of the General Assembly of the Presbyterian Church in the U.S.A.* Third Series, vol. 12, 1933 (Philadelphia: Office of the General Assembly, 1933), 153–54. Patterson, "Robert E. Speer and the Crisis," 155.

58. Robert E. Speer to Margaret B. Speer, 27 March 1933, Speer Papers.
59. Robert E. Speer to Margaret B. Speer, 11 May 1933, Speer Papers.
60. Robert E. Speer to W. Reginald Wheeler, 16 May 1933, Speer Papers. Quoted in Patterson, "Robert E. Speer and the Crisis," 156.
61. "Answer to Dr. Machen and Dr. Monsma," [1933], Speer Papers.
62. "57 to 16" in "Editorial Notes and Comments," *Christianity Today* 4, no. 1 (Mid-May 1933): 1.
63. Robert E. Speer to Margaret B. Speer, 22 May 1933, Speer Papers.
64. Wheeler, *A Man Sent From God*, 220.
65. Ibid., 221, 227; *Minutes of the General Assembly*, 1933, 159; Stonehouse, *J. Gresham Machen*, 480f.
66. Wheeler, *A Man Sent From God*, 227; *Minutes of the General Assembly*, 1933, 159. See John R. Fitzmier and Randall Balmer, "A Poultice for the Bite of the Cobra: The Hocking Report and Presbyterian Missions in the Middle Decade of the Twentieth Century," in Milton J. Coalter, John Mulder, Louis B. Weeks, eds., *The Diversity of Discipleship: Presbyterians and Twentieth-Century Christian Witness* (Louisville, Ky.: Westminster/John Knox Press, 1991), 105–25.
67. Longfield, *The Presbyterian Controversy*, 206. See "Parliamentary Chaos," *Christianity Today* 4, no. 2 (Mid-June 1933): 12.
68. Varg, *Missionaries, Chinese, and Diplomats*, 169. See *Missionary Review of the World* 56, no. Seven (July 1933): 387.
69. "The Foreign Board at the General Assembly," *Presbyterian Banner* 119, no. 49 (8 June 1933): 3–4.
70. "Address at General Assembly," Columbus, 1933, Speer Papers.
71. *Minutes of the General Assembly*, 1933, 159.
72. Longfield, *The Presbyterian Controversy*, 205ff.
73. Robert E. Speer to Elliott Speer, 9 June 1933; Robert E. Speer to Margaret B. Speer, 31 May 1933; Robert E. Speer to Aunt Clara, 31 May 1933; Speer Family Papers.
74. Mackay, "Robert Elliott Speer: A Man of Yesterday Today," 19.
75. Loetscher, *The Broadening Church*, 150. See the *New York Times*, 28 May 1933; H. McAllister Griffiths, "145th Assembly Meets: New Mission Board Announced," *Christianity Today* 4, no. 2 (Mid-June 1933): 13.
76. Robert E. Speer to J. Gresham Machen, 30 April 1929, Speer Papers.
77. Longfield, *The Presbyterian Controversy*, 206–7.
78. Patterson, "Robert E. Speer and the Crisis," 127.
79. Robert E. Speer to David S. Cairns, 11 July 1933, Speer Papers. See Longfield, *The Presbyterian Controversy*, 180; Hutchison, *Errand to the World*, 172f.
80. Patterson, "Robert E. Speer and the Crisis," 157; Hutchison, *Errand to the World*, 172, 174. See Westin, *Presbyterian Pluralism*, 105–8.
81. Robert E. Speer to Elliott Speer, 16 June 1933, Speer Family Papers.
82. Robert E. Speer to Margaret B. Speer, 10 July 1933, Speer Papers.
83. Robert E. Speer to Mark A. Matthews, 25 July 1933, Speer Papers.
84. Robert E. Speer to Margaret B. Speer, 9 October 1933, Speer Papers.
85. Robert E. Speer to Margaret B. Speer, 9 May 1934, Speer Family Papers.
86. Robert E. Speer to Lewis S. Mudge, 20 March 1934; Lewis S. Mudge to Robert E. Speer, 18 April 1934; Robert E. Speer to Lewis S. Mudge, 17 April 1934; in

the Papers of the Office of the General Assembly, Stated Clerk's File. Presbyterian Independent Board of Foreign Missions, 1933–36, in the Presbyterian Historical Society, Philadelphia, Pa.

87. Robert E. Speer to Margaret B. Speer, 9 May 1934, Speer Family Papers.

88. Loetscher, *The Broadening Church*, 151. *Minutes of the General Assembly of the Presbyterian Church in the U.S.A.* Third Series, vol. 13, 1934 (Philadelphia: Office of the General Assembly, 1934), 110–16.

89. Ibid. See Robert E. Speer to Margaret B. Speer, 4 June 1934, Speer Family Papers.

90. "To Our Ministers and Church Sessions," 1 August 1934, Speer Papers.

91. Robert E. Speer to Margaret B. Speer, 4 June 1934.

92. Copies of the overture are in the Macartney Papers and the Speer Papers. See "A Memorandum regarding the Criticisms of the Board of Foreign Missions of the Presbyterian Church, U.S.A. which were presented to The Presbytery of West Jersey on January 15, 1935," Speer Papers.

93. See *Sunday School Times* 97, no. 12 (23 March 1935): 195ff. See Charles G. Trumbull to Robert E. Speer, 22 March 1935, and Robert E. Speer to Charles G. Trumbull, 1 May 1935, Speer Papers.

94. Folder: "Robert Elliott Speer, D.D., LL.D.," Speer Papers.

95. Robert E. Speer to David S. Cairns, 9 August 1935, Speer Papers.

96. Robert E. Speer to Henry W. Rankin, 29 May 1936, Speer Papers.

97. Rian, *The Presbyterian Conflict*, 218.

98. Dallas Morgan Roark, "J. Gresham Machen and His Desire to Maintain a Doctrinally True Presbyterian Church," Ph.D. diss., State University of Iowa, 1963, 63f. For the end of the controversy, see Longfield, *The Presbyterian Controversy*, 209–12, and Loetscher, *The Broadening Church*,148–55. See also Pierard, "Evangelical and Ecumenical," 159–63.

99. James A. Patterson, "The Loss of a Protestant Missionary Consensus: Foreign Missions and the Fundamentalist-Modernist Conflict," in Joel A. Carpenter and Wilbert R. Shenk, eds., *Earthen Vessels*, American Evangelicals and Foreign Missions, 1880–1980 (Grand Rapids: Wm. B. Eerdmans Publishing Co., 1990), 83.

100. "Dr. Robert Elliott Speer's Forty Years of Service," *Presbyterian Banner* 118, no. 18 (29 October 1931): 8.

101. John A. Mackay, "The Missionary Statesman," *Princeton Seminary Bulletin* 42, no. 1 (Summer 1948): 13.

Chapter 14: New Ministries

1. Walter L. Whallon to Dear Mrs. Speer, [1948]; "Abstract of an Address by Dr. Robert E. Speer in Recognition of the Service of Rev. Charles S. Macfarland . . ." 2 December 1930; Robert E. Speer to Margaret E. Hodge, 20 July 1927; Speer Papers.

2. Robert E. Speer to Clara McMurtrie, 7 July 1930, Speer Family Papers.

3. Robert E. Speer to Lucas, 26 July 1937, Speer Papers.

4. Emma B. Speer to Robert E. Speer, 26 August 1937, Speer Family Papers.

5. Robert E. Speer to Dear Helen, 14 December 1938, Speer Family Papers.

6. Robert E. Speer, "The Achievements of Yesterday," 174.
7. Ibid., 180.
8. Ibid., 184.
9. Ibid., 185–86.
10. Speer, *Some Changing and Unchanging Things in Foreign Missions*, 7, 11.
11. Ibid., 14, 17, 19.
12. Leber, "Board Policy During the Crisis Decade," 13.
13. Robert E. Speer to Margaret B. Speer, 26 February 1937, Speer Family Papers.
14. Speer, *One Century Past, Another to Come*, 3.
15. Ibid., 5, 7, 8, 11.
16. Ibid., 13–14. See Ephesians 6:12.
17. Ibid., 15–16.
18. *Presbyterian Banner* 123, no. 48 (27 May 1937).
19. 8 June 1937.
20. Robert E. Speer to Margaret B. Speer, 4 March 1937, Speer Family Papers.
21. Family Card, Speer Family Papers.
22. See Robert E. Speer to Margaret B. Speer, 26 March 1927, Speer Family Papers; Robert E. Speer to Mrs. Charles L. Reed, 9 August 1929, Speer Papers; Robert E. Speer to Margaret B. Speer, 6 June 1928, Speer Family Papers.
23. Emma B. Speer to Robert E. Speer, 4 August 1935, Speer Family Papers.
24. Interview by the author with Constance (Pat) Speer Barbour.
25. Robert E. Speer to Margaret B. Speer, 23 July 1936, Speer Family Papers.
26. Robert E. Speer to Margaret B. Speer, 26 February 1937, Speer Family Papers.
27. Emma B. Speer to Mrs. John J. Eagan, 12 May 1939, Speer Family Papers.
28. Mackay, "Robert Elliott Speer: A Man of Yesterday Today," 20.
29. "Robert Elliott Speer," in *The Record of the Class of 1889* (Princeton University, 1939).
30. Emma B. Speer to Leila Mott, 9 October 1939, Mott Papers.
31. Mark A. Matthews to Robert E. Speer, 22 December 1938, Speer Papers.
32. Robert E. Speer to Lewis S. Mudge, 26 November 1940, the Papers of Lewis Seymour Mudge, 1868–1945, in the Presbyterian Historical Society, Philadelphia, Pa. Hereafter cited as Mudge Papers.
33. Emma B. Speer to Leila Mott.
34. Wheeler, *A Man Sent From God*, 14–16.
35. Robert E. Speer to Lewis S. Mudge, 4 December 1938, Speer Papers.
36. Robert E. Speer to Margaret B. Speer, 24 May 1926; Robert E. Speer to David S. Cairns, 2 July 1937; Speer Papers.
37. Delavan Pierson to Robert E. Speer, 13 October and 9 November 1939, Speer Papers. See form letter, signed by Speer and Pierson, 25 September 1939, Speer Papers.
38. Henry A. Atkinson to Robert E. Speer, 25 January 1939; M. H. Krumbine to Robert E. Speer, 24 September 1941, Speer Papers.
39. Robert E. Speer to William Norbert Nigey, [1940]; Rome A. Betts to Robert E. Speer, 5 September 1940, Speer Papers. See "Emergency Fund for Bibles Asked," *New York Times*, 24 August 1940.
40. John D. Rockefeller, Jr., to Robert E. Speer, 15 October 1940, "Religious Interests," Rockefeller Archives.

41. Howard Chandler Robbins, Reinhold Niebuhr, and Henry Sloane Coffin to Robert E. Speer, 18 August 1941, Speer Papers.
42. *Presbyterian* 110, no. 50 (12 December 1940): 2.
43. Robert E. Speer to Norman Burton Barr, 23 December 1940, Speer Papers.
44. Robert E. Speer, "The Duty of the Church in the Present Crisis," *Presbyterian Tribune* 57, no. 4 (January 1942): 13.
45. Robert E. Speer, "Is the Human Race One?" Speer Papers.
46. Robert E. Speer, *When Christianity Was New* (New York: Fleming H. Revell Co., 1939), 133.
47. Robert E. Speer, *Not Against One Another But Together*, published as a pamphlet, Speer Papers.
48. Robert E. Speer to Lewis S. Mudge, 9 December 1935; Lewis S. Mudge to Robert E. Speer, 11 December 1935, Mudge Papers.
49. Robert E. Speer to Margaret B. Speer, 3 February 1937, Speer Family Papers.
50. Robert E. Speer, "Charge to the President," 6.
51. Gerald W. Gillette, interviewer, "John A. Mackay: Influences on My Life," *Journal of Presbyterian History* 56. no. 1 (Spring 1978): 32–33. Gillette suggests that Mackay and Speer related to each other as brothers.
52. Benjamin F. Farber to Robert E. Speer, 28 April 1939, Speer Papers.
53. Mackay, "Robert E. Speer: A Man of Yesterday Today," 20.
54. "Seminars on Faith and Life," attached to Helen D. Heston to Robert E. Speer, 4 July 1944, Speer Papers. See Robert E. Speer, "Faith and Life Seminars," in David R. Porter, ed., *The Life Work of George Irving* (New York: Association Press, 1945), 59–61.
55. George Irving to Robert E. Speer, 21 November 1939, Speer Papers.
56. "Comments on Seminars," typed manuscript, [1943], Speer Papers.
57. Robert E. Speer to George Innes, 19 May 1943, Speer Papers.
58. Speer, "Faith and Life Seminars," 67.
59. Robert E. Speer to Lewis S. Mudge, in "Princeton Alumni Reports," n.d., Speer Papers.
60. Fay Campbell to Robert E. Speer, [1943], Speer Papers.
61. Robert E. Speer to George Innes, 31 January 1944, Speer Papers.
62. Robert E. Speer to Emma B. Speer, 29 October 1946, Speer Papers.
63. Emma B. Speer to Mrs. John J. Eagan, 19 November 1941, Speer Family Papers.
64. Peter Emmons to Mrs. Speer, n.d., Speer Papers.
65. Robert E. Speer to A. H. Barr, 17 August 1899, Speer Papers.
66. Showalter, *The End of a Crusade*, 203, n. 1.
67. Robert E. Speer, *Nation-Wide Week of Prayer for the Churches*, 8–14 January 1940 (New York: Department of Evangelism of the Federal Council of the Churches of Christ in America, [1940]), issued as a pamphlet, Speer Papers.
68. Speer, *Five Minutes A Day*, "Preface."
69. Interview with Margaret B. Speer and William Speer.
70. Robert E. Speer, "Our Need to Pray," *Adult Bible Class Members Monthly*, March 1936, 5.
71. Robert E. Speer to M. D. Gurley, 26 June 1908, Speer Papers.
72. Speer, *Five Minutes A Day*, 33, 374.

73. Emma B. Speer , "A Letter To My Children—All," Speer Family Papers. See Speer, *Five Minutes A Day*, 228.
74. Robert E. Speer, *The Fellowship of the Spirit*, Easter to Pentecost, 1947 (New York: Federal Council of Churches, Department of Evangelism, 1947), "Interdenominational Edition," published as a pamphlet, Speer Papers.
75. Robert E. Speer to Emma B. Speer, 16 June 1947, Speer Papers.
76. Emma B. Speer to Robert E. Speer, 16 June 1946, Speer Papers.
77. Emma B. Speer to Robert E. Speer, 13 April 1935, Speer Family Papers.
78. Emma B. Speer to Mr. and Mrs. Innes, 16 December 1945, Speer Papers. Emma B. Speer to William Speer, [1933–35], Speer Family Papers.
79. Robert E. Speer, *Seeking the Mind of Christ* (New York: Fleming H. Revell Co., 1926), 5, 79f.
80. Hiram W. Foulkes to Robert E. Speer, 20 June 1939, Speer Papers.
81. "Address By Dr. Robert E. Speer," chapter 1, n. 2.
82. *Presbyterian Tribune* 62, no. 40 (August–September 1947): 6.
83. Ibid.
84. Ibid., 21.
85. Ibid., 19.
86. Carlyle Adams to Robert E. Speer, 27 August 1947, Speer Papers. "From Dr. Speer," *Presbyterian Tribune* 63, no. 1 (October 1947): 38.
87. Wheeler, *A Man Sent From God*, 263.
88. Robert E. Speer to George Innes, 6 November, 1947, Speer Papers.
89. Walter L. Whallon, 22 November 1947, Speer Papers.
90. Wheeler, *A Man Sent From God*, 263. The *Times* printed his obituary on 25 November with the title, "Dr. R. E. Speer Dies: Led Presbyterians."
91. "Edward Stewart McMurtrie," [1925], Brown Notebook, Speer Family Papers.
92. Speer, *Five Minutes A Day*. 141.
93. "Memorial Tributes," Speer Family Papers.
94. "In Memory of Robert Elliott Speer," Speer Family Papers.
95. "Memorial Service for Robert Elliott Speer," Princeton Theological Seminary, Miller Chapel, 7 June 1948; Mackay, "The Missionary Statesman," 10–13; Charles R. Erdman, "The Interpreter of Christ," *Princeton Seminary Bulletin* 42, no. 1 (Summer 1948): 8–10.
96. Wheeler, *A Man Sent From God*, 265–67. See Speer Family Papers.
97. "A Message to his Missionary Friends," Speer Papers.
98. Robert E. Speer to Mrs. Charles L. Reed, 4 March 1927, Speer Papers; Robert E. Speer to Clara McMurtrie, [1927], Speer Family Papers.
99. Lloyd S. Ruland to "Dear Mrs. Speer," 29 December 1947, Speer Papers.
100. John A. Mackay to Mrs. Speer, 31 December 1947, Speer Papers.
101. Jane L. Mackay to Mrs. Speer, 7 December 1947, Speer Papers.
102. John A. Mackay to "Dear Mrs. Speer," 19 July 1948, Speer Papers.
103. John G. Buchanan to Mrs. Speer, 16 October 1948, Speer Papers.
104. Lloyd S. Ruland to Mrs. Speer, 20 October 1948, Speer Papers.
105. Emma B. Speer to Dr. Quay, 25 October 1948, Speer Papers.
106. James K. Quay to "Dear Mrs. Speer," 28 October 1948, Speer Papers.
107. "Princeton to Dedicate New Theological Library Oct. 8," 28 September 1957.
108. John G. Buchanan to Mrs. Speer, 24 December 1951; David L. Crawford to Mrs. Speer, 13 July 1956; James K. Quay to Mrs. Speer, 9 August 1956; John

A. Mackay to Mrs. Speer, 26 September 1956; Speer Papers. Mackay, "Robert Elliott Speer: A Man of Yesterday Today," 20–21. "The Dedication of the Robert E. Speer Library," *Princeton Seminary Bulletin* 51, no. 3 (January 1958): 43–59. On Mackay's authorship of the inscription, see interview with President James McCord, 16 June 1982.

109. John W. Wood to Allen R. Bartholomew, 16 October 1931, Speer Papers.
110. Hugh T. Kerr, "In Memoriam: Robert E. Speer," *Theology Today* 5, no. 1 (April 1948): 93.
111. H. Clay Trumbull to Robert E. Speer, 31 August 1892, Speer Papers.
112. Ibid., 27 August 1892.
113. Emma B. Speer to Robert E. Speer, 13 April 1935, Speer Family Papers.
114. Sherwood Eddy to Mrs. Speer, 1 January 1948, Speer Papers.
115. Unpublished notebook, Speer Family Papers.
116. Kerr et al., "Dr. Robert E. Speer," 4.
117. "Retirement of Dr. Speer," *Minutes of the General Assembly of the Presbyterian Church in the United States of America*, Third Series, vol. 16, 1937 (Philadelphia: Office of the General Assembly, 1937), 201. See Board of Foreign Missions, "China Letter No. 272," Speer Family Papers, 13.
118. W. Reginald Wheeler, "Reminiscences of Robert E. Speer," *Outreach* 2, no. 4 (April 1948): 104.
119. James H. Franklin to Allen R. Bartholomew, 28 October 1931, Speer Papers.
120. John A. Mackay, "Robert E. Speer," *Presbyterian Life*, Preview issue, 17 January 1948. The article is on the inside of the front cover, a space designated for a message from Speer, but which he did not live to write. See Frank Fitt, "Robert E. Speer, Servant of God," *Christian Century* 54, no. 39 (29 September 1937): 1196.
121. Kerr et al., "Dr. Robert E. Speer," 4.
122. Charles P. Robshaw, *The Art and Architecture of the East Liberty Presbyterian Church* (Pittsburgh: East Liberty Presbyterian Church, 1977), 46–49.
123. Samuel McCrea Cavert, "Robert E. Speer, Apostle of Christian Unity," in *Robert Elliott Speer, 1867–1947*, published as a pamphlet, Speer Papers, 20–25. See "Robert E. Speer and Christian Unity," *Federal Council Bulletin* 31, no. 1 (January 1948): 3.
124. Joseph R. Sizoo in Kerr et al., "Dr. Robert E. Speer," 4.
125. Walter Lingle, "Robert E. Speer," 3.
126. The Board of Trustees, "Robert E. Speer Memorial Minute," *Princeton Seminary Bulletin* 42, no. 1 (Summer 1948): 13–15.
127. Arthur J. Brown, "Robert E. Speer Leader for 40 Years," *Presbyterian Magazine* 37, no. 12 (December 1931): 680; J. R. Mott to "Dear Friend," 6 December 1947, Speer Papers. Lucia P. Towne, "Robert E. Speer," 240–41.
128. Frank Mason North to Robert E. Speer, 6 December 1930, Speer Family Papers; John A. Mackay to Mrs. Speer, 19 July 1948, Speer Papers; Henry Sloane Coffin's prayer at the Bryn Mawr Memorial Service, 24 November 1947, Speer Family Papers; Charles R. Watson to Robert E. Speer, 10 May 1922, Speer Papers.
129. John G. Buchanan to Dear Mrs. Speer, 25 November 1947, Speer Papers. See W. B. Anderson to Dr. Bartholomew, 15 October 1931, Speer Papers; Lingle, "Robert E. Speer," 3.

130. Samuel G. Inman to Robert E. Speer, Christmas 1934, Speer Family Papers; Erdman, "The Interpreter of Christ," 9.

131. Mackay, "Robert Elliott Speer: A Man of Yesterday Today," 14.

132. Kerr, "In Memoriam: Robert E. Speer," 94.

133. Eddy, *Eighty Adventurous Years*, 202.

134. Miller, "Christ's Man," 10.

135. Interview with Margaret and William Speer.

136. These documents are in the Speer Family Papers.

137. Wheeler, *A Man Sent From God*, 259.

138. Margaret B. Speer, "RES."

139. Brown, *Memoirs of a Centenarian*, 173. For use of the prophet theme, see: Arthur J. Brown to Margaret B. Speer, 27 November 1947, Speer Family Papers; Goodpasture, "Robert E. Speer's Legacy," 38; Eddy, *Pathfinders of the World Missionary Crusade*, 269.

BIBLIOGRAPHY

I. Interviews and Manuscript Collections

Interviews

The most important interviews were formal ones with the three Speer children who survived their parents. The interviews with Margaret Speer and William Speer took place on 22 March 1984, 9 April 1984, and 8 July 1985, and the interview with Constance (Pat) Speer Barbour was on 19 May 1987. In addition, Margaret Speer was very helpful over the years in responding to inquiries about various aspects of her father's life. Interviews were held with a number of other people who are thanked in the Acknowledgments.

Manuscript Collections

The manuscript collections listed below are those that were used extensively. The most valuable for this study are the ones located in the Robert E. Speer Library at Princeton Theological Seminary, the Miriam Coffin Canaday Library at Bryn Mawr College, and a number of different Record Groups in the Presbyterian Historical Society.

In addition to those listed, the following collections provided some helpful information: the Papers of David Smith Cairns and the Scottish Foreign Mission Records, 1827–1929, in the National Library of Scotland, Edinburgh, Scotland; the Papers of Dwight L. Moody, the Papers of John Haynes Holmes, and the Papers of William Jennings Bryan, all in the Manuscript Division of the Library of Congress, Washington, D.C.; the Dwight L. Moody Papers, the Kenneth Scott Latourette Papers, the Mission Pamphlet Collection and the Henry B. Wright Papers, all in the Archives and Manuscripts of the Yale Divinity School Library, New Haven, Conn.; the Samuel Hall Chester Papers in the Presbyterian Historical Society, Montreat, N.C.; and the Alumni File in the Seeley G. Mudd Manuscript Library, Princeton University, Princeton, N.J. The following Record Groups in the Presbyterian Historical Society also held useful information: the Papers of Hugh Thomson Kerr, Record Group 1; the Papers of John Gresham Machen, Record Group 7; the

Correspondence and Papers, 1931–45, of the Board of Trustees of Princeton Theological Seminary, Record Group 34; the Stated Clerk of the General Assembly, Decision Letters, Mudge, 1921–38, Record Group 17; and the Office of the General Assembly, Stated Clerk File, Presbyterian Independent Board of Foreign Missions, 1933–36, Record Group 20.

Arthur Judson Brown Papers, Archives and Manuscripts, Record Group 2, Yale Divinity School Library, New Haven, Conn.

Charles Rosenbury Erdman Manuscript Collection, Department of Archives and Special Collections, Princeton Theological Seminary Libraries, Princeton, N.J.

Records of the Federal Council of the Churches of Christ in America, 1894–1952, Record Group 18, Records of the National Council of the Churches of Christ, Presbyterian Historical Society, Philadelphia, Pa.

The Papers of Samuel Guy Inman, Manuscript Division, Library of Congress, Washington, D.C.

The Papers of Clarence Edward Macartney, The McCartney Library, Geneva College, Beaver Falls, Pa.

John R. Mott Papers, Archives and Manuscripts, Record Group 45, Yale Divinity School Library, New Haven, Conn.

Papers of Lewis Seymour Mudge, 1865–1945, Record Group 5, Presbyterian Historical Society, Philadelphia, Pa.

Presbyterian Church in the U.S.A., Board of Foreign Missions Records, 1829–95, Record Group 31, Presbyterian Historical Society, Philadelphia, Pa.

Presbyterian Church in the U.S.A., Board of Foreign Missions Records, 1892–1965, Record Group 81, Presbyterian Historical Society, Philadelphia, Pa.

Presbyterian Church in the U.S.A., Stated Clerk of the General Assembly Correspondence and Files, 1921–38, Record Group 125, Presbyterian Historical Society, Philadelphia, Pa.

Rockefeller Family Archives, Religious Interests, Record Group 2, Rockefeller Archive Center, Pocantico Hills, North Tarrytown, N.Y.

Robert E. Speer Papers, Department of Archives and Special Collections, Princeton Theological Seminary Libraries, Princeton, N.J.

Speer Family Papers, Bryn Mawr College Archives, Mariam Coffin Canaday Library, Bryn Mawr, Pa.

Archives of the Student Volunteer Movement for Foreign Missions, Archives and Manuscripts, Record Group 42, Yale Divinity School Library, New Haven, Conn.

Robert Parmelee Wilder Papers, Archives and Manuscripts, Record Group 38, Yale Divinity School Library, New Haven Conn.

II. Books, Pamphlets, and Articles by Robert E. Speer

The following is a complete list of Speer's published books. The Speer Papers contain several unpublished book manuscripts, and the Speer Family Papers contain unpublished manuscripts on daughter Eleanor and son Elliott.

Books

Are Foreign Missions Done For? New York: Board of Foreign Missions of the Presbyterian Church in the U.S.A., 1928.

Christ and Life. New York: Fleming H. Revell Co., 1901.
The Christian Man, the Church and the War. New York: Macmillan Co., 1918.
A Christian's Habits. Philadelphia: Westminster Press, 1911.
Christian Realities. New York: Fleming H. Revell Co., 1935.
Christianity and the Nations. New York: Fleming H. Revell Co., 1910.
The Church and Missions. New York: George H. Doran Co., 1926.
The Finality of Jesus Christ. New York: Fleming H. Revell Co., 1933.
Five Minutes A Day. Philadelphia: Westminster Press, 1943.
George Bowen of Bombay: Missionary; Scholar; Mystic; Saint: A Memoir. Privately printed, 1938.
The Gospel and the New World. New York: Fleming H. Revell Company, 1919.
The Hakim Sahib, The Foreign Doctor: A Biography of Joseph Plumb Cochran, M.D., of Persia. New York: Fleming H. Revell Co., 1911.
Jesus and Our Human Problems. New York: Fleming H. Revell Co., 1946.
John J. Eagan: A Memoir of an Adventurer for the Kingdom of God on Earth. Birmingham, Ala.: American Cast Iron Pipe Company, 1939.
John's Gospel, the Greatest Book in the World. New York: Fleming H. Revell Co., [1915].
The Light of the World. A Brief Comparative Study of Christianity and non-Christian Religions. West Medford, Mass.: Central Committee on the United Study of Missions, [1911].
"Lu Taifu": Charles Lewis, M.D., A Pioneer Surgeon in China. New York: Board of Foreign Missions, Presbyterian Church in the U.S.A., 1930.
The Marks of a Man. New York: Hodder & Stoughton, 1907.
The Master of the Heart. New York: Fleming H. Revell Co., 1908.
The Meaning of Christ to Me. New York: Fleming H. Revell Co., 1936.
A Memorial of a True Life: A Biography of Hugh McAllister Beaver. New York: Fleming H. Revell Co., [1898].
A Memorial of Alice Jackson. New York: Fleming H. Revell Co., [1908].
A Memorial of Horace Tracy Pitkin. New York: Fleming H. Revell Co., [1903].
Men Who Were Found Faithful. New York: Fleming H. Revell Co., [1912].
Missionary Principles and Practice: A Discussion of Christian Missions and of some Criticisms upon them. New York: Fleming H. Revell Co., 1902.
Missions and Modern History: A Study of the Missionary Aspects of Some Great Movements of the Nineteenth Century. 2 vols. New York: Fleming H. Revell Co., 1904.
Missions and Politics in Asia: Studies of the Spirit of the Eastern Peoples, the Present Making of History in Asia, and the Part Therein of Christian Missions. New York: Fleming H. Revell Co., 1898.
Missions in South America. New York: Board of Foreign Missions of the Presbyterian Church in the U.S.A., 1910.
The New Opportunity of the Church. New York: Macmillan Co., 1919.
Of One Blood: A Short Study of the Race Problem. New York: Council of Women for Home Missions and Missionary Education Movement of the United States and Canada, 1924.
One Girl's Influence: A Memorial of Louise Stockton Andrews. Plainfield, New Jersey: Frederick H. Andrews, 1914.
Owen Crimmins: Tales From the Magalloway Country. New York, Fleming H. Revell Co., [1931].

Paul, the All-Round Man. New York: Fleming H. Revell Co., 1909.
Presbyterian Foreign Missions. New York: Board of Foreign Missions of the Presbyterian Church in the U.S.A., 1901.
The Principles of Jesus Applied to Some Questions of Today. New York: Fleming H. Revell Co., 1902.
Race and Race Relations: A Christian View of Human Contacts. New York: Fleming H. Revell Co., [1924].
Remember Jesus Christ. New York: Fleming H. Revell Co., [1899].
Report on China and Japan. New York: Board of Foreign Missions of the Presbyterian Church in the U.S.A., 1926.
Report on India and Persia. New York: Board of Foreign Missions of the Presbyterian Church in the U.S.A., 1922.
Report on Missions in Asia, Persia, China, Japan, Korea. New York: Board of Foreign Missions of the Presbyterian Church in the U.S.A., 1897.
Report on Siam, the Philippines, Japan, Chosen and China. New York: Board of Foreign Missions of the Presbyterian Church in the U.S.A., 1916.
"Re-Thinking Missions" Examined. New York: Fleming H. Revell Co., 1933.
The Second Coming of Christ. Chicago: Winona Publishing Co., 1903.
Seeking the Mind of Christ. New York: Fleming H. Revell Co., 1926.
Servants of the King. New York: Young People's Missionary Movement of the United States and Canada, 1910.
Sir James Ewing. New York: Fleming H. Revell Co., [1928].
Some Great Leaders in the World Movement. New York: Fleming H. Revell Co., [1911].
Some Living Issues. New York: Fleming H. Revell Co., 1930.
South American Problems. New York: Student Volunteer Movement for Foreign Missions, 1912.
Studies in the Book of Acts. New York: International Committee of the Young Men's Christian Associations, [1892].
Studies in the Gospel of Luke. New York: International Committee of the Young Men's Christian Associations, [1892].
Studies of Missionary Leadership. Philadelphia: Westminister Press, 1914.
Studies of the Man Christ Jesus. New York: Fleming H. Revell Co., 1896.
Studies of the Man Paul. New York: Fleming H. Revell Co., [1900].
The Stuff of Manhood: Some Needed Notes in American Character. New York: Fleming H. Revell Co., 1917.
The Unfinished Task of Foreign Missions. New York: Fleming H. Revell Co., 1926.
The Unity of the Americas. New York: Laymen's Missionary Movement, 1916.
When Christianity Was New. New York: Fleming H. Revell Co., 1939.
Young Men Who Overcame. New York: Fleming H. Revell Co., [1905].
A Young Man's Questions. New York: Fleming H. Revell Co., 1903.

Pamphlets

Many of Speer's speeches, sermons, and reports appeared as pamphlets. In addition, excerpts of his books and some of his articles were often printed in this form. The best collection of his pamphlets is in the Speer Papers. The list that follows contains only those cited in the text.

A Call to Prayer. The General War-Time Commission, 1917.

Christian Tithing, A Privilege. Philadelphia: Board of Christian Education, Presbyterian Church in the U.S.A., n.d.

D. L. Moody. E. Northfield, Mass.: Northfield Schools, 1931.

The Deity of Christ. New York: N.p., [1909].

Eleanor Chestnut: A Servant of the King. New York: Women's Board of Foreign Missions of the Presbyterian Church, 1909.

The Federal Council and the Churches. New York: Federal Council of Churches, 1923.

The Fellowship of the Spirit. Easter to Pentecost, 1947. New York: Federal Council of Churches, Department of Evangelism, 1947. "Interdenominational Edition"

How to Preserve Fellowship and Right Understanding Between Japan and the United States. Philadelphia: N.p., 1917.

How to Speak Effectively Without Notes. New York: Fleming H. Revell Co., [1928]. Published in pamphlet form as early as c. 1909.

The Impact of the West Upon the East Must be Christianized. N.p.: Laymen's Missionary Movement, 1910.

The Old, Ever New, Call of Christ. Philadelphia: Office of the General Assembly of the Presbyterian Church in the U.S.A., [1927].

One Century Past, Another to Come. New York: Board of Foreign Missions of the Presbyterian Church in the U.S.A., 1937.

Nation-Wide Week of Prayer for the Churches, 8–14 January 1940. New York: Department of Evangelism of the Federal Council of the Churches of Christ in America, [1940].

The non-Christian Religions Inadequate to Meet the Needs of Men. New York: Board of Foreign Missions of the Presbyterian Church in the U.S.A., 1906.

Not Against One Another But Together. N.p., 1947.

The Place of Missions in the Thought of God. New York: Board of Foreign Missions of the United Presbyterian Church of North America, 1905.

Some Changing and Unchanging Things in Foreign Missions. Privately printed, 1937.

The War and the Religious Outlook. Boston: Pilgrim Press, [1919].

What Constitutes a Missionary Call? N.p., n.d.

The Witness Bearing of the Church to the Nations. N.p., 1919.

The World's Debt to the Missionary. New York: Laymen's Missionary Movement, [1909].

Articles

Speer wrote many articles. The Speer Papers and the Speer Family Papers contain copies of somewhat over twelve hundred. The largest single group of them is in sixteen scrapbooks in the Speer Papers. They range in size from many-page essays to single-page book reviews, letters to editors and brief meditations and prayers. He published in dozens of periodicals over his lifetime, including many of the leading denominational and nondenominational ones. Chapters in books and conference reports are treated as articles. The following list is limited to those cited in the text.

"The Achievements of Yesterday." In *Students and the Christian World Mission,* edited by Jesse R. Wilson, 173–86. New York: Student Volunteer Movement for Foreign Missions, 1936.

"Address by Dr. Robert E. Speer." *Ulster Irish Society and Ulster Club.* Year Book, 1941, 4–14.

"An Appraisal of the Appraisal." *Missionary Review of the World* 56, no. 1 (January 1933): 7–27.

"The Bases of Unity Among Young People and Steps Toward Achievement." In *Church Federation, Inter-Church Conference on Federation*, edited by Elias B. Sanford, 443–53. New York: Fleming H. Revell Co., 1906.

"The Call to a Larger Christian Cooperation," Address of Dr. Robert E. Speer at the Meeting of the Executive Committee in Atlantic City, N.J., 10–12 December 1918. In *Annual Reports of the Federal Council of the Churches of Christ in America*, 1918, 175–93. New York: Missionary Education Movement in the United States and Canada, 1918.

"Charge to the President," Charge at Inauguration of Dr. John A. Mackay as President of Princeton Theological Seminary. *Princeton Seminary Bulletin* 31, no. 1 (April 1937): 2–6.

"The Christ Who Lives in Men." *Christian Century* 42, no. 4 (22 January 1925): 117–20.

"Christianity and Other Religions." *Missionary Review of the World* 25, no. 7 (July 1902): 500–512.

"The closing address of the Convention." In *Student Missionary Enterprise, Addresses and Discussions of the Second International Convention of the Student Volunteer Movement for Foreign Missions*, 28 February–4 March 1894, edited by Max Wood Moorhead, 162–67. New York: Fleming H. Revell Co., [1894].

"The closing remarks of the Convention." In *Report of the First International Convention of the Student Volunteer Movement for Foreign Missions*, 26 February–1 March 1891, 185–88. Boston, Mass.: T. O. Metcalf & Co., [1891].

"The Consciousness of Christ." *Union Seminary Review* 55, no. 2 (February 1944): 93–119.

"Dell Ross, My Dell." *Nassau Literary Magazine* 43, no. 8 (March 1888): 453–63.

"The Duty of the Church in the Present Crisis." *Presbyterian Tribune* 57, no. 4 (January 1942): 9–14.

"The Edinburgh Conference—II." *East and the West* (October 1910), 369–80.

"Elisha B. Swift," *Centennial of the Western Foreign Missionary Society, 1831–1931*. Pittsburgh Presbytery, [1931], 162–88.

"The Evangelization of the World in This Generation." In *The Student Missionary Appeal, Addresses at the Third International Convention of the Student Volunteer Movement for Foreign Missions*, 201–16. New York: Student Volunteer Movement for Foreign Missions, 1898.

"The Evangelization of the World in This Generation." In *Students and the World-Wide Expansion of Christianity, Addresses Delivered Before the Seventh International Convention of the Student Volunteer Movement for Foreign Missions*, 31 December 1913–4 January 1914, edited by Fennell P. Turner, 101–11. New York: Student Volunteer Movement for Foreign Missions, 1914.

"The Faith and Life Seminars." In *The Life Work of George Irving*, edited by David R. Porter, 59–71. New York: Association Press, 1945.

"The Finality of Jesus Christ." *Missionary Review of the World* 56, no. 4 (April 1933): 175–84.

"Foreign Missions or World-Wide Evangelism." In *The Fundamentals*, vol. 12, 64–84. Chicago: Testimony Publishing Co., n.d.

"The Founders and the Foundations." In *Centennial of the Western Foreign Missionary Society, 1831–1931*, 138–62. Pittsburgh Presbytery, [1931].

"The Fulness of the Living Presence of Christ." In *Students and the Modern Missionary Crusade*, 9–15. Nashville: Student Volunteer Movement, 1906.

"Hinduism in Its Holy City," *The Independent* 49, no. 2548 (30 September 1897): 16–17.

"The Indivisibility of the Church's Life." In *United in Service*. Report of the Federal Council of the Churches of Christ in America, 1920–1924, edited by Samuel McCrea Cavert, 14–15. New York: Federal Council of the Churches of Christ in America, 1925.

"Is Identity of Doctrinal Opinion Necessary to Continued Missionary Cooperation?" *International Review of Missions* 12 (October 1923): 497–504.

"The Living Christ." In *Christian Mission in the World Today. Report of the Eleventh Quadrennial Convention of the Student Volunteer Movement*, 175–84. New York: Student Volunteer Movement for Foreign Missions, 1932.

"Looking Through the War Clouds." *Missionary Review of the World* 41 (January 1918): 11–15.

"Men's Question Meeting." In *Students and the Missionary Problem*, 256–59. London, Student Voluntary Missionary Union, 1900.

"The Minister, The Man of One Book." *Princeton Seminary Bulletin* 41, no. 3 (Winter 1948): 22–25.

"Mission Comity." *Churchman* 79, no. 14 (8 April 1899): 511.

"The Missionary Message to the World." *Foreign Missions Conference of North America*, 1929, 36th Annual Conference, edited by Leslie B. Moss, 194–222. New York: Foreign Missions Conference of North America, [1929].

"The National Antipathy to the Negro." *Nassau Literary Magazine* 44, no. 6 (January 1889): 363–67.

"The Need of the Non-Christian World for Christ." *Churchman* 76, no. 25 (18 December 1897): 819–20.

"Our Existing Unity." *Homiletic Review* 89, no. 3 (March 1925): 175–77, 207.

"Our Need to Pray." *Adult Bible Class Members Monthly* (March 1936), 5.

"Paul, The Great Missionary Example." *Student Missionary Enterprise, Addresses and Discussions at the Second International Convention of the Student Volunteer Movement for Foreign Missions*, 28 February–4 March 1894, edited by Max Wood Moorhead, 2–18. New York: Fleming H. Revell Co., [1894].

"The Presbyterian Church and the Evangelization of the World." *Journal of the Department of History* 15, no. 1 (March 1932): 59–71.

"The Presbyterian Churches and Foreign Missions." In *Addresses*, at the Celebration of the Two Hundred and Fiftieth Anniversary of the Westminster Assembly of the Presbyterian Church in the U.S.A., edited by William H. Roberts, 299–322. Philadelphia: Presbyterian Board of Publication and Sabbath-School Work, 1898.

"A Presbyterian View of Catholicity." *Churchman* 83, no. 50 (15 June 1901): 741.

"The Present Situation in the Church as a Whole." In *Christian Unity: Its Principles and Possibilities*, Committee on the War and the Religious Outlook, 123–64. New York: Association Press, 1921.

"Princeton on the Mission Field," *Journal of the Presbyterian Historical Society* 24, no. 2 (June 1946): 100–8.

"The Race Problem and Its Solution." *Christian Endeavor World* 29:18 (26 January 1915): 343–44.

"A Religious Retrospect." *Philadelphian*, June 1887, 336.

"The Resurrection." In *Addresses on General Subjects*. Jerusalem Meeting of the International Missionary Council, 24 March–8 April 1928, 1:135–43. New York and London: International Missionary Council, 1928.

"The Science of Missions." *Missionary Review of the World*, New Series 12, no. 1 (January 1899): 27–37.

"Should the Denominational Distinctions of Christian Lands be Perpetuated on Mission Fields?" *American Journal of Theology* 11, no. 2 (April 1907): 212–16.

"The Significance of the Ecumenical Missionary Conference." In *Ecumenical Missionary Conference*, 1:58–64. New York: American Tract Society, 1900.

"Some Missionary Aspects of the Year 1914." *Missionary Review of the World* 38, no. 1 (January 1915): 7–16.

"The Spiritual Claims of Latin America Upon the United States and Canada." In *Students and the Present Missionary Crisis*, 92–108. New York: Student Volunteer Movement for Foreign Missions, 1910.

"The Supreme and Determining Aim." In *Ecumenical Missionary Conference*, 1:74–78. New York: American Tract Society, 1900.

"The Trend to Christian Unity." *Churchman* 79, no. 4 (28 January 1899): 125.

"Two Hundred and Fifty Years of Foreign Missions." *Journal of the Department of History* 15, nos. 7 and 8 (September–December 1933): 382–91.

"The Uplifted Eye and the Life Laid Down." In *Students and the Modern Missionary Crusade*, 281–84. Nashville: Student Volunteer Movement, 1906.

"The Volunteer Movement's Possible Perils." *Student Volunteer* 1, no. 2 (March 1893): 21–23, and 1, no. 3 (April 1893): 42–43.

"The War's Challenge to Foreign Missions." *Sunday School Times* 56, no. 42 (17 October 1914): 629.

"What This Movement Means," in *The Student Missionary Appeal, Addresses at the Third International Convention of the Student Volunteer Movement for Foreign Missions*, 23–27 February 1898, 141–44. New York: Student Volunteer Movement for Foreign Missions, 1898.

"What This Movement Means?" In *Students and the Missionary Problem*, 187–93. London: Student Volunteer Missionary Union, 1900.

"Why and How to Abolish War." *Sunday School Times* 56, no. 33 (15 August 1914): 504.

"The Work of the Church Today." In *The Church—After the War—What?* edited by Roy B. Guild, 15–30. New York: Association Press, 1919.

III. Official Reports

Many organizations that Speer served published official reports, most of them on an annual basis. In addition, the major ecumenical gatherings, like those at Edinburgh and Jerusalem, published extensive reports of their actions. The documents listed below are those cited in the text.

Addresses on General Subjects. The Jerusalem Meeting of the International Missionary Council, 24 March–8 April 1928. Volume 8. New York and London: International Missionary Council, 1928.

Annual Reports of the Federal Council of the Churches of Christ in America, 1913. New York: National Offices, 1913.

Annual Reports of the Federal Council of the Churches of Christ in America, 1914. New York: National Offices, 1914.

Annual Reports of the Federal Council of the Churches of Christ in America, 1917. New York: Missionary Education Movement of the United States and Canada, 1917.

Annual Reports of the Federal Council of the Churches of Christ in America, 1918. New York: Missionary Education Movement of the United States and Canada, 1918.

Annual Reports of the Federal Council of the Churches of Christ in America, 1919. New York: Federal Council of the Churches of Christ in America, [1919].

Cavert, Samuel McCrea, ed. *The Churches Allied for Common Tasks*. Report of the Third Quadrennium of the Federal Council of the Churches of Christ in America, 1916–1920. New York: Federal Council of the Churches of Christ in America, 1921.

_____, ed. *United in Service*. Report of the Federal Council of the Churches of Christ in America, 1920–1924. New York: Federal Council of the Churches of Christ in America, 1925.

The Christian Life and Message in Relation to Non-Christian Systems of Thought and Life. The Jerusalem Meeting of the International Missionary Council, 24 March–8 April 1928. Vol. 1. New York and London: International Missionary Council, 1928.

Conference on Missions in Latin America, 12–13 March 1913. Lebanon, Pa: Sowers Printing Co., 1913.

Ecumenical Missionary Conference. Report of the Ecumenical Conference on Foreign Missions, Held in Carnegie Hall and Neighboring Churches, 21 April–1 May 1900. 2 vols. New York: American Tract Society, 1900.

Eighth Conference of the Officers and Representatives of the Foreign Missions Boards and Societies in the United States and Canada. New York: Foreign Missions Library, [1901].

Federal Council of the Churches of Christ in America Annual Report, 1923. New York: Federal Council of Churches, 1923.

Foreign Missions Conference of North America. Being the Report of the Twenty-First Conference on Foreign Missions Boards in the United States and Canada. New York: Foreign Missions Conference, [1914].

Foreign Missions Conference of North America: Report of Eighteenth Conference of Foreign Missions Boards in the United States and Canada, 1911. New York: Foreign Missions Library, [1911].

Fourteenth Conference of the Foreign Missions Boards in the United States and Canada. New York: Foreign Missions Library, [1907].

Interdenominational Conference of Foreign Missionary Boards and Societies in the United States and Canada. New York: E. O. Jenkins' Sons Printing House, 1893.

Macfarland, Charles S., ed. *Christian Unity at Work*. Federal Council of the Church of Christ in America in Quadrennial Session at Chicago, Illinois, 1912. New York: Federal Council of the Churches of Christ in America, 1913.

_____, ed. *The Churches of Christ in Council*. Vol. 1, *Library of Christian Cooperation*. New York: Missionary Education Movement, 1917.

_____, ed. *The Churches of Christ in Time of War.* New York: Missionary Education Movement of the United States and Canada, 1917.

Minutes of the General Assembly of the Presbyterian Church in the United States of America. Philadelphia: MacCalla and Company, 1900.

Minutes of the General Assembly of the Presbyterian Church in the U.S.A. Third Series, vol. 4, 1925. Philadelphia: Office of the General Assembly, 1925.

Minutes of the General Assembly of the Presbyterian Church in the U.S.A. Third Series, vol. 5, 1926. Philadelphia: Office of the General Assembly, 1926.

Minutes of the General Assembly of the Presbyterian Church in the U.S.A. Third Series, vol. 6, 1927. Philadelphia: Office of the General Assembly, 1927.

Minutes of the General Assembly of the Presbyterian Church in the U.S.A. Third Series, vol. 8, 1929. Philadelphia: Office of the General Assembly, 1929.

Minutes of the General Assembly of the Presbyterian Church in the U.S.A. Third Series, vol. 12, 1933. Philadelphia: Office of the General Assembly, 1933.

Minutes of the General Assembly of the Presbyterian Church in the U.S.A. Third Series, vol. 13, 1934. Philadelphia: Office of the General Assembly, 1934.

Minutes of the General Assembly of the Presbyterian Church in the U.S.A. Third Series, vol. 16, 1937. Philadelphia: Office of the General Assembly, 1937.

Moorhead, Max Wood, ed. *The Student Missionary Enterprise, Addresses and Discussions of the Second International Convention of the Student Volunteer Movement for Foreign Missions,* 28 February–4 March 1894. New York: Fleming H. Revell Co., [1894].

Moss, Leslie B., ed. *The Foreign Missions Conference of North America,* 1929. 36th Annual Conference. New York: Foreign Missions Conference of North America, [1929].

Ninth Conference of the Officers and Representatives of the Foreign Missions Boards and Societies in the United States and Canada. New York: Foreign Missions Library, [1902].

Report of Robert E. Speer, Secretary to the Presbyterian Board of Foreign Missions, on his visit to the Missions of West and East Persia. New York: Board of Foreign Missions of the Presbyterian Church in the U.S.A., 1897. [Printed for the use of the board].

Report of the Executive Committee of the Student Volunteer Movement for Foreign Missions, 28 February–4 March 1894. Detroit: John Bornman & Son, [1894].

Report of the Fifth Conference of the Officers and Representatives of the Foreign Missions Boards and Societies in the United States and Canada. New York: Foreign Missions Library, [1897].

Report of the First International Convention of the Student Volunteer Movement for Foreign Missions, 26 February–1 March 1891. Boston: T. O. Metcalf & Co., [1901].

Report of the Fourth Conference of the Officers and Representatives of the Foreign Missions Boards and Societies in the United States and Canada. New York: Foreign Missions Library, [1896].

Report of the Seventh Conference of the Officers and Representatives of the Foreign Missions Boards and Societies in the United States and Canada. New York: Foreign Missions Library, [1899].

Report of the Sixth Conference of the Officers and Representatives of the Foreign Missions Boards and Societies in the United States and Canada. New York: Foreign Missions Library, [1898].

Sanford, Elias B., ed. *Church Federation, Inter-Church Conference on Federation*, New York, 15–21 November 1905. New York: Fleming H. Revell Co., 1906.

_____, ed. *Federal Council of the Churches of Christ in America.* Report of the First Meeting of the Federal Council, Philadelphia, 1908. New York: Revell Press, 1909.

The Student Missionary Appeal, Addresses at the Third International Convention of the Student Volunteer Movement for Foreign Missions. New York: Student Volunteer Movement for Foreign Missions, 1898.

Students and the Missionary Problem. Addresses Delivered at the International Student Missionary Conference. London: Student Voluntary Missionary Union, 1900.

Students and the Present Missionary Crisis. New York: Student Volunteer Movement, 1910.

Students and the Modern Missionary Crusade. Nashville: Student Volunteer Movement, 1906.

Turner, Fennell P., ed. *Students and the World-Wide Expansion of Christianity, Addresses Delivered Before the Seventh International Convention of the Student Volunteer Movement for Foreign Missions*, 31 December 1913–4 January 1914. New York: Student Volunteer Movement for Foreign Missions, 1914.

Twelfth Conference of the Foreign Missions Boards in the United States and Canada. New York: Foreign Missions Library, [1905].

Wilson, Jesse R., ed. *Students and the Christian World Mission.* New York: Student Volunteer Movement for Foreign Missions, 1936.

World Missionary Conference, 1910. 9 vols. New York: Fleming H. Revell Co., [1910].

IV. Books

Abrams, Ray H. *Preachers Present Arms.* New York: Round Table Press, 1933.

Ahlstrom, Sydney E. *A Religious History of the American People.* New York: Charles Scribner's Sons, 1965.

Bainton, Roland H. *Christian Attitudes toward War and Peace.* New York: Abingdon Press, 1960.

Baker, Ray Stannard. *Following the Color Line.* New York: Harper & Row Publishers, 1964.

Beaver, R. Pierce. *Ecumenical Beginnings in Protestant World Mission: A History of Comity.* New York: Thomas Nelson & Sons, 1962.

The Book of Confessions. Philadelphia: Office of the General Assembly of the United Presbyterian Church in the United States of America, 1967.

Boyd, Lois A., and Douglas R. Brackenridge. *Presbyterian Women in America: Two Centuries of a Quest for Status.* A Publication of the Presbyterian Historical Society, no. 9. Westport, Conn.: Greenwood Press, 1983.

Braisted, Ruth Wilder. *In This Generation: The Story of Robert P. Wilder.* New York: Friendship Press, 1941.

Brown, Arthur Judson. *Memoirs of a Centenarian*. Edited by William N. Wysham. New York: World Horizons, 1957.

_____. *One Hundred Years*. A History of the Foreign Missionary Work of the Presbyterian Church in the U.S.A. With Some Account of Countries, Peoples and the Policies and Problems of Modern Missions. 2 vols. New York: Fleming H. Revell Co., 1936.

Cable, George W. *The Negro Question*. Garden City, N.Y.: Doubleday Anchor Books, 1958.

Carter, Burnham. *So Much to Learn*. Northfield, Mass.: Northfield Mount Hermon School, 1976.

Cavert, Samuel McCrea. *American Churches in the Ecumenical Movement: 1900–1968*. New York: Association Press, 1968.

_____. *Church Cooperation and Unity in America. A Historical Review: 1900–1970*. New York: Association Press, 1970.

Coleman, Helen Waite Turnbull. *Camp Diamond Story*. Privately printed, 1941.

The Committee on the War and the Religious Outlook. *Christian Unity, Its Principles and Possibilities*. New York: Association Press, 1921.

_____. *Missionary Outlook in Light of the War*. New York: Association Press, 1920.

Conn, Peter J. *Pearl S. Buck: A Cultural Biography*. Cambridge and New York: Cambridge University Press, 1996.

Curtis, Richard K. *They Called Him Mister Moody*. Garden City, N.Y.: Doubleday & Company, 1962.

Doyle, Paul A. *Pearl S. Buck*. New York: Twayne Publishers, [1965].

Eddy, Sherwood. *Eighty Adventurous Years: An Autobiography*. New York: Harper & Brothers Publishers, 1955.

_____. *Maker of Men: The Secret of Character Building*. New York and London: Harper & Brothers Publishers, 1941.

_____. *Pathfinders of the World Missionary Crusade*. New York: Abingdon-Cokesbury Press, 1945.

Ellinwood, Mary G. *Frank Field Ellinwood: His Life and Work*. New York: Fleming H. Revell Co., 1911.

Ernst, Eldon G. *Moment of Truth for Protestant America: Interchurch Campaigns Following World War One*. American Academy of Religion Dissertation Series, no. 3. Missoula, Mont.: Scholars' Press, 1974.

Findley, James F., Jr. *Dwight L. Moody: American Evangelist, 1837–1899*. Chicago & London: University of Chicago Press, 1969.

Fox, Richard Wightman. *Reinhold Niebuhr, A Biography*. New York: Pantheon Books, 1985.

Fraser, Agnes R. *Donald Fraser of Livingstonia*. London: Hodder & Stoughton, 1934.

Frederickson, George M. *The Black Image in the White Mind*. New York: Harper & Row, Publishers, 1971.

The Fundamentals. 12 vols. Chicago: Testimony Publishing Co., 1910–15.

Furniss, Norman F. *The Fundamentalist Controversy, 1918–1931*. Hamden, Conn.: Archon Books, 1963.

Grant, Madison. *The Passing of the Great Race*. New York: Charles Scribner's Sons, 1916.

Guild, Roy B., ed. *The Church—After the War—What?* New York: Association Press, 1919.

Handy, Robert T. *A Christian America: Protestant Hopes and Historical Realities.* New York: Oxford University Press, 1971.

———. *We Witness Together: A History of Cooperative Home Missions.* New York: Friendship Press, 1956.

Hart, D. G. *Defending the Faith: J. Gresham Machen and the Crisis of Conservatism in Modern America.* Baltimore and London: John Hopkins University Press, 1994.

Hatch, Nathan O., and Mark A. Noll, eds. *The Bible in America.* New York: Oxford University Press, 1982.

Hocking, William E., et al. *Re-Thinking Missions: A Laymen's Inquiry After One Hundred Years.* New York: Harper & Bros., 1932.

Hogg, William R. *Ecumenical Foundations: A History of the International Missionary Council.* New York: Harper & Brothers Publishers, 1952.

Hopkins, C. Howard. *John R. Mott 1865–1955: A Biography.* Grand Rapids: Wm. B. Eerdmans Publishing Co., 1979.

Hutchison, John A. *We Are Not Divided.* New York: Round Table Press, 1941.

Hutchison, William R. *Errand to the World: American Protestant Thought and Foreign Missions.* Chicago: University of Chicago Press, 1987.

Iremonger, F. A. *William Temple.* Archbishop of Canterbury, His Life and Letters. London: Oxford University Press, 1948.

Lacy, Creighton. *Frank Mason North: His Social and Ecumenical Vision.* Nashville: Abingdon Press, 1967.

Latourette, Kenneth Scott. *Beyond the Ranges.* Grand Rapids: Wm. B. Eerdmans Publishing Co., 1967.

———. *A History of Christianity.* New York: Harper & Brothers Publishers, 1953.

Loetscher, Lefferts A. *The Broadening Church: A Study of Theological Issues in the Presbyterian Church Since 1869.* Philadelphia: University of Pennsylvania Press, 1954.

Longfield, Bradley J. *The Presbyterian Controversy: Fundamentalists, Modernists, and Moderates.* New York: Oxford University Press, 1991.

Macfarland, Charles S. *Christian Unity in the Making.* New York: Federal Council of the Churches of Christ in America, 1948.

McNeill, John T., and James Hastings Nichols. *Ecumenical Testimony: The Concern for Christian Unity Within the Reformed and Presbyterian Churches.* Philadelphia: Westminster Press, 1974.

Marsden, George M. *Fundamentalism and American Culture, The Shaping of Twentieth-Century Evangelicalism: 1870–1925.* New York: Oxford University Press, 1980.

———. *Understanding Fundamentalism and Evangelicalism.* Grand Rapids: Wm. B. Eerdmans Publishing Co., 1991.

Marty, Martin E. *The Noise of Conflict: 1919–1941.* Vol. 2 of *Modern American Religion.* Chicago and London: University of Chicago Press, 1991.

Miller, Robert Moats. *American Protestantism and Social Issues, 1919–1939.* Chapel Hill, N.C.: University of North Carolina Press, 1958.

———. *Harry Emerson Fosdick: Preacher, Pastor, Prophet.* New York: Oxford University Press, 1985.

_____. *How Shall They Hear Without a Preacher? The Life of Ernest Fremont Tittle.* Chapel Hill, N.C.: University of North Carolina Press, 1971.

Miller, William McElwee. *My Persian Pilgrimage: An Autobiography.* Rev. ed. Pasadena, Calif: William Carey Library, 1995.

Moellering, Ralph L. *Modern War and the American Churches.* New York: American Press, 1956.

Mott, John R. *The American Student Missionary Uprising, or The History and Organization of the Student Volunteer Movement for Foreign Missions.* Published as a pamphlet. August 1889.

_____. *The Evangelization of the World in This Generation.* New York: Student Volunteer Movement for Foreign Missions, 1904.

_____. *The Young Men's Christian Association.* Vol. 4 of *Addresses and Papers of John R. Mott.* New York: Association Press, 1947.

Morse, Richard C. *My Life With Young Men: Fifty Years in the Young Men's Christian Association.* New York: Association Press, 1918.

Myers, Frederic W. H. *Saint Paul.* London: Macmillan & Co., 1928.

Newby, I. A., ed. *The Development of Segregationist Thought.* Homewood, Ill.: Dorsey Press, 1968.

_____. *Jim Crow's Defense: Anti-Negro Thought in America, 1900–1930.* Baton Rouge, La.: Louisiana University Press, 1965.

Nichols, James Hastings. *Democracy and the Churches.* Philadelphia: Westminster Press, 1951.

Padwick, Constance E. *Temple Gairdner of Cairo.* London: Society for Promoting Christian Knowledge, 1929.

Parker, Michael. *The Kingdom of Character: The Student Volunteer Movement for Foreign Missions.* Lanham, Md., New York, Oxford: American Society of Missiology and University Press of America, 1998.

Pierson, Delavan Leonard. *Arthur T. Pierson.* New York: Fleming H. Revell Co., 1912.

Piper, John F., Jr. *The American Churches in World War I.* Athens, Ohio: Ohio University Press, 1985.

Porter, David R., ed. *The Life Work of George Irving.* New York: Association Press, 1945.

Rauschenbusch, Walter. *Christianizing the Social Order.* New York: Macmillan Co., 1921.

_____. *A Theology for the Social Gospel.* New York: Macmillan Co., 1917.

Reimers, David M. *White Protestantism and the Negro.* New York: Oxford University Press, 1965.

Rian, Edwin H. *The Presbyterian Conflict.* Grand Rapids: Wm. B. Eerdmans Publishing Co., 1940.

Robinson, Marion O. *Eight Women of the YWCA.* New York: National Board of the Young Women's Christian Association of the U.S.A., 1966.

Robshaw, Charles P. *The Art and Architecture of the East Liberty Presbyterian Church.* Pittsburgh: East Liberty Presbyterian Church, 1977.

Rouse, Ruth. *The World's Student Christian Federation: A History of the First Thirty Years.* London: SCM Press, 1948.

Rouse, Ruth, and Stephen Charles Neill, ed. *A History of the Ecumenical Movement, 1517–1948.* 2d ed. with rev. bibliog. Philadelphia: Westminster Press, 1967.

Rycroft, W. Stanley. *Memoir of Life in Three Worlds*. Cranbury, N.J.: J. B. Business Services, 1976.

Sanford, Elias B. *Origin and History of the Federal Council of the Churches of Christ in America*. Hartford, Conn.: S. S. Scranton Co., 1916.

Shedd, Clarence P. *Two Centuries of Student Christian Movements*. New York: Association Press, 1934.

Showalter, Nathan D. *The End of a Crusade: The Student Volunteer Movement for Foreign Missions and the Great War*. Lanham, Md., and London: Scarecrow Press, 1998.

Stoddard, Lothrop. *The Rising Tide of Color Against White World Supremacy*. New York: Charles Scribner's Sons, 1920.

Stonehouse, Ned. *J. Gresham Machen: A Biographical Memoir*. Grand Rapids: Wm. B. Eerdmans Publishing Co., 1954.

Strong, Josiah. *Our Country*. New York: Baker and Taylor Co., 1885.

Trumbull, Henry Clay. *Friendship the Master-Passion*. Philadelphia: John D. Wattles, 1892.

_____. *Old Time Student Volunteers*. New York: Fleming H. Revell Co., 1902.

Varg, Paul A. *Missionaries, Chinese, and Diplomats: The American Protestant Missionary Movement in China, 1890–1952*. Princeton: Princeton University Press, 1958.

Wallstrom, Timothy C. *The Creation of a Student Movement to Evangelize the World*. Pasedena, Calif.: William Carey International University Press, 1980.

Westin William J. *Presbyterian Pluralism: Competition in a Protestant House*. Knoxville, Tenn.: University of Tennessee Press, 1997.

White, Ronald C., Jr. *Liberty and Justice for All: Racial Reform and the Social Gospel (1877–1925)*. San Francisco: Harper & Row Publishers, 1990.

Wheeler, W. Reginald. *A Man Sent From God: A Biography of Robert E. Speer*. Westwood, N.J.: Fleming H. Revell Co., 1956.

Wilder, Robert P. *The Great Commission. The Missionary Response: The Student Volunteer Movements in North America and Europe. Some Personal Reminiscences*. London and Edinburgh: Oliphants, [1936].

_____. *The Student Volunteer Movement for Foreign Missions: Some Personal Reminiscences of its Origin and Early History*. New York: Student Volunteer Movement, 1935.

Wright, Henry B. *A Life With a Purpose, A Memorial of John Lawrence Thurston: First Missionary of the Yale Mission*. New York: Fleming H. Revell Co., 1908.

V. Articles

This list contains articles in periodicals and chapters in books and reports that are cited in the text. They are divided into signed and unsigned groups.

Signed

Abrams, Ray H. "The Churches and the Clergy in World War II." *Annals of the American Academy of Political and Social Science* 256 (March 1948): 110–19.

Ainslie, Peter. "American Protestants Getting Together." *Christian Herald* 44 (8 January 1921): 29.

Anderson, Gerald H. "American Protestants in Pursuit of Mission: 1886–1986." *International Bulletin of Missionary Research* 12, no. 3 (July 1988): 98–118.

Barton, James L. "Cooperation Among Christian Forces on the Mission Field." In *Christian Unity at Work*. Federal Council of the Churches of Christ in America in Quadrennial Sessions at Chicago, Illinois, 1912, edited by Charles S. Macfarland, 79–107. New York: Federal Council of the Churches of Christ in America, 1913.

Beaver, R. Pierce. "Missionary Motivation Through the Centuries." In *Reinterpretation in American Church History*, edited by Jerald Brauer, 113–51. Chicago and London: University of Chicago Press, 1968.

The Board of Trustees. "Robert E. Speer Memorial Minute." *Princeton Seminary Bulletin* 42, no. 1 (Summer 1948): 13–15.

Brown, Arthur J. "Robert E. Speer Leader for 40 Years." *Presbyterian Magazine* 37, no. 12 (December 1931): 680.

Buchanan, John G. "Robert E. Speer: The Man." *Princeton Seminary Bulletin* 42, no. 1 (Summer 1948): 5–8.

Buck, Pearl S. "Is There a Case for Foreign Missions?" *Harper's Magazine* 166 (January 1933): 143–55.

————. "The Laymen's Mission Report." *Christian Century* 49, no. 47 (23 November 1932): 1434–37.

Bunyan, John. "He Who Would Valiant Be," *Methodist Hymnal*. Nashville: Methodist Publishing House, 1939.

Campbell, J. A. "The Inadequacy of Non-Christian Religious to meet the need of the World." In *Students and the Missionary Problem. Addresses Delivered at the International Student Missionary Conference*, 26–35. London: Student Volunteer Missionary Union, 1900.

Clarke, Walter Irving. "Moderator Speer in Action at the General Assembly." In *Robert E. Speer: Missionary Statesman*, 13–14. Published as a pamphlet. Philadelphia: General Assembly, 1927.

Clutter, Ronald T. "The Reorganization of Princeton Theological Seminary Reconsidered." *Grace Theological Journal* 7 (1986): 179–201.

Erdman, Charles R. "The Interpreter of Christ." *Princeton Seminary Bulletin* 42, no. 1 (Summer 1948): 8–10.

Fitt, Frank. "Robert E. Speer, Servant of God." *Christian Century* 54, no. 39 (29 September 1937): 1196–98.

Fitzmier, John R., and Randall Balmer. "A Poultice for the Bite of the Cobra: The Hocking Report and Presbyterian Missions in the Middle Decade of the Twentieth Century." In *The Diversity of Discipleship: Presbyterians and Twentieth-Century Christian Witness*, edited by Milton J. Coalter, John Mulder, and Louis B. Weeks, 105–25. Louisville, Ky.: Westminster/John Knox, 1991.

Forman, Charles R. "A History of Foreign Mission Theory in America." In *American Missions in Bicentennial Perspective*, edited by R. Pierce Beaver, 69–140. South Pasadena, Calif.: William Carey Library, 1977.

Foulkes, William Hiram. "A Tribute to Robert E. Speer." *Presbyterian Tribune* 52, no. 27 (30 September 1937): 5–6.

Garrett, Shirley Stone. "Why They Stayed: American Church Politics and Chinese Nationalism in the Twenties." In *The Missionary Enterprise in China and*

America, edited by John K. Fairbank, 283–310. Cambridge, Mass.: Harvard University Press, 1974.

Gillette, Gerald W., interviewer. "John A. Mackay: Influences on My Life." *Journal of Presbyterian History* 56, no. 1 (Spring 1978): 20–34.

Goodpasture, H. McKennie. "Robert E. Speer's Legacy." *Occasional Bulletin of Missionary Research* 2, no. 2 (April 1978): 38–41.

Griffiths, H. McAllister. "145th Assembly Meets: New Mission Board Announced." *Christianity Today* 4, no. 2 (Mid-June 1933): 4, 8–14.

Harder, Ben. "The Student Volunteer Movement for Foreign Missions and Its Contribution to 20th Century Missions." *Missiology: An International Review* 8, no. 2 (April 1980): 139–54.

Harvey, Charles E. "John D. Rockefeller, Jr., and the Interchurch World Movement of 1919–1920: A Different Angle on the Ecumenical Movement." *Church History* 51, no. 2 (June 1982): 198–209.

———. "Religion and Industrial Relations: John D. Rockefeller, Jr., and the Interchurch World Movement of 1919–1920." *Research in Political Economy* 4 (1981): 199–227.

———. "Speer Versus Rockefeller and Mott, 1910–1935." *Journal of Presbyterian History* 60, no. 4 (Winter 1982): 283–99.

Hodge, Margaret E. "Introduction of Dr. Speer," in Robert E. Speer, *One Century Past, Another to Come*, 4.

Homrighausen, Elmer G. "The Finality of Jesus Christ: Robert E. Speer Memorial Lecture." *Princeton Seminary Bulletin* 67, no. 2 (Spring 1975): 1–21.

Hunter, Stanley A. "Minister Appraises Moderator." In *Robert E. Speer, Missionary Statesman*, 5–9. Published as a pamphlet. Philadelphia: General Assembly, 1927.

Hutchison, William R. "Modernism and Missions: The Liberal Search for an Exportable Christianity, 1875–1935." In *The Missionary Enterprise in China and America*, edited by John K. Fairbank, 110–31. Cambridge, Mass.: Harvard University Press, 1974.

Johnson, H. Park. "The Legacy of Arthur Judson Brown." *International Bulletin of Missionary Research* 10, no. 2 (April 1986): 71–75.

Kerr, Hugh T. "In Memoriam: Robert E. Speer." *Theology Today* 5, no. 1 (April 1948): 93–97.

———. "Robert E. Speer: A Question for the Presbyterian Church to Answer." *Presbyterian Banner* 121, no. 45 (9 May 1935): Inside front cover.

Kerr, Hugh Thomson, et al. "Dr. Robert E. Speer." *Presbyterian Banner* 123, no. 48 (27 May 1937): 3–11.

Leavell, Frank H. "Dr. Robert Elliott Speer." *Baptist Student* 11, no. 9 (June 1933): 2.

Leber, Charles T. "Board Policy During the Crisis Decade." In *The Crisis Decade, A History of the Foreign Missionary Work of the Presbyterian Church in the U.S.A., 1937–1947*, edited by Reginald W. Wheeler, 12–23. New York: Board of Foreign Missions of the Presbyterian Church in the U.S.A., 1950.

Lingle, Walter L. "Robert E. Speer." *Christian Observer* 136, no. 1 (7 January 1948): 2–3.

Loetscher, Lefferts A. "Robert Elliott Speer." In *Dictionary of American Biography*, edited by John A. Garraty and Edward T. James, Supplement Four, 1946–50, 763–64. New York: Charles Scribner's Sons, 1974.

514 BIBLIOGRAPHY

Lotz, Denton. "The Watchword for World Evangelization." *International Review of Missions* 68 (April 1979): 177–89.

Lucas, J. J. "A Letter and An Appreciation." *Presbyterian Banner* 124, no. 6 (9 September 1937): 15.

Machen, J. Gresham. "Dr. Robert E. Speer and His Latest Book." *Christianity Today* 4, no. 1 (Mid-May 1933): 15–16, 22–26.

Mackay, John A. "The Missionary Statesman." *Princeton Seminary Bulletin* 42, no. 1 (Summer 1948): 10–13.

_____. "The President's Page." *Princeton Seminary Bulletin* 41, no. 3 (Winter 1948): 26–27.

_____. "Robert E. Speer." *Presbyterian Life*, Preview Issue (17 January 1948): Inside front cover.

_____. "Robert Elliott Speer: A Man of Yesterday Today." *Princeton Seminary Bulletin* 60, no. 3 (June 1967): 11–21.

Mathews, Basil. "The Agenda of Co-operation," A Sketch of the Meeting of the International Missionary Council, Oxford, 9–16 July 1923. *International Review of Missions* 12 (October 1923): 481–96.

Miller, William M. "Christ's Man." *Sunday Times* 108, no. 53 (31 December 1966): 10–12.

_____. "God's Mighty Men: Samuel Zwemer and Robert E. Speer." *Presbyterian Journal* 26, no. 5 (31 May 1967): 7–8, 20.

Miller, William McElwee. "Robert E. Speer: Recruiter With a World Plan." *World Vision Magazine* 11, no. 8 (September 1967): 14–15, 29.

Morrow, William H. "Elliott Speer 1898–1934: The Man." *News*, Northfield Mount Hermon School 24, no. 1 (Winter 1985): 2, 4.

Mott, John R. "Robert Elliott Speer." *Woman's Press* 42, no. 1 (January 1948): 9, 43.

Patterson, James A. "The Legacy of Robert P. Wilder." *International Bulletin of Missionary Research* 15, no. 1 (January 1991): 26–32.

_____. "The Loss of a Protestant Missionary Consensus: Foreign Missions and the Fundamentalist-Modernist Conflict." In *Earthen Vessels, American Evangelicals and Foreign Missions, 1880–1980*, edited by Joel A. Carpenter and Wilbert R. Shenk, 73–91. Grand Rapids: Wm. B. Eerdmans Publishing Co., 1990.

_____. "Robert E. Speer, J. Gresham Machen and the Presbyterian Board of Foreign Missions." *American Presbyterians* 64:1 (Spring 1986): 58–68.

Pierard, Richard V. "Evangelical and Ecumenical: Missionary Leaders in Mainline Protestantism, 1900–1950." In *Re-Forming the Center: American Protestantism, 1900 to the Present*, edited by Douglas Jacobson and William Vance Trollinger, Jr., 150–71. Grand Rapids, Mich. and Cambridge, U.K.: Wm. B. Eerdmans Publishing Co., 1998.

Piper, John F., Jr. "Robert E. Speer: Christian Statesman in War and Peace." *Journal of Presbyterian History* 47, no. 3 (September 1969): 201–225.

_____. "Robert E. Speer: His Call and the Missionary Impulse, 1890–1900." *American Presbyterians* 65, no. 2 (Summer 1987): 97–108.

_____. "Robert E. Speer on Christianity and Race." *Journal of Presbyterian History* 61, no. 2 (Summer 1983): 227–47.

Reifsnyder, Richard W. "Managing the Mission: Church Restructuring in the Twentieth Century." In *The Organizational Revolution: Presbyterians and American Denominationalism*, edited by Milton J. Coalter, John M. Mulder, and Louis B. Weeks, 55–95. Louisville, Ky.: Westminster/John Knox, 1992.

Robert, Dana L. "The Origin of the Student Volunteer Watchword: 'The Evangelization of the World in This Generation.' " *International Bulletin of Missionary Research* 10 (October 1986): 146–49.

Roy, Andrew T. "Overseas Mission Policies—An Historical Overview." *Journal of Presbyterian History* 57, no. 3 (Fall 1979): 186–228.

Sandeen, Ernest. "*The Fundamentals*: The Last Flowering of the Millenarian-Conservative Alliance." *Journal of Presbyterian History* 47, no. 1 (March 1969): 55–73.

Sinclair, John H., and Arturo Piedra Solano. "The Dawn of Ecumenism in Latin America: Robert E. Speer, Presbyterians, and the Panama Conference of 1916." *Journal of Presbyterian History* 77, no. 1 (Spring 1999): 1–11.

Smalley, Martha Lund. "Historical Sketch of the Student Volunteer Movement for Foreign Missions." 6 October 1980, typed manuscript. Archives of the Student Volunteer Movement for Foreign Missions.

Smylie, James H. "Robert E. Speer: Mission Executive and Visionary." In James H. Smylie, Dean K. Thompson, and Cary Patrick, *Go Therefore: 150 Years of Presbyterians in Global Mission*, 46–54. Atlanta: Presbyterian Publishing House, 1987.

Speer, Emma B. "Two Deep Convictions." In W. Reginald Wheeler, *A Man Sent From God: A Biography of Robert E. Speer*, 155–64. Westwood, N.J.: Fleming H. Revell Co., 1956.

Speer, Margaret B. "Marriage and Family." In W. Reginald Wheeler, *A Man Sent From God: A Biography of Robert E. Speer*, 56–69. Westwood, N.J.: Fleming H. Revell Co., 1956.

Stebbins, James. "Prophecy." *Nassau Herald* 25 (1889): 50–51.

Thomas, Winburn T. "Book Review of *The Review of the Gospel* by Rufus Anderson." *Journal of Presbyterian History* 46, no. 2 (June 1968): 155–56.

Tomb, Lynn Stowe. "Elliott Speer 1898–1934: The Mystery." *News*, Northfield Mount Hermon School 24, no. 1 (Winter 1985): 3, 5.

Towne, Lucia P. "Robert E. Speer." *Women and Missions* 14, no. 7 (October 1937): 240–41.

Trumbull, Charles G. "Foreign Missionary Betrayals of the Faith." *Sunday School Times* 97, no. 12 (23 March 1935): 195–99.

Varg, Paul A. "Motives in Protestant Missions, 1890–1917." *Church History* 23 (March 1954): 68–82.

Weigold, Marilyn E. "Emma Bailey Speer." *Dictionary of American Biography*, edited by John A. Garraty, Supplement Seven, 1961–65, 707–09. New York: Charles Scribner's Sons, 1981.

Wheeler, W. Reginald. "The Methods of a Master." *Presbyterian Banner* 123, no. 48 (27 May 1937): 2, 11–12.

_____. "Reminiscences of Robert E. Speer." *Outreach* 2, no. 4 (April 1948): 103–4, 121.

Westin, William. "The Presbyterian Controversy: The Triumph of the Loyalist Center." In *Re-Forming the Center: American Protestantism, 1900 to the Present*, edited by Douglas Jacobson and William Vance Trollinger, Jr., 109–28. Grand Rapids, Mich. and Cambridge, U.K.: Wm. B. Eerdmans Publishing Co., 1998.

Unsigned

"An Illuminating Letter." *Presbyterian* 98, no. 19 (10 May 1928): 19, 27.

"An Unfortunate Start in New York." *Congregationalist and Advance* 103 (7 March 1918): 293.

"The Best Mind of the Church." *Christian Century* 41, no. 52 (25 December 1924): 1673.

"Board Speaks on Report." *Presbyterian Banner* 119, no. 22 (1 December 1932): 14–15.

"Churches to Consider Race Relations." *Federal Council Bulletin* 4 (June–July 1921): 73.

"The Dedication of the Robert E. Speer Library." *Princeton Seminary Bulletin* 51, no. 3 (January 1958): 43–59.

"Denominationalism and Foreign Missions." *Presbyterian Standard* 49, no. 2 (13 January 1909): 2.

"Discovering America's Greatest Preachers." *Christian Century* 41, no. 41 (9 October 1924), 1291.

"Dr. Robert Elliott Speer's Forty Years of Service." *Presbyterian Banner* 118, no. 18 (29 October 1931): 8.

"Dr. Speer Defended." *Congregationalist and Advance* 103 (4 April 1918): 434.

"Dr. Speer Defends China Missionaries." *Continent* 52, no. 14 (7 April 1921): 415.

"Dr. Speer Will Not Be Moderator." *Christian Century* 41, no. 19 (8 May 1924): 607.

"Editorial Notes and Comments." *Christianity Today* 4, no. 1 (Mid-May 1933): 1.

"The Essential Oneness of the Evangelical Churches." *Christian Observer* 108, no. 50 (15 December 1920): 2.

"The Federal Council—Four More Years." *Christian Century* 41, no. 52 (25 December 1924): 1659–60.

"The Foreign Board at the General Assembly." *Presbyterian Banner* 119, no. 49 (8 June 1933): 3–4.

"From Dr. Speer." *Presbyterian Tribune* 63, no. 1 (October 1947): 38.

"Greatness in Preachers." *Christian Century* 42, no. 2 (8 January 1925): 44–45.

"Machen-Speer Debate Historic Event in Presbyterian Church." *Christianity Today* 3, no. 12 (Mid-April 1933): 19–23.

"New Interest in Inter-Racial Problems." *Federal Council Bulletin* 4 (April–May 1921): 60.

"The New President of the Federal Council." *Christian Advocate* 95, no. 50 (9 December 1920): 1635.

"Parliamentary Chaos." *Christianity Today* 4, no. 2 (Mid-June 1933): 12.

"Plans for Organic Union Adopted." *Christian Century* 38, no. 7 (12 February 1920): 16–20.

"Presbyterian Foreign Missions." *Missionary Review of the World* 56, no. 7 (July 1933): 386–87.

"Robert E. Speer a True Patriot." *Presbyterian* 88 (14 March 1918): 4.

"Robert E. Speer and Christian Unity." *Federal Council Bulletin* 31, no. 1 (January 1948): 3.

"Robert E. Speer on the Federal Council." *Presbyterian* 91, no. 2 (13 January 1921): 4.

"Robert E. Speer's Call to Prayer." *Lutheran* 22 (6 December 1917): 3.
"Robert Elliott Speer." *Record of the Class of 1889*, Princeton University, 1939.

VI. Dissertations

Moffett, Samuel Hugh. "The Relation of the Board of Foreign Missions of the Presbyterian Church in the United States of America to the Missions and Church Connected with it in China." Ph.D. diss., Yale University, 1945.

Nykamp, Delwin G. "A Presbyterian Power Struggle: A Critical History of Communication Strategies Employed in the Struggle for Control of the Presbyterian Church, USA, 1922–1926." Ph.D. diss., Northwestern University, 1974.

Patterson, James Alan. "Robert E. Speer and the Crisis of the American Protestant Missionary Movement, 1920–1937." Ph.D. diss., Princeton Theological Seminary, 1980.

Perlman, Daniel. "Stirring the White Conscience: The Life of George Edmund Haynes." Ph.D. diss., New York University, 1972.

Quirk, Charles Evans. " 'The Auburn Affirmation': A Critical Narrative of the Document Designed to Safeguard the Unity and Liberty of the Presbyterian Church in the United States of America in 1924." Ph.D. diss., University of Iowa, 1967.

Roark, Dallas Morgan. "J. Gresham Machen and His Desire to Maintain a Doctrinally True Presbyterian Church." Ph.D. diss., State University of Iowa, 1963.

Roberts, Samuel Kelton. "Crucible For A Vision: The Work of George Edmund Haynes and the Commission on Race Relations, 1922–1947." Ph.D. diss., Columbia University, 1974.

Rosenthal, Lee. "Christian Statesmanship in the First Missionary-Ecumenical Generation." Ph.D. diss., University of Chicago Divinity School, 1989.

INDEX

Abbott Academy, 92, 140
Aberdeen, 203
Acts, 53, 56, 331
Adams, Carlyle, 427, 428
Adopting Act of 1789, 356
Adriatic, 364
Advisory Board of Reference and Co-operation (China), 264
Africa, xiv, 35, 115, 126, 136, 150, 169, 229, 241, 242, 332, 339, 353
African American, 284, 294, 328–30, 332, 335–38, 341. *See also* Negro
Alexander, George, 147
All-India General Conference (1872–73), 259
Allegheny Mountains, 154
America, 207, 240, 270, 271, 284, 288, 289, 298, 305, 311, 312, 328, 330, 332–34, 382
American, 203, 205, 228, 263, 269, 289, 292, 293, 295, 302, 320, 321, 323, 330, 344, 350, 373, 376, 388
American Baptist Foreign Mission Society, 435
American Bible Society, 188, 415, 416
American Board of Commissioners for Foreign Missions, 123, 146, 167, 197, 233, 333
American Christian Literature Society for Moslems, 217
American Colleges in Teheran, 415
American Committee for Non-Participation in Japanese Aggression, 416
American Council on Organic Union of the Churches of Christ, 303
American Episcopal Church (Philippines), 264

American Presbyterian History Window, 431, 435
American Red Cross, 284
American Reformed denomination, 370
American Society for the Study of Oriental Religions, 246
Amos, 56
Anderson, Rufus, 49, 123, 187, 236, 237, 244, 266, 435
Anderson-Venn formula, 186, 191, 206, 212, 240, 262
Andover Theological Seminary, 18, 19, 29
Andrews, Louise, 225
Anglican, 207
Anglo-American, 195
Anglo-Saxon, xv, 328, 330
Animism, 254
Anselm, 424
Apostles' Creed, 50, 52, 360
Arabian, 252, 332
Arch Street Presbyterian Church, Philadelphia, 347
Archbishop of Canterbury, 205
Arden, 96
Are Foreign Missions Done For? 167, 386
Armenians, 318
Arminians, 271, 273
Asbury Park, N.J., 406
Asheville School for Boys, 93
Ashmore, William, 113
Asia, xiv, 126, 136, 150, 167, 168, 169, 171, 172, 176, 188, 217, 218, 228, 229, 241, 242, 247, 261, 262, 333, 339, 411
Atkinson, Henry A., 289
Atlanta, 321, 337
Auburn Affirmation, 386, 387
Augsburg Confession, 50

518